General History, Cyclopedia

and

Dictionary

of

Freemasonry

General History, Cyclopedia
and
Dictionary
of
Freemasonry

Robert Macoy, 33°

Athens ‡ Manchester

EDITOR'S NOTE

Truly fraternally
Robt. Macoy

GENERAL HISTORY,

CYCLOPEDIA

AND

DICTIONARY

OF

FREEMASONRY;

CONTAINING

AN ELABORATE ACCOUNT OF THE RISE AND PROGRESS OF
FREEMASONRY AND ITS KINDRED ASSOCIATIONS—
ANCIENT AND MODERN

ALSO,

DEFINITIONS OF THE

TECHNICAL TERMS USED BY THE FRATERNITY.

By ROBERT MACOY, 33°,

AUTHOR OF

THE BOOK OF THE LODGE, MASONIC MANUAL, TRUE MASONIC GUIDE, VOCAL
MANUAL, ETC.; PAST DEPUTY GRAND MASTER OF NEW YORK AND NOVA
SCOTIA, PAST GRAND SECRETARY OF NEW YORK, GRAND RECORDER
OF THE GRAND COMMANDERY OF NEW YORK, REPRESENTATIVE
OF THE GRAND LODGES OF WISCONSIN, ILLINOIS AND NOVA
SCOTIA, AND THE GRAND COUNCIL OF NEW BRUNSWICK, ETC.

Illustrated with upwards of 300 Engravings.

NEW YORK:

MASONIC PUBLISHING COMPANY,

432 BROOME STREET.

1870.

PREFACE.

TO supply, to some extent, the increasing demand for knowledge, by students in the science of Freemasonry, and to keep step with the irresistible progress of our institution, were the impelling motives that induced the undersigned to undertake the arrangement of a work of this character. Dr. OLIVER's *Dictionary of Symbolical Masonry*, notwithstanding its value and usefulness, falls short of the present wants of the Fraternity. Dr. ALBERT G. MACKEY's *Lexicon of Freemasonry*, better adapted to the requirements of the Fraternity in the United States than any other work of the kind heretofore published, is also deficient in many respects.

The present volume is intended to remedy many of the defects and omissions of its predecessors, and to exhibit, in a form of easy reference, the latest developments and progress of the institution, and the results of more recent investigations. It contains a comprehensive explication of the whole system of Freemasonry, and of kindred or similar associations—ancient and modern—being a careful condensation of all that has ever been written on the subject; intelligible to the Fraternity, and mysterious to the profane. My purpose will be effectually and very satisfactorily answered, if the definitions here given of the technical and other terms of Masonry, shall prove of sufficient value to induce the reader to increase his stock of knowledge by a reference to other works, where the subjects are more thoroughly discussed, or to confirm the more advanced Mason in the truth of those noble principles of the Craft, to the study of which he has devoted his time and talents.

In the preparation of the History of the Masonic Institution, every available means has been adopted to obtain the most reliable information whereon to found a truthful chronicle of its origin and early progress throughout the several parts of the world. The many and almost insurmountable difficulties in arriving at precise dates, when the materials are scattered in different places, or mixed with doubtful circumstances, are sufficient to almost deter any writer from attempting the undertaking. Notwithstanding the uncertainty with which much of the matter of history is surrounded, a diligent and careful examination of the materials, the probabilities of statements possessing the germs of truth were too convincing to be set aside without calm reflection and mature consideration. With these views the history in the accompanying pages is offered to the Fraternity, in the hope that it will prove satisfactory and useful.

I have been greatly assisted in the arrangement of this work by Bro. Aug. C. L. Arnold, LL. D., whose knowledge and correct discrimination upon subjects connected with the history and science of Freemasonry and its kindred associations, will be a guaranty for their correctness. To Bro. John W. Simons, Past Grand Master of New York, whose knowledge of the arcana of Masonry is not excelled by any writer of the present age, I am also indebted for many valuable articles and excellent suggestions. To these and other brethren who have kindly aided me I tender my hearty thanks.

Again asking the fraternal indulgence of the brethren for whatever defects may still be apparent, the work is respectfully submitted to their inspection.

ROBT. MACOY.

GENERAL

HISTORY OF FREEMASONRY.

" Of all the institutions which have been established for the purpose of improving the condition of mankind, Freemasonry stands pre-eminent in usefulness as it is in age. Its origin is lost in the abyss of unexplored antiquity. No historical records, no traditionary accounts, can with certainty point out the precise time, the place, or the particular manner of its commencement. While some have endeavored to discover its footsteps amongst the master-builders and artists engaged in the construction of the first Jewish temple, others have attempted to trace it to the Eleusinian mysteries, which are said to have taught the immortality of the soul and the other sublime truths of natural religion. Some again have ascribed its rise to the sainted heroes of the Crusades; while others have endeavored to penetrate the mysteries of the Druids, and to discover its origin amongst the wise men of that institution."—DE WITT CLINTON.

THE difficulty of arriving at the precise time, place, or circumstance in which Masonry or its true prototype began, has been encountered by every writer upon the subject. Some, over-anxious for the dignity of the fraternity, have represented it as coeval with the world.* Others, more moderate, find its origin in the religious mysteries of the ancient world, and particularly in a supposed branch of those religious associations formed by the architects of Tyre, who, under the name of the "Dionysiac Fraternity," constituted an association of builders, exclusively engaged in the construction of temples and other prominent edifices in Asia Minor, and who were distinguished by the use of secret signs and other modes of mutual recognition. Without adopting any untenable opinions, we are justified in avowing that the institution must have been framed by a people who

* Anderson, Preston, and many other Masonic writers claim for the order the highest antiquity. Preston is particular in his expressions as to the origin of the institution, by saying: "From the commencement of the world, we may trace the foundation of Masonry." He undoubtedly meant that its principles were coexistent with the universe—for he qualifies the preceding sentence by the following expressions: "Ever since symmetry began, and harmony displayed her charms, our order has had a being." Regarding TRUTH as the sun of the Masonic system, around which all the other virtues revolve, we may trace then its origin to GOD—the fountain of all truth, with whom there is no confusion or disorder, but perfect symmetry and harmony. In that sense the origin of Freemasonry may be reconciled with the "commencement of the world."

had made considerable advance in science. The Egyptians, in the time of Moses, were proficient in all the arts and sciences,* as the gigantic works constructed in those early ages, still existing, prove. Their language was mystical, and their priests secured the mysteries of their religion from the knowledge of the vulgar or uninitiated by symbols and hieroglyphics, comprehensible alone to those of their order. The fraternity of ancient Egypt was denominated the Hiero-Laotomi, or Sacred Builders. They were a selected caste, and connected with the government and priesthood, being in fact Masons of the priestly order; whilst the ordinary Masons or artificers were of an inferior caste.† The intent and purpose of those stupendous fabrics, the pyramids, was a great mystery, and a mystery they still remain.

Moses was initiated into the secrets and mysteries of the priestly order when in Egypt, and some have imagined that the Hebrews assisted in the construction of the pyramids; but, in all probability, these wondrous efforts of Masonic skill were hoary with age when the children of Israel settled in the land of Goshen, and were emblems of sublime truths to a civilized nation when Abraham was a wanderer in the wilderness.

By Egyptian colonists, according to our biblical chronology, the arts were carried to Greece two or three centuries before the age of Moses. By the Israelites a purer knowledge of building was carried to the promised land; and when they became a settled people, the remembrance of the beautiful and stupendous edifices they had seen in Egypt, led them to attempt constructions suited to their future home. But it is evident that by the death of their great master, Moses, the Israelites were not in full possession of the knowledge requisite to complete the glorious fabric which the G. A. O. T. U. had in vision to King David directed his son Solomon to erect; as we find by Holy Writ, that "the wisest man" needed the assistance of the King of Tyre. Tyre and Sidon were the chief cities of the Phœnicians: the latter boasts an antiquity anterior to any other whose site can be determined. It was a place of considerable importance in

---

* "The Egyptians are described to us as being the first people who advanced to any high degree of knowledge in astronomy and science; and hence they acquired the means of discovering and proving the existence of the Divinity, and worshipped the Author of those sublime works which they contemplated."—Dr. Ashe.

† Champollion says: "A theocracy or government of priests was the first known to the Egyptians, and it is necessary to give the word *priests* the acceptation that it bore in ancient times, when the ministers of religion were also the ministers of science and learning; so that they united in their own persons two of the noblest missions with which men could be invested—the worship of the Deity, and the cultivation of science."

the time of Joshua, who speaks of it as "great Sidon." Hence it is evident that the Phœnicians were far advanced in the arts of life, when the Israelites reached the promised land. When Solomon was about to build the temple, he communicated to the King of Tyre his wish to enter into an engagement for a supply of timber, knowing, as he said, "that there is not amongst us any that can skill to hew timber like the Sidonians." The answer of the Tyrian king is remarkable: "I will do all thy desire concerning timber of cedar, and concerning timber of fir; my servants shall bring them down from Lebanon unto the sea, and I will convey them by sea in floats, unto the place that thou shalt appoint me, and I will cause them to be discharged there." (1 Kings, v. 8, 9). Solomon was highly pleased with the answer of the Tyrian king, and in return he made him yearly presents of the most costly kinds. Hiram sent him also a man of his own name, a Tyrian by birth, but of Israelitish parentage, who was honored by his king with the title of father, and is called Hiram Abiff,* the most accomplished designer and operator then known in the country, who in Solomon's absence filled the chair as Deputy Grand Master, and in his presence was the Senior Grand Warden, or Principal Surveyor and Master of the work. That no confusion might arise, owing to the great numbers employed, King Solomon selected those of most enlightened minds and comprehensive understandings, religious men, and zealous in good works, as masters to superintend the workmen; men skilful in geometry and proportion, who had been initiated and proved in the mystical learning of the ancient sages—those he made overseers of the work. To carry on this stupendous work with greater ease and speed, Solomon ordered all the craftsmen, as well natives as foreigners, to be numbered and classed as follows, viz:

Harodim, princes, rulers, or provosts	300
Menatzchim, overseers	3,300
Ghiblim, stone-squarers	80,000
The levy out of Israel, at work in Lebanon	30,000
	113,600

Besides the *ish sabbal* or men of burden, the remains of the old Canaanites, amounting to seventy thousand, who are not numbered among the Masons.

* This inspired Master was, without question, the most cunning, skilful, and curious workman that ever lived, whose abilities were not confined to building only, but extended to all kinds of work, whether in gold, silver, brass, or iron. From his designs, and under his direction, all the rich and splendid furniture of the Temple and its several appendages was begun, carried on, and finished.—ENTICK.

The older traditions of Masonry say, "that the only actual Freemasons who were present at the building of the Temple, were the three thousand three hundred overseers, mentioned in 1 Kings, v. 16, added to the three hundred who were called Ghiblimites, and were in fact masters over all the operative Masons employed in the work."

This arrangement produced the happiest effects, and introduced among the fraternity that perfect harmony and universal brotherhood which is so often referred to in our ancient charges.*

Masonic tradition says that the workmen were divided into classes or degrees, and to each class were assigned different methods of recognition.   There is no doubt that there was an organization among the Jews which extended beyond Judea.   The Bible exhibits them mixing themselves with the Tyrians or Dionysian artificers, notwithstanding the ordinary repugnance of the Israelites toward strangers, and that they recognized each other by words and secret signs similar to those employed by natives of other countries.   There was also between the Jews and Tyrians a conformity of allegorical taste, particularly in all that affected sacred architecture.

So perfect was the organization among the vast number of workmen, and so systematic the distribution of labor, that Solomon's Temple, with all its gorgeous splendor and minute ornaments in detail, was finished in little more than seven years from the laying of the foundation-stone; while the Temple of Herod, where the same accurate arrangement did not exist, occupied thirty-six years; that of Diana, at Ephesus, two hundred years; St. Peter's Cathedral at Rome, one hundred and fifty-five years; and St. Paul's in London, thirty-five years in building.

Many of.Solomon's Masons, before he died, began to travel. The royal descendants of King Solomon continued to occupy the throne and patronize the noble art of Freemasonry until the reign of Josiah, the last king of Judah. With no people did the Masons seem to exercise a greater or more beneficial influence than the Gentiles. The Syrians built a lofty temple, and a royal palace at Damascus, and other cities on the coast and throughout Syria.

---

* They were instructed to " salute one another in a courteous manner, calling each other brother; freely giving mutual instruction, as might be thought expedient, without being overseen or overheard, and without encroaching upon each other, or derogating from that respect which was due to any Brother, were he not a Mason; for although all Masons are, as Brethren, upon the same level, yet Masonry takes no honor from a man that he had before; nay, it rather adds to his honor, especially if he has deserved well of the brotherhood."—ANCIENT CHARGES.

About thirty-five years after the death of Solomon, the Temple of Diana, built by some Japhitites, in the days of Moses, was burned down, and the kings of Lesser Asia re-built and ornamented it in the most splendid manner. This temple was regarded by all as pre-eminently magnificent, and hence became the third of the seven wonders of the world.

In the twelfth year of Jotham, king of Judah, A. M. 3256, Sardanapalus was besieged by his brothers Eser and Nabo-nassar, until, in despair, he burned himself, and all his treasure, in the old palace of Nimrod, when the Assyrian Empire was divided between Tiglath Pul Eser and Nabo-nassar. In the days of the latter Prince, who ruled over Chaldea, much attention was given to the study of astrono-my, and so great was the advancement made in the science that after-generations styled this the astronomical era. In one of the degrees of Masonry we have a tradition that after Noah safely landed on Mount Ararat, and offered up sacri-fice to God on an altar which he erected, that he turned his attention to the cultivation of the earth for one hundred years; when, his posterity becoming numerous, he ordered them to disperse themselves and take possession of the earth according to the partition which he made; that they traveled a westerly course until they came to the plains of Shinar, when they counseled together, and, fearing the consequences of a separation, and being desirous to establish for them-selves a name, built the city of Babylon and the Tower of Babel.

We will not attempt to trace Masonry into every country, and point out the various cities that were built or adorned by the traveling Masons who had assisted in the erection of Solomon's Temple, but will be content to look at some of the more prominent places.

Masonry not only flourished in Eastern Asia, but it took a westerly direction also. Boristhenes, in Pontus, was built about the period of which we are writing. Prusias and Chalcedon, in Bithynia, Constantinople (then called Bizan-tium), and Lampsacus, in the Hellespont. The travelers also penetrated into Rome, Ravenna, Florence, and many other cities in Italy; Granada and Malaga, and other cities of Spain; and also on the coast of Gaul.

In A. M. 3416, or B. C. 588, four hundred and sixteen years after the completion of the Temple, the powerful army of Nebuchadnezzar entered Jerusalem, after a protracted siege, and took all the sacred vessels, removing the two famous pillars, Jachin and Boaz, robbed the city and the king's pal-ace of all the riches they contained, and then set fire to the Temple and city, overthrew the walls of the towns, and car-ried away thousands of the people captives to the city of

Babylon, among whom were many of those noble-hearted Giblemites who descended from the builders of Solomon's Temple. And Masonic tradition informs us that they continued to hold secretly their Lodge meetings, and, in this way, taught their children the secrets of Masonry and the principles of the revealed religion of their fathers; for it will be remembered that, previous to the fall of Jerusalem, the power and authority to transcribe the law were confined to the Scribes, and hence but a small portion of the people were in possession of a copy, every copy found having been destroyed by the infidel invader. The captive Jews, therefore, could only perpetuate their religion by teaching it to their children from tradition, as they did Masonry. All the captive Masons were compelled, for the space of fifty-two years, to devote their time, labor, and skill in finishing and ornamenting the buildings which the king of Babylon and his predecessor had commenced, as also the erection of new ones. In this way the Chaldean Masons, who wrought with the captive Jews, perfected themselves in architecture, for the results of their joint labor made Babylon the fourth of the seven wonders of art and the boasted mistress of the world. Thus labored and toiled the true descendants of the children of Israel, borne down with oppression and slavery, and often denied the privilege of worshiping the God of their fathers. But their long sufferings were destined to result in good; for the very opposite effect to that sought by the king of Babylon was the result of their long and painful captivity, for when the proclamation of Cyrus was issued for the liberation of the Israelites, according to the word of God, these architects were better prepared to return to the land they so much loved, and lay the foundation for the rebuilding of the Temple and the city of Jerusalem.

In 536 B. C. the Jews were liberated from Babylonish captivity by Cyrus, king of Persia, who, in the first year of his reign, issued the following proclamation : "Thus saith Cyrus, king of Persia : The Lord God of heaven hath given me all the kingdoms of the earth ; and he hath charged me to build him a house at Jerusalem, which is in Judea. Who is there among you of all his people? his God be with him, and let him go up to Jerusalem, which is in Judea, and build the house of the Lord God of Israel, which is in Jerusalem."

These "glad tidings of great joy" were received by the liberated captives with shouting and praise—for they were permitted to return to their former homes. Forty-two thousand three hundred and sixty of the exiled Jews repaired, in the same year, from Babylon and the neighboring cities to Jerusalem. The leaders of these were Zerubbabel, Joshua, and Haggai, who perform an important part in the Royal Arch degree.

From this period the fraternity of traveling Masons passed into Greece, Rome, Spain, and other countries, where their services could be employed in the erection of the famous edifices for which the ancient world is justly celebrated.

In passing, in this brief outline, from the condition of the fraternity in what we may properly denominate the ancient history, we will endeavor to trace its progress from that period to the more enlightened days of modern architecture, and the cultivation of the arts and sciences, in such chronological order as will give the most concise historical facts in detail—these facts being based upon substantial documents and the principal monuments erected by the traveling operative fraternities or Freemasons. In 715 before the Christian era, the Roman Colleges of Constructors were established, composed of men learned in all the arts and trades necessary for the execution of civil, religious, naval, and hydraulic architecture, with their own laws and judges—laws based on those of the Dyonisian artificers, whose mysteries had spread among the principal peoples of the East. Numa Pompilius, in founding these colleges, made them at the same time civil and religious societies, with the exclusive privilege of building temples and public edifices—their relations to the state and the priesthood being precisely determined by the laws. They had their own jurisdiction and laws; at their head were presidents called Masters, Overseers or Wardens, Censors, Treasurers, Keepers of the Seals, Archivists, and Secretaries; they had their own physicians and serving brethren, and paid monthly dues. The number of members to each college was fixed by law. Composed, principally, of Greek artisans, they surrounded the secrets of their art and doctrines by the mysteries of their country, and concealed them in symbols borrowed from these mysteries and from their own arcana, one of the characteristics of which was the symbolic employment of the utensils of their profession.

710. Numa, the great legislator who founded the colleges, at once assigned them labors of more than ordinary importance. First, the enlargement of the capitol, then the completion of the temples dedicated to the Sun, Moon, Saturn, Mars, and other divinities, commenced under Romulus and other Sabine kings. On the termination of these labors Numa directed the construction of temples to Faith, to Fidelity, to Romulus, and Janus, the god of peace, specially adored by Numa; he caused the city to be fortified, and surrounded it with walls. He also continued labor on the famous temple erected by Romulus to Jupiter, on the spot where his army, about to flee, was induced to fight by the prayer addressed by Romulus to that deity. The great number of temples established in Rome since Romulus are due to the custom that the general-in-chief should erect a temple

to the deity invoked by him in the course of a victorious battle; this also explains the number of temples erected to the same divinity. They were learned in the religious or symbolic teachings of the period as well as in the arts and sciences.

610. Under the reign of the elder Tarquin temples were erected to Jupiter, Juno, and Minerva; he caused the erection of a city wall of hewn stone (614), a sewer for improving the health of the city, and many other public monuments. The first circus was constructed by his order.

580. Servius Tullius again enlarged Rome by the addition of three neighboring eminences, which he surrounded by a wall: he also built temples to Fortune and Diana.

500. Building of the temples of Vesta, Hercules, Pallas, and Minerva, under Junius Drusius.

490. The consuls Sempronius and Minucius cause the building by the colleges of constructors of two temples, one dedicated to Saturn, the other to Mercury: they also establish the Saturnalian feasts.

451. Creation of the law of the Twelve Tables, the VIIIth relating to the colleges of builders.

390. Taking of Rome by the Gauls and destruction of various monuments.

385. The ruined monuments are rebuilt, and new temples constructed under F. Quintius, who dedicated them to Mars, Juno, Health, and Concord.

312. The first paved road was constructed by the colleges, under the orders of Appius Claudius, who had it extended to Capua. The first great aqueduct was built at this time.

290. The temple to Romulus, under the title Quirinus, was built, and in it was placed the first sun-dial, due to the consul Spurius. Carvilius, who also built a temple to *Fortis-Fortuna*, to contain the spoils taken from the Etruscans. A temple in honor of Esculapius is built on an island in the Tiber.

285. The fraternities of builders, as they were then called, attached to the Roman legions, establish themselves in Cisalpine Gaul (Venezia and Lombardy), on the conquest of that country by the Romans; these fraternities, a detachment of which accompanied each legion, were charged with the duty of drawing plans for all military constructions, such as intrenched camps, strategic roads, bridges, aqueducts, dwellings, etc.; they directed the soldiers and laborers in the actual execution of these works; and they also made the instruments of warfare. So far as related to matters directly pertaining to the war, they were under the orders of the generals or chiefs of the legions, but in all other matters enjoyed their peculiar privileges. Composed of artists and learned

men, these fraternities propagated not only a knowledge of the G∴ A∴ O∴ T∴ U∴ but a taste for the proprieties of life, and for literature and the Roman arts, wherever that nation bore its victorious arms. They also taught the vanquished and the oppressed the pacific element of the Roman power—art and civil law.

375. The conquest of nearly all of Cisalpine Gaul (Sardinian States) introduced the building fraternities, never remaining inactive, and ever rebuilding in better style those monuments which the legions had destroyed.

250. While Cisalpine Gaul was being covered with military colonies surrounded by fortifications, executed by the fraternities, who constructed within them habitations and palaces for the military chiefs, other legions push their conquests beyond the Alps, into Transalpine Gaul and Spain. The first causeway was built from Rome through Gaul, to the valley of Ostia.

225. The fraternities of builders continued to follow the legions and fulfil their mission; in Spain they founded *Cordova;* in Gaul *Empodorum,* where they built a famous circus, to which the consul Flaminius gave his name.

220. The Romans, attacked by Hannibal, built, after his retreat, and in memory of that occurrence, a temple to Ridicule. A grand strategic road was constructed by the Roman soldiers, under direction of the colleges. Flaminius, the censor, built a circus in Rome.

210. During the second Punic war the colleges, having nothing to do at Rome, where no buildings were in progress, journeyed to the conquered provinces.

200. The Roman people decided to build a temple to Mars and another to Romulus and Renus, the founders of Rome. These two temples were nearly completed during the same year.

148. The first marble temple was due to General Metellus, who consecrated it to Jupiter, after his victory over the king of Macedonia; he built another temple at his own expense, which he dedicated to Juno; also a remarkable sepulcher, bearing his own name.

125. The legions, having taken possession of Helvetia, fortified themselves, and by gradually enlarging founded a number of cities.

121. A Roman colony, commanded by Marsius, founded Narbonne, which became the principal stronghold of the Romans, until the time of Augustus. The Consul Opimius caused the erection at Rome of the first basilic; to him is also due the elevation of a temple to Concord.

101. Marius, after his victory over the Cimbres and Teutons, caused the erection in Rome, under the special direction

of the architect Musius, of two temples, one dedicated to Honor, the other to Virtue.*

79. Herculaneum, an ancient city, containing many monuments erected by the building fraternities, was buried under the lava of Vesuvius. Pompeii, not less celebrated than Herculaneum, and whose monuments were fully equal to those of Rome, likewise disappeared beneath the ashes and lava from an eruption of Vesuvius in this year.

60. Julius Cesar became master of Transalpine Gaul (France, Belgium, and Switzerland), after ten years of struggles, during which, according to Plutarch, more than 800 Gallic cities were devastated. Cesar gave occupation to the corporations in Gaul as well as others summoned by him to rebuild these cities, aided by his soldiers.

55. Britain, which at this time was partially conquered, received strong re-enforcements of builders sent to establish more extended fortifications. Under command of Julius Cesar, one of the legions pushed forward into the interior of the country, and, to defend themselves, formed an intrenched camp with walls, inside of which, as elsewhere, habitations, temples, and aqueducts appeared. And from it arose *Eboracum* (York), a city celebrated in the history of Freemasonry.

50. While Julius Cesar, pursuing his conquests, destroyed all the Celtic monuments and Druidical altars, Pompey caused the building in Rome of numerous temples and the famous marble amphitheater, capable of holding thirty thousand persons; he also caused the completion by the fraternities of builders of the no less famous highway from Italy across the Alps into Gaul. When Julius Cesar returned to Rome he also built various temples to Mars, Apollo, and Venus. He sent all the colleges actually in Italy to Carthage and Corinth to raise those cities from their ruins.

45. The Roman senate, after the civil war, directed the colleges of constructors to build various monuments in honor of Julius Cesar; among others four temples, to Liberty, Concord, Happiness, and Mercy.

42. The Triumvirs caused a temple to be erected to Isis, and another to Serapis.

37. The Roman legions, stationed on the banks of the Rhine to guard the Gallic country against the continual aggressions of the Germans, found at various points intrenched camps, which became important colonies. Cologne thus be-

---

* Up to this period architecture had preserved the Etruscan character, and the attempts to embellish the temples and other edifices consisted only in ornamenting them with statues and other objects taken from subjugated countries, especially Greece; but from this time forward the predilection of the Romans for Grecian architecture became dominant, and the Etruscan was abandoned.

gan, and was afterward invested with the rights of a Roman city under Claudius.

35. The Pantheon was finished under Marcus Agrippa, who also constructed magnificent baths, which bore his name. The great Cisalpine highway was continued by his orders, under direction of the corporations.

32. The legions established in Paris erected, alongside of the Gallic altars, temples to Isis and Mithra.

30. The reign of Augustus was fertile in splendid monuments. The building fraternities were greatly augmented, and a certain number formed special colleges devoted to naval and hydraulic architecture. The great learning of these men initiated in all arts, the generous principles professed by them, their mysterious organization, surrounded them with so much consideration that many distinguished men sought to participate in their privileges. The most important monuments erected by them at this period were, at Rome, the temple to Jupiter, the theater commenced under the consulate of Claudius Marcellus, the mausoleum bearing the name of Augustus, two triumphal arches also bearing his name, two Egyptian obelisks: in Roman provinces we will only mention the temple of Clitum at Foligni, of Jupiter at Pozuoli, the triumphal arch at Susa. In Gaul a large number of less pretentious monuments ornamented the cities rebuilt or founded by the Romans. A part of the high roads, and notably that of Emporium near the Pyrenees, were due to the orders of Augustus. The friends of this emperor rivaled him in building sumptuous monuments; Statilius Taurus built an amphitheater; Marcus Phillipus a temple to Hercules; Munatius Plancus one to Saturn; Lucius Carnifucius one to Diana; Lucius Cornelius Balbus finished his great theater in stone.

In the first year of the Christian era Augustus caused the building of a temple in honor of his friends Caius and Lucius, the remains of which are known as the square house.

5. The Jewish architects received protection at Rome, where, under Julius Cesar, they were allowed to establish synagogues. Admitted to the colleges of builders, they imparted to them a knowledge of the Hebrew mysteries.

10. Vitruvius Pollio, the celebrated architect, in his works on the subject, mentions the brilliant state of the art at Rome during this period, and speaks of its doctrines as vailed in allegories and symbols.

14. The palace of the Cesars, commenced under Tiberius, continued under Caligula (37), and finished under Domitian (81). Tiberius built a triumphal arch in honor of his brother Claudius Drusus, also one to Augustus and another to Castor.

25. The bridge of Rimini begun by Augustus was finished by Tiberius, who also built temples in honor of Proserpine, Juno, and the goddess of Concord.

41. A superb aqueduct erected under Claudius, bears his name.

43. Detachments of builders from the fraternities along the Rhine were sent by the Emperor Claudius to Britain, where the legions experienced great difficulty in maintaining themselves against the incursions of the Caledonians; they constructed a number of fortresses beyond the camps.

50. At this time architecture reached its culminating point in Rome; the colleges, discouraged by the despotism of the emperors, who gradually deprived them of their privileges, lost their cultivated taste. The monuments of this period were far from attaining the elevated character which placed them among the most sublime creations of human intelligence. The same decay was observed in the Grecian monuments, from which the Romans had borrowed their finest models. The principal cause of this decay was the fact that the most skillful and highly educated architects were sent by Julius Cesar or Augustus into the conquered provinces to build imposing monuments, in order to give the people an elevated idea of the arts and sciences possessed by the conquerors; to inspire them, in short, with admiration. The colleges, concentrating, as they did, among their members most of the acquirements of that time, undoubtedly added as much by their labors to the glory and power of Rome as was contributed by force of arms. Among the architects, or *magistri*, as they were called, of this period, a number busied themselves by writing for the information of their distant brethren works on the theory and rules of their art. The most celebrated of these were Vitruvius Pollio, Fulvitius, Varron, Publius and Septimus. The works of the first only survive.

54. Various temples, baths, and acqueducts constructed under Nero, who, after burning the city of Rome, and destroying many fine monuments, built his celebrated golden palace.

70. Flavius Vespasian constructed the Coliseum, at which 12,000 Jewish prisoners worked. It held 110,000 persons, but was not completed till the reign of Titus (80).

98. Under Trajan was built the famous circus capable of holding 260,000 persons.

120. Under the reign of Adrian many new and costly temples were erected at Rome, particularly the one devoted to the service of Venus. The superb column in honor of Ulpius Trajanus, the emperor, was constructed by the most distinguished of the builders by order of Adrian. He also constructed the mausoleum, known to this day as the castle of St. Angelo. The celebrated architect Apollodorus, to whom was due the honor of arranging the plans of that building, was banished for having uttered some facts not pleasing to

GRAND TRIUMPHAL ARCH OF TITUS, AT ROME.

the emperor. Adrian, with great industry and a display of unusual ability in architectural knowledge, visited the various provinces of his vast empire. In Britain he ordered the construction, by the fraternities of builders, many of which accompanied him, of an immense wall, which, extending from the Tyne to the Gulf of Solway, thus crossing the country from east to west, to protect the military colonies from the continual invasion of the Scots and other clans. Asia is indebted to him for many valuable public monuments; but it was Greece that was particularly favored with his remarkable abilities as an architect, throughout which country he ordered the erection of many of her most celebrated temples, such as the Pantheon and the temples to Jupiter Olympus with its 122 columns.

130. After the fall of the Roman republic all the corpora tions founded at the same time as the colleges of builders, by Numa Pompilius, lost their ancient privileges. The colleges were somewhat restrained by Trajan and Adrian, notwithstanding most of their privileges were left that their talents might still be employed.

140. During the reign of the Emperor Antonius, temples were erected to Mars, besides many others for civic purposes. Another great wall was built in Britain, where the Roman legions were constantly menaced by the marauding bands that then infested the country. About this period the Masonic fraternities, the remains of the ancient Roman colleges of builders, who, in the time of the Christian persecutions ordered by Nero, Domitian, and Trajan, sought refuge in those provinces the most distant from Rome, and which were governed by men more humane than the emperors, that those beautiful masterpieces of architectural grandeur were erected.

166. The greater part of the members of colleges at Rome embraced Christianity. The Emperor Marcus Aurelius, irritated at the progress made by this new doctrine, and determined to destroy it by force, ordered during this year fresh persecutions against the Christians, in consequence of which many of them residing in Gaul took refuge with the corporations in Britain, where greater protection was afforded them than elsewhere. The Christian Masons at Rome sought in the catacombs a secret asylum from the edicts fulminated against them, and an escape from the tortures to which they were condemned. In these dark vaults they met with their co-religionists. During the ten years of persecution under Marcus Aurelius they transformed the catacombs into churches, ornamented with sarcophagi and encaustic paintings; their faith inspired these Christian artists to build chapels and altars on the tombs of the martyrs.

180-275. This period is marked in the history of architecture by one of the most sublime conceptions of the artistic genius of the builders, executed under the reign and by the orders of the Emperor Aurelian—the two temples of Helios at Palmyra, which, in beauty and grandeur, surpass those of Heliopolis. The larger of these temples had 464 columns, many of them from a single block of marble. The total number of columns decorating the two temples and the galleries belonging to them was 1,450.

287–290. Carausius, commander of the Roman fleet, took possession of Britain, and declared himself emperor. To conciliate the Masonic fraternities, then wielding an immense influence in the country, he restored their ancient privileges; since which time they have been called privileged or Free-Masons, to distinguish them from those not thus entitled.

293. Albanus, a converted pagan, was, by order of Carausius, decapitated on account of his faith. In this manner a grand master of Freemasons became the first Christian martyr in Britain.

296. The city of York, in which many Lodges of Freemasons were established, was selected as the residence of Constantius Chlorus, who came to Britain, after the death of Carausius, to assume the control of the government of the country.

300. At this time there were in Rome more than 500 temples, 37 gates and triumphal arches, 6 bridges, 17 amphitheaters and theaters, 14 aqueducts, 5 obelisks, many monumental columns, mausoleums, baths, and sepulchers, all of which were built by the fraternities, or colleges of archi tects.

303. Under the reign of the Emperor Diocletian there were erected, in many of the Roman provinces, numerous aqueducts, temples, and costly baths, by the fraternities that remained in the country. This emperor was particularly distinguished for his atrocious persecutions of the Christians, many of whom were executed with cruelty in the more distant provinces. Notwithstanding the humanity of the ruling governor of Britain, the Christians, of whom a great number were members of the Masonic fraternities, found it necessary to seek refuge in Scotland and many of the adjacent islands, where they were permitted to enjoy their religion and study the arts of architecture. Many of these artisans attached to the colleges established at Rome also fled to the East, or buried themselves within the catacombs—their usual place of refuge in times of religious persecution—where many of them perished.

313. End of the persecutions against the Christians by edict of Constantine, who declared Christianity the religion of the State.

325. The Church of the Lateran at Rome built by order

of Constantine, and one dedicated to St. Paul, in the form of a cross. The form of the Greek cross used by the Christian architects was chosen by them, not because it was ordered by Constantine, but because of its mysterious relation to the religion of all nations, and as a part of their symbolism and the secret teachings of their colleges. It formed the ground-plan of the temple at Jerusalem, and represented unity and trinity. For the general details of their edifices, Solomon's Temple served as a model, being recognized as a masterpiece of architecture, and the first temple erected and dedicated to one God.

360. The Emperor Julian built a magnificent temple and vast baths at Paris, where the remains still exist.

600. Foundation of Canterbury Cathedral and that at Rochester (602).

605. Foundation of St. Paul's Church, London.

620. The corporations are exclusively engaged and directed by the religious orders. An abbot or other ecclesiastic generally presided in the lodges, and was termed venerable, or worshipful Master.

925. At this period every considerable town in Britain had its lodge of Freemasons; but their relations to each other were not intimate, which is explained by the wars and divisions of five centuries and seven kingdoms. During the Danish war, when the monasteries were destroyed, the fraternity suffered an irreparable loss in the destruction of all their documents. Athelstane, grandson of Alfred the Great, educated by the priest-architects, caused his son Edwin to be instructed in the art, and named him Grand Master. He convened a general assembly at York, to whom he submitted a constitution, which was discussed and accepted.

960. On the death of Athelstane the fraternity were again dispersed, many of them passing over to Germany and remaining there, under the name of Brothers of St. John.

1001. In the early years of this period the world was in a measure paralyzed by the idea that the end of time had arrived; but at last, getting the better of their superstitions, especially as the earth continued to revolve on its axis, society awakened from its lethargy, and from that time (1003) our modern civilization may be said to date.

1250. A remarkable period, in which were conceived the plans of those wonderful sanctuaries of the Almighty which are the admiration of posterity for their gigantic dimensions and the harmony of their proportions. The plans of the cathedrals of Cologne, Strasburg, Paris, Rheims, Rouen, Beauvais, Amiens, and others of which the foundations were laid toward the close of the XIIth century, but which were finally executed on a larger scale and in a different style from the original design. The striking analogy between these monuments and those which followed, up to the XVth century, is explained by the bond of fraternity which united the Masons of all countries who had received their instructions from the central school in Lombardy, continued at Cologne and Strasburg, and further by the obedience of the members to the laws which governed them in the construction of all religious edifices, from which they were only allowed to depart in the details of ornamentation.

1272. The construction of Westminster Abbey was completed this year, under direction of the grand master Giffard, Archbishop of York.

1275. A Masonic Congress was convoked by Erwin de Steinbach for the resumption of the long-interrupted labors of the Strasburg cathedral on a grander scale than that upon which the foundations were laid in 1015, and a part of the church erected. Architects from many countries arrived in Strasburg, formed, as in England and according to ancient usage, a Grand Lodge, and bound themselves to observe the laws and regulations of the craft. Near the cathedral was a wooden building (lodge), where the meetings were held and where all matters in relation to the building were discussed. Erwin de Steinbach was elected to preside, and at the meetings held a sword in his hand and was seated on a dais. Words and signs were invented, partly those used in England. Apprentices, Craftsmen, and Masters were received with peculiar symbolic ceremonies, beneath which were concealed or indicated the secrets of architecture.

1310. The construction of the magnificent cathedral of Cologne, begun in 1248, gave to its lodge a certain superiority and made it the school where Masons of other countries came to study this masterpiece. The German Masons, recognizing that superiority, gave it the title of Grand Lodge (*Haupthutte*), and the master architect was regarded as the master of all Masons in Germany.

1312. A small number of Templars, escaped from the persecutions of Philip, king of France, and the Pope, Clement V., took refuge in Scotland, before the death of their Grand Master, Jacques de Molay (1314), and found an asylum in the Masonic lodges.

1314. The Lodge of Kilwinning, in Scotland, founded during the building of the abbey of that name in 1150, assumed the rank of Grand Royal Lodge of Herodom, under authority of Robert Bruce, who also founded an order of the same name for the Masons who had fought for him.

1350. The York Constitutions were revised during the reign of Edward III. In an appendix it is prescribed, among other things, that in future at the making of a brother the Master of the Lodge shall read to him the Constitution and Ancient Charges.

1502. A Lodge of Masters convened June 24, under direction of Henry VII., moved in procession to lay the corner-stone of a chapel at Westminster, bearing the name of Henry VII.

1535. The intelligence spread by the lodges formed out-side of the corporations awakened the suspicions and hatred of the ultramontane clergy, who accused them both openly and in secret of aiding the reform of Luther, who was said to belong to them. They were accused by the priests of seeking to introduce schisms into the Church and sedition among the people, of hatred against the Supreme Pontiff and all sovereigns, and, finally, of a desire to reëstablish the Order of Templars, and to avenge the death of their Grand Master on the descendants of the kings, who were the cause of it. It is said that a convention of these associations was held at Cologne June 24 in this year, at which Herman V., Bishop of Cologne, presided, when they drew up a document announcing their doctrines and the aim of their association, so that if the intolerance of their fellow-citizens should prevent them from maintaining their organization they might propagate their doctrines in other parts of the globe. That document was the Charter of Cologne.

1561. Queen Elizabeth of England, being suspicious of the Masons, sent a detachment of armed men to break up the annual assembly at York. The officers sent for this purpose made so favorable a report that the queen revoked her order, and ultimately became the protectress of the Fraternity.

1607. Freemasonry flourished in England, where, under the reign of James I., who declared himself their protector, it acquired fame and importance, and many gentlemen and persons of mark were initiated. The high consideration accorded the Craft at this period was further augmented by the election of the celebrated architect Inigo Jones to the dignity of Grand Master, who infused great spirit into the lodges.

1646. The Masonic corporations in England, in which for a long time the majority had been composed of learned men, artists, men eminent for knowledge and position, who were received as honorary members, and termed *accepted* Masons, no longer busied themselves with the material and primary object of the association. It was at this time that the celebrated antiquary Elias Ashmole, who founded the museum at Oxford, having been initiated, rectified and composed the formula for the society of Rose-Croix, consisting of ceremonies based on historical allusions, and the communication of signs of recognition after the manner of the

Freemasons. This labor inspired him with the idea of composing new rituals for the Masons, and accordingly he composed and substituted for the rituals in use a new mode of initiation, based, in part, on old Anglo-Saxon and Syriac manuscripts, partly on the Egyptian mysteries, and on what he supposed to have been the form of initiation among the Roman architects. These rituals were adopted by the London lodges, and soon after throughout England.

1650. Freemasonry, in England, took a political bias; after the decapitation of Charles I. the Masons of England, and particularly those of Scotland, partisans of the Stuarts, labored in secret for the re-establishment of the throne destroyed by Cromwell. They used the mystery surrounding their assemblies to lay their plans in security. Unable to admit all Masons to their projects, they composed superior degrees to the initiates, in which they alone unfolded their plans. It was by the influence of these men, placed in high position, that Charles II., initiated during his exile, was raised to the throne in 1660, and it was by this monarch that Masonry was termed *the Royal art*, because it had principally contributed to his restoration.

1663. General assembly at York, Charles II. presiding, who confirmed the Grand Mastership of Henry Jermyn, Count of St. Albans, and conferred on him the Order of the Bath. The assembly passed a series of regulations, all in conformity with past events, and maintained the high degrees. The preponderance of Accepted Masons became more evident; but having no longer to struggle against political events, the superior degrees assumed a universal and humanitarian tendency. Cultivation of the arts and sciences, and sociability, under noble and elevated forms, became the features of their meetings.

1666. The great fire in London, which destroyed forty thousand houses and eighty-six churches, gave a new impetus to architecture. The local craftsmen being unable to meet the demand for labor, others were called in from all countries. They united in a Lodge, under the authority of Sir Christopher Wren, architect of St. Paul's, who furnished plans for rebuilding the city.

1685. James II., Grand Master of the Order of Herodom of Kilwinning, founded by Robert Bruce, King of Scotland, in 1314, in favor of the Freemasons who had fought under his banners, reëstablished the Order of Knights of St. Andrew, which had been suspended, and the possessions of which were confiscated during the Reformation. It was the intention of the king to have made this Order a sign of distinction and reward for Masons in particular, and it is probable that but for his misfortunes he would have returned their property. -

1700. The Masonic corporations, except in England, were dissolved, and even in that country they were no longer busy with operative Masonry.

1703. Notwithstanding the zeal displayed by Grand Master Wren, the number of Masons was continually diminishing. The annual feasts were completely neglected, and the four lodges remaining in London deserted. Differences of opinion among the Fraternity respecting the propriety of extending its privileges to others than those educated in the science of architecture prevented the increase of its membership, and little progress was made until after the death of Grand Master Wren (1716).

1717. The four lodges in London determined to elect a new Grand Master, and form a Grand Lodge. They, therefore, convened a general assembly of the Masons in London and its vicinity, and constituted a central authority under the title of "The Grand Lodge of England," recognizing only the three symbolic degrees. George Payne, elected Grand Master, got together a great quantity of ancient manuscripts, charts, rituals, and documents on the usages of the Fraternity, which, added to those in possession of St. Paul's Lodge, were to form a code of laws and doctrines, certain of which were to be published.

1720. The Grand Lodge having constituted several subordinates, in which many persons of distinction were initiated, the Grand Lodge of York became jealous of its rival, and proscribed its members. About this time the institution met with a severe loss in the destruction of important manuscripts committed to the flames by over-scrupulous members of St. Paul's Lodge, who were alarmed at the proposed publicity about to be given them.

1721. Freemasonry began to extend to the continent. One Lodge was founded at Dunkirk and another at Mons. The Grand Lodge adopted various regulations concerning the government of the lodges, and regularity of their work. The rights of the Grand Master were determined, and he was accorded the right of naming his successor in case of his dismission or non-election. George Payne, having been again elected, gathered such documents as had escaped the flames the preceding year, and from them drew up a historical sketch of the society, which he submitted to the Grand Lodge with certain regulations. This was referred to the committee, who further referred it to Bro. Anderson, and he, after revising it, was authorized to publish it (1722).

1721–1725. Masonry introduced in France, and several lodges constituted.

1729. The activity of the English lodges and their attractiveness stimulated the Masons of Ireland to greater zeal,

and they established a central authority by the name of
" The Grand Lodge of Ireland."

1732. The Grand Lodge at York, to which belonged the
Masons calling themselves ancient, and whose constitution
was more in accordance with the old corporations, recognized the necessity of conforming to the new order of things
as more clearly expressed in the London Constitution.

1733. The first Provincial Grand Lodge in America was
constituted at Boston.

1735. The first persecutions against Masons in modern
times commenced by the States General of Holland, which
interdicted Masonic assemblies.

1736. The Scottish Grand Lodge at Edinburg, in view of
the prosperous state of the English lodges growing out of
their constitution and Grand Mastership, became desirous
of introducing the same system, but was prevented by the
hereditary office of patron, created by James I., for the
Roslin family in 1430. The then Grand Master Baron
Sinclair, of Roslin, consented to resign. The four oldest
lodges in Edinburg called a general assembly, thirty-two
lodges being represented, and the Baron having resigned his
Grand Mastership and all the privileges attached to it, a
regular Grand Lodge was formed, and he was elected its
first Grand Master.

1738. The Pope, Clement XII., issued a bull of excommunication against the Freemasons, which was followed by an
edict of Charles VI., forbidding Masonic meetings in the
low countries of Austria.

August 15, in this year, Frederick II., King of Prussia,
was initiated.

1739. The Grand Lodge of England was accused of
changing the ceremonies and ritual, introducing innovations,
and of having named Provincial Deputies with power to
establish lodges in the South of England, the jurisdiction
of the Grand Lodge of York. A schism was the result,
and a new Grand Lodge was formed with the designation
of " Ancients." The Grand Lodges of Ireland and Scotland sympathized with the ancients, but the moderns were
decidedly the most successful.

In the same year Cardinal Ferraro, in an edict intended to
prevent any misunderstanding of the Papal bull against the
Freemasons, explained it to mean that " no one should dare
to unite, assemble with, or affiliate in, the society, nor be
present at its meetings, under penalty of death and confiscation of their goods, without hope of remission or pardon;
that all proprietors were forbidden to allow any Masonic assembly on their premises under penalty of having their houses
demolished, being fined and sent to the galleys."

1740. At this time there were more than two hundred lodges in France, of which twenty-two were in Paris.

1744. The Lodge of the Three Globes at Berlin, founded by Baron Bielefeld in 1740, was raised to the dignity of a Grand Lodge by Frederick the Great, king of Prussia, who was elected Grand Master, and continued in office till 1747.

1751. At this period Freemasonry had found its way into all civilized countries. Its humane and elevating principles, its dogma of liberty, equality, and fraternity, alarmed the kings and clergy, and they sought to arrest its progress. Edicts were fulminated against it in Russia (1731), its meetings forbidden in Holland (1735), and at Paris (1737, '38, '44, '45), its members arrested and persecuted at Rome and Florence, their meetings forbidden in Sweden, at Hamburg, and Geneva (1738); the Inquisition cast them into prison and caused the executioner to burn the books which treated of its doctrines. The Inquisition also caused knights who had been present at Masonic meetings to be perpetually exiled to Malta (1740). In Portugal, unheard-of cruelties were practiced against them, including condemnation to the galleys, at Vienna (1735); even the Sultan undertook to annihilate them (1748). As a worthy climax to this series of persecutions, Charles, king of Naples, forbid the practice of Masonry in his states; Ferdinand VII., king of Spain, forbid Masonic assemblies under penalty of death; and Pope Benedict XIV. renewed (1751) the bull of excommunication against the Freemasons, issued by Clement XII. in 1738. But all this violence failed to check the progress of the institution, which spread over the face of the globe with a rapidity which nothing could stop. Notwithstanding Benedict's bull, Masonry was openly practiced at Tuscany, Naples, and several other parts of the Italian peninsula. Even at Rome there were lodges which hardly took the trouble to conceal themselves.

1754. A chapter of the high degrees was founded at Paris, by the Chevalier de Bonneville, under the title of Clermont. In it was revived the Templar system, invented by the partisans of the Stuarts.

1755. The Grand Lodge of England first issued individual diplomas.

1756. The English Grand Lodge of France, founded in 1736, and which assumed this title in 1743, cast off its allegiance to England and assumed the title of Grand Lodge of France. The disorders which had arisen under the Grand Mastership of Prince de Clermont were continued, and even augmented. By warrants delivered to Masters of lodges, as well by herself as by the Lodge of St. Andrew of Scotland, at Edinburg, Masonic authorities of all kinds were multiplied in France; illegal warrants were delivered by pretended Masters of lodges; false titles were fabricated; antedated charters, bearing falsehood on their faces, were set afloat without any notice on the part of the Grand Lodge. When she declared her independence she also announced her intention of adhering to the Scottish custom of giving personal warrants to Masters for life, thus putting the climax to the existing disorder. The result was that these Masters governed their lodges according to their own caprice, giving warrants to other Masters at Paris and in the provinces, who, in turn, constituted others; other bodies rivaling the Grand Lodge were formed as Chapters, Councils, Colleges, and Tribunals, at Paris and elsewhere, and they likewise established lodges and chapters. So much confusion resulted that even in France it was not known which was in reality the legitimate body.

1756. Foundation of the National Grand Lodge of Italy, dissolved in 1790. In the same year the Grand Lodge of the United Provinces (Holland) was formed.

1762. Baron de Hunde introduced in Germany the rite of Strict Observance (so-called Templar System), which he had obtained from Paris.

1763. The two factions into which the Grand Lodge of France had been divided in 1761 reunited, but they were unable to stay the tide of disorder which they had previously set in motion.

1764. A person by the name of Johnson, a secret agent of the Jesuits, professing to have plenary powers from the authorities of the Rite of Strict Observance, established chapters of the Templar System particularly at Jena, where he called a Masonic Congress Dec. 25, 1763. He professed to have the sole power of creating knights by virtue of patents from unknown authorities residing in Scotland. He convoked a second congress in 1764, to which the Baron de Hunde was invited, and who at first believed in Johnson's authority; he subsequently, however, exposed him as an impostor, and, at a congress held at Altenberg, in 1765, the Baron himself was elected Grand Master of Templars.

1765. Foundation of the RoyalYork Grand Lodge at Berlin.

1772. Foundation of the Grand Orient of France.

1783. Foundation of the Eclectic Grand Lodge at Frankfort, which promulgated a new rite made up from the variety then existing, and hence called eclectic.

1785. Congress of Paris, called ostensibly to reduce to order the chaos produced by the numerous systems introduced into Masonry. Without good results.

1789. Edict of the Emperor Joseph II. suppressing the lodges throughout his dominions.

1800. The rites and systems of high degrees introduced in the course of the last century, and which had the greatest success were: 1. *The Scottish Rite in Seven Degrees*, brought from England by Doctor Ramsay, in 1736; 2. *The Rite of Swedenborg*, first introduced at Avignon, in 1730; 3. *The System of Strict Observance*, by Baron de Hunde, 1754; 4. *Schroder's Rite* (rectified Rose-Croix) with magic theosophy and alchemy, Berlin, 1766. Subsequently modified and adopted by the Grand Lodge of Hamburg; 5. *Clerks of Strict Observance*, in the interests of Catholicism, 1767; 6. *Swedish Templar Rite*, by Zinnendorf, Berlin, 1767; 7. *Illuminati of Bavaria*, a political society under Masonic forms, 1776; 8. *The Martin System*, a variant of the Scottish rite, 1767; 9. *The Golden Rose-Croix System*, founded in 1616, by Valentine Andrea, a profound philosopher, and revived under Masonic forms in Germany, 1777; 10. *The Scottish Rite in Nine Degrees*, by Fessler, 1798. All these rites or systems, as well as those growing out of them, have either become extinct or been greatly modified.

1804. Foundation of a Supreme Council in France by the Count de Grasse Tilly.

1813. Union of the two Grand Lodges in England. In the act of union it is expressly stated that ancient and true Freemasonry consists of but three degrees: Apprentice, Fellow-Craft, and Master.

1814. Edict of Pius VII. against the Freemasons, pronouncing infamous penalties, even to death and the confiscation of the property of its members. It is needless to add that the accusations contained in this document against the society are entirely without foundation.

1822. Ukase of the Emperor of Russia against the Freemasons.

1824. Edict of the King of Portugal against Masonic assemblies.

1825. Imposing solemnity at Boston in honor of Bro. Lafayette.

1826. The Pope renews the edict of Pius VII. against the Freemasons.

1828. Edict of the king of Spain against the Masonic Fraternity.

1832. Foundation of the Grand Orient of Belgium at Brussels.

1836. Contestations and discussions arose among the German Lodges, especially those at Berlin, in regard to the admission of Israelites. Some lodges refused to initiate them, and others to admit those who had been regularly initiated elsewhere. Addresses were presented by Jewish brethren showing the opposition of this conduct to the true principles of Masonry; but without result, and the same state of affairs continues now.

It seems strange that in these enlightened days a prejudice dating from the middle ages should still sway the minds of men, and stranger still that the Masonic world should not raise its voice against it.

1850. At this period we find Freemasonry spread over the surface of the globe. In Europe it was nearly everywhere flourishing, protected, and respected. England, Ireland, Scotland, Sweden, Denmark, Holland, Prussia, Saxony, the lesser German States, France, Switzerland, and a portion of Bavaria had about 3,000 lodges governed by 21 Grand Lodges. On the other hand, it was prohibited in Russia, Austria, and their dependencies; in the kingdoms of Naples and Sardinia, at Rome, in Tuscany, Spain, and Portugal.

In Africa there were lodges in Algeria, at Alexandria, Cape Town, and other points. In North America it was everywhere known, and lodges were constantly springing up.

In South America, beginning at a later date, it was nevertheless making great progress. It had also been established in Asia and the Ocean islands. So that the number of lodges on the globe were computed at 5,000, of which 3,000 were in Europe, 1,400 in America, and 600 in other parts of the world. Thus, in the course of a century, Freemasonry was propagated over the surface of the globe, scattering in its path the seed of civilization and progress, and impressing on its adepts lessons of truth which have been crystallized into deeds in their intercourse with the world. Little wonder that the partisans of an old and effete order of things, astonished by its peaceful transformations, should oppose, with all their might, the establishment and development of this institution. The influence of Masonry on social progress would unquestionably have been greater had it not, in the last century, been paralyzed by the introduction of numberless incoherent systems, which, essentially contrary to its spirit, destroyed the uniformity and equality on which it rests. These systems gave to Freemasonry a different direction from that indicated by its doctrines, and thus rendering it an object of suspicion to governments, were, in part, to blame for the persecutions levelled against it. It was often abused and assimilated with secret political and religious societies which assumed its name and covered themselves with its mantle to attain an end they dared not avow, such as the Rosicrusians and Illuminati. But when the society shall have got rid of the heterogeneous elements which introduced disorder and hindered its action and influence, nothing can stop the beneficent influence it will exercise on society in general.

The best evidence that may be adduced in favor of the beneficent influence of the institution, is seen in the recent opposition it has elicited from the weak and narrow-minded individuals who make no pretensions to any notion beyond an idea single to a selfish and proselyting ambition. Yet, not withstanding the objections thus raised, the order will move on, spread and flourish. Here we propose to give, in a succinct form, an account of the organization of Grand and Subordinate Masonic bodies, dates of introduction into the several parts of the world, so far as the history could be obtained authentically, and such other facts relative to the progress of Masonry as are deemed worthy of record in a work of this kind.

AFRICA. Freemasonry was introduced into Africa about the year 1736, and is now well known in the European colonies along the coast; the charters for holding lodges emanated from England, France, and the Netherlands. At Monrovia, in the negro state of Liberia, there are lodges of colored Masons, not recognized by the whites, but working under a Grand Lodge of their own.

ALABAMA. Freemasonry was introduced into this State by virtue of charters granted from the Grand Lodges of South Carolina and Tennessee, dates not known.

The GRAND LODGE for the State was organized June 14, 1821.

The GRAND CHAPTER was organized June 2, 1827.

The GRAND COUNCIL of Royal and Select Masters was established in June, 1827.

The GRAND COMMANDERY, Knights Templar, was organized Nov. 29, 1860.

ARKANSAS. The GRAND LODGE of this State was organized Feb. 22, 1832, the centennial anniversary of Washington's birthday.

The GRAND CHAPTER of Royal Arch Masons was organized April 28, 1851.

Hugh de Payens Commandery, Knights Templar, organized Dec. 20, 1853.

ASIA. The introduction of Masonry had its origin in 1728, by warrant from the Grand Lodge of England. The first Lodge was established at Calcutta, by Sir Geo.

Pomfret. In Canton, Hong Kong, Shanghai, and other cities of China, lodges are to be found, working under the English Constitution. In Asia Minor, at Smyrna, two lodges, one working in the English and the other in the German language. In the East Indies there is an English Provincial Grand Lodge, with fifty subordinate lodges. Lodges are established by the Grand Lodge of Scotland in Bengal, Bombay, and Arabia. The Grand Lodge of the Netherlands, and the Grand Orient of France, have subordinate lodges in Java, Sumatra, and Pondichéry. There is scarcely a town in Hindostan in which there is not a Lodge. In the East Indies two Masonic periodicals are published "The Indian Mason," at Bombay, and "The Masonic Record."

AUSTRALIA. Freemasonry was introduced on the islands of this extensive country by the Grand Lodge of England soon after its discovery. There are lodges now established in New South Wales, South Australia, Victoria, Van Dieman's Land, New Zealand, West Australia, Tasmania, the Sandwich Islands, Tahati, and other parts of the territory, by the Grand Lodges of England, Scotland, Ireland, France, and California.

AUSTRIA. The establishment of Freemasonry in Austria was accompanied with great difficulty. The first Lodge was opened in Vienna in 1742, under a warrant from the Grand Lodge of Germany at Berlin. But this body was compelled to cease its meetings through the influence of the papal church authorities. In 1762 several lodges were established in Vienna and Prague, which, notwithstanding the hostility of the church, increased so extensively as to defy its power. The lodges then existing in Bohemia, Hungary, and Transylvania, declared their independence of the Grand Lodge at Berlin, and in 1784 established a Grand Lodge of Austria, with its seat at Vienna.

BAVARIA. The institution of Freemasonry was introduced into Bavaria about the year 1746, and flourished with moderate success until the introduction of the society of the Illuminati, in 1776, when Freemasonry became oppressed because of the attempt of the originator of the Illuminati to engraft his system upon the Masonic rite. In 1784 the lodges voluntarily suspended operations until 1806, when the influence of the institution was again felt throughout the kingdom. The Grand Lodge is located at Munich.

BELGIUM. In 1721 the Grand Lodge of England constituted the first Masonic Lodge in Belgium, at Mons, under the title of Perfect Union. In 1785 there were sixteen lodges established throughout the kingdom. At this period the lodges were composed of the elite of the nation; but, as the sentiments of the brotherhood had become very liberal and patriotic, in May, 1786, the Emperor Joseph II. abolished all the lodges in Belgium except three. Most of them, however, continued their meetings in secret. During the French revolution all the lodges were interdicted, and not until 1798 did they resume operations, but with limited opportunities. In 1814 these lodges declared themselves independent of the Grand Orient of France, and in 1817 organized a Grand Lodge for Belgium and the Netherlands. After the separation of Belgium from the Netherlands in 1830, the latter desired to be entirely independent of the other, which was mutually agreed to. In 1835 most of the lodges placed themselves under the protection of King Leopold. In

1817 the Supreme Council of the Ancient and Accepted Scottish rite was established in Brussels, while the Grand Orient, located also at Brussels, has exclusive control over the symbolic degrees. The two bodies maintain toward each other brotherly intercourse, so that the members of the Grand Orient having the high degrees are considered, on that account, members of the Supreme Council.

BOHEMIA. In 1749 the Grand Lodge of Scotland instituted a Lodge in Prague, Bohemia. The order was highly prosperous until the commencement of the French revolution, when it was suppressed by the Austrian government. On the restoration of peace and the rights of civil law, the Order has been reëstablished, and is highly successful.

BRAZIL. The introduction of Freemasonry into Brazil began as early as 1816; but, owing to the powerful influence of the church authorities, the Order ceased its work until 1820, when several lodges were established there. In 1822 the Grand Orient was founded.

CALIFORNIA. Freemasonry was introduced into this State in 1849 and 1850, by warrants from the Grand Lodges of the District of Columbia, Connecticut, Missouri, and New Jersey. A convention of delegates from all the lodges in the State was held in the city of Sacramento, April 17, 1850, and on the 19th of that month a Grand Lodge for the State of California was established in ample form. Jonathan D. Stevenson was elected Grand Master.

The first Royal Arch Chapter was convened in 1850, and the GRAND CHAPTER of the State was organized May 6, 1854.

The GRAND COMMANDERY, Knights Templar, was founded August 10, 1858.

CANADA. The first lodges in Canada worked under charters from the Grand Lodges of England, Scotland, and Ireland. The first Lodge in Quebec was organized by authority of a warrant from St. John's

Grand Lodge, of Boston, Massachusetts. October 16, 1855, a convention assembled in the city of Hamilton; forty-three lodges were represented, when the subject of an independent organization was calmly discussed, and resolutions adopted, setting forth the circumstances and necessities of a distinct organization. When the convention adopted a Constitution and elected Grand officers, William Mercer Wilson was elected and installed Grand Master. The newly-formed Grand Lodge, however, did not immediately receive the recognition of all the lodges of Canada, and, beside, the Grand Lodge of England showed an unwillingness to surrender her authority. In this unhappy state of affairs, several bodies, claiming partial or absolute jurisdiction, arose, and much confusion prevailed until 1858, when all dissensions happily expired, and the Order in Canada became harmoniously united under one head.

The GRAND ROYAL ARCH CHAPTER of Upper Canada was organized August 27, 1818.

CHILI. The first Masonic Lodge in Chili was constituted about 1840, under charter from the Grand Orient of France. But little is known of it, as it was closed during the political struggle of the republic shortly after it opened. A second commenced its work with a charter from the Grand Orient of France in 1851. A third began with a dispensation from the Grand Lodge of California, working in the York rite, and in the English language; it was kept at work one year and then closed. Four other lodges were subsequently established there—two from the Grand Orient of France, and two from the Grand Lodge of Massachusetts. April 20, 1862, representatives from four lodges met at Valparaiso, in convention, and organized a Grand Lodge for the republic. This Grand Lodge has four lodges under its jurisdiction, and the Grand Lodge of Massachusetts two, to one of which is attached a Royal Arch Chapter. There is also one Lodge acknowledging the jurisdiction of the Grand Orient of France. The Supreme Council of the 33d degree of the Ancient and Accepted Scottish rite for the Southern jurisdiction of the United States, whose East is at Charleston, has instituted bodies of that rite in several parts of the country.

COLOMBIA, NEW GRANADA. Masonry was first established in this republic about the year 1820. The Grand Orient was founded at Carthagenia, June 19, 1833.

COLORADO. Masonry was introduced into this territory in 1859. August 2, 1861, a convention was held in Golden City, by representatives from the three lodges then at labor in the territory, and organized a Grand Lodge. J. M. Chivington was elected the first Grand Master.

COLUMBIA, DISTRICT OF. Freemasonry was introduced into the District of Columbia by warrants from the Grand Lodges of Maryland and Virginia. The GRAND LODGE was established by a convention of delegates from the lodges in the district, December 11, 1810. Valentine Reintzel was elected first Grand Master.

The Royal Arch Chapters belong to the Grand Chapter of Maryland.

The Commanderies of Knights Templar were organized 1825 and 1862, by warrants from the Grand Encampment of the United States.

CONNECTICUT. The introduction of Freemasonry into this State occurred November 12, 1750, by authority of a warrant from the Grand Lodge of Massachusetts. The GRAND LODGE was organized July 8, 1789, by a convention of delegates from fifteen lodges. Pierpont Edwards was elected and installed Grand Master.

The GRAND CHAPTER was organized May 17, 1798; Ephraim Kirby was elected Grand High-Priest.

The GRAND COUNCIL of Royal and Select Masters organized 1819.

The GRAND COMMANDERY, Knights Templar, organized Sept 13, 1827.

CUBA. Freemasonry was introduced into Santiago de Cuba, in 1805, by patent from Count de Grasse, Sov. Grand Inspector General. A Grand Consistory was established in 1806. Since that period Masonry has had but a feeble existence, by reason of the hostility of the Spanish authorities of the island. The Symbolic Grand Lodge, at Santiago, under the title of the Grand Lodge of Colon, was organized Dec. 5, 1859, by the delegates from the three lodges then working in Cuba. Of the earlier history of Freemasonry on this island but little is known. The Ancient and Accepted rite is the acknowledged system of work in the jurisdiction.

DELAWARE. The precise date of the introduction of Freemasonry into this State is not generally known. The lodges, prior to 1806, were held under warrants from the Grand Lodge of Pennsylvania. The GRAND LODGE for the State was organized June 6, 1806.

The GRAND CHAPTER of Royal Arch Masons was established Jan. 19, 1818.

DENMARK. Freemasonry was first introduced into Denmark, at Copenhagen, in 1743, by authority of a warrant from the Grand Lodge at Berlin. In 1745 a warrant was obtained from Lord Cranstoun, Grand Master of England, to establish a Lodge. In 1749 another warrant was obtained from the Grand Lodge of England. From this time lodges multiplied with great rapidity. In 1792, the Landgrave, Charles of Hesse, assumed the title and duties of Grand Master of all the lodges in the kingdom, and thus Freemasonry became a recognized institution of the government. After the death of Charles the Crown Prince, subsequently King Christian VIII., assumed the protectorship of the Danish lodges.

DOMINICANA. The establishment of Freemasonry in this republic was during the year 1845. The Grand Orient was organized at the city of St. Domingo, December 11, 1858.

ECUADOR. Of the introduction of Freemasonry into this republic little is known. In 1857 the Grand Orient of Peru issued charters for a symbolic Lodge, and a chapter of the 18th degree in Guayaquil, which

prospered for about two years, and until the political agitations of the country, and the fierce opposition of the priesthood, compelled the brethren to close their lodges and return their charters to the parent body. There are at the present time (1866) no Masonic bodies in the republic. The Supreme Council of the Ancient and Accepted rite of the Southern jurisdiction of the United States has issued the necessary authority for establishing bodies of the rite in this republic.

ENGLAND. The precise time of the introduction of Freemasonry into England, or Britain, is uncertain. There is intermingled so much of fable with the early accounts of the settlement of that island that no one of the present day can distinguish between the romance and the truth. All history sustains the assumption that its introduction began during the early part of the third century, and was conveyed there by the numerous bands of traveling artisans who perambulated every section of the country where their services could be employed. The first organization of Masons as a distinctive body occurred about A. D. 300, under the protection of the Emperor Carausius, who conferred many privileges on the Masons; granted them a charter, and appointed Albanus, a distinguished Roman general, their Grand Master. Under the auspices of Carausius he labored earnestly for the prosperity of the Craft; convened the annual assemblies, settled the fundamental constitutions; revised the ritual of the Order, and procured them employment and increased wages. Masonry flourished with varied success until the year 926, when King Athelstane became King of England. This king loved and encouraged the Masons, and made his brother Edwin overseer of the Craft, and granted them a charter. "Accordingly, Prince Edwin summoned all the Masons in the realm to meet him in a convention at York, who came and composed a General Lodge, of which he was Grand Master; and having brought with them all the writings and records extant, some in Greek, some in Latin, some in French and other languages, from the contents thereof that assembly did frame the constitution and charges of an English Lodge." From this era we may date the reëstablishment of Masonry in England. For a long time the Grand Lodge at York exercised Masonic authority over all England, and until 1567, when the Masons in the southern part of the island assembled at a Grand Convention, and elected Sir Thomas Gresham, the distinguished merchant, as Grand Master. There were now two Grand Masters in England, who assumed distinctive titles; the Grand Master of the North (York) being called "Grand Master of all England," while he who presided in the South (London) was called "Grand Master of England." Notwithstanding this new appointment of a Grand Master in the South, the General Assembly continued to meet in the city of York, where all the ancient and valuable Masonic records were kept; and to this assembly appeals were made on every important occasion. Masonry flourished and was remarkably prosperous until the early part of the eighteenth century, when, in consequence of the civil war that agitated the country, it became neglected, and fell into decay, particularly in the south of England. Sir Christopher Wren, the Grand Master in the reign of Queen Anne, had become aged, infirm, and inactive, and hence the grand assemblies were entirely neglected. The old Lodge of St. Paul, and a few others, continued to meet regularly, but consisted of few members. To increase their members, a proposition was made, and agreed to, *that the privileges of Masonry should no longer be restricted to operative Masons, but extend to men of various professions, provided they were regularly approved and initiated into the Order.* This is the period when the institution was changed from the operative to the speculative character. In consequence of this resolution many new regulations were established, and the society once more rose into notice and es-

teem. The assembly above alluded to did not fully reëstablish the Grand Lodge of England, but advised that the holding an annual feast should be revived, and that the Grand Master, according to custom, should be chosen. Accordingly, in the third year of the reign of George I., on St. John the Baptist's day, 1717, the annual assembly and feast were held, and Mr. Anthony Sayer was regularly proposed and elected Grand Master. Out of respect to the four old lodges, the only bodies then existing in London, the privileges which they had always possessed under the old organization were reserved to them. The two Grand bodies of York and London kept up a friendly intercourse, and mutual interchange of recognition, until the Grand Master of the latter body, in 1734, granted two warrants of constitution to a number of Masons who had seceded from the former. This unfriendly act was at once condemned by the Grand Lodge at York, and produced a disruption of the harmony that had long subsisted between them. Three years later, in 1738, some disagreeable altercations arose in the Order. A number of dissatisfied brethren separated themselves from the regular lodges, held meetings in different places, for the purpose of initiating persons into Masonry, contrary to the laws of the Grand Lodge. The seceding brethren, taking advantage of the breach between the Grand Lodges of London and York, assumed, without authority, the appellation of "*Ancient Masons.*" These irregular proceedings they pretended to justify under the feigned sanction of the *Ancient* York Constitutions. They announced that the old landmarks were alone preserved by them; that the regular lodges had adopted *new* plans, sanctioned innovations, and were not to be considered as working under the *old* system; they were, therefore, branded with the title of "*Modern Masons.*" They established a new Grand Lodge in 1739, in the city of London, under the name of the "Grand Lodge of Ancient York Masons," and, persevering in the measures adopted, formed committees, held communications, and appointed annual feasts. Under the false appellation of the York banner, they gained the recognition of the Masons of Scotland and Ireland, who, believing the representations made to them, heartily joined in condemning the measures of the regular lodges in London, as tending, in their opinion, to introduce novelties into the society, and to subvert the original plan of Masonry. The two Grand Lodges continued to exist, in opposition to each other, to the great scandal of the Fraternity, until the year 1813, when, by the united efforts of the Duke of Sussex, who was Grand Master of the Grand Lodge termed *Moderns*, and the Duke of Kent, who was Grand Master of the Grand Lodge known as the *Ancients*, the two bodies were happily united with great solemnity, under the style and title of "The United Grand Lodge of Ancient Freemasons of England." In no part of the world is Freemasonry more prosperous or respected than in England.

· FLORIDA. The earliest record of the existence of Freemasonry in Florida, that we can trace, is that a Lodge of Ancient York Masons was organized in the city of St. Augustine, under a warrant granted by the Grand Lodge of the State of Georgia, about the year 1806, to St. Fernando Lodge. But no certain information can be obtained on the subject from the records of the Grand Lodge of Georgia, as a part of the archives of that Grand Lodge, from 1805 to 1817, were destroyed by the great fire which occurred in the city of Savannah, about the year 1818. This Lodge worked, and made Masons, until the year 1811, when it was suppressed by a mandate of the Spanish government. Notwithstanding this pointed opposition to Masonry, a few faithful spirits cherished in their hearts a love for the institution, and, in the year 1820, obtained from the Grand Lodge of South Carolina a warrant for a Lodge to work in the city of St. Augustine, under the style of "Floridan Virtues Lodge, No. 28." But

such was the still prevailing hostility of the Spanish authorities, and from other causes, its existence was not long preserved. The next Lodge, of which we have any knowledge, was a Mark Master's Lodge, called "Union Mark Lodge," established in St. Augustine, in 1822, under a warrant from the Hon. DeWitt Clinton, General Grand High-Priest of the General Grand Chapter of the United States. This Masonic body worked for a short time only, owing, perhaps, to the fact that there was no symbolic Lodge in existence in that city, *to furnish it with material for work;* and to the further fact that Masonry, at that time, had not recovered from the effects of the church prejudices and influences. In 1824 another application was made to the Grand Lodge of South Carolina, by the constitutional number of Master Masons, for a warrant to establish a Lodge entitled "Esperanza Lodge," at St. Augustine. This Lodge, which worked in the Spanish language, became extinct after one year, by the removal of the greater portion of its members to Havana. Its warrant was surrendered to the Grand Lodge, whence it was received. From this time there was no organized Masonry in East Florida, until the establishment of a Lodge in the city of Tallahassee, by a warrant from the Grand Lodge of Alabama, under the title of Jackson Lodge, about the year 1826. The second Lodge was organized in the town of Quincy, by warrant from the Grand Lodge of Tennessee, under the title of Washington Lodge, and the third from the Grand Lodge of Georgia, under the title of Harmony Lodge, in the town of Mariana. On the 5th of July, 1830, delegates from the three lodges in Florida assembled in the city of Tallahassee, for the purpose of organizing a Grand Lodge for the Territory of Florida. After regularly organizing the convention, the necessary resolutions were adopted, and July 6 the Grand Lodge was legally organized, the Grand Lodge was legally organized, the Grand Officers elected and duly installed. Brother John P. Duval, the oldest Past Master present, was elected the first Grand Master. Since this period Masonry has flourished in Florida with remarkable vigor and permanency.

The GRAND CHAPTER of Royal Arch Masons was organized Jan. 11, 1847. This Grand Chapter has ever been an *independent* body—not acknowledging the authority of the General Grand Chapter of the United States.

The GRAND COUNCIL of Royal and Select Masters was organized in January, 1852.

FRANCE. The first Lodge founded in France was at Dunkirk, October 13, 1721, and was called "Friendship and Fraternity;" and about the same time another at Mons, called "Perfect Union." In 1726 Lord Derwentwater established the first Lodge at Paris; it had about five hundred members, and met at a restaurant kept by one Hurre; two others were founded in 1729, and a fourth in 1732, in which the Duke of Aumont was initiated, and which, on that account, took his name. In 1735 Lord Derwentwater received a patent from England, constituting him Provincial Grand Master, which powers he subsequently transferred to his friend Lord Harnouester. In 1736 the four lodges in Paris founded a Provincial Grand Lodge, under the authority of England, and placed Lord Harnouester at the head. In 1738 he was succeeded by the Duke D'Antin, who presided until his death, in 1743, when the Count de Clermont was elected, at which period the body assumed the title of "English Grand Lodge of France." At this time an effort was made to suppress the Fraternity, and Louis XV. issued an edict forbidding the nobility to take part in the society, and threatened with the Bastile any who should have the temerity to accept the Grand Mastership. Notwithstanding the inconvenience attending a residence in the State Prison, and the continued activity of the police, the Craft held its own, and even increased in numbers. The Grand Lodge now cast off its allegiance to the English Grand Lodge, and became the Grand Lodge of France, preserving, however, the usage which prevailed in the parent body of giving warrants to Masters for life, who considered the lodges established by them as personal property. They even sold warrants to other Masters in Paris and the provinces, and these, in turn, constituted other bodies, which set up a rivalry against the Grand Lodge, and produced the utmost degree of confusion, which was more confounded by the Chevalier Ramsay, whose system is credited as the base of all the rites which have since been peddled around the world. The Grand Lodge fell into a state of anarchy on account of the inattention of the Grand Master, who, to rid himself of the direction of affairs appointed proxies: the first was a banker named Baure, who did no better than his master, and he was removed to give place to Lacorne, a dancing master, who took the degrees of Perfection to fit himself for his new dignity. The members of the Grand Lodge, however, refused to associate with him, and he was removed, and succeeded by Chaillon de Joinville, whereupon a schism arose, and the two parties made war upon each other with great bitterness. Each party granted warrants, and a faction under the leadership of Lacorne did likewise; tavern-keepers bought the right to hold lodges; rituals and constitutions were made merchandise, and anarchy reigned supreme. In 1777 the two parties in the Grand Lodge united, but Lacorne and his adherents kept aloof, and caused much trouble, even going so far as to descend to acts of violence, in consequence of which the government closed all the lodges. Secret meetings were, however, held, and charters granted till 1771, when the Count de Clermont died and the Duke de Chartres succeeded to the Grand Mastership. The edict of revocation was withdrawn, and all the charters granted during the suspension were canceled. In 1773 the Grand Lodge changed its title to that of Grand Orient; and March 5, under the gavel of the Duke de Luxembourg, substitute of the Grand Master, adopted "The Statutes of the Royal Order of Freemasonry in France," in which the life Masterships were abolished, and the annual election substituted. Some dissatisfied Masons continued the Grand Lodge of France, and the quarrel went on as before, until both parties were silenced by the terrible events of the Revolution. In 1799 Brother Montaleau being Grand Master, a concordat was signed, and the various factions were united under the direction of the Grand Orient. In 1802, however, new troubles arose with the Philosophical or Scottish rite, which refused obedience to the Grand Orient, and claimed the right to govern and direct the high degrees. Many Masons of distinction, among others the famous Stephen Morin, took part in this movement, and in 1803 the banner of the opposition was fully displayed, and the body took the name of "Scottish General Grand Lodge of the Ancient and Accepted rite;" but in 1804 they united with the Grand Orient. There was, however, still in existence, another body founded in 1802 by the Count de Grasse-Tilly, with the title "Sovereign Grand Inspectors General of the 33d and last degree of the Ancient and Accepted Scottish rite," claiming to have derived authority from the Supreme Council at Charleston. In 1805 the previous concordat was broken, and thus there were again three governing bodies in France. In the same year Joseph Bonaparte was named Grand Master, Cambaceres accepted the position of first assistant, and many persons of distinction were thereby attracted to the Fraternity. In 1814, owing to political events, the Grand Orient found it difficult to maintain its organization, and the bodies of the Scottish rite ceased their meetings altogether. Advantage was taken of this state of affairs by the Grand Orient to assume jurisdiction over all degrees and rites. In 1815, April 9, a new claimant of Masonic authority appeared in the Rite of Misraim, invented and propagated by four brothers, Bedarride by name. This rite applied to the Grand Orient for recognition, but in 1817 was refused.

and finally became so disorderly that the police interfered and closed its halls and operations. At a later period (1838), the Rite of Memphis made its appearance and pursued its labors with varying fortunes—none of them very brilliant—until, on the application of the Grand Hierophant Marcorius de Nègre, it was finally absorbed by the Grand Orient (1862), and its vast system of ninety-six degrees cut down to thirty-three, the dimensions of the Scottish rite. In 1852 Prince Lucien Murat was chosen Grand Master, who proved inefficient, and conferred no honor on the Craft. At the meeting of 1861 violent disputes arose, the majority of the representatives being anxious to get rid of Murat and elect Prince Napoleon in his stead, and the adherents of Murat, as well as himself, being equally anxious to retain the power they had exercised for years to the evident detriment of the society. The clamors reached such a hight that the civil authorities interfered and closed the session before an election was held. The Prince then appointed a committee of five to supervise the affairs of Masonry until the following October, when the Grand Orient was again to be called together for the purpose of electing a Grand Master. The Craft at large, however, refused to acknowledge their authority, and adhered to the council of the Grand Master, who were, in fact, the legal successors of the defunct functionary, and thus, for a time, the Fraternity had two heads. January 11, 1862, Napoleon put an end to this disgraceful state of affairs, and by "the grace of God and the national will" appointed Marshal Magnan Grand Master for three years. At the time of his nomination the Marshal was not a Mason; but he received the whole thirty-three degrees the following day, by communication, in the presence of five Masons, led by Rexes. The whole proceeding was entirely illegal; but there was no help for it, and the Marshal was subsequently installed, and signalized his entrance into official station by decapitating

Rexes and removing those who, with him, had for years mismanaged the affairs of the Grand Orient. He found the Fraternity overwhelmed with debt, and its affairs generally in a state of disgraceful confusion. By the adoption of vigorous measures he reduced this chaos to order, and, at the end of his first term, had succeeded in paying off the floating debt amounting to about $40,000. In 1864 he announced that the Emperor, at his request, had withdrawn his appointment, whereupon the Grand Orient, with unanimity and good taste, elected him for a new term of three years; an honor of which he evidently felt proud, as he signed his edicts thereafter "Elected" Grand Master, etc. May 29, 1865, he died in office, in the 74th year of his age, honored and regretted by the Fraternity he had well and faithfully served. At the succeeding meeting of the Grand Orient General Mellinet, the present Grand Master, was elected. He has appointed on his staff some of the best known and respected citizens of Paris; and we hazard nothing in saying that Masonry in France is at present in a better condition, and its affairs in better hands, than at any time since its introduction into the Empire. At the annual communication for 1865 a new constitution was adopted, which is apparently modeled upon that of New York, and which is decidedly better than any of its predecessors. It recognizes the sovereignty of the lay members, and the great principle of Grand Lodge jurisdiction, for which we have always contended, and which is the subject of difference between the Grand Lodges of America and that of Hamburg. The subject of Masonic reform, by striking out the high degrees, is at present obtaining great consideration in France and throughout Europe, and it is a noteworthy fact that at the adoption of the new constitution a proposition to ignore them entirely only failed by three votes. It is claimed in France that the continuous difficulties which have impeded the progress of the Craft, and brought so much

disgrace upon it, are due to the pitiful intrigues growing out of the many systems of superior degrees which have from time to time been invented and propagated there, and those who are well informed entertain no doubt of the near approach of the day when Masonry in France will return to its primitive organization, and practice only the symbolic degrees. It is also a subject of remark that the lodges in France are gradually falling into the hands of the middle and working classes, and that its social status is likely to be thereby endangered—a fear in which we, on this side of the Atlantic, are not likely to participate; on the contrary we see in it the indication of a healthy growth and a true progress toward the great end of the association—the brotherhood of man.

GEORGIA. The earliest historical record of Freemasonry in Georgia may be found in Preston's Illustrations, during the Grand Mastership of the Earl of Strathmore, in 1733, and is in the following language: "The history of the society at this period affords few remarkable instances of record. Some considerable donations were collected, and distributed among distressed Masons, to encourage the settlement of a new colony, which had been just established at Georgia, America." The next allusion we find by the same author in 1735, who says: "He (Lord Weymouth being then Grand Master) also issued warrants to open a new Lodge at Lisbon, and another at Savannah, in Georgia." Thomas Smith Webb, in his *Freemason's Monitor*, edition of 1805, says: "The Grand Lodge of Georgia is holden by virtue, and in pursuance of the right of succession, legally derived from the Most Noble and Most Worshipful Thomas Thyne, Lord Viscount Weymouth, Grand Master of England, A. D. 1730,* by his warrant, directed to the Right Worshipful Roger Lacey; and by the renewal of the said power by Sholto Charles

---

* This is evidently an error, because Lord Weymouth was Grand Master in 1735, and was succeeded by the Earl of Loudon in 1736.

Douglas, Lord Aberdour, Grand Master of Scotland, for the years 1755 and 1756; and the Grand Master of England for the years 1757 and 1758; as will appear in his warrant directed to the Right Worshipful Grey Elliot. Dec. 16, A. D. 1786, a convention of the several lodges holden in the State assembled at Savannah, when the permanent appointments, which had been theretofore made by the Grand Master of England, were solemnly relinquished, by the Right Worshipful Sam'l Elbert, Grand Master, and the other officers of the Grand Lodge; and certain regulations adopted by which the Grand Officers are now elected annually by the Grand Lodge." At this convention, 1787, William Stephens was elected Grand Master. This Grand Lodge so constituted was afterward incorporated by the legislature of Georgia. The warrant of Solomon's Lodge, as originally issued, was destroyed by fire; therefore its precise date and authority cannot, at this time, be definitely settled.

GERMANY. The earliest history of Freemasonry in Germany is supposed to be closely interwoven with the history of the building associations of the Middle Ages: "as we may easily recognize a strong similarity in the usages, customs and peculiar terms of the Fraternity of Freemasons of the present day, and the '*Stein-Metzen*' (stone-cutters) of Germany. 1. The classification of their members into Masters, Fellow-Crafts, and Apprentices; 2. The government of the society by a certain number of officers; 3. The exclusion of the uninitiated from their meetings; 4. The peculiar qualifications for membership; 5. The equality of all the members of the Craft; 6. Their mutual obligations to relieve suffering; 7. Their peculiar laws, jurisdiction and general regulations; 8. The ceremonies of initiation; 9. The manner of opening and closing their assemblies; 10. The privileges of a Mason's son; 11. The examination of foreign brethren, etc. Taking all these circumstances into consideration, and combining with them

the results of historical investigation, it must be conceded that the modern society is the direct descendant and successor, in an unbroken line, of the operative Fraternity of Masons of the middle ages."[*] In 1733, Preston says, eleven German Masons applied for authority to open a Lodge at Hamburg, under the patronage of the Grand Lodge of England, for which purpose the Grand Master, Lord Strathmore, granted a dispensation to establish a permanent Lodge, concerning which but little is now known. December 6, 1737, a Lodge was established in Hamburg, by authority of the Grand Lodge of England, which, in 1741, assumed the title of "Absalom." August 11, 1738, a deputation of this Lodge was convened at Brunswick for the purpose of initiating the Crown Prince, afterward Frederick II. By this valuable accession of nobility Masonry was greatly benefited throughout Germany. Soon after his initiation, he organized a Lodge in the castle of Rheinsberg, and, in 1740, when Frederick ascended the throne, he conducted the work of a Lodge established at the castle in Charlottenburg. In 1738-39 several Lodges were established in Dresden, and in 1741 the Lodge "Minerva of the Three Palm Trees" was organized at Leipsic. In 1742 the Lodge of Unity was established at Frankfort-on-the Main. In 1741 a Provincial Grand Lodge for Hamburg and Lower Saxony was established. The second Lodge in Hamburg was founded in 1743, under the name of St. George. In 1744 a Lodge under the title "Frederick" was founded at Hanover, which did not, however, enter into active operation until 1746. This Lodge is still in existence. The war of 1750 compelled most of the Lodges to close their work until 1758. About the year 1757 the first Lodge of the system of Strict Observance was established in Naumburg, under the title of the "Lodge of the Three Banners." This system, which claimed to be the true and legitimate succes-

*Findel's History of Freemasonry.

sor of the Order of the Knights Templar, had for a short time an unprecedented popularity. In 1755 a warrant, with ample powers to establish a Provincial Lodge in Hamburg, was received from the Grand Lodge of England. In 1766 another Provincial Grand Lodge was established at Frankfort-on-the-Main, by the Grand Lodge of England. In 1776 the society of Illuminati, a secret political organization, was introduced and spread throughout the country, to the injury of Freemasonry. About the year 1780 the Swedish rite was introduced and practiced by several lodges in Germany. In 1789 an important event took place for the better and more peaceful condition of the Order. Many of the lodges, being dissatisfied with the immense number of rites and high degrees engrafted upon the plain and unpresuming system of Freemasonry, resolved to modify the different elements then in use, and as near as possible to return to the original or primative condition. For this purpose a convention of the lodges of Germany was held in Frankfort, in 1783, at which convention a union was formed under the title of the "Eclectic Union," which had for its material or chief points: 1. The three Masonic degrees alone are acknowledged by all the united lodges; 2. Each Lodge is left free to introduce as many of the higher degrees as it may deem proper, but they must not be compulsory upon the whole association; 3. None of the associated lodges are dependent on the other; they are all equal; 4. The Provincial Lodges of Wetzlar and Frankfort-on-the-Main form a General Directory. In consequence of this independent action of the Provincial Grand Lodge at Frankfort in severing its connection with the Grand Lodge of England, plans were immediately adopted to renew and perpetuate the English authority upon the soil of Germany. In 1789 a new warrant with powers for the establishment of a Provincial Grand Lodge, giving full jurisdiction over the whole of the Upper and Lower Rhine, and the circle of Franconia, was granted by the Grand Lodge of England. During the wars in which the elder Napoleon was the master spirit Masonry occupied a quiet and unobtrusive position throughout the country. Our limited space will not permit us to follow the various incidents of the Fraternity. We must, therefore, refer the Masonic student in his researches to the more elaborate works upon the subject of Masonic history, and which have been prepared with great care by many of the most competent writers of the present age. Freemasonry is in high repute in Germany, embracing within her ample folds the *élite* of the country.

HOLLAND. In 1731, by virtue of a special deputation from Lord Lovel, Grand Master of England, an emergent Lodge was held at the Hague, the Earl of Chesterfield presiding, for the initiation of the Duke of Tuscany, afterward Emperor of Germany. After the ceremony the Lodge was closed. The first regular and permanent Lodge established in Holland was at the same place in 1734. From this Lodge several lodges were formed. In 1756 a convention of all the lodges then working in the country assembled and organized a Grand Lodge. When Holland was united to the French Empire, the Grand Orient of France sought to extend the sphere of her jurisdiction, by ignoring the existence of the lodges in Holland, and founded two lodges of her own creating in Amsterdam. This controversy was of short duration, and the Grand Orient abandoned the effort. In 1863 the Grand Lodge of Holland numbered upward of one hundred lodges upon its rolls.

ILLINOIS. The reliable history of Freemasonry, and of its early introduction into Illinois, is yet to be written, and it is hoped that the subject is of sufficient interest to the cause to induce some enlightened brother, and well versed in the knowledge thereto, to favor the Fraternity with a truthful account of Masonry in this once far western territory. In 1805, six years before the organization of the territorial government, a Lodge was organized at Kaskaskia, the oldest settlement west of the Alleghanies. Other lodges followed, and in those early days, the Lodge-room was the resort of men anxious to profit by the mystic teachings, and enjoy the secret communion of the inner chamber of Masonry. A Grand Lodge, in due time, was formed, which flourished for a time, but succumbed before the anti-Masonic tempest of 1827. From that time forward, until 1840, gloom and obscurity rest upon Masonic records in Illinois. Time, patience, and perseverance, will exhume them. January 20, 1840, a convention of Masons, composed of delegates from several of the subordinate lodges in the State, was held in the town of Jackson, when a resolution was unanimously adopted declaring it expedient to establish a Grand Lodge. The convention adjourned to, and did meet again, April 6 of the same year. The object of the meeting having been fully considered, it was unanimously "*Resolved*, That the several subordinate lodges of Ancient Freemasonry in the State of Illinois here assembled, represented by delegates properly authorized, consider it as a matter of right, and as conducive to the general benefit of Masonry, that a Grand Lodge be established in the State of Illinois, and that they now proceed to establish, organize, and to locate the same accordingly, to be known and designated by the name of the Grand Lodge of Illinois." Abraham Jonas was elected the first Grand Master.

The Grand Chapter was organized April 9, 1850. Wm. B. Warren was elected first Grand High-Priest.

The Grand Council of Royal and Select Masters was organized in 1853. Jas. H. Hibbard was elected the first Grand Master.

The Grand Commandery, Knights Templar, was organized Oct. 27, 1857. Jas. V. Z. Blaney was elected the first Grand Commander.

INDIANA. The Grand Lodge of this State was organized at Carydon, in December, 1817. The first meeting of the Grand Lodge for the election of officers, and the transaction of business, was held Jan.

12, 1818. Alexander Buckner was elected the first Grand Master.

The Grand Royal Arch Chapter was organized in November, 1846.

The Grand Council of Royal and Select Masters was organized in 1853.

The Grand Commandery, Knights Templar, was established May 6, 1854.

IOWA. The introduction of Freemasonry into this Territory, as it was then called, began by authority of letters of dispensation from the Grand and Deputy Grand Masters of Missouri—the first dated Nov 20, 1840, for a Lodge at Desmoines; the second dated Feb. 4, 1841, for a Lodge at Bloomington; the third dated Oct. 10, 1842, for a Lodge at Dubuque. Jan. 2, 1844, delegates from the three lodges met in convention at Iowa City, when the necessary resolutions were adopted, and on the 3d of the same month the Grand Lodge for the Territory was proclaimed. Oliver Cock was elected the First Grand Master.

The Grand Royal Arch Chapter was organized June 8, 1854.

The Grand Council of Royal and Select Masters was organized in 1857.

The Grand Commandery, Knights Templar, was organized June 6, 1864.

IRELAND. Of the early history of Masonry in Ireland so little is known that it would be folly to attempt, in this late day, to discover the footprints of its existence upon that ancient soil. Bro. Michael Furnell, than whom no living Masonic writer is better acquainted with the history of Masonry in Ireland, says : "I furnish a brief abstract of the historic constitution of the Masonic Order in Ireland; and though possessing irrefutable records and data, showing the existence of several self-designated 'Grand Lodges' in past centuries, and though the Lodge No. 1, on the present *legitimate registry*, claims an uninterrupted descent from an independent lodge, which existed from time immemorial, and retains many quaint old documents in her archives, and is by many styled, 'The

First Lodge of Ireland,' yet I leave the task of research into the hazy mist of the past ages, to some more erudite antiquary, taking for granted that those gone-by powers were but by assumption or prescription. The constitution of the present Metropolitan Grand Lodge dates from the year 1729, when the entire Fraternity united in electing the Right Hon. Lord Kingston, Grand Master of Ireland." Since that time many gentlemen of noble birth have occupied the chair, and directed the affairs of Masonry with substantial effect. The Ancient York rite is tenaciously adhered to by this Grand Lodge. In 1809, a charter for the establishment of a Supreme Council of the 33d degree, Ancient and Accepted rite, was granted by the Supreme Council, at Charleston, South Carolina, and creating his Grace, the Duke of Leinster, Grand Commander, *ad vitam*. In 1820 a Council of the Rite of Misraim was instituted, with the Duke of Leinster as the Supreme head. This organization had a very brief existence in this country. The present Grand Master (1866) of the Grand Lodge is the Duke of Leinster, who has held the office since 1813. Within the body of the Grand Lodge is a Grand Conclave of Knights Templar, a Supreme Grand Council of rites, and a Grand Royal Arch Chapter.

ITALY. Freemasonry was first established in this country, at Florence, in 1733, by Lord Charles Sackville, but by what authority is at present unknown. At first the Fraternity was known under the name of the "Company of the Trowel," and, afterward, by the appellation of "*Franchi Muratori*." In 1735 the Grand Duke Francis was initiated. This circumstance gave a fresh and wholesome impetus to the Order; lodges were immediately established in Milan, Verona, Padua, Vicenza, Venice, and Naples. The Fraternity was not long permitted to enjoy entire freedom for the exercise of their privileges. In 1738 Pope Clement XII. issued his famous bull against the Fraternity, which, notwithstanding the influence and power of the Duke,

compelled the brethren, very generally, to close their lodges. For many years only those members who had the courage availed themselves of their right to meet, and in the most secret manner. Persecutions of the most inhuman character were exercised against the members of the Order by the inquisition until 1776, when, through the influence of Queen Caroline, daughter of Francis I., the persecutions ceased, and all the prisoners in charge of the inquisition were released. In 1805 a Supreme Council of the Ancient and Accepted rite was established in Milan by letters patent from Count de Grasse-Tilly. Prince Eugene, viceroy of Italy accepted the office of Sovereign Grand Commander and Grand Master of the Grand Orient of Italy. When Italy was under French rule, then did Masonry begin to rise and thrive. Murat, King of Naples, assisted in the establishment of a Grand Lodge, which was opened with marked splendor and ceremony June 24, 1809. With the fall of Napoleon the persecutions against the Fraternity were renewed, both by civil and ecclesiastical authorities. At this period the secret society known as the CARBONARI (Colliers) arose. This was purely a political organization, which had for its purpose the consolidation of Italy under one scepter, and free it from foreign rule—in the language of the colliers themselves: "Clear the forest of wolves." From 1814 to 1860 Freemasonry was almost extinguished in Italy. The society of the Carbonari absorbed every thought and consideration in the hope that they might free the country from the despotic tyranny of the Bourbons. In 1861 Freemasonry began again to rekindle the fires upon her altars. In Palermo a Grand Orient was founded by Garibaldi, which adopted the Ancient and Accepted Scottish rite. A Supreme Council of the same rite has also been formed in Naples. Within a few years past Masonry in Italy has undergone so many changes that it seems impossible to keep pace with its vast and extensive improvements.

KANSAS. The introduction of Freemasonry into this territory began in 1854, by authority from the Grand Lodge of Missouri. Nov. 14, 1855, delegates from two lodges met for the purpose of organizing a Grand Lodge. This convention, not having the legal number of lodges represented, adjourned until the 27th of the next month; again only two lodges appeared by delegates, when they adopted resolutions, formed a Constitution, proclaimed a Grand Lodge, established and elected Grand Officers. These proceedings having been pronounced illegal, another convention was convened March 17, 1856, when delegates from all the chartered lodges were present, and ratified or reënacted the previous proceedings, and then opened a Grand Lodge for the territory in ample form. Bro. R. R. Rees was elected the first Grand Master.

KENTUCKY. The first regular lodges in Kentucky derived their authority from the Grand Lodge of Virginia. In the year 1800 there were under that authority five regular lodges. But, from their remote situation from their parent Grand Lodge, they were induced to proceed to the establishment of a Grand Lodge for the State of Kentucky; and, in pursuance of an invitation from Lexington Lodge, No. 25, a convention of delegates from all the regular lodges then existing in the State was held at the Masonic Hall, in the town of Lexington, Sept. 8, 1800, when it was resolved that it was expedient and proper to establish a Grand Lodge in the State of Kentucky, and an address, setting forth the motives which impelled the brethren to sever their immediate connection from the parent Grand Lodge of Virginia, was ordered to be prepared. The address was prepared, approved, and forwarded to the Grand Lodge of Virginia; to which that body returned a fraternal and approving reply. The convention met again Oct. 16, 1800, in the same place, and proceeded regularly to establish a Grand Lodge for the State of Kentucky. The delegates then severally

surrendered to the Grand Lodge their respective charters, and received new ones in lieu thereof, under the Grand Lodge there established for the State. Wm. Murray was elected the first Grand Master.

The GRAND ROYAL ARCH CHAPTER was organized Dec. 4, 1817, at the city of Frankfort. James Moore was elected the first Grand High-Priest.

The GRAND COUNCIL of Royal and Select Masters was organized Dec. 10, 1827. Robert Johnson was elected the first Grand President.

The GRAND COMMANDERY, Knights Templar, was established Oct. 5, 1827. Henry Wingate was elected Grand Commander.

LOUISIANA. Freemasonry was first planted upon the soil of Louisiana by the Grand Lodge of South Carolina in 1793; the second Lodge obtained a charter from the Grand Lodge at Marseilles, France, in 1794. In 1800 and 1806 two charters were obtained from the Grand Lodge of Pennsylvania, and one other composed of brethren from St. Domingo. April 18, 1812, a general Masonic convention, composed of delegates from the five lodges, was called. The convention adjourned until June 6, when a constitution was adopted, and, July 11 following, the Grand Lodge was regularly established.

A GRAND CHAPTER was organized March 5, 1813.*

The GRAND ROYAL ARCH CHAPTER, acknowledging the jurisdiction of the General Grand Chapter of the United States, was organized about the year 1828.

The GRAND COUNCIL of Royal and Select Masters was established Feb. 16, 1856.

The Grand Commandery, Knights Templar, was organized February 4, 1864.

* This Grand Chapter was organized by the "Royal Lodges," Concordia and Perseverance, and such officers and members of the Grand Lodge of the State as were Royal Arch Masons. These lodges were originally established in the Island of St. Domingo, under charters from the Grand Lodge of Pennsylvania, with powers to confer all the degrees from Entered Apprentice to Royal Arch inclusive.

MAINE. Until the year 1820 Maine composed a part of the civil and Masonic jurisdiction of Massachusetts. In that year the several lodges, contemplating a political separation of that territory from the commonwealth of Massachusetts, having assembled, by their delegates, at Portland, Oct. 14, 1819, a respectful memorial was drawn up, and subscribed by all the delegates, addressed to the Grand Lodge of Massachusetts, praying their consent to the organization of an independent Grand Lodge in the State of Maine. This request being promptly and generously granted by the Grand Lodge of Massachusetts, the several lodges in Maine were summoned to meet at Mason's Hall, in Portland, June 1, 1820, when a Grand Lodge for the State of Maine was duly and regularly organized. The Hon. William King, Governor of the State, was elected the first Grand Master.

The GRAND ROYAL ARCH CHAPTER of the State was organized in 1821. Robert P. Dunlap was the first Grand High-Priest.

The GRAND COUNCIL of Royal and Select Masters was organized May 3, 1855. Robert P. Dunlap was the first Grand President.

The GRAND COMMANDERY, Knights Templar, was organized May 5, 1852. Charles B. Smith was the first Grand Commander.

MARYLAND. Until the year 1783 the lodges in this State derived their warrants from the Grand Lodge of Pennsylvania, except one at Annapolis, which obtained a charter from the Grand Lodge of Massachusetts in 1750.* On the 17th June, 1783, the first convention was held at Talbot Court House by delegates from the five lodges then working in the State, to take into consideration the propriety of establishing an independent Masonic jurisdiction, when a Master Mason's Lodge was

* August 12, 1750, a charter was granted by the Grand Lodge of Massachusetts to a number of brethren who had petitioned to form a Lodge in Annapolis, Maryland. —*History of Grand Lodge of Massachusetts.* This Lodge is not mentioned in the list of Lodges convened to establish the Grand Lodge.

opened in the usual form, the following resolution was adopted unanimously : *Resolved,* That the several lodges on the eastern shore of Maryland, consider it as a matter of right, and that they ought to form a Grand Lodge, independent of the Grand Lodge at Philadelphia." At a subsequent meeting of the convention, held at the same place, on the 31st of July, Grand officers were chosen, of which John Coats was elected Grand Master and Charles Gardiner was appointed Grand Secretary.

The GRAND CHAPTER, which had, until recently, within its jurisdiction the Chapters of the District of Columbia, was organized in 1812.

MASSACHUSETTS. The introduction of Freemasonry into this country, through warranted lodges, established upon the basis of legal Masonic authority, dates from July 30, 1733. Upon the application of several brethren, Free and Accepted Masons, residing in the town of Boston, Province of Massachusetts, for authority to establish a Provincial Grand Lodge, a warrant was granted by the Right Worshipful Lord Viscount Montacute, Grand Master of Masons of England, dated April 30, 1733, appointing Right Worshipful Henry Price, Provincial Grand Master of New England, and dominions and territories thereunto belonging, with free power and authority to nominate and appoint his Deputy Grand Master and Grand Wardens. On the receipt of this commission, the brethren assembled July 30, 1733, at the "Bunch of Grapes" tavern, State Street, Boston, when the charter of Constitution was read, and the Right Worshipful Grand Master duly invested and congratulated; a Grand Lodge, under the title of "St. John's Grand Lodge," was formed, and the Grand Officers chosen and installed in due and ancient form. A petition was then presented by several brethren, residing in Boston, praying to be constituted into a regular Lodge; and it was voted that the same be granted. This Lodge was styled "The First Lodge in Boston," or "St. John's Lodge."

Thus was Masonry established in North America. In the year 1751 a number of brethren who had traveled, and many of whom had been initiated into the mysteries of the Craft in *ancient* lodges abroad, became emulous to cultivate the royal art in the western world. For this landable purpose they petitioned the Grand Lodge of Scotland for a charter to establish a Lodge. The prayer of the petitioners being granted, they received a dispensation, dated Nov. 30, 1752, from Sholto Charles Donglas, Lord Aberdour, then Grand Master, constituting them a regular Lodge, under the title of "St. Andrew's Lodge, No. 82," to be holden at Boston, in the province of Massachusetts Bay. The establishment of this Lodge was discouraged and opposed by St. John's Grand Lodge, who imagined their jurisdiction infringed by the Grand Lodge of Scotland. They, therefore, refused any communications or visits from such members of St. Andrew's Lodge as had not formerly sat in their lodges, and this difficulty did not entirely subside for several years. The prosperous state of St. Andrew's Lodge soon led to great exertions for the establishment of an ancient Grand Lodge in the Province; and this was effected by the assistance of three traveling lodges, which were holden in the British army, then stationed at Boston, under the title of "The Massachusetts Grand Lodge." Dec. 27, 1769. On this festival, which was celebrated in due form, a commission from the Right Honorable and Most Worshipful George, Earl of Dalhousie, Grand Master of Masons in Scotland, bearing date May 30, 1769, appointing Joseph Warren to be Grand Master of Masons in Boston, New England, and within one hundred miles of the same, was read; whereupon the brethren proceeded, according to ancient usage, to install the Right Worshipful Grand Master Warren, who afterward appointed and invested the other Grand Officers. Nov. 13, 1758, a deputation was granted to the Right Worshipful Edward Huntingford, to hold a Lodge in his Majesty's 28th regiment, stationed at Louisburg. Of the further history of this deputation, or whether a Lodge under its authority was ever organized, we have no authentic record. In 1773, a commission was received from the Earl of Dumfries, Grand Master of Masons in Scotland, dated March 3, 1772, appointing Joseph Warren Grand Master of Masons for the Continent of America. April 19, 1775, hostilities commenced between Great Britain and America. Boston became a garrison, and was abandoned by many of its inhabitants; and the regular meetings of the two Grand Lodges were suspended. June 17, by the contest of this eventful day on the hights of Charlestown, Masonry sustained a heavy loss in the death of Grand Master General Warren, who was slain contending for the liberties of his country. October 6, 1779, a petition of a number of brethren, officers in the American army, praying that this (Massachusetts) Grand Lodge would grant them a charter to hold a traveling Lodge, was read, and Gen. John Patterson, Col. Benjamin Tupper, and Major William Hull, being nominated as Master and Wardens, voted that a dispensation be granted them, under the title of "Washington Lodge," to make Masons, pass Fellow-Crafts, and raise Masters, in any of the United States where there is no Grand Lodge; but in any State where a Grand Master presides they must apply for his sanction. The St. John's Grand Lodge resumed its meetings after Boston was evacuated by the British army, and continued to move in harmony, granting charters for the establishment of new lodges, in various places. Dec. 5, 1791, a committee of the Massachusetts Grand Lodge was appointed to confer with the officers of St. John's Grand Lodge upon the subject of a complete Masonic union throughout this commonwealth, and to report at the next quarterly communication. March 5, 1792, the committee brought in their report, and presented a copy of the constitution and by-laws, and articles of association, as agreed to by St.

John's Grand Lodge, which were read, and receiving the deliberate attention of the grand body, they were unanimously approved. June 9, following, the two Grand Lodges met, agreeably to previous arrangements, unanimously elected Most Worshipful John Cutler Grand Master of the United Grand Lodge, and, thereupon, passed the following resolution: "*Resolved*, That this Grand Lodge shall forever hereafter be known by the name of the Grand Lodge of the Most Ancient and Honorable Society of Free and Accepted Masons, for the Commonwealth of Massachusetts." Thus were the prejudices and contentions so long indulged in most happily removed, and peace and harmony restored to the Order, not only in Massachusetts, but, as far as the original bodies had planted subordinates, in the surrounding country.

MEXICO. Freemasonry has existed for many years in the republic of Mexico, but in a very secluded character. In 1826 a Grand Lodge, with a few subordinates, existed in the city of Mexico, but, through the powerful influence of the church, the Order is not permitted to flourish.

MICHIGAN. Of the early introduction of Freemasonry into this (then) territory, we are unable to furnish any satisfactory data, notwithstanding diligent efforts have been made to obtain historical information. The Grand Lodge was organized at Detroit, June 24, 1826; was incorporated by the legislative council of the territory, in 1827, and, by a formal resolution, adopted in 1829, suspended Masonic labor. A general meeting of the Masons of the State was called for inquiry in 1740; in 1841 the former Grand Officers granted dispensations for several lodges, and in June of the same year, at the constitutional period, the Grand Lodge assembled and was organized by a constitutional number of lodges. General Lewis Cass was the first Grand Master under the original organization.

The GRAND ROYAL ARCH CHAPTER was organized in 1848.

The GRAND COUNCIL of Royal and Select Masters was organized 1858.

The GRAND COMMANDERY, Knights Templar, was organized Jan. 15, 1857.

MINNESOTA. Freemasonry was introduced into this territory by dispensation from the Grand Lodge of Ohio, dated August 4, 1849, to twelve Master Masons, to establish a Lodge, under the title of "St. Paul's Lodge," at St. Paul. Oct. 12, 1850, a dispensation to open a Lodge with the name of "St. John's Lodge," at Stillwater, was granted by the Grand Master of Wisconsin. During the year 1852 a dispensation was granted by the Grand Master of Illinois, to open a Lodge under the title of "Cataract Lodge," at St. Anthony. Feb. 23, 1853, delegates from the three lodges in the territory met in convention at St. Paul and organized a Grand Lodge. A. E. Ames was elected the first Grand Master.

The GRAND CHAPTER was organized Dec. 17, 1859. A. T. C. Pierson was elected the first Grand High-Priest.

The GRAND COMMANDERY, Knights Templar, was organized in 1866.

MISSISSIPPI. The Grand Lodge of Kentucky granted the first charter for a subordinate Lodge in this State, in 1817; afterward the Grand Lodge of Tennessee granted two charters for lodges. July 27, 1818, authorized delegates from the three lodges then working in the State, convened in the city of Natchez, and, being organized, resolved that it was expedient, and highly necessary, to form and organize a Grand Lodge for the State of Mississippi. August 25, following, the convention met again and adopted a constitution for the government of the Grand Lodge, when the lodges surrendered their charters obtained from Kentucky and Tennessee, and received others from the new Grand Lodge. Henry Tooley was elected the first Grand Master.

The GRAND CHAPTER was organized at Vicksburg, May 18, 1846. Benjamin S. Tappen was elected the first Grand High-Priest.

THE GRAND COUNCIL of Royal and Select Masters was organized Jan. 19, 1856. Benjamin Springer was elected the first M. P. Grand Master.

The GRAND COMMANDERY, Knights Templar, was organized Jan. 22, 1857. William H. Stevens was elected the first Grand Commander.

MISSOURI. The first Lodge established in the territory of Upper Louisiana, as this State was originally called, was by authority of a warrant from the Grand Lodge of Pennsylvania, in 1807, in the town of St. Genevieve. This Lodge flourished until 1816, when, owing to the unsettled condition of the country, it ceased to work. In 1809 a constitutional number of brethren obtained another charter from the Grand Lodge of Pennsylvania to open a Lodge in the town of St. Louis. Of the history of this Lodge nothing definite is known. A charter bearing date October 8, 1816, was granted by the Grand Lodge of Tennessee, to open a Lodge in the town of St. Louis, by the name of Missouri Lodge. October 6, 1819, charters were granted to open lodges in the towns of Herculaneum and St. Charles. In 1820 a dispensation from the Grand Lodge of Indiana was granted to form a Lodge in the town of Jackson. Feb. 22, 1821, a convention of delegates from the several lodges assembled in the town of St. Louis for the purpose of consulting upon the propriety of establishing a Grand Lodge for the State. The convention appointed a committee to draft a constitution, and adjourned to meet at the same place April 23, following. Pursuant to notice of adjournment the convention met, organized a Grand Lodge for the State, adopted the Constitution presented by the committee, and elected Grand Officers. Thomas F. Riddick was elected the first Grand Master.

The GRAND CHAPTER was organized May 18, 1846.

The GRAND COMMANDERY, Knights Templar, was organized May 22, 1860. George W. Belt was elected the first Grand Commander.

MONTANA. A Grand Lodge for this territory was organized at Virginia City Jan. 24, 1866. John J. Hull was elected the first Grand Master.

NEBRASKA. The first Lodge established in this territory was by charter from the Grand Lodge of Illinois to Nebraska Lodge, Oct. 3, 1855, at Bellevue; the second by charter from the Grand Lodge of Missouri to Giddings' Lodge, May 26, 1857, at Nebraska City; the third by charter from the Grand Lodge of Iowa to Capital Lodge, June 3, 1857, at Omaha City. Sept. 13, 1857, a convention of authorized delegates from the above Lodges met in Omaha, and established a Grand Lodge for the territory of Nebraska. R. C. Jordan was chosen the first Grand Master.

NEW HAMPSHIRE. The earliest record of the introduction of Masonry into this State will be found upon the books of St. John's Grand Lodge, Boston, and in these words, to wit: "A petition from the brethren residing in Portsmouth, in New Hampshire, for the erection of a Lodge there (June 24, 1734,) was granted, denominated 'The Holy Lodge of St. John's;' which was the beginning of Masonry in New Hampshire." A charter was granted to a number of brethren in Portsmouth by the Massachusetts Grand Lodge, under the name of "St. Patrick's Lodge," bearing date Boston, March 17, 1780. This Lodge continued its meetings until the latter end of 1790, when they ceased working. This Lodge had never acknowledged the jurisdiction of the Grand Lodge of New Hampshire, and the Massachusetts Grand Lodge, by the charter of St. Patrick's Lodge, claimed jurisdiction no longer than till a Grand Lodge should be formed in New Hampshire; therefore, St. Patrick's Lodge was not, at the time of its dissolution, under the jurisdiction of any Grand Lodge. A charter was granted to several brethren at Cornish by the Massachusetts Grand Lodge, dated Nov. 8, 1781. This Lodge met a few times at Cornish, but when that town was claimed by New Hampshire the Lodge removed to Windsor, Vermont, and took the name of Vermont Lodge No. 1. A petition from several brethren, to erect a Lodge at Keene, was read in the Massachusetts Grand Lodge, March 5, 1784, and a charter granted under the designation of the Rising Sun Lodge. This Lodge returned its charter to the Massachusetts Grand Lodge at the formation of the Grand Lodge of New Hampshire. Two other lodges—Faithful and Dartmouth—were chartered by the Massachusetts Grand Lodge, and were surrendered to the parent body after the formation of the New Hampshire Grand Lodge. July 8, 1789, deputies from the several lodges in the State assembled in convention, at Dartmouth, and, after due deliberation, adopted the following: "*Resolved*, That there be a Grand Lodge established in the State of New Hampshire, upon principles consistent with, and subordinate to, the General Regulations and Ancient Constitutions of Freemasonry." The Grand Lodge, being thus organized, proceeded to the election of Grand Officers, when the Hon. John Sullivan, President of the State, was elected Grand Master.

The GRAND CHAPTER was organized in 1819. John Harris was elected the first Grand High-Priest.

The Orders of Knighthood were introduced into this State in 1824.

The GRAND COMMANDERY was organized Aug. 22, 1860. Daniel Balch was elected the first Grand Commander.

NEW JERSEY. Of the exact date of the first existence of Masonry in this State we are compelled, as in several other cases, to say that the truth of history must for a little longer remain in the hidden and undeveloped record of the past. But that it had a name and an existence within the borders of the then colony of New Jersey none who are acquainted with the early history of Freemasonry in this country can doubt. The earliest historical record of the founding of the Order in America is to be found in Preston's Illustrations, under date 1729, the Duke of Norfolk being Grand Master, and in these words: "Established by deputation a Provincial Grand Lodge at New Jersey, in America." The warrant named "Right Worshipful

Brother Daniel Coxe of New Jersey, residing, and about to reside, in the said Provinces of New York, New Jersey, and Pensilvania, Provincial Grand Master, with free power to appoint his Deputy Grand Master and Grand Wardens for the space of two years," etc. This deputation bears date London, June 5, 1730: a certified copy of which is in possession of the Grand Lodge of New Jersey. That Bro. Coxe exercised any of the powers delegated to him we are not informed, nor has any evidence of action on his part been discovered. The first authentic information that we have is that a convention of the Masons in the State was held at the city of New Brunswick, Dec. 18, 1786, when a Grand Lodge was regularly constituted, and the Hon. David Brearley, Chief Justice of the State, was elected the first Grand Master.

The GRAND ROYAL ARCH CHAPTER was organized at Burlington, Dec. 30, 1856. Wm. H. Doggett was elected the first Grand High-Priest.

The GRAND COUNCIL of Royal and Select Masters was organized Nov. 26, 1860.

The GRAND COMMANDERY, Knights Templar, was organized Feb. 14, 1860. Theophilus Fiske was elected the first Grand Commander.

NEW YORK. The first recorded knowledge we have of the establishment of, or the attempt to establish, Freemasonry in the colonies of North America is the deputation granted by the Grand Lodge of England, in 1730, Duke of Norfolk, Grand Master, to Samuel Coxe, for the Provinces of New Jersey, New York, and Pennsylvania. But the fact that Brother Coxe used his authority or performed any Masonic act remains hidden beneath the unexcavated arches of our imperfect history. But the faithful and diligent craftsmen are at work, and we are confident that some valuable memento of the past will yet be the reward of their labors. The first charter for the organization of a Provincial Grand Lodge in New York was granted by the Grand Lodge of England in 1737, during the Grand Mastership of the Earl of Darnley, to Richard Riggs, as Provincial Grand Master. The precise date of this charter and the records of the Grand Lodge were, probably, destroyed during the war of the Revolution. Neither is it known that this Provincial Grand Lodge established any subordinates. In 1747, under the Grand Mastership of Lord Byron, provincial patents were issued for New York. During this period, and up to 1751, Francis Goalet exercised the prerogatives of Provincial Grand Master. For the space of two years we have no knowledge of who exercised the duties of Grand Master. June 9, 1753, a commission was granted by Lord Carysfort, Grand Master of England, empowering George Harrison to superintend the affairs of the Craft as Provincial Grand Master in the Province of New York. He was regularly installed in due and ancient form Dec. 27, 1753. Masonry flourished under his auspices, and several lodges were established in the Province. Sir John Johnson was appointed Provincial Grand Master in 1760 by Lord Aberdour, Grand Master of England, which office he held until the commencement of the war of the Revolution, when he espoused the cause of the British, and it is but fair to presume that he suspended the meetings of the Grand Lodge, took possession of the records, etc., and that they were finally destroyed during the war; as most of the lodges suspended business during the war, and the work of the Craft was transferred to the army or traveling lodges. Sept. 5, 1781, a warrant was granted by the "Ancient Grand Lodge of England," the Duke of Athol, Grand Master, to open a Provincial Grand Lodge in the city of New York, appointing Rev. William Walter Provincial Grand Master. The first meeting of this Grand Lodge was held Dec. 5, 1782, at which nine lodges, then in the city, and six military lodges, connected with the British army, were present. At the close of the war, and the evacuation of the city of New York, by the British army, the military lodges,

and many of the Grand Officers, left the country. Sept. 19, 1783, a meeting of the Provincial Grand Lodge was held, when Bro. Walter resigned and William Cock was unanimously elected Grand Master. At the meeting of Feb. 4, 1784, Bro. Cock resigned, and the Hon. Robert R. Livingston was elected Grand Master. The precise date when the Grand Lodge changed its form from *Provincial* to an *Independent* is not positively known. But it is generally conceded that when the articles of peace were ratified by the two countries, the Provincial title ceased, as a natural and legal result. The history of Masonry in New York has been an eventful one. Yet, notwithstanding these alternating experiences of tranquil calms and raging tempests, the Order of Freemasonry in New York is, to-day, immutable in its principles, unshattered by past convulsions, uninjured by insidious decay, unawed by threatened tumult or turbulent dissension, as securely poised upon a stable base as the everlasting hills.

The GRAND CHAPTER was organized Mar. 14, 1798. DeWitt Clinton was elected the first Grand High-Priest.

The GRAND COUNCIL of Royal and Select Masters was organized 1807.

The GRAND COMMANDERY, Knights Templar, was organized June 18, 1814. DeWitt Clinton was elected the first Grand Commander.

NORTH CAROLINA. Of the existence, or supposed existence, of Freemasonry in this State the earliest record is to be found among the transactions of St. John's Grand Lodge, at Boston, October 2, 1767, to wit: "A dispensation was made out for the Right Worshipful Thos. Cooper, Master of Pitt County Lodge, in North Carolina, constituting him Deputy Grand Master of that Province. And he was commissioned with power to congregate all the brethren there residing, or who should afterward reside in said Province, into one or more lodges as he should think fit, and in such place or places within the same as should most redound to the benefit of Masonry." As the early history

MASONIC TEMPLE AT CINCINNATI, OHIO.

of Freemasonry in every section of this country is of great importance, and that no statement, however small it may appear, should be unnoticed, we copy the following, in the hope of eliciting further and more reliable facts: "In a MS. letter of Robert Williams, Grand Secretary of the Grand Lodge of North Carolina, dated Jan. 9, 1808, and directed to the Grand Secretary of the Grand Lodge of Kentucky, Bro. Williams says: 'The Grand Lodge of North Carolina was constituted by charter, issued from the Grand Lodge of Scotland, in the year 1761, signed by Henry Somerset, Duke of Beaufort, as Grand Master; and attested by George John Spencer, as Grand Secretary. They were among the officers of the Grand Lodge of Scotland, although Beaufort was an English Duke, and Lord Spencer an English Earl.' As the famous altercations between the two Grand Lodges of North Carolina and Kentucky, in relation to the jurisdiction over the territory of Tennessee, in 1807, etc., was finally settled, chiefly by reference to the statements made by Bro. Williams, in relation to the above-named charter, it is a curious fact, that *the persons above-named were not officers of the Grand Lodge of Scotland,* but that the Duke of Beaufort, from 1767 to 1771, was Grand Master of *England!* It is admirable to see what a small amount of Masonic history satisfied our fathers fifty years ago. If Beaufort signed the charter, he must have done so as Grand Master of England. We hope this piece of history will yet be cleared up."[*] Here is another specimen of how Masonic history may be manufactured, when it is necessary to say something, but in the absence of reliable documentary evidence: "We know that a Provincial Grand Lodge was established in North Carolina, in 1771, under the authority of the Grand Lodge of Scotland, which convened alternately in Edenton and Newbern. The archives were deposited at Edenton, which, as we are informed, were destroyed

by the British army, during the Revolution; and, for several years, the meetings of the grand body were suspended, and all knowledge of its early records were lost. We cannot even say whether this Provincial warrant was issued directly by the Grand Lodge of Scotland, as we cannot find the fact stated in the history of that grand body; but we think it not at all difficult to reconcile this seeming defect. We know that, in 1756, the Grand Lodge of Scotland granted a Provincial commission to Col. John Young, who had long acted as Deputy Grand Master over all the Lodges in America and the West Indies. But, as before stated, that warrant was destroyed, and for about ten years no effective attempt was made to reorganize. 'In 1787, the *members of the Craft* assembled at Hillsborough, and compiled a code of laws for the government of the Grand Lodge, and again commenced Masonic labors.' From this it would seem that they did not think themselves incapacitated to reorganize, or resuscitate, the Grand Lodge, or, which is most likely, to form a new Grand Lodge, because the original document of authority had been destroyed."[*] Samuel Johnson, Governor of the State, was elected the first Grand Master.

By the transactions of the General Grand Chapter (meeting of 1847) we learn that a Grand Chapter existed in North Carolina, as a constituent of that grand body, in 1822, but that it had ceased its labors. The Grand Chapter was reorganized June 28, 1847, under the General Grand Chapter of the United States. In 1857 it withdrew and became an independent Grand Chapter.

The GRAND COUNCIL of Royal and Select Masters was organized June 6, 1860.

OHIO. For the introduction of Freemasonry into Ohio we can give no better or more reliable history than that found in the Introduction to the republished transactions of the Grand Lodge. "At the con-

---

[*] "History of Masonry in Kentucky," by Robert Morris, pp. 10, 11.

[*] "History of Freemasonry," by J. W. S Mitchell, p. 576, vol. i.

vention which organized the Grand Lodge delegates from six chartered lodges (the delegate from one Lodge was not admitted—the reason is not stated) appeared as representatives. The lodges were: Union, No. 1; Cincinnati, No. 13; Scioto, No. 2; Erie, No. 47, and Amity, No. 105. Union Lodge, No. 1, at Marietta, derived its charter from the Grand Lodge of Massachusetts.* The strong presumption is that this Lodge is the legitimate successor of the old and honored American Union Lodge organized Feb. 13, 1776, at Roxbury, Massachusetts. As many of its members, after the dispersion of the army, settled at Marietta, Cincinnati Lodge No. 13, at Cincinnati, received its warrant originally from the Grand Lodge of New Jersey, Sept. 8, 1791, under the title of Nova Cesarea Lodge No. 10. Some time between June 24 and Dec. 10, 1805, the members returned their original charter and took one from the Grand Lodge of Kentucky, assuming the title of Cincinnati Lodge No. 13. Scioto Lodge No. 2, at Chillicothe, was organized in 1805, by charter from the Grand Lodge of Massachusetts. Erie Lodge No. 47, at Warren, was organized March 16, 1804, by dispensation from the Grand Lodge of Connecticut. Amity Lodge No. 105, at Zanesville, received its charter from the Grand Lodge of Pennsylvania, about the year 1804. Jan. 8, 1808, a convention of delegates from all the lodges in the State met at Chillicothe to consider the propriety of establishing a Grand Lodge for the State. The convention, in its deliberations, adjourned from day to day, and, on the 7th, the following resolution was unanimously agreed to: "*Resolved*, That a Grand Lodge be formed, to be known and styled the Grand Lodge of Ohio, whose powers

* As the charter, with a portion, if not all, of the records of the Lodge were burned, with the building in which it was held, a few years afterward, very little is known of its history or origin, save that it emanated from the Grand Lodge of Massachusetts. It was brought by the first settlers, and seemed to be in charge, principally, of men belonging to the American army.

shall be to grant charters and dispensations, on proper application, to all such as shall apply, and shall be deemed worthy—and shall have jurisdiction over the same—and shall in all respects be clothed with full powers, as a Grand Lodge, according to ancient and due form, and agreeably to the rules and landmarks of Masonry." General Rufus Putnam, a hero and veteran of the Revolutionary war, was elected the first Grand Master.

The GRAND CHAPTER was organized October, 1816. Samuel Hoyt was elected the first Grand High-Priest.

The GRAND COUNCIL of Royal and Select Masters was organized in 1829.

The GRAND COMMANDERY, Knights Templar, organized Oct. 24, 1843. Michael Z. Kreider was elected the first Grand Commander.

OREGON. Freemasonry was introduced into this territory in 1849 or 1850, by warrants from the Grand Lodge of California. Aug. 16, 1851, a convention was held at Oregon City to take into consideration the subject of forming a Grand Lodge. Three lodges were represented, viz: Multnomah, No. 84; Willamette, No. 11; and LaFayette, No. 15. The Grand Lodge was organized, a constitution adopted, and the officers elected. Berryman Jennings was elected the first Grand Master.

PENNSYLVANIA. The first Lodge of which we have any authentic historical record was established in Philadelphia, in 1734. The deputation granted to Daniel Coxe as Provincial Grand Master for New Jersey, New York, and Pennsylvania, in 1730, naturally leads us to the belief, and particularly when our impression is sustained with notices in the public newspapers of the day, that lodges existed in Philadelphia anterior to 1734. Notwithstanding the doubts and discrepancies existing in regard to the early development of the mystic Order in Pennsylvania, we must content ourselves with the evidences of history as presented to us until the mists that now surround the temple shall be dispelled by the discovery of the truth. The history of St. John's Grand Lodge, at Boston, furnished the following extract: "A petition being presented from Benjamin Franklin and several brethren residing in Philadelphia, June 24, 1734, for a constitution for holding a Lodge there, the R. W. Grand Master (Henry Price), having this year received orders from the Grand Lodge in England to establish Masonry in all North America, was pleased to grant the prayer of the petitioners, and to send them a deputation, appointing the R. W. Benjamin Franklin their first Master; which was the beginning of Masonry in the State of Pennsylvania." July 10, 1749, Franklin received a similar appointment from Thomas Oxnard, Provincial Grand Master of New England, and the successor of Henry Price. In March, 1750, Wm. Allen presented a communication from the Grand Lodge of England as Provincial Grand Master of Pennsylvania. Franklin afterward received a commission from England as Provincial Grand Master. "In 1758, Lodge No. 2 was constituted, by virtue of a warrant from the Grand Lodge of Ancient York Masons of England, the Earl of Blessington, Grand Master, and Laurence Dermott, Grand Secretary."* From the same source as the extract just quoted, we are informed "that a warrant for a Provincial Grand Lodge in Pennsylvania was issued by the Grand Lodge of England, in June 1764, directed to William Ball, as Grand Master. From this period little is known of Masonry in Pennsylvania. The original archives of the Provincial Grand Lodges (for it seems there was more than one) were destroyed during the Revolution, and while Philadelphia was in the hands of the British. In 1779, the Masons of that jurisdiction, feeling the evils resulting from the want of an organized body, requested William Ball to convene the Masons of the State with a view of reorganization. In compliance with their request he summoned the brethren to assemble in Philadelphia, Dec. 20, when Grand Officers were elected—Bro. Ball being chosen Grand Master. Sept. 13, 1786, thirteen lodges, by their Masters and Wardons, met in Philadelphia, and unanimously "*Resolved*, That it would be improper that the Grand Lodge of Pennsylvania should remain any longer under the authority of any foreign Grand Lodge;" whereupon, the Grand Lodge closed *sine die*. On the day following, the delegates of the thirteen lodges assembled in convention, and organized the present Grand Lodge of Pennsylvania, and elected Grand Officers. From the reorganization of this Grand Lodge, down to the present day, the history of Masonry in that jurisdiction has been one uninterrupted course of prosperity and general harmony.

The GRAND CHAPTER was organized Nov. 23, 1795. Until about 1820 this Grand Chapter was in its government under the Grand Lodge, its Grand Master being *ex officio* the Grand High-Priest of the Grand Chapter. It has since been a Grand Chapter with its own elective Grand Officers. It is sovereign and independent, and has never acknowledged the supremacy of the General Grand Chapter of the United States. Previous to the formation of this Grand Chapter, a Master's warrant was sufficient authority for congregating a Chapter, and conferring any degree of Masonry the brethren had knowledge of.

The GRAND COUNCIL of Royal and Select Masters was organized Oct. 16, 1847. Previous to the formation of this Grand Council, it was customary for the Chapters to confer the degrees on those who desired them as honorary degrees.

Masonic Knighthood was introduced into Pennsylvania in 1793.* Prior to 1797 four Encampments were instituted in this State, viz: two in Philadelphia, one in Harrisburg, and one in Carlisle. These bodies were under the authority of the Grand Lodge of Pennsylvania

---

* History of Masonry in Pennsylvania, presented to the Grand Lodge in 1826.

* "History of the Knights Templar of Penn.," by Alfred Creigh, Phila., 1867.

until the 12th of May, 1797, when a Grand Encampment was organized at a convention of delegates from the several Encampments. From this period Templarism has existed as an independent organization.

PERU. As long as the Spaniards held an exclusive and undisputed possession of the country (1536–1782), and the Inquisition lent its aid to a fanatical priesthood, it cannot be a matter of surprise that Masonry was unknown in Peru. The introduction of the Royal Art, or even the fact of being a Mason, would have been a sufficient cause for the banishment, if not the death, of the offender. During the French invasion of Spain (1807–13), and the presence there of the English, many lodges were instituted in that country, and, among the troops sent from Europe to quell the war of Independence in Peru, there were many brethren; these, however, being subjects of Spain, admitted none of the patriots as members, and it was not until the Declaration of Independence, in 1821, when free intercourse was established between Peru and foreign nations, that Freemasonry was introduced among the natives. In 1825, after Peru had achieved her complete independence, lodges were established in Lima and other parts, by authority of letters patent from the Grand Orient of Colombia. From this Grand Orient all the other Masonic bodies in Peru afterward derived their existence. The bodies worked in the Ancient and Accepted Scottish rite. Nov. 2, 1830, a Supreme Council of this rite for the Republic of Peru was established. June 23, 1831, the Masters and Wardens of the symbolic lodges, as well as representatives from the councils, chapters, etc., assembled at the capital and installed themselves into an Independent Grand Lodge under the title of the Grand Lodge of Peru, which was in the same year changed to Grand Orient. The political agitations, which soon after disturbed the peace of the country, caused the lodges to be closed, and an attempt was made to drive Masonry from the country. In 1845, after a recess of some twelve years, a number of brethren assembled and reopened several of the lodges and chapters. Jan. 30, 1849, the Supreme Council was reopened, and lodges under its authority set to work. July 13, 1852, the Grand Orient of Peru was reopened and reconstituted under the title of National Grand Orient of Peru. In 1852 the Supreme Royal Arch Chapter of Scotland granted a charter to hold a Holy Royal Arch Chapter at Callao. This was the first Masonic body of the "Ancient York rite," opened in the Republic. This chapter was not recognized by any of the governing bodies. In May, 1857, an extensive schism broke out among the Fraternity, and many lodges and chapters were instituted by the disaffected party. None of the grand bodies throughout the world acknowledged the schismatics. At the present time (1866) there are no illegal bodies in Peru, except one at Callao —which is only a remnant of the former schisms. There are many lodges and chapters in Lima and Callao, in a healthy and prosperous condition. Beside the lodges and chapters under the Supreme Council, working in the Scottish rite in Lima and Callao, the Grand Lodge of Ireland has two lodges, to one of which a Chapter of Royal Arch is attached, under its jurisdiction, all in Lima. The Grand Lodge of Scotland has, besides the Royal Arch Chapter, a Lodge of symbolic Masonry in Callao. The Grand Lodge of Massachusetts has a Lodge established in Arica. All these bodies, combined, form the Grand Orient of Peru, which admits into its bosom all recognized rites, consistent with the general principles of Freemasonry.

POLAND. Freemasonry began in Poland in 1736, but was almost immediately suppressed through the influence of the church. In 1742–49 many new lodges were established, and in 1766 the institution rose to a high position. In 1780 the Lodge of the Good Shepherd was established by the Grand Lodge of England. In 1784 thirteen lodges, then in the country, met at Warsaw and organized a Grand Lodge. In 1807 the Grand Orient of France founded several lodges in the kingdom. In 1822 a decree of the Emperor Alexander prohibited all secret societies; the brethren of Poland, though deeply grieved, yet submissively closed their lodges, which, since then, have remained closed.

PORTUGAL. The introduction of Freemasonry into this kingdom began at Lisbon, in 1735, by the Grand Lodge of England, but its usefulness was of short duration. The inquisition, that great extinguisher of liberty and enlightenment, had control of this country. Notwithstanding this powerful opposition the Order succeeded in spreading its cheerful influences, and in 1805 a Grand Lodge was organized. In 1807, during the invasion of Portugal by the French troops, Masonry was protected, and until 1810, when a fresh persecution of the Order began, which lasted until about 1837, since which time the Order has been permitted to enjoy some success. There exists in Lisbon a Grand Lodge of Portugal and a Provincial Grand Lodge of Ireland, which are recognized by foreign Grand Lodges.

PRUSSIA. Freemasonry was introduced into Prussia by Frederick II., surnamed the Great. Having been secretly initiated, while crownprince, at Brunswick, he soon after organized a Lodge in the castle of Rheinsberg; and when, in 1740, he ascended the throne he himself wielded the gavel, and conducted the first work with his own hand at the castle in Charlottenburg, June 20. The distinctive title of this Lodge was "The First Lodge," or "The Lodge of the King, our Grand Master." In the same year, Sept. 13, at his instigation, a new Lodge was established in Berlin, which was called "The Three Globes." This Lodge was principally composed of the members of "The First Lodge," which had but a brief existence. In 1744 "the Lodge of the Three Globes" assumed the title of Royal Grand Mother Lodge of the Three Globes, and constituted subordinate lodges at Meiningen, Frank-

fort, Breslau, Halle, etc. The king assumed the office of Grand Master, and continued to bear the title, although during the seven years war, and the cares that government entailed on him, he was prevented from attending to his Masonic duties. In 1747, he appointed the Duke of Holstein-Beck as Vice-Grand Master, when the statutes were revised, and Masonry, which had somewhat declined, again revived. Soon afterward a new Lodge, "*La Petite Concorde,*" was established at Berlin, and, in 1760, a third, "The Three Doves;" the latter being founded by Tilley de Lerney and a number of French prisoners of war. Dissensions soon broke out between these lodges; and then began in Berlin and throughout Germany that lamentable period of Masonry, when the introduction of the French degrees, and the admixture of various systems and new rites, caused such confusion among the Fraternity that the original tendency of the institution was almost extinguished. (To follow the history of Masonry in Prussia through this period, with its thousand changes, systems, schisms, etc., in an intelligible manner, would require too long an article.) In 1765 Zinnendorf became Grand Master of the Grand Lodge of the Three Globes, but the following year abandoned it, and in 1770 instituted at Berlin a new Grand Lodge, called the Grand National Lodge of Germany, for which he obtained royal sanction, and also a constitution from the Grand Lodge of England. In 1772 the Grand Lodge of the Three Globes assumed the title of the "National Grand Mother Lodge for the Prussian States." In the meantime, the Lodge of the Three Doves, which had been founded at Berlin in 1760, and subsequently added to its original title that of "Friendship," separated from its Mother Lodge (the Three Globes) in 1765, and assumed the title of "Royal York of Friendship." In 1798, a royal edict was issued, which, while strictly prohibiting all secret societies, especially excepted the three existing Grand Lodges with their subordinates.

RHODE ISLAND. December 27, 1749, the petition of several brethren residing in Newport was presented to St. John's Grand Lodge at Boston, of which Thomas Oxnard was Grand Master, praying for the incorporation of a regular Lodge there, which, on being read, it was voted that a charter be granted them. This was the beginning of Masonry in Rhode Island. The second Lodge was established at Providence Jan. 18, 1757, under the title of St. John's Lodge, by authority of the same Grand Lodge, Jeremy Gridley being Grand Master, in compliance with the petition of several brethren residing there. Nov. 3, 1790, a report from a joint committee of the two lodges in Rhode Island, proposing a plan for the formation of a Grand Lodge of Rhode Island, was adopted. The constitution of the Grand Lodge was adopted April 6, 1791. Christopher Champlin was elected the first Grand Master. The first charter granted by the Grand Lodge of Rhode Island was in 1799, to certain brethren in Warren, under the name of Washington Lodge No. 3. Notwithstanding the irregularity in the formation of the Grand Lodge by only two subordinates, Freemasonry has always occupied a respectable position in Rhode Island, and her membership has been composed of its best and most honored citizens.

The GRAND CHAPTER was organized March, 1798. Seth Wheaton was the first Grand High-Priest.

The GRAND COUNCIL of Royal and Select Masters was organized Oct. 30, 1860.

The GRAND COMMANDERY, Knights Templar, belonging, jointly, to Massachusetts and Rhode Island, was formed in 1805. Thomas Smith Webb, of R. I., was the first Grand Commander.

RUSSIA. In 1731 the Grand Lodge of England granted a warrant for a Lodge at St. Petersburg, and named Captain John Phillips as Provincial Grand Master. For many years Freemasonry flourished, and gained strength. In 1771 the Order was patronized by the nobility. The Emperor Peter III. conducted the affairs of a Lodge, and was regarded as an expert workman. In 1783 the lodges throughout the empire organized a National Grand Lodge. The society rose to a fullness of splendor, unequaled in any part of the world. But this state of prosperity was not permitted to continue. Politics and religious opinions were permitted to enter the lodge-room; extravagance and speculation became unmanagable among the brotherhood; the church, with powerful influence, and some other causes, compelled the Craft to close their lodges, yet the meetings were occasionally held, but very secluded, until 1808-14, when the Order again flourished with renewed vigor, and until 1822, when, suddenly and most unexpectedly, the Emperor Alexander issued a decree that all the Masonic lodges throughout the empire should be closed, and no others permitted to be founded. The then condition of Poland was alleged as a reason for this. The brethren, with saddened hearts, calmly obeyed the command of their monarch. A few years after the Fraternity ventured again upon their field of philanthropy; gradually reopened their lodges, and resumed their labors, and continue to assemble as Freemasons even to the present day.

SAXONY. The first Lodge was established at Dresden, Saxony, in 1738. In 1741 another was formed at Leipsic, and a third in 1742 at Altenburg. In 1805 a convention of the lodges in Saxony assembled for the purpose of establishing a Grand Lodge; although the rules for its organization were arranged, yet it was not perfected until 1811. The seat of the Grand Lodge is at Dresden. The system of Ancient Craft Masonry and Schroder's rite are the work of the lodges in this country.

SCOTLAND. The early history of Freemasonry in this country, like that of England and Germany, is surrounded with the misty haze of legendary lore. The first reliable information we have touching the Fraternity dates back to the early part of the fifteenth century. They, at that period, acknowledged their king and sovereign as their Grand Master; to his authority they submitted all disputes that happened among the brethren. When not a Mason himself, he appointed one of the brethren to preside as his deputy at their meetings, and to regulate all matters concerning the Craft. In 1430 King James I. was acknowledged as the Royal Grand Master, who regulated the affairs of the Fraternity. In 1441 William St Clair, Earl of Orkney and Baron of Roslin, obtained a grant of the office of Grand Master from King James II. By another grant this office was made hereditary to the said William St. Clair, and his heirs and successors in the barony of Roslin; in which noble family it has continued without interruption till of late years. The Masons held their grand courts, or, in Masonic language, their Grand Lodge assembled at Kilwinning, in the western country, where it is claimed that the Masons of Scotland first held regular and permanent lodges. It is asserted, with great firmness and plausibility, that in this place the royal art first made its appearance. The office of Patron being hereditary in the family of Sinclair of Roslin, he being advanced in years, and having no children, was anxious that the office of Grand Master should not become vacant at his death; therefore he assembled the lodges in and about Edinburg, Oct. 15, 1736, and represented to them how beneficial it would be to the cause of Masonry in general, to have a Grand Master of their own electing, and intimated his intention of resigning his office, and setting the next St. Andrew's day, Nov. 30, as the time for holding such election. On that day thirty-three lodges met, and, having received the resignation of St. Clair, they proceed to the election, and unanimously elected William Sinclair, of Roslin, Grand Master, and this was also the founding of the Grand Lodge of Scotland. The Lodge at Kilwinning, (more generally known as the "Mother Lodge of Kilwinning,") long after the institution of the Grand Lodge,

continued to act independently, and to grant charters to other lodges as formerly. This gave rise to disputes, which it was desirable for the credit of the Fraternity to avoid; and at length, in 1807, Mother Kilwinning Lodge agreed to surrender her authority and acknowledge the Grand Lodge, thereby renouncing all right to grant charters in future. Kilwinning was placed at the head of the roll of the Grand Lodge under the denomination of "Mother Kilwinning," and its Master, for the time being, declared the Provincial Grand Master over the Ayrshire district, and this put an end to all disputes about Masonic precedency. From this time Freemasonry has prospered and increased throughout the country.

Besides the Grand Lodge there are: 1. Supreme Grand Royal Arch Chapter for Scotland; 2. The Royal Order of Scotland, Herodom of Kilwinning, supposed to have been established by King Robert Bruce, in 1314; 3. The General Chapter of the Religious and Military Order of Knights Templar, with various Priories; 4. The Supreme Grand Council of Scotland of the Ancient and Accepted Scottish rite.

SOUTH CAROLINA. There is no evidence, by record or tradition, of the existence of a Masonic Lodge in the Province of South Carolina anterior to the year 1736. Oct. 28, of that year, the first Lodge of Masons in South Carolina was opened in the city of Charleston, then known as "Charles-Town."* In this year John Hammerton was appointed Provincial Grand Master for the Colony, which office he resigned the following year, when he was succeeded by James Græme. The early history of the Order in

* This is the first Lodge that was ever established in the jurisdiction. It received its warrant from Lord Weymouth, the Grand Master of the Grand Lodge of England, with the title of Solomon's Lodge No. 45; afterward it became No. 1. From its organization, in 1736, it continued uninterruptedly to work until 1811, when it suspended labor. In 1817 it was revived, but again became dormant in 1838. It was finally revived, by a new warrant, granted June 25, 1841. It is now in active and successful operation.

South Carolina is shrouded in some doubt, particularly in consequence of the apathy of the brotherhood, and partly by reason of a large fire which occurred in Charleston in 1738. The period of inaction which marked the Order for several years previous to 1754 was, in that year, brought to a happy conclusion, and was followed by an important reaction. In 1754, the Marquis of Carnarvon granted a deputation "to Peter Leigh, Chief Justice of South Carolina, for Carolina." Mr. Leigh proved an efficient officer. He, immediately after his arrival, appointed a Deputy Grand Master and Grand Wardens, and reorganized the Provincial Grand Lodge. Masonry, for a time, flourished with renewed vigor. The Hon. Peter Leigh died Aug. 21, 1759. In 1761 Benjamin Smith was appointed Prov. Grand Master, who resigned the office in 1767. In 1769 the Duke of Beaufort, Grand Master of England, appointed the Hon. Egerton Leigh Provincial Grand Master, which office he held until he left the country, in 1774. In 1777 the Grand Lodge elected the Hon. Barnard Elliott "Grand Master of Masons in this State." This, Dr. Mackey strongly urges, was "the true date of the organization of the Grand Lodge of South Carolina." In 1787 the Grand Lodge became an independent body, and called itself the Grand Lodge of Free and Accepted Masons of South Carolina. In the same year the Grand Lodge of Ancient York Masons was organized. In 1808 the two Grand Lodges united and formed the Grand Lodge of South Carolina. In 1809 the Grand Lodge of Ancient York Masons was revived. In 1817 the final union took place between the Grand Lodge of South Carolina and the revived Grand Lodge of Ancient York Masons, which forms the present Grand Lodge of South Carolina.

The GRAND ROYAL ARCH CHAPTER was organized May 29, 1812. Wm. Young was elected the first Grand High-Priest.

The degrees of Royal and Select Masters were first introduced into South Carolina in the year 1783, and conferred in the Lodge of Perfection, at Charleston, under the authority of the Ancient and Accepted rite. After a time the Supreme Council relinquished its authority over the councils established in the State, and, in 1860, a Grand Council of Royal and Select Masters was established. Albert G. Mackey was elected the first Most Puissant Grand Master.

The order of Knights Templar was introduced into South Carolina about 1780-1803. The exact date is involved in obscurity and doubt. There is but one Commandery (South Carolina Commandery No. 1) in the State.

SPAIN. In 1727 the first Lodge in Spain was established at Gibraltar, by warrant from the Earl of Inchiquin, Grand Master of England; the second at Madrid in 1728, and a third in 1739, at Andalusia. In 1740 Philip V. issued an edict against the Order, and several members of the Fraternity were arrested and condemned to the galleys. Freemasonry was much oppressed in Spain until the year 1807, when Joseph Bonaparte ascended the throne; the Fraternity increased rapidly, and, in 1809, a National Grand Lodge was founded at Madrid, which held its meetings in the same building in which the inquisition had a short time before held its convocations. In 1811, the king, in his capacity of Grand Commander, founded a Grand Chapter of the higher degrees. The Fraternity flourished till the return of Ferdinand VII., who reëstablished the inquisition, and in 1814 the meetings of the Order were prohibited, and many of the Masons persecuted in the most inhuman manner. Between 1845 and 1852 the lodges increased notwithstanding the opposition. A Grand Orient had been organized under the title of "Gran Oriente Hesperico," which acknowledges the Ancient and Accepted rite, and also recognizes the lodges founded by the Grand Lodge. The members of the Order are obliged to use fictitious names to escape the persecutions of the civil authorities. No

Lodge is permitted to possess any written documents, and every six months a new pass-word is selected, and communicated by the Grand Orient; brethren who are strangers are only admitted if personally known to the W. M.

SWEDEN. Freemasonry was introduced into this country in 1735, by charter from the Grand Orient of France, granted to the Governor, Count Sparre. But little is known of this Lodge, as its operations were closed in 1738 by royal decree, forbidding Masons to meet on pain of death. This prohibition was rescinded in 1740, when the Order spread and flourished. It soon enjoyed a position that the brethren did not hesitate to publicly acknowledge their association with the institution. In 1762 King Adolphus Frederick declared himself the protector of the Swedish lodges, and desired to participate in the labors and expenses of the Fraternity. In 1765 Lord Blaney, Grand Master of England, granted a deputation to Brother Charles Fullman, secretary to the English embassy at Stockholm, to establish a Provincial Grand Lodge for Sweden. In 1799 a union of the Grand Lodges of Sweden and England was effected, which was the cause of great rejoicing among the Fraternity. In 1809 Charles XIII. ascended the throne of Sweden, who, May 27, 1811, founded an order of knighthood under the title of "Charles the Thirteenth," for the purpose, as is stated in the manifesto establishing the Order, to do honor to those virtues which are not prescribed by law, and which are seldom offered to the notice of the public. The statutes exacted that this Order, the distinctive badges of which were to be worn openly, should only be communicated to Freemasons; it, therefore, formed the highest degree of Swedish Freemasonry. The reigning king was always to be Grand Master of the Order, and beside the princes of the royal house, the Order could only consist of twenty-seven secular and three ecclesiastical members. Charles XIII. remained an active and zealous member of the Order during his life time. Freemasonry is still protected by the crown, and is, therefore, one of the most respectable institutions in the country.

SWITZERLAND. The introduction of the Order into Switzerland began in 1737, by warrant from the Grand Lodge of England, to Sir George Hamilton, as Provincial Grand Master, by authority of which he established a Provincial Grand Lodge at Geneva. In 1739 the Duke of Montacute, Grand Master of England, granted a warrant to a number of English nobleman to establish a Lodge at Lausanne. Masonry flourished for a short time, when it was prohibited by the civil authorities of Berne. The lodges remained closed for nearly twenty years, when the old Lodge at Lausanne was revived, and flourished for a short period. But soon the old prohibition was again issued against the Order. Internal dissensions also entered the bodies, which, for a time, threatened its total destruction. Four distinct organizations, in spirited opposition to each other, existed at the same time in the republic. During the stormy political events between 1793 and 1803 the lodges remained closed. When Neuenburg and Geneva were ceded to France, the Grand Lodge of Geneva ceased to exist, and all the lodges placed themselves under the Grand Orient of France, which immediately founded new lodges in various parts of the country. Peace, with its harmonious influences, was restored, and Masonry immediately revived. In 1822 a treaty of union was agreed upon between the Grand Orient and the English Provincial Grand Lodge, which assumed the name of the Grand Lodge of Switzerland. In 1844, through the efforts of the powerful and influential Masons of Switzerland, delegates from all the lodges met at Zurich, when the treaty of union was ratified for the newly-founded Grand Lodge under the name of "Alpina." Switzerland displays in the present day great Masonic activity, and the Fraternity therein is much esteemed.

TENNESSEE. Previous to Dec. 27, 1813, the lodges in the State of Tennessee were held under charters from the Grand Lodge of North Carolina, except one which was held under the authority of the Grand Lodge of Kentucky. Pursuant to notice, a convention of delegates from the several lodges in the State assembled at Knoxville in December, 1811, for the purpose of establishing a Grand Lodge, when the following resolutions were adopted: "*Resolved*, That, in the opinion of this convention, the number of lodges of Ancient York Masons in this State, as well as the state of society, require the formation of a Grand Lodge within the same, for the better regulation and extension of the Craft. *Resolved*, That a committee be appointed for the purpose of drawing up an address to the Grand Lodge of North Carolina, soliciting their assent to the establishment of a Grand Lodge in the State of Tennessee." Other resolutions were adopted, of similar effect to the foregoing, and the convention adjourned to meet Dec. 27, 1813, when the Grand Lodge was organized, the officers elected and installed. Thomas Clairborne was elected the first Grand Master.

TEXAS. The introduction of Masonry into Texas began by dispensation from John H. Holland, Grand Master of Louisiana, under the name of Holland Lodge, Dec. 17, 1835, at Brazoria. Soon after hostilities broke out between Mexico and Texas, when the Lodge was obliged to close its operations. Brazoria was abandoned; Gen. Urrea, commander of the Mexican forces, entered the city and took possession of the books, jewels, and everything belonging to the Lodge. Meanwhile the Grand Lodge of Louisiana had issued a charter for Holland Lodge No. 36, and the Lodge was reopened in Oct., 1837, at the city of Houston. Soon after two other lodges, with charters from the Grand Lodge of Louisiana, were established in Texas—Milam, at Nacogdoches, and McFarlane, at San Augustine. Delegates from these, and from Holland Lodge, met in convention at Houston, in the winter of 1837–8,

and the Grand Lodge of the republic was formed. By advice and direction of this body, the three subordinate lodges transferred their allegiance from Louisiana to their own Grand Lodge, surrendered their charters to Louisiana, and received others from Texas. Anson Jones was elected the first Grand Master. Such is the brief sketch of the first establishment of Freemasonry in Texas. It was founded, like our political institutions, amid the stern concomitants of adversity and war; but its foundations were laid broad and deep, and upon them has been raised a superstructure of strength and beauty, symmetrical in its proportions and vast in its dimensions, and which will continue as a beacon to guide and cheer worthy Masons on their journey of life.

TRINIDAD, W. I. Henry Price, Provincial Grand Master of New England, in 1733, on his return to England in 1738, went by way of Antigua, where, finding a number of Masons from Boston, he formed them into a Lodge, gave them a charter and initiated the governor and several gentlemen of high distinction. In 1798 a charter was received from the Grand Lodge of France, for the Lodge United Brothers, which, in 1799, had its warrant renewed by the Grand Lodge of Pennsylvania. This Lodge remained under the jurisdiction of the Grand Lodge of Pennsylvania until 1814, when, in consequence of the war between the United States and Great Britain, communications being interrupted, the brethren petitioned the Grand Lodge of Scotland to take them under their protection, which request was complied with. This Lodge is still in existence, with the No. 251 on the registry of the Grand Lodge of Scotland. A Chapter of Royal Arch Masons has also been established there. The Grand Lodge of England has several lodges at work there. In 1814 a charter was granted by the Royal Grand Conclave of Scotland to the "Trinidad Grand Assembly of Knights Templar, No. 29." Masonry is now in a flourishing condition here.

TURKEY. Freemasonry was introduced into the Ottoman Empire about 1830; but it soon ceased to exist. More recently several lodges have been established at Constantinople, Smyrna, and Aleppo, and particularly among the English settlements. The lodges are prosperous, and an English Provincial Grand Lodge for Turkey has been established recently, with Sir Henry Bulwer as Grand Master.

URUGUAY. The first Lodge was established in this republic in the year 1827, by the Grand Orient of France, under the name of "The Children of the New World." This Lodge is still in existence, having, however, changed its name to that of "The Friends of the Country." There are several Spanish lodges in the republic, governed by the Supreme Council and the Grand Orient of Uruguay, which were established in the year 1855. The lodges under this authority, and the solitary one which retains its allegiance to the Grand Orient of France, are working together in the utmost harmony. Notwithstanding the opposition of the priesthood here, Masonry is fully carrying out its great mission of love.

VERMONT. Of the first introduction of Freemasonry into this State we have, at present, no immediate knowledge, unless the first Lodge is that mentioned in the following statement: "A petition from several brethren, dated at Cornish, (then claimed by Vermont, but now in New Hampshire,) was read in the Massachusetts Grand Lodge, Nov. 8, 1781, praying for the establishment of a Lodge in that place; whereupon, voted that a charter be issued accordingly. This Lodge met a few times at Cornish, but when that town was claimed by New Hampshire the Lodge removed to Windsor, Vt., on the opposite side of Connecticut river, and took the name of 'Vermont Lodge, No. 1.'" Jan. 17, 1785, the Massachusetts Grand Lodge granted a charter to a proper number of Master Masons, residing at Manchester, Vermont, to establish a Lodge at that place. The Grand Lodge was organized Oct. 19, 1794.

The GRAND CHAPTER was organized Dec. 20, 1804. Jonathan Wells was elected the first Grand High-Priest. Reorganized July 18, 1849.

The GRAND COUNCIL of Royal and Select Masters was organized 1854. Nathan B. Haswell was elected the first Grand Master.

The GRAND COMMANDERY, Knights Templar, was organized 1825—was dormant for several years—reorganized Jan. 14, 1852.

VIRGINIA. Writers on the early history of Freemasonry in the United States, particularly of the time when they were colonies of the British government, are often embarrassed in their researches, and are unable to furnish the "tangible proof" of the first introduction of the Order into certain well-established localities among the early settlements of this country. The historian is often sorely perplexed from the fact that the materials within his reach are in many instances only speculations, presumptions, or the—too frequently questionable—statements of "the oldest inhabitant." The difficulty, therefore, of preparing a continuous history of Freemasonry in America lies mainly in the presumptive character of much of the evidence that makes up its record. That there is some cause for this lack of reliable evidence is beyond dispute. The many difficulties that surrounded the habitations of the first emigrants; the wild and unsettled condition of the country; the war of the Revolution, when the merciless foe burned and destroyed every kind of property within his reach; the frequent ecclesiastical and political persecutions which have from time to time been brought against the Order, and the slight interest taken by our predecessors in the preservation of Masonic records—these, with other causes, will, in some measure, account for the scarcity of reliable Masonic data, at the present time. We are led to these reflections after examining the scanty materials which we find for the subject under discussion as well as of that already disposed of. For the matter of this sketch I am indebted to a very able and interesting address on the "History of the Grand Lodge of Virginia, by R. W. JOHN DOVE, M. D." Bro. Dove has been an active member of the Grand Lodge of Virginia for fifty, and its Grand Secretary for more than thirty, years. He says: "The first Lodge of Ancient York Masons was chartered Dec. 22, 1733, in the village of Norfolk, by the title of Royal Exchange Lodge, No. 172. The second Lodge was chartered by the Grand Lodge of Scotland for Port Royal, by the name of Kilwinning Cross, in 1755. The third was chartered by the same Grand Lodge for Petersburg, by the name of Blandford Lodge No. 83, in 1757. The fourth was chartered by the Grand Lodge of Massachusetts for Fredericksburg, July 21, 1758, having some years before obtained a dispensation. The fifth was chartered by the Grand Lodge of England for Hampton, Nov. 6, 1773, by the name of St. Tamany; and, on the same day, by the same grand body, the sixth Lodge was chartered for Williamsburg, by the name of Williamsburg. The seventh was chartered by the same for Gloncester, Nov. 6, 1773, by the name of Botetourt. The eighth was chartered by the Grand Lodge of Scotland for Cabin Point, April 5, 1775, by the name of Cabin Point Royal Arch. Beside these are found on the registry of the Grand Lodge of Scotland that St. John's Lodge No. 111 was constituted at Norfolk in 1741; also there was a Lodge at Falmouth, and one chartered for Yorktown, Aug. 1, 1755, by the Grand Lodge of England. That there were others in the State (military lodges no doubt) is proven by a letter written in 1843, by R. W. John Barney, the Grand Lecturer of Ohio, in which he says: 'Capt. Hugh Maloy, aged ninety-three, is now living in or near Bethel, Clermont Co., who was initiated in 1782, in Gen. Washington's Marquee; Gen. Washington presided in person, and performed the initiatory ceremonies.'" At a convention of delegates from Norfolk, Kilwinning Port Royal Cross, Blandford, Wil-liamsburg, and Cabin Point Royal Arch lodges, met at Williamsburg, Va., May 6, 1777, for the purpose of choosing a Grand Master for the State of Virginia. The convention decided, by unanimous vote, that a Grand Master ought to be chosen to preside over the Craft in Virginia, and a committee was appointed to present, to the Fraternity at large, the reasons for this step. May 13, following, the convention received the committee's report, which presented four reasons for the course contemplated, viz: 1. That the lodges in Virginia were working under *five* distinct and separate authorities, viz: the Grand Masters of England, Scotland, Ireland, Pennsylvania, and America, the last at second hand; consequently, they could not assemble in annual communication to manifest the distinguishing characteristics of Masonry, or settle whatever differences might arise among the respective lodges for want of a common tribunal. 2. No precedent could be found by the committee where Masonry had ever derived any benefit from the foreign appointment of a Grand Master in this country, those officers being but little known and slightly regarded. 3. There was no tribunal for the correction of abuses, and no settled authority for the establishment of new lodges. 4. The Grand Lodges of England, Scotland, and Ireland, having established their own right of election upon the inherent privilege of Masons, distinct from all foreign power whatever, the committee conceive that the Masons of Virginia have the same rights and privileges which Masons in other lands, in all times, heretofore had confessedly enjoyed. After the discussion of this able paper, the convention then adjourned to meet at Williamsburg, June 23, ensuing. Upon that day, the delegates of five lodges assembled, agreeably to adjournment, and declared themselves unanimously of opinion that *a Grand Master of Virginia is essential to the prosperity and dignity of Masonry in general;* but, there not being a majority of the Virginia lodges represented, they declined proceeding at that time to an election. The convention recommended, however, that each lodge petition its own Grand Master (in England, Scotland, etc., as the case might be,) to appoint some one worthy Mason, resident in this State, as Grand Master thereof, with power to resign such authority to a convention of all the lodges when they should meet and elect a Grand Master. And for this purpose the convention recommended that GENERAL GEORGE WASHINGTON, commander-in-chief of the revolutionary army, should be the individual to whom the charter of appointment should be made, but he declined. The convention reassembled, Oct. 13, 1778, four lodges being represented, and adopted a resolution, unanimously, that there was a sufficient number of lodges present to proceed to business. Decided that the power and authority of Cornelius Harnet, as Deputy Grand Master of America, had ceased to exist. John Blair, of Williamsburg, was then unanimously elected Grand Master. He was installed Oct. 30, ensuing, and thus the long-desired object of an Independent Grand Lodge was accomplished.

Royal Arch Masonry was introduced into Virginia under the auspices of Joseph Myers, one of the Inspectors General of the Ancient and Accepted rite, of the southern jurisdiction, at Charleston, S. C. The SUPREME GRAND ROYAL ARCH CHAPTER was organized at Norfolk, May 1, 1808. This grand body is not in affiliation with the General Grand Chapter of the United States.

The GRAND ENCAMPMENT was organized about 1823; was represented in the Grand Encampment of the United States in 1826; soon became dormant. Organized new Grand Encampment in 1845, without approval of the Grand Encampment of the United States. In 1851 united again with the Grand Encampment of the United States; seceded again in 1861; renewed her allegiance to the Grand Encampment of the United States in 1866.

WASHINGTON, TERRITORY OF. A convention of delegates from Olympia Lodge No. 5; Steilacoom Lodge No. 8; Grand Mound Lodge No. 21, and Washington Lodge No. 22, all having received charters from the Grand Lodge of Oregon, met in Olympia, territory of Washington, Dec. 6, 1858, for the purpose of considering the propriety of establishing a Grand Lodge for said territory. The convention appointed the usual officers, and committees, and on the 7th regularly organized a Grand Lodge, adopted a constitution, elected and installed Grand Officers. T. F. McElroy was elected the first Grand Master.

WEST VIRGINIA. A convention of delegates from nine lodges of West Virginia met at Fairmount, on Wednesday, April 12, 1865, when, after the transaction of other business, the convention elected Grand Officers. W. J. Bates was elected Grand Master, and T. H. Logan Grand Secretary. The convention adjourned to meet again May 10, of the same year, when the Grand Officers were installed in ample form, and the Grand Lodge of West Virginia regularly established.

WISCONSIN. The introduction of Freemasonry into this territory began in January, 1843, by dispensations granted to Mineral Point Lodge, at Mineral Point; Melody Lodge, at Platteville; and Milwaukee Lodge, at Milwaukee, by the Grand Lodge of Missouri. A convention of the delegates from the lodges just named assembled at the city of Madison, on Monday, Dec. 18, 1843, when the convention adopted the resolution that it was expedient to form a Grand Lodge in the territory of Wisconsin. A constitution was adopted, officers elected and installed. Rev. B. T. Kavanaugh was elected the first Grand Master.

The GRAND CHAPTER of Royal Arch Masons was founded Feb. 13, 1850. Dwight F. Lawton was elected the first Grand High-Priest.

The GRAND COUNCIL of Royal and Select Masters was organized in 1857. James Collins was elected the first Grand Master.

The GRAND COMMANDERY, Knights Templar, was organized Oct. 20, 1859. Henry L. Palmer, was elected the first Grand Commander.

GENERAL GRAND CHAPTER OF THE UNITED STATES. Until the year 1797 no Grand Chapter of Royal Arch Masons was organized in America. Previous to that period, a competent number of companions of that degree, possessed of sufficient ability, under the sanction of a Master's warrant, exercised the rights and privileges of Royal Arch Chapters, wherever they thought it expedient or proper. This unrestrained mode of proceeding was subject to many inconveniences and of great injury to the society. Fully sensible of the many irregularities to which the Order was exposed, and with the view of preventing these difficulties in the future, in the year 1797, a convention of representatives from the several chapters in the State of Pennsylvania met at Philadelphia, and organized a Grand Chapter for the State. This was the first Grand Chapter in the United States. Actuated by similar motives, Oct. 24, 1797, a convention of delegates from several chapters in the northern States, met at Boston to deliberate upon the propriety of forming a Grand Chapter of Royal Arch Masons for the States of New Hampshire, Massachusetts, Rhode Island, Connecticut, Vermont, and New York. The convention having taken the subject into consideration came to a determination to forward to each of the chapters within the States before mentioned an address, expressive of their opinions. This address was issued, and the convention adjourned to meet again at Hartford, Conn., January 24, 1798. Agreeably to the recommendation of the convention of October, and, as requested by the circular, issued by that body, delegates assembled at the city of Boston, Jan. 24, 1798, from the following chapters, viz: St. Andrew's Chapter, Boston, Massachusetts, instituted 1769; King Cyrus Chapter, Newburyport, Mass., instituted 1790; Providence Chapter Providence, R. I., instituted 1793; Solomon Chapter, Derby, Conn., instituted 1794; Franklin Chapter, Norwich, Conn., instituted 1796; Franklin Chapter, New Haven, Conn., instituted 1796; Hudson Chapter, Hudson, N. Y., instituted 1796; Temple Chapter, Albany, N. Y.; Horeb Chapter, Whitestown, N. Y. The convention, after due deliberation, adopted the following resolution: "*Resolved*, That the delegates who compose this convention, being invested with ample powers, will establish a Grand Royal Arch Chapter, for the States of New Hampshire, Massachusetts, Rhode Island, Connecticut, Vermont, and New York, to be denominated the Grand Royal Arch Chapter of the northern States of America." A constitution was then adopted for the government of Royal Arch Masonry. In 1806 the title of the body was changed to "The General Grand Chapter of Royal Arch Masons for the United States." From this period this grand body has prospered, and its influence spread throughout the whole country. Nearly every Grand Chapter in the United States acknowledges its jurisdiction and authority.

GRAND ENCAMPMENT OF THE UNITED STATES. The convention for organizing the Grand Encampment of the United States was held June 20-1, 1816, in the city of New York, consisting of delegates from the following Encampments, viz: Boston, at Boston, Mass.; St. John's at Providence, R. I.; Temple, at Albany, N. Y.; Montgomery, at Stillwater, N. Y., St. Paul's, at Newburyport, Mass.; Newport, R. I., and Darius Council, at Portland, Maine—when a constitution was adopted and officers chosen. The Hon. DeWitt Clinton, then Governor of New York, was elected the first Grand Master.

Of the early or first introduction of the Masonic Knighthood into this country but little of its true history is known. That it existed previous to 1790 in Pennsylvania is fully authenticated. Tradition affirms that the orders were conferred in some of the army lodges of the revolutionary war.

CYCLOPEDIA OF FREEMASONRY.

A.

AARON. The brother of Moses, who accompanied and assisted him in the great work of emancipating the Jews from Egyptian bondage. He was the first High-Priest of the Hebrew Church, and the dignity of the priesthood was made hereditary in his family. He died on Mount Hor, at the age of 123, and was buried so privately that his sepulcher still continues to be unknown. His son Eleazar succeeded him in the office of High-Priest.

ABACISCUS. In ancient architecture, the checkered or square divisions of the Mosaic pavement. The material of which the ground-floor of King Solomon's Temple was supposed to have been made.

ABACUS. 1. An instrument to facilitate computations in arithmetic; 2. In architecture, a table constituting the upper or crowning member of a column and its capital; 3. A game among the Romans; so called from its being played on a board, somewhat in the manner of chess; 4. A tray or flat board, perforated with holes for carrying cups, glasses, etc.; 5. In the Templar system of Masonic Knighthood it is the name of the Grand Master's staff of office.

"In his hand he bore that singular Abacus."—IVANHOE.

The upper part of the staff is gilt, usually of metal, with a Templar's cross, enameled red, and edged with gold, within a circle; upon the center of the cross a black shield, bearing a silver square. On the circle is the motto of the Order—"IN HOC SIGNO VINCES." Among the early Templars this staff bore a mystic and significant symbolism, and was held in high veneration by the members of the Order.

ABBREVIATIONS, Masonic. The form to which a word, title, or phrase is reduced by contraction and omission. The Masons of Europe are much more addicted to the use of this method of contracting Masonic writing than American Masons. The abbreviations among our foreign brethren are usually distinguished by the use of three periods, placed in the form of a triangle—thus∴ or thus∵—as the writer may prefer. This peculiar form of contraction was first introduced by the Grand Orient of France, in 1774. The following list embraces all the abbreviations commonly made use of by the Fraternity at the present day. When an abbreviation stands for a foreign word or phrase, of which the English explanation is a translation, such word or phrase is given in italics:

A.·. C. M., or A. Y. M. Ancient Craft cr Ancient York Masonry.

A.·. and A.·. S.·. R.·. Ancient and Accepted Scottish rite.

A. D. *(Anno Domini.)* Year of our Lord. The date used in common with all Masonic dates.

A. DEP. *(Anno Depositionis.)* Year of the Deposit. The date used in Cryptic Masonry.

A. G. M. Acting Grand Master.

A. H. *(Anno Hebraico.)* Hebrew year. The date used in the Ancient and Accepted rite. The Hebrew year begins in September, which is the first of Tisri. To find this date add 3760 to the present year—thus 3760+1866=5626. After September 15 add one year more.[*]

A. INV. *(Anno Inventionis.)* Year of the Discovery. Used by Royal Arch Masons. To find this date add 530 to the present year—thus 530+1866=2396.

A. L. *(Anno Lucis.)* Year of Light, or year of the Creation. The common or ordinary date of Masonry, and, like the vulgar era, may be used in all Masonic documents. It is particularly appropriate to Ancient Craft Masonry. To find this date add 4000 to the present year—thus, 4000+1866=5866.

[*] The Jewish people usually employed the era of the Seleucidæ until the fifteenth century, when a new mode of computing was adopted by them. They date from the creation, which they consider to have been 3760 years and three months before the commencement of the vulgar era.

A.·. L.·. G.·. D.·. G.·. A.·. D.·. L'U.·. *(Fr. A la Gloire du Grand Architecte de l'Univers.)* To the Glory of the Grand Architect of the Universe. Usually found on French Masonic documents.

A. L'OR.·. *(Fr. A l'Orient.)* At the East; the location of the Lodge.

A. M. *(Anno Mundi.)* Year of the World. Used with the preceding (A. H.) in documents of the Ancient and Accepted rite.

A. O. *(Anno Ordinis.)* Year of the Order. The date used in the Orders of Masonic Knighthood. To find this date subtract 1118 from the present year—thus 1118—1866=748.

A.·. U.·. T.·. O.·. S.·. A.·. G.·. *(Ad universi terrarum orbis summi Architecti Gloriam.)* To the Glory of the Grand Architect of the Universe. The caption for documents of the Ancient and Accepted rite.

B. L. R. T. Brotherly Love, Relief, and Truth.

B.·. B.·. Burning Bush. Used on documents of the Ancient and Accepted rite.

BR. or BRO. Brother. (Ger. *Bruder* or *Brüder.*) (Fr. *Frère.*)

C.·. C.·. Celestial Canopy. Used on documents of the Ancient and Accepted rite.

C. F. C. Committee on Foreign Correspondence.

C. G. Captain General; Captain of the Guard.

ABB. 71

C. H. Captain of the Host.

COMP. Companion.

D. A. F. Due and Ancient Form.

D. D. G. M. District Deputy Grand Master.

DEG. Degree, or Degrees.

D∴ G∴ B∴ A∴ W∴ (Ger. *Der Grosse Baumeister aller Welten.*) To the Glory of the Grand Architect of the Universe.

D. G. H. P. Deputy Grand High-Priest.

D. G. M. Deputy Grand Master.

D∴ M∴ J∴ (*Deus Meumque Jus.*) God and my right. The motto of the 33d degree, Ancient and Accepted rite.

E. East, the place or emblem of light.

E. A. or E. A. P. Entered Apprentice.

F∴ or FF∴ (Fr. *Frère ou Frères.*) Brother or Brethren.

F. A. M. or F. and A. M. Free and Accepted Masons.

F. C. Fellow-Craft.

F. H. C. Faith, Hope, and Charity.

F∴ U∴ A∴ M∴ (Ger. *Freie und Angenommene Maurer.*) Free and Accepted Mason.

G. Grand; Guard; Guardian; Geometry; Generalissimo.

G. A. Grand Architect; Grand Almoner.

G. C. Grand Chaplain; Grand Chapter; Grand Council; Grand Conductor; Grand Conclave.

G. COM. Grand Commander; Grand Commandery.

G. C. G. Grand Captain General; Grand Captain of the Guard.

G. C. H. Grand Captain of the Host; Grand Chapter of Harodim.

G. E. Grand East; Grand Encampment.

G. G. Grand Geometrician; Grand Generalissimo; Grand Guardian.

G. G. C. General Grand Chapter.

G. H. P. Grand High-Priest.

G. J. W. Grand Junior Warden.

G. K. Grand King.

G. K. S. Grand Keeper of the Seals.

G. L.; GG. LL. (Fr. *Grande Loge; Grandes Loges.*) (Ger. *Gross-Loge; Gross-Logen.*) Grand Lodge; Grand Lodges.

G∴ M∴ (Fr. *Grand Maître.*) Grand Master; Grand Marshal.

G. M. V. Grand Master of the Vails.

G. O. Grand Orient; Grand Orator; Grand Organist.

G. P. Grand Prelate; Grand Pursuivant; Grand Patron.

G. P. K. T. Grand Priory of the Knights of the Temple. The Supreme body in Scotland.

G. P. S. Grand Principal Sojourner.

G. R. Grand Recorder; Grand Registrar.

G. R. A. C. Grand Royal Arch Captain.

G. S. Grand Secretary; Grand Scribe; Grand Sentinel; Grand Steward. (Fr. *Grand Secrétaire.*)

G. S. W. Grand Senior Warden.

G. STD. B. Grand Standard-Bearer.

G. SWD. B. Grand Sword-Bearer.

G. T. Grand Treasurer; Grand Tiler.

G. W. Grand Warder.

H∴ J∴ (Ger. *Heilige Johannes.*) Saints John.

H. K. T. Hiram, King of Tyre.

H. P. High-Priest.

H. R. A. C. Holy Royal Arch Chapter.

H-R-M. Heredom, rite of.

INS∴ GEN∴ Inspector General. One who has received the 33d degree.

I. N. R. I. (*Iesus Nazarenus Rex Iudæorum.*) Jesus of Nazareth, King of the Jews. Motto of the Order of the Knights of Malta.

I. S. Inside Sentinel. An officer in English Lodges.

I. T. N. O. T. G. A. O. T. U. In the name of the Grand Architect of the Universe. Initials usually found on Masonic documents in the English language.

J. D. Junior Deacon.

J. G. D. Junior Grand Deacon.

J. G. W. Junior Grand Warden.

J∴ V∴ S∴ ∴ L∴ N∴ M∴ Q∴ N∴ S∴ C∴ (Fr. *Je vous salue par les noms Maçonniques que nous seul connoissons.*) I salute you by the Masonic names, which we only know.

J. W Junior Warden.

K. C S. Knight of the Order of Charles XIII. of Sweden.

K. K-D-H. Knight Kadosch.

KT. or KNT. Knight.

K. E. P. Knight of the Eagle and Pelican.

K. M. Knight of Malta.

K. R. C. Knight of the Red Cross; Knight of the Rose-Croix.

K. T. or KNT. T. Knight Templar.

L, □; LL, ⌸. Lodge; Lodges.

L. E. T. (*Lux e Tenebris.*) Light out of Darkness.

LT. G. C. Lieutenant Grand Commander.

M∴ (Fr. *Maître.*) (Ger. *Meister.*) (Sp. *Maestro.*) Master; Marshal; Mark.

M. C. Master of Ceremonies; Mark of the Craft.

M.E.G.H.P. Most Excellent Grand High-Priest.

M. E. M. Most Excellent Master.

M∴ K∴ G∴ (Ger. *Maurer Kunst Geselle.*) Fellow-Craft.

M∴ L∴ (Ger. *Maurer Lehrling.*) Entered Apprentice.

M. M. Master Mason; Mark Master; (*Mois Maçonnique.*) Masonic Month. The French Masons begin the year with March. (Ger. *Meister Maurer.*) (Sp. *Maestro Mason.*)

M. W.; M. W. G. M. Most Worshipful : Most Worshipful Grand Master.

N. E C. North East Corner.

No∴ P∴ V∴ D∴ M∴ (Fr. *Noubliez pas vos décorations Maçonniques.*) This abbreviation is used among French Masons, and when placed in the left hand corner of the notice for a meeting of a Lodge means: "Do not forget your Masonic regalia."

O∴ A∴ C∴ (*Ordo ab Chao*) Order out of chaos. A motto of the 33d degree.

O. C. S. Oriental Chair of Solomon.

O. G. Outside Guardian.

Or∴ (*Orient.*) The East. The station of the Master; Orator.

P. C. W. Principal Conductor of the Works.

P. G. M. Past Grand Master; Provincial Grand Master.

P. J. Prince of Jerusalem; Provost and Judge.

P∴ M∴ (Fr. *Maître Passé, ou Ex Vénérable.*) (Ger. *Altmeister* or *Passirmeister.*) Past Master; Perfect Master.

R. A. Royal Arch; Royal Art.

R. A. C, Royal Arch Captain, or Chapter.

R. ✠, or R. C. Rose Cross.

R-s-y C-s. Rosy Cross. The Royal order of Scotland.

R∴ E∴ A∴ et A∴ (*Rite Ecossais Ancien et Accepté.*) Ancient and Accepted Scottish rite.

R. E. G. C. Right Eminent Grand Commander.

R. L., or R. □ (*Respectable Lodge.*) Worshipful Lodge.

R. O. S. Royal Order of Scotland.

R. W. Right Worshipful.

R. W. M. Right Worshipful Master. The title of a Provincial Grand Master in England, and of the Master of a Lodge in Scotland.

Sec. Secretary.

S∴ C∴ S∴ G∴ I∴ G∴ Supreme Council Sovereign Grand Inspectors General.

S. G. D. Senior Grand Deacon.

S. G. W. Senior Grand Warden.

S∴ G∴ I∴ G∴ Sovereign Grand Inspector General. A member of the 33d degree.

S. M. Secret Master; Select Master; Secret Monitor; Sovereign Master. Speculative Masonry.

S∴ P∴ R∴ S∴ Sublime Prince of the Royal Secret.

SS. John. Saints John.

S. S. (*Sanctum Sanctorum.*) Holy of Holies.

SSS. (Fr. *Trois fois Salut.*) Thrice Greeting, or thrice Welcome; salutation. Often found in French Masonic documents.

Surv.∴1ᵉʳ. (Fr. *Premier Surveillant.*) Senior Warden.

Surv.∴ 2ᵉ. (Fr. *Second Surveillant.*) Junior Warden.

S. W. Senior Warden.

T.∴ C.∴ ou V.∴F.∴ (Fr. *Très cher ou Vénérable Frère.*) Dearest or Venerable Brother.

T. G. A. O. T. U. The Grand Architect of the Universe.

Treas. Treasurer.

T.∴ S.∴ (*Trés Sage.*) Wisest. The presiding officer in the French rite.

V.∴ (*Vénérable.*) Worshipful. The title of the Master in France.

V.∴ L.∴ (Fr. *Vraie Lumière.*) True Light.

W.∴ M.∴ (Ger. *Würdiger Meister.*) Worshipful Master.

⬜. This symbol is often substituted for the word Lodge.

⬛. This symbol represents the plural—Lodges.

△. The delta is the emblem of the Chapter.

✝ Passion Cross. The prefix to the signature of a Knight Templar.

⬛ Templar's Cross, used before the signature of an officer of a State Grand Commandery.

✚ Patriarchal Cross, used before the signature of an officer of the Grand Encampment of the United States.

✚ Cross of Salem, used before the signature of the Grand Master of Knights Templar.

When these crosses are used on documents relating to Templar Masonry, they should be made in red ink.

Besides the generally current abbreviations given above, other short methods of statement are frequently employed in particular cases. The meaning of unexplained contractions will be sufficiently obvious from the connection in which they may stand.

ABDITORUM. In Archæology, a secret place, where important documents may be concealed and preserved. The two columns at the entrance of Solomon's Temple were supposed to be used for this purpose.

ABELITES. So called from Abel, the son of Adam. 1. It was the appellation of a sect in Northern Africa, which professed a certain form of gnosticism. 2. This was the name also of a secret, or quasi Masonic Society, which sprang up in Germany about the year 1746. A pamphlet called "The Abelite," setting forth the character and purposes of the Order, was published at Leipzig, in the same year. From this it appears that it was founded on the highest principles of Christianity, morality, and philanthropy. It had secret signs, ceremonies, pass-words, and symbols, and was, for a short time, remarkably popular; but it never extended beyond the country in which it originated. The motto of the Order was "Sincerity, Friendship, and Hope."

ABIB. The name given to green ears of corn by the Jews, and was adopted as the name of the first month of their ecclesiastical year—our March—because, at that time, corn was in the ear. This month was afterward called Nisan.

ABIF. A Hebrew word, signifying "his father." It is often used in the Scriptures as a title of honor. It was given to Hiram, the Tyrian builder, probably on account of his distinguished skill.

ABLUTION. Washing, or, literally, a washing off, i. e., making one clean from all pollution. In the ancient mysteries it constituted a part of the preparation for initiation, and was a symbolical representation of moral purification. The ceremony is known in some of the degrees of the Ancient and Accepted rite.

ABSENCE. The signification usually applied to this term is that of being absent by permission, for a specified time, during the regular meetings of the Lodge, and in such a manner as not to interfere with the harmony or working of the body. Long or continued absence from the Lodge meetings is contrary to the duties inculcated by the ancient charges of the Order, which prescribe, as a rule, "that no Master or Fellow could be absent from the Lodge, especially when warned to appear at it, without incurring a severe censure, until, it appeared to the Master and Wardens that pure necessity hindered him."

ACADEMIE DES ILLUMINES D'AVIGNON. *Academy of the Illuminati of Avignon.* This society, was established at Avignon, in 1785. It admitted both sexes to membership, and the teachings of its ritual were a mixture of the Hermetic Philosophy and Swedenborgian ideas.

ACADEMIE DES SUBLIMES MAITRES DE L'AN-NEAU LUMINEUX. *Academy of the Sublime Masters of the Luminous Ring.* This is the name of a high degree introduced into the Lodge of Douay, France, in 1815, by the Scotch Baron Grant, of Blairfindy, who was a member of Contract Social Lodge, and Chief of the Scottish Philosophical rite. He formed the eighth and highest degree known in the Lodge of Douay into three Orders. In one of the first Orders of this Academy, they employed themselves in a study of the true history of Freemasonry, but in the third they explained the various sciences, and applied themselves to the acquirement of the highest wisdom.

ACADEMIE DES VRAIS MACONS. *Academy of True Masons.* This was a French Chapter of the high degrees, with Alchemistical tendencies, which, in 1778, was founded at Montpellier, by Boileau, the distinguished pupil of Pernetti. This rite had six degrees beyond the symbolic degrees of Ancient Craft Masonry, which were essential for admission, but not practiced. In it the Hermetic Science was taught. The degrees were: 1. The True Mason; 2. The True Mason in the Right Way; 3. The Knight of the Golden Key; 4. The Knight of the Rainbow; 5. The Knight of the Argonauts; 6. The Knight of the Golden Fleece.

ACADEMY OF ANTIQUITY, or of the Mysteries. An Alchemistical Brotherhood, with a Masonic form, founded at Rome, by Thoux de Salverte, in the sixteenth century, and at Warsaw, Poland, in 1763.

ACADEMY OF SAGES. A society for the interpretation and propagation of the high degrees, introduced into France in 1776, by the Scotch Mother-Lodge of the Philosophical rite.

ACANTHUS. An herbaceous plant—vulgar name, bearsbreech—bearing large whitish flowers, and pinnatifid leaves. A species of it is found in the East, and is supposed to be the beautiful classic plant of antiquity, to which Masonic tradition attributes the model of the Grecian architect who invented and formed the leaves of the Corinthian Capital; and the idea of so applying it was derived from the following incident: "It happened that a basket, covered with a tile, was left upon the crown of the root of an Acanthus plant, which when it began to grow, finding itself unable to arrange its leaves in the usual manner, turned them up around the sides of the basket, until, encountering the under side of the tile, they gradually curved back in the form of a volute."

ACCHO, or Acre. An ancient city, situate on the coast of the Mediterranean sea, thirty miles south of Tyre. During the Crusades this place was usually known to Europeans by the name of Acon; afterward, from the occupation of the Knights of St. John of Jerusalem, as St. Jean d'Acre, or simply Acre. It was the last fortified place in the Holy Land wrested from the Christians by the Turks.

ACCLAMATION. An exclamation of admiration, approval, welcome, or reverence among Masons. In French Lodges the expression is "*vivat.*" In the Ancient and Accepted rite it is "*Housa,*" or "*Hoshea,*" and in English Lodges "*So mote it be.*"

ACCOLADE. An interesting ceremony formerly used in conferring the honors of knighthood, by the King, the Grand Master, or other authorized person laying his arms about the neck of the young knight, and embracing him. This familiar expression of regard was the practice before the introduction of the more stately act of touching, or gently striking, with the sword, the neck or shoulder of the kneeling knight. The present ceremony of conferring the honors of Masonic knighthood, is evidently derived from it. The custom is of great antiquity, and is regarded by some writers as the blow which the Roman slave received on manumission.

ACELDAMA. *Field of Blood.* A small piece of land, lying on the south side of Jerusalem, called also Potter's Field, which was used as a cemetery for strangers. In the time of the crusades it was appropriated as a burial-place for pilgrims, and since, it has been used for the same purpose by the Armenians. It is referred to instructively in the lessons of the Templars' degree.

ACHISHAR. An officer having charge of the household of Solomon. Allusion is made to him in the degree of Select Master.

ADEPT, from the Latin *Adeptus.* A name given to members of the Order of the Illuminati. The Rosicrucians also employed the titles of *Adeptus Adoptatus, Adeptus Coronatus,* and *Adeptus Exemptus.* The title of Prince Adept is given to the chief of the Consistory of the 28th degree.

ADHUC STAT. *It stands yet.* A Latin motto which is often found on Masonic medallions.

ADONIS, THE MYSTERIES OF. Adonis is supposed by some to be identified with Osiris, the grand figure in the Egyptian mysteries; and the mystical rites, celebrated by his priests, and performed at initiations, are thought to be the same as, or a reproduction of, the mysteries of Isis. There are, indeed, some points of resemblance; but there are also radical differences. They were both slain, but Osiris met his death by the deliberate machinations of Typhon, or Evil, while Adonis was killed by a wild boar. The meaning of the myth of

Osiris is plain enough. The struggle between Osiris and Typhon was the eternal struggle between Truth and Error, the destruction of Osiris by Typhon represents the temporary triumph of Evil over the Good, and his return to life and the downfall of Typhon show forth the final triumph of virtue over vice, of life over death. The myth of Adonis is not so comprehensive, and all parts of the legend are not so readily interpreted. The mysteries of Adonis were celebrated throughout all the countries of Syria, and formed a part of the ceremonies of the Tyrian architects, by whom they were introduced into Judea. Duncan, in his "Religions of Profane Antiquity," says: "The objects represented in these mysteries were the grief of Venus and the death and resurrection of Adonis. An entire week was consumed in these ceremonies; all the houses were covered with black drapery; funeral processions traversed the streets, while the devotees scourged themselves, uttering frantic cries. The orgies were then commenced, in which the mystery of the death of Adonis was depicted. During the next twenty-four hours, all the people fasted, at the expiration of which time the priests announced the resurrection of the god. Joy now prevailed, and music and dancing concluded the festivals." Some writers regard the story of Adonis as an astronomical allegory, representing the seasons of the year, and the transition through which the earth passes, in consequence of these changes. But the rites had, undoubtedly, a deeper meaning, and related to the supreme ideas of religion. The early Christian writers evidently regarded them as having relation to the great Christian mystery. Fermicius, who lived in the fourth century, says: "On a certain night an image is placed upon a bed, and is mourned over by many with sorrowful cries. Then, when wearied by this simulated grief, light is brought in, and the mouths of those who were weeping are anointed by a priest, who breathes forth in a low murmur: 'Trust ye, disciples! for the god having been saved, out of his sufferings, salvation shall be ours.'"

ADOPTIVE MASONRY. A name given to certain degrees resembling Masonry, and Masonic in spirit, which have, at times, been invented for ladies who have claims upon the Order of Freemasonry, through relatives who are members of it. Adoptive Masonry first made its appearance in France, in the early part of the 18th century, and there is still a legal and regular branch of the institution in that country. The French rite has four degrees: 1. Apprentice; 2. Companion; 3. Mistress; 4. Perfect Mistress. The officers of a Lodge of Adoption are a Grand Master and a Grand Mistress; an

Orator; an Inspector, and Inspectress; a Depositor and Depositrex; a Conductor and Conductress. They wear blue collars, with a gold trowel pendant therefrom, white aprons, and gloves. The members also wear the jewel of the Order, which is a golden ladder with five rounds, on the left breast. Many of the most distinguished ladies of Europe have been, and are now, members of this Order. Among them were the Duchess of Bourbon, the Empress Josephine, Lady Montague, Duchess Elizabeth Chesterfield, and the Empress Eugenie. The Adoptive Lodges were at first rapidly diffused throughout all the countries of Europe except the British empire. But the American Adoptive rite is better adapted to the United States, and has excited considerable interest, and found many powerful advocates in this country. It consists of five degrees, as follows: 1. Jephthah's daughter, or the Daughter's degree, illustrating respect to the binding force of a vow; 2. Ruth, or the Widow's degree, illustrating devotion to religious principles; 3. Esther, or the Wife's degree, illustrating fidelity to kindred and friends; 4. Martha, or the Sister's degree, illustrating undeviating faith in the hour of trial; 5. Electa, or the Benevolent degree, illustrat-

SEAL OF THE ORDER OF THE EASTERN STAR.

ing charity and courage, with patience and submission under wrongs. All the degrees together are called the "Rite of the Eastern Star," and are very beautiful and impressive. Ladies who have received these degrees have a ready and efficient means of commanding the services of Freemasons whenever and wherever they may need them. The moral teachings of the Eastern Star degrees are excellent, and cannot fail to make a good impression. Notwithstanding there is among some Masons a strong feeling against any form of Adoptive Masonry, it cannot be questioned that the spirit of the age demands something of the kind. Masons cannot find a surer safeguard and protection for their wives, sisters, and daughters, than is furnished by the American Adoptive rite or Order of the Eastern Star. To the objection that the degrees are not Masonic, it may be replied that they are as much so as any degree outside of the Symbolical Lodge. All degrees above the first three are Masonic, only by adoption.

ADORATION. Worship, the expression of that supreme reverence which a man should feel toward his Creator. Although in different parts of the world the attitudes of worship differ, in some respects, yet there is a strong resemblance between them. One may bow his head, another may kneel, and others may bend the body toward the earth, or throw themselves prostrate thereon, with the face downward, the act is still the same, a symbol most expressive of dependence, and reverence, and filial obedience.

AFFILIATED. A word that designates a Mason as a member of some Lodge. A Mason who does not belong to any Lodge is styled "Non-Affiliated."

AFFILIATION. Initiation indicates the first reception of a person into a Masonic Lodge; affiliation denotes the reception of one already a Mason into some other Lodge than the one in which he received the Light.

AFRICAN MASTER BUILDERS. A secret society with a Masonic form which came into being about the year 1756, and ceased to exist in 1786. It professed to be devoted to the discovery of truth, and the cultivation of virtue, and was a very worthy and respectable order. They set forth that: "When the architects were by wars reduced to a very small number, they determined to travel together into Europe, and there to form, together, new establishments. Many of them came to England with Prince Edward, son of Henry III., and were shortly afterwards called into Scotland by Lord Stewart. Their installation in this kingdom falls about the Masonic year 2307." They received the protection of the King of Sweden in 1125, of the King of England in 1190, and of Alexander III., of Scotland, in 1284. There were five initiations into their Apprentice's degree: 1. The Apprentice to the Egyptian Secret, *Menes Musae*; 2. The Initiation into the Egyptian Secret; 3. The Cosmopolite; 4. The Christian Philosopher; 5. The Lover of Truth. The higher degrees followed these, of which there were three. They had Chapters, whose officers were chosen for life.

AGAPE. *Love-feast.* A banquet of charity, among the early Christians. St. Chrysostom thus describes its origin and purpose: "At first Christians had all things in common; but when that equality of possession ceased, as it did even in the Apostle's time, the Agape, or love-feast, was instituted instead of it. Upon certain days, after the religious services were closed, they met at a common feast, the rich bringing provisions, and the poor, who had nothing, being invited. These meetings were held in secret." The Agape cannot but call to mind the Table-lodges of Freemasonry, and, in truth, these owe their origin to the love-feasts of the primitive Christians. A distinguished German scholar, A. Kestner, professor of Theology at Jena, published a work in 1819, entitled, "The Agape, or the Secret World-Society—*Welt-bund*, of the primitive Christians"—i.e., a society apart from their spiritual organization—"founded by Clemens, at Rome, in the reign of Domitian, having a hierarchical constitution, and a ground system of Masonic symbolism, and mysteries." In this work he establishes the fact of a direct connection between the Agape and the Table-loge of Freemasons.

AGATHOPADES, The Order of. This Order was founded in Brussels about the middle of the fifteenth century, and aimed to avoid, equally, the fanaticism of both the Catholic and Protestant churches. Many persons, distinguished by rank and talent, became members. Among them, it is claimed, were the Prince of Epinoi, the Duke of Bournon-ville, Marshal Moritz, of Saxony; P. P. Rubens and Voltaire. The old Brotherhood became extinct in 1837, at the death of the Advocate, Pins, who, a few months before that event, initiated his friend Schayes, through whom the Order of the New-Agathopades was constituted Sept. 29, A. D. 1846. The Chief of the Society bears the peculiar name of "Hog," and all the members are called by the name of some wild beast. The motto of the Order is "*Amis comme cochons*," and the *Pentastigma* (. : .) is the holy sign.

AGENDA. A Latin participle, signifying "things to be done." In Masonry it means small books in which certain virtues or precepts are written, and which it is the duty of all Masons to inculcate and practice.

AGNUS DEI. *Lamb of God.* The name of an amulet, and also of the seal of the old Order of Knights Templar, and the jewel of the Generalissimo.

ALCHEMY. The art of changing base metals into gold. Among the things that men the most earnestly desire are the means of physical comfort or luxury—that is to say wealth, and freedom from disease, and long life. The hope of discovering among the secrets of Nature the art of making gold, and that magic liquor, which would secure perpetual youth, called the Elixir of Life, gave birth to the science of Alchemy. A class of Hermetic philosophers arose who prosecuted their researches with ardor and seriousness; for it is not necessary to assume that the Alchemists were imposters. They were enthusiasts, and taught their doc-trines through mystical images and symbols. To transmute metals they thought it necessary to find a substance which, containing the original principle of all matter, should possess the power of dissolving all its elements. This general solvent, or *menstruum universale*, which, at the same time, was to possess the power of removing all the seeds of disease out of the human system, and renewing life, was called the "Philosopher's Stone"—*Lapis Philosophorum*—and its possessors were styled *Adepts*. The more obscure the ideas the Alchemists themselves had of the appearances resulting from their experiments the more they endeavored to express themselves in symbolical language, which they afterward employed to conceal their secrets from the uninitiated. The science of Alchemy is as old as the history of philosophy itself. The Egyptian Hermes, the son of Anubis, who was ranked among the heroes, has been claimed as its author, and many books on the subject of magic are to be attributed to him, though not on sufficient grounds. The name, however, is Arabian, and it is well known that the Arabs prosecuted the science with ardor, and to their labors many valuable discoveries in chemistry are to be attributed. Paracelsus, Roger Bacon, Basilius, Valentinus, and many other distinguished men were believers in the art. And even to this day science cannot positively decide that the Philosopher's Stone is not within the circle of possibilities. Alchemy has been more or less connected with Freemasonry since the middle of the last century, chiefly through the Rosicrucians. One of the most interesting degrees in Freemasonry—"Adepts, or Knights of the Eagle and the Sun"—is founded on this Hermetic Philosophy, and cannot be understood without a study of the mystic science of the Alchemists.

ALCORAN. The sacred book of the Mahommedans, or rather *a* sacred book; for they recognize the old Hebrew Scriptures as of greater authority. The Alcoran contains the revelations made to Mahommed, his doctrines and precepts. In a Masonic Lodge of Mahommedans it should lay on the altar as the Bible does in a Lodge of Christians.

ALLAH. The Arabic name of God. The Alcoran describes his character and attributes thus: "He alone is self-existent; has no rival; is from everlasting to everlasting; fills the universe with his presence; is the center in which all things unite, as well the visible as the invisible; is infinite; Almighty, all-wise, all-merciful, tender-hearted, and his decrees are unchangeable."

ALMOND–TREE. The tree of which Aaron's rod, that budded, was a branch. Its flowers were pure white.

ALMONER. A name formerly applied to an official in religious and monastic orders, whose business was to distribute alms. It is also the title of an officer in the Templar System.

ALOADIN. Prince of the Assassins, or Arsacides, commonly called the Old Man of the Mountain. He was Sheik of a Syrian tribe, professing the Mahommedan religion, but blindly devoted to the will of their chief. Many fabulous stories are related of him, from whose followers the word assassin is derived. [See art. Assassin.]

ALPHABET OF ANGELS. The Jewish mystics affirmed that the patriarchs had a knowledge of such an alphabet, communicated to them by the angels themselves. Several degrees in the Scottish rite allude to this alphabet.

AMALTHEA. The name of the horn of the Cretan goat. It is the mythological horn of plenty—" Cornu Copia"—which signifies an abundance of things necessary to life. It is the jewel of the stewards of a Lodge of Master Masons.

AMAZONS, Order of. A system of Androgyne Masonry, which for a time excited some interest in South America during the last century.

AMBURVALIA. Religious festivals among the Romans. They had an agricultural reference. The rites were celebrated in the latter part of May, and consisted of processions through the fields, and solemn invocations of the goddess Ceres, that she would bless the labors of the husbandmen, and grant them an abundant harvest.

AMENTHES, or Amenti. In the Egypthian Mythology, the place of departed spirits, corresponding to the Hades of the Greeks. It was also the place of judgment where Osiris presided, and announced the decisions of eternal justice.

AMERICAN MYSTERIES. There unquestionably existed among the more enlightened of the Aborigines of the Western Continent fraternities which were bound together by mystic ties and formed a kind of rude Freemasonry. The Peruvian and Mexican mysteries resembled very strongly the rites of the ancient nations of Northern Europe.

AMULET. A piece of stone or metal, or other substance, marked with certain figures, which people wear about their persons as a protection against danger, etc. The name, as well as the thing, comes from the East. It is from the Arabic, hamail, a locket—anything hung around the neck. Among the Turks and other nations every person thinks an

Amulet necessary to safety. Amulets were in vogue among the Greeks, the Egyptians, and Romans. They were introduced into Christendom by the Basilideans. The Amulets of this sect were stones with the mystic word Abraxas engraved upon them. They were highly valued by the Jews; and in past times Christians have worn them, having the mark of a fish or a symbol of the Savior. In many quasi Masonic societies they have been largely used, and are not wholly unknown in Masonry itself—*e. g.*, the Tyrian Signet, H. T. W. S. S. T. K. S.

ANDERSON, JAMES, D. D., was born at Edinburg, Scotland, August 5, 1662. The time of his death is uncertain; but, from the most reliable sources at our command, it is believed that he died in 1738. He was a man of a high order of literary talent. His first work was an "Essay showing that the Crown of Scotland is Imperial and Independent," for which the Parliament of Scotland gave him a vote of thanks. At what time, or in what Lodge, Bro. Anderson became a Mason is not known. At the meeting of the Grand Lodge at London, September 29, 1721, he was ordered to arrange and more fully digest the old Gothic Constitutions into a new and better method than had before existed. This duty he performed most satisfactorily to the Grand Lodge and the Fraternity, and the work was issued in 1723, under the title, "The Constitutions of the Freemasons; containing the History, Charges, Regulations, etc of that most Ancient and Right Worshipful Fraternity. For the use of the Lodges." In 1738, a second edition, enlarged and corrected, was published under his supervision. These are regarded as the basis of Masonic Constitutions for the government of the Fraternity to the present time. He was, for many years, Grand Chaplain of the Grand Lodge. His most elaborate work was a folio volume entitled, "Royal Genealogies; or, the Genealogical Tables of Emperors, Kings, and Princes, from Adam to these times. London, 1732."

ANDREW, DAY OF ST. November 30 is sacred to this Saint, and on this day the Scottish Lodges, and many others, hold their festivals and elect their officers. The Grand Lodge of Scotland was organized Nov. 30, 1736.

ANDREW DEGREE, OR ANDREW'S MASONRY. Degrees of Scottish Masonry, introduced into France and Germany by the followers of the Pretender, in 1736. "The Apprentice of St. Andrew," and "the Companions of St. Andrew," form the 4th degree of the Swedish system; "Master of St. Andrew" is the 5th degree of the same. "The Favorit

Brothers of St. Andrew," and also "The Knights of the Purple Band," make the 9th degree of Swedish Masonry.

ANDREW, St. Brother of St. Peter, one of the Twelve Apostles. The Russians hold him in the highest reverence, as also do the people of Scotland, and the Freemasons of that country honor him as one of their patrons. Tradition says that he was crucified on a cross, shaped thus **X**. In both countries there is an order of knighthood named in his honor.

ANDROGYNAL MASONRY. [*See* ADOPTIVE MASONRY.]

ANOINTING was a custom extensively practiced among the Hebrews and other oriental nations, and its omission was significant of mourning. They anointed the hair, head, and beard, and sometimes the feet. It was a customary mark of respect to guests. Kings and High-Priests were anointed at their inauguration. This ceremony indicated their being set apart and consecrated to the service of God. The custom of anointing with oil or perfume was common among the Greeks and Romans, and is practiced in the higher mysteries of the Masonic institution with sublime effect.

ANTIQUITY OF FREEMASONRY. Notwithstanding much that is claimed as true in Masonic history, by enthusiastic brothers, must fall before the stern tests of sound philosophical criticism, yet the high antiquity of the institution is incontestably established. A part of the ritual of Freemasonry originated in Egypt, and was engrafted on the system of the Sidonian builders. This society also adopted a portion of the rituals of Eleusis and Adonis, and through this Order Freemasonry was introduced into Judea, and constructed Solomon's Temple. We fail to find a vestige of Masonry among the Jews previous to this period. In the time of Numa Pompilius, King of Rome, a branch of the Order of Hiram appeared in Italy, and formed the Collegia Fabrorum and Artificum. This society of builders continued in uninterrupted succession till the downfall of the Roman empire, when its members spread over all Europe, a portion of whom settled in Britain. Here the society had a plain and tangible history till 1717, when the Brotherhood laid aside its operative character, and it became entirely speculative.

APIS. A bull to which divine honors were paid in Egypt. It was necessary that he should be black, with a triangle of white on his forehead, a white spot in the shape of a crescent on his side, and sort of knot, like a beetle, under his tongue. When one was found, he was fed four months in a building

BROS. WASHINGTON AND LAFAYETTE.

MASONIC APRON PRESENTED TO GEN. WASHINGTON
BY MADAME LAFAYETTE.

facing the East. At the new moon he was led to a splendid ship, with great solemnity, and conveyed to Heliopolis, where he was fed forty days more by priests and women. After this no one was permitted to approach him. From Heliopolis he was taken to Memphis, where he had a temple, two chapels to dwell in, and a large court for exercise. He had the gift of prophecy. The omen was good or bad as he went into one chapel or the other. Notwithstanding all this reverence, he was not suffered to live beyond 25 years. His death caused universal mourning. He was an important symbol in the mysteries of Isis.

APRON. The pure white lambskin apron is to the operative Mason an ancient and spotless emblem. The investiture of this symbol of the purity of the order, being the first gift bestowed upon the candidate, is made in behalf of the whole Fraternity, while the recipient, in return, is required to keep himself pure in all his actions, so that he may prove to the world that it is "more honorable than the star or garter," or any other order that can be conferred upon him. It is worn by operative Masons to protect their garments from injury, spot, or stain. The investiture of the candidate with the apron, among the primitive Masons, formed an essential part of the ceremony of initiation, and was attended with rites equally significant and impressive. This badge received

a characteristic distinction from its peculiar color and material. With the Essenian Masons, it was accomplished by a process bearing a similar tendency, and accompanied by illustrations not less imposing and satisfactory to the neophyte. He was clothed in a long white robe, which reached to the ground, bordered with a fringe of blue ribbon, to incite personal holiness, and fastened tightly round the waist with a girdle, to separate the upper from the lower parts of the body. With feet bare and head uncovered, the candidate was considered the personification of modesty and humility, walking in the fear of God. The Masonic Apron is a pure white lambskin, 15 inches wide and 13 inches deep, with a flap of triangular shape about 5 inches deep at the point, square at the bottom. For the symbolic degrees the trimmings are blue, and in the Royal Arch degree the trimmings are scarlet, or blue and scarlet.

ARCADE DE LA PELLETERIE. A nickname of the so-called Orient of Clermont, or old Grand Lodge of France, before its union with the Grand Orient, 1799.

ARCH. Part of a circle. In architecture a construction supported by its curve. The Arch is a prominent idea in the ritual of Royal Arch Masonry.

ARCH OF ENOCH explained in the degree of the Knights of the Ninth Arch, the ritual of which says: "Enoch was the seventh in descent from Adam, and lived in the fear and love of his Maker. Being inspired by the Most High, and in commemoration of a wonderful vision, this holy man built a nine-fold temple under ground, and dedicated the same to God. He was assisted in the construction of this subterranean temple by Jared, his father, and Methuselah,

his son, without being acquainted with his motives. This happened in that part of the country which was afterward called Canaan, or the Holy Land." The engraving here used is copied from an old Masonic publication, and appears to allude to this event.

ARCH OF STEEL. In the Templar system, and also the French, the Arch of Steel is formed during certain ceremonies, by the members, arranged in two ranks, with their swords raised and crossed.

ARCHÆOLOGY. From the Greek words *Arche*, the beginning, and *Logos*, word, *i. e.*, a discourse concerning the primitive times; in other words, the science of antiquities. This science is peculiarly interesting to Freemasons, inasmuch as through the investigations of Archæologists the antiquity of Masonry is vindicated.

ARCHIMAGUS. In other words, *Chief of the Sages*, and High-Priest of the Chaldean Mysteries. In the ceremony of initiation he represented Ormuzd, the god of beauty, light, and truth, and the rite was intended to illustrate the struggles of that god with Ahriman, the god of darkness and evil, and his final victory over him.

ARCHITECTURE. The art of construction or building, according to certain proportions and rules, determined and regulated by nature, science, and taste. It is divided into

THE FIVE ORDERS OF ARCHITECTURE.

three distinct branches—civil, military, and naval. The art of building had its origin in the desire implanted in man to procure protection from the outward elements and the vicissitudes of the changing seasons. There is something divine in man, which prompts him to look beyond the mere supply of his necessities, and to aim continually at higher objects. He, therefore, soon expected from his habitation and his temples more than mere utility. He aimed at elegance, and architecture became by degrees a fine art, differing essentially, however, from the other fine arts in these respects: 1. That it is based on utility; 2. that it elevates mathematical laws to rules of beauty, correct proportion, and perfect symmetry. It is difficult, perhaps now impossible, to fix the exact period of the invention of architecture, as every art is perfected by degrees, and is the result of the labors of many. In the early ages of the human race, the habitation must have been rude and imperfect; yet each nation, at every age, possessed its peculiar style of architecture, and marked its character by its symbolic monuments. Among such monuments we should place, as the chief, the Temple of Solomon, from which the true knowledge of architecture became diffused throughout the world. Thus through ages has the institution been transmitted; and though deprived of its operative character, it is none the less efficient in its symbolism and importance. The working-tools of an operative Mason have, therefore, become our symbols. There are five orders of architecture, viz: The Doric, the Tuscan, the Ionic, the Corinthian, and the Composite.

AREOPAGUS. The hill of Mars, the seat of the supreme tribunal of Athens, which was also called Areopagus. This famous court had sovereign jurisdiction over all the affairs of Grecian society, and from its decrees there was no appeal. In Freemasonry, the name in France and Belgium is applied to a council or assembly of the 30th degree of the Scotch rite.

ARGENT. French for *silver*. An heraldic term used in describing coats of arms, thus: The arms of the Company of Freemasons in the reign of King Henry IV. "Azure, on a chevron, between three castles, *Argent*."

ARGONAUTS, ORDER OF. An Androgyne Masonic Society founded in Germany, in 1775, by some members of the Strict Observance. Its chief officer was called Grand Admiral, the place of meeting was called a *ship*, and all the appointments were named from various parts of a vessel. The motto of the Order was: "*Es lebe die Freude*," they live to promote happiness. The seal was a silver anchor inlaid with green.

ARK OF THE COVENANT. The sacred chest, or coffer, which Moses constructed by command of God, wherein were deposited the two tables of stone on which were graven the Ten Commandments, Aaron's rod, and a pot of manna. The ark was a symbol of the Divine presence, and a protec-

tion to the people, so long as they adhered to the articles of
the covenant, which the ark contained. It was made of
shittim-wood, covered with plates of gold; nearly four feet
in length, and two feet three inches in width and height. On
the top of it, all round, ran a kind of gold crown. It had
four rings of gold, two on each side, through which staves
were put, whereby it was carried. These also were overlaid
with the finest gold, and were not to be removed from the
rings. The lid of the ark, glistening with gold, was called

the Mercy-seat; and upon its opposite ends were two golden
cherubim, fronting each other, with their wings so extended as to cover the Mercy-seat. It was borne from place
to place during the journeys of the Israelites, with great
solemnity, and deposited in the most sacred places in the
tabernacle. It was finally placed by Solomon in the Holy of
Holies, and was supposed to have been lost at the destruction of the temple by the Chaldeans. The idea of the concealment of an ark and its accompanying treasures always
prevailed in the Jewish sect. The use of this sacred symbol,
and the important moral lessons its discovery inculcates, are
exceedingly interesting to Royal Arch Masons.

ARK AND DOVE. An American degree, sometimes given
as a preparation for the Royal Arch. The appellation
Noachite, by which it is sometimes designated, is improperly
applied. The term Noachite belongs to the 21st degree of
the old English system, and the 35th of the rite of Misraim.
Dr. Oliver conjectures that it was derived from a more
ancient degree called the "Ark Mariner," and was of an
honorary character.

ARK MARINER, Royal. This is a speculative degree given in a Royal Arch Chapter. It is founded on the Mosaic account of the deluge, which is explained through questions and answers. This degree, however, is considered modern, and to have first appeared toward the end of the last century.

ARMS OF FREEMASONRY. The armorial bearings of the order have undergone some changes in the lapse of ages, varying more or less from the original, in consonance with the country or the times. They are described in several works on heraldry as follows: " *The Company of Masons*, being otherwise termed Freemasons of ancient standing, and good reckoning, by means of affable and kind meetings, at divers times did frequent this mutual assembly in the time of King Henry IV., viz: the 12th of his reign. Their arms, azure on a chevron, between three castles, argent, a pair of compasses somewhat extended of the first, were granted by William Hawkslow, Clarencieux King of Arms."—GUILLAM. *The Arms of the Operative or Stone Masons*. Azure on a chevron between three castles argent, a pair of compasses somewhat extended of the first. Crest, an arm extended,

grasping a trowel, proper. Supporters, two beavers, proper.
—DERMOTT. The arms of the Grand Lodge of England, and
used by several of the Grand Lodges of this country, are
similar to those adopted by Royal Arch Masons, which are
described as follows: Party per cross vert, voided or; in the
first quarter azure, a lion rampant or, for the tribe of Judah,
in the second or, an ox passant sable, for Ephraim; in the
third or, a man erect proper, for Reuben; in the fourth
azure, a spread eagle or, for Dan. Crest, an ark of the covenant; supporters, two cherubim, all proper; motto, Holiness
to the Lord. The banners which adorn the Royal Arch Chapters of England, representing the twelve tribes of Israel, are
as follows: Scarlet, a lion couchant, for Judah; blue, an ass
crouching beneath its burden, for Issachar; purple, a ship,
for Zebulon; yellow, a sword, for Simeon; white, a troop of
horsemen, for Gad; green, an ox, for Ephraim; flesh-color,
a vine, by the side of a wall, for Manasseh; green, a wolf, for
Benjamin; purple, a cup, for Asher; blue, a hind, for Naphtali; green, an eagle, for Dan.

ASAROTA. A kind of pavement in variegated colors, used
by the ancients for floors of temples.

ASIATIC SYSTEM, OR BROTHERS OF ASIA. A Masonic sect
with somewhat mystical theories, which arose in Germany
about the year 1780. It explained somewhat fancifully the
symbols, rites, and words of Freemasonry. There were
several degrees, all more or less tinctured with the speculations of the Rosicrucians and hermetic Masonry.

ASPIRANT. A seeker of Masonic light, who has applied
for admission to the mysteries of the Order, and, having been
accepted, is preparing himself for the induction.

ASS. An emblem of stupidity and ignorance. In the
Egyptian system it represented the uninitiated, ignorant,
and profane.

ASSASSINS. A secret order of Ishmaelites, professing the
Mahommedan religion, and yet at heart repudiating all
religions. They had a remarkable organization, were noted
for their daring bravery, but were still nothing more nor
less than a band of plunderers and cut-throats.

ASTROLOGY bears the same relation to astronomy as
alchemy does to chemistry. It is the art of reading the
future and discovering the destinies of mortals by the stars.
Many learned men have been believers in the art, as Tycho
de Brahe and Kepler. It held a high place in the hermetic
system of Masonry.

ATELIER. French for *workshop*. In symbolic Masonry it is the name of the Lodge, and also in many of the higher degrees, especially in France and Germany. In the French and Scotch rites it denotes council, tribunal, consistory, college, court, and areopagus.

ATHERSADA. A Persian word meaning the strong hand. This name in the Septuagint is given to the Persian governors of Jerusalem who accompanied Zerubbabel and Nehemiah. (*See* Esdr. ii. 63; Neh. vii. 65–70.) In the Order of Heredom of Kilwinning, it was the appellation of the chief of the Order; and in French Masonry it is the official name of the head of a Chapter.

ATHOL MASONS. The seceders from the Grand Lodge of England, in 1739, having assumed the title of "Ancient Masons," and organized a Grand Lodge, elected the Duke of Athol, then Grand Master of Scotland, Grand Master of the new Grand body. Hence they were called Athol Masons.

AZURE. Sky-blue. The appropriate color of the symbolic Lodge. A favorite color in heraldry; employed in blazonry.

B.

BAAL. A Hebrew or Canaanitish name signifying lord. The Phœnicians or Sidonians who went into Judea to build Solomon's Temple carried with them the mysteries of Baal represented by the sun, and many of the decorations of the temple referred to his system of worship. The sun was a significant symbol of the Tyrian architects, and also of the Druids, as it is now of the Masonic Brotherhood.

BACHELOR. A low rank of knighthood, yet the most ancient. It does not often appear now except in heraldic description in connection with knightly or social rank. It was originally accounted the first of military dignities, and the foundation of all honors. The word was added to the dignity of knighthood by King Henry III. of England, because the title died with the person to whom it was given, and did not descend to his posterity. It is now conferred indiscriminately on persons in civil or military stations, and may be granted even to a child as soon as he is baptized.

BAHRDT'S RITE. A system of Freemasonry consisting of six degrees, introduced into some of the Lodges of Germany by Carl Friedrich Bahrdt, a learned divine, and author of a large number of works on theology, ethics, philology, etc. His system found for a time many adherents, but is not now practiced.

BALDACHIN. The canopy which is placed over the oriental chair in the Master's Lodge, and also denotes the covering of the Lodge itself, which is a symbol of the star-decked heavens, and a sign of the universality of Freemasonry. In Pritchard's catechism we meet with the following: "What has the Lodge for a covering?" Answer: "The vaulted skies of various colors, or the clouds." It is remarked by Klause that the "sense of this beautiful system of symbols is not well understood. Some think that the primitive Lodge was not covered above, and that the skies were literally its covering; hence the ceiling of a Lodge-room is generally made to represent the celestial planisphere." The Baldachin, in this sense, is also a symbol of the extent of Freemasonry; for as the skies, with their troops of stars, spread over all regions of the earth, so Freemasonry holds in its embrace all the world, and reaches through all time.

BALUSTER. A small column or pilaster. In the higher degrees of the French system, proclamations and decrees are thus named.

BALUSTRADE. A row of balusters. Although archæological researches have failed hitherto to discover this architectural invention among the ruins of ancient buildings, yet it is difficult to conceive that an arrangement of such obvious utility should be wholly unknown to the architects of antiquity.

BAND. A ribbon worn around the neck of the officers of Grand Lodges, and also of individual Lodges, to which are attached the official jewels. The color of the band differs in different Lodges, but blue is predominant.

BANNER-BEARER. In the high degrees of the French and English systems, a Lodge-officer whose duty is well enough described by the word itself.

BANNERET. 1. A small banner; 2. a justice of the peace; 3. in the Knight-Templar system an officer who, together with the Marshal, led all warlike enterprises; 4. in France and England the word formerly designated an order of knighthood of great dignity. The title is now extinct.

BANQUET. The custom of banqueting after Lodge meetings is now very generally abolished in American Lodges, except upon installation nights, or, on the festivals of the Sts. John, on the 24th June and the 27th of December, when social gatherings of the brethren take place similar to the carnival meetings of other bodies. The brethren are enjoined not to convert the hours of recreation and refreshment into that of abuse or intemperance.

BAPHOMET. Among the charges preferred against the Order of the Knights of the Temple was that of worshiping an idol or image called Baphomet. The word is probably a corruption of Mahomet, and the image itself, with its mystical embellishments, was without doubt a cabalistic talisman, which the Templars had brought from the East, and which had some connection with the hermetic philosophy of the Arabians. That it was an object of worship among the members of that Order there is not a shadow of proof.

BAREFEET. Putting off the shoes has a threefold signification in Scripture. First, it was usual to put them off in token of mourning and grief, as David is said to have gone from Jerusalem barefoot, when he fled from Absalom. Secondly, it signified the yielding of one's right to another, and is so prescribed in Deuteronomy, and matured by Boaz; the third, was a token of respect and reverence, as appears by the command of God to Moses, and the reason assigned for it was that the ground whereon he stood was holy, or sanctified by God's immediate presence. *See* DISCALCEATION.

BASILICA. By this name market-houses and halls of justice, erected after the fashion of religious edifices and Christian churches, were called in the middle ages. These buildings were of an oblong rectangular form, with a narrow side suitable for a semicircular niche. Anderson, in his Book of Constitutions, remarks that " Our modern temple has arisen from the Basilica, having the same interior arch."

BATON. A staff or truncheon, about two feet long, generally ornamented or gilt at each end, and the middle enveloped in a scroll; it is usually carried in the right hand, and is the distinguishing mark or emblem of authority of Marshals in Masonic and other processions. The badge of a Marshal in a subordinate Lodge is two cross batons, and that of the Marshal in the Grand Lodge two cross batons encircled in a wreath.

BEAUSEANT. The name given to the banner which the ancient Knights Templar carried before them to battle. It was divided across the center—the upper half being black, and the lower half white, intended to signify that they were fair and favorable to the friends of Christ, but black and terrible to his enemies. The idea is quite an oriental one, white and black being always used among the Arabs metaphorically, in the sense above indicated. Their customary salutation is, "May your day be white!"—*i. e.*, May you be happy! *Beauséant* was not merely the name of the banner, but it was also the battle-cry and the most sacred oath of the emplars, in allusion to the seal, whereon two brethren were represented as riding on one horse, which was considered by the order as a "fair seat"—*bien seant*—that is, as a seal of true fraternal alliance. The seal of this Order was always accompanied with the word *Beauséant*—both standing in close relationship. It would seem natural, therefore, to refer the word to this token of brotherly love, where two Templars were represented as united in close friendship, and seated on one horse. This device, then, "*the fair seat*," "*beau séant*," served as a symbol of intimate union, the word was adopted as their battle-cry and the name of their banner, and finally it formed an appropriate formula of oath, signifying "*By the fraternal bond of the Temple Order—Beauséant.*"

BELLS were the most notable ornaments on the robe of the chief pontiff of the Hebrews. "And it shall be unto Aaron to minister, and his sound shall be heard when he goeth in into the Holy Place before the Lord, and when he cometh out, that he die not."

BORDER. The ornaments of a Lodge are said to be the Mosaic pavement, the indented tessel, and blazing star. The indented tessel represents the beautiful border that embellished the outer edges of the Mosaic pavement. This border consisted of small stones of various colors, artistically arranged, so as to produce the most pleasing effect.

BRAHMINS. The members of the priestly caste in Hindostan are thus named. They are a well educated class, for the most part, and many among them are distinguished for learning. In this respect they are superior to many of the missionaries who have been sent there to convert them. They were early celebrated for their attainments in philosophy and science, and their ideas have entered largely into the various philosophical systems of the West.

BRASSART. A piece of armor worn by the Knights Templar, to protect the upper part of the arm, from the elbow to the shoulder.

BREASTPLATE. A splendid piece of ornamental embroidered cloth, of the same material of which the ephod was made, ten inches square, and worn by the Jewish High-

Priest on his breast, when dressed in full sacerdotal vestments. The front was set with twelve precious stones, in golden sockets, arranged in four rows, three in each row, on each of which was engraved the name of one of the twelve tribes of Israel. On the first row a *sardius*, red, for Judah; a *topaz*, pale green, for Issachar; an *emerald*, green, for Zebulon; on the second row a *carbuncle*, deep red, for Reuben; a *sapphire*, deep blue, for Simeon; a *jasper*, green, clouded with white, for Gad; on the third row, a *ligure*, dull red, for Ephraim; an *agate*, gray, spotted with different colors, for Manasseh; an *amethyst*, purple, for Benjamin; on the fourth row a *chrysolite*, pale green, for Dan; an *onyx*, bluish white, for Asher; a *beryl*, bluish green, for Naphtali. The breastplate was double, or composed of two pieces, forming a kind of purse or bag, in which, according to the learned rabbins, the Urim and Thummim (Light and Truth), were inclosed. It was fastened at the four corners, those at the top to each shoulder, and a golden ring at the end of a wreathed chain; those below, to the girdle of the ephod, by four blue ribbons, two at each corner. This ornament was never to be severed from the priestly garments; and it was called the "Memorial," being designed to remind the priest how dear those tribes should be to him whose names he bore upon his heart. It was also named "the Breastplate of Judgment," because it was believed that by it was discovered the judgment and the will of God, or because the high-priest who wore it was revered as the fountain of justice, and put it on when he exercised his judicial capacity in matters of great importance, which concerned the whole nation.

BRIDGE. In the higher degrees of Freemasonry the Bridge has a Masonic use, and is an important symbol.

BROTHERLY KISS. At the close of their meetings the first Christians were accustomed to kiss each other; this took place also at the holy evening banquet—agape—of the community of brothers and sisters. To this practice the Apostles Paul and Peter refer in their epistles: "Greet each other with the holy kiss"—"*philēmate agiō*," Rom. xvi., 16, 1 Pet. v., 14. This holy kiss, as a sign or token of brotherly love, is found likewise as a venerable custom in many Lodges, particularly in Europe, where the Master greets with a kiss each newly-initiated member.

BROTHERS OF THE BRIDGE. A charitable and religious Brotherhood, which arose in the south of France in the mediæval age, the members of which devoted themselves to the work of building bridges, roads, hospitals, the maintaining ferries, and otherwise providing for the comfort and protection of travelers and pilgrims. Two bridges, in particular, are mentioned as having been constructed by them;

that of "Bon-Pas," three miles from Avignon, and the bridge over the Rhone, "Pont-St.-Esprit," in the department of Gard, which was commenced Aug. 21, 1265. Pope Clement III. granted them peculiar favors in consideration of their works of mercy and humanity. The peculiar token or jewel of the Order was a pick-axe worn upon the breast. RAMSAY, in a discourse published in Paris, 1741, affirms that this Order united or established relations with the Knights of St. John of Jerusalem, and afterward with the Roman builders, and thus establishes a direct connection between them and Freemasonry. Many of the high degrees of the French system have borrowed some of their decorations from the Order of the Brothers of the Bridge.

BURIAL. The right to be conducted to the last resting-place on earth, by his brethren, and to be committed to the grave with the ceremonies of the society, belong alone to Master Masons. Among the old regulations is the following: " No Mason can be interred with the formalities of the Order, unless it be at his own special request, communicated to the Master of the Lodge of which he died a member— foreigners and sojourners excepted; nor unless he has been advanced to the third degree of Masonry, from which there can be no exception."

BURNING BUSH. In the ceremonies of the Royal Arch degree, the Burning Bush is represented. It was on Mount Horeb that the angel of the Lord appeared to Moses in a burning bush, not one leaf of which was consumed. Here it was that the un-utterable name, which was never known or heard of before GOD told it to Moses, was revealed. Supreme Councils of the Ancient and Accepted Rite, date their documents "near the B. B." or "Burning Bush"—this being the great source of true Masonic light, and the place whence all Masonic instruction must emanate.

BY-LAWS. The power of framing its own by-laws is inher-ent in every Subordinate Lodge, provided they are made in accordance with the ancient statutes and regulations of the Grand Lodge. As the validity of by-laws rests on the author-ity of the Grand Lodge, it is required that they should first be submitted for approval.

C.

CAABA. The name of a talismanic and sacred stone, which has been an object of reverence among the Arabians from time immemorial. Previous to the time of Mohammed it was the recipient of divine honors; but after the remarkable conversion of those idolaters to theism, by the labors of the Prophet, he consecrated it as a symbol of the Eternal Mysteries, and an emblem of the perpetual duration of the truth that "God is one and his name one." Many fabulous stories are told of the building in which it is enclosed; but although all relating to its origin are too absurd for belief, yet it is certain that it is a temple of very great antiquity. The Caaba is not an object of worship among the Mohammedans; for they are more strict and earnest in opposition to idolatry than ever were the ancient Hebrews. It is simply the type of invisible verities and virtues which should be objects of the profoundest reverence. The pilgrims who visit Mecca march around the mystic stone in procession, and salute it with kisses, and believe that its very touch imparts a divine influence—efficacious—at the same time curing the diseases of the body and working a moral purification of the heart.

CABAL. From the French *Cabale.* It means, primarily, a society of men who profess to have a knowledge of secret things. Politically, it signifies a clique of unprincipled politicians; and, in the reign of Charles II., was applied to the ministers of that monarch, Clifford, Ashley, Buckingham, Arlington, and Lauderdale, because their initials form the word.

CABIRI. Gods, or deified heroes, held in great esteem by the Phrygians. The secret ceremonies performed in their sacred grottoes were called the mysteries of the Cabiri. Herodotus and Strabo both speak of these rites; and it is probable that most of the mysteries of antiquity were only variations of the Phrygian, which were celebrated in the obscurity of night, and with the most profound secrecy. These rites were spread through all the cities of Syria, and it has been said that Hiram, King of Tyre, was a High-Priest of these mysteries, and through him the leading feature of the Cabirian initiation was incorporated into Masonry, and perpetuated in the legend of the third degree. Many conjecture that the Order of the Essen, or the Essenes, grew out of the Cabirian rites.

CABUL. A country in Galilee ceded to Hiram, King of Tyre, by Solomon, as a reward for his assistance in building the temple. The history of this event is given in the degree of Intimate Secretary of the Ancient and Accepted rite.

CALENDAR. An almanac—a method of marking exactly the division of the years, starting from some great epoch. Thus Christian nations reckon their time from the birth of Christ, while those of the Mohammedan faith reckon theirs from the hegira, or, the flight of Mohammed from Mecca. The Masonic era commences with the creation of the world *(Anno Mundi)*, or, asonically expressed, *Anno Lucis*, year of light, or year of the Lodge. Between the creation of the world and the advent of Christ 4000 years intervene; thus A. D. 1866 added to 4000 gives the Masonic year, 5866. The Rite of Misraim adopts the chronology of Archbishop Usher, which adds 4 years to the common era, and makes 5870 the Masonic year. The Scotch rite employs the Jewish chronology; thus the Hebrew year 5826 is the A. L. of Scotch Masonry. This rite also adopts the Hebrew manner of dividing the year into months, and closes the year Sept. 17, and begins the new on the 17th (Tisri, 1st). The York rite commences the year with Jan. 1; the French with March 1. The Royal Arch degrees begin their computation with the year in which Zerubbabel began to build the second temple, which was 530 years before Christ. So that 530+1866=2396, the Masonic year of the Royal Arch. The Royal and Select Master's degree reckons time from the year in which Solomon's Temple was completed, viz: 1000 years before Christ. Thus, 1000+1866=2866, the year of the Royal and Select Master. The Knights Templar compute time from the founding of the Order, A. D. 1118; so that A. D. 1866—1118= 748 the year of the Order of the Temple. Others (Strict Observance) commence their reckoning from the destruction of the Templars, in 1314; therefore, A. D. 1866—1314= 552. The following will place these Masonic years directly before the eye: A. D. 1866=A. L. 5866, the common Masonic year; A. D. 1866=A. L. 5870 of the Rite of Misraim; A. D. 1866= A. M. 5826 of the Scottish rite; A. D. 1866=A. I. 2396 of the Royal Arch; A. D. 1866=A. D. 2866 of the Royal and Select Master; A. D. 1866=A. O. 748 of the Templars; A. D. 1866= A. O. 552 of the Strict Observance.

CALLED, OR CALLING OFF. This term can have but one application, and denotes the ceremony which summons the Craft from labor to refreshment. To "call off" for any other purpose is neither legal nor Masonic.

CALLED, OR CALLING ON. When the brothers are summoned to their labors, after the hours of refreshment, the summons is designated by the term "calling on."

CANCELLARIUS. An office in Templar Masonry of the middle ages. Each Province and Prefect had its Chancellor; he conducted the correspondence; was also properly the custodian of the mysteries, and had to instruct the newly-initiated knights in regard to their duties.

CANDLESTICK, GOLDEN. The candelabrum which Moses was commanded to make for the tabernacle, after the model shown him on the Mount. The material of which it was made was fine gold, of which an entire talent—(about $2,000)—was expended on the candelabrum and its appendages. The mode in which the metal was to be worked is described by a term which appears to mean *wrought* with the hammer, as opposed to *cast* by fusion. It consisted of a base; of a shaft rising out of it; of six arms, which came out by threes from two opposite sides of the shaft; of seven lamps which were supported on the summits of the

CANDLESTICK, ARK AND FURNITURE.

central shaft and the six arms. The arms were adorned with three kinds of carved ornaments, called cups, globes and blossoms. Its lamps were supplied with pure olive oil, lighted every evening, and extinguished every morning. It was placed in the Holy Place, on the south side (*i. e.*, to the left of a person entering the tabernacle), opposite the table of shew-bread. In the first temple there were ten candelabra of pure gold, five on the north and five on the south side, within the Holy Place. These were carried away to Babylon. In the second temple there was but one, resembling that of the tabernacle. This was carried, with other spoils, to Rome, on the destruction of Jerusalem; it was lodged in Vespasian's temple to Peace, and copied on the triumphal arch of Titus. The seven-branched candlestick is an indispensable emblem in the Royal Arch degree, also in several of the degrees of the Ancient and Accepted rite.

CAPITULAR DEGREES. The appellation, in France, of certain degrees of the Scotch rite, from the 4th to the 18th, inclusive, and which the French rite has contracted to four. These degrees are divided into four series, viz: First series, 4th degree (Scotch rite), Secret Master; 5th, Perfect Master; 6th, Intimate Secretary; 7th, Provost and Judge; 8th, Intendant of the Building. Second series, 9th degree (Scotch rite), Master Elect of Nine; 10th, Grand Elect of

Fifteen; 11th, Sublime Knight Elect. Third series, 12th degree (Scotch rite), Grand Master Architect; 13th, Knight of the Royal Circle ; 14th, Scotch Elect. Fourth series, 15th degree (Scotch rite), Knight of the East; 16th, Prince of Jerusalem; 17th, Knights of the East and West; 18th, Knight of the Rose Cross.

CAPTAIN-GENERAL. In a Commandery of Knights Templar the third officer, and who, in the absence of the Commander and Generalissimo, presides over the same. By virtue of his office, he is one of the representatives of his Commandery in the Grand Commandery. His station is on the left of the Commander; his jewel, a level surmounted by a cock, emblematic of courage; his duties are to see that everything is properly prepared for the conclave, and to communicate all orders from the Council.

CAPTAIN OF THE HOST. The fourth officer in a Chapter of Royal Arch Masons; his station is at the right, in front of the Council; his duty corresponds with that of a Marshal, having charge of the Chapter when in procession; to receive orders from the Council, and see that they are properly executed. The preservation of the essential traits of the ancient customs, usages, and landmarks of Royal Arch Masonry is entrusted to his charge.

CARAUCIUS. A Roman Emperor who patronized the Masons of Great Britain, A. D. 300. A Roman knight, named Albanus, being much interested in the prosperity of the Craft, influenced the Emperor to confer on the Brotherhood peculiar privileges. He granted the Masons a charter, and Albanus became their Grand Master, during whose administration many of their fundamental constitutions were settled, and the ritual revised.

CANEPHOROS. The bearer of the round flat basket, containing the sacred cake, chaplet, frankincense, and the implements of sacrifice, usually a young Athenian maiden, who walked in the processions of the Dionysia, Panathenea, and the other public festivals, in which all marriageable women offered small baskets to their favorite deities. The attitude in which they appear in works of art was a favorite one with the ancient artists and familiarly described by classic authors; the figure elevates both arms to support the basket carried on the head.

CARBONARI, or COLLIERS. A political society, with a Masonic form, which, for a long time, exercised a powerful influence in Italy. The date of its origin is unknown. It was inspired with the noblest ideas of liberty and religious freedom, and labored for the regeneration of Italy, the emancipation of the conscience, and the purification of religion. Botta, in his "*Historia d'Italia*," says that during the reign of Murat most of the republicans joined the Order, and in one month the society was increased by the addition of over six hundred thousand members. The essence of the oath of administration was, "Hatred to all tyrants." There were four degrees. The place of meeting was called *baraca*, i. e., hut or lodge, the exterior parts were called the *wood*; the interior was called the *vendita* or *colliery*. The confederation of all the lodges was called the *Republic*. The religious character is revealed in the following statute: "Every Carbonaro has the natural and inalienable right to worship the Almighty according to his own sense of duty and the dictates of his own conscience. The grand idea of the society has at last triumphed; it has united the Italian States, and given them free institutions. No society has ever existed which succeeded so well in working out its ideal.

CARPET. A kind of map, on which are pictured the emblems illustrative of the several degrees of Freemasonry, and by reference to which the neophytes are instructed. They were formerly traced upon the floor, hence the term carpet.

CASTELLAN. In Germany, a steward or superintendent of Masonic buildings. He has charge of the furniture of the Lodge, and also has the direction of the "Agape, or Table-lodge."

CENTAINE, ORDRE DE LA. *The Order of the Century.* An Androgyne system of Masonry, which came into notice, at Bordeaux, A. D. 1735.

CENTER OF UNITY. The central force or authority which keeps a society or order of men together. In most organizations, the center of unity is a visible material power. In the Papal Church, it is the hierarchy of Rome. But the Masonic center of unity is not material nor visible. It is an internal principle or sentiment, which dwells in all its parts, and binds them all altogether in one harmonious whole. By virtue of the omnipotence of this principle the Masonic Order has resisted all attacks from without, and all treachery within, and is more powerful than ever before.

CENTER, OPENING ON. The explanation usually given of this phrase is not satisfactory. It is too far-fetched and fanciful. A better exposition may be found by a reference to kindred societies, and especially ancient orders that are now represented either wholly or in part by Freemasonry. Let it be observed that a Lodge of Entered Apprentices or of Fellow Crafts is never said to be "opened on the center," but only a Master Mason's Lodge. The reason for this is obvious. The Apprentice Lodge is the exterior circle; the Fellow-Craft, the inner circle; the Master Mason's Lodge, the center. While in the first two the truth is but partially revealed, and is seen through a shadowy vail, in the third circle—the Master Mason's Lodge—the great center of Masonic Light— it shines with cloudless luster. "Opening on the center" simply means opening in the interior or central circle of Freemasonry. The intelligent Mason is referred to the Constitution of the Order of Essenes, of the Pythagoreans, and the "Apostolical Constitutions," and "Arcana Disciplina," of the primitive church.

CEPHAS. A Græco-Syriac word, meaning stone; the same as petros. In the Masonic degree of Royal Master it is used in connection with the cubical stone.

CERCLE, Social. *Social Circle.* An order which sprang up at Paris, in 1790, and endeavored, though happily without effect, to tempt the Masonic Brotherhood to play an important part in the French Revolution. The society published a journal, called " *The Mouth of Iron,*" the object of which was, as it claimed, "to establish a universal confederation of the friends of truth."

CHAMBER OF REFLECTION. A room used in the Templar system; also in the Ancient and Accepted rite, where, before initiation, the candidate is left, surrounded with gloomy and somber emblems, to reflect on the solemn responsibilities he is about to assume.

CHANCELLOR. The name of an officer in a Council of Knights of the Red Cross.

CHAOS, or Cahos. The 1st and 2d names of the 49th and 50th degrees of the Rite of Misraim.

CHAPTER, General Grand. This supreme body is composed of the principal officers of the State Grand Chapters and the past officers of the General Grand Chapter. The General Grand Chapter of the United States was organized in 1798.

CHAPTER, Grand. An organization consisting of the officers of the subordinate chapters under its jurisdiction and the past officers of the Grand Chapter.

CHARLES XIII., Order of. An Order of Knighthood, instituted by Charles the Thirteenth, King of Sweden, May 27, 1811, as an encouragement and reward for social and benevolent efforts to the advantage of the people, and particularly to those who may need assistance. The order is conferred only on the members of the Masonic Fraternity who have attained to a high rank in the institution in Sweden. In the original statutes instituting the order, the King said: "To give to this society (the Masonic) an evidence of our gracious sentiments toward it, we will and ordain that its first dignitaries, to the number which we may determine, shall in future be decorated with the most intimate proof of our confidence, and which shall be for them a distinctive mark of the highest dignity." The King of Sweden is the perpetual Grand Master, and the number of knights is limited to 27. Knights can be installed only on Jan. 28. Carlisle, in his *"Account of the Orders of Knighthood,"* says: "The King, who is always Master of the Order, is bound to wear it, as well as the heir apparent and the Princes of the House of Sweden, appointed to that dignity by the King. It is also conferred upon thirty native Swedes, being 36 years of age, appointed by the King, of whom three are of the Ecclesiastical Order." The badge is a cross of four points, of ruby red, with a golden border, surmounted by the regal crown. In the center of the obverse, on a white ground, are the initials of the royal founder, viz: the number XIII., between two C's, intertwined with each other; on the reverse, in a triangle, the letter B. It is worn pendant to a red watered ribbon.

CHARTER. In Freemasonry, a document issued by a Grand Lodge, or Chapter, or other grand body, to a certain number of members, empowering them to organize a Lodge or Chapter, etc., and confer degrees. A Lodge can never be opened for labor unless the Charter is present; and it is the right of every visiting brother to see it before he enters the Lodge.

CHASIDEES, Chasidim. A class or order of men mentioned in the 1st Book of Maccabees, chap. vii., 13. The Septuagint designates it by the Greek name *Assidai.* The word means skilled in all wisdom, human or divine. This association was composed of the great and learned men of Israel, who were eminent for their charitable and peaceful dispositions; and their superior knowledge of the law; especially were they distinguished by their ardent zeal for the purity and preservation of the temple. Dr. Oliver sees in this Order a kind of Masonic society, and Scaliger thinks the Chasidim were the predecessors of the Essenes.

CHIEF OF THE TABERNACLE. The 23d degree of the Ancient and Accepted rite. This is the first of a series of three degrees giving a full description of the setting up of the Tabernacle in the wilderness, its form, materials, furniture, etc., the sacerdotal and sacrifical ceremonies performed by the Priests in their worship of the Deity, as described in the instructions delivered to Moses in Exodus xxix and xl. The ceremonies of this degree commemorate the institution of the order of the High-Priesthood in Aaron and his sons Eleazar and Ithamar. Assemblies in this degree are styled Courts. The hangings are white, supported by red and black columns, by twos, placed at intervals. The court represents an encampment of the twelve tribes, in the desert, near Sinai. The standards of the tribes, made after the accompanying model, are planted round the room near the walls, in the following order: In the east, that of Judah; the color of the standard being crimson, in stripes or waves; and the device a lion, couchant, between a crown and scepter. Next to Judah, on the side toward the north, that of Issachar; color, greenish yellow; device, an ass, couchant, beneath its burden. Next to Judah, on the side toward the south, that of Zebulon; color, light green; device a ship. Next toward the south, that of Simeon; color, yellow; device, a naked sword. In the south, that of Reuben; color, a brilliant crimson; device, a man. Next to Reuben, on the side toward the west, that of Gad; color, bluish-green; device, a field covered with stars. Next toward the west, that of Manasseh; color, variegated, like agate; device, a vine running over a wall. In the west, that of Ephraim; color, variegated, like opal; device a bull. Next toward the north that of Benjamin; color violet; device a wolf. Next toward the north, that of Asher; color, blue; device, a tree in full leaf. In the north, that of Dan; color, that of the gold-stone; device, an eagle, holding a serpent in his beak. Next to Dan, toward the east, that of Naphtali; color, bluish-green; device, a female deer running at speed. In the center of the Court is a representation, reduced in size, of the Tabernacle of Moses, described in Exodus, chapters xxvi and xxxvi. The furniture of the Court consists of an altar of

sacrifice; a laver, or large basin of bronze, filled with water; the table of shew-bread; the seven-branched candlestick; an altar of incense, and the ark of the covenant. On the altar of incense are the roll of the Book of the Law and a poniard; and on the Book of the Law, the square and compasses. The presiding officer sits in the east, represents Aaron, and is styled Most Excellent High Priest. The Wardens sit in the west, and represent his two sons, Eleazar and Ithamar, and are styled Excellent Priests. The Orator, Secretary and Treasurer sit on the east of the tabernacle, the Master of Ceremonies on the west of it, the Captain of Guards on the south of it, and the Sentinel on the north. The other officers and members sit on the north, south and west of it. All except the three first officers are styled Worthy Levites. Aaron is dressed in full priestly robes. The Wardens wear the same dress, except the breastplate and the miter, instead of which they wear plain turbans of white linen. The High-Priest and Wardens do not wear aprons. The other officers and members wear white aprons lined with scarlet, and bordered with red, blue and purple ribbons. In the middle is painted or embroidered the golden candelabrum with seven lights. They also wear a red leather belt, fringed along the lower edge with gold; from which hangs a small silver censer, or ornamented cup, with a long handle, the end whereof, on which the cup sits, is shaped like an open hand. This is also the form of the jewel of the degree. For receptions an extra apartment is required, with an altar, a feeble light, and other appropriate emblems.

CHIVALRY. This word indicates an institution which arose in Europe very soon after Christianity had destroyed the old religions and brought most of the nations under its benignant influence, and seems to owe its existence to several elements. Its military and outward form was derived from the Equestrian Order of ancient Rome. Its system of symbols, and ceremonies, and fraternal bonds was contributed by the Masonic Order, and the spirit of reverence for woman, which it cultivated so earnestly, and illustrated with so many brilliant examples, was derived from the Teutonic and Scandinavian nations. In all countries of the world, except the north of Europe, woman had ever been regarded as a slave. But Tacitus informs us that the Teutons and Northmen held that there was something divine in the female sex, and therefore regarded woman with a love which approached to reverence. In the worship which they paid to the goddess Frigga, they expressed their devotion to the sex. Frigga was the type of woman deified and enthroned in the hearts of men. Thus the Romans and Scandinavians, and Masons, contributed equal parts in the creation of this institution. The Rite of Induction was in the Masonic form; and the Order was divided into three circles, corresponding to the three degrees of ancient Masonry. These three circles or degrees were those of Page, Squire, and Knight. The ceremony of reception took place in a room called a chapter, and strongly resembled the Masonic rites. The Knight, at the time of his full investiture, bound himself, by a solemn oath, to protect the weak, defend the right, love God, and reverence and shield from harm the female sex. The influence of the institution on the manners of society was very salutary. It disenthralled woman; invested her with the charms of romance, and threw around her a drapery of poetic beauty. It elevated love from the character of an instinct to that of a sublime sentiment. It created the troubadours, and called into being, in European society, music and poetry, the most powerful agencies of human civilization. [*See* KNIGHTHOOD.]

CHRONOLOGY. From *Chronos*, time, and *Logos*, a word or discourse, i. e., the science of time, or rather the science of computing time and arranging dates. The chronology of Christians dates from the nativity of Christ—*Anno Christi*. The Romans began their computation, *Anno Urbis*, from the building of the city. Masons date their documents, *Anno Mundi*, year of the world, or *Anno Lucis*, year of light. [*See* CALENDAR.]

CLAY GROUND. A piece of land remarkable for the character of its clay; situated between Succoth and Zeredatha, about 35 miles from Jerusalem. The pillars and sacred vessels of the Temple were cast there by Hiram Abiff.

CLEFTS IN THE ROCKS. The country around Jerusalem is mountainous and broken, and abounds in caves and clefts, which afford convenient hiding-places for robbers and assassins.

CLERICI ORDINIS TEMPLARIORUM. A name adopted by the Strict Observance system after the close of the seven years' war. The author of this arrangement was a person by the name of Stark. For a time this new system of Temple-Masonry flourished and drew to itself considerable attention, but, at length, it fell into disfavor and passed into obscurity.

CLERMONT, CHAPTER OF. Under this name the Chevalier de Bonneville founded, in 1754, at Paris, a chapter of the high degrees.

COCK. This fowl was considered by the ancients as the companion of Mars. He is a symbol of courage and vigilance. His image is the jewel of the Captain General of a Commandery of Knights Templar.

COLLEGES, IRISH; OR IRISH CHAPTERS. These Chapters were established at Paris about the year 1730, and soon spread over the whole of France. Their object was to propagate a form of the Ancient and Accepted rite; but they were soon superseded by the Scottish Chapters.

COLLOCATIO. Anciently, a ceremony at the funerals of Greeks and Romans, who were accustomed to place the corpse, laid on a bier, near the threshold of the house, that all might see whether he had met his death by violence or not.

COMMANDER. In councils or assemblies of the high degrees, this is the common name of the Chief of the Order. The presiding officer of a Commandery of Knights Templar is called Eminent Commander. His official jewel is a passion cross surrounded by a halo of rays.

COMMANDERY. An assembly of Knights Templar. It must consist of at least nine members, authorized by a dispensation or charter from some competent power to confer the degrees of knighthood. The officers are a Commander, Generalissimo, Captain General, Prelate, Senior Warden, Junior Warden, Treasurer, Recorder, Standard-Bearer, Sword-Bearer, Warder, three Guards, and a Sentinel.

COMMANDERY, GRAND. A body of Knights Templar, formed by three or more subordinate Commanderies in a state or province, and which exercises jurisdiction over all the Councils of the Red Cross, and the Commanderies of Knights Templar and Knights of Malta.

CONCLAVE. A secret assembly. The college of cardinals is thus called when assembled, especially for the election of a Pope. The name is also given to a Commandery of Knights Templar, when in session.

CONCORD, ORDER OF. Several societies have borne this name, but the first one that could lay any claim to a Masonic character was the "Order of Concord," or of "United Hosts." This was a fraternity founded on Masonic principles, in 1696, by the Prince of Nassau. Prince Swartzburg-Rudolstadt founded another of the same name, which admitted ladies to membership, in 1718, and in 1759 another arose in Hamburg, where it still flourishes.

CONFERENCE. In Europe, particularly on the continent, intelligent Masons are in the habit of meeting occasionally for the purpose of consulting together in regard to the interests of Freemasonry. These assemblies they call Conferences. In the last century the most important ones were those of Copenhagen, Hamburg, and Mattisholm.

CONGRESS, MASONIC. A modern name for assemblies like those described in the preceding article.

Congress of Washington, convoked in the year 1822, at the call of several Grand Lodges, for the purpose of recommending the establishment of a General Grand Lodge of the United States. The effort was an unsuccessful one.

Congress of Baltimore, convoked in the year 1843, with the object of establishing a uniform system of work. Perhaps there was not, in any of the preceding Congresses, a greater instance of failure than in this, since not a year elapsed before the most prominent members of the Congress disagreed as to the nature and extent of the reforms which were instituted; and the Baltimore system of work has already become a myth.

Second Congress of Baltimore, convoked in the year 1847, the object being again to attempt the establishment of a General Grand Lodge. This Congress went so far as to adopt a "Supreme Grand Lodge Constitution," but its action was not supported by a sufficient number of Grand Lodges to carry it into effect.

Congress of Lexington, convoked in 1853, at Lexington, Ky., for the purpose of again making the attempt to form a General Grand Lodge. A plan of constitution was proposed, but a sufficient number of Grand Lodges did not accede to the proposition to give it efficacy.

Third Congress of Paris, convoked by order of Prince Murat, in 1855, for the purpose of effecting various reforms in the Masonic system. At this Congress, ten propositions, some of them highly important, were introduced, and their adoption recommended to the Grand Lodges of the world. The meeting has been too recently held to permit us to form any opinion as to what will be its final results.

North American Masonic Congress, convened in the city of Chicago, Sept. 13, 1859, at the call of a large number of prominent members of the Fraternity, for the purpose of organizing a General Grand Lodge of the United States. The Convention held two sessions, adopted articles of confederation, which proposed that the Congress should meet triennially; take cognizance of all cases of difference which may have arisen between two or more Lodges; consult and advise on questions of Masonic law and jurisprudence, without power of enforcement of its decrees. No subsequent session was held; the project, therefore, failed of establishing any definite results.

CONSECRATION, ELEMENTS OF. Corn, wine, and oil are the materials used by Masons for consecrating purposes. Corn is the symbol of nourishment; wine is the symbol of refreshment, and oil is the symbol of joy. They are also emblematic of peace, health, and plenty.

CONSECRATION is the act of solemnly dedicating a person or thing to the service of God. It was one of the most widely-spread religious ceremonies of the ancient world. The ceremonies of consecrating a Lodge-room are imposing and necessary, and should be performed before the purposes of Freemasonry can be consistently exercised.

CONSERVATOR, GRAND. The name of an officer of the Grand Orient of France. He was a counselor of the Grand Master, and in some cases could restrain his action. This appellation was also given to a triumvirate of three Grand Conservators of the Grand Orient, in 1814, when Joseph Napoleon, then Grand Master, and his adjunct, Prince Cambaceres, were called away by public duties.

CONSISTORY. The name given to an assembly or organization of Masons in the higher degrees, especially of the Ancient and Accepted rite, and the Rite of Misraim.

CONSOLIDATION LODGES: About the middle of the past century a large number of Scottish Lodges, with alchemistical tendencies, were constituted under this name. One of the most interesting of our Masonic degrees was derived from them.

CONTRACT, SOCIAL, i. e., SOCIAL CONTRACT. A Lodge, or rather a union of lodges, for purposes of instruction, founded in Paris about the year 1776. It made a new arrangement of the degrees.

CONVENTION. A Masonic convocation, now called a Congress, was formerly designated by this name. The following are the principal Conventions, mentioned in chronological order:

Convention at York. In the year 926, Prince Edwin, a brother of King Athelstane, of England, convoked a Masonic Convention at the city of York, which, under the name of a General Assembly, established the celebrated Gothic constitutions, which are the oldest Masonic document extant. These constitutions have always been recognized as containing the fundamental law of Masonry. Although transcripts of these constitutions are known to have been taken in the reign of Richard II., the document was for a long time lost sight of until a copy of it was discovered in the year 1838, in the British Museum, and published by Mr. J. O. Halliwell.

First Convention of Strasburg, convoked at Strasburg, in 1275, by Edwin Von Steinbach, master of the work. The object was the continuation of the labors on the cathedral of Strasburg, and it was attended by a large concourse of Masons from Germany, England, and Italy. It was at this Convention that the German builders and architects, in imitation of their English brethren, assumed the name of *Freemasons,* and took the obligations of fidelity and obedience to the ancient laws and regulations of the Order.

First Convention of Ratisbon, convoked in 1459, by Jost Dotzinger, the master of the works of the Strasburg cathedral. It established some new laws for the government of the Fraternity in Germany.

Second Convention of Ratisbon, convoked in 1464, by the Grand Lodge of Strasburg, to define the relative rights of, and to settle existing difficulties between, the Grand Lodges of Strasburg, Cologne, Vienna, and Berne.

Convention of Spire, convoked in 1469, by the Grand Lodge of Strasburg, for the consideration of the condition of the Craft, and of the edifices in course of erection by them.

Convention of Cologne, convoked in 1535, by Hermann, Bishop of Cologne. It was one of the most important conventions ever held, and was attended by delegates from nineteen Grand Lodges; it was engaged in the refutation of slanders at this time circulated against the Fraternity. The result of its deliberations was the celebrated document known as the "Charter of Cologne."

Convention of Basle, convoked by the Grand Lodge of Strasburg, in 1563, principally for the purpose of settling certain difficulties which had arisen respecting the rights of the twenty Lodges which were its subordinates. Some new regulations were adopted at this Convention.

Second Convention of Strasburg, convoked by the Grand Lodge of Strasburg, in 1564. It appears to have been only a continuation of the preceding one at Basle, and the same matters became the subjects of its consideration.

Convention of London, convoked by the four Lodges of London, at the Apple-tree tavern, in February, 1717. Its history is familiar to all American and English Masons. Its results were the formation of the Grand Lodge of England, and the organization of the institution upon that system, which has since been pursued in England and in this country.

Convention of Dublin, convoked by the Lodges of Dublin, in 1730, for the purpose of forming the Grand Lodge of Ireland.

Convention of Edinburgh, convoked in 1736, by the four Lodges of Edinburgh, for the purpose of receiving from Sinclair, of Roslin, his abdication of the hereditary Grand Mastership of Scotland, and for the election of a Grand Master. The result of this Convention was the establishment of the Grand Lodge of Scotland.

Convention of the Hague, convoked by the Royal Union Lodge, in 1756 and the result was the establishment of the National Grand Lodge of the United Provinces.

First Convention of Jena, convoked in 1763, by the Lodge of Strict Observance, under the presidency of Johnson, a Masonic charlatan, but whose real name was Becker. In this Convention the doctrine was first announced that the Freemasons were the successors of the Knights Templar, a dogma peculiarly characteristic of the rite of Strict Observance.

Second Convention of Jena, convoked in the following year, 1764, by Johnson, with the desire of authoritatively establishing his doctrine of the connection between Templarism and Masonry. The empirical character of Johnson or Becker was here discovered by the celebrated Baron Hunde, and he was denounced, and subsequently punished at Magdeburg by the public authorities.

Convention of Altenberg, convoked in 1765, as a continuation of the preceding. Its result was the establishment of the Rite of Strict Observance, and the election of Baron Hunde as Grand Master.

Convention of Brunswick, convoked in 1775, by Ferdinand, Duke of Brunswick. Its object was to effect a fusion of the various rites; but it terminated its labors, after a session of six weeks, without success.

Convention of Lyons, convoked in 1778, by the Lodge of *Chevaliers bienfaisants*. Its object was to produce a reform in the rituals of the Masonic system, but it does not appear to have been sagacious in its means, nor successful in its results.

Convention of the Lovers of Truth, held at Paris, in 1784, under the auspices of the "Lodge of the United Friends." The Duke of Brunswick, St. Martin, and the celebrated Mesmer, were active participants in its discussions.

Convention of Wolfenbuttel, convoked in 1778, by the Duke of Brunswick, as a continuation of that which had been held in 1775, and with the same view of reforming the organization of the Order. However, after a session of five weeks, it terminated its labors with no other result than an agreement to call a more extensive meeting at Wilhelmsbad.

Convention of Wilhelmsbad, convoked in 1782. Its avowed object was the reform of the Masonic system, and its disentanglement from the confused mass of rites with which French and German pretenders or enthusiasts had sought to overwhelm it. Important topics were proposed at its commencement, but none of them were discussed, and the Convention was closed without coming to any other positive determination than that Freemasonry was not connected with Templarism, or in other words, that, contrary to the doctrine of the rite of Strict Observance, the Freemasons were not the successors of the Knights Templar.

Conventions at Paris, convoked in 1785 and 1787, with the laudable view of introducing a reform in the rituals and of discussing important points of doctrine and history. Both Conventions closed, after sessions of several months, without producing any practical result.

From the foregoing lists, it wil. be seen that a large number of the Masonic conventions and congresses which have been held were productive of little or no effect. Others of them, however, such, for instance, as those of York, of Cologne, of London, and a few others, have certainly left their mark, and there can, we think, be but little doubt that a general convention of the Masons of the world, meeting with an eye single to the great object of Masonic reform, and guided by a spirit of compromise, might be of incalculable advantage to the interests of the institution at the present day.

CONVOCATION. The meetings of Chapters of Royal Arch Masons and Councils of Royal and Select Masters are called Convocations. The term is applied to several of the bodies of the higher grades.

CORNUCOPIA, or the HORN OF PLENTY. A source whence, according to the ancient poets, every production of the earth was lavished. In the Masonic system it is the symbol of joy, peace and plenty. It is the official jewel of the Stewards of the Lodge.

CORRESPONDENCE. Intercommunication between lodges. The duty of attending to this is usually assigned to an officer called Corresponding Secretary. In the Masonic Grand Bodies the subject is in charge of a committee.

CORYBANTES. Priests who are supposed to have derived their origin from Corybas, who appointed them to perform religious service to his mother, the goddess, Cybele; in the island of Crete and Phrygia. The ceremonies bore a strong resemblance to those of the Cabiri.

COTYS, MYSTERIES OF. Cotys was a goddess worshiped at Corinth and Chios. Her mysteries were celebrated in the night.

COUNCIL. An appellation given to assemblies of many of the higher degrees of Freemasonry, as "Council of Royal and Select Masters; Council of the Trinity," etc.

COUSINS, Collier, the Good. An old order which flourished in the western part of France. Their book of laws, ritual, and catechism, were a mixture of religious and mystical ideas.

COVERING. [*See* Baldachin.]

CREATED. In the orders of chivalry the recipient of the honor of knighthood is said to be "created." The term is used in the degrees of Red Cross, Knights Templar, and Knights of Malta.

CREED. Articles of faith. The "Creed" of a Mason is simple. It is belief in a God "in whom we live, and move, and have our being."

CROSS-LEGGED. The effigies on the tombs of the ancient Knights Templar are always represented with the legs crossed, in allusion to their character as Knights of the Cross. Consequently, in the sixteenth century, when some Knights Templar in Scotland joined the Masonic Lodge, at Stirling, they were called cross-legged Masons.

CROW. An instrument of iron used to raise heavy substances. Employed as a symbol in Royal Arch Masonry.

CROWN, Princesses of the. A system of Adoptive Masonry which appeared in Saxony, in 1770. It flourished for a short time, and then became extinct.

CULDEES. An order which at one period had establishments in almost every part of Great Britain and Ireland. Some derive the name from the Latin *cultor Dei*, a worshiper of God. Others, however, think they can trace its origin to the Gaelic *kyldee*, from *cylle*, a cell, and *dee*, a house, that is a building composed of cells. They were much persecuted, and lived in as retired a manner as possible. A society of them settled at York, and were found there by King Athelstane on his return from Scotland, in 936. They are described as holy men—"*viros santæ vitæ et conversationes honestæ dictos adhuc Calideas.*" Fessler thinks he has discovered a connection between them and the building corporations of Great Britain, and thus brings them into the category of Masonic societies.

D.

DACTYLI. Priests of Cybele in Phrygia; so-called because they were five in number, thus corresponding with the number of the fingers, from which the name is derived. To them is ascribed the discovery of iron, and the art of working it by means of fire. Their ceremonies were similar to those of the Corybantes and Curetes, other priests of the same goddess in Phrygia and Crete. Their number appears to have been originally three: Celmis (the smelter), Damnameneus (the hammer), and Acmon (the anvil). Their number was afterward increased to five, ten (male and female), fifty-two, and one hundred.

DADUCHI. Priests of Ceres, who, at the feasts and sacrifices of that goddess, ran about the temple with lighted torches, delivering them from hand to hand, till they had passed through the whole company.

DAIS. The platform or raised floor in the East, on which the presiding officer is seated. In a Lodge the dais should be reached by three steps; in a Royal Arch Chapter by seven.

DEACONS. In the constitutional list are two officers known as Senior Deacon and Junior Deacon. Their duties are a general superintendence over the security of the Lodge; the introduction of distinguished visitors and strangers; assist in the ceremonies of the Order; carry messages about the Lodge, and to see that proper accommodations are afforded to every member. The S. D. should be appointed by the Master, and the J. D. by the Senior Warden, as they are the special messengers of those two officers. There is no knowledge of these officers in Masonry prior to 1777 in this country, and still more recently in England.

DEATH. That event in the life of man which marks the transition from the material and visible to the invisible and spiritual world. In point of fact, there is no such thing as death—it is simply a progress, or a change in the manner of existence. The ancients were more earnest believers in immortality than the moderns. With them immortality was a fact which admitted of no doubt; consequently all the literature of the old Pagans deals largely with the awful mysteries of eternity. It invariably represents the future life as a continuation of this.* In the mysteries, and also in

* Dr. Oliver has allowed himself to repeat the assertions of ignorant and prejudiced minds in his article on this subject. Both of the authors to whom he refers, and from whom he makes quotations, were earnest believers in immortality. These quotations are garbled extracts.

Freemasonry, death has a symbolical meaning. It signifies
the end of a profane and vicious life—a life of stupidity and
ignorance—and the introduction to a life of virtue, and to the
enjoyments of knowledge; in other words, to that higher
sphere of intellectual and moral perfection which is the result
of those labors and trials which are symbolically represented
in the initiation.

DEBATE. An exchange of opinions or a war of words.
Freemasonry forbids all improper debates in the Lodge, i. e.,
the discussion of those ideas which divide men into religious
and political sects. Seeking the harmony and concord of
society it tolerates no practice which would destroy its object.
Fraternal debates on literary, scientific, and philosophical
subjects are always in order, in a Masonic Lodge, when they
tend to the improvement of the brethren.

DECALOGUE. The ten commandments or precepts delivered by God to Moses on Mount Sinai. They are engraved
on two tables of stone, and are important symbols in the
ceremonies of the Royal Arch degree.

DECANUS. An honorary officer in the Knights Templar
system of Baron Hunde. In the absence of the Grand
Master and the Prior, he presided as chief of the Chapter.
When a vacancy occurred in the office of Grand Master, he
was one of four vicars who governed a province.

DELTA. The name of the fourth letter of the Greek
alphabet. In form it is a triangle ($\triangle$), and was considered
by the ancient Egyptians a symbol of fire, and also of God.
In the Scottish and French systems, and also that of the
Knights Templar, the triangle or delta is a symbol of the
Unspeakable Name.

DEMIURGE. *A handicraftsman.* The name given in the
cosmogony of the Gnostics to the creator or former of the
world of sense. He was conceived as the archon or chief
of the lowest order of the spirits or æons of the pleroma;
mingling with chaos, he formed in it a corporeal animated
world. He created man, but could impart to him only his
own weak principle, the *psyche* or sensuous soul; therefore
the highest, the really good God, added the divine rational
soul, or *pneuma*. But the power of evil in the material body,
and the hostile influence of the merely sensuous demiurge,
prevented the development of that higher element. The
demiurge, holding himself to be the highest God, could not
bring his creatures to the knowledge of the true godhead;
as the Jehovah of the Jews, he gave them the imperfect law

of Moses, which promised merely a sensuous happiness, and even that not attainable; and against the spirits of the *hyle*, or world of matter, he sent only a psychical, and therefore powerless Messiah.

DEPUTATION-LODGES. Assemblies composed of deputations from several lodges who meet for the purpose of accomplishing some common object deemed important to the interests of all concerned. These lodges afforded opportunities for intelligent Masons to exchange thoughts, and in the last century were useful in purging the institution of many customs and practices which were foreign to it. The Deputation-Lodge, we believe, is not known in the United States.

DEPUTY. An officer appointed by the Grand Master to represent him in a certain Masonic district. In the United States he is styled District Deputy Grand Master.

DEUS MEUMQUE JUS. *God and my Right.* Motto of the Supreme Council 33d degree of the Ancient and Accepted Scottish rite.

DEVICE. A badge, in heraldry, derived from the old French word *deviser*, to talk, to discourse familiarly; probably so-called because a symbol united with a word or words describes more graphically and forcibly what is desired than any other invention possibly could. A device is, therefore, a painted metaphor, and is used on banners, seals, medals, shields, armorial bearings, etc. Almost every degree in Freemasonry has its device, as *Adhuc Stat, Deus Meumque Jus,* etc. All knightly orders have their devices—that of the French Order of the Star, founded in 1351, was a star with the words: "They show to kings the way to the stars."

DIEU LE VEUT (French). *God wills it.* The battle-cry of the Crusaders, and, in imitation of them, a common expression in the Knight Templar system.

DIGNITAIRES (French). *Dignitaries.* In French Lodges the first five officers are called by this name, and in the Grand Lodge the same are styled Grand Dignitaries.

DIMIT. From the Latin *dimitto.* To permit to go. The act of withdrawing from membership. The dimission of a Mason from his Lodge does not cancel his Masonic obligations to the Order. He is still subject to the imperative law —*once a Mason, always a Mason.*

DIONYSIAN ARCHITECTS. Priests of Bacchus, who is also named Dionysus. Becoming skilled in the science of architecture they founded the order of Sidonian Builders, a considerable period before the time of David, King of Israel. From this society—which built the Temple of Solomon—sprung the Roman Colleges of Architects, and these, in thei. turn, gave birth to the building corporations of the middl ages, from which the present order of Freemasonry is derived. Thus the society of Dionysian Builders is the connecting link between Modern Masonry and the Ancient Mysteries.

DIONYSIAN MYSTERIES. The ceremonies of this order of mystagogues appear to have been a mixture of the rituals of the Egyptian mysteries and the Cabriri. The ritual of Freemasonry preserves, in its central circle, the leading features of the Dionysian institution. Hiram and Dionysus, or Bacchus, are names, representing and illustrating in their history and experience, the same ideas. The initiation was a symbolical progress, from the dark, dead, and frigid North to the refulgent East—a pilgrimage

> "Through darkness dread, and terrors wild,
>   And horrors that appall,
> To Bacchus' shrine, where splendors mild
>   Around the 'accepted' fall."

The moral teaching of these mysteries was the same as that of the Mysteries of Isis, *which see.*

DIPLOMA. From the Greek *diploŏ*, I fold up; literally a letter folded but once. It signifies a document signed and sealed, conferring certain rights and privileges on the holder. In Freemasonry this would designate a certificate of membership, and of good standing, issued by a Lodge to its members, to be used by them when traveling among strangers. These documents have been in vogue since 1663, and in some jurisdictions traveling brothers, who are strangers, are not permitted to visit Lodges, if they are not provided with one. The great body of Masons, however, seem reluctant to make the presentation of a diploma a necessary condition of admission to the Lodge as a visitor

DIRK, or DAGGER. An attribute of the clothing or costume of the members of the Degree of the elect—the 4th degree of the French rite—and of the Knights Kadosch—the 30th degree of the Ancient and Accepted rite.

DISCALCEATION. Denuding or making bare the feet as an act of religious reverence. This custom appears to have been universal among ancient nations, and is, at least, as old as the time of Moses; for it is said, Exod. iii. 5, that the angel of the Lord called to Moses from the burning bush.

"Draw not nigh hither; put off thy shoes from off thy feet; for the place whereon thou standest is holy ground." But among all peoples the custom was observed as an act of reverence and a sign of humility. Even among Christians the practice has prevailed. An Ethiopian bishop, an envoy from the King of Abyssinia to John III., Portugal, is represented as saying: "*Non datur nobis potestas adeundi templum nisi nudibus pedibus*," i. e., "The power or privilege of going into the temple is not given us unless we go with naked feet."

DISCIPLINA ARCANA. The name given to the secret ritual and practices of the first Christian Church. The disciples of Christ had scarcely formed themselves into a brotherhood, before the instinct of self-preservation compelled them to retire into secrecy, and throw over themselves and all their proceedings the vail of mystery. The ancient documents known as the "Apostolical Constitutions and Canons" often speak of the *Disciplina Arcana*, or secret discipline of the most ancient church. Irenæus, Tertullian, Clemens, Origen, and Gregory, of Nyssa, also furnish abundant proofs that the primitive church was a secret society. Indeed, so well known was this peculiar organization that nearly all ancient writers, Christian or Pagan, have noticed the fact. Lucian of Samosata speaks of Christ as a magician who established new mysteries. Pliny, also, informs us that the Christians were persecuted in the reign of Trajan, not on account of their religion, but as a secret society, under a general law of the empire which prohibited all "secret associations." The arcana of the primitive disciples were comprised in four circles, which the neophyte was required to traverse before he could participate in the most sacred mysteries of the church. The central light of truth shone in its full splendor only on those who had attained to the highest degree. They were styled: 1. *Oi pistoi*, the Faithful; 2. *Photizomenoi*, the Enlightened; 3. *Memue menoi*, the Initiated; 4. *Teleioumenoi*, the Perfect. The terms *mustai*, and *musta gogetoi* are often used in this connection, and, in short, all the phraseology which profane writers employ in describing an initiation into their mysteries. Indeed the right of baptism itself has an evident relation, as Cyril of Jerusalem represents, to the initiatory rites of Isis, Eleusis, Samothrace and Phrygia.[*]

DISTRICT DEPUTY. [*See* DEPUTY.]

[*] Cyril, Hierosol, Catech, Mystagog, 5, *et seq*, *et Jamieson*, Manners of Primitive Christians.

DOVE, Knights and Ladies of the. A kind of Adoptive or Androgynal Masonry which appeared in France, a. d. 1784.

DRAGON, Knights of the. A degree in Knight-Templarism, which was popular in Strasburg, Lyons, and Bordeaux from 1766 to 1783. It had a history and a cypher of a peculiar character.

DRUIDS. An order of priests resembling the Brahmins of India, whose principal seat was in Great Britain. The name seems to have been derived from the Greek *drus*—the oak—or from *derw* the Celtic word for the same tree, which they held in the highest reverence, as a symbol of wisdom and strength. They were divided into three *castes*. 1. Those who were peculiarly priests, and directed the public worship. 2. The prophets, who foretold future events. 3. The *vates*, holy singers, bards, or poets. According to Julius Cæsar,* they were the learned men and philosophers of the Gauls and Celts, and possessed great authority also in the government of the State. The instruction of the people—save in the art of war—was intrusted to them. Their teachings were often communicated in verse, and had a double sense. They believed in the immortality of man, and the transmigration of souls, and a restoration of all to purity and happiness. Their reverence for the parasitical plant—mystletoe—amounts almost to worship. At a certain season of the year the Arch-druid ascended the oak, on which it was usually found, and cut it with a golden knife. This was the holiest thing in nature, and a panacea for every disease. Their temples and altars were constructed of unhewn stones, and the former had no roofs or coverings. Their ceremonies were symbolical, which has led some writers, as Lawrie, Preston, Hutchinson, and Oliver, to see a connection between them and Freemasonry.

DUE FORM. When a Lodge is constituted, and its officers installed, or any Masonic service is performed, such as laying corner-stones, consecrating halls, by the Grand Master and his officers, it is said to be done in ample form; if by deputies of the Grand Master, it is said to be done in due form.

DUE GUARD. The "due guard" of Masonry teaches every brother to set a watch over his words, his acts, and his thoughts, and constantly warns him to remember his solemn obligations, and never to forget the penalty of broken vows and violated faith.

* Cæsar, Bell, Gall.

E.

EAGLE, KNIGHT OF THE AMERICAN. A quasi-military degree in Texas, and the Western States.

EAGLE, KNIGHT OF THE BLACK. The name of a Prussian Order founded in 1701; also of the 38th degree of the Rite of Misraim, the 66th of the Metropolitan Chapter of France, and of the 27th degree of the Primitive Scotch rite.

EAGLE, KNIGHT OF THE RED. A title in the French *Ordre de la Sincerité*.

EASTERN STAR, ORDER OF THE. An American adoptive system of Freemasonry. It was introduced into this country in 1778, and since that time thousands of persons have participated in its ceremonies. The theory of the Order of the Eastern Star is founded upon the Holy writings. Five prominent female characters, illustrating as many Masonic virtues, are selected, *adopted* and placed under Masonic protection. Its obligations are based upon the honor of the female sex, and framed upon the principles of Equality and Justice. Those who are entitled to receive the degrees are Master Masons, their wives, widows, sisters and daughters. [*See* ADOPTIVE MASONRY.]

ECLECTIC MASONRY. Soon after the convention of Wilhelmsbad, 1782, some German Masons, with the celebrated Baron Knigge at their head, conceived the idea of such a reform in the system of degrees as would confine Freemasonry, in its original and legitimate character, to the three symbolical degrees, governed by the English constitution of 1721, and in this way escape from the tyrannical usurpations of the Circles of the Strict Observance. The Lodges, however, according to this plan, were allowed to select or choose any of the higher degrees, and work them as a kind of amusement or recreation. This invention did not meet with the success anticipated, and has nearly disappeared. It was never introduced into the United States.

ECOSSAIS (French), *Scotch*. A term applied to the Ancient and Accepted rite, and the name of the fifth degree of the French system. This system has a very curious history, and at different times has promulgated nearly a hundred degrees, and through their agency all sorts of ideas and theories of a mystical character were propagated by their inventors. The apocryphal degrees, however, have gradually been discarded.

EGYPTIAN MYSTERIES. According to Herodotus, the secret institution of Isis, with its wonderful mysteries and imposing ceremonies, made its appearance simultaneously with the organization of Egyptian society and the birth of Egyptian civilization. At first the initiation into these mysteries was, probably, simply a mystic drama, representing the progress of man, from a barbarous to a civilized state, and his advancement and struggles through gloom and toil, toward the supreme perfection, whether in time or eternity. This is seen in the hieroglyphical representation of the judgment of Amenti. It is a picture of an ordeal or scrutiny to which the candidate was subjected preparatory to initiation. The ceremony of initiation itself was a progress through gloom and terror, and all possible mortal horrors, to scenes of indescribable beauty and glory. The principal seat of the mysteries was at Memphis. They were of two kinds —the Greater and the Less; the former taught by the priests of Osiris and Serapis, the latter by those of Isis. The candidate was required to furnish proofs of a pure and moral life as an evidence that he was fitted for admission or enrollment. When these conditions were fulfilled, he was required to spend a week in solitude and meditation, abstain from all unchaste acts, confine himself to a light diet, and to purify the body by frequent ablutions and severe mortifications of the flesh. Being thus prepared, the candidate was ordered to enter the pyramid during the night, where he had to descend on his hands and knees through a narrow passage without steps, until he reached a cave-like opening, through which he had to crawl to another subterranean cave, on the walls of which he found inscribed the following words: "The mortal who shall travel over this road alone, without hesitating or looking behind, shall be purified by fire, by water and by air, and if he can surmount the fear of death he shall emerge from the bosom of the earth; he shall revisit the light, and claim the right of preparing his soul for the reception of the mysteries of the great goddess Isis." At the same time three priests, disguised in masks resembling the heads of jackals, and armed with swords, sought to frighten him, first by their appearance and noise, and after-

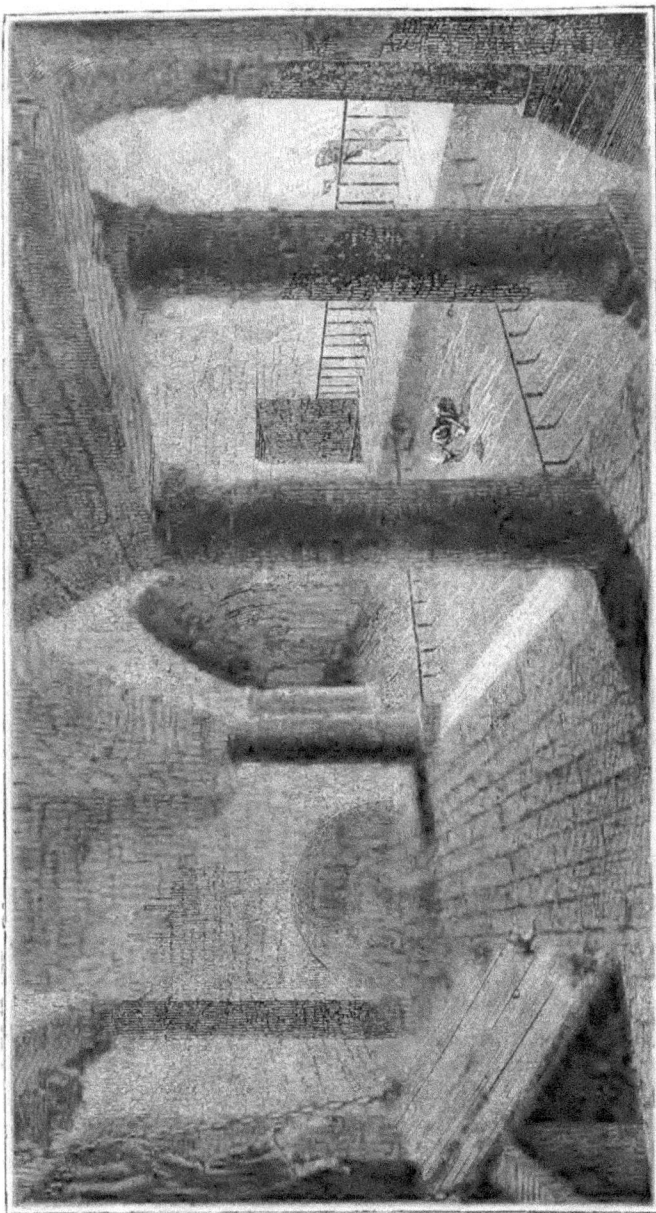

NEOPHYTE PASSING THROUGH THE GREATER EGYPTIAN MYSTERIES.

ward by enumerating the dangers that waited him on his journey. If his courage did not fail him here, he was permitted to pass on to the Hall of Fire. This was a large apartment lined with burning stuffs, and whose floor was a grate painted flame color; the bars of this grate were so narrow that they offered scarcely room enough for him to cross. Through this hall he was obliged to pass with the greatest speed to avoid the effects of the flames and heat. Having overcome this difficulty, he next encountered a wide channel fed from the waters of the Nile. Over this stream he had to swim, with a small lamp, which furnished all the light that was afforded him. On reaching the opposite side, he found a narrow passage leading to a landing place about six feet square, the floor of which was made movable by mechanism underneath. On each side were walls of rough stone, and behind wheels of metal were fixed. In front was a gate of ivory, opening inward, and preventing any farther advance. On attempting to turn two large rings annexed to the door, in hopes of continuing his journey, the wheels came into motion, producing a most terrific and stunning effect, and the floor gave way, leaving him suspended by the arms over apparently a deep abyss, from which proceeded a violent and piercing current of cold air, so that the lamp was extinguished, and he remained in complete darkness. In this process of trial, it will be observed that the candidate was exposed to the action of the four great purifying elements---Earth, Fire, Water and Air. After the risk of falling into an unknown depth had continued for a moment or two, the floor resumed its original position, the wheels ceased to revolve, and the door of ivory flew open, disclosing the sanctuary of Isis, illuminated with a blaze of light, where the priests of that goddess were assembled drawn up in two ranks, clothed in ceremonial dresses, and bearing the mysterious symbols of the Order, singing hymns in praise of their divinity, who welcomed and congratulated him on his courage and escape from the dangers which had surrounded him. The entrance to the sanctuary was constructed in the pedestal of the triple statue of Isis, Osiris and Horus; and the walls were ornamented with various allegorical figures, symbols of the Egyptian mysteries, among which were particularly prominent: 1. A serpent throwing an egg out of its mouth; a symbol of the production of all things by the heat of the sun. 2. A serpent curled up in the form of a circle, holding its tail in its mouth; an allusion to eternity, and to the uninterrupted revolution of the sun. 3. The double tau, which is meant to represent the active and passive power of nature in the generation of all things.

There he was made to kneel before an altar, and required
o pronounce the following solemn obligation : "I swear
never to reveal to any uninitiated person the things that
I have seen in this sanctuary, nor any of the mysteries
which have been or shall be communicated to me. I call on
all the deities of earth, of heaven, and of the infernal
regions, to be witnesses of this oath; and I trust that their
vengeance will fall on my head should I ever become a
villain so base and perjured." He was then retained for
several months in the temple, where moral trials of different
kinds awaited him. The object of this was to bring out all
the traits of his character, and to test his fitness for his
vocation. After he had passed through this trial, then came
what was called his *Manifestation.* This consisted of a
number of ceremonies, of which the novice was the subject
during the space of twelve days. He was dedicated to
Osiris, Isis and Horus, and decorated with the twelve consecrated scarfs (*stolæ*) and the Olympic cloak. These scarfs
were embroidered with the signs of the Zodiac, and the
cloak with figures that were symbolic of the starry heavens
as the abode of the gods and happy spirits. A crown of palm
leaves was placed upon his head, and a burning torch in his
hand. Thus prepared, he was again led to the altar, where
he renewed his oath. Now came the time when he had a
right to appear as victor before the people, and to this end
they prepared for him a solemn procession, called the
Triumphal March of the Initiated, which was proclaimed by
heralds in every quarter of the city. On the morning of
the day appointed for the ceremony, the priests assembled
in the temple, when the most precious treasures belonging
to the sanctuary were displayed, and repaired to the chapel
of Isis to bring a sacrifice to the goddess, covered with a
vail of white silk, and embroidered with golden hieroglyphics, and this again concealed beneath a black gauze.
After the sacrifice, the procession left the temple and moved
westward. First in the train came an image of Isis seated
upon a triumphal car drawn by six white horses, next to
which walked the priests in the order of their rank, dressed
in their most gorgeous attire, and carrying the sacred
symbols, the utensils of the temple, the books of Thot, and
the sacred tablet of Isis, which was a silver plate with the
hieroglyphics that referred to the mysteries of this goddess
engraved on it. The priests were followed by all the native
and foreign adepts, dressed in white linen garments. The
newly-initiated walked in their midst, distinguished by a
white vail which extended from his head down to his
shoulders. All the houses of the streets through which the

procession passed were decorated as on festal occasions. Flowers and perfumes were everywhere thrown over the person of the novice, and his arrival greeted with shouts of rejoicing. After his return to the temple, he was placed upon an elevated throne, before which immediately afterward a curtain descended. While the priests chanted during the interval hymns in favor of the goddess, he divested himself of his holiday suit, and assumed the white linen garb which he was henceforth to wear. The curtain was now again raised, and the renewed shouts of the spectators greeted him as an adept. The ceremonies concluded with a festival, which lasted three days, during which the newly-made brother occupied the seat of honor. At a subsequent period the Mysteries were augmented by the introduction of the tragedy of Osiris. The ceremony consisted of funereal rites, expressive of the wildest grief on account of his death; a search for his body, which is at last found, the return of Osiris to life, and the destruction of Typhon, his assassin. Osiris was the symbol of truth or goodness; Typhon of error or evil—the murder of Osiris signified the temporary subjugation of virtue, and his resurrection the ultimate triumph of the good. This was the parent of all those Grecian rites which represent a death and a resurrection, and whose principal features are perpetuated in the legend of the Sidonian builders. These Mysteries exercised a powerful influence over the Egyptian mind. They gave unity to the Egyptian character, consistency to their religious establishments, stability to their political institutions, and vigor and directness in the pursuits of philosophy, science and art.

ELECT OF PERIGNAN. A degree of the French rite, nearly identical with the degrees Elected Knights of Nine, and Illustrious Elected of Fifteen, in the Ancient and Accepted rite.

ELECT OF TRUTH, or LODGE OF PERFECT UNION, was the name given to a rite adopted in the Lodge Perfect Union, at Rennes, in France, about 1779, and for a time extended to other cities. The object of the system was to throw aside the Templar degrees, and everything that related to magic, alchemy and the cabala. It was divided into three classes, which contained fourteen degrees; the first class comprising the Entered Apprentice, Fellow-Craft, Master and Perfect Master; the second, the Elect of Nine, Elect of Fifteen, Master Elect, Minor Architect, Second Architect, Grand Architect, Knight of the East, Rose Croix; and the third class, Knight Adept and Elect of Truth. This rite has ceased to exist.

ELECTA. The name of the fifth degree of the Order of the Eastern Star. She was a lady of high repute in Judea, and illustrates the Masonic characteristics of bevevolence and hospitality in the American Adoptive rite.

ELECTED COHENS. The Rite of "Elected Cohens," or "Priests," was founded some time between 1754 and 1760 by Martinez Paschalis, by whom it was introduced into the Lodges of Bordeaux, Marseilles and Toulouse. Of its principles very little is known, but it is said to have been divided into two classes; in the first of which was represented the fall of man from virtue and happiness, and in the second his final restoration. It consisted of nine degrees: Entered Apprentice, Fellow-Craft, Master Mason, Grand Elect, Apprentice Cohen, Fellow-Craft Cohen, Master Cohen, Grand Architect, and Knight Commander. Clavel tells us this rite was rather popular among the *littérateurs* of Paris for a short time, but it has now ceased to exist.

ELECTED KNIGHTS OF NINE. Called by the French "Master Elect of Nine." The body is termed a Chapter. The presiding officer represents King Solomon, and is styled "Thrice Illustrious." The room represents the audience chamber of King Solomon; it is illuminated by nine lights of yellow wax. The apron is of white lambskin, spotted with red, and lined and bordered with black. On the flap is painted or embroidered an arm holding a dagger; and in the middle of the apron an arm holding a bloody head by the hair. The sash is a broad black watered ribbon, worn from

JUDGMENT HALL.

ELECTED KNIGHTS OF NINE.

the right shoulder to the left hip. At the lower end of this are the nine red rosettes, four on each side and one at the bottom; and from the end of the sash hangs the jewel, which is a dagger, its hilt of gold, and its blade of silver. The object of this degree is to exhibit the mode in which a certain workman, who, in order prematurely and improperly to obtain the knowledge of a superior degree, engaged in an execrable deed of villainy, received his punishment. It exemplifies the truth of the maxim that the punishment of crime, though sometimes slow, is ever sure; and it admonishes us, by the historical circumstances on which it is founded, of the binding nature of our Masonic obligation. The symbolic colors in the regalia are white, red, and black; the white being emblematic of the purity of the Knights, the red of the atrocious crime committed, and the black of grief for its results. In the French rite this is the 4th degree; it requires three chambers, and in some respects has similitude to the 11th degree of the Ancient and Accepted rite, being also preparatory to the degree of Sublime Knight Elect.

ELEPHANTA. An island, called by the natives Gharipoor, situated between the west coast of Hindostan and Bombay. It is celebrated for its wonderful cave, and Hindoo mythological inscriptions. The largest of the excavations on this island is nearly square, measuring 133 by 132 feet; and immediately fronting its main entrance stands a bust or third-length of a three-headed deity, with a height of 18 feet, and a breadth of 23. It was the seat of the ancient mysteries of India.

ELEUSINIA. The name by which the rites and ceremonies originally celebrated at Eleusis were known, and by way of eminence called *"The Mysteries."** These, like the Egyptian

* Amidst all the institutions which have been denominated Mysteries, those of Eleusis hold the highest rank, equally imposing from their origin and their results: they alone appear in relation with the primitive source of religious ideas, and alone formed the mysticism of polytheism. Never did the ancients by the name of mysteries so thoroughly understand any other than the Eleusinian. The others, with a few exceptions, were nothing more, originally, than the mysterious practices of selfish and interested persons, the object of whose mission was accomplished in the deception of a confiding and credulous people. The mysteries of Eleusis had *alone*, and within its own organization, attained the object of every great religious association. All Greece hastened to be initiated; and Plato, who had penetrated into the secrets of the sanctuary, did not speak of them without admiration. "The knowledge of nature," says St. Clemens of Alexandria, "is taught in the *Great Mysteries*." If it were possible to lift the vail which covers the mysteries of Eleusis, we should possess a key to the mysteries of Egypt and of the East; a clue; which, having once been found, would lead on to the last moments of polytheism. The time when the mysteries of Eleusis were founded

mysteries, were of two kinds—the lesser and the greater, which were also *esoteric* and *exoteric**—held at different periods of the year, and at different places; the lesser, which was introductory to the greater, being celebrated at Agræ, on the banks of the Ilyssus; the greater at Eleusis, a town of Attica in Greece. They were subsequently extended into

is equally uncertain as the name of their founder. Tertullian attributes them to Musæus; St. Epiphany to Cadmus and Inachus; while Clemens of Alexandria informs us, that the mysteries were traced to an Egyptian named Melampus. Some declare that one Eumolpus was the founder and first Hierophant of the mysteries; and others believe that Orpheus introduced them from Egypt into Greece. The writers, however, most worthy of credit, ascribe to Ceres herself the foundation of the Eleusinian mysteries. We shall not here repeat the different fables that have been told concerning the manner in which Ceres established these mysteries. By attributing them to the goddess or to Earth, the epoch of their foundation was removed beyond the bounds of history, and the impossibility of ascertaining it was acknowledged. An uncertainty still more great hangs over the year of their institution; those who have discussed this subject offering various opinions, all equally deficient in proofs and even in the appearance of probability. Meiners and Dupuis have already shown that this research is no less frivolous than useless. In support of the assertion here made, we shall observe, that the *lesser* mysteries having undoubtedly preceded the *great*, the epoch of their true development should be that of the organization of the Grecian republics. It is, therefore, infinitely more interesting to study the mysteries in their maturity than in their infancy. We may remark also, that however remote the date of their transmigration from Egypt, however symbolical the name of Ceres, the mysteries must have been anterior to the epoch which has been assigned for their foundation, if we consent to place the germ of them in the festivals and popular practices of those who first inhabited Greece, and who, like them, had issued from the East. The religion of the Greeks was not formed without successive acquisitions; and of their worship and of their ceremonies much had been transmitted to them by the Egyptians. The mysteries of Ceres, according to Lactantius, very strongly resemble those of Isis. The Attic Ceres is the same as the Egyptian Isis, who, in the time of Herodotus, was the only divinity in Egypt honored by the celebration of mysteries. From these, therefore, we may partly derive the mysteries of Ceres : but this depository of ideas can have developed itself but slowly; and it was late in assuming those mystic forms which always announce a maturity of thought. In this we clearly see the ordinary progress of the human mind, that departs from the idea of infinitude, and ranges through an immense space ere it resumes its station before this same idea, which seems to embrace the two extremities of its career.—OUVAROFF, *Essay on the Mysteries of Eleusis.*

*The mysteries of Eleusis were divided, like the philosophy of the ancients, into two parts; the one *esoteric*, the other *exoteric ;* and these two parts were the *greater* and the *lesser* mysteries. It is generally allowed that the lesser were the more ancient, and this progression is consistent with the nature of things. M. de St. Croix, supported by Meursius, regards the lesser mysteries as preparatory ceremonies. It is, however, more probable that the greater and lesser mysteries were absolutely distinct. Some writers contend that the lesser mysteries were celebrated annually and the greater once in five years. On this point, though, there is no absolute authentic information.

Italy and even to Britain.* These mysteries were instituted in honor of Ceres and Proserpine, and commemorated the search of Ceres after her daughter Proserpine, who had been

CERES, TRIPTOLEMUS, (on the car of CERES,) PROSERPINE AND CYBELE.
From an ancient Etruscan vase.

forcibly carried by Pluto to the infernal regions. The exoteric celebration of the greater mysteries occupied nine days, chiefly devoted to sacrifices, processions and other acts of worship; and during this period the judicial tribunals were closed; an armistice was proclaimed; private enmities were hushed; and death was decreed by the Athenian senate against any one, high soever in rank, who should disturb the sanctity of the rites. The esoteric ceremonies of initiation into both the lesser and greater mysteries were conducted by four priests of the most illustrious families of Greece, called the Hierophant or Mystagogue, who wore the emblems of the supreme deity; the Daduchus, or Torch-bearer, who was a type of the sun; the Hiero-Ceryx, or Sacred Herald, who enjoined silence on those who were candidates for initiation, and commanded the profane to withdraw; the Altar-Minister, who attended at the altar, and bore the symbol of the moon; Basileus, or king, who judged and punished those who disturbed the

* The mysteries of Eleusis, celebrated at Athens in honor of Ceres, swallowed up, as it were all the others. All the neighboring nations neglected their own, to celebrate those of Eleusis; and in a little while all Greece and Asia Minor were filled with the initiates. They spread into the Roman Empire, and even beyond its limits, "those holy and august Eleusinian Mysteries," said Cicero, "in which the people of the remotest lands are initiated." Zosimus says that they embraced the whole human race, and Aristides termed them the common temple of the whole world.---PIKE, *Gnosticism and Mysteries.*

solemnities. Besides these leading ministers, there was a multitude of inferior priests and servants. Priestesses were also mentioned in connection with these rites. The examination of those who had been purified by the lesser mysteries, and who were preparing for the greater, was exceedingly rigorous. All foreigners, all who had even involuntarily committed homicide, all who had been declared infamous by the laws, or had been guilty of a notorious crime, were excluded. Women and children were admissible; and a child, styled the "Child of Holiness," whose innocence, it was believed, of itself endowed him with capacity to fulfill the requirements of the mysteries, was selected to conciliate the deity in the name of the initiated. The ceremonies of admission were performed at night. Into this branch of the mysteries the qualifications for initiation were maturity of age, perfectness in physical conformation, and purity of conduct.* The postulant was held under a solemn obligation to conceal whatever he saw or heard within the hallowed precincts; and he who violated the obligation was not only put to death, but devoted to the execration of all posterity. Crowned with myrtle, and enveloped in robes, which from this day were preserved as sacred relics, the neophyte was conducted beyond the boundary impassable to the rest of men. Lest any should be introduced not sufficiently prepared for the rites, the Herald proclaimed, "*Far from hence the profane, the impious, all who are polluted by sin!*" If any such were present, and did not instantly depart, death was the never-failing doom. The skins of new-slain victims were now placed under the feet of the novice; he was thus duly prepared, and amid the singing of hymns in honor of Ceres, he passed on, when soon the whole scene changed; utter darkness surrounded him; a low deep sound rose from the earth; the lightning flashed, mighty winds were heard, terrific thunder broke forth, and specters glided through the vast obscurity, moaning, sighing and groaning. Mysterious shades, the messengers of the infernal deities—Anguish, Madness, Famine, Disease, and Death—flitted around; and the explanations of the Hierophant, delivered in a solemn voice, added to the horrors of the scene. This was intended as a representation of the infernal regions, where misery had its seat. As they advanced, amidst the groans which issued from the darkness were distinguished

* Purity of morals and elevation of soul were required of the initiates. Candidates were required to be of spotless reputation and irreproachable virtue. Nero, after murdering his mother, did not dare to be present at the celebration of the mysteries; and Antony presented himself to be initiated, as the most infallible mode of proving his innocence of the death of Avidius Cassius.—PIKE, *Gnosticism and Mysteries.*

those of the suicides—thus punished for cowardly deserting the post which the gods had assigned them in this world. But the scene which the novice had heretofore beheld seemed to be a sort of purgatory, where penal fires and dire anguish, and the unutterable horrors of darkness, were believed, after countless ages of suffering, to purify from the guilt acquired in this mortal life. Suddenly the bursting open of two vast gates, with a terrific sound, dimly displayed to his sight, and faintly bore to his ears, the torments of those whose state was everlasting—who had passed the bounds beyond which there is no hope. On the horrors of this abode of anguish and despair a curtain may be dropped; the subject is unutterable. Onward proceeded the novice, and was soon conducted into another region; that of everlasting bliss, the sojourn of the just—of those who had been purified and whose minds had been enlightened by "the Holy Doctrine."* This was ELYSIUM—the joys of which were equally unutterable, equally incomprehensible, to mortals not admitted into these mysteries. Here a vail was in like manner thrown over this scene, and the ceremonies were closed. These rites inculcated the doctrine of one God, and the dignity and destiny of the human soul; they instructed the people in the knowledge of nature and of the universe, and taught them to see the presence of the Eternal in the splendor and beauty of the natural world. It is evident that these mysteries constituted the great educational institution of ancient Greece. They formed the Grecian mind, and led in the development of Grecian ideas. Nearly all ancient writers speak of their eminent utility and salutary influence. Arrien, Pausanias, Euripèdes and Cicero, unite their testimony in their favor, and speak of them as peculiarly calculated to "reform the manners, and perfect the education of mankind."

ELEUTHERIA. A festival celebrated at Platæa, in honor of Jupiter Eleutherius, or the asserter of liberty, by delegates from almost all the cities of Greece. There was also a festival of the same name observed by the Samians, in honor of the god of love. Slaves also, when they obtained their liberty, kept a holiday, which they called Eleutharia.

ELU. A French participle, signifying "elected." It is the 4th degree in the French rite, and resembles in its teachings the degree of " *Maitre elu des neufs.*"

---

* The Holy Doctrine is held by all the mystic ceremonies of the ancients, not only to purify the heart from sin, and expel ignorance from the mind, but to insure also the favor of the gods, and to open the gates of immortal felicity to the initiated.

EMPERORS OF THE EAST AND WEST. An order calling itself a "Council of Emperors of the East and West" was instituted in Paris, A. D. 1758. Its adepts styled themselves "Sovereign Prince Masons—Substitutes General of the Royal Art—Grand Superintendents and Officers of the Grand and Sovereign Lodge of St. John of Jerusalem." The rite consisted of 25 degrees, the first 19 of which were the same as those of the Scottish rite. The 20th was named Grand Patriarch Noachite; the 21st, Key of Masonry; 22d, Prince of Lebanon; 23d, Knight of the Sun; 24th, Kadosh; 25th, Prince of the Royal Secret. This rite had some success, and was propagated in Germany, particularly in Prussia, and was accepted by the Grand Lodge of the Three Globes. The assumption that Frederick II., King of Prussia, ever had any connection with it will not be acknowledged by the intelligent Mason.

ENCAMPMENT. [See COMMANDERY.]

ENCAMPMENT, GRAND. [See COMMANDERY, GRAND.]

ENCAMPMENT, GRAND. The Grand Encampment of the United States was organized on the 22d of June, 1816. It consists of a Grand Master, Deputy Grand Master, Grand Generalissimo, Grand Captain General, Grand Prelate, Senior Grand Warden, Junior Grand Warden, Grand Treasurer, Grand Recorder, Grand Standard-Bearer, Grand Sword-Bearer, Grand Warder, Grand Captain of the Guards; all Past Grand Masters; all Past Deputy Grand Masters; all Past Grand Generalissimos, and all Past Grand Captains General of the Grand Encampment of the United States. Likewise, all Grand Commanders, Past Grand Commanders, Deputy Grand Commanders, Grand Generalissimos, and all Grand Captains General of each State Grand Commandery that acknowledges the jurisdiction of the United States Grand Encampment. Also, the first three officers of each Commandery that holds its charter immediately from the Grand Encampment of the United States. No person shall be eligible to any office in the Grand Encampment of the United States, unless he shall be at the time a member of some subordinate Commandery under the general or immediate jurisdiction of the Grand Encampment of the United States. Its conclaves are held triennially, on the second Tuesday of September, at such place as may have been previously designated.

EPHOD. A vestment worn by the Jewish high-priest over the tunic and the robe. It was without sleeves, and open below the arms on each side, consisting of two pieces, one of which covered the front of the body and the other the back, and reaching down to the middle of the thighs. They were joined together on the shoulders by golden buckles set with gems, and two large precious stones set in gold, on which were engraved the names of the twelve tribes of Israel, six on each stone, according to their order. The material of which the ephod was wrought was extremely costly and magnificent; gold, blue, purple, scarlet, and fine twined linen, with rich embroidery. A girdle or band, of one piece with the ephod, fastened it round the body. Just above this girdle, in the middle of the ephod, and joined to it by golden chains, rings, and strings, rested the square oracular breast-plate, originally intended to be worn by the high-priest exclusively. Ephods of an inferior material were in use among the ordinary priests. Even David, when bringing the ark of the covenant to Jerusalem, was "girt with a linen ephod." The Jews had a peculiar superstitious regard for this garment, and employed it in connection with idolatrous worship, and held that no worship, true or false, could subsist without its presence.

EPOPTÆ. A Greek word, formed from *epi* and *optamai*, I see, or rather, look upon. It was the name given to those who were initiated into the greater mysteries of Eleusis, to distinguish them from the *mustæ*—disciples—who had only been received into the lesser. It signifies the "spectators of the mysteries," or the illuminated. Epopt was also used by the Illuminati, to distinguish the members of the sixth degree.

EQUES. Latin for *Knight*. In the system of Strict Observance, established in Germany, in 1754, by Baron von Hund, it designated all the members of the sixth degree. On being invested with the honor of knighthood they received an order-name, an escutcheon, and a device.

ESOTERIC. Greek, *Esotéritos*. That which is secret, revealed only to the initiated. In the secret societies of the ancients, the doctrines were divided into the *esoteric* and *exoteric*; the former for the initiated, who were permitted to look upon the most sacred mysteries of the arcana; and the latter for the uninitiated, who remained in the outer court.

ESPERANCE-LOGES (French), *Lodges of Hope*. Under the name of Knights and Ladies of Hope, an order was organized in France early in the last century, and established Lodges bearing this title. This was the commencement of that system now known as Adoptive Masonry (q. v.).

ESQUIRE. Anciently the person that attended a Knight in time of war, and carried his shield. In the days of chivalry this title was honorable, and generally borne by persons of good family. Heads of ancient families were considered esquires by prescription; and hence originated the use of the word, in the present day, as a common addition to the names of all those who live in the rank of gentlemen. It is a title in the English Knights Templar system.

ESTHER, Hebrew name HADASSAH. A damsel of the tribe of Benjamin, born during the exile, and whose family did not avail itself of the permission to return to Jerusalem, under the edict of Cyrus. The reigning king of Persia, Ahasuerus, having divorced his former queen, Vashti, search was made throughout the empire for the most beautiful maiden to be her successor. The choice fell on Esther, who found favor in the eyes of the king, and was advanced to the station of queen. Her Jewish origin was perhaps at the time unknown; when she avowed it to the king, she seemed to be included in the doom of extirpation which a royal edict had pronounced against all the Jews in the empire. This circumstance enabled her to turn the royal indignation upon Haman, the chief minister of the king, whose resentment against Mordecai had led him to obtain from the king this monstrous edict. The laws of the empire would not allow the king to recall a decree once uttered; but the Jews were authorized to stand on their defense; and this, with the known change in the intentions of the court, averted the fearful consequences of the decree. The Jews established a yearly feast called PURIM, in memory of this deliverance, which is observed among them to this day. Such is the substance of the history of Esther, as related in the book which bears her name. Esther is also the title of the third degree of the order of the Eastern Star, which illustrates the Masonic characteristic of fidelity to kindred and friends in the American Adoptive rite.

EUNUCH. The physical and moral deterioration which emasculation produces in men is of a most marked character. The whole nature is degraded. The affections are blunted, generous dispositions are destroyed, the intellect is impaired, and the man is entirely incapacitated for performing any deeds which require a high and magnanimous disposition. For this reason they were excluded by the Jewish law from "the congregation of the Lord," and for this reason cannot be received into the Masonic brotherhood.

EXPERT. The name of an officer in French Lodges, who superintends the examination of visiting brothers. The office is not known in the United States. Strangers seeking admission to the Lodge are usually examined by a committee of brothers appointed by the Master.

F.

FAMILY-LODGES. The same as Conference-lodges—peculiar to Germany.

FECIALES. A number of priests at Rome, employed in declaring war and making peace. When the Romans thought themselves injured, one of the sacerdotal body was empowered to demand redress, and, after the allowance of thirty-three days to consider the matter, war was declared, if submissions were not made, and the Fecialis hurled a bloody spear into the territories of the enemy in proof of intended hostilities.

FELICITÉ, ORDER OF. A society with a Masonic form, established at Paris A. D. 1742, by some naval officers. It admitted females. Its official titles and the names of its degrees were borrowed from the nomenclature of the sea, and its initiation represented a "voyage." It was a symbolical journey in search of the Island of Happiness. The seal of the Order was an anchor, suspended from three silken cords, and its pass-word was *schalom lecka,* i. e., "peace be with thee." It had four degrees viz: 1. Cabin-boy;

2. Patron; 3. Commander; 4. Vice-Admiral. In 1748 it was merged in a new organization, called the "Knights and Ladies of the Anchor."

FEMALE DEGREES. About the year 1730 societies imitating Freemasonry for the admission of women were instituted in France. By whom they were invented or who first introduced them history or tradition does not enlighten us. They are evidently the product of the French mind. The forms of these associations were, however, not definitively settled until 1760; and they were not recognized or sanctioned by the administrative authority of Masonry until the year 1774, when the Grand Orient of France established a new system called the "Rite of Masonic Adoption," which was placed under the control of the Grand Orient. Rules and regulations were thenceforth provided for the government of these bodies, one of which was that no men should be permitted to attend them except regular Freemasons, and that each Lodge should be placed under the charge, and held under the sanction and warrant of some regularly-constituted Masonic Lodge, whose Master, or, in his absence, his Deputy, should be the presiding officer, assisted by a female President or Mistress. At first these organizations adopted divers names and rituals; some of which were ingenious and chaste, while others were puerile, and sometimes of a character not to merit countenance. In 1743 the emblems and vocabulary were nautical—an orient was called a *Roadstead*, and a Lodge, *Squadron*—and the sisters made the fictitious voyage to the island of Felicity, under the *sails* of the brethren. In 1747, the Chevalier Beauchaine, the most famous and zealous of the Masters in Paris, the same who had established his Lodge in a *cabaret*, where he slept, and for six francs gave at one sitting all the degrees of Masonry, instituted the order of Woodcutters; the ceremonies whereof were borrowed from the society of the Carbonari, or Coal-burners, which had been previously established in Italy. The Lodge was styled a Woodyard, and was supposed to represent a forest. The officers were known by the following titles: Father Master, President; Cousin of the Oak, God-father; Cousin of the Elm, Introductor; Cousin of the Beech, Keeper of the Wine; Cousin of the Service-tree, Keeper of the Bread; Cousin of the Yoke-Elm, Guard of Hospitality; Cousin of the Maple, Guard of the Chair; Cousin of the Ash, Guard of Honor. The brethren and sisters were called Cousins, and the candidate was called a Brick. This rite had an extraordinary success; the meetings were held in a large garden, in the quarter of New France, out of Paris; the most distinguished men and women of

France went there in crowds, wearing blouses and petticoats of frieze, and heavy wooden shoes, and indulged in all the fun and noisy merriment of the common people. Upon a reception, the Father Master sat on a log of oak, his left elbow resting on a table; a slouched hat and a crown of oak leaves were on his head. Round his neck was a cordon of green silk, at the end of which hung a wedge of box-wood. He held an axe in his hand, and a pipe in his mouth, and was dressed in coarse linen. All was so arranged as to call the attention of the adepts to the lower classes of society, to make them acquainted with their poverty and misery, and induce them to labor to improve their lot. Among these people, apparently so utterly disinherited by fortune, were nevertheless practiced virtue, friendship, love and gratitude. The design of this degree was to call the attention of the candidates, who then belonged chiefly to the noblesse, or the rich Bourgeoisie, and who were soon to be called on to regenerate France, to their true relations to the people. All these mysteries, all these odd ceremonies tended to impress the minds of the candidates, to instruct them, and to bring the higher and lower classes together, in the bonds of equality and fraternity. Other societies of both sexes succeeded this, such as the orders of the *Hatchet*, of *Fidelity*, the forms of which more fully resembled those of the ordinary Freemasonry. In 1775 a Lodge of Masonic Adoption was instituted at Paris, with imposing solemnities, under the auspices of the Lodge of St. Anthony, and in which the Duchess of Bourbon presided, and was installed Grand Mistress. This rite consisted of four degrees, viz: 1. Apprentice; 2. Companion; 3. Mistress; 4. Perfect Mistress. In 1785, under the patronage of several members of the Court of France, the Lodge "La Candeur" was opened at Paris, as Grand Mistress of which the Duchess of Bourbon was installed with unusual pomp and solemnity. The revolution checked the progress of Adoptive Lodges; but they were revived in 1805, when the Empress Josephine presided over a Lodge at Strasburg. For some years past the rite of Adoption has been confined to the limits of Paris, as a distinct and recognized institution. At the meeting of the Grand Orient of France, in 1866, formal application was made to have the degrees of Adoptive Masonry reorganized and administered by that body.

FERALIA. A festival in honor of the dead, observed at Rome the 17th or 21st of February. It continued for eleven days, during which time presents were carried to the graves of the deceased, marriages were forbidden, and the temples of the gods were shut.

FERLÆ. Solemn religious festivals celebrated by the early Romans. They met on the Alban mount, where, under the direction of the magistrates of Rome and the several cities, they offered sacrifices to Jupiter, and under sanction of this ceremony took oaths to preserve their mutual friendship and alliance. It continued but one day originally, but in process of time four days were devoted to its celebration, and during that time it was unlawful for any person to work. The days on which the *feriæ* were observed were called by the Romans *festi dies*, because dedicated to mirth, relaxation and festivity.

FESSLER'S SYSTEM, or, as it is sometimes called, "Fessler's Rite." This is the most elaborate, learned and philosophical illustration and application of the Masonic degrees. Bro. Fessler was a professor of the civil law and Deputy Grand Master of the Lodge Royal York à l' Amitie, at Berlin. He was a man of profound learning, and took great interest in all things pertaining to Masonry. He at first undertook to destroy the high degrees, but finding it impracticable, he accepted, in 1798, an appointment to revise and rectify them. He thus created nine degrees, the first three of which, Apprentice, Fellow-Craft and Master Theosoph, are the symbolic degrees, with slight variations. After these came 4th, the Holy of Holies; 5th, Justification; 6th, Celebration, 7th, The True Light, or Passage; 8th, The Country, or Fatherland; 9th, Perfection. The last degree was never completed; and the six last were taken from the rituals of the Rose Croix of Gold, those of the Strict Observance, of the Chapter Illuminatus of Sweden, and the Ancient Chapter of Clermont. It is said that the system, though incomplete, was approved by Frederic William in 1797. It is at present practiced by only a small number of Lodges in Prussia.

FEUILLANTS. 1. A Masonic order, governed by the statutes of St. Bernard; 2. A kind of Androgynous Masonry.

FIDELITÉ, Order of. One of the many forms of Adoptive Masonry which appeared in France during the last century. It was instituted at Paris, about 1748, and was styled "The Order of Knights and Ladies of Fidelity." It flourished for a long period, and was propagated considerably in Germany and on the continent.

FIDES. Latin for *faith* or *faithfulness*, that is to say, fidelity. It was also the name of a goddess among the Romans, who presided over contracts, sanctified oaths, and punished their violation. Numa Pompilius, the second King of Rome, 714 to 672 B. C., is said to have erected temples, and consecrated altars to her service. The goddess was usually represented by two hands joined together, or by two figures holding each other by the right hand.

FIELD-LODGES. Also called "Army Lodges," "Traveling Lodges," "Military Lodges." These are Masonic bodies organized in armies, and which move with them. They are eminently useful in relieving the monotony of the soldier's life, and mitigating the horrors of war. In the war of the American Revolution they were found in both of the belligerent armies, and also in the civil war of 1861-5. During the Bonapartean wars they sustained and illustrated the principles of Freemasonry in the allied and French armies.

FINANCE. The funds of a Lodge are deposited with the Treasurer, who pays them out on the order of the Master, and with the consent of the brethren. According to an ancient practice the funds are first received by the Secretary, who transfers them to the Treasurer, taking his receipt for the same. His yearly accounts are examined by an auditing committee.

FIVE SENSES. The brain is wonderfully adapted by its perfect system of nervous sympathy to give the intellectual powers their force, and enable the mind to receive perceptions of every object in the wide creation, that comes within the sphere of *hearing, feeling, smelling, tasting,* and *seeing ;* these being the five human senses explained in the lecture of the Fellow-Craft's degree.

FLOORING. A large chart on which the emblems of the second degree are painted, for the purpose of illustrating the instructions given to neophytes. It is the same as the Master's Carpet, and is called "flooring," because these emblems were formerly delineated on the floor.

FORESTERS. Several societies have borne this name, with symbols and ritual borrowed from the various departments of woodcraft. They styled themselves "Colliers," "Woodcutters," and "Sawyers." The most extensive of these brotherhoods is the "Ancient Order of Foresters," known in England and the United States.

FORM OF THE LODGE. The form of a Masonic Lodge is said to be a parallelogram or oblong square—its greatest length being from East to West—its breadth from North to South. A square, a circle, a triangle, or any other form but that of an oblong square, would be eminently incorrect and unmasonic, because such a figure would not be an expression of the symbolic idea which is intended to be conveyed. At the Solomonic era—the era of the building of the Temple at Jerusalem—the world, it must be remembered, was supposed to have that very oblong form, which has been here symbolized. If, for instance, on a map of the world, we should inscribe an oblong figure whose boundary lines would circumscribe and include just that portion which was known and inhabited in the days of Solomon, these lines running a short distance North and South of the Mediterranean sea, and extending from Spain in the West to Asia Minor in the East, would form an oblong square, including the southern shore of Europe, the northern shore of Africa, and the western district of Asia, the length of the parallelogram being about sixty degrees from East to West, and its breadth being about twenty degrees from North to South. This oblong square, thus inclosing the whole of what was then supposed to be the habitable globe, would precisely represent what is symbolically said to be the form of the Lodge, while the Pillars of Hercules in the West, on each side of the straits of Gades or Gibraltar, might appropriately be referred to the two pillars that stood at the porch of the Temple.

A Masonic Lodge is, therefore, a symbol of the world. This symbol is sometimes, by a very usual figure of speech, extended, in its application, and the world and the universe are made synonymous, when the Lodge becomes, of course, a symbol of the universe. But in this case the definition of the symbol is extended, and to the ideas of length and breadth are added those of hight and depth, and the Lodge is said to assume the form of a double cube.* The solid contents of the earth below and the expanse of the heavens above will then give the outlines of the cube, and the whole created universe be included within the symbolic limits of a Mason's Lodge.—MACKEY.

FRANKS, ORDER OF REGENERATED. In the last half of the year 1815, a political brotherhood, with forms borrowed from Freemasonry, was organized in France, and had for its motto, "For God, the King, and Fatherland." It flourished for a short time.

FREEMASONRY, DEFINITIONS OF. The definitions of Freemasonry have been numerous, and they all unite in declaring it to be a system of morality, by the practice of which its members may advance their spiritual interest, and mount by the theological ladder, from the Lodge on earth to the Lodge in heaven. Subjoined are a few of the most important definitions:

"Freemasonry is a beautiful system of morality, vailed in allegory, and illustrated by symbols."—HEMMING.

"The grand object of Masonry is to promote the happiness of the human race."—WASHINGTON.

"Masonry is an art, useful and extensive, which comprehends within its circle every branch of useful knowledge and learning, and stamps an indelible mark of preëminence on its genuine professors, which neither chance, power, nor fortune can bestow."—PRESTON.

"Freemasonry is an establishment founded on the benevolent intention of extending and conferring mutual happiness upon the best and truest principles of moral life and social virtue."—CALCOTT.

"Freemasonry is an institution calculated to benefit mankind."—ANDREW JACKSON.

"Freemasonry is a moral order, instituted by virtuous men, with the praiseworthy design of recalling to our remembrance the most sublime truths, in the midst of the most innocent and social pleasures, founded on liberality, brotherly love and charity."—ARNOLD.

"I have ever felt it my duty to support and encourage the principles of Freemasonry, because it powerfully develops all social and benevolent affections."—LORD DURHAM.

"From its origin to the present hour, in all its vicissitudes, Masonry has been the steady, unvarying friend of man."—REV. ERASTUS BURR.

* The form of a Lodge should always be an oblong square, in length, between the East and West; in breadth, between the North and the South; in hight, from earth to heaven; and in depth, from the surface to the center. This disposition serves to indicate the prevalence of Freemasonry over the whole face of the globe, guarded by its laws, and ornamented by its beautiful tenets. Every civilized region is illuminated by its presence. Its charity relieves the wretched; its brotherly love unites the Fraternity in a chain of indissoluble affection, and extends its example beyond the limits of the Lodge-room, to embrace, in its ample scope, the whole human race, infolding them in its arms of universal love. The square form was esteemed by our ancient operative brethren as one of the Greater Lights, and a component part of the furniture of the Lodge. The double cube is an expressive emblem of the united powers of darkness and light in the creation.

"The study of Freemasonry is the study of man as a candidate for a blessed eternity. It furnishes examples of holy living, and displays the conduct which is pleasing and acceptable to God. The doctrine and examples which distinguish the Order are obvious, and suited to every capacity. It is impossible for the most fastidious Mason to misunderstand, however he may slight or neglect them. It is impossible for the most superficial brother to say that he is unable to comprehend the plain precepts, and the unanswerable arguments which are furnished by Freemasonry."—OLIVER.

"Freemasonry is an institution based on that never-failing charity which upholds universal love, calms the troubled sea of our evil passions, and leaves a smooth surface, in which all men, who are sincere and conscientious worshipers of God, and unexceptionable in moral deportment, may unite, bless each other, and rejoice in practically realizing the sublime sentiment that

God hath made mankind one
　　Mighty brotherhood,
　Himself their Master, and the
　　World his Lodge."—DR. J. BURNS.

"Freemasonry is an ancient and respectable institution, embracing individuals of every nation, of every religion, and of every condition in life. Wealth, power and talents, are not necessary to the person of a Freemason. An unblemished character and a virtuous conduct are the only qualifications for admission into the Order."—LAURIE.

"Freemasonry is an institution founded on eternal reason and truth; whose deep basis is the civilization of mankind, and whose everlasting glory it is to have the immovable support of those two mighty pillars, science and morality."—DR. DODD.

"I highly venerate the Masonic institution, under the fullest persuasion that where its principles are acknowledged, and its laws and precepts obeyed, it comes nearest to the Christian religion, in its moral effects and influence, of any institution with which I am acquainted."—REV. FRED. DALCHO.

"Freemasonry is a science of symbols, in which, by their proper study, a search is instituted after truth—that truth consisting in the knowledge of the divine and human nature, of God and the human soul."—DR. A. G. MACKEY.

"Masonry superadds to our other obligations the strongest ties of connection between it and the cultivation of virtue, and furnishes the most powerful incentives to goodness."—DE WITT CLINTON.

"Freemasonry is an order whose leading star is philanthropy, and whose principles inculcate an unceasing devotion to the cause of virtue and morality."—LA FAYETTE.

"Freemasonry is an institution essentially philanthropic and progressive, which has for its basis the existence of God and the immortality of the soul. It has for its object the exercise of benevolence, the study of universal morality, and the practice of all the virtues."—Constitution Grand Orient of France.

"I regard the Masonic institution as one of the means ordained by the Supreme Architect to enable mankind to work out the problem of destiny; to fight against, and overcome, the weaknesses and imperfections of his nature, and at last to attain to that true life of which death is the herald, and the grave the portal."—JOHN W. SIMONS.

"It is noble in its administration; to think and let think, beyond the narrow contracted prejudices of bitter sectarians in these modern times. It is general or universal language, fitted to benefit the poor stranger, which no other institution is calculated to reach by extending the beneficent hand."—LORENZO DOW.

"The prosperity of Masonry as a means of strengthening our religion, and propagating true brotherly love, is one of the dearest wishes of my heart, which, I trust, will be gratified by the help of the Grand Architect of the universe."—CHRISTIAN, King of Denmark.

"The precepts of the Gospel were universally the obligations of Masonry."—REV. DR. RUSSELL.

"Masonry is one of the most sublime and perfect institutions that ever was formed for the advancement of happiness, and the general good of mankind, creating, in all its varieties, universal benevolence and brotherly love."—DUKE OF SUSSEX.

"For centuries had Freemasonry existed ere modern political controversies were ever heard of, and when the topics which now agitate society were not known, but all were united in brotherhood and affection. I know the institution to be founded on the great principles of charity, philanthropy, and brotherly love."—BULWER.

"Everything which tends to combine men by stronger ties is useful to humanity; in this point of view, Masonry is entitled to respect."—LA LANDE.

"I think we are warranted in contending that a society thus constituted, and which may be rendered so admirable an engine of improvement, far from meriting reproach, deserves highly of the community."—REV. DR. MILNE.

"Charity, or brotherly kindness, is as much a Masonic as it is a Christian virtue."—REV. DR. SLADE.

"A Mason's Lodge is a school of piety. The principal emblems are the teachers."—REV. DR. NORVAL.

"The aims of Freemasonry are not limited to one form of operation, or one mode of benevolence. Its object is at once moral and social. It proposes both to cultivate the mind and enlarge and purify the heart."—REV. J. O. SKINNER.

"The Masonic system exhibits a stupendous and beautiful fabric, founded on universal piety. To rule and direct our passions; to have faith and love in God, and charity toward man."—STEPHEN JONES.

"There are Great Truths at the foundation of Freemasonry—truths which it is its mission to teach—and which as constituting the very essence of that sublime system which gives to the venerable institution its peculiar identity as a science of morality, and it behooves every disciple diligently to ponder and inwardly digest.—ALBERT PIKE.

"Its *laws* are reason and equity, its *principles* benevolence and love; and its *religion* purity and truth; its *intention* is peace on earth; and its *disposition* good-will toward man."—REV. T. M. HARRIS.

FRENCH RITE. The French or Modern rite was established by the Grand Orient of France about the year 1786, to preserve the high degrees; and for the purpose of simplifying the system the number was reduced to seven, viz: Entered Apprentice, Fellow-Craft, Master Mason, Elect, or First Order of Rose Croix, Scotch Order, or Second Order of Rose Croix, Knight of the East, or Third Order of Rose Croix, and the Rose Croix, or *ne plus ultra.* The peculiar signs and secrets of the two first symbolical degrees under this rite are in reverse of those adopted by the Grand Lodge, or Supreme Council of the Ancient and Accepted rite, of France, in which the practice is the same as in our own Grand Lodge. In the 3d degree the Lodge has a very solemn appearance, being hung with black drapery, and displaying many somber and awe-inspiring emblems. The Master is designated *Très Respectable* (Very Worshipful), and the members Venerable Masters; all the brethren appear covered. In the 4th degree there are three chambers—the Room of Preparation, the Council Chamber, and the Cavern. The lesson inculcated in this degree is intended forcibly to imprint on the mind of its recipient the certainty with which punishment will follow crime. The 5th degree requires also three chambers, the second of which is most elaborately furnished and decorated with various Masonic attributes; in the East is a triangular pedestal, on which is placed the cubical stone; in the center of the chamber is a column, and by it a table, having upon it the corn, wine, and oil; and in the North is a sacrificial altar. The Lodge is illuminated by twenty-seven lights, in three groups of nine each; it represents the Temple completed, and its whole appearance is most gorgeous. The Lodge is denominated Sublime; the presiding officer is *Très Grand* (Very Great), and the brethren are Sublime Masters. The 6th degree also requires three chambers; the second, which is called the Hall of the East, represents the council of Cyrus at Babylon, and is composed of that prince, seven principal officers, and other Knights. The decoration is green, and requires fifteen lights. Behind the throne is a transparency, representing the vision of Cyrus, in which he received the injunction, "Restore liberty to the captives." The candidate, in passing from the second to the third chamber, has to cross a bridge of timber over a stream choked with rubbish; and having at length arrived at the last, or western chamber, he perceives the Masons reposing among the ruins of Jerusalem. The room is hung with red, and illuminated by ten groups of candles of seven each. In the center is the representation of the ruined Temple. The Sovereign Master represents Cyrus; the chief Officer, Daniel the Prophet. The badge is of white satin, bordered with green; the sash, of water green, is worn from left to right; the jewel is the triple triangle, crossed by two swords. The 7th degree is precisely like that of the 18th degree of the Ancient and Accepted rite. A rite, slightly differing from the preceding, and called the "Ancient Reformed rite," is now practiced in Holland and Belgium.

FRÈRES PONTIVES. A community of operative and speculative Masons, who, as a religious house of brotherhood, established themselves at Avignon, at the close of the twelfth century; they devoted themselves, as the name denotes, to the construction and repair of stone bridges. It is on record that the community existed as late as 1590. John de Medicis, who was Master in 1560, may perhaps have been a son of Cosmo, Duke of Florence, who died 1562, and was made a cardinal shortly before.

FRIENDLY ADMONITIONS. As useful knowledge is the great object of our desire, let us diligently apply to the practice of the art, and steadily adhere to the principles which it inculcates. Let not the difficulties that we have to encounter check our progress, or damp our zeal; but let us recollect that the ways of wisdom are beautiful, and lead to pleasure. Knowledge is attained by degrees, and cannot everywhere be found. Wisdom seeks the secret shade, the lonely cell, designed for contemplation. There enthroned she sits, delivering her sacred oracles. There let us seek her, and pursue the real bliss. Though the passage be difficult, the farther we trace it the easier it will become. Union and harmony constitute the essence of Freemasonry; while we enlist under that banner, the society must flourish, and private animosities give place to peace and good fellowship. Uniting in one design, let it be our aim to be happy ourselves, and contribute to the happiness of others. Let us mark our superiority and distinction among men, by the sincerity of our profession as Masons; cultivate the moral virtues, and improve in all that is good and amiable.

FRIENDLY SOCIETIES. Associations with some Masonic features, formed chiefly among mechanics for mutual protection and assistance. They help their members in sickness and misfortunes, and at their death furnish assistance to their families. The most important of these societies, and the most efficient in its organization, is the Ancient and Independent Order of Odd Fellows. All of them seem to have borrowed their idea of mutual relief from the Masonic brotherhood.

FRIENDS, ORDER OF PERFECT. A society of distinguished Masonic *Savans* in Germany, in the last century, the chief spirit of whom was Knigge. The society was sometimes called "The Seven Allies."

FUNERAL SERVICES. No Mason can be interred with the ceremonies of the Order, unless it be by his own request, made while living to the Master of the Lodge of which he died a member; nor unless he has been raised to the third degree of Masonry; sojourners and officers high in the Order excepted. A dispensation has first to be obtained from the Grand Master before any public procession can be allowed to take place.

FURNITURE OF THE LODGE. Every well-regulated Lodge is furnished with the Holy Bible, the Square, and the Compasses. These constitute the furniture of the Lodge— being the three Great Lights of Masonry. The first is designed to be the guide of our faith; the second to regulate our actions; and the third to keep us within proper bounds with all mankind.

G.

This letter is deservedly regarded as one of the most sacred of the Masonic emblems. Where it is used, however, as a symbol of Deity, it must be remembered that it is the Saxon representative of the Hebrew *Yod* and the Greek *Tau*—the initial letters of the name of the Eternal in those languages. This symbol proves that Freemasonry always prosecuted its labors with reference to the grand ideas of Infinity and Eternity By the letter G—which conveyed to the minds of the brethren, at the same time, the idea of God and that of Geometry—it bound heaven to earth, the divine to the human, and the infinite to the finite. Masons are taught to regard the Universe as the grandest of all symbols, revealing to men, in all ages, the ideas which are eternally revolving in the mind of the Divinity, and which it is their duty to reproduce in their own lives and in the world of art and industry. Thus God and Geometry, the material worlds and the spiritual spheres, were constantly united in the speculations of the ancient Masons. They, consequently, labored earnestly and unweariedly, not only to construct cities, and embellish them with magnificent edifices, but also to build up a temple of great and divine thoughts and of ever-growing virtues for the soul to dwell in. The symbolical letter G—

> * * * "That hieroglyphic bright,
> Which none but craftsmen ever saw,"

and before which every true Mason reverently uncovers, and bows his head—is a perpetual condemnation of profanity, impiety and vice. No brother who has bowed before that emblem can be profane. He will never speak the name of the Grand Master of the Universe but with reverence, respect and love. He will learn, by studying the mystic meaning of the letter G, to model his life after the divine plan; and, thus instructed, he will strive to be like God in the activity and earnestness of his benevolence, and the broadness and efficiency of his charity. "The letter G occupies a prominent position in several of the degrees in the American system; is found in many of the degrees of the Ancient and Accepted Scottish rite; in Adonhiramite Masonry; and, in fact, in every one of the many systems in which the people of the sixteenth and seventeenth centuries were so prolific in manufacturing. Wherever we find this recondite symbol in any of the Masonic rites, it has the same significance—a substitute for the Hebraic *jod*, the

initial letter of the Divine name, and a monogram that
expressed the Uncreated Being, principle of all things; and,
inclosed in a triangle, the unity of God. We recognize the
same letter G in the Syriac *Gad*, the Swedish *Gud*, the
German *Gott*, and the English *God*—all names of the Deity,
and all derived from the Persian *Goda*, itself derived from
the absolute pronoun signifying *himself*. The young Fellow-
Craft is the representative of a student of the sciences, and
to him the letter G* represents the science of Geometry."

GAVEL. An emblem in the degree of Entered Apprentice.
It is a hammer with an edge such as is used by stone-masons
to break off the corners of stones, in preparing them for the
builder's use.   In the Masonic system it is employed as a
symbol by which the Mason is constantly admonished to
divest his mind and conscience of all the vices and errors
of life, thereby fitting his body as a living stone for that
building, "that house not made with hands—eternal in the
heavens."   It is also an emblem of authority, and is used
by the Master in governing the Lodge.   It is sometimes
erroneously confounded with the setting-maul, which is quite
a different instrument.   The name gavel is probably derived
from the German *Giebel*, the gable or apex of the roof –
which its edge resembles.
The form of the gavel used
by the presiding officer of
a Masonic Lodge varies in
different sections of the
country, as displayed in the
annexed engravings, viz:—
1. Is   sometimes   found
among our French and
Spanish brethren, and is
familiarly known as the
president's hammer; 2. The
setting-maul, which is frequently found in use ; 3.
The stone-mason's hammer.

FORMS OF GAVELS USED IN MASONIC BODIES.

This is the appropriate emblem of authority in the hand
of the Master of the Lodge.   The gavel is also called a
Hiram, *which see.*

*"In my own opinion, the letter G, which is used in the Fellow-Craft's
degree, should never have been permitted to intrude into Masonry; it
presents an instance of absurd anachronism, which would never have
occurred if the original Hebrew symbol had been retained. But being
there now, without the possibility of removal, we have only to remember
that it is in fact but the symbol of a symbol."—MACKEY.

GENERALISSIMO. A title conferred by the French, on the commander-in-chief of a grand division of an army. This dignity was first assumed by Cardinal Richelieu on the occasion of his leading the French army into Italy. In the Knights Templar system the second officer of a Commandery. He is the assistant of the Grand Commander, presides in his absence, and is *ex-officio* a member of the Grand Commandery. His jewel is a square surmounted with a paschal lamb.

GENUFLEXION. A bending of the knee, or kneeling. The act of kneeling has, among all people, and in all ages, been a token of reverence, a sign of dependence, supplication, and humility.

GIBEON. A city of Judea which was situated in a northerly direction from Jerusalem. It had a place of worship peculiarly sacred, perhaps the seat of the Tabernacle. Hence the name is used symbolically in France, as the apellation of the Master, who must have a pure heart, in which the High and Holy One may dwell. In the Swedish ritual it is also used in the same sense.

GIBLEMITE. The Giblemites were the people of Gebal or Giblos, a city on the coast of Phœnicia, between Tripoli and Berytus, called Byblos by the Greeks and Romans, now known by the name of Jiblah. At the present time it is but little more than a mass of ruins, which are sufficiently magnificent to indicate its former greatness and beauty. Indeed it was famous in former times for the skill of its masons and builders, who excelled all others in the knowledge of architecture. They are frequently mentioned in Scripture as "stone-squarers," a term applied to them as being eminently distinguished in that kind of work. The people of the ancient city of Gebal were famous for their worship of Adonis, who was believed to have been wounded by a wild boar while hunting on Mount Libanus. The river Adonis, whose waters are at some seasons as red as blood, passes by it; and when this phenomena appeared the inhabitants lamented the death of Adonis, pretending their river to be colored with his blood.

GILEAD. A part of the ridge of mountains which runs south from Mount Lebanon, on the east of Palestine. They gave their name to the whole country which lies on the east of the sea of Galilee. Gilead is the name of the keeper of the seals, in the Scottish degree of the Sacred Vault of James VI.

GNOSTICISM, ᴏʀ Gɴᴏsᴛɪᴄs, from the Greek word, *gnôsis*, knowledge. This name was assumed by a philosophical sect which sought to unite the mystical notions of the East with ideas of the Greek philosophers, and teachings of Christianity. The system has features which show conclusively that it was a development of the old Persian or Chaldean doctrine. According to the gnostics, God, the highest intelligence, dwells in the fullness of light, and is the source of all good; matter, the crude, chaotic mass of which all things were made, is like God, eternal, and is the source of all evil. From these two principles, before time commenced, emanated beings called æons, which are described as divine spirits. The world and the human race were created out of matter by the æons and angels. They made the body and sensual soul of man, of this matter; hence the origin of evil in man. God gave man the rational soul; hence the constant struggle of reason with the senses. What are called gods by men—as Jehovah, the god of the Jews—they say are only æons or creators, under whose dominion man becomes more and more wicked and miserable. To destroy the power of these malicious gods, and redeem man from the thraldom of matter, God sent the most exalted of all æons—Christ—who, in the form of a dove, descended upon a Jew—Jesus—and revealed, through him the doctrines of Christianity; but before the crucifixion of Jesus separated from him, and at the resurrection of the dead will be again united with him, and lay the foundation of a kingdom of the most perfect earthly felicity, to continue a thousand years. There have been no gnostic sects since the fifth century; but many of their principles and ideas reappear in later philosophical systems. There are some traces of gnosticism in several parts of Freemasonry, particularly in the degree of the Adepts of the Eagle or Sun, and also in the rite of the mystic Mason. Fessler, and his friends Krause and Mossdorf, were much interested in gnosticism, and Fessler's rite is tinctured with some of its ideas.

GOD. The highest and most perfect intelligence in which all things exist, and from which all things depend. The belief in God is not the result of teaching, not the result of the exercise of reason, not a deduction from the order and regularity of the universe; for faith in a Supreme Being was universal among men in the infancy of the race, and before the human mind was capable of that power of analysis, or had attained to that degree of science which this study of the universe and of the laws of nature supposes. As the notion of an Infinite Being transcends the circle of sensible and material objects, and is clearly beyond the power of a finite being to create, therefore, that notion must have been communicated directly to man by God himself. Man believes in a God, therefore God exists; because, were there no God the notion of such a being could not exist. The crowning attribute of man, and what distinguishes him from the brute, is not the faculty of reason; for *that*, the brute has in common with man; but the power of seeing and aspiring to the ideal. Thus man had no sooner looked upon the grandeur, and glory, and beauty of the world, than he saw enthroned far above the world that which was vaster, more beautiful, more glorious than the world, the IDEAL, that is to say, God. Therefore, Freemasonry accepts the idea of God, as a supreme fact, and bars its gates with inflexible sternness against those who deny his existence. *No atheist can become a Mason.*

GOLGOTHA. *The place of Skulls.* A retired spot near Jerusalem, commonly called Calvary, where Jesus was crucified, and which contained his sepulcher. The word is found in the Swedish, and also in the Templar rite.

GOTHIC CONSTITUTIONS. These comprise all the statutes, laws, and regulations enacted for the government of Masons, from the convention of York, A. D. 926, down to the revival, A. D. 1717. These were revised by Dr. Anderson, and published for the first time in 1722.

GRAND BODIES, MASONIC. The organization of Grand bodies for the government of Masonry in its representative character is of recent date, as compared with the age of the institution. Every Lodge or body of Masons was originally independent, as "a sufficient number of Masons not less than seven met together within a certain district, with the consent of the sheriff or chief magistrate of the place, were empowered at this time to make Masons and practice the rites of Masonry without warrant of constitution. The privilege was inherent in them as individuals." The custom prevailed in the early period of Masonic history for the brethren to assemble annually for the purpose of consulting on the general concerns of the Craft. At these yearly meetings the Grand Master, or Grand Patron of the Order for the kingdom or province, was elected by the whole brotherhood then assembled. These gatherings were called *Annual Assemblies,* and were attended by members of the Craft without regard to grade or position. At a general assemblage of the Fraternity of England in 1717, adopted a regulation that every Lodge, except the four old Lodges then existing, should thereafter obtain a warrant from the Grand Lodge.

DEGREE OF PERFECTION.

GRAND ELECT, PERFECT AND SUBLIME MASON.

GRAND ELECT, PERFECT AND SUBLIME MASON.
The 14th degree of the Ancient and Accepted rite, sometimes
called the "Degree of Perfection." In France it is called
"Grand Scotch Mason of Perfection of the Sacred Vault
of James VI." The degree is considered to be the
ultimate rite of ancient Masonry, as it is the last of the
Ineffable degrees that refer to the first temple. The Masons
who had been employed in constructing the temple acquired
immortal honor. Their association became more uniformly
established and regulated after the completion of the temple
than it had been before. In the admission of new members
their prudence and caution had produced great respect, as
merit alone was required of every candidate. With these
principles firmly established many of the Grand Elect left
the temple after its dedication, and, traveling into other
countries, disseminated the knowledge they had acquired,
and instructed in the sublime degrees of ancient Craft
Masonry all who applied and were found worthy. The
Lodge is styled the Secret Vault. The hangings are crimson,
with white columns at regular intervals. 24 lights—9 in the
East; 7 in the West; 5 in the South; and 3 in the North. The
apron is white, lined with crimson; in the middle is a square
flat stone, in which is an iron ring. The collar is crimson; the
jewel, a gold compass, open on a circle of forty-five degrees;
between the legs of the compass is a medal representing the
sun on one side, on the other the flaming star. On the circle is
engraved the figures 3, 5, 7, 9. The compass is surmounted
with a pointed crown. The ring of alliance is of gold. On
the inside is engraved: "Virtue unites what death cannot
separate;" with the name and date of initiation of the owner.

GRAND INQUISITOR COMMANDER. The 31st degree
of the Ancient and Accepted rite. It is not an historical degree, but is simply administrative in its character;
the duties of the members being to examine and regulate
the proceedings of the subordinate lodges and chapters.
The meeting is designated a "Sovereign Tribunal," and is
composed of nine officers, viz: a Most Perfect President, a
Chancellor, a Treasurer, and six Inquisitors—one being
elected to perform the functions of Inspecting Inquisitor.
The decoration of the Lodge is white, with eight golden
columns; on the dais above the presiding officer's throne are
the letters J. E.; there is also an altar covered with white
drapery. In the East, on a low seat, is placed a case containing the archives of the Order, covered with blue drapery,
having on its front a large red cross; on the right of the altar
is the table of the Chancellor, on the left that of the Treasurer.
The floor of the Sovereign Tribunal is covered by a painting,

the centre of which represents a cross, encompassing all the attributes of Masonry. There is no apron; the members wear a white collar, on which is embroidered a triangle with rays, having in its center the figures 31, to which is suspended the jewel—a silver Teutonic cross. In France the regulations direct a white apron, with *aurore* (yellow) flap, embroidered with the attributes of the degree.

GRAND LODGES, Jurisdiction of. At first there were no clear nor well defined notions in regard to the territorial jurisdiction of Grand Lodges. Until within a few years each Grand Lodge claimed the right to constitute lodges in any part of the world. At the time of the breaking out of our revolutionary war the Grand Lodges of England, Ireland, and Scotland had lodges in Massachusetts and other colonies. The principle, however, is now well settled that the Grand Lodge of a Province or State has exclusive jurisdiction within such territory, and that no other Grand Lodge can legally charter lodges therein. A Grand Lodge is supreme over its own affairs. There is no Masonic authority or power above it: it is subject only to the unchangeable laws of the Order, the acknowledged constitutions, and the Ancient Landmarks.

GRAND LODGES, Organization of. A Grand Lodge consists of the Master and Wardens of all the lodges under its jurisdiction and such Past Masters as may be elected members. The officers are a Grand Master, Deputy Grand Master, Senior Grand Warden, Junior Grand Warden, Grand Treasurer, Grand Secretary, Grand Chaplain, Senior Grand Deacon, Junior Grand Deacon, Grand Stewards, Grand Marshal, Grand Standard Bearer, Grand Pursuivant, Grand Sword Bearer and Grand Tyler. In a country or state where there is no Grand Lodge three or more legal lodges may meet in convention and organize a Grand Lodge. Then these lodges surrender their charters to the Grand Lodges from which they received them, and take others from the new Grand Lodge.

GRAND MASTER ARCHITECT. The 12th degree of the Ancient and Accepted rite. In this the principles of operative Masonry become prominent; it is a purely scientific degree, in which the rules of architecture and the connection of the liberal arts with Masonry are dwelt upon. Although the lectures on the Fellow-Craft degree illustrate architecture from the same point of view, the subject is susceptible of great extension, and under the "Grand Master Architect" numerous details illustrative of the temple dedicated to the Most High by the wisest man might be worked out. In the absence of distinct information upon many points, there is some exercise for the imagination in furnishing a complete description of Solomon's Temple, which was an astonishing and magnificent work for the time in which it was built; and it seems to have been distinguished from all other temples of remote antiquity by its sumptuousness of detail. The principal officers of this degree are the Master, denominated Thrice Illustrious, and two Wardens. The body is styled chapter, and is decorated with white hangings, strewed with crimson flames; the ornaments are the columns of the five orders of architecture, and a case of mathematical instruments. The jewel is a heptagonal medal of gold. In each angle, on one side, is a star, enclosed in a semicircle. In the center, on the same side, is an equilateral triangle, formed by arcs of circles, in the center of which is the letter א. On the reverse are five columns or different orders of architecture. This is suspended by a blue ribbon.

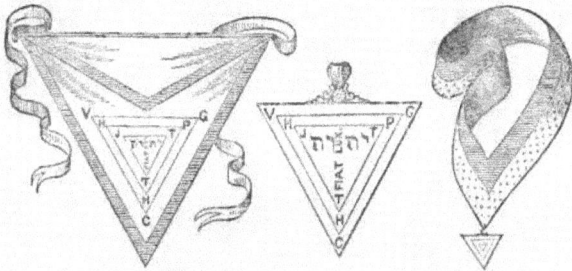

GRAND MASTER OF ALL SYMBOLIC LODGES. The 20th degree of the Ancient and Accepted rite. This degree affords a thorough exemplification of the philosophical spirit of the system of Freemasonry. Philosophy and Masonry, being one and the same principle, have the same object and mission to attain—the worship of the Great Architect of the universe, and the disenthralment of mankind. Here the candidate is charged with the responsible duties of instructor of the great truths of the universality of Masonry, inspired by an upright and enlightened reason, a firm and rational judgment, and an affectionate and liberal philanthropy. This degree bears the same relation to Ineffable Masonry that the Past Master's degree does to the symbolic degrees. Veneration, Charity, Generosity, Heroism, Honor, Patriotism, Justice, Toleration, and Truth are inculcated. The body is called a Lodge; the hangings are blue and gold. The presiding officer is styled Venerable Grand Master, and is seated in the East. A Lodge cannot be opened with less than nine members. In the East is a throne, ascended by nine steps, and surmounted by a canopy; the Lodge is lighted by nine lights of yellow wax. The apron is yellow, bordered and lined with blue; the sash is of broad yellow and blue ribbon, passing from the left shoulder to the right hip; the jewel is a triangle, of gold, on which is engraved the initials of the sacred words.

GRAND PONTIFF. The 19th degree of the Ancient and Accepted rite. The degree is founded on the mysteries of the Apocalypse, relating to the new Jerusalem, as set forth in the Revelation of St. John, XXI. and XXII., which it illustrates and endeavors to explain. The assembly is styled a chapter; two apartments are required. The presiding officer is styled Thrice Puissant Grand Pontiff. The members are called Faithful Brothers. The jewel is an oblong square, of solid gold, with the letter A engraved on one side, and Ω on the other.

GRAND PRIORY. The title applied to the head of the Templars in Scotland. It is synonymous with Grand Encampment, Conclave, etc.

GRAND SCOTTISH KNIGHT OF ST. ANDREW. The 29th degree of the Ancient and Accepted rite. It is also called "Patriarch of the Crusades," in allusion to its supposed origin during those wars, and it is also sometimes known by the name of "Grand Master of Light." This degree is devoted to toleration and freedom of man in the great moral attributes. It inculcates equality—representing the poor Knight equal to the monarch, and exhibits the requisites of knighthood; protection to the defenseless and innocent; the possession of virtue, patience, and firmness—and represents the Knight as the exponent of truth, and one alike without fear and without reproach. The assembly is called a chapter. Two apartments are required. In the first apartment the hangings are crimson, supported by white columns. During the reception this room represents the court of Saladin, the great Sultan of Egypt and Syria. The second apartment should be a well-furnished room, decorated in the eastern style. The presiding officer is styled Venerable Grand Master. The Knights are all dressed in crimson robes, with a large white cross of St. Andrew on the breast. The jewel is two interlaced triangles, formed by arcs of large circles, with the concave outward, of gold, and enclosing a pair of compasses open to twenty-five degrees. At the bottom, and to one of the points is suspended a St. Andrew's Cross, of gold, surmounted by a Knight's helmet; on the center of the cross is the letter ה, inclosed in an equilateral triangle, and this again in a ring formed by a winged serpent; between the two lower arms of the cross may be suspended a key.

H.

HAIL, or HELE. The Masonic word usually spelt hail is more properly the old English word hele, from the ancient German *hehlen*, to conceal. From this comes our word hell, corresponding to the Greek hades, and the Hebrew sheol, the invisible, the unseen.

"These words thou shalt publish and these thou shalt hele."—ESDRAS.

Hele—pronounced hale—should be used in the catechism. The fact that this Saxon word is found in the ritual of Freemasonry proves the relation and connection between the modern system of Freemasonry and the German Building Corporations.

HALLELUIAH. *Praise the Lord.* Expression of applause in the Apprentice degree of Misraim, in the degree of Sublime Scotch, Heavenly Jerusalem, and others.

HAND CLAPPING. Among Masons the common expression of applause, approval, and agreement. Its use is universal in the Order.

HARMONY, ORDER OF. An order embracing both men and women, founded in 1788, by Grossinger, under the auspices of Augusta, Countess of Staff. The Duchess of Newcastle was Grand Mistress. They bound themselves by a solemn oath to be eternally faithful to the obligations of friendship and love.

HARMONY, Order of Universal. A new French rite which, in 1806, arose out of a stock company, through which they hoped to cultivate an East Indian trade. It could not have less than 26 degrees, with military rank up to marshal of the empire.

HARODIM. In 2d Chronicles, ii. 18, it is recorded that Solomon "set three score and ten thousand people to be bearers of burdens, and four score thousand to be hewers in the mountains, and three thousand six hundred overseers to set the people at work." These overseers were called Harodim, or Princes.

HARPOCRATES. Among the Greek writers he was compared with Apollo, and identified with Horus, the Egyptian god of the sun, the youngest son of Osiris and Isis. Both were represented as youths, and with the same attributes and symbols. He was believed to have been born with his finger in his mouth, as indicative of secrecy and mystery. The Greeks and Romans worshiped him as the god of quiet life, repose and secrecy. He is described by Plutarch as lame in the lower limbs when born, to indicate the weak and tender shootings of corn. He also symbolizes the sun when in its early or feeble condition. He is sometimes represented, in sculpture, as a child wearing the skull cap or *pschent*, the crown of the upper and lower world, and holding in his hands the whip and crook, to expel evil influences. He is also represented mounted upon a ram, which carries a ball upon its head; his left hand is armed with a club, while he presses the two fore-fingers of the right hand upon his lips, as the symbol of silence, and intimates that the mysteries of religion and philosophy ought never to be revealed to the profane or uninitiated. Being armed with the club identifies him as the Hercules of the Egyptians.

HAT. Among the Romans the hat was a sign of freedom. Formerly Masons wore hats in the Lodge, as a symbol of freedom and brotherly equality. In English and American Lodges it is now exclusively an attribute of the Master's costume.

HEAL. An act of a legally constituted body of Masons by which a person who has been irregularly admitted to the mysteries of Freemasonry is made a lawful Mason. When the person to be "healed" has been initiated into a self-constituted or false lodge he can be healed only by a reinitiation. Members, however, of schismatic Lodges may be recognized as legitimate by the action of a Grand Lodge. There is a difference between a clandestine (or sham) Lodge and one that is simply schismatic. The founders and members of the first are impostors; the latter are regular Lodges, but from some cause or other not recognized by the legitimate Masonic authorities.

HECATESIA. An annual festival observed by the Stratonicensians in honor of Hecate. The Athenians paid particular attention to this festival, and worshiped this goddess under the name of Diana, who was deemed the patroness of families and of children. From this circumstance statues of the goddess were erected before the doors of the houses, and upon every new moon a public supper was always provided at the expense of the richest people, and set in the streets, which the poorest of the citizens were permitted to enjoy.

HECATOMBOIA. An ancient festival, celebrated in honor of Juno, by the Argians and people of Ægina. A hundred bulls were sacrificed as an offering to the goddess, whence its name. The flesh of the animals was distributed among the poor citizens of the country.

HECATOMPHONIA. A solemn sacrifice offered by the Messenians to Jupiter, when any of them had killed an hundred enemies.

HERMANDAD. *Brotherhood.* This Spanish society was founded A. D. 1295, in the cities of Castile and Leon. It was based on the Masonic principle of secrecy, having ceremonies of admission, secret signs of recognition, and secret places of meeting, where causes were tried and offenders against justice were judged and punished. It invested itself in a garment of mystery, and the blow of justice fell from its hand surely and swiftly, like the bolt of lightning. It sought not only to punish crime, but to prevent it. It warned every nobleman who showed a disposition to wrong a citizen of the certain destruction that awaited him if he persisted. Should he rob or injure a member of the Order, or a citizen, and refuse to make restitution, or give security for better conduct in future, his cattle, his vineyards and gardens were destroyed. The mysterious power of this terrible but righteous brotherhood penetrated every place—through barred and bolted gates and armed sentinels—and often dealt its retributions in the royal presence itself. Of the utility of this Spanish Fraternity there cannot be a doubt, and its beneficial effects in those stormy times were immeasurable. Its ideas were justice, absolute justice, in the administration of the laws' and equality in society and before God.

HERMAPHRODITE. This word is often used, although improperly, in Masonic lodges; for in the human species there is no such thing. Among the lower races such monsters are sometimes found, though rarely.

HERMETIC MASONRY. The Hermetic philosophy was introduced into the Masonic system very early in the 18th century, and for a time was very popular with the most distinguished members of the Order. It even now constitutes the substance of one degree, and is taught in the philosophical and moral lodges of the degree of Prince Adepts. [*See* ALCHEMY.]

HERODEM, ROYAL ORDER OF. Dr. Oliver claims that this Order was instituted by Robert Bruce, after the battle of Bannockburn, which took place on St. John's day, 1314. He says: "The Royal Order of H. R. D. M.—Herodem—had formerly its seat at Kilwinning, and there is reason to think that it and St. John's Masonry were then governed by the same Grand Lodge. But during the 16th and 17th centuries Masonry was at a very low ebb in Scotland, and it was with the greatest difficulty that St. John's Masonry was preserved. The Grand Chapter of H. R. D. M. resumed its functions about the middle of the last century, at Edinburg; and in order to preserve a marked distinction between the Royal Order and Craft Masonry, which had formed a Grand Lodge there in 1736, the former confined itself solely to the two degrees of H. R. D. M. and R. S. Y. C. S., i. e., Herodem and Rosycross." It is more probable, however, that Chevalier Ramsay had more to do with the creation of this Order than Robert Bruce. This appears to be the opinion of Ragon. Something of the nature of this Rite may be gathered from the following extracts, taken from the lectures:

Ques. In what place was the Grand and Holy Order of H. R. D. M. first established?

Ans. Upon the holy summit of Mt. Moriah, in the kingdom of Judea

Ques. What qualifications are requisite for admission into this sublime Order?

Ans. Patience, prudence, firmness, justice.

Ques. Where was it afterward reëstablished?

Ans. At I-colm-kill, and afterward at Kilwinning, where the King Scotland presided in person as Grand Master.

Ques. Why was it reéstablished, and why were changes made?

Ans. To reform the abuses and correct the errors which had been introduced among the brethren of the first three degrees.

In the third section we find the following:

Ques. What symbol in Masonry represents the Son of Man?

Ans. The corner-stone.

Ques. What is the corner-stone?

Ans. It is the stone which the builders rejected, and which is now become the principal stone of the corner, or the most perfect model by which the workmen can fashion their moral jewels.

Ques. How do you know it to be the most perfect model?

Ans. By three grand principles of Masonry.

Ques. Will you name them?

Ans. Fraternal love, assistance, and truth.

Ques. Why fraternal love?

Ans. Because no person can show more love for his brethren than he who is ready to sacrifice himself for them.

Ques. Why the second?

Ans. Because he has come to deliver us from slavery and sin.

Ques. Why the truth?

Ans. Because he is himself the truth in his own essence.

Ques. What is his name?

Ans. Immanuel.

Ques. What does it signify?

Ans. God with us.

These extracts afford a very clear view of the tone and spirit of the entire ritual of the Royal Order of H. R. D. M. There is no reason for believing that this Order has any connection with that of the Culdees, notwithstanding that monastic society once had an establishment at I-colm-kill.

HERODEN. This word is identical with Heredom, Haeredom, Haeredum. It is thought by some to be derived from the Greek words *"ieras domos,"* i. e., holy house. In the catechism of the degree of Grand Architect it is a name given to a mountain near Kilwinning.

Ques. What do they call these mountains?

Ans. Mount Moriah in the land of Gibeon, Mount Sinai, and the mountain of Heroden.

Ques. Where is the mountain of Heroden?

Ans. Between the west and north of Scotland, at the end of the ecliptic, where the first Lodge of Masonry was erected.

It is inferred from this that King Robert I. of Scotland united the Knights Templar with St. Andrew's Order of the Thistle, and called it the Order of Heroden, or of the Holy House, i. e., Holy Temple.

HEROINE OF JERICHO. An adoptive degree conferred on the wives and widows of Royal Arch Masons. It was never widely propagated, and is now almost entirely superseded by the American Adoptive rite of the Eastern Star.

HIEROPHANT. The chief director of the ceremonies and expounder of the doctrines in the mysteries of Eleusis. No one but a descendant of Eumolpus could hold this office. It was necessary for him to have the experience and gravity of age, and to be perfect in his physical organization. In the inferior mysteries, he introduced the novice into the Eleusinian temple, and initiated those who had undergone the final probation into the last and great mysteries. He represented the Creator of the world, and explained to the novice the various phenomena that appeared to him. In the great mysteries, he was the sole expounder of the secrets of the interior of the sanctuary, and of those esoteric doctrines which it was the only object of the institution to communicate to its adepts. No person was permitted to pronounce his name in the presence of an uninitiated person. He sat in the East, and wore, as a symbol of authority, a golden globe, suspended from his neck. He was also called Mystagogue.

HIGH PLACES. It seems natural to man to regard mountains and high places with a certain degree of reverence; and the sentiment of religion has always, and everywhere, impelled him to consecrate them as places of worship. Solomon went to Mount Gibeon to offer sacrifice, because it was a high place. The Druids, too, were partial to hills, and erected their altars on their highest summits. And thus Masons are said to have met on "lofty hills or in low valleys" in the olden time, when the earth, with its carpet of variegated flowers, was literally the mosaic pavement, and the star-decked heavens the only covering of the Lodge.

HIGH-PRIESTHOOD. The order of the High-Priesthood is conferred only on Past High-Priests of Chapters, as an honorary degree, and corresponds to that of Past Master.

HIRAMITES. A name sometimes given to Freemasons as disciples or followers of Hiram, the Tyrian Builder.

HOLY GHOST, ORDER OF. 1. An order of male and female hospitallers. It was founded in the twelfth century by Guy, son of the Count of Montpellier, for the relief of the poor, the infirm, and foundlings. He took the vows himself, and gave a rule to the order. Pope Innocent III., confirmed it in 1198, and founded a hospital at Rome. The dress of both sexes is black, with a double white cross of twelve points on the left breast. 2. The principal military order in France, instituted in 1574, by Henry III. The revolution of 1830 swept it away. Several brotherhoods have borne this name, which is also known in some Masonic systems.

ANCIENT CHARACTERS OF THE INSCRIPTION.

HOLINESS TO THE LORD. An inscription worn on the forehead of the High-Priest, as described in Exodus xxxix. 30: "And they made the plate of the holy crown of pure gold, and wrote upon it a writing like to the engraving of a signet, HOLINESS TO THE LORD."

HONORABLE. In former times a title given to the degree of Fellow-Craft, on account of its scientific character.

HONORARY DEGREE. A degree like that of Past Master, or the Order of the High-Priesthood, conferred as a reward for official service.

HONORARY MASTER. An honorary title given to learned and worthy brothers, who have not filled the oriental chair, as a recognition of their Masonic science and worth. An honor not known in the United States.

HONORS, GRAND. A peculiar ceremony among Masons by which they applaud, or express their agreement, satisfaction or sorrow. They are divided into private and public. The first can only be given in a Master's Lodge, and cannot be described here. The public grand honors, as their name imports, do not partake of this secret character. They consist of clapping of the hands three times, in rapid succession, and are given on all public occasions in which the ministrations of the Fraternity are required, in the presence of the profane as well as the initiated. The funeral grand honors are given in the following manner: Both arms are crossed on the breast, the left uppermost, and the open palms of the hands touching the shoulders; the hands are then raised above the head, the palms striking each other, and then made to fall sharply on the thighs, with the head bowed. This is repeated three times. While the honors are being given the third time, the brethren audibly pronounce the following words—when the arms are crossed on the breast:—"We cherish his memory here;" when the hands are extended above the head—"We commend his spirit to God who gave it;" and when the hands are extended toward the ground—"And consign his body to the earth."

HOST, Captain of the. Among the Jews a military rank. In a Royal Arch Chapter the title designates a kind of master of ceremonies.

I.

I-COLM-KILL. An island, situated near the Hebrides, in a southerly direction therefrom. In ancient times it was the seat of the Order of Culdees, and contains the ruins of the monastery of St. Columba, which was founded A. D. 565. Here the Rite of Herodem, it is claimed, originated.

IDIOT. This word did not always have the meaning which is now attached to it. It is derived from the Greek, *idiōtēs*, which signified a private citizen. In Sparta it denoted one who felt no interest, and took no part, in public affairs, and hence came to mean an ignorant person. It was used in this sense in the middle ages, and this is its Masonic meaning. The modern meaning—fool—would be out of place; for it would be as absurd to establish a rule that no fool should be made a Mason as it would be to enact a law that no horse, or infant, or dead man, should be admitted to the mysteries of Freemasonry. The word means, masonically, not a fool, but a listless, indifferent, ignorant, fellow, who could only be a disgrace to the Craft.

ILLUMINATI OF AVIGNON. This system was organized as a species of Masonry intermingled with the reveries of Swedenborg, somewhere about the year 1760, by Pernetti (who was a Benedictine Monk), and the Baron Gabrianca, a Polish nobleman. Very little is known of the institution, and it might have been forgotten but for the Marquis de Thormé, in 1783, taking up the system that had been adopted in the Avignon Lodge, and from it framing what is now known as the Swedenborg rite—*which see.*

ILLUMINATI, or the Enlightened. During the second half of the eighteenth century, among the numerous secret societies which were more or less connected with Freemasonry there was not one that attracted so much attention, received the support of so many distinguished men, and created so rich a literature, as this. It was founded in 1776 by Adam Weishaupt, professor of law, at Ingolstadt, a man of great originality and depth of thought, and remarkable for the earnestness of his character. The objects which he sought to effect by this association were the highest and noblest ever entertained by the human mind. He desired to assert the individuality of man as a fundamental principle—and hence was an apostle of civil and religious liberty—to discover the means of advancing human nature to a state of higher perfection—to bind in one brotherhood men of all countries, ranks, and religions, and to surround the persons of princes with trustworthy counselors. Apostles, styled Areopagites, were sent into various parts of Europe to make converts, and in a short time the Order was flourishing in Germany, Holland, and Milan. Protestants, rather than Catholics, were preferred as members. The degrees were eight in number: 1. Novice; 2. Minerval; 3. Illuminatus Minor; 4. Illuminatus Major; 5. Knight; 6. Priest; 7. Regent; 8. King. Attracted by the liberality of its doctrines, and the grandeur of its objects, large numbers of illustrious Masons, and among them the celebrated author Knigge, became active members of it. In 1784 the society was dissolved by order of the Bavarian government. No association of men was ever more calumniated and misrepresented than the Order of Illuminati. It is common to dismiss them with the remark that they were "a body of men united together for the purpose of destroying society and religion," whereas, they were men of the profoundest religious convictions, and only desired such a reform in politics as would give man a greater degree of freedom, and afford him larger opportunities and facilities for the development of his faculties. It is humiliating to see that some Masonic writers have repeated the infamous calumnies of those high-priests of the lying fraternity, Robison and Baruel, in regard to them. If they were infidels and anarchists, then the whole American people are; for they were only inspired with, and sought to propagate, the ideas which we hold in the highest reverence, and have embodied in our institutions. This name has been borne by other orders, as the religious society of the Alombrados, in Spain, founded in the sixteenth century; the Order of Guerinets, in France, in the seventeenth; and many others before and since.

ILLUSTRIOUS ELECT OF FIFTEEN. The 10th degree of the Ancient and Accepted rite. The body is called a chapter. The decorations are black, sprinkled with red and white tears; there are 15 lights, 5 in the East, and 5 before each Warden, and 1 in the center—all of yellow wax. The officers are: Thrice Illustrious, Senior and Junior Inspectors, Orator, Secretary and Treasurer, Hospitaller, Master of Ceremonies, and Captain of the Host. This degree is devoted to the same objects as the Elective Knights of Nine—the conclusion of the punishment of the traitors, who, just before the completion of the temple, had committed an infamous crime.

IMMANUEL. A name applied to Christ, and means "God with us."

INDIA, MYSTERIES OF. The leading idea of the India philosophy is that a state of absolute quiescence or rest constitutes the most perfect bliss, and that it can be attained only by the most complete self-abnegation. This idea naturally grows out of the pantheistic nature of their religion. They believe in unity existing in all things, and all things in unity; God in the universe, and the universe in God; and regard nature as a revelation of the divine intelligence. Everything is thus the perpetual transformation or metamorphosis of God. This doctrine is taught in all their mysteries, and upon this theory rests the idea of the reciprocal influence of worlds upon each other, and their central light, and the conception of the universe as a perpetual creation, as does, likewise, the belief in metempsychosis, or the transmigration of souls after death. Beginning and end are mingled, and mind and matter are continually striving for predominance in the universe, which, therefore, exhibits an eternal struggle between good and evil, light and darkness. The notion of God taught in the highest Hindoo mysteries is pure and elevated. He is called *Brahm*, *Atma*, *Bramatma*. Before the creation he reposed in silence, and absorbed in himself. "This world," says Menou, "was all darkness, undiscernible, undistinguishable, altogether as in profound sleep, till the self-evident and visible God, making it manifest with five elements, and other glorious forms, perfectly dispelled the gloom. He, desiring to raise up various creatures by an emanation from his own glory, first created the waters, and impressed them with the power of motion; by that power was brought the wondrous egg, bathed in golden splendors and blazing like a thousand suns, from which sprang Brahma, the self-existing, the parent of all rational beings. In the Hindoo mysteries God is represented under three forms: Vishnu, Siva, and Brahma; for that is the order in which the three are expressed by the letters A U M, that form the mysterious and ineffable name, OM, which is never spoken, but is the object of silent and constant contemplation. The Lingam is worshiped in these rites the same as the Phallus in the Egyptian. The Lotos, too, is a sacred attribute in these mysteries, as it was in those of Isis. The whole initiation represented the same idea as the Egyptian. The eternal combat between the opposing forces of good and evil, of light and dark, and the ultimate triumph of the former, is the leading feature of both, showing conclusively, that the Egyptian system, which is the parent of the Grecian, Roman, and, consequently, of our Masonic system, was itself the offspring of the old Indian mysteries. The most celebrated temples where these rites were performed were those of Elora, Salsette, and Elephanta.

INDUCTION. In a Council of the "Illustrious Order of the Cross," the word has a significance similar to the following. The word also occurs in a Lodge of Past Masters, wherein the newly-elected Master is inducted into the oriental chair of King Solomon.

INDUCTION, Rite of. Those acts and ceremonies by which the novice is first introduced into the Lodge are called by this name. They are highly instructive when properly explained, and have an important symbolical meaning.*

INEFFABLE. *Unutterable.* The ineffable degrees, so-called, are the eleven conferred in a Lodge of Perfection, known as the second series of degrees in the Ancient and Accepted rite. The third series are historical, and conferred in a Council of Princes of Jerusalem. The fourth series are philosophical, and conferred in a Chapter of Rose Croix de H.-R.-D.-M. The fifth series are chivalric, historical, and philosophical, and are conferred in a Consistory of Sublime Princes of the Royal Secret. The last grade is official, and is conferred in the Supreme Council of the thirty-third degree.

INFLAMED URN. An emblem in the alchemistical degree of "*Knight of the Sun or Black Eagle.*" It teaches that the Hermetic Mason should, by his knowledge and virtue, exercise an influence on the world as acceptable as the perfume of the burning urn.

INFORMATION, Lawful. No stranger can be permitted to visit a Lodge until he has been examined and tried in the usual form, unless some brother present *knows* him to be a Mason, by previous trial, or by having met him in a legally constituted Lodge, and vouches for him. This voucher, by a known brother, is called "lawful information." The examination of strangers should be made by intelligent Masons

* The Rite of Induction signifies the end of a profane and vicious life— the *palingenesia* (new birth) of corrupted human nature—the death of vice and all bad passions, and the introduction to a new life of purity and virtue. It also prepares the candidate, by prayer and meditation, for that mystic pilgrimage, where he must wander through night and darkness, before he can behold the golden splendors of the Orient, and stand in unfettered freedom among the Sons of Light. The rite further represents man in his primitive condition of helplessness, ignorance, and moral blindness, seeking after that mental and moral enlightenment which alone can deliver his mind from all thralldoms, and make him master of the material world. The Neophyte, in darkness and with tremblings, knocks at the portals of the Lodge, and demands admission, instruction, and light. So man, born ignorant, and helpless, and blind, yet feeling stirring within him unappeasable longings for knowledge, knocks at the doors of the temple of science. He interrogates Nature, demands her secrets, and at length becomes the proud possessor of her mysteries.

who know how to be, at the same time, thorough and courteous. An examination may be careless and inefficient through an excess of modesty on the part of the examining officer, or it may be needlessly rigid and pedantic. Both of these extremes should be avoided.

INNOVATIONS. These can never be permitted in Freemasonry. As it was in the beginning, so it is now, and so it must forever remain. This is particularly true of symbolic Masonry. It has resisted all attempts of *reformers*, as these innovators style themselves, to add to, or take from, or introduce, changes. The high degrees are developments of the first three, and complete the fabric in all its beauty. Among the innovators who, in the last age, attempted to change the character of the Masonic rites, Cagliostro and the Chevalier Ramsay were the chief. But their efforts were unavailing, and their inventions soon forgotten.

I. N. R. I., i. e., *Jesus Nazarenus Rex Iudæorum.* Jesus of Nazareth, King of the Jews, the inscription which was placed upon the cross of the Savior. In the Philosophical Lodge they represent Fire, Salt, Sulphur, and Mercury. In the system of the Rosicrucians they had a similar use: "*Igne Natura Renovatur Integra*"—"by fire nature is perfectly renewed." This idea is also found in the degree of "Knights Adepts of the Eagle or the Sun."

INTENDANT OF THE BUILDING, sometimes called MASTER IN ISRAEL. The 8th degree in the Ancient and Accepted rite. The body is called a Lodge, and its decorations are crimson; the room is lighted with 27 lights, arranged in three groups of 9 each, and each group forming a triple triangle; on the altar are 5 other lights. The Master is styled Thrice Potent, and represents King Solomon. This degree was instituted to supply the loss of the chief architect of the temple.

INTIMATE SECRETARY. The 6th degree of the Ancient and Accepted rite. The place in which the Lodge is held represents the audience chamber of King Solomon. It is hung with black, strewed with white tears. There are but three officers, who represent King Solomon, King Hiram, and a Captain of the Guards. The ceremony and legend are intended to preserve the remembrance of an instance of unlawful curiosity, the due punishment of the offender being averted only in consideration of his previous fidelity. The degree also teaches that Masons should cultivate the virtues of Silence, Justice, Humanity, and Secrecy; and that in the execution of justice they should not be unmindful of mercy.

IRISH DEGREES. These degrees appeared in France between the years 1730-40. They had a political element, and were intended to aid the Pretender in his efforts to regain the English throne. There were three degrees: Irish Master, Perfect Irish Master, and Puissant Irish Master.

ISIAC TABLE. A monument of ancient Egypt, on which is represented the worship of the goddess Isis, with her ceremonies and mysteries. It is a square table of copper, covered with silver mosaic, skillfully inlaid. The principal figure of the central group is Isis. This table is said to be now in the royal museum at Turin.

ISIS. The chief goddess in the Egyptian mysteries, the symbol of nature, and mother and nurse of all things. Diodorus says that Osiris, Isis, Typhon, Apollo and Venus were the children of Jupiter and Juno. Osiris, who identical with the Dionysus (Bacchus) of the Greeks, married Isis, the moon, and they both made the improvement of society their especial care. Men were no longer butchered, after Isis had discovered the valuable qualities of wheat and barley, and Osiris had taught how to prepare them. Isis and Osiris were undoubtedly persons superior in mind and intelligence to the age in which they lived, who organized society, and contributed largely to the improvement of mankind, on which account the gratitude of after ages elevated

ISIS AND HORUS.

them to the rank of gods. Her priests were bound to observe perpetual chastity. Her festivals were celebrated in all parts of Egypt, Greece and Rome. In her terrestrial character, she wears upon her head the throne which represents her name; in her celestial, the disc and horns, or tall plumes, and nursing Horus. The mysteries of Isis are interesting to Masons, as being the foundation of those of the Sidonian builders, or Dionysian architects, which have contributed so many elements to the Masonic rites.

IVORY KEY. A symbol in the Philosophical Lodge, or degree of Knights Adept of the Eagle or the Sun. It teaches that one should exercise due caution in opening his heart, and expressing his opinions. The Ivory Key, with the letter Z on the wards, in black, is the jewel of the degree of Secret Master, Ancient and Accepted rite.

J.

JACHIN, (יָכִין). The name of one of the brazen pillars placed at the porch of Solomon's Temple. It signifies, "*he that strengthens*," or "*will establish*." The other pillar was called Boaz, (בֹּעַז), "*in strength*"—the two words signifying "*in strength shall this my house be established.*" *

JEHOVAH (יְהֹוָה). The name of God, ineffable and mysterious, which God declared to Moses, from the burning bush on Mount Horeb. Its ancient pronunciation was *Yahveh*; its meaning is HE IS, the same as I AM, the person only being changed. In reply to the request of Moses that God would reveal to him his name, "God said unto Moses, I AM THAT I AM."—EX. III. 14. Thus it denotes the self-existence, independence, immutability, and infinite fullness

* "Stieglitz, in his work '*On Ancient German Architecture*,' gives an illustration of two celebrated pillars, as they are now standing in the cathedral of Wurzburg, one of the oldest cities of Germany, and formerly

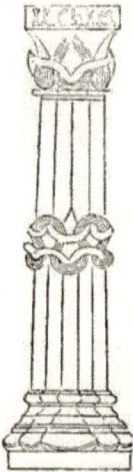

capital of Franconia. He dates them from the time of the construction of the old cathedral, in 1042, by the Fraternity of Steinmetzen, the peculiar form and ornamentation of the capitals and bases being characteristic of the architecture of that period. They were originally situated, like the brazen columns of Solomon's Temple, on either side of the porch—*Jachin* on the right, and *Boaz* on the left; but at the present time they are placed in an inverse position, within the body of the cathedral, not far from the main entrance, on either side of a Gothic door-way, leading to a small vaulted chamber. He says, that 'they were intended to bear a symbolic reference to the Fraternity, which reference is revealed to the initiated in their peculiar proportions, in the ingenious construction and combination of the shafts and capitals, as well as by the names sculptured on the abacus.' Bernewitz, disagreeing with Stieglitz in his explanation of the symbolism of these pillars, says, that 'the artist intended by them to represent God and man.' *Boaz* is tripartite, and yet constitutes but one whole (*Trinity*); the central portion of the shaft reënters within itself (*God without beginning or end*). *Jachin* consists of only two actual parts, *Body and Soul*, which are united by a mysterious entwined bond or tie. The interior of these pillars is invisible. The inner man is likewise invisible—unfathomable. The lower portion of the shaft rises from the earth, and again returns thither; (*so shall the dust return to the earth as it was;*) while the upper portion returns again within itself, and is bound with an endless band (*the spirit, being also without beginning or end, waits hopefully for its union with the everlasting spirits above; it embraces eternity, and is by it embraced*)."—STEINBRENNER, *Hist. of Masonry.*

of the divine Being. It never has the article before it, nor
is it found in the plural form. The Jews, with a deep
reverence for the Deity, never pronounce this name; and
whenever it occurs in the Hebrew Scriptures, they substitute
for it, in reading, the word ADONAI, *Lord*, or ELOHIM, *God*.
That Jehovah is specifically the God of the Hebrews is clear
from the fact, that the heathen deities never receive this
name; they are always spoken of as *Elohim*. Moreover, the
altars, the sacrifices, the festivals, the tabernacle, the temple,
the priesthood and the prophets, all belong emphatically to
Jehovah. The word is sometimes called the TETRAGRAMMATON,
(from the Greek *tetra*, four, and *gramma*, letter,) as it was
among some ancient nations, the mystic number four, which
was often symbolized to represent the Deity, whose name
was expressed in several languages by four letters. The
investigation of this subject is exceedingly interesting tc
Royal Arch Masons.

JEPHTHAH'S DAUGHTER. The name of the first degree
of the Order of the Eastern Star, or American Adoptive
rite. It illustrates, in a beautiful and impressive manner,
the ready obedience of a child to the obligations of the
parent; of the sacredness of a solemn vow or promise, and,
at the same time, the great care, deliberation and discretion
with which it should be formed and offered. Its symbolical
color is blue. There is a touching and thrilling interest in
the history of Jephthah's daughter. The Scriptures give a
simple statement of facts and circumstances, without orna-

ment or impassioned comments, and the narrative excites
the deepest attention. The question has often been propounded, *What was the precise nature of Jephthah's vow?*
Amidst all the uncertainty which may attend the interpretation of this question, there is enough to stamp character
upon it, and to invest it with peculiar interest. Important
moral and spiritual lessons are involved in it. Painful as is
the impression produced by the thought of the young,
lovely, and only daughter sacrificed at the hands of her
father in the fulfillment of a rash and unlawful vow, yet,
under that impression, relief is at once afforded as we sympathize with the spirit and mark the conduct of the destined
victim, and we acknowledge Jephthah's daughter—the beautiful Adah—as one of the illustrious heroines of Scripture,
in the most appropriate sense of the term. The incidents
of the degree are recorded in the book of Judges, chap. xi.

JERUSALEM. *Habitation* or *foundation of peace*. The most
famous and important city of Palestine. The old traditions
and natural prepossessions both of Jews and Christians
connect it with that Salem of which Melchizedek was king.
It is situated on elevated ground south of the center of the
country, about 37 miles from the Mediterranean, and about
24 from the Jordan. About a century after its foundation,
it was captured by the Jebusites, who extended the walls,
and constructed a castle, or citadel, on Mount Zion. By
them it was called Jebus. In the conquest of Canaan,
Joshua put to death its king, Adonizedek, and obtained
possession of the town, which was jointly inhabited by Jews
and Jebusites until the reign of David, who expelled the
latter, and made it the capital of his kingdom, under the
name of Jebus-Salem, or Jerusalem. Its highest historical
importance dates from the time of David, who transported to
it the ark of the covenant, and built in it an altar to the
Lord. The building of the temple by King Solomon was
the consummation of the dignity and holiness of Jerusalem,
which was further enlarged, strengthened and beautified by
this king and by his successors. After the death of Solomon
(B. C. 975), it suffered a diminution of political importance
through the revolt and secession of the ten tribes. It was
pillaged (B. C. 972), by Shishak, king of Egypt, and by
Athaliah (B. C. 884), and finally (B. C. 588), it was taken, after
a siege of three years, by Nebuchadnezzar, who razed its
walls, and destroyed the temple and palaces, and carried all
the holy vessels of the temple, together with thousands of
captives, to Babylon. Having been rebuilt after the Captivity
(B. C. 536), it was again taken and pillaged under Ptolemy
Lagos (B. C. 320), and under Antiochus Epiphanes (B. C. 161).

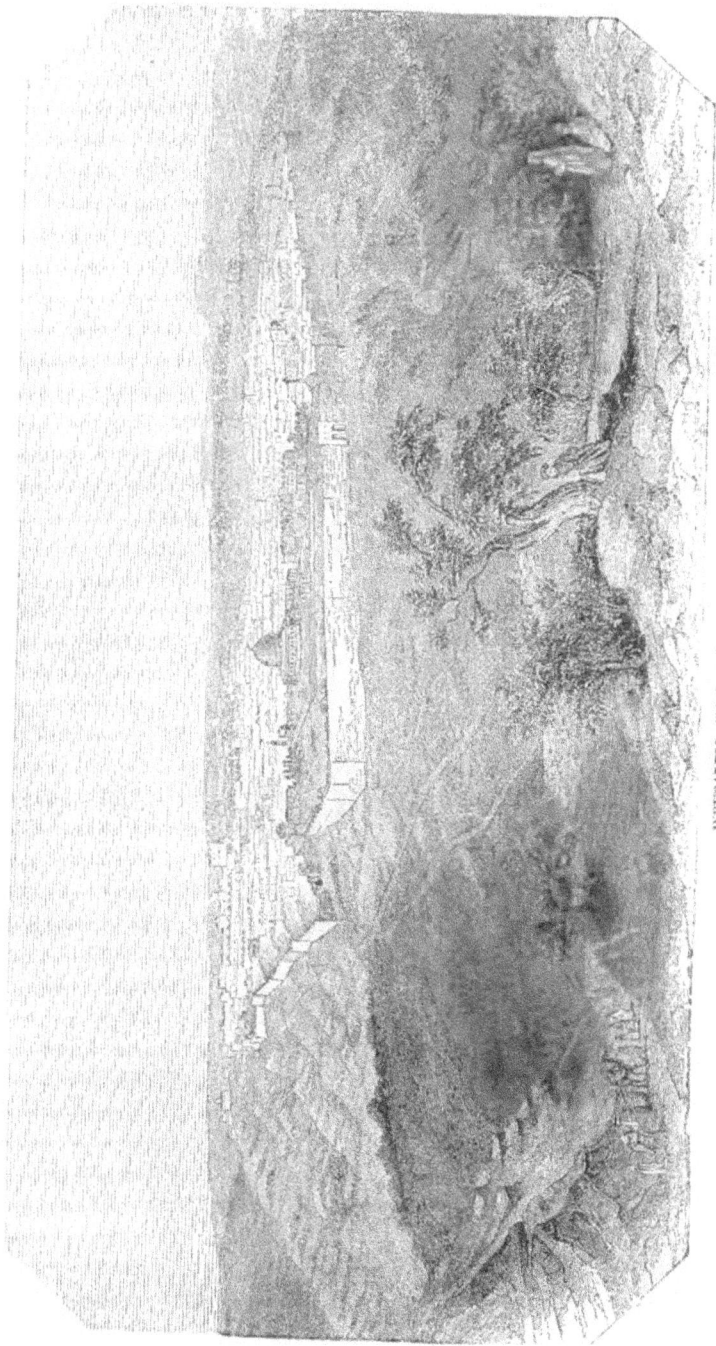

JERUSALEM, FROM MOUNT OLIVES.

Pompey took the city (B. C. 63), put 12,000 of the inhabitants to the sword, and razed the walls to the ground, sparing, at the same time, the treasures of the sanctuary. A few years later (B.C. 51) it was pillaged by Crassus; and from these beginnings date the continued series of Roman aggressions, which terminated in the complete destruction of the city and dispersion of the Jewish race, under Vespasian and Titus, A. D. 70.

JERUSALEM, HEAVENLY. *The City of God.* In several of the higher degrees the Heavenly Jerusalem is frequently alluded to, and occupies a prominent place. In the fifth section of the 2d degree of the Rite of Herodem the Thersata says: "Brothers, may we all, whether present or absent, so labor that we shall come at last to Mount Zion, to the city of the living God; the *Heavenly Jerusalem* * * * *, where the sun shall set no more, nor the moon deprive us of her light, and where the days of our affliction, and the fatigues of our pilgrimage shall find an end." This celestial city is also referred to in the 19th degree of the Ancient and Accepted rite.

JERUSALEM, NEW. Some professors of the doctrine of Swedenborg formed a society in London under this name, having relations with a mystical-magnetical-spiritual brotherhood, in Stockholm. It had some Masonic symbols, and its spirit is seen in some of the degrees of the Swedish rite.

JESUITS, ORDER OF. This celebrated society was founded in 1534, by Ignatius Loyola, a Spaniard of ardent imagination and earnest spirit, and was confirmed by Pius III. in 1540. There can be but little doubt that he intended it to be a mystical and contemplative association, resembling, in many things, the colleges of Egyptian priests; and the original objects of the Order, as promulgated by Loyola, were certainly entitled to respect. To defend and propagate the faith, to educate the young, to assist each other, to renounce the honors of the world, and ecclesiastical dignities; such was the basis upon which was erected a fabric that destroyed itself as soon as it lost sight of its first ideal, and ceased to be what it promised at the commencement of its career. The Jesuits appear to have taken the Egyptian priests for their model. Like them, they were the conservators and interpreters of religion. The vows, they pronounced, bound them to their company, as indissolubly as the interest and politics of the Egyptian priests fixed them in the sacred college of Memphis. Like those ancient priests, they subjected all who aspired to membership in the

Order to the severest trials; like them, they sent forth missionaries to propagate and interpret the faith; they were the counselors of princes, and the educators of statesmen. But the Order lost its power, and received the condemnation of the world as soon as it became the ally of despots and made a traffic of the rights of man. After the Order of Jesus had fallen from its high estate, and became merely a secret society of political agitators and intriguers, some ardent and enthusiastic men conceived the idea of superseding it by a new Order that should retain all the good of the old, and be better adapted to the circumstances of modern times, and the wants of modern society. The Society of the Illuminati and that of the Rosecrucians were formed with this aim and purpose. The adepts of the Illuminati were governed by rules nearly identical with those of the Jesuits, and the whole machinery of the two orders was constructed after the same idea.

JEWELS. Every Lodge is furnished, symbolically, with six jewels; three movable and three immovable. The three immovable jewels are the square, level, and plumb; they are so-called because they are the permanent and unchangeable jewels of the Lodge, and can never be taken or removed from their proper places. They belong, permanently and immovably, to the three principal offices and chairs. The movable jewels are the rough ashlar, the perfect ashlar, and the trestle-board. Jewels are the names applied to the emblems worn by the officers of Masonic bodies as distinctive badges of their offices. For the purpose of reference, the jewels used by the several Masonic bodies most popular in the United States are herewith described:

SYMBOLIC LODGE.
OF SILVER.

Past Mast. wears a compass, opened on a quarter circle, sun in center.

This jewel may be of silver or gold, or of silver and gold.

Master wears a	square.	
S. War.	"	level.
J. War.	"	plumb.
Treasurer	"	cross-keys.
Secretary	"	cross-pens.
S. Deacon	"	square and compass, sun in the center.
J. Deacon	"	square and compass, quar. moon in the center.
Stewards	"	cornucopia.
Mast. of Cer.	"	cross-swords.
Chaplain	"	open Bible.
Marshal wears		cross-batons.
Organist	"	lyre.
Tyler	"	sword.

GRAND LODGE.
OF GOLD OR YELLOW METAL (suspended within a circle).

Past Grand Mast. wears a compass, opened on quarter circle, triangle in the center.

G. Mast. wears a		compass, opened on a quar. circle, sun in center.
Dep. G. Mast.	"	square.
S. G. War.	"	level.
J. G. War.	"	plumb.
G. Treas.	"	cross-keys.
G. Sec.	"	cross-pens.
G. Chaplain	"	open Bible.
G. Marshal	"	scroll and sword crossed.

LODGE JEWELS.

PAST MASTER.

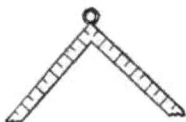

MASTER.

SENIOR WARDEN.

JUNIOR WARDEN.

TREASURER.

SECRETARY.

SENIOR DEACON.

JUNIOR DEACON.

STEWARDS.

MASTERS OF CEREMONIES.

CHAPLAIN.

TILER.

GRAND LODGE JEWELS.

GRAND MASTER.

DEP. GR. MASTER.

SEN. GR. WARDEN.

JUN. GR. WARDEN.

GR. TREASURER.

GR. SECRETARY.

GR. CHAPLAIN.

GR. MARSHAL.

GR. STANDARD BEARER.

GR. SWORD BEARER.

GR. STEWARDS.

GR. DEACONS.

GR. PURSUIVANT.

GR. LECTURER.

GR. TILER.

CHAPTER JEWELS.

HIGH-PRIEST.

KING.

SCRIBE.

CAPT. OF THE HOST.

PRINC. SOJOUR.

R. A. CAPT.

MASTS. OF THE VAILS.

TREASURER.

SECRETARY.

CHAPLAIN.

STEWARDS.

SENTINEL.

COMMANDERY JEWELS.

COMMANDER.

GENERALISSIMO.

CAPT. GEN.

PRELATE.

SEN. WARDEN.

JUN. WARDEN.

TREASURER.

RECORDER.

STAND. BEARER.

SWORD BEARER.

WARDER.

GUARDS.

G. Std. B. wears a	banner.
G. Sword B. "	straight sword.
G. Stewards "	cornucopia.
G. Deacon	dove, bearing olive branch.
G. Pursuiv. "	sword and trum't crossed.
G. Tyler "	cross-swords.

ROYAL ARCH CHAPTERS.

H. P. wears a	miter.
King "	level, surmounted by a crown.
Scribe "	plumb, surmounted by a turban.
Capt. of Host "	triangular plate, inscribed with a soldier.
Princ. Sojr. "	triangular plate, inscribed with a pilgrim.
R. A. Captain "	sword, with signet ring.
Mast. of Vails "	swords.
Treasurer "	cross-keys.
Secretary "	cross-pens.
Chaplain "	open Bible.
Sentinel "	cross-swords.

All the above jewels for Grand or Subordinate Chapters are of yellow metal, and suspended within an equilateral triangle.

ROYAL AND SELECT MASTERS.

G. Mast. wears a	trowel and square.
Hir. of Tyre "	trowel and level.
C'dr. of Wks. "	trowel and plumb.
Treasurer "	trowel and cross-keys.
Recorder "	trowel and cross-pens.
Capt. of Grd. "	trowel and bat. ax.

Cond'r. wears a	trowel, with scroll and baton.
Sentinel "	trowel and sword.

Of yellow metal, and suspended within an equilateral triangle.

COMMANDERY OF KNIGHTS TEMPLAR.

Em't Commander wears a passion cross, with rays of light at the crossings.

Gen'simo wears	sq'e., surmounted by paschal lamb.
Capt. Gen. "	level, surmounted by a cock.
Prelate "	triple triangle with a passion cross in each.
Sen. War. "	hollow square and sword.
Jun. War. "	eagle and flaming sword.
Treasurer "	cross-keys.
Recorder "	cross-pens.
Stand. B. "	plumb, surmounted by a banner.
Sword B. "	triangle and cross-swords.
Warder "	square plate, with trumpet and cross-swords.
Guards "	square plate, with battle-ax.
Sentinel "	sword.

The jewels for Grand Commandery are the same, enclosed within a circle, and all of yellow metal.

A description of the jewels belonging to the Ancient and Accepted rite may be found attached to the name of each degree, respectively, in this work.

JOABERT. The companion of Solomon and Hiram. The name appears in several of the high degrees in connection with the above-mentioned illustrious Masons.

JOACHIM, Order of St. An offspring of the Order of true and perfect friendship of St. Jonathan. It was composed of Knights and ladies, and, in 1804, had its seat in Bamberg. One of the vows of the members required them to believe in the Trinity and avoid waltzing.

JOHANNITE MASONRY. The lodges of symbolical Masonry which were formerly dedicated to King Solomon are now dedicated to St. John the Baptist and St. John the Evangelist. Hence the first three degrees are called Johannite Masonry.

JOPPA. One of the most ancient seaports in the world; on the Mediterranean sea, about 35 miles north-west of Jerusalem. Here the materials for building the first and second temples, sent from Lebanon, Tyre and other places, were landed, and conveyed to Jerusalem. Its harbor is shoal and unprotected from the winds; but on account of its convenience to Jerusalem, it became the principal port of Judea, and is still the great landing-place of pilgrims and travelers to the Holy Land. The place is now called Jaffa. The peculiarly hilly and even precipitous character of Joppa is preserved in the traditions of the degree of Mark Master, and a benevolent moral deduced, in accordance with the entire instructions of the grade.

JUDAH. The fourth son of the patriarch Jacob, whose descendants became the most distinguished of the twelve tribes. On account of this the whole of Palestine is sometimes called Judea, or the land of Judah. The device on the banner of this tribe was a lion. It appears in the symbolism of Freemasonry.

JUDAH AND BENJAMIN. Of the twelve tribes of Israel, which were carried away captive by Nebuchadnezzar, only two (Judah and Benjamin) ever returned to Palestine. No traces of the lost tribes have ever been found.

K.

KADOSH. A Hebrew word, signifying *holy, consecrated, separated;* the designation of the 30th degree of the Ancient and Accepted rite, or Knight of the White and Black Eagle. [*See* KNIGHT OF KADOSH.] There are several degrees bearing this name, but they all seem to be allied to the Knights Templar system. In the history of the high degrees we find: 1. The Knight Kadosh; 2. Kadosh of the Chapter of Clermont; 3. Philosophical Kadosh; 4. Kadosh Prince of Death; 5. Kadosh of the Scottish rite. It is also the name of the 10th degree of Martin's system; the 24th of the Council of Emperors of the East and West; 9th of the Scotch Philosophical rite, and 65th of the system of Misraim.

KALAND, Brothers of. A lay brotherhood which originated in Germany in the thirteenth century. The name is derived from the Latin word *kalendæ*, which, among the ancient Romans, designated the first day of the month. On this day the brethren assembled to pray for their deceased friends, and to meditate and discuss religious, moral, and philosophical subjects. The meeting was closed with the *agape*, or Table-lodge.

KILWINNING. A small town in Scotland, of no importance or influence, but which fills a large place in Masonic history, although it is doubtful whether the greater portion of the Masonic events said to have transpired there ever existed, except in the regions of the imagination. As Kilwinning, however, was the seat of a monastery, founded in 1140, it is not unlikely that a Lodge of Masons might have been organized there at that time; although there are no authentic records existing showing this to be the fact. Thory—Acta Latamorum—says that: "Robert Bruce, King of Scotland, under the title of Robert I., created the Order of St. Andrew of Chardon, after the battle of Bannockburn, which was fought June 24, 1314. To this Order was afterward united that of Heroden, for the sake of the Scotch Masons, who formed a part of the thirty thousand troops with whom he had fought an army of one hundred thousand Englishmen. King Robert reserved the title of Grand Master to himself and his successors forever, and founded the Royal Grand Lodge of Herodem at Kilwinning." The whole subject of the connection of Kilwinning with the history of Freemasonry is involved in great obscurity; but it is generally believed by Masons that the first Lodge in Scotland was opened at Kilwinning at the time of the building of the abbey. [*See* Herodem.]

KING. In the Chapter of Royal Arch Masons, he is the second officer, and represents Zerubbabel, governor of Judea, and a lineal descendant of the royal race of King David. In the Lodge of Mark, Past and Most Excellent Masters, the King acts as Senior Warden.

KING OF THE SANCTUARY. An honorary or side degree. A Mason can only receive this degree from five Masters of Lodges, who have each served a year in that office without interruption. No King of the Sanctuary can confer this degree, until after the expiration of nine years from the time of receiving it, unless he who presided at his reception knowing him to be the only person in possession of the degree, in the place where he resides, relieves him of this restriction before finally parting with him permanently;

and this is moreover to be done in the presence of those who assisted at his reception.

KNIGHT. 1. A young servant, or follower; a military attendant; 2. A young man when admitted to the privilege of bearing arms; hence one of a certain chivalric or feudal rank; a champion; 3. One on whom knighthood is conferred by the sovereign or authorized military power, or, masonically, within the body of a just and legally constituted Commandery of Knights Templar, entitling the recipient to be addressed as Sir Knight.

KNIGHTHOOD, Masonic. There is much difference of opinion as to the origin of this branch of the Masonic Institution, and without attempting to show that the form of conferring the order is identical with that of the gallant and devoted soldier-monks of the Crusades, it cannot be controverted that their Institution possessed some features of similarity to Freemasonry. The connection between the Knights Templar and the Masonic Institution has been repeatedly asserted by the friends and enemies of both. Bro. Lawrie says: "We know the Knights Templar not only possessed the mysteries, but performed the ceremonies, and inculcated the duties of Freemasons;" and he attributes the dissolution of the Order to the discovery of their being Freemasons, and assembling in secret to practice the rites of the Order. He endeavors to show that they were initiated into the Order by the Druses, a Syrian Fraternity which existed at that date, and indeed now continues. In a French MS. ritual of about 1780, in the degree of Black and White Eagle (30th), the transmission of Freemasonry by the Templars is most positively asserted. The history of the Templars and their persecution is minutely described in the closing address, and the Grand Commander adds: "This is, my illustrious brother, how and by whom Masonry is derived and has been transmitted to us. You are now a Knight Templar, and on a level with them." The Order of the Temple, in the twelfth century, was divided into three classes: Knights, Priests, and Serving Brethren. Every candidate for admission into the first class must have received the honor of knighthood in due form, and according to the laws of chivalry, and consequently the Knights Templar were all men of noble birth. The second class, or the Priests, were not originally a part of the Order, but by the bull of Pope Alexander, known as the bull *omne datum optimum*, it was ordained that they might be admitted, to enable the Knights more commodiously to hear divine service, and to receive the sacraments. Serving Brothers,

like the Priests, were not a part of the primitive institution.
They owed their existence to the increasing prosperity and
luxury of the Order. Over this society, thus constituted, was
placed a presiding officer, with the title of Grand Master.
His power, though great, was limited. He was in war the
commander-in-chief of all the forces of the Temple. In his
hands was placed the whole patronage of the Order, and as
the vicegerent of the Pope, he was the spiritual head and
bishop of all the clergy belonging to the society. He was,
however, much controlled and guided by the chapter, without whose consent he was never permitted to draw out or
expend the money of the Order. The Grand Master resided
originally at Jerusalem; afterward, when that city was lost,
at Acre, and finally at Cyprus. His duty always required
him to be in the Holy Land; he, consequently, never resided
in Europe. He was elected for life from among the Knights
in the following manner: On the death of the Grand Master,
a Grand Prior was chosen to administer the affairs of the
Order until a successor could be elected. When the day,
which had been appointed for the election, arrived, the
chapter usually assembled at the chief seat of the Order;
three or more of the most esteemed Knights were then
proposed, the Grand Prior collected the votes, and he who
had received the greatest number was nominated to be the
electing Prior. An Assistant was then associated with him
in the person of another Knight. These two remained all
night in the chapel, engaged in prayer. In the morning,
they chose two others, and these four, two more, and so on
until the number of twelve (that of the Apostles) had been
selected. The twelve then selected a chaplain. The thirteen
then proceeded to vote for a Grand Master, who was elected
by a majority of votes. When the election was completed,
it was announced to the assembled brethren, and when all
had promised obedience, the Prior, if the person was present,
said to him: "In the name of God the Father, the Son, and
the Holy Ghost, we have chosen, and do choose thee, Bro. N.,
to be our Master." Then, turning to the brethren, he said:
"Beloved sirs and brethren, give thanks unto God, behold
here our Master." The mode of reception into the Order
is described to have been exceedingly solemn. A novitiate
was enjoined by the canons, though practically it was in
general dispensed with. The candidate was received in a
chapter assembled in the chapel of the Order, all strangers
being rigorously excluded. The Preceptor opened the business with an address to those present, demanding if they
knew any just cause or impediment why the candidate should
not be admitted. If no objection was made, the candidate
was conducted into an adjacent chamber, where two or

ADMISSION OF A NOVICE TO THE VOWS OF THE ORDER OF THE TEMPLE.

three of the Knights, placing before his view the rigor and austerities of the order, demanded if he still persisted in entering it. If he persisted, he was asked if he was married or betrothed, had made a vow in any other order, if he owed more than he could pay, if he was of sound body, without any secret infirmity, and free? If his answers proved satisfactory, they left him and returned to the chapter, and the Preceptor again asked, if any one had anything to say against his being received. If all were silent, he asked if they were willing to receive him. On their assenting, the candidate was led in by the Knights who had questioned him, and who now instructed him in the mode of asking admission. He advanced, and kneeling before the Preceptor, with folded hands, said: "Sir, I am come before God, and before you and the brethren; and I pray and beseech you, for the sake of God, and our sweet Lady, to receive me into your society and the good works of the order, as one who, all his life long, will be the servant and slave of the order." The Preceptor then inquired of him if he had well considered all the trials and difficulties which awaited him in the order, adjured him on the Holy Evangelists to speak the truth, and then put to him the question which had already been put to him in the preparation-room, further inquiring if he was a Knight, and the son of a Knight and gentlewoman, and if he was a priest. He then asked him the following questions: "Do you promise to God, and Mary, our dear Lady, obedience, as long as you live, to the Master of the Temple, and the Prior who shall be set over you? do you promise chastity of the body? do you further promise a strict compliance with the laudable customs and usages of the order now in force, and such as the Master and Knights may hereafter add? will you fight for and defend, with all your might, the Holy Land of Jerusalem, and never quit the order but with the consent of the Master and Chapter? and lastly, do you agree that you never will see a Christian unjustly deprived of his inheritance, nor be aiding in such a deed?" The answers to all these questions being in the affirmative, the Preceptor then said: "In the name of God, and of Mary, our dear Lady, and in the name of St. Peter of Rome, and our Father the Pope, and in the name of all the brethren of the Temple, we receive you to all the good works of the order, which have been performed from the beginning, and will be performed to the end, you, your father, your mother, and all those of your family whom you let participate therein. So you, in like manner, receive us to all the good works which you have performed and will perform. We assure you of bread and water, the poor clothing of the order, and labor and toil enow." The Preceptor then took the white mantle, with its ruddy cross, placed it about his neck, and bound it fast. The Chaplain repeated the 133d Psalm : "Behold, how good and how pleasant it is for brethren to dwell together in unity !" and the prayer of the Holy Spirit, "*Deus qui corda fidelium;*" each brother said a *pater*, and the Preceptor and Chaplain kissed the candidate. He then placed himself at the feet of the Preceptor, who exhorted him to peace and charity, to chastity, obedience, humility, and piety, and so the ceremony was ended. The secret mysteries of the Templars, most of the historians say, were celebrated on Good Friday; and what those mysteries were, we discover from those who still carry them on as their successors—the order as kept up in France and other countries on the continent—not the Masonic institution. They are accustomed in these secret rites to act over the events which took place on Thursday, Friday and Saturday of the Holy Week, and then solemnize with great pomp the resurrection of Christ. One writer, Rosetti, distinctly asserts that the Templars were a branch of the Masonic institution, whose great object in that age was the overthrow of the papal tyranny, and the monstrous fabric it had erected of idolatry, superstition, and impiety; and hence he traces the determination of the Pope to crush, at all hazards, the order of the Temple, with all its daring innovations. Though there is a great probability, if not a certainty, that Masonry was a leading feature in the Templar institution, we are inclined to believe that the mysteries of the craft were the only secrets of their practice. The wonderful architectural and engineering works which, both in Asia and Europe, were constructed under the direction of the Templars and Hospitallers—more particularly the former—are, it seems to us, very striking evidence of the Masonic origin of the Knights. Gervase of Canterbury, who wrote in the twelfth century, speaks of both French and English artificers, skillful to work in stone and in wood, who traveled in guilds or societies, for the purpose of proffering their services wherever the architect's and builder's art required to be exercised. These were the only men who possessed the requisite knowledge, and from their ranks kings and princes frequently impressed by violence workmen whom they required to construct their palaces or fortresses. They were the operative Freemasons, to whose surpassing skill and knowledge of the laws of beauty and just proportion we are indebted for the magnificent cathedrals which adorn many parts of Europe. They met in Lodges close tiled from the vulgar gaze, and pursued the practice of their mystic rites under the sanction of the throne and the church. The traveling bodies of Freemasons, which we have mentioned, consisted of brethren well skilled in every branch of knowledge; among their ranks were many learned ecclesiastics, whose names survive to the present day in the magnificent edifices which they assisted to erect. The Knights of the Temple, themselves a body of military monks, partaking both of the character of soldiers and priests, preserved in their Order a rank exclusively clerical, the individuals belonging to which took no part in warfare, who were skilled in letters, and devoted themselves to the civil and religious affairs of the Order; they were the historians of the period, and we know that all the learning of the time was in their keeping, in common with the other ecclesiastics of their day. From the best information we are possessed of regarding the Order, we believe there can be little doubt that these learned clerks introduced the whole fabric of Craft Masonry into the system of knighthood, and that not only was the speculative branch of the science by them incorporated with the laws and organization of the Knights, but to their operative skill were the Templars indebted for their triumphs in architecture and fortification. We have shown that the early Freemasons were the architects of all structures above the hovels of the peasantry; and we have endeavored to trace to Masonic influence the eminence attained in structural science by the various knightly orders. In our opinion, there is little room to doubt that the practice of Masonry soon became a prominent feature of the Order, and that Masonic secrets alone were the far-famed mysteries of the Templars. As it is evident that these pursuits would not in the eyes of the world appear to further the original objects of the chivalric orders, we cannot be surprised that the knights made no profession of their Masonic studies; perhaps, even at that remote period, there was a well-grounded fear of the animosity which has been since so fearfully developed in the church of Rome against all secret societies. That power has ever trembled at the progress of liberality and science, knowing full well that in proportion as the intellect of man is strengthened by freedom of thought, her influence, founded upon blind superstition and puerile credulity, must gradually disappear from the earth. In illustration of the alarm of the papal church at societies of this kind, we will refer, though not strictly belonging to our subject, to the Academy of Secrets, established in Italy in the sixteenth century, by Baptista Porta, for the advancement of science. This association was called *I Secreti*, and was accessible only to such as had made some new discovery (real or supposed) in physical science. Porta did not content himself with this private means of instruction and education; he also, to the utmost of his power, promoted public academies, wherein were taught the then recondite sciences of chemistry, optics, and natural history. His voluminous works extended his fame, and he was visited by the learned from all parts of Europe. Such a man, in that age, could not escape the notice and pressing attentions of the Holy Church. Writing, of course, much that was perfectly incomprehensible to the ignorant priests of the time, he was summoned to Rome to answer for his conduct and opinions.

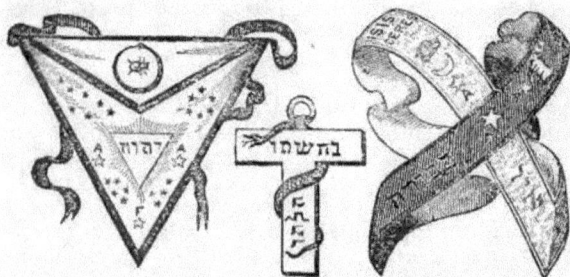

KNIGHT OF THE BRAZEN SERPENT. The 25th degree of the Ancient and Accepted rite. The history of this degree is founded upon the events described in the Book of Numbers xxi. 6–9.* The body is styled the Council, and represents the camp of the Israelites in the wilderness, after the death of Aaron. The camp, standards, and tabernacle with its court, are arranged as in the 23d and 24th degrees. In the East is a transparency on which is painted a cross, with a serpent coiled round it and over the arms. The teaching and moral of the degree is FAITH. The presiding officer represents Moses, and is styled "Most Puissant Leader." The candidate is called "A Traveller." The hangings of the council are red

* "And the Lord sent fiery serpents among the people, and they bit the people; and much people of Israel died. Therefore, the people came to Moses, and said, We have sinned, for we have spoken against the Lord, and against thee; pray unto the Lord, that he take away the serpents from us. And Moses prayed for the people. And the Lord said unto Moses, make thee a fiery serpent, and set it upon a pole: and it shall come to pass, that every one that is bitten, when he looketh upon it, shall live. And Moses made a serpent of brass, and put it upon a pole, and it came to pass that if a serpent had bitten any man, when he beheld the serpent of brass, he lived." The ritual says that Moses, in obedience to the divine command, placed the brazen serpent upon the *tau*, and every one who looked upon it was directed to pronounce the word *hatathi*, "I have sinned;" and having done this, he was immediately healed.

and blue. The jewel is a tau cross, of gold, surmounted by a circle—the *Crux Ansata*—round which a serpent is entwined, suspended by a red ribbon. The legend states that this degree was founded during the time of the crusades in the Holy Land, as a military and monastic order, and gave it the name it bears, in allusion to the healing and saving virtues of the brazen serpent* among the Israelites in the wilderness—it being part of the obligation of the Knights to receive and gratuitously nurse sick travelers, protect them against the attacks of the infidels, and escort them safely through Palestine.

KNIGHT OF THE CHRISTIAN MARK, AND GUARD OF THE CONCLAVE. According to the traditions of this degree it was first created at Rome by Pope Alexander, for the defense of his person and the Holy See. Circumstances, however, occurred which rendered some changes necessary, and he called on the worthy Knights of St. John to assist him, as they were well known to be faithful and zealous followers of the Lord. That no stranger should gain admission and discover the secrets of this august assembly, the Order of the Christian Mark was conferred on the members. The motto of the Order is *"Christus regnat, vincit, triumphat,"* Christ reigns, conquers, and triumphs. *"Rex regum, et Dominus dominorum."* King of kings, and Lord of lords. The body is called a conclave. The officers are: 1. Invincible Knight; 2. Senior Knight; 3. Junior Knight; 4. Six Grand Ministers; 5. Recorder; 6. Treasurer; 7. Conductor; 8. Guard The jewel is a triangular plate of gold with seven eyes engraved on one side, and the letter G within a five-pointed star on the other.

KNIGHT OF CONSTANTINE. This degree, sometimes, but improperly, styled "Knight of Constantinople," is an auxiliary or side degree; the legend thereof refers to the time of Constantine Perphyrogenitus, who became Emperor A. D. 911. It may be conferred on any Master Mason in good standing, by any one who is legally in possession of it, with the aid of at least five other Master Masons who are also Knights of the degree. The body is styled a Preceptory and the presiding officer is called Preceptor.

* The brazen serpent which Moses set up was preserved as a memorial of the miracle till the time of Hezekiah—more than 700 years—who, in extirpating idolatry, "removed the high places, and brake the images, and cut down the groves, and brake in pieces the brazen serpent that Moses had made; for until those days the children of Israel did burn incense to it." This was a bold measure; for some kings, however determined on the extirpation of idolatry, would have hesitated at the destruction of that which was certainly in itself an interesting memorial of a remarkable manifestation of the power of God.

KNIGHT OF THE EAST OR SWORD. The 15th degree of the Ancient and Accepted rite. It refers to those valiant Masons who, with trowels in hand and swords by their sides, were ever ready to construct and defend the Holy City and Sanctuary. It is founded on the circumstance of the assistance rendered by Darius to the Jews, who, liberated from their captivity by Cyrus, had been prevented by their enemies from rebuilding the temple. This degree requires three apartments, styled Hall of the West and Hall of the East, between which must be an ante-chamber or passage, representing the road from Jerusalem to Persia. The first apartment represents the encampment of the Masons among the ruins of Jerusalem. The hangings are crimson. The room is lighted with 70 lights, disposed in groups of 7 each, in commemoration of the 70 years captivity. The second apartment represents the council chamber of Cyrus, King of Persia, and should be decorated according to the customs of the Orientals. In the ante-room, separating the two apartments, must be a solid bridge, resembling stone, with a representation of running water under it. The jewel, of gold, is three triangles, one within the other, diminishing in size, and inclosing two naked swords, crossed hilts downward, resting on the base of the inner triangle. From Scripture and tradition is derived the following legend of this degree: The Knights of the East derive their origin from the captivity, when the whole land was a "desolation and an astonishment," and the nation did "serve the King of Babylon seventy years." And when the seventy years were accomplished, the Israelites were restored to liberty by Cyrus, in fulfillment of the prophecy of Jeremiah. Cyrus permitted the Jews to return to Jerusalem for the purpose of rebuilding the temple, and he caused all the holy vessels

and ornaments which had been carried away by Nebuzaradan
to "be restored, and brought again into the temple which
is at Jerusalem, every one to his place, and place them in
the house of God" (Ezra vi. 5). The king committed the
charge of the holy vessels, as well as of the returning captives,
to Sheshbazzar, the prince of Judah; this is the Babylonian
name of Zerubbabel, who was of the royal line of David.
When the Israelitish captives were assembled they numbered
42,360, exclusive of slaves and servants amounting to 7,337.
This traditional history relates that Zerubbabel, for the protection of his people, armed 7,000 Masons, and placed them in
the van to repel such as should oppose their march to Judea.
Their march was unimpeded as far as the banks of the
Euphrates, where they found an armed force opposed to their
passage. A conflict ensued, and the enemy was cut to pieces
or drowned at the passage of the bridge. The emblematic
color of the degree is in allusion to this circumstance. The
journey occupied four months, and in seven days from their
arrival the work of restoring the temple was commenced.
The workmen were divided into classes, over each of which
a chief, with two assistants, was placed. Every degree of
each class was paid according to its rank, and each class had
its distinctive modes of recognition. The works had scarcely
commenced before the workmen were disturbed by the
neighboring Samaritans, who were determined to oppose the

THE SOLDIER MASONS BUILDING THE SECOND TEMPLE.

reconstruction of the
edifice. Zerubbabel
therefore ordered, as
a measure of precau-
tion, that the Masons
should work with a
sword in one hand
and a trowel in the
other, that they might
be able at any moment
to defend themselves
from the attacks of
their enemies. The
second temple occu-
pied about 20 years in its construction, and was consecrated in a like manner to that of the Temple of Solomon.
Those Masons who constructed it were created by Cyrus
Knights of the East, and hence the title of this degree. This
degree appears in both the French rites; in the Grand
Orient it is the 6th; in both it is termed Knight of the East.
The assembly is called a Council. Everything bears a
Hebrew character; there are the candlestick with seven
branches, the brazen sea, and the table of shewbread, etc.

The Chief of the Council is designated Sovereign, and represents Cyrus, King of Persia. Zerubbabel and two others
receive the authority from the King of Persia to rebuild the
Holy City and Sanctuary.

THE TRACING-BOARD OF THE DEGREE.*

KNIGHTS OF THE EAST AND WEST. The 17th degree
of the Ancient and Accepted rite. It is entirely philosophical, and makes no pretense in its history with Freemasonry.
Its origin dates back to the time of the crusades; that in
1118—the same year that the Order of the Temple was

* The Tracing-board of the degree is a heptagon within a circle, the
upper portion forming a rainbow. At the angles of the heptagon, on the
outside, are the initials of the seven words which are on the capitals of the
columns; at the angles, on the inside, are the initials of the seven words
which are on the bases of the columns. Near the center of the heptagon
is the figure of a man in a long white robe, with a golden girdle round
his waist, and standing on a section of the globe; hair and beard white
as snow; his right hand extended, holding seven stars surrounding the ⌐;
his head encircled by a glory emanating from a delta; a two-edged flaming
sword in his mouth. Around him stand seven golden candlesticks, with
candles burning; and over each of these, one of the letters E. S. P. T. S.
P. L., the initials of the names of the seven churches—Ephesus, Smyrna,
Pergamos, Thyatria, Sardis, Philadelphia, Laodicea. The sun and moon
are also depicted, and the basin and chafing dish.

instituted—eleven Knights took the vows of secrecy, friendship, and discretion, between the hands of the Patriarch of Jerusalem. The Lodge-room is in the shape of a heptagon, hung with crimson, sprinkled with stars of gold. In each angle is a square column; on the capitals of which are the initials, respectively, of the following words: Beauty, Divinity, Wisdom, Power, Honor, Glory, Force; and on the bases of these columns are the initials, respectively, of the words Friendship, Union, Resignation, Discretion, Fidelity, Prudence, and Temperance. On each column is a brilliant light. Bodies of this degree are called Preceptories. The Master is styled Venerable, and represents John the Baptist. The jewel is a heptagonal medal of gold and silver. On one side are engraved, at the angles, the same letters as are upon the square columns, with a star over each. In the center of it on the same side, is a lamb, lying on a book with seven seals; on the seals are, respectively, the same letters. On the reverse side are two swords crosswise, points upward, and the hilts resting on an even balance; in the corners are the initials of the seven churches.

KNIGHT OF THE HOLY SEPULCHER. St. Helena, daughter of Coylus, King of Great Britain, visited Jerusalem in 296, in search of the cross and sepulcher of Christ. Having been, as it is said, successful, she instituted this order in 302, which was confirmed by Pope Marcellinus in 304. The duties enjoined on the Knights were; 1. Feed the Hungry; 2. Give drink to the thirsty; 3. Clothe the naked; 4. Visit and ransom captives; 5. Harbor the homeless, and give the widow and orphan where to lay their heads; 6. Visit and relieve the sick; 7. Bury the dead.

KNIGHT KADOSH, or KNIGHT OF THE WHITE AND BLACK EAGLE. The 30th degree of the Ancient and Accepted rite. There are several degrees known as Kadoshes. The French rituals mention seven: 1. That of the Hebrews; 2. That of the first Christians; 3. That of the Crusades; 4. That of the Templars; 5. That of Cromwell, or the Puritans; 6. That of the Jesuits; 7. The Grand Veritable Kadosh, "apart from every sect, free of all ambition, which opens its arms to all men, and has no enemies other than vice, crime, fanaticism, and superstition." Its ritual furnishes the history of the destruction of the Templars by the united efforts of Philip of France and Pope Clement V. In this degree, when there is a reception, four apartments are used. In the first and second apartments, the Lodge is termed Council; in the third, Areopagus; in the fourth, the Senate. The presiding officer is styled Most Illustrious Grand Commander. The jewel is a Teutonic cross, and is thus described, in heraldic language: "A cross potent sable, charged with another cross double potent or, surcharged with an escutcheon, bearing the letters J. B. M.; the principal cross surmounted by a chief, azure semé of France." On the reverse, a skull transpierced by a poniard. The stated meetings of all councils of Kadosh are held January 6; on Good Friday; on Ascension day, and on November 2, in each year. No one of these is ever, on any account, to be omitted.

KNIGHTS AND LADIES OF THE DOVE. In the year 1784 a secret society of both sexes was framed on the model of Freemasonry; its meetings were held at Versailles under the title of *Chevaliers et Chevalières de la Colombe.* Its existence was of brief duration.

KNIGHTS OF MALTA. The Knights of St. John of Jerusalem, afterward known as Knights of Rhodes, and finally called Knights of Malta. This society was organized as a military order about the year 1048, for the protection of pilgrims who visited Jerusalem. They became eminent for their devotion to the cause of religion, their boundless charity, and noble hospitality; rapidly increased in numbers and in wealth. After long and bloody contests with the infidels they were finally driven from Palestine, when they took possession of Cyprus, which they soon lost again, and hen established themselves on the island of Rhodes; at which time (1309) they took the name of Knights of Rhodes. They held this island for a period of two hundred years, when they were attacked by the Turks and driven from it. After this disaster they successively retired to Castro, Messino, and other places, until, in 1530, when the Emperor Charles V. bestowed upon them the island of Malta, on the condition of their defending it from the depredations of the Turks and pirates who then infested the Mediterranean. At this time they assumed the title of Knights of Malta, by which name they have ever since been known. In 1565, the island of Malta was besieged by Soliman II. and thirty thousand Turkish soldiers, on which occasion the Knights suffered immense loss, from which they never entirely recovered. After one of the most persistent and noble defenses known in modern warfare, the brave Knights were overcome, the fort of St. Elmo was taken, and the island was, for a time, in the hands of the infidels. At length the promised succor came; the viceroy of Sicily, with a large army, reached the island in safety, the troops disembarked; and, though the Turks still possessed the advantage of numbers, a panic seized them,

DEFENSE OF FORT SAINT ELMO, MALTA, AGAINST THE TURKS, IN 1565, BY THE KNIGHTS OF MALTA, UNDER THE COMMAND OF JOHN DE LA VALETTE, GRAND MASTER.

and they fled. Joy and triumph succeeded to danger and dread. This may justly be regarded as the last great event in the military history of the Order of St. John. The siege was raised Sept. 8, 1565, and so late as the year 1784, at Malta on that day, an annual procession was solemnly made in memory of their deliverance. June 9, 1798, the island of Malta was taken by the French, under Bonaparte. In the same year the Knights chose Paul I., Emperor of Russia, as Grand Master, who took them under his protection. Upon the reduction of the island by the English, in 1800, the chief seat of the Order was transferred to Catania, in Sicily, whence in 1826, it was removed by authority of the Pope to Ferrara. The last public reception of the Order took place at Sonneburg in 1800, when Leopold, King of Belgium, Prince Ernest, and several other noblemen were created Knights according to the long-established customs of the Order. The assembly is called a Council. The officers are: 1. Commander; 2. Generalissimo; 3. Captain General; 4. Prelate; 5. Senior Warden; 6. Junior Warden; 7. Treasurer; 8. Recorder; 9. First Grand; 10. Second Grand; 11. Standard Bearer; 12. Warder; 13. Sentinel. The Order must be conferred in an asylum of a legal Commandery of Knights Templar, or in a Council of the Order of Malta, regularly convened for the purpose, distinct from, and after, the Templar's Order. The ancient ceremonies of reception were simple and impressive: "The novice was made to understand that he was 'about to put off the old man, and to be regenerated;' and having received absolution, was required to present himself in a secular habit, without a girdle, in order to appear perfectly free on entering into so sacred an engagement, and with a burning taper in his hand, representing chastity. He then received the holy communion, and afterward presented himself 'most respectfully before the person who was to perform the ceremony, and requested to be received into the company of Brothers, and into the Holy Order of the Hospital of Jerusalem.' The rules of the Order, the obligations he was about to take upon himself, and the duties that would be required of him being explained, he, with great solemnity, vowed and promised 'to render henceforward, by the grace of God, perfect obedience to the Superior placed over him by the choice of the Order, to live without personal property, and to preserve his chastity.' The brother who received him then said as follows: 'We acknowledge you the servant of the poor and sick, and as having consecrated yourself to the service of the church.' To which he answered: 'I acknowledge myself as such.' He then kissed the book and returned it to the brother, who received him, in token of personal obedience. He was then invested with the mantle of the Order, in such a manner as that the cross fell on his left breast. A variety of other minor ceremonies followed, and the whole was concluded with a series of appropriate and solemn prayers." The Order of the Knight of Malta is conferred in a Commandery of Knights Templar, and is acknowledged in the United States as one of the orders of Masonic knighthood.

KNIGHT OF THE MEDITERRANEAN PASS, some times called KNIGHT OF ST. PAUL. An honorary degree, conferred on Knights Templar and Knights of Malta. Its ceremonies are very impressive, and its organization into councils, governed by appropriate officers, assimilates its forms to that of one of the regular degrees of Masonry. The ritual of this degree informs us that it was founded about the year 1367, in consequence of certain events which occurred to the Knights of Malta. In an excursion made by a party of these Knights in search of forage and provisions, they were attacked while crossing the river Offanto (the ancient Aufidio), by a large body of Saracens, under the command of the renowned Amurath I. The Saracens had concealed themselves in ambush, and when the Knights were on the middle of the bridge which spanned the river, they were attacked by a sudden charge of their enemies upon both extremities of the bridge. A long and sanguinary contest ensued; the Knights fought with their usual valor, and were at length victorious. The Saracens were defeated with such immense slaughter that fifteen hundred of their dead bodies encumbered the bridge, and the river was literally stained with their blood. In commemoration of this event, and as a reward for their valor, the victorious Knights were affranchised in all parts of the Mediterranean coasts, that is to say, had free permission to pass and repass, wherever and whenever they pleased, from which circumstance the degree, which was then founded, received its name of "Mediterranean Pass." It will be seen from these details that there is no real connection between this degree and that given under the same name to Royal Arch Masons, although there is some internal evidence that the latter was surreptitiously obtained from, and is only a corruption of, the former. [See MEDITERRANEAN PASS.]

KNIGHT OF THE NINTH ARCH, sometimes called the ANCIENT ROYAL ARCH OF SOLOMON. The 13th degree of the Ancient and Accepted rite. The ceremonies of this degree afford abundant information on certain points, in which the sacred volume is not entirely free from obscurity, and these have reference to the mode in which Enoch, notwithstanding the destruction caused by the deluge, and the lapse of ages, was enabled to preserve the true name in its purity; that it might eventually be communicated to the first possessors of this degree. The body is called a Chapter, and represents the audience chamber of King Solomon. The hangings are alternately red and white. The presiding officer is styled "Thrice Potent Grand Master," and represents King Solomon. The apron and collar are purple, bordered with white. The jewel is a gold triangle: on one side is engraved the delta of Enoch, surrounded with rays; on the obverse is a representation of two persons letting down a third through a square opening into an arch. Around this device are the letters: "R. S. R. S. T. P. S. R. I. A. J. S., Anno Enochi, 2995.'

KNIGHTS AND NYMPHS OF THE ROSE. An Order of Adoptive or Androgynous Masonry, established in Paris toward the close of the eighteenth century; but its existence was brief. A full history of the ceremonies are furnished for the benefit of the curious. The place of meeting was called "The Temple of Love." It was ornamented with garlands of flowers, and hung round with escutcheons, on which were painted various devices and scenes of gallantry. There were two presiding officers, the man being styled Hierophant, the female the High-Priestess. The former initiated men, the latter women. The Conductor Assistant of the men was called Sentiment, that of the women Discretion. The Knights wore a crown of myrtle; the Nymphs a crown of roses. The Hierophant and High-Priestess wore, in addition, a rose-colored scarf, on which were embroidered two devices within a myrtle wreath. One dull taper was the only light during the initiation; at the closing business the hall was illuminated by numerous wax candles. When a candidate was to be initiated, he or she was taken in charge by Sentiment or Discretion, divested of all weapons, jewels, or money, hoodwinked, and loaded with chains, and conducted to the door of the Temple of Love, where admission was demanded by two knocks. When admitted and presented, the candidate was asked his or her name, country, condition in society, and having answered these questions was asked, "What are you now seeking?" to this the answer was, "Happiness." The interrogatory then proceeds a little further, "What is your age?" and the candidate has, if a male, to reply, "The age to love;" the female, "The age to please and to be loved." The candidate's feelings and opinions on matters of gallantry are further probed, and all being satisfactory, the chains are removed and replaced by garlands of flowers, which are called "the chains of love." After some other probationary exercises of a like character, the O B is administered: "I promise and swear by the Grand Master of the Universe

never to reveal the secrets of the Order of the Rose, an
should I fail in this my vow, may the mysteries I shall receiv
add nothing to my pleasures, and, instead of the roses (
happiness, may I find nothing but thorns of repentance
The candidates were then conducted to the mysterious grove
in the neighborhood of the Temple of Love, and during th
time there spent, slow and delicious music in march sty!
is played. These trials ended, the novice is next con
ducted to the altar of mystery, placed at the foot of th
Hierophant's throne, and there incense is offered to Venu
and her son Cupid; a brief space spent there, and after son
more ceremonies of a like character, the bandage is remove
from the novitiate's eyes, and with delicious music, and in
brilliantly lighted apartment, the signs and secrets al
communicated.

KNIGHT OF THE RED CROSS. This degree is int
mately connected with the circumstances related in the Roya
Arch degree, and cannot be conferred upon any one who he
not been exalted to that sublime degree. Its history date
from the close of the captivity of the Jews at Babylon, whe
Cyrus, King of Persia, at the solicitation of Zerubbabel, th
Prince of Judah, restored the Jews to liberty, and permitte
them to return to Jerusalem, to rebuild their city and templ
The ceremonies of the degree forcibly illustrate some of th
difficulties and interruptions encountered by them in the
labors. A full history of the degree will be found i
Josephus, and in the 3d and 4th chapters of the first Boc
of Esdras. It is the initiatory grade to the Templar's degre
The body is called a Council. The presiding officer is style
Sovereign Master.

KNIGHT OF THE ROYAL AXE, OR PRINCE OF LIBANU
The 22d degree of the Ancient and Accepted rite. The legen
of this degree informs us that it was instituted to recor
the memorable services rendered to Masonry by the might
cedars of Lebanon, as the Sidonian architects cut down th
cedars for the construction of Noah's ark. Our ancier
brethren do not tell us how the Israelites had the woc
conveyed to them from the land of promise to the mou
tains in the wilderness. They say, however, that th
descendants of the Sidonians were employed in the sam
place, in obtaining materials for the construction of th
ark of the covenant; and also, in later years, for buildin
Solomon's Temple; and, lastly, that Zerubbabel employe
laborers of the same people in cutting cedars of Lebano
for the use of the second temple. The tradition adds tha
the Sidonians formed colleges on Mount Libanus, and alwa

adored the G. A. O. T. U.* Bodies of this degree are styled Colleges. There are two apartments; the first representing the workshop at Lebanon, with axes, saws, mallets, planes, wedges, and such like implements. The room should be lighted with lamps or candles. In this apartment the Senior Warden presides, and is styled Master Carpenter. He and all the brethren wear blouses and aprons. The second apartment represents the council-room of the round table. It is hung with red, and lighted with 36 lights, arranged by sixes and each 6 by twos. In the center of the room is a round table around which the brethren sit; on the table are plans and mathematical instruments. The presiding officer is Chief Prince, who is styled Thrice Puissant. The

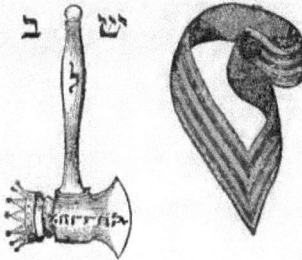

sash, to be worn from right to left, is a broad rainbow-colored ribbon, lined with purple. The apron is white, lined and bordered with purple; in the middle a round table is painted, on which are mathematical instruments, and plans unrolled. On the flap is a serpent with three heads. The jewel is a golden axe, crowned, having on the blade and handle the initials of several personages illustrious in the history of Masonry.

KNIGHT OF THE SUN, or Prince Adept. Sometimes known by the names "The Philosophical Lodge," "Prince of the Sun," "Key to Masonry." It is the 28th degree of

* Sidon was one of the most ancient cities of the world, and even in the time of Homer, the Sidonians were celebrated for their trade and commerce, their wealth and prosperity. The allusion to the "Colleges" on Mount Libanus may have some reference to the secret sect of the Druses, who still exist in that country, and whose mysterious ceremonies, travelers affirm, have considerable affinity to Freemasonry.

the Ancient and Accepted rite, and is strictly philosophical and scientific. The ceremonies and lecture, which are of great length, furnish a history of all the preceding degrees, and explain in the fullest manner the various Masonic emblems. The great object of the degree is to inspire men with the knowledge of Heavenly Truth, which is the pure source of all perfection, and as this virtue is one of the three great tenets of Masonry it deserves commendation. The body is styled a Council, and consists of not less than ten members. The walls should be painted to represent the open country, mountains, plains, forests and fields. The chamber is lighted by a single light, a great globe of ground glass, in the South; this represents the sun. The only additional light is from the transparencies. In the East is suspended a transparency, displaying the sign of the macrocosm, or of the seal of King Solomon—the interlaced triangles; one white and the other black. In the West is

suspended a transparency displaying the sign of a microcosm, or the pentagram traced on a pure white ground with lines of vermilion, and with a single point upward. Many other transparencies, symbolizing objects of great importance, are appropriately arranged around the chamber, particularly the accompanying figures, which are placed in the North. On the right hand of the presiding officer, in the East, on a gilt pedestal, is a *Caduceus*, gilded, the upper part of it a cross, surmounted by a globe; and with two serpents twining around it, their heads rising above the cross. The ceiling should represent the heavens, with the crescent moon in the West, the principal planets, and the stars, in the constellations Taurus and Orion and those near the polar star. The presiding officer is styled Father Adam. The Warden sits in the West, and is called Brother Truth; there are seven other officers, who are styled Brothers Gabriel, Auriel, Michael, Camaliel, Raphael, Zaphiel and Zarakhiel. The collar is a broad white watered ribbon; on the right side is

painted or embroidered an eye, in gold. The apron is of pure white lambskin, with no edging or ornament, except the penta-gram, which is traced on the middle of it with vermilion. The jewel is a medal of gold, on one side a full sun, on the other a globe. When the degree is con-ferred, no jewel or apron is worn.

KNIGHTS TEMPLAR. The natural desire of visiting those holy places which have been sanctified by the presence, and rendered memorable by the sufferings of the founder of the Christian religion, drew, during the early ages of Christianity, crowds of devout worshipers and pilgrims to Jerusalem. To such a height did this religious enthusiasm arrive that, in 1064, not less than 7,000 pilgrims assembled from all parts of Europe around the holy sepulcher. The year following Jerusalem was conquered by the wild Turco-mans, three thousand of the citizens were massacred, and the command over the holy city and territory was confided to the Emir Ortok, the chief of a savage pastoral tribe. Under the iron yoke of these fierce northern strangers, the Christians were fearfully oppressed; they were driven from their churches and plundered, and the patriach of the holy city was dragged by the hair of his head over the sacred pavement of the Church of the Resurrection, and cast into a dungeon, to extort a ransom from the sympathy of his flock. The intelligence of these cruelties aroused the religious chivalry of Christendom; "a nerve was touched of exquisite feeling, and the sensation vibrated to the heart of Europe." Then arose the wild enthusiasm of the Crusades, and men of all ranks, and even priests and monks, were animated with the "pious and glorious enterprise" of rescuing the holy sepulcher of Christ from the foul and polluting abomi-nations of the heathen. When the intelligence of the capture of Jerusalem by the Crusaders (A. D. 1099) had been conveyed to Europe, the zeal of pilgrimage blazed forth with increased fierceness. The infidels had, indeed, been driven out of Jerusalem, but not out of Palestine. The lofty mountains bordering the sea coast were infested by warlike bands of fugitive Musselmen, who maintained themselves in various impregnable castles and strongholds, from whence they issued forth upon the high roads, cut off the communication between Jerusalem and the seaports, and revenged themselves for the loss of their habita-tions and property by the indiscriminate pillage of all travelers. To alleviate the dangers and distresses to which they were exposed, nine noble gentlemen, who had greatly distinguished themselves at the siege and capture of Jerusalem, formed a holy brotherhood in arms, and entered into a solemn compact to aid one another in clearing the highways, and in protecting the pilgrims through the passes and defiles of the mountains, to the Holy City. Warmed with the religious and military fervor of the day, and animated by the sacredness of the cause to which they had devoted their swords, they called themselves the *Poor Fellow-soldiers of Jesus Christ.* In 1118 Baldwin II., King of Jerusalem, granted them a place of habitation within the sacred inclosure of the temple on Mount Moriah; thenceforward they became known by the name of "THE KNIGHTHOOD OF THE TEMPLE OF SOLOMON." The views and exertions of the Order now became more extensive, and it added to its profession, of protecting poor pilgrims, that of defending the kingdom of Jerusalem, and the whole eastern church, from the attacks of infidels. Hugues de Payens was chosen by the Knights to be the superior of the new religious and military society, by the title of "The Master of the Temple," and he has, consequently, generally been called the founder of the Order. The name and reputation of the Order spread rapidly through Europe, and many princes, nobles, and gentlemen of the best houses of France, Germany, Italy, and England, became members of it. In 1128 they received rules and regulations for their governance from the Pope, which had been expressly arranged for them by St. Bernard. The illustrious Order of the Temple has, through many vicissitudes, survived to our times; and, indeed, of late years a great, and we may say an astonishing, influence has been exercised in the Masonic Craft by this brotherhood in England, on the continent of Europe, and in the United States. Notwithstanding the persecution the Order was subjected to, consequent upon the machinations of Philip le Bel and Pope Clement, it continued to exist, if not to flourish. Jaques de Molay, the martyred Grand Master, in anticipation of his fate, appointed his successor to rule the Fraternity, and from that time to the present there has been an uninterrupted succession of Grand Masters. It is true that as years passed on, and clouds arose still more ominous to the existence of the society, the Templars were amalgamated with their ancient brothers in arms, the Knights of Malta. The Knights Templar degree is highly valued in all countries, and its ritual is nearly identical. The candidate for its honors must be a Royal Arch Mason, and as such he presents himself at the Commandery—as the bodies are called—in the character and garb of a pilgrim, cr palmer, as they were designated in the Holy Land; he figuratively undergoes seven years' travel, and then seven years' warfare, when, having conducted himself courageously through his trials, he is finally admitted into the Order. There is not a vestige of Freemasonry, as such, in the degree, save the absolute necessity of candidates having been admitted into the Royal Arch. The throne is situated in the East, above which is suspended a white banner, on which is painted a red passion cross, edged with gold and irradiated at the crossings with rays of light; on the right and left are two sky-blue banners, on one of which is painted a Paschal Lamb and a red Templar's Cross, with the words "The will of God." On the other, the emblems of the Order are displayed. The symbolic colors of the Order are white and black, properly interspersed with gold and silver. The Grand Standard of the Order is displayed in the West, in charge of the Standard-bearer. The Beauseant, or battle-flag of the Ancient Templars, is displayed in the South, in charge of the Senior Warden. The following is the Templar uniform adopted by the Grand Encampment of the United States, September, 1862: *Full Dress*—Black frock coat, black pantaloons, scarf, sword, belt, shoulder-straps, gauntlets and chapeau, with appropriate trimmings. *Fatigue Dress*—Same as full dress, except for chapeau a black cloth cap, navy form, with appropriate cross in front, and for gauntlets white gloves. In the United States, the assembly is called a Commandery, and has the following officers: 1. Eminent Commander; 2. Generalissimo; 3. Captain General; 4. Prelate; 5. Senior Warden; 6. Junior Warden; 7. Treasurer; 8. Recorder; 9. Standard-Bearer; 10. Sword-Bearer; 11. Warder; 12. Three Guards; 13. Sentinel. Commanderies are dedicated to Saint John the Almoner. The candidate receiving this Order is said to be "dubbed and created a Knight of the valiant and magnanimous Order of Knights Templar." The motto of the Order is, "*In hoc signo vinces*"—in this sign we conquer.

KNIGHT OF THE THREE KINGS. An honorary or side degree of high moral character. Its history connects it with the completion and dedication of the first temple. The presiding officer represents King Solomon. It is intended, by an appropriate ceremony and interesting legend, to portray the beauty of that harmony and peace which should exist among all Masons, and it has been often used in a judicious manner, and on appropriate occasions, to reconcile differences among Masons, and to subdue that spirit of strife which will sometimes exhibit itself in despite of the philanthropic lessons of our Order. It may be communicated by one Master Mason to another, but to be conferred in ample form the presence of at least five Knights is necessary.

KNIGHT OF THE TRIPLE CROSS. This Order was founded in 1080. It is held in a Sovereign Council. The Master is styled Grand Commander; the Wardens Sublime Knights; the Master of Ceremonies Grand Esquire, and the other members Knights. The jewel is three crosses arranged in a square. History—In 1080, Solyman, Prince of the Turks, established the seat of his Empire, or rather of his tyranny, at Nicopolis, in Syria Minor. Among many pilgrims who then resorted to the holy places of Palestine a Frenchman, named Pierre Clement, made the journey to Jerusalem, in 1093, and then, conferring with Simon the patriarch, offered to convey letters from him to the Pope and all the western princes, to arouse them to expel from the Holy Land those barbarians and infidels. The good patriarch accepted his offer, and entrusted to him all the letters for which he asked. Pierre Clement embarked without delay, and repaired to the court of the Pope, where he presented the letters of the patriarch to Urban II., who sent him into all the provinces on either side of the Alps, to negotiate with the princes, and publicly to preach the crusades. All who were made acquainted with the designs of the Pope exhibited much zeal for so holy an undertaking; but Urban thought it fitting to convoke a council, in which he himself presided. During this council, which was held in 1095, he addressed the members in the great hall of the city, and so excited the council, that all cried out together, as if in concert, "*Dieu le Veut!*" The Pope willed that a cry, which was so good an omen, should become the device of the whole army, be borne on the flags and standards, and be the war-cry of the soldiery, and even of their captains in battle, to animate each other to deeds of daring. And he determined that those who enlisted in this service should wear a red cross upon the right shoulder, to show that they were the soldiers of him who had conquered the cross. Many princes took up the cross, and they were conjointly the chiefs of that holy enterprise, without any one of them claiming to have the right to command the others.

KNIGHT OF THE TRUE LIGHT. A mystical Order founded in Austria, A. D. 1780, probably by Baron Hans Heinrich and some of his friends. Its ritual and teachings were a mixture of the mysteries of Rosicrucians and Asiatic brothers. It had five degrees: 1. Knight Novice of the third year; 2. Knight Novice of the fifth year; 3. Knight Novice of the seventh year; 4. Levite; 5. Priest. This Order belongs to the Hermetic or Alchemistical system of Masonry.

L.

LABARUM. The imperial standard of Constantine the Great, Emperor of Rome, which he caused to be formed in commemoration of the vision of the cross in the heavens. It

is described as a long pike surmounted by a golden crown, inclosing a monogram which contains the two first letters of the name of Christ, and is at the same time a representation of the figure of the cross. The silken banner which depended from it was embroidered with the figure of Constantine and his family. The labarum is engraved on some of his medals with the famous inscription, EN TOYTΩ NIKA; and it was preserved for a considerable time, and brought forward at the head of the armies of the emperor on important occasions as the palladium or safe-guard of the empire.*

LABYRINTH. A place full of inextricable windings. In the ancient mysteries the passages through which the initiate made his mystical pilgrimage.

* Dr. Oliver, in his "Historical Landmarks," (Am. ed., p. 89,) furnishes the following illustration and explanation of the vision of Constantine: "The Red Cross of Constantine commemorates the following circum-

stance, which is attested by Eusebius: The army of Constantine being on the march to meet the enemies of the cross, it happened one evening when the sun was declining, and the emperor was engaged in devotion, that there suddenly appeared a pillar of light in the heavens like a cross, whereon was an inscription expressed in letters formed by a configuration of stars—TOYTΩ NIKA, *in this overcome.* Constantine was not a little startled at this sight, and so was the whole army that beheld it. They looked upon it as an inauspicious omen, and even the emperor himself was confounded. But at night our Lord appeared to him in a dream, with the cross in his hand, commanding him to make a royal standard like that which he had seen in the heavens, and cause it to be borne before him in his wars as an ensign of victory."

"Constantine, in his contest with Maxentius, and on his march to Rome, is said to have seen in the sky a luminous cross with the inscription, ἐν τούτῳ νικα, by this, conquer; and on the night before the last and decisive battle with Maxentius a vision is said to have appeared to Constantine in his sleep, bidding him inscribe the shields of his soldiers with the sacred monogram of the name of Christ. The miracle of his conversion to Christianity was commemorated by the imperial standard of the *labarum*, at the summit of which was the monogram of the name of Christ."--SMITH'S CLASSICAL DICTIONARY.

LANDMARKS, MASONIC. Literally, and in a general sense, anything by which the boundary of a property is defined. In ancient times the correct division of lands was an object of great importance. Stones, trees, and hillocks were the usual landmarks. The removal of a landmark was considered a heinous crime by the Jewish law, as may be judged by the denunciation of Moses: "Cursed be he that removeth his neighbor's landmark." Of the nature of the landmarks of Masonry there has been some diversity of opinion; yet the conviction has become settled that the true principles consti-tuting landmarks are those universal customs of the Order which have gradually grown into permanent rules of action, and originally established by competent authority, at a period so remote that no account of their origin is to be found in the records of Masonic history, and which were considered essential to the preservation and integrity of the institution, to preserve its purity and prevent innovation. Dr. Albert G. Mackey, who has devoted much study and attention to the subject, enumerates the following as the unchangeable Landmarks of Masonry:

"1. The modes of recognition are, of all the landmarks, the most legiti-mate and unquestioned. They admit of no variation; and if ever they have suffered alteration or addition, the evil of such a violation of the ancient law has always made itself subse-quently manifest. An admission of this is to be found in the proceed-ings of the late Masonic Congress at Paris, where a proposition was presented to render these modes of recognition once more universal—a proposition which never would have been necessary if the integrity of this important landmark had been rigorously preserved.

"2. The division of symbolic Masonry into three degrees is a landmark that has been better preserved than almost any other, although even here the mischievous spirit of innovation has left its traces, and by the disruption of its concluding portion from the third degree, a want of uniformity has been created in respect to the final teaching of the Master's order; and the Royal Arch of England, Scot-land, Ireland, and America, and the 'high degrees' of France and Ger-many, are all made to differ in the mode of which they lead the neo-phyte to the great consummation of all symbolic Masonry. In 1813, the Grand Lodge of England vindicated the ancient landmark, by solemnly enacting that Ancient Craft Masonry consisted of the three degrees of Entered Apprentice, Fellow-Craft, and Master Mason, including the Holy Royal Arch. But the disrup-tion has never been healed, and the landmark, although acknowledged in its integrity by all, still continues to be violated.

"3. The legend of the third de-gree is an important landmark, the integrity of which has been well preserved. There is no rite of Masonry, practiced in any country or language, in which the essential elements of this legend are not taught. The lectures may vary, and, indeed, are constantly changing, but the legend has ever remained sub-stantially the same. And it is necessary that it should be so, for the legend of the temple builder constitutes the very essence and identity of Masonry. Any rite which should exclude it, or materially alter it, would at once, by that exclusion or alteration, cease to be a Masonic rite.

"4. The government of the Frater-nity by a presiding officer called a Grand Master, who is elected from the body of the Craft, is a fourth landmark of the Order. Many persons ignorantly suppose that the election of the Grand Master is held in consequence of a law or regulation of the Grand Lodge. Such, however, is not the case. The office is indebted for its existence to a landmark of the Order. Grand Masters are to be found in the records of the institution long before Grand Lodges were established; and if the present system of legislative government by Grand Lodges were to be abolished, a Grand Master would still be necessary. In fact, although there has been a period within the records of history, and, indeed, of very recent date, when a Grand Lodge was unknown, there never has been a time when the Craft did not have their Grand Master.

"5. The prerogative of the Grand Master to preside over every assembly of the Craft, wheresoever and whensoever held, is a fifth landmark. It is in consequence of this law, derived from ancient usage, and not from any special enactment, that the Grand Master assumes the chair, or, as it is called in England, 'the throne,' at every communication of the Grand Lodge; and that he is also entitled to preside at the communication of every subordinate lodge, where he may happen to be present.

"6. The prerogative of the Grand Master to grant dispensations for conferring degrees at irregular times is another, and a very important, landmark. The statutory law of Masonry requires a month, or other determinate period, to elapse between the presentation of a petition and the election of a candidate. But the Grand Master has the power to set aside or dispense with this probation, and to allow a candidate to be initiated at once. This prerogative he possessed, in common with all Masters, before the enactment of the law requiring a probation, and, as no statute can impair his prerogative, he still retains the power, although the masters of lodges no longer possess it.

"7. The prerogative of the Grand Master to give dispensations for opening and holding lodges is another landmark. He may grant, in virtue of this, to a sufficient number of Masons, the privilege of meeting together and conferring degrees. The lodges thus established are called 'lodges under dispensation.' They are strictly creatures of the Grand Master, created by his authority, existing only during his will and pleasure, and liable at any moment to be dissolved at his command. They may be continued for a day, a month, or six months; but whatever be the period of their existence, they are indebted for that existence solely to the grace of the Grand Master.

"8. The prerogative of the Grand Master to make Masons at sight is a landmark which is closely connected with the preceding one. There has been much misapprehension in relation to this landmark, which misapprehension has sometimes led to a denial of its existence in jurisdictions where the Grand Master was, perhaps, at the very time substantially exercising the prerogative, without the slightest remark or opposition. It is not to be supposed that the Grand Master can retire with a profane into a private room, and there, without assistance, confer the degrees of Freemasonry upon him. No such prerogative exists, and yet many believe that this is the so-much-talked-of right of 'making Masons at sight.' The real mode and the only mode of exercising the prerogative is this: The Grand Master summons to his assistance not less than six other Masons, convenes a Lodge, and without any previous probation, but on *sight* of the candidate, confers the degrees upon him, after which he dissolves the Lodge, and dismisses the brethren. Lodges thus convened for special purposes are called 'occasional lodges.' This is the only way in which any Grand Master within the records of the institution has ever been known to 'make a Mason at sight.' The prerogative is dependent upon that of granting dispensations to open and hold lodges. If the Grand Master has the power of granting to any other

Mason the privilege of presiding over lodges working by his dispensation, he may assume this privilege of presiding to himself; and as no one can deny his right to revoke his dispensation granted to a number of brethren at a distance, and to dissolve the Lodge at his pleasure, it will scarcely be contended that he may not revoke his dispensation for a Lodge over which he himself has been presiding within a day, and dissolve the Lodge as soon as the business for which he had assembled it is accomplished. The making of Masons at sight is only the conferring of the degrees by the Grand Master, at once, in an occasional Lodge, constituted by his dispensing power for the purpose, and over which he presides in person.

"9. The necessity for Masons to congregate in lodges is another Landmark. It is not to be understood by this that any ancient Landmark has directed that permanent organization of subordinate lodges which constitutes one of the features of the Masonic system as it now prevails. But the Landmarks of the Order always prescribed that Masons should, from time to time, congregate together for the purpose of either operative or speculative labor, and that these congregations should be called Lodges. Formerly these were extemporary meetings called together for special purposes, and then dissolved, the brethren departing to meet again at other times and other places, according to the necessity of circumstances. But warrants of constitution, by-laws, permanent officers and annual arrears are modern innovations wholly outside the Landmarks, and dependent entirely on the special enactments of a comparatively recent period.

"10. The government of the Craft, when so congregated in a Lodge by a Master and two Wardens, is also a Landmark. To show the influence of this ancient law, it may be observed, by the way, that a congregation of Masons meeting together under any other government, as that for instance of a president and vice-president, or a chairman and sub-chairman, would not be recognized as a Lodge. The presence of a Master and two Wardens is as essential to the valid organization of a Lodge as a warrant of constitution is at the present day. The names, of course, vary in different languages, the Master, for instance, being called 'Venerable' in French Masonry, and the Wardens, 'Surveillants,' but the officers, their number, prerogatives and duties are everywhere identical.

"11. The necessity that every Lodge, when congregated, should be duly tiled, is an important Landmark of the institution, which is never neglected. The necessity of this law arises from the esoteric character of Masonry. As a secret institution, its portals must, of course, be guarded from the intrusion of the profane, and such a law must, therefore, always, have been in force from the very beginning of the Order. It is, therefore, properly classed among the ancient Landmarks. The office of tiler is wholly independent of any special enactment of Grand or Subordinate Lodges, although these may and do prescribe for him additional duties, which vary in different jurisdictions. But the duty of guarding the door, and keeping off cowans and eavesdroppers, is an ancient one, which constitutes a Landmark for his government.

"12. The right of every Mason to be represented in all general meetings of the Craft, and to instruct his representatives, is a twelfth Landmark. Formerly, these general meetings, which were usually held once a year, were called 'General Assemblies,' and all the Fraternity, even to the youngest Entered Apprentice, were permitted to be present. Now they are called 'Grand Lodges,' and only the Masters and Wardens of the subordinate lodges are summoned. But this is simply as the representatives of their members. Originally, each Mason represented himself; now he is represented by his officers. This was a concession granted by the Fraternity about 1717, and of course does not affect the integrity of the Landmark, for the principle of representation is still preserved.

The concession was only made for purposes of convenience.

"13. The right of every Mason to appeal from the decision of his brethren in Lodge convened, to the Grand Lodge or General Assembly of Masons, is a Landmark highly essential to the preservation of justice, and the prevention of oppression. A few modern Grand Lodges, in adopting a regulation that the decision of subordinate lodges, in cases of expulsion, cannot be wholly set aside upon an appeal, have violated this unquestioned Landmark, as well as the principles of just goverment.

"14. The right of every Mason to visit and sit in every regular Lodge is an unquestionable Landmark of the Order. This is called 'the right of visitation.' This right of visitation has always been recognized as an inherent right, which inures to every Mason as he travels through the world. And this is because lodges are justly considered as only divisions for convenience of the universal Masonic family. This right may, of course, be impaired or forfeited on special occasions by various circumstances; but when admission is refused to a Mason in good standing, who knocks at the door of a Lodge as a visitor, it is to be expected that some good and sufficient reason shall be furnished for this violation of what is in general a Masonic right, founded on the Landmarks of the Order.

"15. It is a Landmark of the Order that no visitor, unknown to the brethren present, or to some one of them as a Mason, can enter a Lodge without first passing an examination according to ancient usage. Of course, if the visitor is known to any brother present to be a Mason in good standing, and if that brother will vouch for his qualifications, the examination may be dispensed with, as the Landmark refers only to the cases of strangers, who are not to be recognized unless after strict trial, due examination or lawful information.

"16. No Lodge can interfere in the business of another Lodge, nor give degrees to brethren who are members of other lodges. This is undoubtedly an ancient Landmark, founded on the great principles of courtesy and fraternal kindness, which are at the very foundation of our institution. It has been repeatedly recognized by subsequent statutory enactments of all Grand Lodges.

"17. It is a Landmark that every Freemason is amenable to the laws and regulations of the Masonic jurisdiction in which he resides, and this although he may not be a member of any Lodge. Nonaffiliation, which is, in fact, in itself, a Masonic offense, does not exempt a Mason from Masonic jurisdiction.

"18. Certain qualifications of candidates for initiation are derived from a Landmark of the Order. These qualifications are that he shall be a man—shall be unmutilated, free-born, and of mature age. That is to say, a woman, a cripple, or a slave, or one born in slavery, is disqualified for initiation into the rites of Masonry. Statutes, it is true, have from time to time been enacted, enforcing or explaining these principles; but the qualifications really arise from the very nature of the Masonic institution, and from its symbolic teachings, and have always existed as Landmarks.

"19. A belief in the existence of God, as the Grand Architect of the Universe, is one of the most important Landmarks of the Order. It has been always deemed essential that a denial of the existence of a Supreme and Superintending Power is an absolute disqualification for initiation. The annals of the Order never yet have furnished or could furnish an instance in which an avowed atheist was ever made a Mason. The very initiatory ceremonies of the first degree forbid and prevent the possibilty of so monstrous an occurrence.

"20. Subsidiary to this belief in God, as a Landmark of the Order, is the belief in a resurrection to a future life. This Landmark is not so positively impressed on the candidate by exact words as the preceding; but the doctrine is taught by very plain implication, and runs through the whole symbolism of the Order. To believe in Masonry, and not to believe in a resurrection, would be an absurd anomaly, which could only be excused by the reflection, that he who thus confounded his belief and his skepticism was so ignorant of the meaning of both theories as to have no rational foundation for his knowledge of either.

"21. It is a Landmark that a 'Book of the Law' shall constitute an indispensable part of the furniture of every Lodge. I say, advisedly, *Book of the Law*, because it is not absolutely required that everywhere the Old and New Testaments shall be used. The 'Book of the Law' is that volume which, by the religion of the country, is believed to contain the revealed will of the Grand Architect of the Universe. Hence, in all lodges in Christian countries, the Book of the Law is composed of the Old and New Testaments; in a country where Judaism was the prevailing faith, the Old Testament alone would be sufficient; and in Mohammedan countries, and among Mohammedan Masons, the Koran might be substituted. Masonry does not attempt to interfere with the peculiar religious faith of its disciples, except so far as relates to the belief in the existence of God, and what necessarily results from that belief. The Book of the Law is to the speculative Mason his spiritual trestle-board; without this he cannot labor; whatever he believes to be the revealed will of the Grand Architect constitutes for him this spiritual trestle-board, and must ever be before him in his hours of speculative labor, to be the rule and guide of his conduct. The Landmark, therefore, requires that a Book of the Law, a religious code of some kind, purporting to be an exemplar of the revealed will of God, shall form an essential part of the furniture of every Lodge.

"22. The equality of all Masons is another Landmark of the Order. This equality has no reference to any subversion of those gradations of rank which have been instituted by the usages of society. The monarch, the nobleman, or the gentleman is entitled to all the influence, and receives all the respect which rightly belong to his exalted position. But the doctrine of Masonic equality implies that, as children of one great Father, we meet in the Lodge upon the level—that on that level we are all traveling to one predestined goal—that in the Lodge genuine merit shall receive more respect than boundless wealth, and that virtue and knowledge alone should be the basis of all Masonic honors, and be rewarded with preferment. When the labors of the Lodge are over, and the brethren have retired from their peaceful retreat, to mingle once more with the world, each will then again resume that social position, and exercise the privileges of that rank, to which the customs of society entitle him.

"23. The secrecy of the institution is another, and a most important, Landmark. There is some difficulty in precisely defining what is meant by a 'secret society.' If the term refers, as, perhaps, in strictly logical language it should, to those associations whose designs are concealed from the public eye, and whose members are unknown, which produce their results in darkness, and whose operations are carefully hidden from the public gaze—a definition which will be appropriate to many political clubs and revolutionary combinations in despotic countries, where reform, if it is at all to be effected, must be effected by stealth—then clearly Freemasonry is not a secret society. Its design is not only publicly proclaimed, but is vaunted by its disciples as something to be venerated—its disciples are known, for its membership is considered an honor to be coveted—it works for a result of which it boasts—the civilization and refinement of man, the amelioration of his condition, and the reformation of his manners. But if by a secret society is meant—and this is the most popular understanding of the term—a society in which there is a certain amount of knowledge, whether it be of methods of recognition, or of legendary and traditional learning, which is imparted to those only who have passed through an established form of initiation, the form itself being also concealed or esoteric, then in this sense is Freemasonry undoubtedly a secret society. Now this form of secrecy is a form inherent in it, existing with it from its very foundation, and secured to it by its ancient Landmarks. If divested of its secret character, it would lose its identity, and would cease to be Freemasonry. Whatever objections may, therefore, be made to the institution, on account of its secrecy, and however much some unskillful brethren have been willing in times of trial, for the sake of expediency, to divest it of its secret character, it will be ever impossible to do so, even were the Landmark not standing before us as an insurmountable obstacle; because such change of its character would be social suicide, and the death of the Order would follow its legalized exposure. Freemasonry, as a secret association, has lived unchanged for centuries—as an open society it would not last for as many years.

"24. The foundation of a speculative science upon an operative art, and the symbolic use and explanation of the terms of that art, for purposes of religious or moral teaching, constitute another Landmark of the Order. The Temple of Solomon was the cradle of the institution, and, therefore, the reference to the operative Masonry, which constructed that magnificent edifice, to the materials and implements which were employed in its construction, and to the artists who were engaged in the building, are all competent and essential parts of the body of Freemasonry, which could not be subtracted from it without an entire destruction of the whole identity of the Order. Hence, all the comparatively modern rites of Masonry, however they may differ in other respects, religiously preserve this temple history and these operative elements, as the substratum of all their modifications of the Masonic system.

"25. The last and crowning Landmark of all is that these Landmarks can never be changed. Nothing can be subtracted from them—nothing can be added to them—not the slightest modification can be made in them. As they were received from our predecessors, we are bound by the most solemn obligations of duty to transmit them to our successors. Not one jot or one tittle of these unwritten laws can be repealed; for, in respect to them, we are not only willing, but compelled to adopt the language of the sturdy old barons of England—'nolumus leges mutari.'"

Dr. Oliver, than whom no Masonic writer is better qualified to render a correct opinion on this important subject, favors us with these as the Landmarks of Freemasonry:

"In the absence of positive evidence we will endeavor to ascertain, on the authority of ancient documents, what were considered Landmarks by the Craft at the earliest period on record, as they were collected and handed down to us in the Lectures which were used during the last century.

"1. OPENING AND CLOSING THE LODGE.—To begin with the beginning: The opening and closing of the Lodge include many important Landmarks, which are absolutely indispensable to the integrity of the Order. For instance, if a Lodge be opened in the absence of a stipulated number of brethren; or by any other than the proper officers, and unaccompanied by the prescribed batteries or reports; if this essential ceremony be performed without enumerating the principal and assistant officers, together with a description of their several duties, and including a reference to the cardinal points of the compass; if it be done in an untiled Lodge, or without the brethren appearing in Order as Masons; or if the solemn invocation to T. G. A. O. T. U. be omitted; then the meeting would forfeit the character of a Lodge of Masons, its transactions would be illegal, and the brethren would become liable to an indictment for irregularity and a violation of the established Landmarks. At the closing of the Lodge, similar ceremonies have been transmitted to us from the most ancient times, and their observance invests the proceedings with solemnity and decorum; until the members are finally dismissed with an exhortation to fidelity—which is an unchangeable Landmark—and they depart in peace, harmony, and brotherly love.

"2. MEET ON THE LEVEL AND PART ON THE SQUARE.—This Landmark was originally introduced into the lectures, to show that the Order, although confessedly based on the principle of equality, is not the exponent of that species of communism which would destroy rank, equalize property, and reduce society to the common level of a savage state. Nor do its members look forward to the period which was so ardently desired by Condorcet, 'when the sun shall shine on none but free men; when a man shall recognize no other master than his reason; when tyrants and their slaves—when priests, together with their stupid and hypocritical agents, will have no further existence but in history or on the stage.' It is only when the Lodge is open that the brethren, without any reference to a diversity of rank, are equal; and during the process of working the lectures, each bears the burden assigned to him by the Master for the furtherance of that common object the acquisition of knowledge. But having met on the level, they part on the square.

"3. CONCERNING CANDIDATES.— By studying the Landmarks, an industrious brother will acquire an accurate knowledge of the boundaries within which his investigations ought to be confined. And for want of some such incipient training, many a zealous Mason has abandoned the Order in despair. There is one rule respecting candidates which every brother ought to understand distinctly, as an inalienable Landmark in Masonry; that *no one can, under any circumstances, invite his friend to become a Mason*, because

a disappointed candidate would then have it in his power to say that he had been inveigled into the Order for the sake of the fee; which would bring upon it a scandal, rather than a benefit. Every person who offers himself for initiation is, therefore, bound by another stringent Landmark, which the Grand Lodge of England has invested with the authority of a law, solemnly to declare that he has not been biased by the solicitations of friends, or by any mercenary or other unworthy motive; and that his request for admission is made from a favorable opinion of the institution, and a desire of knowledge. Thus, in the beautiful language of the lectures, he must freely and voluntarily ask, if he would have; seek, if he would find; and knock, if he wishes the door of Masonry to be opened for his admission into the Order.

"4. ADMISSION OF CANDIDATES.— To prevent disappointments of this nature from being of frequent occurrence, another Landmark directs the brethren of a Lodge to proceed with great deliberation in the admission of candidates, by making a strict perquisition, before the ballot is taken, into the character they sustain among their neighbors and friends. This may be ascertained with sufficient accuracy by a careful examination of their antecedents, and the testimony of those with whom they have been connected in the affairs of business or the pursuits of pleasure. The most ancient Landmarks that we are acquainted with provide that 'the son of a bondman shall not be admitted as an apprentice, lest his introduction into the Lodge should cause dissatisfaction among the brethren;' and that the candidate must be of good morals, without blemish, and have the full and proper use of his limbs; for 'a maimed man,' as the York Constitutions express it, 'can do the Craft no good.' By the assistance of these plain and simple directions, added to others which have been subsequently enjoined by Speculative Grand Lodges, no difficulty can arise in estimating the qualifications of a candidate for initiation.

"5. **The Ballot.**—Every facility is afforded for making the necessary inquiries. The laws and Landmarks equally provide that, before a candidate can be admitted, he must be proposed in open Lodge, and a notice to that effect served on each individual member in the ensuing summons, with his name, occupation, and place of abode, distinctly specified. And to afford ample time for deliberate investigation, the ballot cannot legally be taken, except in cases of emergency, till the next regular lodge-night; when, if approved, the candidate may receive the first degree; because it is presumed that every brother, before he records his vote, has made due inquiry, and is perfectly satisfied that the candidate possesses the necessary qualifications to become a good and worthy Mason.

"6. **Preparation.**—Every existing institution is distinguished by some preliminary ceremony of admission which is inaccessible to those who are unable to establish an indisputable claim to participate in its privileges. The approved candidate in Freemasonry having sought in his mind and asked of his friend, its tiled door is now about to be opened and its secrets disclosed. The preparation is accompanied by ceremonies which, to a superficial thinker, may appear trifling and undignified, although they embody a series of references to certain sublime matters, which constitute the very essence of the institution, and contribute to its stability and permanent usefulness, if, in accordance with the advice of St. Paul, everything be done decently, and in Order. But ceremonies, considered abstractedly, are of little value, except as they contribute their aid to impress upon the mind scientific beauties and moral truths. And this is the peculiar characteristic of Freemasonry, which, although its rites and observances are studiously complicated throughout the whole routine of its consecutive degrees, does not contain a single ceremony that is barren of intellectual improvement; for they all bear a direct reference to certain ancient usages recorded in the Book which is always expanded on the pedestal in the East.

"7. **The Badge.**—In the lodges of the last century, some trifling varieties existed in the arrangements during the process of initiation; for a perfect uniformity, however desirable, had not been attained. To explain them here would be superfluous, and, perhaps, not altogether prudent. Suffice it to say that in some lodges the investiture took place before the candidate was entrusted with the peculiar secrets of the degree, while others practiced a formula similar to that which was enjoined at the Union in 1813. The Senior Warden performed the duty, and recommended the candidate to wear the apron as a badge of innocence and bond of friendship, in the full assurance that if he never disgraced that badge it would never disgrace him. There are other elementary Landmarks embodied in the initiation, but they are so well known and generally understood that it will scarcely be necessary to enumerate them, much less to go into the detail of a particular illustration, which, indeed, would be unauthorized, and constitute, if not a legal offense against the Constitutions of Masonry, at least a moral infringement of the O. B.

"8. **Tests of Industry.**—Every candidate at his initiation, should carefully note the particulars of the ceremony; and if there should happen to be some things which appear to his inexperience unnecessary, and others that he cannot exactly comprehend, he may conceive it to be within the bounds of probability that they will admit of a satisfactory explanation. For it is scarcely to be supposed, even by the most obtuse intellect, that in the nineteenth century educated men would meet together periodically to waste their time in unprofitable discussions; to lend the sanction of their names to propagate a fiction, or to engage in pursuits which lead to no advantageous result. Let the candidate use the means at his disposal to remove all false impressions, by studying his elementary exercise—

the tests of the first degree, which are enjoined by the authority of many Grand Lodges—and ought to be by all—as a proof of his industry, and a desire of knowledge; for they are intended to convey some preliminary insight into our allegorical system."

John W. Simons, in his excellent and popular work on the "Principles and Practice of Masonic Jurisprudence," offers the following to be the Landmarks of Masonry, in the proper sense of the term:

"1. A belief in the existence of a Supreme Being, and in the immortality of the soul.

"2. That the moral law, which inculcates, among other things, charity and probity, industry and sobriety, is the rule and guide of every Mason.

"3. Respect for, and obedience to, the civil law of the country, and the Masonic regulations of the jurisdiction where a Mason may reside.

"4. That new-made Masons must be free-born, of lawful age, and hale and sound at the time of making.

"5. The modes of recognition, and, generally, the rites and ceremonies of the three degrees of Ancient Craft Masonry.

"6. That no appeal can be taken to the Lodge, from the decision of the Master, or the Warden occupying the Chair in his absence.

"7. That no one can be the Master of a Warranted Lodge till he has been installed and served one year as Warden.

"8. That when a man becomes a Mason he not only acquires membership in the particular Lodge that admits him, but, in a general sense, he becomes one of the whole Masonic family; and hence he has a right to visit, masonically, every regular Lodge, except when such visit is likely to disturb the harmony or interrupt the working of the Lodge he proposes to visit.

"9. The prerogative of the Grand Master to preside over every assembly of the Craft, within his jurisdiction, to make Masons at sight in a regular Lodge, and to grant Dispensations for the formation of new lodges.

"10. That no one can be made a Mason, save in a regular Lodge, duly convened, after petition, and acceptance by unanimous ballot, except when made at sight by the Grand Master.

"11. That the ballot for candidates is strictly and inviolably secret.

"12. That a Lodge cannot try its Master.

"13. That every Mason is amenable to the laws and regulations of the jurisdiction in which he resides, even though he be a member of a particular lodge in some other jurisdiction.

"14. The right of the Craft at large to be represented in Grand Lodge, and to instruct their representatives.

"15. The general aim and form of the society, as handed down to us by the fathers, to be by us preserved inviolate, and transmitted to our successors forever."

Bro. Rob. Morris, in his "Code of Masonic Law," deduces these boundaries, marks of distinction, or immemorial laws, as the unalterable landmarks:

"1. The Masonic Landmarks are unchangeable and imperative.

"2. Masonry is a system, teaching, symbolically, piety, morality, science, charity and self-discipline.

"3. The Law of God is the rule and limit of Masonry.

"4. The civil law, so far as it accords with the Divine, is obligatory upon Masons.

"5. The Masonic Lodge and the Masonic institution are one and indivisible.

"6. Masonic qualifications regard the mental, moral, and physical nature of man.

"7. Personal worth and merit are the basis of official worth and merit.

"8. The official duties of Masonry are esoteric.

"9. The selection of Masonic material and the general labors of the Masonic Craft are exoteric.

"10. The honors of Masonry are the gratitude of the Craft and the approval of God.

"11. Masonic promotion, both private and official, is by grades.

"12. The Grand Master may have a Deputy.

"13. The head of the Lodge is the Master, duly elected by the Craft.

"14. The medium of communication between the head and the body of the Lodge is the Wardens, duly elected by the Craft.

"15. Obedience to the Master and Wardens is obligatory upon the members.

"16. Secrecy is an indispensable element of Masonry.

"17. The Grand Lodge is supreme in its sphere of jurisdiction, and controls both the subordinate lodges and individual Masons, but always subject to the Ancient Landmarks."

The Constitution of the Grand Lodge of New York sets forth, in a concise and masterly manner, the following as the Landmarks of the Order:

"1. That belief in the Supreme Being, 'The Great Architect of the Universe,' who will punish vice and reward virtue, is an indispensable pre-requisite to admission to Masonry.

"2. That the moral law which inculcates charity and probity, industry and sobriety, and obedience to law and civil government, is the rule and guide of every Mason, and to which strict conformity is required.

"3. That obedience to Masonic law and authority, being voluntarily assumed, is of perpetual obligation, and can only be divested by the sanction of the supreme government in Masonry.

"4. That the rites and ceremonies (which include th' *unwritten language*) of the true system of the Ancient York rite, and which constitute a part of the body of Masonry, are immutable, and that it is not in the power of any man, or body of men, to make innovations therein.

"5. That contention and lawsuits between brethren are contrary to the laws and regulations of Masonry.

"6. That charity is the right of a Mason, his widow, and orphans, when poor and destitute, to demand, and the duty of his prosperous brother to bestow.

"7. That Masonic instruction is, like charity, a reciprocal right and duty of Masons.

"8. That the right to visit, masonically, is an absolute right, but may be forfeited or limited by particular regulations.

"9. That men made Masons must be at least twenty-one years of age, free-born, of good report, hale and sound, not deformed or dismembered, and no woman, no eunuch.

"10. That no one can be made a Mason except in a lawful Lodge, duly convened, acting (except when made by the Grand Master at sight) under an unreclaimed Warrant or Dispensation, and at the place therein named.

"11. That the Grand Master may make Masons at sight, in person, and in a lawful Lodge, and may grant a dispensation to a Lodge, for the same purpose; but in all other cases a candidate must be proposed in open Lodge, at a stated meeting, and can only be accepted at a stated meeting following, by the scrutiny of a secret ballot, and an unanimous vote, and must pay a fixed price before admission.

"12. That the ballot for candidates or for membership is strictly and inviolably secret.

"13. That a petition to be made a Mason, after being presented and referred, cannot be withdrawn, but must be acted upon by report of committee and ballot.

"14. That a ballot for each degree separately is an undeniable right, when demanded.

"15. That initiation makes a man a Mason; but he must receive the Master Mason's degree, and sign the By-Laws, before he becomes a member of the Lodge.

"16. That it is the duty of every Master Mason to be a contributing member of a Lodge.

"17. That a Lodge under dispensation is but a temporary and inchoate body, and is not entitled to representation in the Grand Lodge, and those who work it do not forfeit their membership thereby in any other Lodge, while it so continues, but such membership is thereby suspended.

"18. That the Master and Wardens of every warranted Lodge must be chosen annually by its members, and if installed, cannot resign their offices during the term for which they were elected; and are, of right, and inalienably, representatives in, and members of, the Grand Lodge; and in case they do not attend the Grand Lodge a proxy may be appointed by the Lodge to represent it in the Grand Lodge, who in such case shall have three votes.

"19. That no one can be elected Master of a warranted Lodge (except at its first election) but a Master Mason who shall have served as Warden.

"20. That no appeal to the Lodge can be taken from the decision of the Master, or the Warden occupying the chair in his absence.

"21. That every Mason must be tried by his peers; and hence the Master cannot be tried by his Lodge.

"22. That Masonic intercourse with a clandestine or expelled Mason is a breach of duty, and an offense against Masonic law.

"23. That a restoration to the privileges of Masonry by the Grand Lodge does not restore to membership in a Subordinate Lodge.

"24. That a Mason who is not a member of any Lodge is still subject to the disciplinary power of Masonry.

"25. That the disciplinary powers of a Lodge may not be exercised for a violation of the moral law (as distinguished from the law of the land) until the offender has been thrice admonished by the Master or Wardens of his Lodge.

"26. That a failure to meet by a Lodge for one year is cause for the forfeiture of its Warrant.

"27. That it is the duty, as well as the right, of every warranted Lodge to be represented in the Grand Lodge at its annual Communication.

"28. That a Grand Lodge has supreme and exclusive jurisdiction, within its territorial limits, over all matters of Ancient Craft Masonry.

"29. That no appeal lies from the decision of a Grand Master in the chair, or his Deputy or Warden occupying the chair in his absence.

"30. That the office of Grand Master is always elective, and should be filled annually by the Grand Lodge.

"31. That a Grand Lodge, composed of its Officers and of Representatives, must meet at least once in each year to consult and act concerning the interests of the Fraternity in its jurisdiction.

"Besides these, there are various Landmarks, which constitute the frame-work of the government of the Fraternity; and the indispensable discharge of various duties and relations growing out of them; and also those matters regulating and attending the ceremonies and work of Masonry, which are not proper to be written; and various other duties and rights more fully set forth in the "ANCIENT CHARGES," being a part of the Constitutions of Freemasons."

Dr. Mitchell, in his "History of Freemasonry," disposes of the subject of Landmarks in the following brief manner:

"The Landmarks of Masonry are those immemorial laws which have been handed down from age to age, and from generation to generation, no one knowing whence they originated, and no one having the right to alter or change them, but all Masons being bound by a fair and liberal construction of them. They consist of the written and unwritten fundamental laws of the society. The unwritten Landmarks comprise all those essential rituals and teachings of the lodge-room, and which can be learned nowhere else. The written Landmarks are six in number, and are to be found under the head of 'The Old Charges of a Freemason,' first published in 1723, by order of the Gr. Lodge of England.'

Bro. Luke A. Lockwood, in his work entitled "Masonic Law and Practice," gives the following as the Landmarks:

1. Belief in the existence of a Supreme Being, in some revelation of his will, in the resurrection of the body and in the immortality of the soul.

2. The obligations and modes of recognition, and the legend of the third degree.

3. The inculcation of the moral virtues, of benevolence and of the doctrines of natural religion, by means of symbols derived from the Temple of King Solomon and its tradition, and from the usages and customs observed, and from the implements and materials used in its construction.

4. That Masons must obey the moral law and the government of the country in which they live.

5. That the Grand Master is the head of the Craft.

6. That the Master is head of the Lodge.

7. That the Grand Lodge is the supreme governing body within its territorial jurisdiction.

8. That every Lodge has an inherent right to be represented in Grand Lodge by its first three officers, or their proxies.

9. That every Lodge has power to make Masons, and to administer its own private affairs.

10. That every candidate must be a man, of lawful age, born of free parents, under no restraint of liberty, and hale and sound, as a man ought to be.

11. That no candidate can be received except by unanimous ballot, after due notice of his application and due inquiry as to his qualifications.

12. That the ballot is inviolably secret.

13. That all Masons, as such, are peers.

14. That all Lodges are peers.

15. That all Grand Lodges are peers.

16. That no person can be installed Master of a Lodge unless he be a Past Warden, except by dispensation of the Grand Master.

17. That the obligations, means of recognition, and the forms and ceremonies observed in conferring degrees are secret.

18. That no innovation can be made upon the body of Masonry.

19. That the Ancient Landmarks are the Supreme Law, and cannot be changed or abrogated.

The late Bro. Charles Scott, in "The Keystone of the Masonic Arch," thus discusses the character of Landmarks:

"The ancients set great value upon the landmarks or boundaries of their property. To deface or remove any of them was regarded as a grievous offense. * * * * Even among the heathen the landmark was sacred—so sacred, they made a deity of it. * * * * The 'sons of light' have their landmarks; and so clearly may they be traced that a friend may always be distinguished from a foe. The better opinion is that the rites, forms, or ceremonies are enumerated among our landmarks; also our universal or common laws. These laws cannot be repealed or modified, and are, or ought to be, the same in every Lodge. Any attempt to repeal or alter them would be a violation of Masonic faith; for it is a fundamental principle of our ancient constitution that no innovation can be made in the body of Masonry, and every member of the Fraternity is religiously obligated to observe and enforce it."

To maintain the present standing of our order; to secure its vigorous existence, and extend its benefits, much depends upon the vigilance with which we watch over its concerns, and the means employed to preserve its Ancient Landmarks from innovation, and its principles from corruption.

LAVER, Brazen. Moses was directed to make, among other articles of furniture for the services of the tabernacle, a laver of brass. It was held as a vessel of great sacredness, in which water was kept for the ablutions of the priests before entering upon the actual discharge of their sacred duties of offering sacrifices before the Lord. In the ancient mysteries the laver with its pure water was used to cleanse the neophyte of the impurities of the outer world, and to free him from the imperfections of his past or sinful life. It is a necessary article in many of the higher degrees, for the ablution of the candidate in his progress to a higher and purer system of knowledge.

JEWISH PRIEST AND LAVER.

LAY BROTHERS. An order bearing this name, and appearing to have some connection with the corporations of builders and stone masons, was founded in the 11th century. It became a numerous body, the members of which were divided into two classes. They were skilled in all the arts, especially those connected with architecture. There was also an order of Lay Brothers in the Strict Observance.

LAZARUS, Order of. 1. A Sardinian Order of Knighthood. 2. The memory of a monk of this name belonging to the 9th century is celebrated, February 21, by the Roman church, because neither the threats nor violence of Theophilus, Emperor of Constantinople, could prevent him from painting images of the Saints. This monk afterward became the patron of the sick, particularly of lepers, and in Palestine was instituted the "United Order of St. Lazarus and of our beloved Lady of Mt. Carmel"—the members of which were called Knights Hospitallers of St. Lazarus of Jerusalem. The founder of this Order is unknown. Its object was the care of the sick and of poor pilgrims. Lewis VII. of France introduced it into Europe, where it established numerous hospitals for the same class of diseased persons. 3. This is also the name of a Masonic degree, the members of which wear an emerald cross upon the breast.

LEVITICON. Name of the Ritual-book of the Parisian New Templars, in which the secret instructions of the Order, and the ceremonial forms for the reception of members, in the several degrees, are preserved.

LEWIS, or Louveteau. The words Lewis and Louveteau, which, in their original meanings, import two very different things, have in Masonry an equivalent signification—the former being used in English, and the latter in French, to designate the son of a Mason. The English word *lewis* is a term belonging to operative Masonry, and signifies an iron cramp, which is inserted in a cavity prepared for the purpose in any large stone, so as to give attachment to a pulley and hook, whereby the stone may be conveniently raised to any hight, and deposited in its proper position. In this country the lewis has not been adopted as a symbol of Freemasonry, but in the English ritual it is found among the emblems placed upon the tracing-board of the Entered-Apprentice, and is used in that degree as a symbol of strength, because by its assistance the operative Mason is enabled to lift the heaviest stones with a comparatively trifling exertion of physical power. Extending the symbolic allusion still further, the son of a Mason is in England called a *lewis*, because it is his duty to support the sinking powers and aid the failing strength of his father, or, as Oliver has expressed it, "to bear the burden and heat of the day, that his parents may rest in their old age, thus rendering the evening of their lives peaceful and happy." By the constitutions of England, a lewis may be initiated at the age of eighteen, while it is required of all other candidates that they shall have arrived at the maturer age of twenty-one. The Book of Constitutions had prescribed that no Lodge should make "any man under the age of twenty-one years, *unless by a dispensation* from the Grand Master or his Deputy." The Grand Lodge of England, in its modern regulations, has availed itself of the license allowed by this dispensing power, to confer the right of an earlier initiation on the sons of Masons. The word *louveteau* signifies in French a young wolf. The application of the term to the son of a Mason is derived from a peculiarity in some of the initiations into the ancient mysteries. In the mysteries of Isis, which were practiced in Egypt, the candidate was made to wear the mask of a wolf's head. Hence, a wolf and a candidate in these mysteries were often used as synonymous terms. Macrobius, in his *Saturnalia*, says, in reference to this custom, that the ancients perceived a relationship between the sun, the great symbol in these mysteries, and a wolf, which the candidate represented at his initiation. For, he remarks, as the flocks of sheep and cattle fly and disperse at the sight of the wolf, so the flocks of stars disappear at the approach of the sun's light. The learned reader will also recollect that in the Greek language *lukos* signifies both the sun and a wolf. Hence, as the candidate in the Isiac mysteries was called a wolf, the son of a Freemason in the French lodges is called a young wolf or a *louveteau*. The louveteau in France, like the lewis in England, is invested with peculiar privileges. He also is permitted to unite himself with the order at the early age of eighteen years. The baptism of a louveteau is sometimes performed by the Lodge of which his father is a member, with impressive ceremonies. The infant, soon after birth, is taken to the lodge-room, where he receives a Masonic name, differing from that which he bears in the world; he is formally adopted by the Lodge as one of its children, and should he become an orphan, requiring assistance, he is supported and educated by the Fraternity, and finally established in life. In this country, these rights of a lewis or a louveteau are not recognized, and the very names were, until lately, scarcely known, except to a few Masonic scholars.—MACKEY.

LIBATION. Latin *libatio*, from *libare*, to *pour out*. Properly a drink offering. Libations were frequent at meals among the ancient Greeks and Romans, and consisted generally of wine, though libations to the dead consisted sometimes of blood or milk. In sacrifices, the priest was first obliged to taste the wine, with which he sprinkled the victims, and caused those to do the same who offered the sacrifice. They consisted in offerings of bread, wine, and salt. Libations are in use in several of the high degrees of Freemasonry, particularly in the Templar system.

LIBERTAS. The name of the Goddess of Liberty among the ancient Romans. According to Hyginus, she was the daughter of Jupiter and Juno. Crowned with a diadem and covered with a vail, she personifies liberty in general. The modern Libertas, or Goddess of Liberty, is a female figure, the head covered with a cap. The cap has always been a symbol of liberty, and in the Masonic brotherhood it is also a sign of equality, and hence, in former times, the figure of Libertas was often found among the decorations of the Lodge, and Masons wore their hats while engaged in the labors of the Craft.

LIBERTINE. By this name is designated a person who is governed by no principle, and restrained by no laws of morality and virtue, who selfishly and basely seeks his own gratification and advancement, at whatever cost to others. Such a man is, of course, in every sense unfit to be a Mason. In the Ancient Charges it is laid down as a fundamental rule that "a Freemason is obliged by his tenure to obey the moral law; and if he rightly understands the art he will never be a stupid atheist nor an irreligious *libertine*." Here the word implies a person who rejects all religious truths, i. e., an infidel.

LILY OF THE VALLEY. A side degree in the Templar system of France.

LINGAM. The symbol of the creating and producing power, sacred in the Egyptian, Grecian, and Indian myste · ries. [*See* PHALLUS.]

LOWEN. It is difficult to ascertain the exact etymology of this term. The word occurs in the Ancient Charges of the Lodge of Antiquity, London, as follows: "Twelvethly: That a Master or Fellow make not a mould stone, square, nor rule to no *lowen*, nor let no *lowen* work within their lodge, nor without to mould stone." It is evident the word is employed to designate an ignorant, reckless, wild fellow, wholly unsuited to be the companion of Masons. It may be the old Saxon word *löwen*, lion, sometimes used as a general term for wild beasts. Hence, metaphorically, it may properly be applied to an ignorant, stupid, brutish person.

LUSTRATION. A purification, or ceremony of expiation, and also, in the Mysteries, of preparation. The word is derived from *lustrare*, to expiate. A solemn purification or consecration of the Roman people, by means of a *sacrificium lustrale*, was performed after every census. It consisted of a bull, a sow, a sheep or ram—*suoveta urilia.* The ram was dedicated to Jupiter, the swine to Ceres, and the bull to Mars. This solemn act was called *lustrum condere.* In Masonry the word means a purification, and is of a moral character, although in some degrees an actual lustration by water is performed.

LUX. Latin for *Light.* It is applied to Freemasonry because Masonry is a fountain of intelligence and wisdom. It has been a favorite word in the symbolism of all mystic orders.

LUX E TENEBRIS. *Light out of Darkness.* This device teaches that when man is enlightened by reason he is able to penetrate the darkness and obscurity which ignorance and superstition spread abroad.

L. V. C. LABOR VIRIS CONVENIT. *"Labor is useful to men."* A device in the Templar system of Baron Hunde, which was engraved on the inside of the rings worn by the Knights, and also upon their seals and escutcheons. It is also the device of the "Scottish Lodge of Nine Sisters," in Brunswick.

LYONS, THE SYSTEM OF. The name applied to the reformed ritual and regulations adopted by the "*Chevaliers bienfaisants de la Sainte Cite,*" benevolent Knights of the Holy City, at the convention of Lyons, A. D. 1778.

M.

MACBENAC. A word well known to Masons. It is derived from the Hebrew, and signifies *"He lives in the* Son."

MAGIANS. The name of the members of the priestly order among the ancient Medes and Persians. The word is of Indian origin, being derived from *mag*, which, in the Pehlvi language, signifies *priest*. In the last half of the seventh century before Christ, Zoroaster reformed and reorganized the order, and divided the members into three classes or degrees: 1. Herbeds, or Apprentices; 2. Mobeds, or Teacher and Master; 3. Destur Mobeds, or Perfect Master. The Magians claimed to have the gift of prophecy, a supernatural wisdom, and power to control the secret forces of nature. They were held in the highest reverence among the people, and no transaction of importance took place without or against their advice. Hence their almost unbounded influence in private as well as in public life; and, quite apart from the education of the young princes being in their hands, they also formed the constant companions of the ruling monarchs. Their mode of life was of the simplest and severest, befitting their station. The food, especially of the lower classes, consisted almost entirely of flour and vegetables; they wore white garments, slept on the ground, and were altogether subjected to the most rigorous discipline. The initiation consisted of the most imposing and mysterious ceremonies. Purifications of several months duration, and fastings of the severest test, had to precede it; and it was long before the candidate could be led into the realms of the dead, where all is darkness and misery, thence to the higher stages of glory and perpetual life. Gradually, however, their influence, which once had been powerful enough to raise them to the throne itself, began to wane, and in the course of time, its members dwindled down to the number of seven, and finally to extinction. In the seventeenth century an order of Magians was established in Florence, and still later a sub-division of the order of Rosicrucians bore this name. We find, also, the appellation *Magus* applied to the 8th degree, or the 1st degree of the Grand Mysteries of the Illuminati, to the 9th and last degree of the German, Gold and Rose-Cross, and to the 7th grade of the Clerical system of the Strict Observance. Thory also mentions a *Sovereign Magus* of the 5th degree of the Clerical-Cabalistic system.

MAGNA CHARTA. The great charter, so called, obtained by the English barons from King John, June 5, 1215, and confirmed by his successor, Henry III. It has been viewed by after ages as the basis of English liberties. Its most important articles are those which provide that no freeman shall be taken or imprisoned or proceeded against, "except by the lawful judgment of his peers or by the law of the land," and that no scutage or aid should be imposed in the kingdom (except certain feudal dues from tenants of the crown), unless by the authority of the common council of the kingdom. The remaining and greater part of it is directed against abuses of the king's power as feudal superior.

MAHER-SHALAL-HASH-BAZ. A mystical name that was to be given to one of the sons of the prophet Isaiah. which he had previously written by divine command, on a tablet, the meaning of which is: "*He hasteth to the spoil; speed to the prey.*" A prophetic intimation of the speedy invasion and victory of the Assyrians over Syria and Israel. As a warrior, devoted to the cause of honor and justice, we should be ever ready to hasten to the relief of the destitute and oppressed.

MAITRESSE AGISSANTE. (*M.·. A.·.*) In the Egyptian system of Cagliostro, this title, "Acting Mistress," is given to the presiding sister.

MAKE. When a candidate is initiated into the mysteries of the order, he is said to be made a Mason. An expression in use among the operative Masons in the ancient times. It is a term synonymous with the word "initiate."

MALLET. One of the working tools of a Mark Master; an instrument of practical architectural labor. As an emblem of morality it is synonymous with the common gavel of the Entered Apprentice.

MANES. In Roman antiquity, the gods of the lower world; the benevolent deities; generally applied to the souls of the departed. According to Apuleius, the Manes were originally called Lemures, and consisted of two classes—the *Lares* and the *Larvæ;* the former of whom were the souls of those who had led virtuous lives, and the latter of those who had lived improperly. At a later period the term *Manes* came to be a general designation for both.

MARK. The Mark-Master's medal, or the Tyrian Signet, which Hiram is said to have sent to King Solomon. It is in the form of a keystone, and has engraved upon it a circle—the emblem of an eternal compact of friendship— and a mark or device chosen by the possessor. A Mark-Mason who receives this mark from a destitute brother is bound by the most solemn obligations to assist him to the extent of his ability. In this respect it resembles the

"Ring of Hospitality," and the "Tessaræ" among the ancients, with whom hospitality was considered a most sacred duty. Individuals often entered into contracts of friendship, binding themselves and descendants to assist and protect

each other in adverse circumstances; and, as was the case among the Greeks, ratified the alliance by breaking a ring into two parts, each party taking one half. The visitor was kindly received, clothed, and entertained. After nine days, if the stranger had not previously made himself known, the question was put to him, "who and whence art thou?" If, in reply, he could show the half of the broken ring, he was welcomed still more warmly.

Among the early Christians, *marks* were in general use, and in the existing circumstances of the Brotherhood were of the highest importance and utility. In Rev. ii. 17 allusion is made to the Christian *mark*, as follows: "To him that overcometh will I give a white stone, and in it a new name written, which no man knoweth, saving he that receiveth it." That is, "To him who passes triumphantly through all the trials, discipline, and proofs of discipleship, will I give the mystical stone, which will secure to him protection and assistance, and brotherly love, in this world; and in the world to come, will open to him the eternal mysteries, and admit him to a more perfect fellowship in the grand circle of the just.

MARKMAN. The name of a Masonic degree which is not now in use. The markmen were Wardens at the building of Solomon's Temple.

MARK OF THE CRAFT. According to the traditions of the Mark Master's degree, each Mason employed in building the Temple of Solomon was required to place a peculiar mark upon his work, to distinguish it from that of others. It is probable that this has always been the practice with the various corporations of builders from the earliest periods down to quite modern times. Most of the edifices constructed in the middle ages, particularly those of Strasburg, Worms, Rheims, bear these marks, which appear to have been of two classes, viz: monograms, which belonged to overseers; and emblems, as the trowel, mallet, square, etc., that belonged to the workmen. A writer, describing the walls of the fortress of Allahabad, in the East Indies, erected A. D. 1542, says: "The walls are composed of large oblong blocks of red granite, and are almost everywhere covered with Masonic emblems, which evince something more than mere ornament. They are not confined to any particular spot, but are scattered over the walls of the fortress, in many places as high as thirty or forty feet from the ground. It is quite certain that thousands of stones on the walls, bearing these Masonic symbols, were carved, marked, and numbered in the quarry before the erection of the building.

MARSHAL. A term, in its origin, meaning a groom or manager of the horse, though eventually the king's marshal became one of the principal officers of state in England. In France, the highest military officer is called a marshal, a dignity which originated early in the thirteenth century. Originally, the *Maréchal de France* was the first companion of the king, and commanded the vanguard in war; in later times, the command became supreme, and the rank of the highest military importance. After the deposition of Louis XVI. the dignity of marshal ceased; but was revived by Napoleon, with the title of Marshal of the Empire. 2. An officer known to Masonic bodies, whose duty is to have charge of processions and other public ceremonies. As a badge of special distinction he wears a scarf and carries a baton.

MARTHA. The name of the fourth degree of the order of the Eastern Star, or American Adoptive rite. It illustrates undeviating friendship and the power of faith to console the heart in seasons of affliction. Its symbolical color is **green**, representing at the same time, the immortality of the soul and of its affection. The incidents of the degree are recorded in John xi. 26.

MARTINISTS. The members of a philosophical and mystical form of Freemasonry were called by this name, from the founder of the rite, the Marquis de Saint Martin.* The adepts of this order were earnest, pious, and remarkably modest men, and, although they promulgated ideas, startling in that material and skeptical age, were never fanatical in their advocacy of them, nor ill-tempered when ridiculed. Like the Rosicrucians, the Illuminati, and some other similar societies, they aspired to a higher and more positive philosophy, and sought a foundation for the ideas of religion and morality in the eternal fitness of things, and the interior experiences of the soul, rather than in tradition. They believed that the very existence of religious ideas in the human mind demonstrated their eternal truthfulness; for all subjective notions must be the reflex of an *objective* reality. Thus the vast orb of the sun is mirrored in the tiny dew-drop. The reflected image of the sun is a demonstration of the sun's existence. In like manner the notion of God that exists in the mind is a reflex of God himself, and could no more exist in the mind were there no God than the image of the sun could be found in the dew-drop if there were no sun. Like Goethe, they believed that *" Die geisterwelt ist nicht verschlossan"*—"the world of spirits is not shut." It was their belief that an invisible sphere—a world of superior intelligence—environs man; that beneficent spirits are always near him, the constant companion of his actions, and witnesses of his thoughts; that the highest science—all the ideas

* Louis Claude de Saint Martin was born at Amboise, of a noble French family, in 1743, and died in 1803. He adopted the *nom de plume* of *"le Philosophe inconnu,"* which we read Philosopher of the unknown. He possessed vast original genius and metaphysical insight, and as a thinker he digested and assimilated, in a masterly manner, whatever he found to his taste. The first and most valued of his numerous writings was a work entitled *Des Erreurs et de la Vérité*, published at Lyons, in 1775, in which may be found, under the most enigmatic style, that ancient doctrine which so universally prevails, of a good and a bad principle, of an ancient state of perfection of man, of his fall, and of the possibility of his restoration. For many years he devoted his best energies to reforming the system of his teacher, Martinez Paschalis, the founder of the sect of Martinists; and to that end instituted a new system that became famous under the name of Martinism, which had its center at Lyons, in the Lodge of Beneficent Knights. This rite was extended into the principal cities of France, Germany and Russia. Saint-Martin, like many other of the noblesse of France, suffered by the French revolution, and, being implicated in a conspiracy, owed his life to the revolution of Thermidor.

of religion, art, and philosophy—are revelations of this over-world, whose ineffable splendors are ever streaming downward to meet humanity, which, impelled by its immortal needs, is aspiring upward to the fountain of light. The Order of St. Martin was a modification of a society founded by Paschalis, at Marseilles, 1754. It had ten degrees, divided into two divisions, called "Temples." Those of the 1st temple were Apprentice, Fellow-Craft, Master, Ancient-Master Elect, Grand Architect, and Mason of the Secret. Those of the 2d temple were the Prince of Jerusalem, Knights of Palestine and Kadosch. The object of the initiation was the regeneration of men, and the instructions to neophytes embraced the whole circle of human knowledge.

MASON, Etymology of. The speculations of many Masonic writers respecting the origin and derivation of this word are too puerile to be repeated. It is evidently the German "metzen" to cut. In Germany the operative Masons were called "stein-metzen," stone-cutters, and sometimes "mauern," wall-builders. The term Mason is simply the German word anglicized, by softening the tz sound.

MASONIC COLORS. Every grade of Masonry is furnished with its peculiar and emblematic color. An important and mystic meaning has always been applied to colors, and they are used as the distinguishing mark of different nations. The colors best known, and almost universally adapted to Masonry, are seven, viz:

1. BLUE. This is the great color of Masonry. It is the appropriate tincture of the Ancient Craft degrees. It is to the Mason an emblem of universal friendship and benevolence, teaching us that in the mind of a brother those virtues should be as extensive as the blue arch of heaven itself. It is, therefore, the only color, except white, which should be used in a Master Mason's Lodge. Besides the three degrees of Ancient Craft Masonry, this color is also to be found in several other degrees, especially of the Ancient and Accepted rite, where it bears various symbolic significations; all, however, more or less related to its original character, as an emblem of universal friendship and benevolence. This tincture was held in high veneration among all the nations of antiquity. It symbolically expressed heaven, the firmament, truth, constancy, and fidelity.

2. PURPLE, being formed by a due admixture of blue and scarlet, is intended to remind us of the intimate connection and harmony that exists between symbolic Masonry and the Royal Arch degree. In the religious services of the Jews purple is employed on several occasions. It is one of the colors of the curtains of the tabernacle, and is symbolical of the element of water. It is also used in the construction of the ephod and girdle of the High Priest, and the cloths for divine service. Among the Gentile nations of antiquity purple was considered rather as a color of dignity than of veneration, and was deemed an emblem of exalted office. Pliny says it was the color of the vestments worn by the early kings of Rome, and it has ever since, even to the

present time, been considered as the becoming insignia of regal or supreme authority.

3. SCARLET, RED, or CRIMSON, for it is indifferently called by each of these names, is the appropriate color of the Royal Arch degree, and symbolically represents the ardor and zeal which should actuate all who are in possession of that sublime portion of Masonry. Scarlet was used as one of the vails of the tabernacle, and was an emblem of the elements of fire. Scarlet was, among the Jews, a color of dignity, appropriated to the most opulent or honorable. In the middle ages, those Knights who engaged in the wars of the crusades, and especially the Templars, wore a red cross as a symbol of their willingness to undergo martyrdom for the sake of religion. Scarlet is in the higher degrees of Masonry as predominating a color as blue is in the lower. These three colors—BLUE, PURPLE, and SCARLET—were called, in the early English lectures, the old colors of Masonry," and were said to have been selected "because they are royal, and such as the ancient kings and princes used to wear; and sacred history informs us that the vail of the temple was composed of these colors."

4. WHITE is one of the most ancient as well as most extensively diffused of the symbolic colors. It is to be found in all the ancient mysteries, where it constituted, as it does in Masonry, the investure of the candidate. It always, however, and everywhere has borne the same signification, as the symbol of purity and innocence. White was the color of one of the curtains of the tabernacle, where it was a symbol of the element of earth. Among the ancients the highest reverence was paid to this color. It was, in general, the garment of the Gentile as well as of the Hebrew priests in the performance of their sacred rites. It is regarded as the emblem of light, religious purity, innocence, virginity, faith, joy, and life. In the judge, it indicates integrity;

in the sick man, humility; in the woman, chastity. We see, therefore, the propriety of adopting this color in the Masonic system, as a symbol of purity. This symbolism commences in the York rite, where the lambskin or white apron is presented to the Entered Apprentice as an emblem of purity of life and rectitude of conduct, and terminates in the Ancient and Accepted rite, where the Sovereign Inspectors of the 33d degree are invested with a white scarf as an emblem of that virtuous deportment, above the tongue of all reproach, which should distinguish the possessors of that exalted grade.

5. BLACK. As white is universally the emblem of purity, so black, in the Masonic ritual, is constantly the symbol of grief. This is perfectly consistent with its use in the world, where black has, from remote antiquity, been adopted as a garment of mourning. In Masonry this color is confined to but a few degrees, but everywhere has the same single meaning of sorrow. Black is in the world the symbol of the earth, darkness, mourning, wickedness, negation, death, and was appropriate to the Prince of Darkness. White and black together signify purity of life, and mourning or humiliation.

6. GREEN, as a Masonic color, is confined to a few of the degrees. It is employed as a symbol of the immutable nature of truth and victory. In the *evergreen* the Master Mason finds the emblem of hope and immortality. In all the ancient mysteries, this idea was carried out, and green symbolized the birth of the world, and the moral creation or resurrection of the initiate.

7. YELLOW. Of all the Masonic colors, yellow appears to be the least important, and the least used. It is a predominating color in a few of the degrees of the Ancient and Accepted rite. It was a significant symbol of the sun, of the goodness of God, of initiation or marriage, faith, or faithfulness. In an improper sense, yellow signifies inconstancy, jealousy, and deceit.

MASON'S DAUGHTER. This degree, conferred on Master Masons, their wives, sisters, and daughters, in some things resembles the degree of Martha of the American Adoptive rite. The Scripture lesson of the degree is selected from the 11th and 12th chapters of the Gospel of St. John.

MASTER OF CAVALRY. An officer in a Council of the Knights of the Red Cross, equivalent to the Senior Warden in the Commandery. His position is in the south, on the right of the first division when separately formed, and on the right of the whole when formed in line.

MASTER OF CEREMONIES. An officer first instituted at the court of England, in 1603, for the more honorable reception of Ambassadors and persons of distinction. This officer is found in most of the Lodges in England and on the continent, and has lately found a place in the Lodges of the United States. He assists the Senior Deacon when conducting the candidate, and performs the duties usually belonging to the office of Steward.

MASTER OF DISPATCHES. The Recorder of a Council of the Knights of the Red Cross.

MASTER OF FINANCES. The name of the Treasurer in a Council of Red Cross Knights.

MASTER OF INFANTRY. An officer known in the Council of the Knights of the Red Cross, equivalent to the Senior Deacon in a Lodge, or Junior Warden in a Commandery. His station is in the north, on the right of the second division when separately formed, and on the left of the whole when formed in line.

MASTER OF A LODGE. The presiding officer of a Lodge of Freemasons, whose style is "Worshipful." In the whole series of offices recognized by the Masonic institution, there is not one more important than that of the Master. Upon the skill, integrity and prudence of the presiding officer, depend the usefulness and welfare of the Lodge. To become the Master of a Lodge, with the title "worthy and well qualified," is a legitimate object of ambition for every young brother who takes an interest in the prosperity of the society. The powers of the Master are very great; far more varied and positive than those of any organization now in existence. From his decisions there can be no appeal to the Lodge; he is amenable for his conduct to the Grand Master or the Grand Lodge. Equally important with the proper qualifications for the discharge of the duties of the Master, are experience, a thorough knowledge of the ritual and the parliamentary rules of the Craft, the service of a full term as a Warden, except in the case of a newly-constituted Lodge, when there is no Warden or Past Master to serve; a legal election; a compliance with the covenants of the installation service and induction into the oriental chair. The prerogatives of the Master of a Lodge are: 1. To congregate or assemble his Lodge; 2. To preside therein; 3. To fill temporary vacancies in office; 4. To regulate the admission of visitors; 5. To control and terminate discussions; 6. To determine all questions of order and the order of business, without appeal, except to the Grand Lodge or Grand Master; 7. To appoint all committees; 8. To open and close the Lodge; 9. To be the custodian of the warrant; 10. To order the issuing of summonses, and compel the attendance of members; 11. To give the casting vote in case of a tie, in addition to his own vote: 12. To sign all drafts upon the Treasurer for the payment of Lodge expenses, with the consent of the Lodge; 13. To refuse to initiate a candidate, if, in his judgment, such initiation would be improper; 14. In company with the Senior and Junior Wardens, to represent the Lodge at all communications of the Grand Lodge; 15. To appoint the Senior Deacon, and such other officers as may be prescribed in the by-laws of the Lodge; 16. To install his successor and assist in conferring the official Past Master's degree. His duties are— to attend all communications of the Lodge; to open the Lodge at the time designated in the by-laws, and close it at a reasonable hour; to preserve order in the Lodge; to obey, enforce and defend the landmarks, the laws and edicts of the Grand Lodge, the orders of the Grand Master, and the by-laws of the Lodge; to preserve the charter of the Lodge, and transmit it to his successor; to perform the ritualistic work of Masonry, and instruct the brethren; to cause an investigation into all Masonic offenses committed by the initiated candidates, by members of the Lodge, or by Masons residing within the jurisdiction of the Lodge; to visit the sick, and perform the Masonic burial service over the remains of a deceased member of the Lodge; to perfect himself in the ritual, laws and usages of the order; to use his best endeavors to preserve and promote peace and harmony in the Lodge, and, by his Masonic deportment in and out of the Lodge, be a good example to the brethren. He is exempt from discipline for his official acts, except to the Grand Lodge. He cannot dimit or resign during his term of office, for if a vacancy should occur in the office of Master, by death or removal from the jurisdiction, the Senior Warden assumes, by virtue of immemorial practice, all the prerogatives and responsibilities of that officer. His jewel is the square, because, as that instrument is dedicated to the Master, and is the proper Masonic emblem of his office, it symbolically teaches him official and individual responsibilities, to regulate his actions by rule and line, and to harmonize his conduct by the principles of morality and virtue, so that no ill-feeling or angry discussions may arise to impair the harmony and good fellowship that should ever distinguish a Masonic Lodge, for he

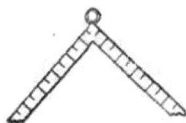

> "Who wears the SQUARE upon his breast,
> Does in the sight of GOD attest,
> And in the face of man,
> That all his actions will compare
> With the Divine, th' unerring square,
> That squares great virtue's plan."—MORRIS.

The jewels, furniture and other property of the Lodge are in his charge, and he has a general control over all its affairs.

MASTER OF THE PALACE. The title of an officer in a Council of Red Cross Knights. He is the Captain General in a Commandery of Knights Templar.

MASTERS OF THE VAILS. In a Royal Arch Chapter three officers whose duties are to guard the blue, purple and scarlet vails of the tabernacle. Each is armed with a sword, and carries a banner of a color corresponding with that of the vail before which he is stationed. Their jewel is a sword within a triangle.

MAUSOLEUM. A general designation of any superb and stately sepulchral monument. The name is derived from the tomb erected at Halicarnassus by Artemisia, to the memory of her husband Mausolus, king of Caria, B. C. 353. It was one of the most magnificent monuments of the kind, and was esteemed one of the seven wonders of the world. When the Knights of St. John of Jerusalem, in 1404, took possession of the site of Halicarnassus, then occupied by a small village called Cleesy, while excavating among the ruins for building materials, they discovered a large chamber with marble pilasters, and with richly inlaid panels. The sarcophagus of the founder was also discovered; fragments of lions, dogs, etc., and a beautiful sculpture of a horse, have been found.

Mausoleums of rare beauty and strength, bearing Masonic symbols and sentiments of fraternal affection, have been erected in several parts of Europe and America.

MEDALS, MASONIC. This term is applied to pieces of metal, of various forms, but generally similar to coins, not intended for circulation as money, or means of exchange, struck and distributed in commemoration of some important event. The study and a thorough knowledge of medals recognized by the Craft, especially those bearing emblems and perpetuating valuable Masonic historical eras or events, are indispensable to prevent our ancient legends, traditions and history from falling into decay or passing into oblivion. So far as our investigations have extended in Masonic medals or numismatics, there is nothing extant in this department earlier than the eighteenth century. This may be explained from the fact that before that period the ancient or operative form of the institution existed; then Masons made their medals of mighty blocks of stone; their symbols were wrought in the ground-plans of extensive and beautiful edifices; their marks were deeply cut upon the living rocks "with an iron pen and lead in the rock forever." The first Masonic medal of which we have any account (an impression of which will be seen in the accompanying engraving) was struck about A. D. 1733. Its history is substantially as follows: In 1733 a Lodge was established at Florence, by Lord Charles Sackville, son of Lionel Granville Sackville, great grandson of Thomas

Sackville, who, in 1561, was Grand Master of the Masons acknowledging the jurisdiction of the Grand Lodge at York. This Lodge was not founded by regular authority; certainly there was no order for it by the Grand Lodge of England, then governed by James Lyon, Earl of Strathmore. The formation of the Lodge, however, was the origin of this medal, a copy of which exists in the valuable collection of Ma-

sonic medals in possession of the Lodge *Minerva of the Three Palms*, at Leipsic. The *obverse*, not given here, has a bust of Lord Sackville, with the inscription, "Carolvs Sackville, Magister, Fl." The *reverse* exhibits Harpocrates, the god of silence, who, as the son of Isis and Osiris, stood

MASONIC MEDALS.

Struck in 1832.

Struck in 1812.

STRUCK IN 1833.

STRUCK IN 1825.

STRUCK IN 1811.

STRUCK IN 1787.

STRUCK IN 1774.

STRUCK IN 1771.

STRUCK IN 1763.

STRUCK IN 1771.

STRUCK IN 1655.

STRUCK IN 1797.

STRUCK IN 1774.   STRUCK IN 1781.

at the entrance of most Egyptian and Roman temples, in his well-known attitude, leaning upon a broken column, with the fore-finger of his right hand, the emblem of silence, upon his lips, and holding in his left arm the cornucopia, filled with the rich fruits of the earth. The cubic block, around which are grouped the stone-hammer, the compasses, the square, the level, the chisel, the plumb and mallet, is at his feet. The thyrsus, staff and the serpent, rest behind him. The motto is *Ab Origine*, "from the beginning." An immensely large number of Masonic medals have been struck, for as many memorable occasions, during the past century; a brief notice of which would be very far beyond our limits to give. Medals are frequently given to brothers as a reward for efficient official services and distinguished Masonic virtues.

MEDITERRANEAN PASS. An honorary or side degree conferred on Royal Arch Masons. Its legend and ritual are identical with the more imposing and interesting degree of the Knight of the Mediterranean Pass, from which this is supposed to be extracted.

MELCHIZEDEK. Pontiff-king of Salem, and prototype of Christ. The name and his history are referred to in the Order of the High-Priesthood; also, in the 5th degree of the Asiatic Brothers, and in the Order of the Illuminati.

MELEK-MELOCHIM. *King of Kings.* A sacred word in several of the higher degrees of the French rite.

MELITA. The ancient Greek name of the Island of Malta; referred to in the Order of the Knights of Malta.

MEMPHIS, Rite of. Sometimes called the Oriental rite. A modification of the rite of Misraim, organized in Paris, in 1839, by Messieurs Marconis and Mouttet. It afterward extended to Brussels and Marseilles, thence to New York. It was composed of 90 working and 6 official degrees. For a time it excited some interest in Paris, and then fell into obscurity until 1860, when it was reorganized, the 96 degrees reduced to 30, and then merged into the Grand Orient of France, where it is permitted to slumber. It may now be regarded as extinct.

MENATZCHIM, Council of. The principal degree in the French rite of the "Vieille Bru" was called by this name. The word is Hebrew, and means consoler, or comforter. The overseers at the building of the Temple were called Menatzchim.

MENU, INSTITUTES OF. The name given to the most celebrated code of Indian civil and religious law; so called from
Menu, Menou, or Manu, the son of Brahma, by whom it is
supposed to have been revealed. The Hindoos, themselves,
ascribe to this system the highest antiquity; and many of
the most learned Europeans are of opinion that of all known
works there is none which carries with it more convincing
proofs of high antiquity and perfect integrity. Sir W. Jones
assigns the date of its origin somewhere between Homer
and the Twelve Tables of the Romans; and Schlegel asserts
it as his belief that it was seen by Alexander the Great in a
state not materially different from that in which we possess
it. The Institutes of Menu are of a most comprehensive
nature: they embrace all that relates to human life; the
history of the creation of the world and man; the nature of
God and spirits; and a complete system of morals, government and religion.

MESMERIAN MASONRY. A name applied to a Masonic
rite invented by some of the disciples of Mesmer, A. D. 1784.

MINUTES. Records of the transactions at each meeting
of the Lodge. These proceedings—that is, all which it is
lawful to write—should be carefully entered on the records,
and at the opening of the next meeting, read to the brethren,
that errors, if any, may be corrected.

MISCHCHAN, MISCHPHERETH, MISCHTAR. Hebrew terms,
signifying *Tabernacle, Most Powerful,* and *Fountain,* used as
sacred words, in several of the high degrees of the French
rite.

MISRAIM, RITE OF. This rite was introduced into France
near the commencement of the present century. It made
considerable progress, and, in 1817, application was made on
the part of its friends, to the Grand Orient, to accept it as a
legitimate branch of Masonry. The application was denied,
partly on the ground that the antiquity of the rite had not
been proved, and partly because of the 90 degrees which its
ritual comprised 68 were already included in the French
system. The rite of Misraim is interesting and instructive,
but many of its degrees are too abstruse to be popular. The
initiation is a reproduction of the ancient rite of Isis, and
represents the contests of Osiris and Typhon, the death,
resurrection, and triumph of the former, and the destruction
of the latter. There are 90 degrees, divided into four series
—symbolic, philosophical, mystical and cabalistic, and again
divided into seventeen classes.

The traditions of this system are full of anachronisms, historical events and characters, separated by hundreds of years, being made to figure on the same scene, at the same time. The work entitled "*De l'Ordre Maçonnique de Misraim,*" published at Paris, in 1835, by Mons. Marc Bedarride, purporting to give the history of the Order, is a mere romance, and full of puerilities. Nevertheless, many of the degrees are highly interesting and instructive.

MITHRA, Mysteries of. The Sun-God in the ancient Zend religion, and mediator between Ormuzd, the god of light, and Ahriman, the god of darkness, through whom the latter with his kingdom of evil will be destroyed, and the former will establish his empire of light and happiness throughout the universe. His symbols are the sun—type of truth and justice—on his head; the mace—emblem of power—in his hand, or the sacrificing dagger, and the bull of the world, on whose back he lies. The mysteries of Mithra were dramatic and scenic illustrations of the Persian religion, and were divided into seven degrees. The principal dogmas, as revised by Zoroaster, are as follows: From the beginning there have existed two beings, Ormuzd and Ahriman, the principles of the universe. Ormuzd is pure eternal light, the spirit of beauty and love, and original source of all perfection. Ahriman was also originally of the light, and so far good; but as he envied the light of Ormuzd he obscured his own, became an enemy to Ormuzd and the father of evil, and of all evil beings who joined him in a contest with the good. Ormuzd and Ahriman performed the work of creation at different epochs, and brought into existence various species of beings. Ormuzd created the community of good spirits; first six immortal spirits of light; then twenty-eight subordinate spirits, representatives of the months and days; and, at last, a multitude of human souls. Ahriman produced a number of bad spirits, six *arch-devs*, spirits of darkness, and innumerable *devs* of lower rank. The good dwell with Ormuzd in light. Ahriman lives with his creatures in the kingdom of darkness. 3,000 years Ormuzd ruled alone; after which he created material beings, in their various degrees; at last man, and after the labor celebrated the first festival of creation with the good spirits. Again he ruled in this world of innocence and happiness 3,000 years. In the next period of equal length begins the contest between light and darkness, Ormuzd and Ahriman, who in a continual struggle divide the dominion of the world. The following 3,000 years extend and confirm the power of Ahriman; afterward his power declines; the *devs* sink to nothing; their former prince, through the influence of Mithra, the mediator, does homage to Ormuzd, and the empire of darkness and vice disappears. The dead arise, and all darkness, sin, and misery are ended forever. The initiation into the mysteries of Mithra and the entire ceremonial of the seven degrees were symbolical representations of the everlasting struggle between good and evil, their alternate triumph and defeat, until at last evil is overwhelmed in a final overthrow, and the splendor of truth fills, and the songs of triumphant virtue resound through, all worlds. The rites of Mithra seem to combine some of the features of the Indian, Egyptian, and Cabirian mysteries. They were widely extended through Asia and Europe, and it is said that traces of the worship of Mithra are found at the present time in those parts of Germany that were anciently under the dominion of the Romans.

MITRE. The sacred covering for the head of the Jewish High-Priest. It was made of fine linen or silk of a blue color, wrapped in several folds, in the manner of a Turkish turban. In front and around the base of the mitre, as a band, secured with blue ribbon, was a plate of pure gold, called the "plate of the holy crown of pure gold," upon which is inscribed "HOLINESS TO THE LORD." This important vestment was worn by the High-Priest on occasions of solemn and imposing services only. This is the proper form of the mitre which should be worn by the High-Priest in a Royal Arch Chapter when officiating in the ceremonies of the Royal Arch degree, and when dressed in the other appropriate priestly garments.

MONITOR. A name given to books which contain the charges, regulations, emblems, and exoteric ceremonies of Freemasonry. Numerous works of this character have been published, some of them very valuable; works arranged on the principle that "*the initiated know what is meant*," which, by ingenious methods of suggestions, places before the mind of the intelligent Mason the whole ritual of the order, with its profound and varied meanings, while it reveals nothing to the profane.

MONUMENTS, SEPULCHRAL AND MASONIC. An emblem erected over the grave, to mark the resting-place and per-

petuate the memory of the dead. In the earliest ages and
among the eastern nations, it was the practice to place the
remains of the dead in excavated sepulchres, with monumental structures over them. Egypt, Palestine, Greece,
Persia and Rome abounded with monuments of this character. In Egypt the monarch's burial-place began to be
excavated as soon as he ascended the throne, and the
excavation and decoration went on year by year until the
king's death, when it was suddenly broken off, the tomb
thus becoming an index both of the king's magnificence and

of the length of his reign. Masonic monuments, as memorials
of fraternal affection, and rewards of well-merited honor
are often erected over the remains of the illustrious dead,
with appropriate hieroglyphic symbols, or the following
emblematic legend delineated thereon: A virgin weeping
over a broken column, with the book open before her; in her
right hand a sprig of acacia, in her left an urn; Time is
behind her with his hands enfolded in the ringlets of her

hair. The weeping virgin symbolizes the unfinished state of
the temple; the broken column, that one of the principal
supporters of Masonry has fallen; the open book implies
that his memory is recorded in every Mason's heart; the
sprig of acacia refers to the discovery of his remains; the
urn shows that his ashes have been carefully collected, and
Time behind her implies that we are rapidly passing from
life to a blessed immortality.

MOPSES. From the German *mops*, a young mastiff. It is
intended to indicate the mutual fidelity and attachment of
the brethren—those virtues being characteristic of the noble
animal. This order originated in the following manner: Pope
Clement XII. having issued a bull against the Freemasons
in 1738, the people were alarmed, and hesitating to join a
society which had been thus proscribed, formed another on
the same principle, which would afford them equal gratification, without subjecting them to the thunders of the Vatican.
Freemasonry was the model, with pretensions of devotion
to the papal hierarchy, and thus, under the assumed appellation, they evaded the papal denunciation. Some of the
most illustrious personages in Germany countenanced and
extended their patronage to the scheme; many of the princes
of the empire became its Grand Masters. In 1776 this organization assumed an androgynous character, and admitted
females to its ceremonies and offices. The ceremonies of
this order were highly interesting. It had forms of initiation,
signs, pass-words and tokens, and other marks of recognition; and the symbols admitted of an intellectual and moral
explanation.

MORNING STAR, KNIGHT OF. This degree is a modification of the Kadosh, according to the nomenclature of
Fustier, which is preserved in the archives of the "Lodge of
the Philosophical rite."

MOSAIC WORK. The Mosaic pavement, so frequently
alluded to in the rituals of the order as the ornaments of a
Lodge, are the productions of artistic designs, by setting
small and variously shaped stones, glass or wood of different
colors, so as to give the effect of painting. The floor of the
tabernacle and the pavement of Solomon's temple were thus
ornamented. Mosaic or tesselated pavements were common
among the ancients; the Egyptians, the Greeks and especially the Romans most ingeniously decorated the floors and
walls of their temples in this manner. In commemoration
of the flooring of the temple and tabernacle, the Mosaic
pavement is always preserved as an ornament of the Masonic
Lodge, with the blazing star in the center, and the beautiful

tesselated border* surrounding the whole, as a symbol of
the manifold blessings and comforts which constantly surround us. The Mosaic pavement of a Lodge is placed there
as an emblem of the vicissitudes of human life; that however prosperity may favor us with smiles to-day, it is
uncertain how long it will continue to bless us. Adversity
may come when we least expect it, and penury and distress
may follow joy and pleasure. The latter period of life may
be subjected to want and misery, when we are most unfit to
encounter it; and instead of resting in peace after a long
and troublesome journey, we may be compelled again to
encounter the burden and heat of the day.

MOSQUE OF OMAR, or the Noble Sanctuary. This
splendid edifice on Mount Moriah, covers a portion of the

* The indented tessel is a border of stones, of various colors, around
the pavement. *Tessel*, from the Latin tessela, means a small square
stone, and to *indent* is to cut or notch a margin into inequalities resembling teeth, a tesselated border is, therefore, a notched border of
variegated colors. A limited number of samples of Mosaic work is
represented in the above engraving.

space once occupied by the more brilliant Temple of Solomon. It is believed to have been commenced by the Caliph Omar, the first of that name, and father-in-law of Mahomet, between the years 638 and 644, and very much enlarged, beautified and enriched, in fact, quite rebuilt by the Caliph Abd-el Melek, in 686. It was seven years in building: the Moslems believe it to stand over the rock on which Jacob

INTERIOR VIEW OF THE MOSQUE OF OMAR.

was sleeping when he saw the vision of the heavenly ladder; but it is still more sacred to them, as to us, from having been the sacred rock beneath the altar of Solomon's Temple, whereon the daily sacrifice was offered. During the time of the Latin kingdom in Jerusalem this mosque became a Christian cathedral, where the service was daily sung and an altar erected on the summit of the rock. The building was called by the Crusaders the "Temple of the Lord." The fanciful and intricate patterns of the porcelain walls of the mosque, the graceful letters of the inscription round it, and the tracery of the windows are still more beautiful on a closer inspection—nothing can be more perfect of their kind, or more peculiarly charming than the harmony of the colors; the windows are filled with stained glass of the very richest and most brilliant colors, that even the palmiest days of the médieval ages could produce in Europe. Two rows of columns encircle the center, forming a double corridor, and support the clerestory and the dome: these columns have evidently belonged to some other building—their capitals are mostly of acanthus leaves. The rock itself is enclosed in a metal screen of lattice work about six feet high, and to it, we are told by the Bordeaux Pilgrim, in 333, the Jews came every year, anointing the stone with oil, wailing and rending their garments, thus proving its authenticity in their minds; it had been for many years polluted by an equestrian statue of the Emperor Adrian elevated on the very rock itself. The Bordeaux Pilgrim specially mentions that this rock adored by the Jews was *pierced:* below it is the "noble cave" spoken of in the Mishna, into which the blood, etc., from the altar drained, and descended thence by a conduit into the valley of Siloam, the gardens of which were enriched by this drainage.*

* Dr. JAMES T. BARCLAY, for many years a resident missionary in Jerusalem, and favorably known in Europe and this country, for the valuable discoveries he has made in the temple enclosure, to which he was admitted by special firman, gives the following description of the Mosque of Omar, in his invaluable work, "THE CITY OF THE GREAT KING:" "The superb edifice called by Moslems Kubbet es-Sakhrah (Dome of the Rock), and by Franks the Mosk of Omar, is situated rather below the middle of the platform—being nearest to the western side, and farthest from the northern. The lower story, or main body of the building, is a true octagon, of sixty-seven feet on a side; but the central and elevated portion is circular. A more graceful and symmetrical dome than that which covers the building is perhaps nowhere to be found; and the lofty bronze crescent that surmounts the whole gives a pleasing architectural finish. * * * * * Immediately beneath the center of the dome is the venerated rock about which so much has been written. In the estimation of the Jew, this is by far the most hallowed spot on earth; for, according to the Rabbins, this is the identical rock upon which Jacob pillowed his head, and set it up for a pillar and poured oil upon the top of it; and he called the name of that place Bethel—House of God. It is the general belief, also, that it is the threshing floor of Araunah the Jebusite—the spot where the faith of Abraham was so sorely tried in his determined obedience to God to offer up Isaac; and the site of the Holy of Holies of the temple—which glowed beneath the divine manifestation of Deity in the Shekinah. * * * * * When the rock was brought to light by Omar, it was exhumed beneath an immense mound of rubbish and dirt. But it had previously been crowned by Hadrian's splendid Temple of Jupiter Capitolinus. The present noble structure over and around it is undoubtedly the work of the munificent Khaliff Abd-el Melek, though often supposed to be a Christian edifice. * * * * * There are various recesses cut in the rock, both above and

MOST EXCELLENT. The honorary title of the High-Priest of a Chapter of Royal Arch Masons.

MOST EXCELLENT MASTER. The title of the 6th degree of Masonry. It illustrates the dedication of the Temple by Solomon.

MOST WORSHIPFUL. The title of the presiding officer of a Grand Lodge, and sometimes applied to the body.

MUSIC. A combination or succession of sounds, so arranged as to please the ear.* The pleasure derived from music arises from its exciting agreeable sensations, and raising pleasing mental images and emotions. Apart from words, it expresses passion and sentiment, and linked to words, it loses its vagueness and becomes a beautiful illustration of language. This science is truly congenial to the

below, indicating the spots where Abraham, Elijah, David, Solomo and other renowned Hebrews were in the habit of praying; and a praye offered there, even by us *infidels*, as all Christians are termed, they say, must be effectual. * * * * * The Moslem tradition concerning the Sakhrah is that fell it from heaven about the time that the spirit of prophecy was imparted. This holy stone, they say, wished to accompany the prophet in his nocturnal flight to heaven, and actually started; but in response to the great prophet's prayers, the angel Gabriel was dispatched to stay its flight; and so firm was the grasp by which it was retained, that the impression of the angel's hands are to be seen there to this day. They allege also that the mosk contains the scales for weighing the souls of men, the shield of Mahommed, the birds of Solomon, the pomegranates of David, the saddle of el-Borak, and an original copy of the Khoran, the parchment leaves of which are four feet long. A well of soul-refreshing water is also alleged to exist there. A green slab of marble is also shown, formerly nailed down by eighteen silver nails, three of which still remain. This, it seems, is a kind of chronological table; a nail having been withdrawn for each grand epoch in their history, and when the last nail takes its flight, the consummation of all things will occur. Such are a few of their legends concerning the marvelous rock. They serve, at least, to exhibit the puerility of Moslem ideas, and the strength of their credulity."

* Lucretius ascribes the invention of music to the whistling of the winds in hollow reeds. Franckinus, to the various sounds produced by the hammers of Tubal Cain. Cameleon Poutique and others to the singing of birds; and Zarlino to the sound of rushing waters. It is, however, agreed that music was first reduced to rules by Jubal, sixth in descent from Cain, who was "the father of all such as handle the harp and organ" (B. C. 1800). The flute, and harmony and concord in music were invented by Hyagnis, B. C. 1506. Vocal choruses of men are first mentioned B.C. 556. Pythagoras maintained that the motions of the twelve spheres must produce delightful sounds inaudible to mortal ears, which he called "the music of the spheres." St. Cecilia, a Roman lady, is said to have excelled so eminently in music that an angel was enticed from the celestial regions by the fascinating charms of her melody; and from this tradition she has been esteemed as the patroness of music and musicians.

nature of man; for by its powerful charms the most discordant passions may be harmonized, and brought into unison; but it never sounds with such seraphic harmony as when employed in singing hymns of gratitude to the Creator of the universe. In praise of this science the great poet of nature says,

> "The man that hath no music in himself,
> Nor is not mov'd with concord of sweet sounds,
> Is fit for treasons, stratagems, and spoils;
> The motions of his spirit are dull as night,
> And his affections dark as Erebus:
> Let no such man be trusted."

MUSTARD SEED, Order of. This order was founded by Count Zinnendorf in 1739, under the title of *The Association of Moravian Brothers of the Order of Religious Freemasons*, afterward styled *The Order of the Grain of Mustard Seed.* It belongs to the department of mystic Masonry. The rite is drawn from the parable of the mustard seed (Mark iv.), where Jesus compares the kingdom of God to a grain of mustard seed, which, though the smallest of all seeds, sends forth so great branches that the birds of heaven may repose under its shadow. It had two mottoes—one engraved on a ring, "No one of us lives for himself;" and the other, "What was it before? nothing," was engraved on a cross of gold, which the members wore as the jewel of the order, suspended from a green watered ribbon.

MYSTAGOGUE. In the Eleusinian mysteries, the official who introduced the candidates for initiation, showed the interior of the temple, and explained the doctrines, bore this name. Hence any one who deals in mysteries is called Mystagogue.

MYSTERIES. Since the establishment of the Christian church among all civilized nations the moral and religious instruction of the people has been confided to its care. The church, although *one*, yet among different nations exists in a great variety of forms—forms adapted to the peculiar wants and genius of the people whose improvement it seeks to advance. Previous to the advent of the church this great work was accomplished among the civilized nations of antiquity by organizations which are designated under the general name of Mysteries. It appears that all the perfection of civilization, and all the advancement made in philosophy, science, and art among the ancients are due to those institutions which, under the vail of mystery, sought to illustrate the sublimest truths of religion, morality and virtue, and impress them on the hearts of their disciples. Although history speaks of several institutions of the kind, as the Eleusinian mysteries, the mysteries of Mithra, etc., yet all had a common origin, and a like purpose, and never exhibited a greater variety of forms than the Christian church. The principal of these mysteries are: 1. The Indian Mysteries; 2. The Egyptian; 3. The Orphic; 4. The Cabirian; 5. The Phrygian or Samothracian; 6. The Eleusinia; 7. The Sidonian or Dionysian; 8. Pythagorean.* The civilization, and the social institutions of India, Egypt, Greece, and Syria, and the degree of enlightenment in religion, morality, and science, to which they attain can be traced directly to the salutary influence of the Mysteries. From the foregoing it will be seen that—to a certain degree following the opinion of many of the early Christian fathers—they realized the idea of a church. As none but the just and virtuous were eligible to membership, the initiated were—at least were reported to be—the wisest and best of all countries, and constituted the ancient Pagan Ecclesia—if one may so speak—the church, or assembly of the wise and good; a body competent to teach and enforce the everlasting truths of religion. Their chief object was to teach the doctrine of one God, the resurrection of man to eternal life, the dignity of the human soul, and to lead the people to see the shadow of the deity, in the beauty, magnificence, and splendor of the universe. By the most solemn and impressive ceremonies they led the minds of the neophytes to meditate seriously the great problems of human duty and destiny; imbued them with a living sense of the vanity and brevity of life, and of the certainty of a future state of retribution; set forth in marked contrast the beauty of virtue and truth, and the deep bitterness and tormenting darkness of vice and error; and enjoined on them, by the most binding obligations, charity, brotherly love, and inflexible honor, as the greatest of all duties, the most beneficent to the world, and the most pleasing to the gods. They also, by these rites—rites magnificent and impressive, and startling, by sudden transitions and striking contrasts—rites commencing in gloom and sorrow, and ending in light and joy, dimly shadowed forth the passage of man from barbarism to civilization, from ignorance to science, and his constant progress onward and upward through the ages, to still sublimer elevations. The trembling and helpless neophyte, environed with terror and gloom, and pursuing his uncertain and difficult way through the mystic journey of initiation, which terminated in light and confidence, was a type or representative of humanity marching upward from the gloom and darkness of the primitive state

* See articles on the above under their proper heads.

of barbarism, to a high degree of enlightenment, of social refinement and perfection. The mystic ceremony was, therefore, emblematical of the progressive development of man, and was intended as an aid to that development. The initiatory rituals of Orpheus, of the Cabiri, and of Isis, typifying thus the development of man and the progress of society, were in a sense prophetic announcements of a golden age to come—a more perfect state, where virtue, triumphant over vice, and truth, victorious over error, would be installed on the throne of the world, and direct all human actions and relations. The idea which these rites presented of future retribution is not in harmony with modern opinions, at least so far as most of our Protestant communions are concerned. All the ancient systems of religion and philosophy held that all punishment was purgatorial*—a means of purification—and consequently finite and limited in its character and duration, and was graduated according to the degree of moral turpitude attached to each offense. Hence, in the initiation, the neophyte represented the progress of the soul through the various stages of discipline, upward from the receptacles of sorrow to Elysian beatitude and purity. In all these rites, indeed, the idea seemed to prevail that man, society, humanity, could be perfected only by the ministry of gloom and suffering. The soul's exaltation, and highest good and truest repose, were to be approached only by the way of tears, and sacrifice, and toil. Those mystic dramas symbolized the profoundest mysteries of the soul—the deepest experiences of the human heart. They taught that through darkness and difficulty, in the midst of obstacles and opposition, man should ever struggle upward and onward—onward from the shadowy vale of doubt, and fear, and perplexity, to the golden Orient, whence comes the light of eternal truth! Some writers have contended that the mysteries, and, indeed, all the myths of antiquity, have no reference whatever to religious ideas, or to a spiritual sphere, but are merely allegorical representations of the phenomena of the physical world. Dupuis† explains all the mysteries in this way, and carries his theory so far as finally to assert that Christ is only an astronomical sign, and that the mystical woman of the Revelations, whom St. John describes as "clothed‡ with the sun, and the moon under her feet, and on her head a crown of twelve stars," is but the constellation Virgo! That portions of the Isianic and Cabirian mysteries had reference to astronomical ideas is undoubtedly true; but this fact by

* Vide Enfield's History of Philosophy. Also Guigniant: *Religions de l'Antiquité considereés principalement dans leur Tronnes Symboliques et Mythologique.*
† Origin des tous les cultes.　　‡ Rev. xii. 1.

no means justifies the conclusions of Dupuis and others, that they have no spiritual reference at all. On the contrary, it was the deep, earnest, and positive faith of the ancients, in the unseen and spiritual, which led them to blend in this manner—unfortunately so foreign to our modern habits of thinking—the ideas of science with those of religion. And here we fall far below the ancients. We have divorced science and philosophy from religion, and seem to regard them as quite different and distinct things, the deplorable results of which are seen in our modern systems of education, which are entirely material, and end in skepticism, if not in absolute irreligion. On the other hand, the ancients contemplated the universe from the religious point of view. All the phenomena of life—all the motions of the heavenly bodies—the whole stupendous spectacle of the world—revealed to them the presence of an unseen Intelligence. Hence, their religion embraced all the facts of physical science ; art and philosophy were necessary parts of religion, and reposed on a spiritual basis. Hence, instruction with them was religious and moral. And were they not right? The mysteries were established for human instruction; and there all the sciences were studied with reference to a higher sphere of thought. Nature, with all its laws, its motions, and its mysteries, which science attempts to explore, was, in their views, only a shadow or reflex, or projection, of the more substantial verities of the unseen—the eternal world; philosophy itself was religion. Such was education among the ancients, so far as it went. It was eminently religious. Hence the dramas, represented in the mysteries, and in the rites of initiation, took note at the same time of the facts of science and the verities of religion. And because these dramas and rites shadowed forth some of the phenomena of nature, and the motions of the heavenly bodies, we are not to infer that those who celebrated them had no faith in God, accountability, or a future life; but rather, on the contrary, that those old Grecians and Egyptians saw in all the phenomena of nature—in all the motions of the starry spheres, and in all the miracles of the world—the awful shadow of that mysterious One, who, although infinite and indivisible, yet in some manner incomprehensible to human intelligence, individualizes himself to every human thought, and localizes himself in every place. The mysteries were established then to assist the education and development of man. And with this intention the mystagogues employed every resource to stimulate the moral energies and awaken the noble instincts of those they sought to elevate. The ancients all claimed for these mysteries a divine origin.

Bacchus, in Euripides,* responds to the questions of Pentheus, who demanded from whom he received his new worship and his mysteries, that he received them from the son of Jupiter. All the ancient educators of the race affirmed the same of their teachings. Rhadamanthus says that he received from heaven the laws that he gave to the Cretans.† Minos shut himself up in a sacred cave, to compose his code of laws, which he affirmed were revealed to him by the divinity. Zoroaster, the Persian Seer, claims also to have been divinely inspired.‡ He separated himself from society, and gave himself up to sacred meditations. He invoked the supernal powers, and at length the light of a heavenly inspiration descended upon his soul, and a divine messenger visited him and instructed him in celestial things. Thus, according to Chandemér, he received from heaven the Zend Avesta, that great depository of sublime maxims so revered by the ancient Persians. Ardheshir, desiring to reform the religious code of his kingdom, appointed one of the sages to accomplish the work. The new reformer, not wishing to make innovations which might not be authorized by heaven, invoked the aid of the spiritual powers. He sunk away into a mysterious sleep, and experienced an ecstacy, during which his soul seemed to go forth out of his body. At the end of seven days he awoke, and declared that he had been in communication with the unseen world of spirits, and employed a scribe to write the new revelations which he had received from the gods. Pythagoras§ also professed to receive the divine direction in the foundation of his famous society. He affirms of himself what Titus Livius‖ asserts of Numa, viz: that the secrets of nature, which others knew by opinion and conjecture, were communicated to him by the direct interposition of the gods, and that Apollo, Minerva, and the Muses, had often appeared to him. Whatever we may think of these professions and claims to a divine enlightenment, on the part of the ancient reformers, we cannot but respect that faith and piety which always led them to refer all wisdom and virtue to a divine influence. Their maxim seemed to be that whatever is useful to men is divine. And as the mysteries and the rules of virtue, which they cultivated and enforced, were useful to humanity, they were, of a consequence, providential institutions created by the will of the Eternal. After what we have now said, it cannot be difficult to see clearly the true end and purpose of the mysteries, the first and greatest fruits of which were, according to the

* Euripid: Bacch., p. 460.   † Strabo 1, x. p. 476.
‡ Hyde do vet, Pers. p. 317.   § Phil: I. i. c. 1 Vit. Apoll.
‖ Plut· Vita Numa.

ancients, to civilize savage people, soften their ferocious manners, render them social, and prepare them for a kind of life more worthy of the dignity of man. Cicero places, in the number of supreme benefits which the Athenians enjoyed, the establishment of the mysteries of Eleusis, the effect of which was, he tells us, to civilize men, and to make them comprehend the true principles of morality, which initiate man into an order of life which is alone worthy of a being destined to immortality. The same philosopher, in another place, where he apostrophizes Ceres and Proserpine, says that we owe to these goddesses the first elements of our moral life, as well as the first aliment of our physical life, viz: the knowledge of the laws, the refinement of manners, and the examples of civilization, which have elevated and polished the habits of men and of cities. Their moral end was well perceived by Arrien, who tells us that all these mysteries were established by the ancients, to perfect our education and reform our manners. Pausanias,[*] speaking of the Eleusinia, says that the Greeks, from the highest antiquity, had established them as an institution the most effectual to inspire men with the sentiments of reverence and love for the gods. And among the responses that Bacchus[†] makes to Pentheus, whose curiosity is excited by his mysteries, he tells him that this new institution merits to be widely known, and that one of the greatest advantages resulting from it is the proscription of all impiety and crime. From the above it appears that the mysteries must have been of the highest utility in advancing the civilization of our race, in promoting the arts, and stimulating a taste for science and letters. We have seen that the cultivation of music commenced with the establishment of the mysteries, and formed a great portion of the ceremonies. Sculpture and painting were encouraged, and received their first impulse in these institutions. Literature and philosophy were pursued with ardor by the disciples of Orpheus and Eumolpus, and through them religion shed a benign and gentle radiance over all of life. Through the mysteries society received wise and wholesome laws, and that moral and mental impulsion which raised Greece to the summit of human greatness. The drama also owes its birth to these institutions. The first plays, symbolical of man and his progress, his struggles, his trials, his labor, his combats and triumphs, were performed within the secret enclosures, secure from the intrusion of profane eyes. The ceremonies were themselves dramas, shadowing forth, more or less perfectly, the great truths of God, of nature, and the soul, pointing man forward to his great destiny, acquainting him

---

*Paus. Phoc. p. 384.   † Euripid: Bacch vi. p. 460.

with the conditions of moral perfection, and aiding him in advancing toward it.

MYSTIC MASON, RITE OF THE. The eighteenth century, if considered in connection with its intellectual activity, the immense progress made in the sciences and arts, and in relation to the general advancement of the human mind, must be recognized as the most remarkable epoch in the history of the world. It was the golden age of science, and of scientific men. And yet, such were the negative character of its speculations, and the habit that prevailed, of studying the mysteries of the universe, and investigating the laws of nature, apart from the ideal, or without reference to a higher sphere of thought, that the human mind became almost entirely materialized, and at last sunk into the abyss of skepticism. But unbelief is not natural to the heart of man; and even when the intellect is cursed with the demon of infidelity, the heart yearns with deeper intensity to penetrate the occult realms of nature, and hold communion with the awful mysteries of those invisible regions which have no boundaries, and on which philosophy and science, that are simply material, can throw no light. Thus, toward the end of the last century—an age noted at the same time for its splendid achievements in science, and its fearful harvest of irreligion—numerous sects of Mystics arose, particularly on the European continent, whose doctrines, however crude and extravagant, were the solemn protest of the heart against the skeptical spirit of the times, and the agonizing cry of the soul for a more intimate communion with the infinite. Many of the first minds of the age were moved by this impulse, and sought peace and quiet, and consolation, and hope, in the golden realm of the ideal. The Rosicrucians, Illuminati, the Order of St. Martin, and many bodies strictly Masonic, entered with ardor into these high speculations, which were so well calculated to exalt, refine, and expand the soul, and fill it with a divine enthusiasm. To these men the worlds revolved in a sea of light—the emanation from the infinite mind—the natural and spiritual were united in an everlasting embrace. Myriads of spiritual beings walked the earth, and dwelt with men, and occupied themselves with human affairs, as in the days of old. Whatever we may think of some of their theories and operations, it cannot be denied that they accomplished a great work in arresting that furious tide of atheism which threatened, at one time, to sweep all things into its horrible abysses of darkness and despair, and in establishing a harmony between reason and the profoundest mysteries of religion. It was at this time that the "Rite of the Mystic Mason" made its appearance.

Its character is strictly Masonic. It recognizes the three symbolical degrees as the groundwork of its system. It has a strong infusion of Swedenborgian ideas, repudiates all Sadducean doctrines, and asserts the existence of angels and spirits, their constant presence with men, and invokes them in the Lodge, at the commencement of labor. Like the 28th degree of the Scotch rite, it is somewhat alchemistical. It believes the Philosopher's Stone and the Elixir of Life among the possibilities of science. Thus, in the instructions of the 2d degree, the disciple is informed that Solomon learned, by the opening of the first and second circles, the art of purifying—that is, transmuting metals, wherewith to enrich and embellish his temple. This rite consists of three degrees: 1. Mystic Apprentice; 2. Mystic Fellow-Craft; 3. Mystic Master. Something of their character may be learned from the following extracts taken from the lectures:

Ques. Are you a Mystic Apprentice?

Ans. I know the northern part of the Temple of Solomon, and the four quarters of the circle.

Ques. How were you received a Mystic Apprentice?

Ans. By striking three blows with the gavel upon——

Ques. What else have you done?

Ans. I have invoked the spirits who preside there, by pronouncing their names.

Ques. Can you repeat them?

Ans. Mahir is that of the East, over the part of the South; Haouzay is spirit of the West, over the part of the North; and Mahal Marainto is the spirit of the East, over the same part.

Ques. What is Masonry?

Ans. The knowledge of the covenants of God with men.

Ques. What signify the four spirits?

Ans. They represent to us that without the assistance of the guardian angels, that God has given to all men to direct their conduct, we cannot succeed in any undertaking.

In the instructions of the 2d degree we find the following:

Ques. Are you a Mystic Fellow-Craft?

Ans. I know the column of Boaz.

Ques. What are the five perfect points of Masonry?

Ans. To build temples to virtue, and dungeons to vice; to know the relations of man with his creator; to practice faithfully his precepts; penetrate into those mysteries it is permitted us to discover, and to employ our knowledge for the instruction and improvement of mankind.

N.

NABIIM, COLLEGES OF THE. Among ancient nations instruction was confined to the few, and generally the schools were controlled entirely by the priests. Moses was educated in a priestly school, in Egypt; Cyrus in a seminary, under the direction of the magi—the Indian Bramins imparted instruction in secret schools. In Palestine those conversant with Hebrew, science, and the Scriptures, taught in the colleges of the Nabiim, or schools of the prophets and rabbins.*

NAHARDA, BROTHERHOOD OF. The Hebrew Rabbins relate that the captive tribes of Israel, during their exile from their own country, after the destruction of the first temple, in order to strengthen the bonds of fraternity, and to enjoy the consolations of friendship, founded a brotherhood at Naharda, on the banks of the Euphrates. On the return of the Jews from the captivity, Zerubbabel, Jeshua, and Esdras, carried away all the secret knowledge which was so carefully preserved within the closed recesses of this mysterious institution with them to Jerusalem, and established in that city a similar society for the same purpose.

NAPOLEON MASONRY. This brotherhood was founded at Paris, 1816, by the adherents of the Emperor Napoleon. Its ritual comprised three degrees: 1. Knight; 2. Commander; 3. Grand Elect. This last was divided into three classes, viz: 1. Secret Judge; 2. Perfect Initiate; 3. Knight of the Oaken Crown. All of them had reference to Napoleon. In the catechism of the degrees we find the following questions and answers:

Ques. How many stories had the temple?
Ans. Eight.

* These institutions are said to have been established by the prophet Samuel, to counteract the progress of the spurious Freemasonry which was introduced into Palestine before his time. They were seminaries in which the most talented and pious youths of Israel were educated to become the future teachers of the nation. For this purpose young men of superior capacity were invited to enter these institutions from all parts of Israel; the system of instruction comprising a thorough knowledge of the law and writings of Moses, natural philosophy, music, and poetry and as this last was altogether devoted to celebrate the power and goodness of God, Samuel, in the 99th Psalm, is enumerated amongst those worthies who promoted divine knowledge. After the death of Samuel, the Nabiim spread widely over the land, and similar lodges or seminaries were founded in every part of Israel. In the days of Elijah three of these institutions are spoken of; and though little is known of their internal economy, their rites and ceremonies being strictly concealed, there can be no doubt that they were in many respects similar to our Masonic lodges, and in some of their features they bore a resemblance to the collegiate institutions of our own country.

Ques. What were their names?
Ans. Adam, Eve, Noah, Lamech, Naamah, Phaleg, Obal, Orient—the initial letters of Napoleon.
Ques. What is your age?
Ans. I have lived only ten years, i. e., 1804–14.

General Bertrand was elected the first Grand Master, without his knowledge, and in his absence the Order was governed by a Supreme Commander and two Lieutenants.

NARBONNE, RITE OF. Primitive Rite, or Philadelphians— *Friendly Brothers*—of Narbonne. This Order was established at Narbonne, 1780, under the name of "First Lodge of St. John." In 1784 it entered into relations with the Philaletheans, at Paris, and was deeply occupied with the Hermetic Philosophy. It had ten degrees, the higher ones strongly alchemistical—divided into three classes, viz: 1st class, 1. Apprentice; 2. Fellow-Craft; 3. Master. 2d class, 4. Perfect Master; Elect; Architect; 5. Sublime Scotch; 6. Knight of the Sword; Knight of the East; Prince of Jerusalem. 3d class, 7. 1st Chapter of Rose-Croix; 8. 2d Chapter of Rose-Croix; 9. 3d Chapter of Rose-Croix. In this, Masonic and physical science, philosophy, and whatever can contribute to the improvement and happiness of mankind, were made objects of special study. 10. 4th Chapter, called Brothers Rose-Croix of the Grand Rosary. The brothers of this degree devoted themselves chiefly to an investigation of the sciences of Ontology, Psychology, Pneumatology, in a word, all those sciences that are named occult or secret. Their professed object was the general enlightenment of man, and his reëstablishment in his primitive rights.

NEBUZARADAN. According to Gesenius the name means "Prince and Lord of Nebo." He was the chief of the lifeguard of Nebuchadnezzar, and general of his armies. He captured and sacked Jerusalem, burned the temple, and carried most of the inhabitants to Babylon. In the degrees of Knight of the East and West and Prince of Jerusalem the second Overseer bears this name, and also in the degree of Sovereign Prince of Masonry it is an important word.

NEKAM-NEKAH; also NEKAM-NETAR OR NEHAM-NATOR. A Hebrew expression, equivalent to "Vengeance is accomplished, the punishment has been executed." The word is found in several of the higher degrees of Masonry.

NEOKOROS. A name derived from the Greek "*neōs* and *koreō*," keeper or warder of the temple. The Priest of the 2d class in the Egyptian Mysteries bore this name.

NEOPHYTE. From *neós*, young, and *phuton*, plant. In the Eleusinia and other mysteries a newly-initiated person was thus designated. Among the early Christians the name meant a new convert from paganism; in the monasteries a novice; a title sometimes applied to the candidate for the privileges of Freemasonry.

NE VARIETUR. *That it may not be changed.* When a brother receives a certificate from his Lodge he is required to write his name on the margin, so as to guard against imposture. Should a person claim to be a Mason, and present a certificate to a Lodge he desired to visit, he would be asked to write his name in a book kept for the purpose. If the writing corresponded with the name—that is, was a *fac simile* of it—it would be a proof of the brother's identity; but if the hand writing were different it would be a proof that the person was an impostor, and had either stolen or found the certificate. These words, "ne varietur," refer to this practice.

NEW TEMPLARS. A name given to a Masonic society organized in France, in the early part of the present century, and which claims to be legally descended from the ancient Order of Knights Templar. These pretensions, however, are not recognized. The ritual has five degrees, as follows: 1. Initiati; 2. Intimi Initiati; 3. Adepti; 4. Orientales Adepti; 5. Magni aquilæ nigræ sancti Johannis Apostoli Adepti. These are mere Masonic degrees disguised under latin names. The Order, however, is respectable in point of numbers and the character of the members who are affiliated with it; and its objects, the enlightenment and improvement of mankind, and the relief of the suffering, are certainly worthy of approval.

NINE, THE—that is, the nine muses. In the ritual of the "Royal Order of Herodem of Kilwinning," the following questions and answers are found in the 2d section of the catechism of the first degree:

Ques. How many Knights are necessary to constitute a Chapter of the Royal Order of Herodem?

Ans. Nine.

Ques. Why?

Ans. For three reasons.

Ques. Will you tell me the first?

Ans. Because there are three divisions in numbers which teach us so to number our days as to apply ourselves to wisdom.

Ques. Will you give me the second?

Ans. Because there are nine muses in harmony, which refine and polish human nature.

Ques. Will you name them to me?

Ans. Calliope, Clio, Euterpe, Melpomene, Terpsichore, Erato, Polyhymnia, Urania, and Thalia.

Ques. Will you give me the third reason?

Ans. Because there are nine orders of angels in the celestial hierarchy.

Ques. Will you name them?

Ans. Cherubim and Seraphim, Thrones, Dominions, Principalities, Powers, Virtues, Archangels and Angels.

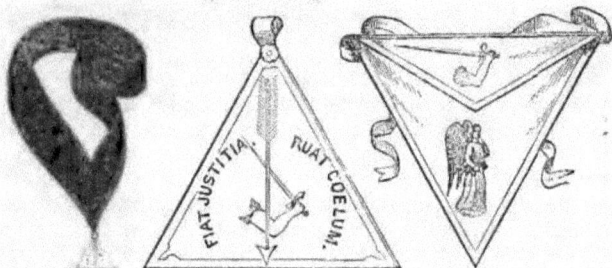

NOACHITE, or PRUSSIAN KNIGHT, sometimes called The Very Ancient Order of Noachites. The 21st degree of the Ancient and Accepted rite. The traditional history of this degree is carried back to an early period; for it commemorates the destruction of the Tower of Babel. It is founded upon the immutable principles of Justice. The meeting is called Grand Chapter, and must be held in a retired place, on the night of the full moon, in each month. The place is lighted by a large window or opening, so arranged as to admit the light of the moon, the only light allowed. The presiding officer sits facing the moonlight; he is styled Lieutenant Commander; the other officers are Warden, Knight of Eloquence, Knight of the Chancery, Knight of the Finances, Master of Ceremonies, Warder, and Standard-Bearer. The sash, worn from right to left, is a broad black ribbon; the jewel is a golden triangle traversed by an arrow, point downward; on the jewel is an arm upraised, holding a naked sword, and around it the motto *"Fiat Justitia, Ruat Cœlum."*

NOAH, PRECEPTS OF. Certain commandments transmitted to the present time, in documents of the ancient stonemasons, bear this name. They require: 1. The renunciation of all idols; 2. The worship of the true God; 3. The commission of no murder; 4. Freedom from the crime of incest; 5. The avoidance of theft; 6. The practice of justice; 7. The abstaining from flesh with blood in it.*

* The Rabbins affirm that God gave Noah and his sons certain precepts, which contain the natural duty common to all men; the observance of which, alone, will be sufficient to save them. The Hebrews would not suffer any stranger to dwell in their country unless he would conform to them. Maimonides says that the first six of these precepts were given by Adam; the seventh was added by Noah. What inclines us to doubt of their antiquity is that no mention is made of these precepts in Scripture, in Onkelos, in Josephus, or in Philo; nor in any ancient father.—CALMET.

NOMINATION. Literally the act of designating a person as a candidate for any particular office. Nominations for office are, by the usages of Masonry, unlawful, and should be so declared by the presiding officer whenever attempted. The election of officers in a lodge to be strictly within the rules of Masonic consistency must be conducted upon the principles of secrecy. Fitness for a proper discharge of the duties of the office should be the only qualification to entitle the candidate, for Masonic preferment, to the suffrages of his brethren; and the brother so elected will be more honored in the silent yet appreciative action of his brethren than by an open showy acclamation.

NORMAL, from the Latin *Norma.* A square for measuring right angles; employed by masons, carpenters, builders, etc., to prove that the angles are true. It was formed in its original adaptation, by the ancient operative craft, in two ways; either by two rules joined together at right angles, or by a flat piece of board with a right angle cut out of it. The illustrations are from ancient sculptured monuments.

NORTH. In the Masonic symbolism the North is the place of darkness. Intelligent Masons understand why this is so. On this word *L'Encyclopedie Maçonnique* thus speaks: "We believe it was to England that Freemasonry was first transported by the Saxons. It here took a new language, new forms modified upon the ancient. It cast its roots deep in that classic land of modern liberty. At a later period it was transplanted into France, where its authentic existence dates only from 1725; we know not whether it came then for the first time, or whether it was a return from a long exile produced by the catastrophe of the Templars. We owe this benefit to an Englishman, Lord Derwentwater, who returned to his country to die for his king. Let us remark, besides, that during the last age the North has been the true East of light! It is in the British Islands, and in the north of Germany that liberty of thought, elevated ideas, Philosophy and Masonry, in fine, have the most numerous partisans; and we can easily make a *climatic* scale of the philosophical spirit."

NOVICE, Novitiate. 1. The same as Neophyte. 2. In the Knight Templar system of Baron Hunde, and also in the Swedish rite this word was the name of the 5th degree. 3. In the Order of *Chevaliers de la St. Cité* certain members were distinguished by this name.

O.

OBELISK. From the Greek *obeliskos* and *obelos*. Schauberg, in his *Handbuch der Symbolik die Freimaurerei*, says: "It was a frequent custom in Egypt to place before the main entrance to a temple two high obelisks, which obelisks were called 'the rays of the sun.'" This species of temple ornaments belongs to the oldest and most simple monuments of Egyptian architecture, and are high four sided pillars, diminishing as they ascend. It is probable that these monuments were first built before the time of Moses. There are still several obelisks in Egypt; at Alexandria, at Matarea, and at Thebes. The two finest are at Luxor, at the entrance of the temple. These Egyptian obelisks are generally constructed of red granite, from 30 to 100 feet in hight, and occupy at their base a space of from 4½ to 12 feet square. Some are plain, while others are adorned on all sides with hieroglyphics. Of their origin nothing is known with certainty. Probably the first images of the gods, which at an early period were nothing but stones of a pyramidical form, furnished the idea of them. According to Herodotus they were first raised in honor of the sun, and meant to represent its rays. This is confirmed by their name and form. They might also have been raised to perpetuate the memory of certain events, since the hieroglyphics contained the praises of the gods and kings, or inscriptions relating to their religious notions. They were generally hewn out of a single stone in the quarries of Upper Egypt, and brought on canals to the place of their erection. Old quarries are still found there with obelisks already hewn out, or with places whence monuments of this form must evidently have been taken out. The two columns, Jachin and Boaz, which stood at the entrance of Solomon's Temple, were *fac similes* of these Egyptian obelisks, and from them arose the fashion in the middle ages of surmounting cathedrals and churches with two towers.

OBLATE. In ecclesiastical antiquities, 1. A person who, on embracing a monastic order, had made a donation of all his goods to the community. 2. One who is dedicated to a religious order by his parents from an early period of his life. 3. A layman residing as an inmate in a regular community to which he had assigned his property. In France, in ancient times, the king possessed the privilege of recommending a certain number of *oblati*, chiefly invalided soldiers, to monasteries, whom they were bound to maintain. In several parts of Europe Masonic asylums are established for the express purpose of maintaining the orphans of deceased Master Masons, and the indigent of the Order, upon similar principles to the above.

OBSECRATO. In Roman antiquity, a solemn ceremony performed by the chief magistrates of Rome, to avert any impending calamity. It consisted of prayers offered up to the gods, whom they supposed to be enraged. So exact were they in observing the prescribed form on these occasions that a person was appointed to read it over to the man who was to pronounce it, and the most trifling omission was held sufficient to vitiate the whole solemnity.

OCCULT. Something secret, hidden, or invisible, as the occult quality of matter. The ceremonies of Masonry are among the occult mysteries.

ODD-FELLOWS, INDEPENDENT ORDER OF. This Fraternity, fashioned after the model of the Masonic Brotherhood, is a widely-extended and influential society. Its motto is "Friendship, Love, and Truth." It first appeared in England, near the close of the last century, and at that time was a social and mutual relief society. It continued to increase until 1840, when, perhaps, the Order in England was in its highest stage of prosperity. It was introduced into the United States as early as 1799, at which time a Lodge was constituted in Connecticut. In 1802 it made its appearance in Baltimore, and in 1806 in New York. It did not, however, attract any attention till 1814, when Thomas Wildey, who is styled the "Father of American Odd-Fellowship," became an earnest propagator of the Order, and founded lodges in a large number of important places. In 1821 the Grand Lodge of Maryland, and of the United States, was formed, and in 1822 the institution assumed its present form. A peculiar feature of the Order is its system of benefits, or of health insurance. In addition to the fees of admission a quarterly tax is collected from its members, which, together, form a fund of relief; and when a brother is sick he receives from his Lodge a certain sum per week, ranging from $3 to $8, or such a sum as the by-laws of the Lodge have determined on. There is, also, a funeral benefit which is paid to the family of a brother in the event of his death. The organization of the Order in the United States stands thus: 1. The Subordinate Lodge, which has five degrees; 2. The Patriarchal or Encampment grade, which has three degrees; 3. The Grand Lodge of a State; 4. The Grand

Encampment of a State; 5. Grand Lodge of the United States;
6. Grand Encampment of the United States. The Order has a
system of symbolism of a highly interesting character, and a
ritual instructive and impressive. In the United States the
Order has had a brilliant career, and awakened, at times, a
large degree of enthusiasm. Its excellent moral teachings,
the intelligence and character of its members, and the salutary
influence it has exercised in the community, have made it
one of the most popular institutions of the age.

ODINIC MYSTERIES. The northern mythology, in the
systematic condition in which we now possess it, is the work
of Scalds—that is, of the ancient minstrels of Denmark,
Sweden, Norway, and Iceland. Religion and civilization
here, as is often the case, sprang from poetry, and were
propagated and nourished, and improved by the mysteries.
The rites of Odin had an Oriental origin. Odin was the
name of the supreme god of the Scandinavians. It appears
from the northern chronicles that in the first century of the
Christian era Sigge, the chief of the Aser, an Asiatic tribe,
emigrated from the Caspian sea and the Caucasus into
northern Europe. He directed his course northwesterly
from the Black sea to Russia, over which, according to the
tradition, he placed one of his sons as a ruler, as he is said
to have done over the Saxons and the Franks. He then
advanced through Cimbria to Denmark, which acknowledged
his fifth son Skiold as its sovereign, and passed over to
Sweden, where Gylf, who did homage to the wonderful
stranger, and was initiated into his mysteries, then ruled.
He soon made himself master here, built Sigtuna as the
capital of his empire, and promulgated a new code of laws,
and established the sacred mysteries. He, himself, assumed
the name of Odin, founded the priesthood of the twelve
Drottars (Druids?) who conducted the secret worship, and
the administration of justice, and, as prophets, revealed the
future. The secret rites of these mysteries celebrated the
death of Balder, the beautiful and lovely, and represented the
grief of gods and men at his death, and his restoration to life.
The neophytes were instructed in regard to the creation of the
heavens and earth, of man and woman, by three Drottars, who
are called the "High," the "Equally High," and the "Highest."
They discoursed to the initiates of the mysteries of the world,
of day and night, of the sun and moon, of the golden age,
of the winds and seasons, of the gods and goddesses, of the
destinies, the twilight of the gods, the conflagration and
destruction of the world. The ceremony of initiation ended
with a sublime representation of the restoration of the
universe, the return of all things to purity, harmony, and

pcacc. The wonderful ash tree Yggdrasil, on which the earth is supposed to rest, was the most notable and significant symbol in these mysteries. Dr. Oliver seems to think that it is the analogue of Jacob's Ladder, but without sufficient

reason. It was the symbol of universal life. According to the ancient Edda, it stands over the well of time; its branches extend over the world, its top reaches above the heavens. It has three roots, one among the gods, another among the giants, and a third under Hela. Near the middle root is the fountain of wisdom—the well of Hymir. Near the heavenly root is the sacred fountain by which the gods hold their council and make known their decisions. From this fountain rise three beautiful maids—the Norns or Fates—whose names are Urdur, the Past; Verdandi, the Present; and Skuld, the Future. On the top of the tree, immediately under its lofty branches, sits an eagle with a hawk, the symbol of watchfulness, between his eyes, which possesses great power and wisdom; the squirrel Ratatösk (mischief) runs up and down the tree, fanning strife between the eagle and the serpent at the root, by whispering to the one what the other says; four harts, which represent the four winds, roam through its branches and bite the buds; the serpent Nidhögge (darkness) is perpetually gnawing at its roots; the trunk of the tree decays, but the holy maidens constantly water its roots from the sacred fountain, that it may not wither. The city on the mountain is *Asgard*, the name of the abode of the gods, access to which is only gained by crossing the bridge *Bifröst*—the rainbow. On one end of the bridge is a citadel in which dwells *Heimdall*, the warden appointed by the gods to watch without ceasing, that no enemy cross or even approach it. At the foot of the hill of *Asgard* lies *Midgard*—middle earth—the dwelling place of mortals. The earth thus formed is round and flat, and the arched heaven above is supported by four dwarfs called *Austri*, east; *Vestri*, west; *Northri*, north; and *Suthri*, south. The sea forms a belt around the earth, and beyond this belt is *Jotenheim*, the abode of the giants. Incessant warfare is carried between the wicked giants who live in the gloomy region and the noble heroes of *Asgard*, who defend the inhabitants of *Midgard* from their invasions. These rites were celebrated periodically, in the temple of Thor, at Upsal, Sweden, and in that of Frigga, on the Island of Rugen. They exercised a profound influence on the life and thought of the Scandinavian people. They taught the immortality of man, and this conviction of eternity so possessed the Northmen that they sought, rather than avoided, death. Looking forward to the golden-roofed palace of heroes, the glorious *Valhalla*, the residence of Odin, gleaming in the splendor of an everlasting morning, where, as they were taught by their mysteries, they should join the innumerable company of the brave, whom the beautiful Valkyræ had previously conducted thither, they stood, undismayed, in the face of the most appalling dangers, and, with joyful songs, entered the gloomy shades of the valley of death.

OFFERINGS, The Three Grand. Offerings are gifts which man brings to the Deity, thus symbolically giving himself. up to him. This was the first mode of openly recognizing the divinity, and a principal part of the service of God in all the religions of antiquity; and even to this day the inhabitants make offerings to the Supreme being, as they make presents to their temporal lords. The idea that God has physical wants, and finds pleasure in food, drink, and perfumes, was the origin of such offerings, which took their character from the mode of life of those who presented them. The three grand offerings referred to in Masonry were those of Abraham, David and Solomon, which were presented on Mount Moriah. There Abraham offered up his son Isaac; there David built an altar, and offered thereon peace and burnt offerings to regain the favor of the Almighty, and move him to stay the plague which was destroying the people; and there Solomon, at the consecration of the temple, presented costly offerings to the Lord. These are the three grand offerings of Freemasonry.

OHEB-ELOAH. A Hebrew expression, which denotes "*one whom God loves.*" It is a sacred word in several Masonic degrees. In the 30th degree of the Ancient and Accepted rite the symbolical ladder with seven steps has these words upon the right side.

OPENING OF THE LODGE. All rites and ceremonies should have for their aim the instruction and improvement of those concerned. They should be simple in character, adapted to the purposes designed, and easy of performance; they should be performed with earnestness, precision, correctness, and in proper time. The ceremony of opening a Lodge is important, instructive and impressive. To conduct this ceremony with propriety ought to be the peculiar study of all Masons, especially of those who have the honor to preside in our assemblies. To those who are thus dignified, every eye is directed for regularity of conduct and behavior; and from them other brethren, less informed, may naturally expect to derive instruction. From a share in this ceremony no Mason is exempted; it is a general concern, in which all must assist. This is the first request of the Master, and the prelude to business. Precisely at the appointed time, the presiding officer should take the chair, and give the proper signal, then every officer should repair to his proper station, and the brethren appropriately clothe themselves and take their seats. Punctuality in this matter is of the highest importance. Our first care is directed to the external avenues of the Lodge; and the officers, whose province it is to discharge that duty, are required to execute the trust with fidelity. "In the ancient mysteries (those sacred rites which have furnished so many models for Masonic symbolism), the opening ceremonies were of the most solemn and impressive character. The sacred herald commenced the initiatory ceremonies by the solemn formula: 'Depart hence, ye profane!' to which was added a proclamation which forbade the use of any language that might be deemed of an unfavorable character to the approaching rites." At the opening of the Lodge two purposes are effected; the Master is reminded of the dignity of his character and position, and the brethren of the respect and veneration due to him in their sundry stations. These are not, however, the only advantages resulting from a due observance of the ceremony; a reverential awe for the Deity is inculcated, and the eye is fixed on that object from whose radiant beam alone light can be derived. Hence, in this ceremony, we are taught to adore the Great Architect of the universe, and to supplicate that the labors then begun may be continued in peace and closed in harmony. A Lodge must always be opened on the third degree, and in due form, for the transaction of any business, except for initiating and passing a candidate into the mysteries of the first and second degrees. The first business after opening, if it be a *regular* communication, is the reading of the minutes of the previous communication, for the information of the brethren. The transactions of the evening should always be read before the Lodge is closed, that the brethren may know that they have been properly recorded, and then duly approved.

OPERATIVE MASONRY. The physical wants of man originally compelled the establishment of operative Masonry. When by transgression man forfeited his primeval home and was obliged to seek shelter from the storms and from the winds, from the cold and from the heat, in winter, the caves of the earth—in summer, the bower of twined foliage, would be his dwelling; next, his inventive mind did conceive the rude tent, then the cabin, afterward the house and the splendid palace, the adode of elegance and skill. Masonry, in its character as an operative art, is familiar to every one; as such, it is engaged in the application of the rules of architecture to the construction of public and private edifices. It abounds in the use of technical terms, and makes use of implements and materials which are peculiar to itself. It is the popular theory that the operative Masons were the founders of the system of speculative Masonry, in which they applied the language and ideas of their art of building to a spiritual and religious sense. At first operative Masonry existed simply as an art of building. Then the operative Masons, with the assistance of learned and pious men, invented the speculative science, or *Freemasonry*, and then each became an integrant part of one undivided system. Not, however, that there ever was a time when every operative Mason, without exception, was acquainted with or initiated into the speculative science. There are, even now, thousands of skillful (operative) stone-masons who know nothing of the symbolic meaning of the implements they employ. Speculative Masonry, now known as Freemasonry, is, therefore, the scientific application and the religious consecration of the rules and principles, the technical language and the implements and materials, of operative Masonry to the worship of God as the Grand Architect of the universe, and to the purification of the heart and the inculcation of the dogmas of a religious philosophy.

OPHITES. An Egyptian Gnostic brotherhood, sometimes called "Brothers of the Serpent," because the serpent was an important symbol in their mysteries. It made its appearance in the second century, and held, in common with the Valentinians, the doctrines of the two principles, of æons and of the theogony therewith connected. They were peculiar by the reverence in which they held the serpent, a living one being employed in their ceremonies. It was an emblem of wisdom—*sophia*— and not, as in other systems, a symbol of evil.

ORANGEMEN. This name was first used by the Catholics of Ireland as an apellation of their Protestant countrymen, who adhered to the house of Orange. It has since been assumed by a political order which was founded in 1794. In 1795 the rules and regulations of the Lodges were published by Thomas, who had privately been made a Mason at Dyon, in the county of Tyrone. At first the order had but one degree; later—1796—the purple degree was added by John Templeton, and still later that of "Markman," and "Heroine of Jericho." The ritual is Masonic in its character, and the organization of the society imitates the Masonic model. The object of the society is to defend the interests of Protestants in Ireland, and propagate Protestant ideas among the Irish. The initiate is required by a solemn oath to renounce all allegiance to the Pope and sympathy with popery, and to declare his unwavering loyalty to the Protestant dynasty of Great Britain.

ORATOR. An officer in most of the degrees of the Ancient and Accepted and French rites. His duties are to explain the history and lectures of the degrees to the cand-date during the ceremony of initiation.

ORDER. Lexicographers thus define this word, "a regular government; a society of dignified persons, distinguished by marks of honor; a religious fraternity." The military orders are societies, the members of which are bound by certain vows and rules, and distinguished by particular badges. They originated from the institutions of chivalry and the ecclesiastical corporations, and were in the beginning fraternities of men, who, in addition to particular duties enjoined by the law of honor, united for the performance of patriotic, charitable, or religious purposes. The oldest Christian orders of which history speaks are the order *Sanctæ* ampullæ, which Clovis founded in the year 499; the Order of the Oak, which Garcias Ximenes, King of Navarre, founded in 722, and the Order of the Genet, the date of whose origin is uncertain. The first orders after these arose during the time of the crusades, and were an example for all future orders. From societies, established under certain rules, for the cure of sick persons as well as the diffusion of the Christian religion, first proceeded the religious military orders, of which the oldest is the Order of St. John of Jerusalem. Their rules are similar to the laws of the monastic orders. The celebrated Order of Templars arose at this period, and distinguished itself by its zeal and bravery through the whole duration of the crusades. The Orders of St. John and of the Knights of the Temple are reproduced in the orders of Masonic Knighthood. The name, order, is applied to a vast number of societies, secular and religious, and also to a considerable number in which the secular and religious are united. Of these Freemasonry is the most ancient and most distinguished. In the *Manuel du Franc Maçon* we find the following reasons why Freemasonry is entitled to be called an order: "An order is a body whose character is known, its practices observable, its rules fixed, its purposes declared, its utility proved, and whose credit is found in the protection of the government. It enters not into the principles of Masonry to unvail its mysteries to the public; but the kings who are members of the order attest that its mysteries would be honored if they were revealed. Its rules are fixed. No one is received into its circle who is not well-born and of good reputation. Its purpose is plain to all; to love God, serve the country, and do good to all. Its utility is proved by its excellent precepts, and the services it renders to humanity. Its credit is not doubtful, since it is protected by sovereigns, and everywhere the title of Freemason is a powerful recommendation. Freemasonry is, therefore, an Order. Religion is a virtue which moves us to render to God the worship that is his due. Freemasons adore the Grand Architect of the universe, therefore, the Order of Freemasonry is religious in its teachings and practice. Freemasonry is an art, since it draws, historically, its origin and illustration from the building of the Temple of Solomon. The art is royal, since Solomon was the conductor of the labors and the chief of the workmen, and the princes and kings who are Masons, are, as Masons, simple artisans. Freemasonry is a society, for its members are elected and are brothers. This society is perfect; for it has existed from time immemorial, and its principles are immutable."

ORDER-NAME. In the Orders of Strict Observance, the Illuminati, and the Royal Order of H-R-D-M. of Kilwinning, each member received at his reception a kind of baptismal name expressive of some quality or virtue. Thus Baron Knigge, in the Strict Observance, bore the name of "*Cygno.*"

ORDO AB CHAO. *Order out of Chaos.* A motto of the Supreme Council, thirty-third degree of the Ancient and Accepted rite.

ORIENT. From the Latin participle "*Oriens,*" rising, i. e., the rising of the sun—*the East.* The Lodge, being a source of light, is called the Orient or East. A Grand body is called the Grand East; thus the Grand Lodge of France is called "Grand Orient." This title is applied to most of the Grand bodies in Europe.

ORIENTAL CHAIR OF SOLOMON. In the East, the seat of the Master in a symbolical Lodge. When the Master of the Lodge is installed he is said to be inducted into the oriental chair of King Solomon.

ORIFLAMME. The ancient royal standard of France. Originally it was the church banner of the abbey of St. Denis, which was presented by the Lord Protector of the convent whenever it was necessary to take up arms for the preservation of its rights and possessions. It was a piece of red silk—hence the name—fixed on a golden spear, in the form of a banner, and cut into five points, each of which was adorned with a tassel of green silk. The banners of several orders imitating the ceremonies of Freemasonry are of this description, and sometimes bear the name Oriflamme upon them.

ORNAMENTS OF A LODGE. The Mosaic pavement, the indented tessel, and the blazing star, are called the ornaments of a Lodge.

ORNAN. A Jebusite, from whom David purchased the threshing-floor on Mount Moriah, on which to erect an altar to God—2d Chron. xxi. 18–25. The site of the threshing-floor afterward became the location of the temple.

ORPHIC MYSTERIES. The founder of these mysteries— Orpheus—lived about forty years before the Trojan war. His mysteries were of the Egyptian type, he having been initiated by the priests of Egypt, to which country he went in search of wisdom. The Orphic rites were of a mystical and philosophical character, and, in after ages, united with the Pythagorean, were widely diffused in both Europe and Asia. The Orphic mysteries were the fountain of Grecian civilization. Through their influence the untamed tribes of Greece were trained to the habits of civilized life, and were united in towns and cities, and instructed in useful arts. In his mystic society commenced the development of those great ideas which regenerated that celebrated country, placed it at the head of the civilization of the world, and made it preëminent in science, literature, philosophy, and poetry, and in all the arts that enrich society and embellish life. These rites were the foundation of the mysteries of Eleusis. The Orphic poems embrace the whole cycle of the esoteric religious principles, and the doctrines of the mysteries.

OSIRIS, LEGEND OF. In the articles Isian and Egyptian mysteries we have given an account of this chief figure in the Egyptian mythology. Most writers who have expressed opinions on this subject seem to think that the legend has solely an astronomical sense, and simply means the contest between light and darkness, the conservative and destroying powers of nature. Thus, when the sun—Osiris—sets, darkness—Typhon—appears to triumph, and when the sun rises Typhon or darkness is vanquished, and so the eternal contest goes on. During the last age it was a fashion among the material philosophers to explain all ancient mythology, and the mysteries in this manner, in order to show that they had no religious sense. This was carried so far that even Christ was declared to be nothing but a symbol of the sun, and the twelve apostles were the twelve signs of the zodiac! We cannot admit that the Osirian myth is to be explained solely from the astronomical point of view. It had a higher meaning, and shadowed forth the great mystery of the world, the conflicts of good and evil, of vice and virtue, and announces that even through persecution and death, justice and truth, and virtue, shall advance to a perfect victory; and that the night of death shall yield to an immortal day.

OVERSEER. In the system of Strict Observance, and several others, each of the first two officers of the Lodge, after the Master, is called "Overseer." The name is also given to the Senior and Junior Wardens in English Lodges. In a Mark Master's Lodge three officers bear this title, namely: Master, Senior and Junior Overseers. The duties of these officers are performed by the three Masters of the Vails. Their official emblem is a square.

P.

PALESTINE. 1. The Land of Canaan—Judea. There are two periods in the history of this country which are peculiarly interesting to Freemasons, viz: that which included the reign of Solomon, during which the temple was built, and the one when that country was the theater of the exploits of the crusades, from which time many knightly orders date their existence. The Christian kingdom of Jerusalem was founded in 1099, by the Crusaders. Its constitution was European: a patriarchate, four archbishoprics, several earldoms and baronies, and three orders of knighthood, were instituted; an army of from 12,000 to 20,000 men was kept on foot; and the mosque built by the caliph Omar, in 638, upon the site of Solomon's Temple, was changed into a magnificent cathedral. During this period the order of Knights Hospitallers of St. John of Jerusalem arose, and also that of the Knights Templar. 2. Palestine has been styled the Father-land of the Masonic orders; and a large number of degrees derive their names from its cities and other noted localities, and events that have transpired in its history.

PALLADIUM, Order of the. The date of the origin of this society is unknown. It first appeared at Douay, France. Its ritual and statutes are ascribed to Fenelon; the rules admitted both sexes to membership; its professed objects were spiritual and moral improvement. The male members were called the "Companions of Ulysses," and the female the "Sisters of Penelope." The seal of the order was a heart, crowned with flowers, upon an altar, ornamented with a garland, with a branch of laurel at the right, and another of palm, at the left. Upon the heart was the inscription: "*Je sais aimer,*" I know how to love. This device and the intimacy which prevailed between the Companions of Ulysses and the Sisters of Penelope indicate with sufficient plainness the certain end and principal object of the order of the Palladium. Its existence was of short duration.

PANATHENÆA. One of the famous festivals of Greece, celebrated at Athens in honor of Athene, patron goddess of the city, and intended to remind the people of Attica of their union into one community by Theseus. Before the time of Theseus, or before the formation of the Attic confederacy, this festival was celebrated only by the citizens of Athens, and called simply *Athenœa*. According to tradition, the Athenæa owed its origin to King Erichthonius, about 1506 or 1521 B. C. The later Panathenæa appears to have been a double festival. All writers who mention it speak of a Lesser or Greater Panathenæa, the former held annually, the latter every fourth year. Both took place in the month *Hecatombœon* (July), and lasted several days. The Lesser Panathenæa was celebrated with gymnastic games, musical compositions, declamations, and a torch-light race in the evening, the whole concluding with the sacrifice of an ox contributed by every one of the Athenian boroughs, from which the whole company enjoyed a sumptuous entertainment. During the celebration, no person was permitted to appear in dyed garments. The prize of the victors was a vessel filled with oil, from the sacred tree on the Acropolis. The Greater Panathenæa only differed from the Lesser in being more solemn and magnificent. Homeric poems were sung; dramatic representations were given, and on the last day of the festival a splendid procession took place, in which Athene's (Minerva) sacred garment was carried. This garment was woven by a select number of virgins called εργασκαι, from ἐργον, *work*. It was of a white color, without sleeves, and embroidered with gold. Upon it were described the achievements of the goddess, particularly her victories over the giants. This garment was carried in procession in such a manner as to give it the appearance of the sail of a vessel, to the temple of Ceres Eleusiania, thence to the citadel, where the *peplus* was placed upon the statue of Minerva, which was laid upon a bed strewed and artistically decorated with flowers. Not alone the Athenians, but the whole population of Attica poured forth on this occasion. It was usual to set all prisoners at liberty, and to present golden crowns to such as had deserved well of their country.

PANTHEISTIC BROTHERHOOD. Toland, in his celebrated essay, "Pantheisticon," describes a fraternity whose ritual, as well as principal features, had a strong likeness to Freemasonry; and, thereby, the society gained much credit, but its pretensions to a Masonic character were exposed on the establishment of the Grand Lodge in London, A. D. 1717, and the society was soon abandoned.

PAROLE. It is well known that the order of Odd-Fellows, in addition to its permanent and unchangeable pass-words, has an annual traveling "word," and also term pass-words. The Masonic fraternity in the United States has no arrangement of this kind. But the order in France has a system of this character. The *parole* is of two kinds "*mot de semestre*"—half-yearly word—and "*mot annuel*"—annual word—the first of which is given to all the Lodges at the semi-annual festival of the brotherhood, and the second is communicated to the higher orders in November.

PASSED. A word used to describe the advancement of an Entered Apprentice to the degree of Fellow-Craft. It alludes to his passage between the symbolical columns and through the porch to the middle chamber of the temple.

PAST HIGH-PRIEST, an honorary title by which a companion who has served in the office of High-Priest for the official term of one year is known. The honors and special privileges pertaining to the office are conferred in a convention called the Order of High-Priesthood, composed of present and past High-Priests, which is held to be the bond of brotherly love that unites those who have been elevated to the highest station in a Royal Arch Chapter by their companions, and are engaged in one common task of preserving the landmarks of the order unimpaired, and in protecting, by their high authority, the integrity and honor of the institution. The jewel of a Past High-Priest consists

 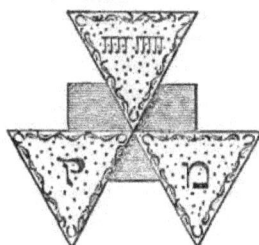

OBVERSE. REVERSE.

of a plate of gold in the form of a triple triangle, a breast-plate being placed over the point of union. In front, on the face of each triangle is inscribed, with the tetragrammaton, יהוה; on the other side the upper triangle has the following mystical notation, ▰▰▰ ▰▰▰▰; the two lower triangles have the Hebrew letters מ and ק inserted upon them. Each side of each triangle should be one inch in length, and may be ornamented at the fancy of the wearer. The breastplate may be plainly engraved or set with stones.

PAST MASTER. The name of a degree conferred on Masters of Lodges before they can assume the duties of the chair. The same degree is also the second of the series known as the Royal Arch degrees. This somewhat anomalous arrangement has led to a confusion of ideas, and considerable controversy in regard to the rights of these two classes of Past Masters. Is a brother who has received the degree of Past Master in a Royal Arch Chapter, but who has never been elected to nor installed into the office of Master of the Blue Lodge, eligible to the elective offices in the Grand Lodge? The constitutions of most Grand Lodges confine the honors of official station to Past Masters. The point to be determined is what construction must be put on this term Past Master, as used in the constitutions. Does it refer solely to those who have actually passed the oriental chair, or does it include others who are not actual Past Masters, but who are entitled to the name, from the fact that they have received the degree in the Royal Arch Chapter? It would seem to be a plain conclusion that, as neither the Grand Lodges nor their subordinates know anything of such a body as the Chapter, the authors of those constitutions could have had no reference to the Chapter whatever, nor to any of its degrees. When designating those who should be eligible to office in the Grand Lodge, they *must* have had in their minds those, and only *those*, who had actually served a term as Master of a Blue Lodge. In point of fact, the degree of Past Master is out of place in the Chapter, and has no right there. It belongs to the Blue Lodge, and should be conferred only upon actual Masters of Lodges when installed into office. As a degree of the Lodge, used as above, it is fit and proper. In the Chapter it has no significance nor pertinence whatever—it is simply an act without meaning, and mars greatly the beauty of Royal Arch Masonry. The degree, itself, furnishes strong internal evidence that it never was intended for any persons but Masters of Lodges. It deals solely with the duties of Masters and with Masonic labors which belong exclusively to Blue Lodges, and is nothing more nor less than the beginning of the installation service.

PASTOPHORAI. From the Greek words *pastos*, a couch or chest, and *pheró*, I bear, equivalent to couch-bearers. The priests of the first class in the Egyptian mysteries bore this name. In the performance of certain ceremonies they carried an image of a god—Osiris—whose allegorical death had been represented on an enclosed couch, or rather, perhaps, in a kind of coffin. This title was also applied to other persons who carried images of their deities through the public streets for the purpose of eliciting charity.

PATENT. A warrant of constitution conferring privileges, and by the authority of which societies and companies exercise their peculiar functions. All Masonic bodies work under a patent or charter, derived from some legitimate authority having full power to grant the same. It must be confessed that not a few of the Masonic patents and charters of the last century were forgeries. The one that Baron Hunde laid before the Convention of Kohlo, June, 22, 1772, was written in cipher, and no person has ever yet been able to explain or read it. It was examined, however, by Firks, Lestwitz, De Bruggen and Hohenthal, who pronounced it legitimate, and Kessler, in a funeral oration pronounced over the deceased Grand Master, relates that the Brothers Smith brought it from England or Scotland about the year 1754! Many other patents and charters that are sometimes spoken of had an origin equally lofty in the clouds of doubt and ambiguity.

PATMOS, KNIGHT OF. A degree which belongs to a series of degrees that the ancient Grand Encampment of Templars in Scotland conferred. It is historical, and has reference to the banishment of St. John and the visions of the Apocalypse.

PATRIARCH. From the Greek *patria,* family, and *archōn,* head or chief. The heads of the antediluvian families, and the three fathers of the Hebrew race, are thus designated. The celebrated Charter of Cologne speaks of an unknown or invisible Patriarch, and also a Supreme Master Elect, who are to be recognized as the legitimate governors of the Craft. The name is found also in the encampment degrees of the Order of Odd Fellows; in several of the high grades of Freemasonry, and in the 20th degree of the Councils of the Emperor of the East and West. At Paris there is an officer who bears the name of Grand Patriarch.

PATRON. A protector. The Latin *patronus* signified, in the Roman Republic, a patrician, who had plebeians called *clients* under his immediate protection, and whose interests he supported by his authority and influence. The history of Freemasonry in Great Britain shows that the Order, at a very early period, recognized the king as its patron, or some one appointed by the king to represent him. The constitutions of York also ordained that "All legitimate societies"— of Masons—"shall labor under a patron." Charles I. was patron of the English Masons from 1625 to 1644. The changed circumstances of the times, the growth of democratic ideas, and the overwhelming political power now possessed by the masses of the people, have rendered the expression, "patron of Masonry," very nearly an obsolete notion.

PELICAN. It was formerly believed that this bird, when food could not be found, would sacrifice itself to its young and nourish them with its own blood. Hence the Pelican nourishing its young ones with its blood has often been used by various societies as a symbol of self-sacrificing benevolence. Ragon says that in the hieroglyphic language the Eagle signified a wise, and the Pelican a benevolent, man, and therefore concludes that the Eagle and Pelican of the Rose Croix degrees symbolize perfect Wisdom and perfect Love.

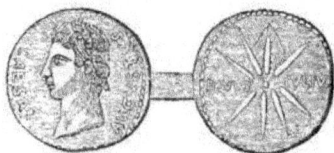

PENNY. The Greek *drachma*, or Roman *denarius*, was the name of the coin mentioned in the parable of the "vineyard," with which the laborers were paid for their day's work. "Every man received a penny." The value of this coin was twelve to fourteen cents United States currency. It plays an important part in the degree of Mark Master.*

PERFECTIONISTS. This was the name that Weishaupt first gave to that branch of the order which was afterward exchanged for that of Illuminati.

PERFECTION, DEGREE OF. Also called Grand Elect, Perfect and Sublime Mason. The French style it *Grand Ecossais de la voûte sacrée de Jacques VI.* It is the 14th degree of the

---

* An erroneous impression prevails respecting the real value of money in olden times, on account of our associations with its present value. A *penny,* equivalent to twelve or fourteen cents, seems to us to be a mean compensation for ten or twelve hours toil in the vineyard, and the *two pence* (Luke x. 35) affords very equivocal evidence to our minds of generosity in the good Samaritan; but when it is considered how much of the comforts and necessaries of life these apparently trifling sums could obtain, the case appears differently. As lately as the year 1351 the price of labor was regulated in England by act of Parliament, and "haymakers, corn-weeders, without meat, drink, or other courtesy" (in modern phrase, finding themselves,) were to have a penny a day. In many places these were the highest wages paid for any kind of agricultural labor, some kinds being still less. The pay of a chaplain in England, in 1314, was three half pence, or about three cents a day. At the same time wheat was sixteen cents a bushel, and a fat sheep only twelve cents. A penny a day under such circumstances would not be inconsiderable wages. In the time of Christ a penny or Roman denarius would have bought, it is estimated, at least ten times more than it would have done in England in the year 1780—and prices then were very much lower than at the present day.—BIBLE DICTIONARY.

CHAMBER OF DEATH.—PERFECT MASTER.

TOMB OF HIRAM.

Ancient and Accepted rite, and the 20th of the Rite of Misraim. Chevalier Ramsay and other political associates of the Pretender were undoubtedly the authors of the degree.

PERFECTION, Rite of. A French system founded by De Bonneville, 1754, which assumed that the Freemasons were the lineal descendants of the Templars, and therefore that all Masons were Knights Templar. It had 25 degrees. Stephen Morin and others introduced some modifications and additions into the rite, and transplanted it in the United States under the name of the Ancient and Accepted rite.

PERFECT MASTER. The 5th degree of the Ancient and Accepted rite. The legend of this degree is founded upon the circumstances of King Solomon's efforts in establishing appropriate obsequies as a grateful tribute of respect to the memory of a worthy departed brother. The Master is styled Most Venerable, and represents Adoniram. The hangings are green; in each corner of the room is a white column; the altar is covered with a black cloth, strewed with tears. The apron is white lambskin, lined and bordered with green; in the center of which is painted, within three circles, a square stone, on which the letter J is inscribed; the flap of the apron is green, symbolically to remind the neophyte that, being dead in vice, he must hope to revive in virtue. The jewel is a compass open to 60 degrees, the points on the arc of a circle. The solemn ceremonies of an interment take place during the progress of this degree.

PERFECT UNION, Lodge of. A new arrangement of Masonic degrees which made its appearance in France during the latter part of the last century, under the auspices of the Lodge of Perfect Union at Rennes. It received the title of the Elect of Truth, and had 14 degrees, divided into three classes. This rite is but a modification of the Rite of Perfection.

PERSECUTION. No society or order of men has been the object of greater abuse or more malicious misrepresentation and unreasonable persecution than that of Freemasonry. Even among the Jews, not many years after the building of the temple, Freemasons were accused of idolatry, the temples where they practiced their mysteries were destroyed, and many of them were put to death. This arose in a great degree from the ignorance of the Jews of that age. They misapprehended the lofty ideas of their greatest king and wisest sage, Solomon, and were made to believe, after his death, that the symbolical decorations of the temple were of a profane and idolatrous character. They were also taught to distrust the liberal views entertained in regard to other nations, and saw in his friendly and fraternal intercourse with Hiram of Tyre, and other distinguished Gentiles, a departure from the strictness of the Hebrew faith. During the life of Solomon the company of Hiram continued to practice their rites unmolested; but after his death a strong and bitter opposition sprang up against them. Their mysteries, not being understood, were called "abominations," and a general movement for the extermination of the Sidonian architects was organized. This ancient persecution of the Sidonian Masons finds its parallel in the persecutions of modern Masons by the Roman Church and other religious bodies. In 1738, Pope Clement XII. fulminated his celebrated bull against the Order, in which he shows himself as fanatical and ill-informed in regard to the nature of Freemasonry as those who headed the persecutions of the Sidonians among the ancient Jews. He says: "We have learned that a society has been formed under the name of Freemasons, into which persons of all religions and all sects are indiscriminately admitted, and whose members have established certain laws which bind themselves to each other, and which, in particular, compel their members, under the severest penalties, by virtue of an oath taken on the Holy Scriptures, to preserve an inviolable secrecy in relation to everything that transpires in their meetings." The bull concludes with a command to all bishops to inflict on Masons "the penalties which they deserve, as people greatly suspected of heresy, having recourse, if necessary, to the secular power." The "penalty" here alluded to is plainly enough explained by the following transcript from an edict published in the following year: "No person shall dare to assemble at any lodge of the said society, nor be present at any of their meetings, under pain of *death* and confiscation of goods, the said penalty to be without pardon." This bull, however, failed to stay the progress of the institution, and when Benedict XIV., 1751, renewed it, and ordered its enforcement, his proclamation was treated with derision and contempt. In Germany, Spain, Turkey, Portugal, France and Switzerland the order has, at times, been persecuted, but it has outlived all opposition, and is now master of those who once trampled it under foot. The anti-Masonic movement in the United States is familiar to all. It was a real benefit to Masonry, and has overwhelmed its authors with infamy and scorn. But the last (and we hope it will be the last) and probably the most ridiculous attempt at persecuting the Masonic institution emanated from the *Secret Consistory* of the Vatican, by Pope Pius IX., September 25, 1865, in the form of a Papal Allocution to his "Venerable Brethren." This dreadful anathema pronounces, *ex-cathedra*, that Freemasonry is "monstrous, impious and criminal, full of snares and frauds—a dark society; the enemy of the Church and of God, and dangerous to the security of kingdoms; inflamed with a burning hatred against religious and legitimate authority; desirous of overthrowing all rights human and divine," etc. It may not be necessary to waste much time or space to the refutation of the charges displayed in this silly and odious papal address. Such accusations against a public body of men spread over the whole surface of the civilized world and in all classes of society, among whom may be numbered monarchs, princes, senators, prelates, and the great and good of all countries, accompanied by the awful sentence of eternal perdition, are detestable, and not worthy of any serious notice. The Pope and his venerable brethren do not like Freemasonry. Very well; nobody blames them for that; and least of all, the members of the Masonic Order; for it is not a proselytizing institution. He objects to it because it is a *secret* society. Very well! Has Romanism no secrets? Then it has no confessional, and it never had an inquisition. Why this Allocution, in which secret societies are subjected to such severe invective, was actually delivered in his own *Secret* Consistory. But as the Roman Church is hostile to freedom of conscience, its doctrines are therefore incompatible with the tolerant and liberal principles of Freemasonry. We shall patiently await another (although another may never occur) "Thunder from the Vatican," but in the meantime the Order of Freemasonry must move on.

PERSEVERANCE, ORDER OF. An Order of Knights and Ladies, which was founded at the Court of Louis XV., A.D 1771, by the Polish Countess, Potoska, Count Brostosky, and the Marquis de Seignelay. Its existence was short.

PERSIAN PHILOSOPHICAL RITE. A new system of Masonry which arose at Paris in the year 1819. It was not much encouraged, and has now ceased to exist. Little is known of its ritual, and whether the three symbolic degrees were essential to its members, or whether they were included in the fanciful names of the degrees adopted, we are unable to learn. It consisted of seven degrees, viz: 1. Listening Apprentice; 2. Companion Adept, Esquire of Benevolence; 3. Master of the Sun—from the 29th degree of the Scotch rite; 4. Architect of all Rites, Knight of the Philosophy of the Heart—enthusiasm; 5. Knight of Eclecticism and of Truth; 6. Master Grand Shepherd; 7. Venerable Grand Elu.

PHALLUS. An image of the *virile* member, which, fastened to a pole, was carried in the religious processions of many of the nations of antiquity. It was not an object of worship, as some have thought, but was reverenced as a symbol of the male productive principle. This symbol, under the name of Lingam, was first employed in the Indian Mysteries; thence it was introduced into Egypt, and made still more conspicuous in the Mysteries of Isis. The legend of Osiris relates that, on being overcome by Typhon, his body was dismembered, and the several parts of it—and among them the virile member—were concealed by Typhon in the four quarters of the globe. Isis, after a long search, succeeded in finding all the members except the one in question, and of this she made a wooden image, which was carried in the processions peculiar to the festivals of Osiris, as an emblem of the productive energies of nature. In the Grecian Mysteries, also, it was used in the same sense, and traces of it are even found among the Jews. The Phallus was not associated in the minds of the people with any low, vulgar or lascivious ideas, but rather represented, as we have before observed, that plastic power, that creative force of nature, that mysterious and inexhaustible fountain of life from which all things proceed. This sign has been prominently associated with the symbol of the *Point within a Circle*.

PHI BETA KAPPA. An order composed of students in American colleges. The first society of the kind was, we believe, organized by the members of William and Mary's College in Virginia, and under the auspices of Thomas Jefferson. It has a sign, grip and word, and a silver medal, which serves as a token of membership; on one side of which, under *six stars*, the number of colleges where the Order is in vogue, and above a *hand*, are engraved the initials Φ. B. K.; while on the other is marked the date of its foundation, "S. P., December 5, 1776." The letters S. P. stand for *Societas Philosophiæ*. The three Greek initials signify *"Philosophia biou Kubernētes"*—Philosophy, the guide of life.

PHILADELPHIANS. This was the appellation of a lodge erected at Narbonne, France, in which the Rite of Narbonne and also the Primitive rite had their seats. This rite claims to rest upon a scientific study of Masonry. Thory—*"Histoire du Grand Orient"*—says: " *Suivant l'ecrit: notion générale sur le caractère et l'objet du rite primitif, le regime est formé par trois classes de Maçons, qui reçoivent dix degrés d'instruction. Ces dégrés, ou classes ne sont pas la designation de tels ou tels grades, mais des denominations de collections, qu'il suffit de* *derouler autant qu'elles en sont susceptible, pour en faire jaillir un nombre presque infini de grades."* Thus, for example, the 4th degree, under the titles of Perfect Master, Elect, Architect, designates an acquaintance with the greater part of the degrees analogous to them.

PHILALETHEANS. This name—a compound Greek word—signifying the "Friends or Lovers of Truth," was given to an order which originated in the *"Loge des Amis Reunis,"* A. D. 1773. The rite or system of degrees was divided into twelve classes:

1. Apprentice.
2. Fellow-Craft.
3. Master.
4. Elect.
5. Scottish Knight.
6. Knight of the East.
7. Knight of the Rose-Croix.
8. Knight of the Temple.
9. Unknown Philosopher.
10. Sublime Philosopher.
11. Initiated.
12. Philalethean, Lover of Truth, or Master of all Degrees.

Like the sect of St. Martin, it had a mystical formation, but most of its teachings were of an elevated character, and discussed the profoundest questions of philosophy in an able manner. It attracted the attention of many distinguished men, who became active members of it; among whom were Count de Gebelin, Dutrousset d'Héricourt, the Landgrave Fredrich Ludwig of Hessen Darmstadt, Baron Gleichen, Abbe Rozier, etc. The soul of the Order was Savaletto de Langes, who was also its founder.

PHILOCHOREITES, ORDER OF. This was a secret society composed of men and women, founded by some officers connected with the French army, in Spain, A. D. 1808, and was afterward carried by them into France. It was also diffused by the Spanish army through many other parts of Europe. It was a system of Adoptive Masonry, with initiation and mysteries. The Lodge was styled the Circle. Each Knight bore an Order name.

PHILOSOPHERS UNKNOWN, ORDER OF. This Order, sometimes called also the Order of Unknown Philosopher-Judges, was a Masonic society, and had two degrees. It belonged to the Templar-Jesuitical system, and its tendency, on the whole, was unmasonic, although it wrapped itself in a Masonic form. The jewel of the Order was a dagger, with the words *Tais* and *Revenge.*

*According to the MSS. "a general idea of the character and objects of the Primitive Rite," the system includes three classes of Masons who receive ten degrees of instruction. These classes are not the designation of such and such degrees, but of collections, which, being properly developed, may produce an infinite number of degrees.

PHILOSOPHICAL DEGREES. The degrees, above the 18th, are distinguished by this name; but why they should be thus named it is difficult to explain. Only one of them —the 28th, or Knight of the Sun—can lay any claim to the appellation. Nearly all the rest are historical and moral, and are, for the most part, amplifications of preceding degrees. During the last century, however, there were several philosophical rites practiced among Masons, but they have gradually been dropped. Only one—the 28th—of our system remains. The name Philosopher is given to a large number of degrees in several Masonic rites. In the *Lodge of des Amis Reunis* we find the degrees of Cabalist Philosopher, Philosopher of the Grand Circle, Hermetic Philosopher, and Philosopher of Hermes. Elsewhere we find Cabalistic Philosopher, Cabalistic Philosopher of the Sublime number Five, Christian Philosopher—degree of the African Architects, Grand Mistress Philosopher—in the Chapter of the Dames of Mt. Tabor, Grand Philosopher, Perfect Mason Philosopher, Perfect Master Philosopher, Sublime Philosopher, Philosopher of the Sublime number Nine, Philosopher of Samothrace, etc. The foregoing by no means completes the list, but these will serve to show the character of the Masonic mind during the last half of the 18th century. There was a yearning for the attainment of the highest truth, and these rites, with their multifarious degrees, were considered as so many steps leading thereto.

PHILOSOPHIC SCOTCH RITE. This system was established in Paris, and adopted by the Grand Lodge in 1776. Some few years previously a Mason named Pernetti founded a rite, to which he gave the name of "Hermetic, or Sublime Masters of the Luminous Ring," the object of the contriver being to instruct his disciples, not only in the higher degrees of Masonry, but also in the art of transmuting metals and preparing the elixir of life. Pernetti had for a pupil a physician named Boileau, who did away with the alchemy, and made it more purely Masonic, and then gave this reformed rite the name above affixed to it. This rite, which Clavel says is still practiced in France, has twelve degrees, the three degrees of Ancient Craft Masonry being necessary pre-requisites, though they do not form a part of the rite. The degrees are: 1, 2, and 3, Knight of the Black Eagle or Rose-Croix, divided into three parts; 4. Knight of the Phœnix; 5. Knight of the Sun; 6. Knight of Iris; 7. True Mason; 8. Knight of the Argonauts; 9. Knight of the Golden Fleece; 10. Grand Inspector, Perfect Initiate; 11. Grand Inspector, Grand Scotch Mason; 12. Sublime Master of the Luminous Ring. The doctrine taught in this rite was that

Freemasonry was founded by Pythagoras; and the lectures consisted of an explanation of the philosophy and peculiar doctrines of the Samian sage, asserting, for instance, that the symbols he adopted in his secret instruction were chiefly derived from geometry; thus, the right angle was an emblem of morality and justice; the equilateral triangle was a symbol of God, the essence of light and truth; the square referred to the divine mind; the cube was the symbol of the mind of man after it had been purified by acts of piety and devotion, and thus prepared for mingling with the celestial beings. The point within a circle, and the dodecahedron or figure of twelve sides, were symbols of the universe; the triple triangle was an emblem of health; and the letter Y a representation of the course of human life, in which there were two diverging paths, the one of virtue leading to happiness, and the other of vice conducting to misery.*

PHILOSOPHY OF MASONRY. This expression opens an immense field for the intelligent Mason to explore, and one so rich in materials that it can never be exhausted. The Philosophy of Freemasonry involves the history of its origin, an inquiry into the ideas that lie at its base, an investigation of its peculiar form, an analytical study of its several degrees, and a development of the ideas which are illustrated by its ritualistic emblems, myths and allegories, and which speak through its sublime system of symbols. Freemasonry has now arrived at a period in its history when the prosperity of the Order imperatively demands a deeper insight into its character and teachings. In this country, for nearly half a century, Masons have occupied themselves merely with the outward and material forms of the institution. Not knowing in what ideas the system had its birth, what truths were symbolized by the rites, what notions were intended to

* Pythagoras, in pursuit of knowledge, traveled into Chaldea and Egypt, and is said to have been instructed in the sacred lore of the Hebrews, either by the Prophet Ezekiel or Daniel. Dr. Oliver asserts that he was initiated into the Jewish system of Freemasonry, and that "his mysteries were the most perfect approximation to the original science of Freemasonry which could be accomplished by a philosopher bereft of the aid of revelation." Jamblicus relates, as evidence of their brotherly love and of their means of mutual recognition, the following incident: A Pythagorean, traveling in a distant country, fell sick and died at a public inn. Previously to his death, however, being unable to compensate the landlord for the kindness and attention with which he had been treated, he directed a tablet, on which he had traced some enigmatical characters, to be exposed on the public road. Some time after another disciple of Pythagoras passed that way, perceived the tablet, and learning from the inscription that a brother had been there sick and in distress, and that he had been treated with kindness, he stopped and reimbursed the innkeeper for his trouble and expense.

be illustrated by its symbols, they have not been able to rise to a true appreciation of its sublime spirit and profound significance. The superior intelligence and culture of the present age require more than this. The questioning spirit of the times demands a reason for this and for that; it cannot rest in a dead form, an outward sign. Masons should acquaint themselves with the philosophy of Masonry, seek and find the *sense* of its rites, study its symbols until they see them all aglow with infinite and eternal truths. "Symbols are the speech of God," and through them Eternity looks into Time, and the Infinite holds communion with the finite, the divine with the human—through them the mysterious currents of life from the over-world stream into our human world of prosaic reality, and light it up with a living glory. There is that latent in Freemasonry which makes it exactly the institution most needed in this age. But to be an effective agent in elevating and advancing man to a more perfect condition, the *sense* of its mysteries must be better understood by Masons, its philosophy must be studied, and its grand and ancient emblems and symbols must be made to speak their immortal meanings as of old. In other words, Freemasonry must be idealized. Masonic literature is exceedingly poor in works touching upon this point. The lectures of Ragon, "*Cours Philosophique*," in France, and the "*Rationale and Ethics of Freemasonry*," by Arnold, in the United States, are the only works we have any knowledge of in this department.

PHŒNIX. A Phœnix, burning, with the words written beneath, "*Perit ut vivat*"—he dies that he may live—alluding to Jacques de Molay, was adopted as the seal of the Order of the Temple, according to the account of the Baron Hunde, by Harris, the second Grand Master after Molay, A. D. 1313; or according to Starck's assertion by Aumont, Molay's successor, 1312–13.

PLATONIC ACADEMY. An institution having Masonic emblems, which was founded at Florence, 1480, during the reign of Cosmo de Medici. It was devoted to the study of the Platonic Philosophy.* Clavel supposes—drawing his conclusions from the Masonic symbols that adorn their hall, which yet exists—that they were a society of Masons, who, even at that early period, had abandoned the operative for the speculative art.

* Plato believed God to be an infinitely wise, just and powerful Spirit; and that he formed the visible universe out of preëxistent amorphous matter, according to perfect patterns or ideas eternally existent in his own mind. Philosophy he considered as being a knowledge of the true nature of things, as discoverable in those eternal ideas after which all things were fashioned.

PLENTY. Literally denoting a full or adequate supply; an abundance. As an emblem of Masonry it is symbolized by a sheaf of wheat (commonly called corn), suspended near a waterfall. The Hebrew word *Shibboleth*, which occupies an important part in the ceremonies of the Fellow-Craft's degree, signifies an ear of corn, also a rapid stream or flow of water. In the Eleusinian Mysteries the goddess Ceres was represented with a flaming torch in her right and an ear of corn in her left hand, and a wreath about her head, as emblems of peace and plenty. This goddess is nearly always represented thus; several gems and medals are now extant, where the ears of corn appear with her image.

POMEL. Literally a round knob. The term is used to designate the globes which rested on the summit of the pillars that stood at the entrance of the temple.

PONTIFEX. This title was borne by the members of one of the great colleges among the ancient Romans, instituted by Numa, for the purpose of preserving and cultivating the highest order of knowledge, particularly of a religious character. Their duties embraced the regulation of all the religious rites and ceremonies (public and private) of the state. They were a self-elected body down to the latter ages of the republic, when the power of election was sometimes held by the people. It was finally vested in the emperors, who added as many to their number as they thought fit. The chief of the pontifices was called the Pontifex Maximus. His station was one of great dignity and power, as he not only had supreme authority in religious matters, but, in consequence of the close connection between the civil government and religion of Rome, he had also considerable political influence.

PRELATE. An officer in a Council of Red Cross Knights and Commandery of Knights Templar, whose title is "Excellent." His duties are to officiate at the altar and rehearse the lessons of divine inspiration. His position is at the right of the Generalissimo in the East. His jewel is a triple triangle, with a passion cross in the center of each, which is the emblem of the Eternal Jehovah, and is to remind him of the importance of the sacred trust reposed in him.

PRIEST, Hebrew, *Cohen.* One who officiates in the public worship of God, especially in making expiation for sin, being "ordained for men in things pertaining to God, to offer both gifts and sacrifices for sins." In the Old Testament the priesthood was not annexed to a certain family until after the promulgation of the law by Moses. Before that time the first born of each family, the fathers, the princes, the kings, were the priests in their own cities, and in their own houses. In the solemnity of the covenant, made by the Lord with his people, at the foot of Mount Sinai, Moses performed the office of mediator, and young men were chosen from among Israel to perform the office of priests. But after the Lord had chosen the tribe of Levi to serve him in his tabernacle, and the priesthood was annexed to the family of Aaron, the right of offering sacrifices and oblations to God was reserved to the priests of this family. The High-Priest was at the head of all religious affairs, and was the ordinary judge of all difficulties that belonged thereto, and even of the general justice and judgment of the Jewish nation. God had appropriated to the person of the High-Priest the oracle of his truth; so that when he was habited in the proper ornaments of his dignity, and with the Urim and Thummim, he answered questions proposed to him, and God disclosed to him secret and future things. He was forbidden to mourn for the death of any of his relations, even for his father or mother; or to enter into any place where a dead body lay, that he might not contract or hazard the contraction of uncleanness. He had the privilege of entering the sanctuary only once a year, on the day of solemn expiation, to make atonement for the sins of the whole people. In general, no priest who had any corporeal defect could offer sacrifice, or enter the holy place to present the shew-bread. The consecration of Aaron and of his sons was performed by Moses in the desert, with great and imposing solemnities. The garments worn by the High-Priest consisted of the following articles: Short linen drawers; over this was a shirt or tunic of fine linen, embroidered, reaching to the feet, and with sleeves extending to his wrists; over this again was another garment called the robe of the ephod, woven entire, blue, with an ornamented border around the neck, and a fringe at the bottom, made up of pomegranates and golden bells. Above all these vestments was placed the ephod, made without sleeves, and open below the arms on each side, consisting of two pieces, one of which covered the front of the body, and the other the back, and reaching down to the middle of the thighs. They were joined together on the shoulders by golden buckles set with

HIGH-PRIEST IN FULL ROBES.

gems, and two large precious stones set in gold, on which were éngraved the names of the twelve tribes of Israel, six on each stone, according to their order. The material of which the ephod was wrought was extremely costly; of blue, purple, scarlet, and fine-twined linen, with rich golden embroidery; also a girdle of fine linen, woven with blue, purple, scarlet and gold, passed twice around the body. Just above the girdle, on the breast of the ephod, and joined to it by golden chains attached to rings at the upper corners, was suspended the breastplate, which was made of the same rich material as the ephod; it was about ten inches square; the front of which was set with twelve precious stones, on each of which was engraved the name of one of the sons of Jacob; these stones were divided from each other by golden partitions, and set in four rows. Upon his head was the miter. This was made of fine linen or silk, blue, wrapped in several folds, in the manner of a Turkish turban. In front, and around the base of the miter, as a band, secured with blue ribbon, was a plate of gold, called the "plate of the holy crown of pure gold," upon which was inscribed, "HOLINESS TO THE LORD," in Hebrew characters. These vestments should be worn by the High-Priest of a Royal Arch Chapter at every convocation, and when worn each of them will convey to the possessor important lessons of symbolical instruction. The various colors of the robes are emblematic of the graces and virtues which should adorn the human mind; the white, of innocence and purity; the scarlet, of fervency and zeal; the purple, of union; and the blue, of friendship. The miter is to remind him of the dignity of his office, and the inscription on its plate to admonish him of his dependence on God. Lastly, the breastplate, upon which is engraved the names of the twelve tribes, is to teach him that he is always to bear in mind his responsibility to the laws and ordinances of the institution, and that the honor and interests of the Chapter and its members should always be near his heart.* In the United States the High-Priest is the first officer of a Chapter of Royal Arch Masons. He represents Joshua, the High-Priest, who, with his com-

* According to Josephus the ancient Jews gave an interesting symbolical interpretation to the several parts of these vestments. He says, that being made of linen signified the earth; the blue denoted the sky, being like lightning in its pomegranates, and in the noise of its bells resembling thunder. The ephod showed that God had made the universe of four elements, the gold relating to the splendor by which all things are enlightened. The breastplate in the middle of the ephod resembled the earth, which has the middle place of the world. The sardonyxes declare the sun and moon. The twelve stones are the twelve months or signs of the zodiac. The miter is heaven, because blue.

panions, Zerubbabel, Prince of Judah, and Haggai, the
scribe, assisted in building the second temple.

PRIMITIVE SCOTCH RITE. This system was first introduced at Namur, in 1770, and consisted of thirty-three
degrees, mostly taken from the Scottish series of Heredom.
Its principal author was Bro. Marchot, an eminent advocate
at Nivelles. It never extended beyond Namur. Clavel says it
is principally practiced in Belgium, and has its see at Namur,
in the Lodge *de La Bonne Amitie.*

PRIMITIVE SCOTCH RITE, or the Philadelphi of
Narbonne, was established at Narbonne, on the 19th of April,
1780. It consisted of three classes of Masons, who received
ten degrees of instruction—a degree meaning a certain
amount of instruction, and some of them including several
Masonic degrees. Thus, the first class had for its three
degrees, the three symbolic degrees in all the rites; the
second class had for its first (4th) degree the Perfect Master,
Elu and Architect; for its second (5th) the Sublime Scottish;
for its third (6th) the Knight of the Sword, Knight of the
East and Prince of Jerusalem; while the third class had for
its four degrees, all being in the Chapter of Rose Croix,
instruction in all branches of knowledge, especially Masonic,
physical, philosophical, psychological and occult. This rite
was reconstituted in the Low Countries in 1819.

PRINCE OF JERUSALEM. The 16th degree of the
Ancient and Accepted rite. The history of this degree is
founded upon the incidents that occurred during the building of the second temple, at which time the Jews were
much annoyed by the constant and malicious interference
of the Samaritans, their ancient enemies. This degree is
closely connected with, and a continuation of, the degree of
the Knight of the East and Sword, to which the reader is
referred for a more detailed statement. There should be
two principal apartments in addition to the ante-room. The
first apartment represents the court of Zerubbabel at
Jerusalem. The hangings are of saffron color, except the
East, which is hung with white, blue, red, and violet colors,
in stripes. The second apartment represents the council
chamber of Darius, King of Persia. The hangings are green,
the throne and canopy saffron color. In it is no Masonic
furniture. The Senior Warden presides and represents
Darius, King of Persia, dressed in royal robes, and wearing
a crown. In the first apartment the presiding officer represents Zerubbabel, and is styled Most Illustrious. The apron
is of crimson, lined and edged with saffron color. On the
flap is an equal balance, held by a hand of Justice. In the

middle of the apron, a representation of the second temple. The jewel is a medal of gold; on which is engraved a hand, holding an equal balance; a double-edged sword, surrounded by five stars; on one side of which is the letter D, and on the other the letter Z, the initials of Darius and Zerubbabel. The Princes of Jerusalem are sometimes styled "Chiefs of Masonry," and are authorized to visit and inspect all lodges of inferior degrees.

PRINCE OF MERCY, or Scotch Trinitarian. The 26th degree of the Ancient and Accepted rite. It is a highly philosophical degree, and its ritual very impressive; its title clearly designates its character and intention. The body is styled a Chapter. The hangings are green, supported by 9 columns, alternately white and red; upon each of which is a chandelier, holding 9 lights. Near the altar is a statue of white marble, the figure of a virgin, covered with thin gauze. This represents Truth, and the palladium of the Order of the Princes of Mercy. The presiding officer is styled Most Excellent Chief Prince. The jewel is an equilateral triangle of bars of gold, with a flaming heart, of gold, in the center. On the heart are the letters I. H. S; and on the respective sides of the triangle, W on the right, F on the left, and H on the bottom. The jewel is suspended from a small collar of narrow watered purple ribbon, and hangs on the left breast.

PRINCE OF ROSE CROIX, sometimes called Knight of the Eagle and Pelican. The 18th degree of the Ancient and Accepted rite. It is the most ancient, interesting, and most generally practiced of the philosophical degrees of Masonry. It is found in all the principal rites, and where it does not exist by name its place is supplied by others, whose symbols do not differ materially from it. To those who have not gone beyond the symbolic degrees, the name is perhaps more familiarly known than any other of the higher degrees. Of its origin nothing satisfactory is known. Baron Westerode, in 1784, supposes it to have been instituted by the Knights Templar in Palestine, in the twelfth century, and asserts that Prince Edward, afterward King Edward I., was then admitted into the Order, under the auspices of Raymond; he also says that the Order was derived from Ormesius, its founder, an Egyptian priest, who had been converted to Christianity. Ragon has elaborately investigated the subject, and attributes its origin to a pious and learned monk, named John Valentine Andreä, who flourished in the latter part of the 16th century; and the same author says that Andreä, grieved at seeing the principles of Christianity forgotten in idle and vain disputes, and that science was made subservient to the pride of man instead of contributing to his happiness, passed his days in devising what he supposed to be the most appropriate means of restoring each to its legitimate, moral and benevolent tendency. Clavel affirms that the degree was founded by the Jesuits, for the purpose of counteracting the insidious attacks of freethinkers upon the Romish faith, but offers no evidence in support of his assertion; when, in fact, they were the great enemies of Masonry, and so far from supporting it wrote a treatise against the Order. Oliver says that "the earliest notice that he finds of this degree is in a publication of 1613, entitled *'La Reformation universelle du monde entier avec la fama fraternitalis de l'Ordre respectable de la Rose-Croix.'"* And he adds: "It was known much sooner, although not probably as a degree in Masonry; for it existed, as a cabalistic science, from the earliest times, in Egypt, Greece, and Rome, as well as among the Jews and Moors in times more recent."† The

* Landmarks, vol. ii. p. 63 n. 35 Am. ed.

† There is a tradition among the Masons of Scotland, that after the dissolution of the Templars, many of the Knights repaired to Scotland and placed themselves under the protection of Robert Bruce, and that after the battle of Bannockburn, which took place on St. John the Baptist's day, in the year 1314, this monarch instituted the Royal Order of Heredom and Knight of the Rosy-Cross, and established the chief seat of the Order at Kilwinning. From that Order, it seems to us by no means improbable that the present degree of Rose-Croix de Heroden may have taken its origin. In two respects, at least, there seems to be a very close connection between the two systems: they both claim the kingdom of Scotland and the Abbey of Kilwinning as having been at one time their chief seat of government, and they both seem to have been instituted to give a Christian explanation to Ancient Craft Masonry. There is, besides, a similarity in the names of the degrees of "Rose-Croix de Heroden," and "Heredom and Rosy-Cross," amounting almost to an identity, which appears to indicate a very intimate relation of one to the other. The subject, however, is in a state of inextricable confusion, and we confess that after all our researches we are still unable distinctly to point to the period when, and to the place where, the present degree of Rose-Croix received its organization as a Masonic grade. No matter, however, where precisely it received its origin, nor who has the honor of having been its inventor, it is at least certain that the degree of Rose-Croix is to be placed among the most ancient of the higher degrees of Masonry; and that this antiquity, in connection with the importance of its design and the solemnity of its ritual, has given to it a universality in the Masonic world, inferior only to the degrees of Ancient Craft Masonry. It is to be found, as we have already said, in nearly all the rites, under some name and in some modification, and in many of them it is placed at the summit of the ritual.

ceremonies of the degree are of the most imposing and impressive character. Its ritual is remarkable for elegance of diction, while the symbolic teaching is not only pleasing, but consistent, figuratively expressing the passage of man through the valley of the shadow of death, accompanied and sustained by the Masonic virtues—FAITH, HOPE, and CHARITY —and his final reception into the abode of light, life, and immortality. VIRTUE and HUMILITY are the foundations and characteristics of this sublime degree. "A man's life," it has been beautifully said, "is laid in the loom of time, to a pattern which he does not see, but God does; and his heart is a shuttle. On one side of the loom is sorrow, and on the other joy; and the shuttle, struck alternately by each, flies back and forth, carrying the thread, which is white or black, as the pattern needs, and in the end, when God shall lift up the finished garment, and all its changing hues shall glance out, it will then appear that the deep and dark colors were as needful to beauty as the light and high colors." Some writers have labored to give an exclusive Christian character to this degree; but the following words of one of the most eminent students of Masonry, and an ardent admirer of the Ancient and Accepted rite, may very properly be quoted,* and a study of the ritual will further prove the correctness of the remarks: "If anywhere brethren of a particular religious belief have been excluded from this degree, it merely shows how gravely the plans and purposes of Masonry may be misunderstood; for, whenever the door of any one degree is closed against him who believes in one God and the soul's immortality, on account of the other tenets of his faith, that degree is no longer Masonry." Bodies of this degree are styled Sovereign Chapters. In cases of reception, there are three apartments, beside the ordinary reception room. The presiding officer is styled Most Wise Master. The recipient is created and constituted "a Knight of the Eagle and Pelican, and Prince of the Order of Rose-Croix." To give the degree full effect music is required. The Knights are dressed in black, with black gloves and a sword. The collar should be reversible, of velvet or silk, crimson on one side and black on the other; plain, without device or embroidery on the crimson side, and with a passion-cross of scarlet on the black side. The apron is, on one side, white satin, bordered with crimson; on the other, black velvet. On the white side is painted or embroidered the pelican side of the jewel. On the black side is a red passion-cross. The jewel hangs at the bottom of the collar, or is suspended to a narrow crimson watered

* Albert Pike.

ribbon on the breast. The jewel is a compass, its points resting on the segment of a circle; at the bottom, on one side, is an eagle, with its wings extended and head slightly

OBVERSE.   REVERSE.

depressed; and on the other a pelican piercing its breast to feed its young, which are in a nest beneath it; between the legs of the compass is a red cross, and above a red rose in full bloom; on the summit of the compass is an antique crown. On the segment of the circle are the letters I. N. R. I. The jewel is of gold, with the pelican and eagle of silver. In this jewel are included the most important symbols of the degree. The cross, the rose, the pelican, and the eagle, are all important symbols, the explanation of which will go far to a comprehension of what is the true design of the Rose-Croix degree.

PRINCE OF THE TABERNACLE. The 24th degree of the Ancient and Accepted rite. It is intended to illustrate the directions for constructing the tabernacle, which God ordered Moses to build, the particulars of which may be found in the 25th chapter of Exodus. This was a movable chapel, and so contrived as to be taken to pieces and put together at pleasure, for the convenience of carrying it from place to place, during the wandering of the Israelites in the

wilderness for forty years. The body is styled a Court.
The presiding officer represents Moses, and is called Most
Puissant Leader. The second officer represents Eleazar, the
High-Priest, the son of Aaron. The candidate represents
Phinehas, the son of Eleazar the High-Priest. Two apartments are required when conferring the degree. The
hangings are red and black. The jewel is the letter ℵ suspended from a violet colored watered ribbon. This degree
is most intimately connected with, and should be considered a
continuation of, that of the Chief of the Tabernacle. The
especial duties of a Prince of the Tabernacle are to labor
incessantly for the glory of God, the honor of his country,
and the happiness of his brethren; to offer up thanks and
prayers to the Deity in lieu of sacrifices of flesh and blood.

PRINCIPAL OFFICERS. A term applied to the Worshipful Master and the Senior and Junior Wardens. They
are called the three principal officers of the Lodge.

PRINCIPAL SOJOURNER. An officer in a Chapter of
Royal Arch Masons. He represents the leader of a party of
Jews, who sojourned in Babylon for a time
after the departure of Zerubbabel with the
main body, and who subsequently came up
to Jerusalem to assist in rebuilding the
temple. His duties in the Chapter are
similar to those of the Senior Deacon in
the symbolic Lodge. He wears a black
robe, with a rose-colored border, and a

slouched hat and pilgrim's staff. His station is on the left,
in front of the Council. His jewel is a triangular plate, on
which a pilgrim is engraved.

PRINCIPALS. The first three officers in an English Royal
Arch Chapter are the First Principal, who represents Zerubbabel, the prince of the people; the Second Principal, who
represents Haggai, the prophet; and the Third Principal,
who represents Joshua, the High-Priest.

PROVOST AND JUDGE. The 7th degree of the Ancient and Accepted rite. The legend of this degree is founded upon the principles of Impartiality and Justice. After the death of the Grand Master Workman of the temple, King Solomon, for the purpose of strengthening his means of preserving order among the vast number of craftsmen engaged in the construction of the temple, appointed seven Provosts and Judges, in order that all complaints among the workmen might be heard, disputes settled, and justice administered. The apartment represents the middle chamber of King Solomon's Temple; the hangings are red, with a sky-blue canopy in the East. The room is lighted with 5 lights, 1 in each corner, and 1 in the middle. The presiding officer is styled Venerable Chief Provost and Judge. The apron is white, edged with red; in the middle is a pocket, with a red and white rosette. On the flap is painted, or embroidered in gold, a key. The sash is crimson, worn from right to left; from it hangs the jewel, which is a key of gold.

PROXY (contracted from *Procuracy*). The agency of one person who acts as a substitute for another, or as his principal; authority to act for another, or for a body, especially in a legislative body. Every Lodge is entitled to be represented in its Grand Lodge, by its Master and Wardens. Should these, or either of them, be unable to attend the Grand Lodge at any communication, a brother or brothers may be appointed. Such substituted representatives, in the absence of their principal, succeed to all his powers and privileges, but in his presence they cannot act. Persons appointed proxies must be Master Masons, and members of some subordinate Lodge under the jurisdiction of the Grand Lodge, and must be furnished with a written certificate of their appointment, under the seal of the Lodge or party appointing them. A proxy cannot appoint a proxy. An officer of the Grand Lodge cannot, as such officer, appoint a proxy, unless the constitution specifically give him such power. The Grand Master is the only officer who has the power or right of appointing his proxy, for any purpose, unless such power be granted by the particular constitution. In the selection of an agent for the proper discharge of a Masonic duty, preference should always be given to able and experienced Masons; it is, therefore, suggested that as a general rule a Master or Past Master should have the preference.

PRUDENCE. One of the four cardinal virtues, the practice of which is beautifully explained in the Entered Apprentice degree.

PYTHAGORAS, Symbols of. The esoteric or secret instructions of Pythagoras were explained with the aid of symbols, as the readiest and most efficient method of impressing upon the mind of the candidate for the mysteries the sublime truths and moral lessons for which the school of that justly celebrated philosopher was distinguished. A few of the most important symbols are here explained. The *Equilateral Triangle*, a perfect figure, was adopted among the ancient nations as a symbol of Deity, the principle and author of all sublunary things; the essence of Light and Truth, who was, and is, and shall be. The *Square* comprehends the union of the celestial and terrestrial elements of power; and was the emblem of Morality and Justice. The *Tetractys* was a sacred emblem, which was expressed by ten jods disposed in the form of a triangle, each side containing four. This was the most expressive symbol of Pythagoras.

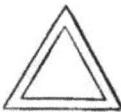 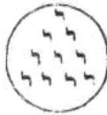 

TRIANGLE.   TETRACTYS.   CUBE.

On it the obligation to the aspirant was propounded; and it was denominated the Trigonon mysticum, because it was the conservator of many awful and important truths, which are explained as follows: The one point represented the *Monad*, or active principle; the two points the *Duad*, or passive principle; the three points the *Triad*, or the world proceeding from their union; the four, the *Quarternary*, or the liberal sciences. The *Cube* was the symbol of the mind of man, after a well-spent life in acts of piety and devotion, and thus prepared by virtue for translation into the society of the

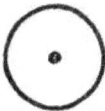   

POINT WITHIN A CIRCLE.   DODECÆDRON.   TRIPLE TRIANGLE.   47TH PROBLEM.

celestial gods. The *Point within a Circle* was the symbol of the universe. The use of this emblem is coeval with the first created man—the creation was the circle and himself the center. The *Dodecædron*, or figure of twelve sides, was also a symbol of the universe. The *Triple Triangle*—a unity of perfectness—was a symbol of health, and was called Hygeia. The *Forty-seventh proposition of Euclid* was invented and explained by Pythagoras, and is so extensively useful that it has been adopted in all Lodges as a significant symbol of Freemasonry. The letter Y was a symbolical representation of the course of human life. Youth, arriving at manhood, sees two roads before him, and deliberates which he shall pursue. If he meet with a guide that directs him to pursue philosophy, and he procures initiation, his life shall be honorable and his death happy. But if he omits to do this, and takes the left hand path, which appears broader and better, it will lead to sloth and luxury; will waste his estate, impair his health, and bring on an old age of infamy and misery.*

PYTHIAN FESTIVAL. One of the four great national festivals of Greece, celebrated every fifth year in honor of Apollo, near Delphi. Their institution is variously referred to Amphictyon, son of Deucalion, founder of the council of Amphictyons, and Diomed, son of Tydeus; but the most common legend is, that they were founded by Apollo himself, after he had overcome the dragon Python. The festivities were similar to those at Olympia, and the victors were rewarded with costly gifts, fruits of various kinds, medals prepared for the purpose, and garlands of laurel, etc.

* PYTHAGORAS, the celebrated philosopher, was born at Samos, about 540 B. C. His father, Mnesarchus, was a person of distinction, and therefore the son received that education which was best calculated to enlighten his mind and invigorate his body. Like his contemporaries, he was made acquainted with poetry and music; eloquence and astronomy became his private studies, and in gymnastic exercises he often bore the palm for strength and dexterity. At an early age he left his native country and began his travels in pursuit of knowledge; he visited Egypt, Chaldæa and India, where he gained the confidence of the priests, and availed himself of an understanding of the mysteries and symbolic writings by which they governed the princes as well as the people of those countries; and after he had spent many years in gathering all the information which could be collected from antique traditions concerning the nature of the religions and the immortality of the soul, he revisited his native island. The tyranny of Polycrates, at Samos, disgusted the philosopher, who was a great advocate of national independence; and, though he was a great favorite of the tyrant, he retired from the island and settled in the town of Crotona, in Southern Italy, where he founded a sect which received the name of *The Italian*, or Pythagorean Fraternity; and he soon saw himself surrounded by a great number of pupils, which the recommendations of his mental, as well as his personal accomplishments, had procured. Pythagoras was, perhaps, the most virtuous, and taught the purest doctrines of all the heathen philosophers. He distinguished himself particularly by his discoveries in geometry, astronomy and mathematics; and it is to him that the world is indebted for the demonstrations of the 47th proposition of the first book of Euclid's elements, about the square of the hypothenuse. The time and the place of the death of this great philosopher are unknown; yet many suppose that he died at Metapontum, about 487 B.C.; and so great was the veneration of the people of Magna Græcia for him that he received the same honors as were paid to the immortal gods, and his house became a sacred temple.

Q.

QUALIFICATIONS OF CANDIDATES. The Masonic institution, like other societies, is composed of individual members, which, in the aggregate, make up a body or Lodge. As the source of power is, primarily, vested in the members, it is important to consider who should compose the body or be admitted into the Order. The qualifications which are indispensable in a candidate for initiation into the mysteries of Freemasonry are four-fold in their character—*Moral, Physical, Intellectual* and *Political.*

The Moral character is intended to secure the respectability of the Order, because, by the worthiness of its candidates, their virtuous deportment and good reputation, will the character of the institution be judged, while the admission of irreligious libertines and contemners of the moral law would necessarily impair its dignity and honor.

The Physical qualifications contribute to the utility of the Fraternity, because he who is deficient in any of his limbs or members, and who is not in the possession of all his natural senses and endowments, is unable to perform, with pleasure to himself or credit to the Fraternity, those peculiar labors in which all should take an equal part. He thus becomes a drone in the hive, and so far impairs the usefulness of the Lodge, as "a place where Freemasons assemble to work, and to instruct and improve themselves in the mysteries of their ancient science."

The Intellectual qualifications refer to the security of the Fraternity; because they require that its mysteries shall be confided only to those whose mental developments are such as to enable them properly to appreciate, and faithfully to preserve from imposition, the secrets thus entrusted to them. It is evident, for instance, that an idiot could neither understand the hidden doctrines that might be communicated to him, nor could he so secure such portions as he might remember, in the "depository of his heart," as to prevent the designing knave from worming them out of him; for, as the wise Solomon

has said, "a fool's mouth is his destruction, and his lips are the snare of his soul."

The Political qualifications are intended to maintain the independence of the Fraternity; because its obligations and privileges are thus confided only to those who, from their position in society, are capable of obeying the one, and of exercising the other without the danger of let or hindrance from superior authority.

Of the Moral, Physical and Political qualifications of a candidate there can be no doubt, as they are distinctly laid down in the Ancient Charges and Constitutions. The Intellectual are not so readily decided. These essential qualifications may be briefly summed up in the following axioms:

Morally, the candidate must be a man of irreproachable conduct, a believer in the existence of God, and living "under the tongue of good report."

Physically, he must be a man of at least twenty-one years of age, upright in body, with the senses of a man, not deformed or dismembered, but with hale and entire limbs as a *man* ought to be.

Intellectually, he must be a man in the full possession of his intellects, not so young that his mind shall not have been formed, nor so old that it shall have fallen into dotage; neither a fool, an idiot, nor a madman; and with so much education as to enable him to avail himself of the teachings of Masonry, and to cultivate at his leisure a knowledge of the principles and doctrines of our royal art.

Politically, he must be in the unrestrained enjoyment of his civil and personal liberty, and this, too, by the birthright of inheritance, and not by its subsequent acquisition, in consequence of his release from hereditary bondage.

The Lodge which strictly demands these qualifications of its candidates may have fewer members than one less strict, but it will un doubtedly have better ones. ※

But the importance of the subject demands for each class of the qualifications a separate section, and a more extended consideration. Dr. Oliver, in his "Institutes of Masonic Jurisprudence," enumerates the following as the qualifications of candidates, according to the English Book of Constitutions, and we here show how easily our transatlantic brethren can change a provision which has, from time immemorial, been regarded as an unchangeable landmark:

"1. Every candidate for the honors of Masonry ought to lead an uncorrupt life, and do the thing which is right, always speaking the truth from his heart; to use no deceit in his tongue, nor to do evil, or slander his neighbor. He must be lowly in his own eyes, and give due honors to good and pious men. If he swears unto his neighbor he must not disappoint him, even though it should subject himself to temporary inconvenience, neither must he lend money to his brother on exorbitant usury, or take reward against the innocent. In conformity with this primitive recommendation, our constitutions pronounce that 'every candidate must be a free man, and his own master, and at the time of his initiation, be known to be in reputable circumstances. He should be a lover of the liberal arts and sciences, and have made some progress in one or other of them.'

"In 1763, the worthy candidate was described to be one 'who to a well-informed and accomplished mind added elegance of manners and a conduct guided by principle; one who would not have injured the rights of the meanest individual; who contracted no debts that he could not pay, and thought every breach of morality unbecoming the character of a gentleman, and who studied to be useful to others so far as his opportunity or abilities enabled him.' This standard of qualification may be considered rather high, and, indeed, it is, and ought to be, so in an institution which plumes itself on its moral tenden-

cies, and maintains a leading position amongst the existing societies which are professedly devoted to works of benevolence and charity. It would be well if the Masters of Lodges were to give themselves the trouble of examining, more particularly than they generally do, whether their candidates are able to substantiate a valid claim to these preliminary qualifications.

"2. According to the customs and regulations of our ancient brethren, every candidate was formerly required to be 'a free man, born of a free woman.' This formula was originally considered to be an unchangeable landmark; but on the extinction of negro slavery by the British parliament, the following arguments were used at a Grand Lodge, holden Sept. 1, 1847, in favor of its alteration. The Grand Master (Earl of Zetland) requested the brethren to consider the propriety of remodeling the form by which a candidate for initiation declares himself to be *free born*. 'There are,' he said, 'at the present moment, many men in Jamaica and other places who are free by the law of emancipation, and yet, their mothers having been slaves, they cannot conscientiously sign such a declaration, knowing it to be untrue; and in the absence of that preliminary act, we cannot initiate them. I should be glad to see it altered, and, therefore, move that in future we substitute the words *free agent* for *free born*, and that the declaration be thus revised.' The amendment was unanimously adopted.

QUESTIONS OF KING HENRY VI. This curious document, which has been printed in many works on Masonry, has elicited a vast amount of discussion among Masonic writers as to its genuineness. It first appeared in the "Gentlemen's Magazine" for 1753, where it purports to be a reprint of a pamphlet of 12 pp., published in 1748, in Frankfort, Germany. It is entitled "Certayne questyons, with answeres to the same, concernynge the mystery of Masonrye; writtene by the hande of Kynge Henrye the Sixthe of the name, and faythfullye copyed by me, Johan Leylande, Antiquarius, by the commande of his Highnesse." The magazine above referred to states that this document was copied by one John Collins, from a MS. in the Bodleian library, and to have been enclosed in a letter from John Locke, the celebrated metaphysician, to Thomas, Earl of Pembroke, dated May 6, 1696. For the still further preservation of this singular paper, it is here repeated, together with the explanatory notes of Mr. Locke:

Ques. Whatt mote ytt be?*

Ans. Ytt beeth the skylle of Nature, the understondynge of the myghte that ys hereynne, and its sondrye werkynges; sonderlyche, the skylle of reckenyngs, of waightes and metynges, and the true manere of façonnynge al thyngs for mannes use; headlye, dwellinges, and buyldynges of alle kindes, and all other thynges that make gudde to manne.

Ques. Where dyd ytt begynne?

Ans. Ytt dydd begynne with the ffyrste menne yn the este,† which were before the‡ ffyrste menne of the weste; and comyinge westlye, ytt hathe broughte herwyth alle comfortes to the wylde and comfortlesse.

Ques. Who dyd brynge ytt westlye?

Ans. The Venetians,* whoo beynge grate merchaundes, comed ffyrste ffromme the este ynn Venetia, for the commodyte of merchaundysynge beithe este and weste bey the redde and myddlonde sees

Ques. Howe comede ytt yn Englonde?

Ans. Peter Gower,† a Grecian journeyedde ffor kunnynge yn Egypte, and in Syria, and yn

---

* What mote ytt be?] That is, what may this mystery of Masonry be? The answer imports. That it consists in natural, mathematical, and mechanical knowledge. Some part of which (as appears by what follows) the Masons pretend to have taught the rest of mankind, and some part they still conceal.

†‡ Ffyrste menne yn the este, &c.] It should seem by this, that Masons believe there were men in the east before Adam, who is called the "ffyrste manne of the weste;" and that arts and sciences began in the east. Some anthors of great note for learning have been of the same opinion; and it is certain that Europe and Africa, (which, in respect to Asia, may be called western countries,) were wild and savage, long after arts and politeness of manners were in great perfection in China and the Indies.

* The Venetians, &c.] In the times of monkish ignorance it is no wonder that the Phœnicians should be mistaken for the Venetians. Or, perhaps, if the people were not taken one for the other, similitude of sound might deceive the clerk who first took down the examination. The Phœnicians were the greatest voyagers among the ancients, and were in Europe thought to be the inventors of letters, which, perhaps, they brought from the east with other arts.

† Peter Gower.] This must be another mistake of the writer. I was puzzled at first to guess who Peter Gower should be, the name being perfectly English; or how a Greek should come by such a name. But as soon as I thought of Pythagoras, I could scarce forbear smiling, to find that philosopher had undergone a metempsychosis he never dreamt of. We need only consider the French pronunciation of his name, Pythagore, that is, Petagore, to conceive how easily such a mistake may be made by an unlearned clerk. That Pythagoras travelled for knowledge into Egypt, &c., is known to all the learned; and that he was initiated into several different Orders of priests, who in those days kept all their learning secret from the vulgar, as is well known. Pythagoras also made every geometrical theorem a secret, and admitted only such to the

everyche londe, whereas the Venetians hadde plaunted maçonrye, and wynnynge entraunce yn al lodges of maçonnes, he lerned muche, and retournedde, and woned yn Grecia Magna,[*] wacksynge and becommynge a myghtye wyseacre,[†] and gratelyche renowned, and her he framed a grate lodge at Groton,[‡] and maked manye Maçonnes, some whereoffe dyde journeye yn Fraunce and maked manye Maçonnes; wherefromme, yn processe of tyme, the Arte passed in Engelonde.

Ques. Dothe Maçonnes descouer here artes unto odhers?

Ans. Peter Gower, whenne he journeyede to lerne, was ffyrste made,[§] and anonne techedde; evenne soe shulde all odhers beyn recht. Natheless Maçonnes hauethe|| alweys, yn everyche tyme, from tyme to tyme, communycatedde to mannkynde soch of her secrettes as generallyche myghte be usefulle; they hauthe keped back soche allein as shulde be harmfulle yff they comed

knowledge of them as had first undergone a five years' silence. He is supposed to be the inventor of the 47th proposition of the first book of Euclid, for which, in the joy of his heart, it is said he sacrificed a hecatomb. He also knew the true system of the world, lately revived by Copernicus; and was certainly a most wonderful man. See his Life by DION HAL.

* GRÆCIA MAGNA, a part of Italy formerly so called, in which the Greeks had settled a large colony.

† WYSEACRE.] This word at present signifies simpleton, but formerly had a quite contrary meaning. Wiseacre, in the old Saxon, is philosopher, wiseman, or wizard; and having been frequently used ironically, at length came to have a direct meaning in the ironical sense. Thus Duns Scotus, a man famed for the subtilty and acuteness of his understanding, has, by the same method of irony, given a general name to modern dunces.

‡ Groton.] Groton is the name of a place in England. The place here meant is Crotona, a city of Grecia Magna, which in the time of Pythagoras was very populous.

§ Ffyrste made.] The word MADE I suppose has a particular meaning among the Masons; perhaps it signifies initiated.

|| Maçonnes hauethe—communycatedde, &c.] This paragraph hath something remarkable in it. It contains a justification of the secrecy so much boasted of by Masons, and so much blamed by others; asserting that they have in all ages discovered such things as might be useful, and that they conceal such only as would be hurtful either to the world or themselves. What these secrets are, we see afterwards.

yn euylle haundes, oder soche as ne myghte be holpynge wythouten the techynges to be joynedde herwythe in the lodge, oder soche as do bynde the fres more stronglyche togeder, bey the proffyte and commodyte com yuge to the confrerie herfromme.

Ques. Whatte artes haueth the Maçonnes techedde mankynde?

Ans. The artes agricultura,[*] architectura, astronomia, geometria, numeres, musica, poesie, kimistrye, governemente, and relygyonne.

Ques. Howe commethe Maçonnes more techers than odher menne?

Ans. The hemselfe hauthe allein in arte of ffyndynge neue artes,[†] whyche arte the ffyrste Maçonnes receaued from Godde; by the whyche they fyndethe what artes hem plesethe, and the treu way of techynge the same. Whatt odher menne doethe ffynde out, ys onelyche bey chaunce, and herfore but lytel I tro.

Ques. What dothe the Maçonnes concele and hyde?

Ans. Thay concelethe the arte of ffyndynge neue artes, and thatt ys for here owne proffytte, and preise:[‡] thay concelethe the arte of kepynge secrettes,[§] that soe the worlde may-

* The artes agricultura, &c.] It seems a bold pretence, this of the Masons, that they have taught mankind all these arts. They have their own authority for it; and I know not how we shall disprove them. But what appears most odd is, that they reckon religion among the arts.

† Arte of ffyndynge neue artes.] The art of inventing arts must certainly be a most useful art. My Lord Bacon's Novum Organum is an attempt towards somewhat of the same kind. But I much doubt, that if ever the Masons had it, they have now lost it; since so few new arts have been lately invented, and so many are wanted. The idea I have of such an art is, that it must be something proper to be employed in all the sciences generally, as alegabra is in numbers, by the help of which now rules of arithmetic are, and may be found.

‡ Preise:] It seems the Masons have great regard to the reputation as well as the profit of their Order; since they make it one reason for not divulging an art in common, that it may do honour to the possessors of it. I think in this particular they show too much regard for their own society, and too little for the rest of mankind.

§ Arts of kepynge secrettes.] What kind of an art this is, I can by no means imagine. But certainly such an art the Masons must have; for though, as some people suppose, they should have no secret at all, even that must be a secret, which, being discovered, would expose them to

eth nothynge concele from them. Thay concelethe the arte of wunder-werckynge, and of foresayinge thynges to comme, that so thay same artes may not be usedde of the wyckedde to an euyell onde. Thay also concelethe the arte of chaunges,[*] the wey of wynnynge the facultye of Abrac,[†] the skylle of becommynge gude and parfyghte wythouten the holpynges of fere and hope; and the universelle longage of Maçonnes.[‡]

the highest ridicule; and therefore it requires the utmost caution to conceal it.

[*] Arte of chaunges.] I know not what this means, unless it be the transmutation of metals.

[†] Facultye of Abrac.] Here I am utterly in the dark.

[‡] Universelle longage of Maçonnes.] An universal language has been much desired by the learned of many ages. It is a thing rather to be wished than hoped for. But it seems the Masons pretend to have such a thing among them. If it be true, I guess it must be something like the language of the Pantomimes, among the ancient Romans, who are said to be able, by signs only, to express and deliver any oration intelligibly to men of all nations and languages. A man who has all these arts and advantages is certainly in a condition to be envied; but we are told that this is not the case with all Masons; for though these arts are among them, and all have a right and an opportunity to know them, yet some want capacity, and others industry, to acquire them. However, of all their arts and secrets, that which I most desire to know is, "The skylle of becommynge gude

Ques. Wylle he teche me thay same artes?

Ans. Ye shalle be techedde yff ye be werthye, and able to lerne.

Ques. Dothe all Maçonnes kunne more then odher menne?

Ans. Not so. Thay onlyche haueth recht and occasyonne more then odher menne to kunne, butt manye doeth fale yn capacity, and manye more doth want industrye, that ys pernecessarye for the gaynynge all kunnynge.

Ques. Are Maçonnes gudder men than odhers?

Ans. Some Maçonnes are not so virtuous as some odher menne; but, yn the most parte, thay be more gude then they would be yf thay war not Maçonnes.

Ques. Dothe Maçonnes love eidher odher myghtlye as beeth sayde?

Ans. Yea verylyche, and yt may not odherwise be: for gude menne and true, kennynge eidher odher to be soche, doeth always love the more as they be more gude.

[Here endethe the questyonnes and awnswares.]

and parfyghte;" and I wish it were communicated to all mankind, since there is nothing more true than the beautiful sentence contained in the last answer, "That the better men are, the more they love one another:" Virtue having in itself something so amiable as to charm the hearts of all that behold it.

This document has always been regarded as authentic, and even the life of Leland asserts its genuineness. But this has recently been disputed by Mr. J. O. Halliwell, the distinguished antiquarian, in a work entitled, "The Early History of Freemasonry in England," published in London, 1844.[*]

[*] "It is singular," says Mr. Halliwell, "that the circumstances attending its publication should have led no one to suspect its authenticity. A few years since I was at the pains of making a long search in the Bodleian Library, in the hope of finding the original, but without success; and I think there is little doubt but that this celebrated and well-known document is a forgery. In the first place, why should such a document have been printed abroad? Was it likely that it should have found its way to Frankfort, nearly half a century afterward, and been published without any explanation of the source whence it was obtained? Again the orthography is most grotesque, and too gross ever to have been penned either by Henry the Sixth or Leland, or both combined. For instance, we have Peter Gowere, a Grecian, explained in a note by the fabricator—for who else could have solved it?—to be Pythagoras! As a whole, it is but a very clumsy attempt at deception, and is quite a parallel to the recently discovered one of the *first Englishe Mercurie*. Let us add that Freemasonry is not in any degree dishonored by the rejection of this evidence from its history.

QUESTIONS TO CANDIDATES. Before the candidate for the privileges and mysteries of Freemasonry can be admitted to a participation in its ceremonies he is required to give his free and full assent to the following questions, respecting the motives that influenced his desire to become a Mason:

1. Do you seriously declare, upon your honor, that, unbiassed by the improper solicitation of friends, and uninfluenced by mercenary motives, you freely and voluntarily offer yourself a candidate for the mysteries of Freemasonry.

2. Do you seriously declare, upon your honor, that you are prompted to solicit the privileges of Freemasonry by a favorable opinion conceived of the institution, a desire of knowledge, and a sincere wish of being serviceable to your fellow-creatures?

3. Do you seriously declare, upon your honor, that you will cheerfully conform to all the ancient usages and established customs of the Fraternity?

4. Do you solemnly declare, upon your honor, that you have never petitioned any other Lodge for initiation and been rejected?

R.

RABBI, or **RABBONI.** A Hebrew word signifying *Teacher* or *Master.* The ancient Jews employed it as a title to designate their learned men, particularly the professors in the schools of the Nabiim or Prophets. Gamaliel, the celebrated Pharisee, and preceptor of St. Paul, was one of these. This title was never formally bestowed on more than seven persons. In John xx. 16, Christ is thus called: "Jesus saith unto her, Mary. She turned herself, and saith unto him, Rabboni, which is to say, *Master.*" It is an important and significant word in Freemasonry.

RAMSAY, ANDREW MICHAEL, better known as the CHEVALIER DE RAMSAY, was born at Ayr, Scotland, June 9, 1686. He was the son of a baker, in good circumstances, and received a liberal education, first at the school of his native place, and afterward at the University of Edinburgh. Becoming dissatisfied with the condition of affairs, particularly of the religious character, in Scotland, he repaired to the continent, and at the University of Leyden, he made the acquaintance of Mr. Poiret, a mystic divine, who induced him to adopt the doctrines of that system of theology. In 1710, he visited the celebrated Fenelon, Archbishop of Cambray, who had imbibed the fundamental principles of mysticism, and by that amiable prelate he was persuaded to become a Roman Catholic. Fenelon's influence procured him the appointment of preceptor to the Duke de Chateau-Thiery and the Prince de Turenne, where he was made a knight of the Order of St. Lazarus, and about the same time became a member of the Masonic Fraternity, in which he soon became a conspicuous and active member. He was also one of the most faithful and zealous adherents of the Pretender (James III.), of whose son he was for a time the tutor; in this position he sought to identify the influence and progress of Freemasonry with the fortunes of the house of Stuart. For this purpose he endeavored to obviate the objections of the French nobility to the mechanical origin of the institution, by asserting that it arose in the Holy Land during the Crusades, as an order of Chivalry.* In the year 1740, he delivered his celebrated discourse at Paris, in which he set forth his theory in regard to the origin of Freemasonry, as follows, viz: "That the first Freemasons were a society of knights, who had devoted themselves to the purpose of rebuilding the sacred edifices which had been destroyed by the Saracens; that the latter, with a view of preventing the execution of this pious design, sent emissaries among them, who, disguised as Christians, mingled with the builders, and paralyzed their efforts; that the knights, having discovered the existence of these spies, became more careful in the future, and instituted certain signs and words for the purpose of guarding against them; and, as many of their workmen were new converts to Christianity, they adopted certain symbolic ceremonies, in order more readily to instruct their proselytes in the new religion. Finally, the Saracens becoming more powerful, the Knight Masons were compelled to abandon their original occupation; but, being invited by a King of England to remove into his dominions, they accepted the invitation, and there devoted themselves to the cultivation and encouragement of the arts of Architecture, Sculpture, Painting, and Music. Ramsay attempted to support his theory by the fact of the building of the College of Templars, in London, which edifice was actually constructed in the 12th century by the fraternity of Masons who had been in the holy wars." In 1728, Ramsay attempted a Masonic reform according to this system. He proposed to the Grand Lodge of England to substitute, in place of the three symbolic degrees, three others of his own invention; those of *Scotch Mason, Novice and Knight of the Temple,* which he pretended were the only true and ancient degrees, and had their adminis-

---

* "The constitutions of English Masonry appeared too coarse for the refined taste of our neighbors, and they must make it more like the occupation of a gentleman. Therefore, the degrees of Apprentice, Fellow-Craft, and Master, were called symbolical; and the whole contrivance was considered either as typical of something more elegant, or as a preparation for it."—*Robison.*

trative center, from time immemorial, in the Lodge of St.
Andrew, at Edinburgh. His proposition was at once rejected by the Grand Lodge of England, which has ever
been averse to any innovations in Ancient Craft Masonry.*
He, however, carried his degrees to Paris, where they met
with astonishing success, and gave rise to all those higher
grades which have since been known by the name of the
Ancient Scottish Rite, and which afterward became so popular on the continent, and gave birth to innumerable other
degrees. These first degrees, introduced by Ramsay, were
called "Scottish Degrees," because they were supposed to
have been instituted by James II., in Scotland, in 1688.
The incorrectness of this assertion is, however, historically
proven; for in the records of the Grand Lodge of Scotland,
we find no mention of any other than the three symbolic
degrees prior to the year 1763. In this year, we find the
first mention of the *Royal Arch Degree* in Scotland, whither
it had been introduced from England, where it had already
been practiced as early as 1752. Thus, prior to 1763, all
these pretended *Scottish* degrees were absolutely unknown
in Scotland, and could not therefore have been instituted
there in 1688. During a visit to his native country, he
offered to settle an annuity on his relations, but they indig-
nantly refused to accept it, on the ground of his having
renounced the Protestant religion. After his return to
France he resided at Pontoise, a seat of the Prince de
Turenne, in whose family he continued, in the capacity of
intendant, till his death, which happened at St. Germain-de-
Laye, May 6, 1743. He was the author of several works
which were very popular.

RECEIVED. In the first degree of Masonry the candidate,
on being initiated, is described as "*entered*;" in the second
degree, as "*passed*," and in the third, as "*raised*." The
word "*received*" is used in the sixth, or Most Excellent
Master's degree, to express the same condition.

RECHABITES. A religious order among the ancient
Jews, instituted by Jonadab, the son of Rechab, from whom
they derived their name. It comprised only the family and
posterity of the founder, who was anxious to perpetuate
among them the nomadic life; and, with this view, prescribed
to them several rules, the chief of which were—to abstain
from wine, from building houses, and from planting vines.
These rules were observed by the Rechabites with great
strictness. (See Jer. xxxv. 6.) In modern times, societies

* Kloss contradicts this, and says that he was only once in England,
and that in 1730, to receive the degree of Doctor of Law.

bearing the name of Rechabites, for the avowed object of abstaining from the use of wine, and promoting the cause of temperance, have been organized in various parts of the world, particularly in the United States.* Many of these recent organizations have adopted ceremonies of initiation, pass-words, grips, etc.

RECORDER. Literally, the chief judicial officer of a borough or city, exercising within it, in criminal matters, the jurisdiction of a court of record; one who enrolls or records. Masonically, an officer in a Commandery of Knights Templar, and a Council of Royal and Select Masters, who has charge of the records and seal of those bodies; his duties are equivalent to those of the Secretary of a symbolic Lodge.

RECTIFIED RITE. This right came from and was a modification of the system of the Templars. It was adopted in 1782, by the Lodges of Strict Observance *(Rite Templier)*; but was subsequently practiced only by some Scottish Directories, the last of which, that of Zurich, was in existence and working as late as 1844. It may be regarded as extinct, since that Directory has been united with the National Grand Lodge of Berne, and has formed with it a new power, styled Grand Lodge of Alpina, sitting alternately at Berne and Zurich. It works the modern English rite; but some of the Lodges under it have reserved to themselves the power of giving the higher degrees that are conferred in foreign countries, not to propagate them, but by way of historical instruction, and to enable their members to be admitted to visit all bodies working the high degrees.

REFLECTION, Chamber of. A room adjoining the asylum of a Commandery of Knights Templar in which the candidate is placed during the ceremonies of the order. In the French and Ancient and Accepted rites the candidate is placed in this room, where he remains for serious reflection, and until he is introduced into the higher and more sublime mysteries of initiation.

REFORMED RITE. This was a reformation of the Rite of Strict Observance, which had been established in 1754, rejecting the connection which the latter had with the Knights Templar. The Reformed rite was established by an assembly of Masons at Wilhelmsbad, under the auspices

---

* In 1851 the Grand Lodge of the United States, Independent Order of Odd Fellows, established a degree specially for the use of the wives of the members of the order, called the *Degree of Rebekah*, which has become very popular throughout this country in connection with that widely extended institution.

of Ferdinand, duke of Brunswick, in the year 1782, assuming
in the first instance, the title of the "Order of Beneficent
Knights of the Holy City." M. de St. Martin's system was
merged into this; and the Lodges that had adopted Martinism adopted the Reformed rite. The ritual of initiation
is divided into two parts; the External Order, comprising
the three symbolic degrees, and the Internal Order, composed
of three degrees, forming a religious system based on
chivalry. These two orders are connected by an interme-
diate degree, the Scotch Master of St. Andrew, in which
candidates were selected for the Beneficent Knights of the
Holy City. This system produced different Directories,
styled "Scottish," having special names and particular
magistral sees, and each exercising, within its jurisdiction,
a pretended Masonic Supremacy. These distinct establishments, united by the same principles, the same doctrines,
and the same Masonic formulas, styled themselves "The
French Tongue," *Langue Française.* They corresponded
with Chambéry, which had the Directory of Italy, or of
Austrian Lombardy. Many Provinces of France, among
others Alsac, Franche-Comte, Dauphiné and Provence, had
Lodges constituted by these Directories. The rite was
extended into Switzerland. Its supreme body is at Zurich,
under the title of the "Directory of Switzerland."

REFORMED HELVETIC RITE. The same as the rite
described in the preceding article, with some changes introduced by Mon. Glayre, of Switzerland, who carried the rite
into Poland in 1784, where it was adopted by the Grand
Orient. It is still practiced, but to a limited extent, in that
country.

REINSTATED. This term is applied to a Mason who has
been expelled or suspended from the Lodge of which he
was a member. On his restoration he is restored to all the
rights and privileges of the Fraternity. No other Lodge
than the one which inflicted the punishment has the power
to restore to membership in a Lodge. The Grand Lodge,
which is the supreme authority within the territorial jurisdiction, has the power to restore an expelled Mason to the
privileges of the order, on proper application being made to
that body.

REJECTION. In the United States an applicant for initiation can be received only by a unanimous vote. One black
ball ensures rejection, and the rejected candidate can apply
to no other Lodge for admission, without the consent of the
one which first received his proposition. In the absence of

any local regulations to the contrary a candidate who has been rejected may renew his application at any time when he may have reason to expect a more favorable consideration of his petition.

RELAXED OBSERVANCE, Clerks of. This system grew out of a schism which occurred in the order of the Strict Observance, at Vienna, in 1767. The new order had as chiefs, among others, the Baron von Caven and the preacher Stark.* They pretended to have exclusive possession of the secrets of the association, and to know the *mysterious cavern* in which were hidden the riches of the ancient Templars. The *régime* comprised ten degrees: 1. Apprentice; 2. Fellow-Craft; 3. Master; 4. African Brother; 5. Knight of St. Andrew; 6. Knight of the eagle, or Master Elect; 7. Scottish Master; 8. Sovereign Magas; 9. Provincial Master of the Red Cross; 10. Magus, or Knight of Splendor and Light. The last degree was divided into five parts, viz: Knight Novice of the third year; Knight Novice of the fifth year; Knight Novice of the seventh year; Knight Sevite, and Knight Priest. Von Stark, by means of this new system, exercised a powerful influence among the Knights and Commanders of the several branches of Templars then existing in France, Germany and Russia. The rite met with great success until 1800, when the Mother Lodge Royal York à l' Amitié, at Berlin, declared that it renounced the high degrees, and would thenceforward work only the symbolic degrees. The same schism produced the High Observance, in which they dealt with alchemy, magic, the cabala, divinations, and other fanciful practices; and the Exact Observance, in which the teaching partook of that of the two first Observances, that had for their bases the systems of Jesuitism and catholicism.

RELICS. The name given in theological and historical nomenclature to what may be in general described as the personal memorials of those among the dead who have been distinguished during life by eminent qualities. The term is also applied to certain emblems of mortality in the Templar system of Masonry, which, in connection with the Holy Scriptures, teach us that a faithful reliance in the truth revealed in that sacred volume will afford us consolation in the gloomy hour of death, and secure to us inevitable happiness in the world that is to come.

* John Aug. von Stark, commonly called the *Preacher*, a man of brilliant intellect and great ambition, was born at Schwerin, October 29, 1741, graduated with the highest honors at Göttingen; initiated in a French Military Lodge in 1763; died 1816.

RELIGION. "Speculative Masonry is so far interwoven with religion as to lay us under obligations to pay that rational homage to the Deity which at once constitutes our duty and our happiness. It leads the contemplative mind to view with reverence and admiration the glorious works of creation, and inspires him with the most exalted ideas of the perfection of his divine Creator." That Freemasonry should be spoken of as a religious institution, or as imparting religious instruction, undoubtedly sounds strange to those who think religion must necessarily be confined to a particular set of theological dogmas, or, in other words, be sectarian. But why should it be thought necessary to make religion traverse simply the narrow circle of sectarian ideas? Is it not a degradation to confine it to so limited a sphere? The Masonic idea is that religion is absolute, everlasting and unchanging; that it is not a dogma, or a collection of dogmas, but rather reverence and humility before the awful Ideas of Infinity and Eternity; a sense of subjection to the great law of Justice which stretches through the universe, and of obligation to love and serve man on earth, and God in heaven. The ideas of God, retribution, a future life—these great facts of religion are not the property of any one sect or party; they form the groundwork of all creeds. Religion, we have said, is everlasting and immutable. It is the same yesterday, to-day, and forever. Sectarianism is but the material framework, changeable and perishable, which men in different ages and countries have raised around it. This material and human investiture of sectarian dogmas changes with the times and seasons; but *that* religion, in the light of which all Masons, whatever their particular creed, desire to walk—that religion, sent forth into the world with the awful sanction of the DEITY upon it, which, as an Ancient says, "is to visit the widow and the fatherless in their afflictions, and keep one's self unspotted from the world"—that religion, the essence of which is to love God supremely and our neighbors as we love ourselves, can never change; being absolute, it can never pass away, and it may be taught, with all its obligations, duties and hopes, and all its beautiful applications to life, without being trammelled by any sectarian dogmas whatever. About religion, in its absoluteness, neither men nor sects ever dispute or quarrel. No; it shines over the human soul clear and bright, like the eternal stars, visible to all; and always, and everywhere, has her voice been heard, consoling the sorrowful, fortifying the weak, and bidding the sons of men aspire to a celestial communion. Such is the Masonic idea of religion. Freemasonry recognizes God as immanent in all created things, working in each blade of grass, and swelling bud, and opening flower, and looks upon all the sciences as so many divine methods through which the Infinite Artist reveals his mysteries to man. Should any Masonic brother, or any other, think that we are claiming too much for Freemasonry in this respect, we have only to ask him to turn to the "charges" and "lectures" published in our books, to find abundant proofs of what we assert. There we read: "The universe is the temple of the Deity whom we serve: Wisdom, Strength and Beauty are around his throne, as pillars of his works; for his wisdom is infinite, his strength is omnipotent, and his beauty shines forth through all his creation." Ancient Freemasonry invariably united all the sciences to the religious sentiment. Of Arithmetic it says: "All the works of the Almighty are made in number, weight, measure, and, therefore, to understand them rightly, we ought to understand arithmetical calculations, and be thereby led to a more comprehensive knowledge of our great Creator." "Astronomy," it says, "is that sublime science which inspires the contemplative mind to soar aloft and read the wisdom and beauty of the Creator in the heavens. How nobly eloquent of God is the celestial hemisphere, spangled with the most magnificent symbology of his infinite glory." Discoursing of Geometry, it says, "By it we discover the power, wisdom and goodness of the Grand Artificer, and view with delight the order and beauty of his works and the proportions which connect all parts of his immense universe." Freemasonry, therefore, in the spirit of true reverence, consecrates all to God—the worlds with their sublime mysteries, and the human mind with its mighty powers and the sciences which it has discovered and explained.

REPEAL. A resolution adopted at a regular meeting of a Lodge, cannot be repealed or reconsidered at any special or extra session.

REPRESENTATIVES, Grand Lodge. The system of Representatives in Grand Lodges originated in the United States, with the Grand Lodge of New York. The system has now become almost universal throughout the world, and much good is being accomplished from its influence, as producing a closer union between the various Masonic bodies thus represented. The Masonic costume is that of the Grand Lodge they represent, and they are also entitled to bear a banner with the name and colors peculiar to the body represented.

RIGHT-HAND. In Freemasonry, the right hand is an emblem of fidelity, and hence, in the fraternal greetings of the Order, it plays a conspicuous part. In the ancient Roman, Collegia Fabrorum, a goddess—Fides or Fidelity—was worshiped by the members. She was symbolically represented by two right hands joined, or by two female figures holding each other by the right hands. The Jewish historian, Josephus, speaking of the Persians and Parthians, relates an incident where the right hand was given as a pledge of security, and says, in regard to the custom : "This is of the greatest force there, with all these barbarians, and affords a firm security to those who hold intercourse with them; for none of them will deceive, when once they have given you their right hands; nor will any one doubt their fidelity when that is once given, even were they before suspected of injustice."

RIGHT SIDE and Left Side. The ancients held that the right side possessed some peculiar excellence above the left, and hence the Latin words "dexter," right, and "sinister," left, also convey the sense of lucky, or good; and unlucky, or evil. The right side has always been considered the place of honor, and the Scriptures abound in passages illustrative of this idea—as in Matt. xxv. 33-4: "And he shall set the sheep on his right hand, but the goats on the left. Then shall the king say to those on his right hand, Come ye blessed of my Father," etc.

RITE. This word is defined to be a formal act of service established by law, precept or custom; a symbolical ceremony and method of representing ideas. Freemasonry, although uniform and immutable, in its principles and general laws, exists, nevertheless, in a variety of methods or forms, which are called rites. These differences, however, are unimportant, and do not affect in the least the fundamental plans of the Order, nor disturb its interior harmony; for Masons, whatever may be the legal rite which they profess, recognize no less, as brothers, Masons of a different rite. These remarks will apply with great force to a member of the Symbolic Lodge—a Master Mason—who is, in all rites and in all countries, acknowledged as such, and entitled to all the privileges which that universal degree confers. Until within a recent period, there was but one system, known as Ancient Craft Masonry, consisting of only three degrees—Entered Apprentice, Fellow-Craft and Master Mason. Many rites and systems have sprung up in various parts of Europe, but without permanent existence. The following list will serve to show to what extent the ingenuity and industry of man may be exerted to gratify his personal interest or vanity. Very few of these degrees or rites are now practiced:

1. *York Rite.* This system is the most ancient, simple, and scientific, having existed from time immemorial. It derives its name from the city of York, in the north of England, where, in 926, the first Grand Lodge of England was organized. In this, the present rite of pure Masonry, originally consisted of the three primitive degrees, Entered Apprentice, Fellow-Craft, and Master Mason, under the title of Ancient Craft Masonry. To them have been added, in modern times, four other degrees, viz: Mark Master, Past Master, Most Excellent Master, and the Royal Arch. The York rite is the most extensively diffused of the rites, embracing four-fifths of the Masons of the habitable globe. It is the predominating rite in England, Scotland, Ireland, their dependencies, and the United States of America, and is practiced, in a modified form, by several of the European Grand Lodges. From this arose—

2. *The English Rite*, adopted by the United Grand Lodge of England and Wales, at the union in 1813, and is now practiced by the Lodges under that jurisdiction.

3. *Ancient and Accepted Rite*, or Ineffable degrees; first known in France, in 1758, as the Emperors of the East and West, with twenty-five degrees. Subsequently these degrees were increased to thirty-three, under the title of Ancient and Accepted Scottish Rite, at the city of Charleston, where, in the year 1801, a Supreme Council for the southern portion of the United States was organized. In 1807 another Supreme Council was established in New York, for the northern portion of the United States. These two bodies are now (1867) in active operation, one in New York and the other in Charleston. This rite, except the York, is the most widely diffused throughout the world.

4. *Rite of Strict Observance*, a system of degrees of immense popularity for many years, in Germany, founded by Baron Von Hund, in 1754.

5. *Chapter of Clermont*, with seven degrees, organized in France about the year 1750, by the Chevalier de Bonneville. This was the first system of what is now termed the "high degrees." From this sprang—

6. *The Rite of Perfection*, the first of the series of the Ineffable degrees, established in 1754.

7. *French*, or *Modern Rite*, was established by the Grand Orient of France, about the year 1786.

8. *Rite of Elected Cohens*, or Priests, was founded some time between 1754 and 1760, by Martinez Paschalis. in France.

9. *Rite of St. Martin*, or Martinism, was instituted by the Marquis de St. Martin, at Lyons, France, about the year 1767.

10. *Elect of Truth*, or Lodge of Perfect Union, founded and practiced for a short period at Rennes, in France, during a portion of the last century.

11. *Emperors of the East and West*, established in Paris, about 1758; the members were at first called "Sovereign Prince Masters, Substitutes General of the Royal Art, Grand Superintendents and Officers of the Grand and Sovereign Lodge of St. John of Jerusalem." This rite had twenty-five degrees, and is the parent of the Ancient and Accepted Scottish Rite.

12. *Philosophic Scotch Rite* was established in Paris, by a physician named Boileau, in 1774; it was adopted by the Grand Lodge in 1776.

13. *Order of African Architects* was established in Germany, by a Prussian named Bancherren, with the approbation of Frederick II., in 1767.

14. *Rite of Philalethes*, or Searchers after Truth, was organized by Sal-

valette de Langes, at Paris about the year 1775.

15. *Illuminati of Avignon* was introduced into Paris by a Benedictine monk, named Pernetti, and Baron Gabrianca, a Polish nobleman, about 1760.

16. *Rite of Swedenborg* was framed from the system of the Illuminati of Avignon, by the Marquis de Thomac, in 1783. This rite is still practiced in some parts of Sweden.

17. *Rite of Zinnendorff*, which was a modification of the Swedenborgian and other rites, was promulgated by Count Zinnendorff, in Germany, in 1767.

18. *Reformed Rite*, established in 1782, at Wilhelmsbad. The members of this rite assumed the title of "Order of Charitable Knights of the Holy City."

19. *Reformed Helvetic Rite* was introduced into Poland in 1784, by Bro. Glayre. The Grand Orient of Poland adopted it.

20. *Order of True Masons*, an offshoot of the Hermetic Rite" of Pernetti, was formed at Montpelier, in France, in 1778.

21. *Adoniramite Rite* was established in France, during the latter part of the last century. The exact date of its rise, and the name of its founder, are at present unknown.

22. *Fessler's Rite*, established by the Lodge "Royal York of Friendship," at Berlin, in 1798, is still practiced to some extent.

23. *Rite of Mizraim.* This rite was first introduced in 1805, at Milan, Italy, and was said to have been brought from Egypt by a learned philosopher of that country, named Ananiah. It was established in Paris in 1814, but has never been recognized by the Grand Orient of France or any other Grand body.

24. *Rite of the Grand Royal Mother Lodge of the Three Globes.* On the 13th of September, 1740, a number of brethren residing in Berlin, Germany, established "by royal authority, and without demanding a charter from any other Grand Lodge," the Lodge of the "Three Globes," which, in 1744, became

the "Grand Royal Mother Lodge of the Three Globes," of which the king, Frederick II., was recorded as Grand Master. This is the popular and prevailing rite practiced in Prussia.

25. *Persian Philosophic Rite* was founded in France about the year 1819. It was not much encouraged, and has now ceased to exist.

26. *Order of the Temple.* This order flourished for a brief period in France, during the early part of the present century. The members claimed a regular descent from the Knights Templar of Palestine.

27. *Order of Charles XIII.* This order was instituted by Charles the Thirteenth, King of Sweden, in 1811, into which distinguished Masons were admitted.

28. *Rite of Memphis* was established in Paris, in 1839, by J. A. Marconis and E. A. Montet. It was a variation of the Rite of Misraim, and its existence was very brief.

29. *Rite of Mopses* was founded in 1740, in Germany. In 1776 it became an androgynous order, and admitted females as members.

30. *Royal Order of Heredom and Rosy Cross*, said to have been founded by King Robert Bruce at Kilwinning, after the battle of Bannockburn, in 1314. This order is confined exclusively to Scotland, and is given only to those who have attained high positions in the Fraternity.

31. *The Swedish Rite*, or that practiced by the sanction of the Grand Lodge of Sweden, was founded upon the above order.

32. *Schrœder's Rite* was first established at Marburgh, Germany, in 1766. This rite is still practiced in some parts of Germany.

33. *Primitive Rite of Narbonne* was established in that city in 1780. The degrees were selected from other rites, and were chiefly of a philosophic character, assuming as their object the reformation of intellectual man, and his restoration to his primitive rank of purity and perfection.

34. *Frères Pontives*, an association of operative and speculative Ma-

sons, established at Avignon, in 1178. Their principal employment was the building and repairing stone bridges.

35. *Order of Mustard Seed*, or the Fraternity of Moravian Brothers of the Order of Religious Freemasons, was instituted in Germany, in 1739.

36. *The Knight of Malta*, as a Masonic grade, was established in England, in the early part of the seventeenth century.

37. *Council of the Trinity* was an independent Masonic system, in which were conferred a number of Christian degrees. This order was established by St. Helena, the mother of Constantine, A. D. 326, when on her visit to Jerusalem.

38. *Rosaic Rite* was instituted in Germany, during the last century. It was for a short time exceedingly popular, but was superceded by the Rite of Strict Observance.

39. *Bahrdt's Rite* was established at Halle, Germany, about the close of the eighteenth century, Its prosperity was of short duration.

40. *Knights and Ladies of the Dove.* An organization founded at Versailles, France, in 1784, into which ladies were introduced. It soon ceased to exist.

41. *Eclectic Rite.* This system was established at Frankfort, Germany, by Baron de Knigge, having for its object the abolition of the high grades, or philosophical degrees, which had, at that period, increased to an extraordinary number. It is clear the Baron did not succeed in his endeavors, as many of the degrees he attempted to destroy are still flourishing, while his rite is very little known.

42. *Grand Chapter of Harodim*, an institution revived, (it is supposed, by Bro. Wm. Preston,) in London,

in 1787. It was a school of instruction, organized upon a peculiar plan, and the lectures were divided into sections, and the sections into clauses. Its teaching embodied the whole art of Masonry.

43. *Knight of the Mediterranean Pass*, an independent and honorary degree, established in 1367, and conferred only on Knights Templar as Knights of Malta.

44. *Knight of Constantine*, like the preceding, is an honorary, or side degree, and only occasionally conferred.

45. *Knights and Nymphs of the Rose.* This was an order of Adoptive Masonry, invented toward the close of the eighteenth century, by M. de Chaumont, at Paris. It had a brief existence.

46. *Order of the Roman Eagle* was established at Edinburgh, in 1784. Its ritual was in Latin.

47. *Adoptive Rite*, or, as it is sometimes called, *Androgynous Masonry*, for the initiation of males and females, was first established in France about 1730, under the title of Lodges of Adoption, which were, in consequence of their great popularity, recognized by and placed under the control of the Grand Orient in 1774. In America, there are several androgynous degrees, such as the Good Samaritan, the Heroine of Jericho, the Mason's Daughter, and the Order of the Eastern Star, the last of which is extensively propagated throughout the United States.

48. *Order of the Illuminati.* A secret society, instituted in Bavaria, by Adam Weishaupt, in conjunction with several other men of high intellectual attainments, in 1776. It flourished for a brief period, and was suppressed in 1784, by order of the Bavarian Government.

ROSAIC RITE. One of the numerous Masonic forms which arose in Germany during the last century. Its author was a clergyman by the name of Rosa. Through the influence of Baron de Prinzen, it was extensively propagated, and continued to flourish until the superior popularity of the rite of Strict Observance threw it into the shade.

ROSE. Harpocrates, the god of silence, was sometimes represented with a crown of roses; consequently, the rose is properly regarded as a symbol of silence and secrecy. The rose, cross, and pelican are the emblems of the Rose Croix degree. Ragon says, respecting the first two, that they were Egyptian symbols, the cross signifying immortality, and the rose secrecy, and hence they together mean the "secret of immortality." The rose has no reference to Christ. The theory that the Book of Canticles, in which the phrase "Rose of Sharon" is found, is an allegorical description of Christ and his Church, has long since been rejected by all well-instructed divines.

ROSE CROIX RECTIFIÉ. In the articles "Herodem" and "Prince of Rose Croix," the reader will find the traditions which profess to give the history and origin of the degree of Rose Croix, which is the eighteenth of the series known as the Scotch Rite, Ancient and Accepted. It is an instructive and interesting grade, in many respects resembling the degree of the Royal Arch, of the York rite. But the form and dogma of this degree are such that it must be confined to those who profess the Christian religion. The Rose Croix revised (*rectifié*), on the contrary, is more comprehensive, and while it is overflowing with the positive spirit of Christianity, it is so constructed that men of all beliefs can receive it. As practiced in France, the ceremonies of reception are divided into three parts.

ROSY CROSS, Brothers of. A secret society bearing this name became known in Europe at the beginning of the seventeenth century. Its object was the reformation of state, church, and individuals, and the study of philosophy and science. At that time alchemy occupied, in a large degree, the attention of the learned, and it is not strange that the Rosicrucians should follow the fashion of the age. It was pretended that the order was founded in the fourteenth century by a person named Christian Rosenkreuz, who was said to have lived long among the Brahmins, in Egypt, etc.; but the real founder is believed to have been Andreä, a German scholar, of the latter part of the sixteenth century, whose object was to purify religion, which had been degraded by the scholastic philosophy. Others think that he only gave a new character to a society founded before him, by Agrippa von Neltesheim. Krause says that Andreä occupied himself from early youth with the plan of a secret society for the improvement of mankind. In 1614 he published his famous "Reformation of the Whole Wide World," and *"Fama Fraternitatis."* Christian enthusiasts and alche-

mists considered the society, poetically described in those
books, as one really existing; and thus Andreä became the
author of the later Rosicrucian fraternities, which extended
over Europe and were even brought into connection with
Freemasonry. Bailey, in his Dictionary, inclines to the
opinion that Rosenkreuz was the real founder of the order.
He says: "A German gentleman, educated in a monastery,
having learned the languages, traveled to the Holy Land
A. D. 1378, and being at Damascus, and falling sick, he had
heard the conversation of some Arabs and other Oriental
philosophers, by whom he is supposed to have been initiated
into this mysterious art. At his return into Germany he
formed a society, and communicated to its members the
secrets he had brought with him out of the East, and died in
1484. They were a sect or cabal of hermetical philosophers,
who bound themselves together by a solemn secret which
they swore inviolably to observe, and obliged themselves, at
their admission into the order, to a strict observance of
certain established rules. They pretended to know all
sciences, and especially medicine, of which they published
themselves the restorers; they also claimed to be masters of
important secrets, and, among others, that of the philosopher's
stone; all which they affirmed they had received by tradition
from the ancient Egyptians, Chaldeans, Magi and Gymnoso-
phists. They pretended to protract the period of human life,
by means of certain nostrums, and even to restore youth.
They are also called the Invisible Brothers, because they
have made no appearance, but have kept themselves *incog.*
for several years." Notwithstanding the flippant description of Bailey, and the vile calumniations of Barruel, the
Order of the Rosy Cross was eminently respectable, and its
purposes praiseworthy. Its ideas, like those of the Illuminati,
were in advance of the age, and, however objectionable to
such advocates of political and religious despotism, as Robison, Barruel, *et al.*, are precisely those principles which
we, as a nation, have embodied in our institutions and laws,
and of which we are justly proud. The Rosicrucians *did*
fraternize with the Freemasons, and it was a very respectable companionship. The twenty-eighth degree of Freemasonry must have been composed by Freemasons who
were also members of the Order of the Rosy Cross. The
ritual of the Rosicrucians had nine degrees: 1. Zelator;
2. Thericus; 3. Practicus; 4. Philosophus; 5. Adeptus Junior;
6. Adeptus Major ; 7. Adeptus Exemptus ; 8. Magister;
9. Magus. From this Order originated the " German,"
" Gold Rose-Croix," and also the " Asiatic Brothers." The
Masonic degree of "Sovereign Prince of Rose-Croix" has no
connection with the Rosicrucians.

ROYAL ARCH. Sometimes, and more properly, called the HOLY ROYAL ARCH. The fourth of the series of degrees conferred in a Royal Arch Chapter, and the seventh in grade known as the York rite, as practiced in the order wherever that rite is established. Dr. Oliver says that it is "a degree indescribably more august, sublime and important than any which precede it; and is, in fact, the summit and perfection of ancient Masonry. It impresses on our minds a belief in the being of God, without beginning of days or end of years, the great and incomprehensible Alpha and Omega, and reminds us of the reverence which is due to his Holy Name." The late distinguished brother, Salem Town, has left on record a brief summary of the symbolism inculcated in Capitular Masonry. "In advancing to the *fourth* degree," he says, "the good man is greatly encouraged to persevere in the ways of well-doing even to the end. He has a name which no man knoweth save he that receiveth it. If, therefore, he be rejected, and cast forth among the rubbish of the world, he knows full well the Great Master Builder of the universe, having chosen and prepared him as a lively stone in that spiritual building in the heavens, will bring him forth with triumph, while shouting grace, grace to his divine Redeemer. Hence opens the *fifth* degree, where he discovers his election to, and his glorified station in, the kingdom of his Father. Here he is taught how much the chosen ones are honored and esteemed by those on earth, who discover and appreciate the image of their common Lord. This image being engraven on his heart, he may look forward to those mansions above, where a higher and most exalted seat has been prepared for the faithful, from the foundation of the world. With these views the *sixth* degree is conferred, where the riches of divine grace are opened in boundless prospect. Every substantial good is clearly seen to be conferred through the great atoning sacrifice. In the *seventh* degree the good man is truly filled with heartfelt gratitude to his heavenly benefactor, for all those wonderful deliverances wrought out for him while journeying through the rugged paths of human life. Great has been his redemption from the Egypt and Babylon of this world. * * * Such is the moral and religious instruction derived from the order of the Masonic degrees." This degree brings to light many important matters of great interest to the Craft, which were, for the space of four hundred and seventy years, buried in darkness, and without a knowledge of which the Masonic character cannot be complete. The incidents on which the degree is founded, may, in part, be understood from the following brief statement: Soon after the close of Solomon's glorious reign, the kingdom of Jerusalem—the house of David, was divided. Ten of the tribes separated themselves, and took the name of the kingdom of Israel, leaving the tribes of Judah and Benjamin to constitute the kingdom of Judah. Each of these two kingdoms suffered a distinct captivity. That of Israel is called the Assyrian, and that of Judah the Babylonish captivity; only in the latter captivity is our subject interested. The Jews being thus divided, in the reigns of Jehoiachin and Zedekiah, Nebuchadnezzar, king of the Chaldees, then reigning at Babylon, with a large army, laid seige to Jerusalem, and after a severe struggle reduced it. He caused the city to be leveled to the grouud, the royal palace to be burned, the temple pillaged, and the inhabitants carried captive to Babylon.* They remained in captivity for seventy years, or until the time of Cyrus, king of Persia, who, in the first year of his reign, issued his proclamation, which liberated the Hebrew captives, and permitted them to return to Jerusalem, to "rebuild the city and house of the Lord." The circumstances connected with the captivity of the Jews, its termination, their liberation, and their return over the *rough and rugged roads* to the ancient city of their fathers, the holy cause in which they were engaged—that of rebuilding the temple—the labors performed, and the valuable discoveries brought to light by the zealous workmen, with many other equally interesting incidents are rehearsed in the degrees of the Royal Arch, Knights of the Red Cross, and Knights of the East and West. The children of Judah, after their arrival at Jerusalem, erected a tabernacle, similar in form to that of Moses. Tradition, however, informs us that the tabernacle of Zerubbabel differed from that of Moses in many particulars. The most Holy Place of the original tabernacle contained the ark of the covenant, the table of shew-bread and the golden candlestick, and the whole structure was designed for the worship of God. That of Zerubbabel was used as a temporary place of worship, and the sanctuary was also used for the meetings of the Grand Council, consisting of Joshua, Zerubbabel and Haggai. This tabernacle, according to the Masonic tradition, was divided into apartments by cross vails of blue, purple, scarlet and white, at which guards were stationed. The ostensible object of the degree is to recover the lost word—the Master Mason being . . . . . .

---

*A Masonic tradition informs us that the captive Jews were bound by their conquerors with triangular chains, and that this was done by the Chaldeans as an additional insult, because the Jewish Masons were known to esteem the triangle as an emblem of the sacred name of God, and must have considered its appropriation to the form of their fetters as a desecration of the Tetragrammaton.

RESTORATION OF THE TABERNACLE BY ZERUBBABEL AND HIS COMPANIONS.

The seventy years which had been foretold by the prophets to be the duration of Judea's captivity, had just expired. Cyrus, King of Persia, in the first year of his reign, inspired by God, a love of justice, and prompted by the counsels of the wise men among the Jews, issued a royal decree for the liberation of the Hebrew captives then in Babylon, permitting them to return to Jerusalem to rebuild their city and temple. A large proportion of the people of the tribes of Judah and Benjamin, with the Priests and Levites, under the leadership of Zerubbabel, Joshua and Haggai, joyfully accepted the privilege of returning to the city of their fathers, and immediately departed. On their arrival at Jerusalem they dispersed themselves according to their tribes and families into their several cities, and began to build habitations for shelter. They also erected a Tabernacle and set up an altar for Divine service, near the ruins of King Solomon's Temple. This Tabernacle was also used for the meetings of the Grand Council; for the reception of proper workmen, and to deliberate upon the best means of rebuilding the city and temple.

in a secret vault, which for a period of nearly five centuries was unknown, it being beneath the first temple, and brought to light by the workmen who were sent to prepare the foundation for the second temple. The degrees conferred and composing the system of Royal Arch Masonry are: 1. Mark Master; 2. Past Master; 3. Most Excellent Master; 4. Royal Arch. The officers are: 1. The High-Priest, whose title is *Most Excellent*, who represents Joshua, the first High-Priest of the Jews, after their return from the Babylonian captivity; 2. The King, whose title is *Excellent*, represents Zerubbabel, a Prince of Judah, who was the leader of the first colony of Jews that returned from the captivity to rebuild the temple; 3. The Scribe, whose title is, also, *Excellent*, represents Haggai, the prophet; 4. The Captain of the Host, who represents the general of the troops; 5. The Principal Sojourner, represents the leader of a party of Jews, who sojourned in Babylon for a time after the departure of Zerubbabel with the main body, and who subsequently came up to Jerusalem to assist in rebuilding the temple; 6. The Royal Arch Captain, represents the captain of the king's guards; 7. Grand Master of the Third Vail; 8. Grand Master of the Second Vail; 9. Grand Master of the First Vail; 10. Treasurer; 11. Secretary; 12. Sentinel; and a Chaplain may be appointed. The jewels of a Chapter are of gold or yellow metal, within a triangle, and suspended from a collar. The symbolic color of the Royal Arch degree is scarlet. Candidates receiving the degree are said to be "exalted to the most sublime degree of the Royal Arch." A Royal Arch Chapter represents the Tabernacle erected by our ancient brethren near the ruins of King Solomon's Temple. Chapters are dedicated to Zerubbabel. The appropriate badge and clothing of a Royal Arch Mason, are a jewel, an apron and a sash. The jewel, worn on the left breast, suspended from a scarlet ribbon, is a double triangle within a circle; in the center of the two triangles a sun with diverging rays, within a triangle, and underneath, or suspended to this, the triple tau. On the intersecting triangles and outer circle the following words are engraved—on the *obverse*—on the circle, "Si talia jungere possis sit tibi scire satis"—*If you are able to unite these things your knowledge is sufficient.* On the triangles — "Εὑρήκαμεν," "Invenimus"—*We have found it;* "Cultor Dei"—*Worship of God;* "Civis Mundi"—*Citizen of the world.* On the ribbon under the circle, "Nil nisi clavis deest" —*Nothing is wanting except the key. Reverse*—on the circle: "Deo, Civitati, Fratribus, Honor, Fidelitas, Benevolentia"— *For God, for the State, for the Brethren, Honor, Fidelity, Benev-*

olence. On the triangles—Wisdom, Peace, Strength, Concord, Truth, Beauty. On the ribbon under the circle—Exalted, (with date). The intersecting triangles denote the elements

OBVERSE.   REVERSE.

of fire and water, the circle, infinity and eternity, and the sun within the triangle is an emblem of Deity. So important is the triple tau considered, that it is called "the emblem of all emblems, and the grand emblem of Royal Arch Masonry." The apron is of white lambskin (13×15 inches, or

nearly square,) lined and bound with scarlet, or lined with scarlet and bound with blue and scarlet tesselated; on the flap the triple tau within a triangle, and all within a circle, as delineated in the engraving. The sash, worn from right to left, is the tesselated blue and scarlet ribbon, four inches wide, with no ornament except a metal or embroidered triple tau, triangle and circle, at the crossing. "The true origin of the Royal Arch is an important question that has lately engaged the attention of Masonic writers. Some have asserted that it was brought by the Templars from the Holy Land; others say that it was established as a part of Templar Masonry in the sixteenth century; and others again assert. that it was unknown before the year 1780. Dr. Oliver, in a work of profound research on this subject, says that 'there exists sufficient evidence to disprove all their conjectures, and to fix the era of its introduction to a period which is coeval with the memorable schism among the English Masons about the middle of the last century.'* It seems to me as the result of a careful examination of the evidence adduced, that, before the year 1740, the essential element of the Royal Arch constituted a part of the third degree, and that about that year it was severed from that degree and transferred to another, by the schismatic body calling itself 'the Grand Lodge of England according to the old Constitutions.'"† It may now be said that never before since the existence of the order was there so general a demand among intelligent Masons for veritable and substantial information on the history of Freemasonry, particularly in regard to this branch of the order. For more reliable information the reader is referred to the most valuable work on the subject of Royal Arch Masonry that has ever been published in this country.‡

* "Some Account of the Schism which took place during the last century among the Free and Accepted Masons in England, showing the Presumed Origin of the Royal Arch Degree."

† MACKEY's *Lexicon of Freemasonry.*

"The date of the organization of this body has been variously stated. Dr. MACKEY gives the date as 1739. PIERSON, in his ' *Traditions,*' gives it as having occurred about 1753. PRESTON asserts that the seceders continued to hold their meetings without acknowledging a superior until the year 1771, when they chose for their Grand Master the Duke of Athol, then Grand Master elect of Scotland. SANDYS, in his ' *Short View,*' says they (the ancients) established their Grand Lodge in London in 1757. In certain testimony taken by a commission in England, for use in the New York Masonic difficulty some years since, Bro. WHITE, at that time the Venerable Grand Secretary of the Grand Lodge of England, says, under oath, in answer to a question, that the Athol or *Ancient* Grand Lodge was formed in 1752. This ought to settle the question.".— GOULD.

‡ *Guide to the Royal Arch Chapter:* a complete Monitor for Royal Arch Masonry; with full instructions in the degrees of Mark Master, Past Master, Most Excellent Master and Royal Arch, according to the text of the Manual of the Chapter. By JOHN SHEVILLE, P. G. H. P., and JAMES L. GOULD, G. H. P. Together with a Historical Introduction, Explanatory Notes and Critical Emendations. To which are added Monitorial Instructions in the Holy Order of High Priesthood in Royal Arch Masonry, with the Ceremonies of the Order.

ROYAL ARCH CAPTAIN. An officer in a Chapter of the Royal Arch degree. He represents the Captain of the King's Guards. His station is in front of the Council, and at the entrance of the fourth vail. His duties, in some respects, are similar to those of the Junior Deacon in the Symbolic Lodge.

ROYAL ARCH OF ENOCH. The same as the degree of Knights of the Ninth Arch.

ROYAL MASTER. The first of the degrees in the Council, or Cryptic system. It is immediately associated with the degree of Select Master, and, with it, is explanatory of the Royal Arch degree, and was originally conferred in a Chapter of Royal Arch Masons. Its ritual is highly interesting.

ROYAL ORDER OF SCOTLAND. This is an order composed of two parts, viz: that of H.-R.-M. and R.-S.-Y. C.-S. The former took its rise in the reign of David I., King of Scotland, and the latter in that of King Robert the Bruce. The last is believed to have been originally the same as the Most Ancient Order of the Thistle, and to contain the ceremonial of admission formerly practiced in it. The Order of H.-R.-M. had formerly its chief seat at Kilwinning; and there is reason to suppose that it and the Grand Lodge of St. John's Masonry were governed by the same Grand Master. The introduction of this order into Kilwinning appears to have taken place about the same, or nearly the same period as the introduction of Freemasonry itself into Scotland. The Culdees, as is well known, introduced Christianity into Scotland, and, from their known habits, there were good grounds for believing that they preserved among them a knowledge of the ceremonies and precautions adopted for their protection in Judea. In establishing this degree in Scotland, it is more than probable that it was done with the view to explain, in a correct Christian manner, the symbols and rites employed by the Christian Architects and Builders; and this will also explain how the Royal Order is purely catholic,—not Roman Catholic, but adapted to all who acknowledge the great truths of Christianity, in the same way that Craft or Symbolic Masonry is intended for all, whether Jew or Gentile, who acknowledge a Supreme God. The second part, or R.-S.-Y. C.-S., is an order of knighthood, and perhaps the only genuine one in connection with Masonry, there being in it an intimate connection between the sword and the trowel. The lecture consists of a figurative description of the ceremonial both of H.-R.-M. and R.-S.-Y. C.-S., in simple rhyme, modernized, of course, by oral tradition, and breathing the purest spirit of Chris-

CRYPT.—ROYAL MASTER.

tianity. These two degrees constitute, as has been already said, the Royal Order of Scotland. Lodges or Chapters cannot legally meet elsewhere, unless possessed of a charter from it, or by dispensation from the Grand Master or his Deputy. The office of Grand Master is vested in the person of the King of Scotland, (now of Great Britain,) and one seat is invariably kept vacant for him, in whatever country a Chapter is open, and cannot be occupied by any other member.

RULE. A well-known instrument by which measurements are made or straight lines are drawn. It is employed as an important emblem in the degree of Past Master, admonishing the newly-elected Master to punctually observe his duty, press forward in the path of virtue, and, neither inclining to the right nor to the left, in all his actions to have eternity in view.

S.

SAINT JOHN THE ALMONER, born at Cypress, A. D. 550, was made patriarch of Alexandria, A. D. 606, and died Nov. 11, 616. He has no connection with Freemasonry, and is mentioned here merely because Commanderies of Knights Templar and the 30th degree (Kadosh), Ancient and Accepted rite, claim that it is to him, and not to St. John the Baptist and St. John the Evangelist, that Masonic bodies are dedicated. "*Celui a qui elles sont dediees est St. Jean l'aumônier, qui etait le Grand Maitre des chevaliers de St. Jean de Jerusalem, au xiii e siecle, et qui a toujours ete le plus bel ornement de l'Ordre, et le patron des Templiers.*"* It requires no little credulity, and some imagination, to believe that a man who died A. D. 616 was Grand Master of the Knights of St. John A. D. 1250!

SAINT JOHN THE BAPTIST, Disciples of. A society which has existed in Asia for many hundred years, but the exact date of its origin is unknown. Tradition asserts that it was founded by the immediate disciple of John the Baptist, who fled from Judea directly after the latter was beheaded. Their religious and philosophical doctrines have a mystical character. Their moral system is pure and elevated, and the highest virtues are inculcated and rigidly practiced. Their priests are divided into three degrees. They have some peculiarities which remind one of the early Christian Brotherhood, especially their "*Agape*," or love-feast, which is the prototype of the Masonic Table-lodge.

---

* "He to whom they are dedicated is St. John the Almoner, who was the Grand Master of the Knights of St. John of Jerusalem, in the 13th century, and who was always the greatest ornament of the order and patron of the Templars."

SAINT JOHN THE BAPTIST, Knight of. A division of Templar Masonry which, toward the end of the last century arose in Ireland, flourished for a brief period, and then became extinct.

SAINT JOHN, Favorite of. The 7th degree of the Swedish rite, and also of the imperial Grand Lodge of Prussia. Oliver calls it the 6th in the series comprised in the degrees of the Knights of the East and West.

SAINT JOHN, or Holy Saint John of Jerusalem. This expression, so common in our Lodges, is, by its needless tautology, offensive alike to the ear and to a refined literary taste. Holy and Saint are the same word, both signifying the same thing. The French Masons do not say "*Saint Saint Jean,*" nor in the German Lodges do we hear the phrase, "Heiligen Saint, i. e., Heiligen Johann," but simply "*Saint Jean,*" and "*Heiligen Johann.*"

SAINTS JOHN, Festivals of. The 24th of June is consecrated to Saint John the Baptist, and the 27th of December to Saint John the Evangelist. It is the duty of Masons to assemble on these days, and by a solemn invocation of the past, renew the ties and strengthen the fraternal bonds that bind the present to the brotherhood of the olden time.

SAMARITAN, Good. An androgynous degree in Masonry. It is an impressive and interesting degree, founded on the well-known parable. It is communicated to the wives of Royal Arch Masons.

SANCTUARY. That part of the Temple at Jerusalem which was the most secret and most retired; in which was the ark of the covenant, and wherein none but the High-Priest might enter, and he only once a year, on the day of holy expiation. The same name was also given to the most sacred part of the Tabernacle, set up in the wilderness, which remained until some time after the building of the Temple.

SCANDINAVIAN MYSTERIES. These rites were introduced into the north of Europe, near the beginning of the Christian era, by Sigge, a Sythian priest and chieftain, who is known in the Northern mythology by the name of Odin. The principal feature of the initiation seems to have been a modified form of the Isianic rite. Balder was slain by Loke, with a branch of mistletoe, and the initiation represented a search for his body. The myth preserved in the "Ancient Edda," which describes the descent of Odin into the regions of Hela, seeking for his murdered son, conveys a very clear idea of the ceremony. The candidate meets with difficulties and troubles of the most appalling kind, but finally reaches the palace "roofed with golden shields," which resounds with songs of triumph. Balder, physically, represents the sun, and, morally, the truth, and Loke is a symbol of winter, and also of evil. Thus here, again, is seen an attempt to illustrate the everlasting conflict between Truth and Error, Good and Evil, in which, after divers defeats, Truth and Goodness gain the empire of the universe.

SCHRÖDER'S RITE. In 1766, a person bearing this name established at Marburgh a Chapter of "True and Ancient Rose-Croix Masons," which met with so much success that he was encouraged to introduce into a Lodge at Sarrebourg certain mystical and alchemistical degrees. This system recognized the three symbolical degrees as the foundation of Masonry, and, at one time, was considerably disseminated. The rite is still acknowledged as legitimate Masonry by the Grand Lodge of Hamburg, under which, it. is said, there are several Lodges now at work.*

SCOTCH MASON. In the French, or modern rite, the fifth degree. It is intended to throw light on the events which are the subject of the Royal Arch degree, and, in substance, is nearly identical with the degree of Select Master.

SCOTCH RITE, more familiarly known as the Ancient and Accepted Scottish rite. The degrees of this rite are, for the most part, elaborated from the system invented by Ramsay, who claimed that he found them in Scotland, where

* "Louis Schröder, of Hamburg, with Ignace Fessler, of Berlin, took up the old English rituals, toward the end of the 18th century, and they together determined to introduce them into the German Lodges, wherein the higher degrees had become so dangerous. In their place they desired to introduce the Masonic degrees of Symbolism and Light. A profound investigation as to the origin, genius and history of Freemasonry, and an exposition of the different systems of the Lodges and of their higher degrees, necessarily awakened in the brethren a more general desire to simplify the object and constitution of the society, and to guard for the future against the invasions of a mystical and dangerous reverse. Schröder introduced these degrees without any ceremony of reception, so that they might not have even the appearance of the higher degrees. Fessler preserved particular ceremonies. The latter, though beautiful and solemn, resembled those of the Roman Catholic worship; their founder, who probably retained a secret liking for it, being, perhaps, unconscious of the Fast. The Grand Lodge of Hamburg constituted itself, according to the system of Schröder, at the beginning of the present century; and many Lodges have since followed its example; as also the Grand Lodge Royal York, of Friendship, at Berlin, has, since 1800, made great progress in propagating the system of Schröder with the improvements of Fessler."—BONRICK. *Hist. de la Fr. Mag.*

they had been planted by Knights of the Temple and of Malta, on their return from Palestine. It is needless to say that these pretensions have no foundation in truth. The Councils and Lodges of this rite are governed by Supreme

Councils of Grand Inspectors General, of which there are two in the United States, one at Charleston, S. C., and the other at Boston, Mass. This rite is, next to the York, the most extensively diffused throughout the Masonic world. It consists of thirty-three degrees, divided as follows:

Symbolic Lodge.

1. Entered Apprentice.
2. Fellow-Craft.
3. Master Mason.

Lodge of Perfection.

4. Secret Master.
5. Perfect Master.
6. Intimate Secretary.
7. Provost and Judge.
8. Intendant of the Building.
9. Elected Knights of the Nine.
10. Illustrious Elect of the Fifteen.
11. Sublime Knights Elected of the Twelve.
12. Grand Master Architect.
13. Knights of the Ninth Arch, or Royal Arch of Solomon.

14. Grand Elect, Perfect, and Sublime Mason.

Council of Princes of Jerusalem.

15. Knights of the Sword, of the East, or of the Eagle.
16. Prince of Jerusalem.

Chapter of Rose-Croix.

17. Knight of the East and West.
18. Knight of the Eagle, Knight of the Pelican; or, Sovereign Prince Rose-Croix.

Consistory of Princes of the Royal Secret.

19. Grand Pontiff; or, Sublime Ecossais.
20. Venerable Grand Master of all Symbolic Lodges.
21. Noachite; or, Prussian Knight.

22. Knight Royal Axe; or, Prince of Libanus.
23. Chief of the Tabernacle.
24. Prince of the Tabernacle.
25. Knight of the Brazen Serpent.
26. Prince of Mercy; or, Scottish Trinitarian.
27. Sovereign Commander of the Temple.
28. Knight of the Sun ; or, Prince Adept.
29. Grand Scottish Kn't of St. Andrew; or, Patriarch of the Crusades.
30. Knight Kadosch.
31. Grand Inquiring Commander.
32. Sublime Prince of the Royal Secret.

Supreme Council.

33. Sovereign Grand Inspectors General.

SCRIBE. Among the Jews, Scribes were officers of the law. There were *civil* and *ecclesiastical* scribes. The former were employed about any kind of civil writings or records. The latter transcribed, studied and explained the Holy Scriptures. In the traditions of the Royal Arch degree, Haggai, the scribe, occupies an important place in the Council of the Chapter, and should be regarded as the secretary of the king.

SECRECY. Freemasonry, in laying its foundations in secrecy, follows the Divine order of Nature, where all that is grand and beautiful and useful is born of night and mystery. The mighty labors which clothe the earth with fruits and foliage and flowers are "wrought in darkness." The bosom of Nature is a vast laboratory, where the mysterious work of transmutation of substances is perpetually going forward. There is not a point in the universe, the edges of which do not touch the realms of night and silence. God himself is environed with shadows, and "clouds and darkness are round about his throne;" yet his beneficence is felt, and his loving Spirit makes itself visible through all worlds. So Freemasonry works in secrecy, but its benignant fruits are visible in all lands. Besides, this principle of secrecy furnishes a mysterious bond of unity and strength, which can be found nowhere else. The objection often urged against the Order on account of this peculiar feature is too puerile to be considered.

SECRET SOCIETIES. All the great associations of antiquity, the objects of which were to civilize and improve the condition of mankind, were secret societies. They were called "MYSTERIES." The mysteries of India, Egypt, Greece, etc., were secret orders—great educational institutions, established for the advancement of men in wisdom and virtue. The wide extension of the secret principle at the present time, and the immense number of secret philanthropic societies which cover all lands, prove that there must be some wants, universally felt, to which political institutions do not respond; some elements of human nature not represented therein, which are the cause and groundwork of these secret orders. When society and governments are oppressive or imperfect—and all are imperfect, when they do not provide for all the moral, intellectual, and physical needs of men,—the earnest, the loving, the hoping, who, dissatisfied with the present, invoke the future; and the weak, who are crushed to the earth by the oppressive laws which govern all industrial arrangements, become disgusted with these conditions, and fly to the embrace of some secret order, where a higher ideal is revealed, and the prophecy of a better state is announced. We conclude, then, that secret societies have their origin in the deepest and most pressing wants of humanity. They grow out of a social arrangement which is unjust and unequal, and point forward to a time when justice and love shall possess and govern the earth.

SECRET MASTER. The 4th degree of the Ancient and Accepted rite, and the first of the Ineffable degrees, conferred in the Lodge of Perfection. The body is styled a Lodge. The hangings are black, strewed with white tears. The Lodge is illuminated with eighty-one lights, the square of nine. On the altar the Book of Constitutions, closed; and on that lies a key of ivory. No working-tools are used, for the reason that the labors on the Temple are suspended after the death of . . . . The Master represents King Solomon, and is styled Puissant Master. The East represents the Holy of Holies of the first Temple at Jerusalem, with its appropriate decorations and furniture. The sash is a broad blue watered ribbon, worn from right to left. The apron is white, edged with black; the flap is blue, with an open eye embroidered or painted on it. Two branches, one of laurel and the other of olive, cross each other in the middle of the apron, and at the crossing is the letter Z, embroidered in gold. The gloves are white, turned over, with black at the wrists. The jewel of the degree is an ivory key, on which is engraved the letter Z, referring to Zadoc, who was the High-Priest in the reigns of David and Solomon. The duty of a Secret Master is to keep a careful watch over the conduct of the Craft in general; to practice virtue, shun vice, and remain in silence.

SANCTUARY OF THE TEMPLE.

SECRET MASTER.

SECRET MONITOR. An interesting and useful side degree, founded on the history of the covenant of friendship which was entered into by David and Jonathan, an account of which is given in the 1st book of Samuel, 20th chapter.

SELECT MASTER. The second degree in the Council known as the Cryptical branch of Masonry. It accounts for the concealment of important mysteries at the building of the first Temple, which were preserved and brought to light at the erection of the second Temple, and furnishes the history which connects the incidents of Ancient Craft Masonry with those of the Royal Arch.

SENSES. Man is brought into communication with the external world by means of five senses, or organs of perception. Seeing, Hearing and Feeling are often referred to in Masonic instructions. They are explained in the degree of Fellow-Craft.

SENTINEL. In Chapters of Royal Arch Masons, and Councils of some other degrees, the Tiler, or guardian of the door, bears this name.

SHIBBOLETH. The Hebrew word שִׁבֹּלֶת signifies an ear of corn and a stream or flood of water. The name given to a test or criterion by which the ancient Jews sought to distinguish true persons or things from false. The term originated thus: After the battle gained by Jephthah over the Ephraimites, (Judges xii.,) the Gileadites, commanded by the former, secured all the passes of the river; and, on an Ephraimite attempting to cross, they asked him if he was of Ephraim. If he said no, they bade him pronounce the word *Shibboleth*, which the Ephraimites, from inability to give the aspirate, gave *Sibboleth*. By this means he was detected as an enemy, and immediately slain. In modern times this word has been adopted into political and other organizations as a pass or watchword.

SIDE DEGREES. Certain degrees having no real connection with Freemasonry, invented by enthusiastic brethren, are thus designated. Some of them are conferred for their supposed utility, and others for the harmless amusement they afford. The degree of Secret Monitor belongs to the first class, and that of the Knight of Constantinople to the second.

SIGNET. A sign, token, or seal. Formerly, rulers had seals or signets with which they invested their ministers, as signs that they acted by royal authority. The signet of

King Solomon, or rather of Hiram, known among Masons, is said to have been a token of friendship which the King of Tyre sent to the Hebrew monarch.

SIX PERIODS, The Grand Architect's. God is said to have created the earth in six days, and rested on the seventh. The "Grand Architect's Six Periods" refer to that event. Hence Masons are instructed to labor during the six days of the week, and devote the seventh to rest, devotion and meditation. These important periods in the world's history, and the manifestation of the Almighty's power and goodness are often and eloquently portrayed during the ceremonies of the Fellow-Craft's degree.

SKIRRET. In the English ritual, one of the working-tools of a Master Mason. It is an instrument usually made of wood, shaped like a letter T, and acts on a center pin, from which a line is drawn, chalked and struck, to mark out the ground for the intended edifice. In a speculative sense, it points out that straight and undeviating line of conduct laid down in the sacred volume.

SOLOMON. This celebrated monarch was the son of David by Bathsheba, through whose influence he inherited the Jewish throne, in preference to his elder brothers. During his long and peaceful reign—from b. c. 1015 to 975—the Hebrews enjoyed their golden age. His remarkable judicial decisions, and his completion of the political institutions of David, showed a superiority of genius which gained him the respect of the people. By building the Temple, which plays so important a *rôle* in the symbolism of Freemasonry, exceeding as it did, in splendor and beauty, all former works of architecture, he gave to the Hebrew worship a magnificence that bound the people more closely to the national rites. He was truly a great ruler; but, while the Jews were naturally proud of the glory which his great qualities reflected on the nation, his enlarged and liberal views with regard to intercourse with foreign peoples deeply offended the national bigotry. The decorations of the Temple were thought by many to be pagan emblems, and, finally, they accused him openly of idolatry. Solomon is often styled "the first Grand Master of Masons." This cannot be true. He might have been, and probably was, the first Grand Master of Masons in Judea; for Masonry was not known in that country until it was introduced by the Masons of Tyre and Sidon, who built the Temple. Solomon must have been made a Mason at that time, unless he

DECORATIONS FOR LODGE OF SORROW.

had been previously admitted into the society at Tyre or Sidon. To Solomon, however, belongs the honor of having brought the Masonic institution to the knowledge of the Hebrews, through the agency of the Tyrian architects. Yet the society seems not to have made much progress among that people, and even Solomon's great name and patronage could not secure it from misrepresentation and persecution. And this is not strange. A Jew of that age could not comprehend, much less appreciate, the cosmopolitan character and liberal spirit of such an institution. Consequently, the Masons—called, in the Scriptures, Sidonians—were often the objects of bitter persecution. Of the writings ascribed to Solomon, the "Proverbs," and the book entitled the "Wisdom of Solomon," are the best. The latter Protestants have unwisely pronounced apocryphal; for, in a purely religious point of view, it is the most instructive and valuable book in the Old Testament series.

SORROW LODGES. In this country Lodges of Sorrow are somewhat rare. They are, however, of very frequent occurrence in Europe, particularly in Germany, where, shortly after the death of a worthy brother, the "*Trauer Loge*" is held, when the virtues, memory, and intellectual qualifications are commemorated, and the funereal rites of an impressive character are performed. The custom is eminently proper, and strictly in accordance with the fraternal principles of Freemasonry, and one which should be as universal as the extent of the institution itself. On these occasions the Lodge-room should be appropriately draped in black, and the several stations covered with emblems of mourning. On the Master's pedestal is a skull and lighted taper. In the center of the room is placed a catafalque, which consists of a rectangular platform, about six feet long by four wide, on which are two smaller platforms, so that three steps are represented. On the third one should be an elevation of convenient height, on which is placed an urn. The platform should be draped in black, and a canopy of black drapery may be raised over the urn. (*See engraving.*) At each corner of the platform will be placed a candlestick, bearing a lighted taper, and near it, facing the East, will be seated a brother, provided with an extinguisher, to be used at the proper time. During the first part of the ceremonies the lights in the room should burn dimly. Arrangements should be made to enable the lights to be increased to brilliancy at the appropriate point in the ceremony. On the catafalque will be laid a pair of white gloves, a plain lambskin apron, and, if the deceased brother had been an officer, the appropriate insignia of his office. When the Lodge is held in memory of several brethren, shields bearing their names are placed around the catafalque. Vocal and instrumental music are indispensable to the proper effect of the ceremonies. Brethren should wear dark clothing, and no insignia but the white lambskin apron and white gloves.

SOVEREIGN COMMANDER OF THE TEMPLE, sometimes called KNIGHT COMMANDER OF THE TEMPLE, is the 27th degree of the Ancient and Accepted rite. The assemblage is called a Chapter. The degree is entirely chivalric. The presiding officer is styled Commander-in Chief; the Wardens are called Marshal and Turcopilier; the members are designated Knights Commanders. The hangings are scarlet, with black columns at intervals, on each of which is a branch holding a light. The hangings and columns are so arranged as to give the room the form of a circle; in the center of which is a large round table, covered with the emblems of the degree; around the table the members sit. In front of the East is a candelabrum, with three circles of lights, one above the other. In the upper circle are six lights; in the second nine, and the third twelve. The jewel is a golden triangle, on which is engraved the letters I. N. R. I.; it is suspended from the collar, which is of white watered ribbon, edged with red; embroidered on each side in black and gold, is the Teutonic cross. This order was founded in 1190, in Palestine, and on the 23d of February, 1192, it was solemnly approved and confirmed by Pope Celestine III. This was the origin of the once famous military order of Teutonic Knights. All the French writers who have investigated the history of this degree concur in connecting it with the Knights Templars, and it certainly has much of the character of that order. Vassal expresses the following opinion of the degree: "The 27th degree does not deserve to be classed in the Scotch rite as a degree, since it contains neither symbols or allegories that connect it with initiation. It deserves still less to be ranked among the philosophical degrees. I imagine that it has been intercalated only to supply an hiatus, and as a memorial of an order once justly celebrated."

SOVEREIGN GRAND INSPECTOR GENERAL. The 33d and ultimate degree of the Ancient and Accepted rite. It is not certainly known when or where this grade originated.

The theory which ascribes it to the King of Prussia has long since been discarded by intelligent Masons. The number of Inspectors in a kingdom or republic must not exceed nine. These organized in a body, constitute the Supreme Council, which claims jurisdiction over all the Ineffable and Sublime degrees. The presiding officer is styled Sovereign Grand Commander. The sash is white, edged with gold, and suspended from the right shoulder to the left hip. At the bottom is a red and white rose, and on the part crossing the breast is a delta, with rays transversed by a poniard, and in the center the number 33. The jewel is a black, double-headed eagle, crowned, and holding a sword in his claws. The beak, claws, crown and sword are of gold. The motto of the degree is "*Deus meumque jus*," "God and my right."

SPHINX. In antiquity, an emblematical figure, composed of the head and breasts of a woman, and the body of a lion, and said to be the Egyptian symbol of mystery. This supposition arises most naturally from the fact that these symbols are always found at the entrance of the Egyptian temples. Also, a fabulous monster, said to have infested the country around Thebes. According to mythological history, its father was Typhon, the gigantic son of Terra, and it was sent by Juno to afflict the Thebans, which it did by proposing enigmatical questions to persons, whom it killed if they could not expound them. The Egyptian Sphinx had no wings; these appendages were added by the Greeks. As a symbol of mystery, silence and antiquity, it has been adopted as a Masonic emblem.

STANDARD. A staff with a flag or colors, under which men are united or bound for some common purpose. From the earliest antiquity all nations have been in the habit of using peculiar standards or banners, by which they were distinguished from each other in peace, and rallied to action in war. The ancient Egyptians were, probably, the first to adopt the use of the standard to distinguish their people or a particular tribe during their wars, or when performing their ceremonies publicly. They are frequently mentioned in the Old Testament. The earliest Roman standard was a bundle of straw fixed to the top of a spear. This was succeeded by figures of animals—the horse, the boar, etc.—all of which soon gave place to the eagle, which continued to be the Roman ensign, and was afterward assumed by the German, and since by the French emperors of the Napoleonic dynasty. Standards are frequently carried in Masonic processions, with appropriate devices painted or embroidered thereon. The standard appropriate to the Order, and that which is designated as the principal or general standard of symbolic Masonry, is described as follows: "The escutcheon, or shield on the banner, is divided into four compartments, or quarters, by a green cross, over which a narrower one of the same length of limb, and of a yellow color, is placed, forming what is called a cross *vert* voided *or;* each of the compartments formed by the limits of the cross is occupied by a different device. In the first quarter is placed a golden lion, on a field of blue, to represent the standard of the tribe of Judah; in the second, a black ox, on a field of gold, to represent Ephraim; in the third, a man, on a field of gold, to represent Reuben; and, in the fourth, a golden eagle, on a blue ground, to represent Dan. Over all is placed, as the crest, an ark of the covenant, and the motto is 'Holiness to the Lord.'"

STANDARD OF SYMBOLIC MASONRY.

ROYAL ARCH STANDARD.

Besides this, there are six other standards proper to be borne in processions, the material of which must be white, bordered with blue fringe or ribbon, and on each of which is inscribed one of the following words:

FAITH, HOPE, CHARITY, WISDOM, STRENGTH, BEAUTY. In the Royal Arch degree, as recognized in this country, there are five standards. The Royal Arch Captain carries a white standard, which is emblematic of a purity of heart, and rectitude of conduct. The standard of the Grand Master of the third vail is scarlet, emblematic of fervency and zeal, and is the appropriate color of the Royal Arch degree. The standard of the Grand Master of the second vail is purple, which is emblematic of union, being a due mixture of blue and scarlet, the appropriate colors of the Symbolic and Royal Arch degrees; and this teaches us to cultivate the spirit of harmony and love between brethren of the Symbolic, and companions of the Sublime degrees, which should ever distinguish the members of a society founded upon the principles of everlasting truth, and universal philanthropy. The standard of the Grand Master of the first vail is blue, the peculiar color of the Ancient Craft, or Symbolic degrees, which is emblematic of universal friendship and benevolence. In the Royal Arch degree, as practiced in the Chapters of England, twelve standards are used, illustrating the twelve tribes of Israel, which are as follows: Judah, scarlet, a lion couchant; Issachar, blue, an ass crouching beneath its burden; Zebulon, purple, a ship; Reuben, red, a man; Simeon, yellow, a sword; Gad, white, a troop of horsemen; Ephraim, green, an ox; Manassah, flesh-colored, a vine by the side of a wall; Benjamin, green, a wolf; Dan, green, an eagle; Asher, purple, a cup; Naphtali, blue, a hind. The banner or grand standard of the Order of Masonic knighthood is of white silk, six feet in height and five feet

GRAND STANDARD OF KNIGHTS TEMPLAR.

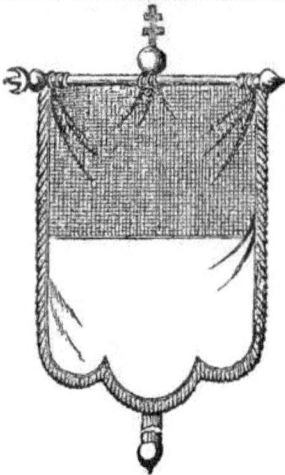

BEAUSEANT OF THE KNIGHTS TEMPLAR.

in width, made tripartite at the bottom, fastened at the top to the cross-bar by nine rings; in the center of the standard, a blood-red Passion Cross, edged with gold, over which is the motto, "*In hoc signo vinces*," and under, "*Non nobis Domine, non nobis, sed Nomini tuo da Gloriam!*" The cross to be four feet high, and the upright and bar to be seven inches wide. On the top of the staff, a gilded globe or ball, four inches in diameter, surmounted by the Patriarchal Cross, twelve inches in height. The Beauséant, or the battle-flag of the Ancient Knights Templar, is of woolen or silk stuff, six feet in height, and five feet in width, made tripartite at the bottom, fastened at the top to the cross-bar by nine rings. The upper half of the standard is black, and the lower half white. The grand standard of the Ancient and Accepted rite is of white silk, three-and-a-half feet long, by two-and-a-half feet wide, edged with gold, gold fringe and tassels. In the center, the double-headed eagle, under which, on a blue scroll, the motto, in letters of gold. "*Deus Meumque Jus.*" On the upper part of a triangle, irradiated, the figures 33 in the center.

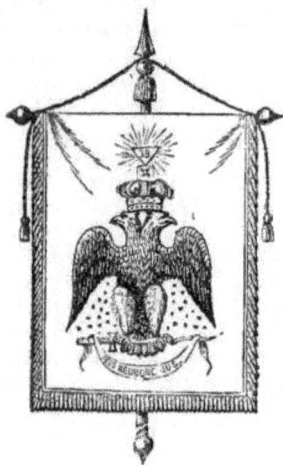

THE STANDARD OF THE ANCIENT AND ACCEPTED SCOTTISH RITE.

STATISTICS OF FREEMASONRY. Although, strictly speaking, this word "statistics" has reference to the present condition, resources and influence of whatever nation or society one may have under consideration, we shall depart a little from these limits, and introduce a few items which we deem important, that belong more properly to the history of the institution. Masonry now has gained a foothold and influence in nearly every country on the face of the earth. It exists to-day, and exercises an immense power in every country of Europe; its Lodges cover the American continent, are found in Northern and Southern Africa, in the East and West Indies; indeed, the Freemason can hardly travel into any part of the world but he will find Lodges to receive him, and fraternal sympathy and assistance. if he is sick or in distress. In no country, however, excepting England and Germany, has the Order a connected history reaching beyond the year of the revival, A. D. 1717. In the former kingdom the records of the Fraternity have been so well preserved that we gather from them a pretty correct view of its administration and condition through a long period of years.

STANDARD-BEARER. An officer in Grand Lodge; also in a Commandery of Knights Templar. His duty is to have charge of the banner of the order in processions.

STEWARDS' LODGE. The Grand Stewards' Lodge, in some jurisdictions, is a kind of court of adjudication for hearing complaints—considering applications for charity—and, in some instances, trying and punishing Masonic offenses. The Stewards' Lodge was founded in England, 1735, under the Grand Mastership of Lord Weymouth. It was entitled to twelve representatives in the Grand Lodge.

STRICT OBSERVANCE, RITE OF. This was the third attempt at innovation upon the purer systems of Freemasonry by the Jesuits. It encouraged in its adepts the hope of coming into possession of the wealth of the ancient Templars. The chronological history of its Grand Masters is nothing more than the history of the generals of the Jesuits. It was established in Germany, in 1754, by Baron von Hund (Charles Gotthelf), and a few of his associates. Six degrees only were conferred. They were, 1. Apprentice; 2. Fellow Craft; 3. Master Mason ; 4. Scotch Master ; on the trestle-board of this degree were represented a lion, emblem of fearlessness, courage and calm fortitude; a fox, the symbol of prudence; an ape, signifying the faculty of imitation, and a sparrow-hawk, typical of swiftness. The Scotch Master, having been found worthy of advancement, was then received in the fifth degree as a Novice; and in the sixth was created a Knight Templar. This latter degree was divided into three branches, viz : *Armiger,* those who were not of noble birth or rank; *Socii et Amici,* or those who were already Knights of some order, and *Equites,* or Knights. Each *Armiger, Socius* or *Eques,* received on his initiation a knightly name, coat of arms and motto. Von Hund afterward instituted a seventh degree, styled *Eques Professus,* which he surrounded with an unusual amount of mystery, and conferred the degree on those only who could be of the greatest service to him or his schemes. The whole of Europe was apportioned into nine "Provinces," the seventh of which included the northern part of Germany, between the Elbe and Oder. The order was subordinate to a Grand Master, who was supposed to be unknown to all, except a few of the privileged knights, Von Hund being in reality the head of

the order. The superior officer of each Province was termed
"*Heermeister*," Von Hund assuming command of the seventh
Province, under the distinctive title of *Carolus Eques ab Ense*.
The Lodges were called Commanderies, the Masters being
styled, "*Commendatur domus*." The Masters were subordinate
to the *Prefects*, and these again to *Sub-priors and Priors*.
The seats of these officers were called by names taken from
the rolls of the old Knights Templar and Knights of Malta.
The Preceptory of Hamburg was termed Foenack; Copenhagen, Eydendorp; Brunswick, Brunopolis, etc. Many plans
were concocted and attempted, in order to furnish a revenue
to these office-holders. While Von Hund was in Paris, he
actually contemplated the establishment of colonies in North
America and on the coast of Labrador, and afterward in
Russia. In 1768, he endeavored to dispose of his property
to the order, at a very low price, in order to furnish dwellings
for the officers, but, owing to the mistrust of the brethren,
the arrangement fell through, and this plan cost him more
than one-half his wealth. In 1766 a brother, by the name
of Schubarth, proposed a so-called "Economical Plan," by
which he proposed a regular system of graduated assess-
ments upon the Lodges, a sort of sliding-scale of fees, which,
on paper, presented a beautiful design and an enormous
result. The plan, however, failed, a large majority of the
brethren not being sufficiently credulous to embark in the
speculation. Some Lodges, however, who had, in accordance
with the plan, commenced the collection of a fund for the
above purpose, soon found themselves enabled to erect
handsome halls for their accommodation, and thus laid the
foundation for acquiring considerable property. Von Hund,
as "Heermeister" of the seventh Province, dwelt at Sonnen-
burg, on his own estates, from whence he governed his
Province and issued his decrees. This order was well
organized, gave proof of great strength and exercised a
powerful influence over all similar organizations during its
existence throughout Europe. The Provincial Grand Lodge
of Hamburg, which had been constituted by the Grand
Lodge of England in 1740, went over to the Strict Observance in 1765, and each of its members was obliged to sign
an act of obedience, abjuring its former system of York
Masonry, and vowing implicit obedience and allegiance to
the superiors of the order. The latter, fearing lest they
might be persecuted in some way, as being the successors
of an order which had been abolished by royal command,
and desirous of insuring the existence of their order, began
now to look around for some noble patron. The first reigning prince who acceded to their wishes was the Margrave

Charles Alexander, of Bayreuth, who was received as *Eques a Munimento* in 1766, and appointed as *Protector Ordinis in Franconia.* He arranged elegant rooms in his chateau at Anspach for the accommodation of the chapters, and had in contemplation the restoration of the *Order of the Swan*, (an order which flourished in the fifteenth century,) as a cloak beneath which should be concealed the actual Order of Templars. This plan was, however, suddenly abandoned, for what reason is not known. In the year 1767, a certain Dr. Stark, rejoicing in the cognomen of *Frater Archidemides ab aquila fulva*, made his appearance at Wismar, and pretended that he and some of his friends belonged to another branch of the Templar order, viz: the *Clerical* or ecclesiastical branch, who alone possessed the true secrets of the order, and that he had been invested with full powers by his superiors to take charge of the secular brethren. He exhibited a patent, in which he was styled *"fils et frère des pères de la famille des Sçavans l'Ordre des Sages par tous les générations de l'univers,"* and which empowered him to initiate those whom he deemed worthy. The *clerks*, as they styled themselves, pretended to be descendants of the pious Essenes, who employed themselves in the study of the secrets of nature, and who had attained the highest perfection in this secret knowledge. After the institution of the Order of the Temple in the Holy Land, they became acquainted with some of the members of that order, among whom was a nephew of St. Bernard, by name Andreas Montisbarrensis. They then united with this order, obtained a rule from St. Bernard, and chose Andreas as their first ecclesiastical Prior. These clerical brethren became the guardians of the laws and mysteries of the order, and to them mainly was due its future importance and wealth. At the dissolution of the order, their most secret documents and treasures were rescued by the Knight John Eures, and a part of these were still in their possession. Stark brought with him rituals, instructions, and other manuscripts, interlarded with Latin and old French sentences, which he pretended to have received in Auvergne, and which contained the forms and ceremonies of initiation of the Novices and Knights, as practiced in the French and Italian provinces. At that date, however, (1765-73,) no trace of the Strict Observance was to be found in those countries. It is most likely that Stark received his knowledge of the higher degrees in St. Petersburg, (1763-65,) and manufactured the rituals to suit himself. Toward the end of the year 1770, Duke Ferdinand, of Brunswick, was initiated as *socii et amici* into the Strict Observance, or so-called Order of Templars; and, in the following year, his brother, the reigning Duke Charles, was likewise initiated. These initiations reanimated the spirit of the whole order, which had for some time shown signs of being about to fall to pieces. In May, 1772, a general convention of the officers and deputies of the seventh Province was held at Kohlo, at which the *clerical branch* was also represented. Von Hund, by request, presented his patent, which, although no one was able to decipher, was pronounced genuine. The *clerical branch* was acknowledged by an act of union, signed on either part, and Duke Ferdinand was chosen *Magnus Superior Ordinis and Grand Master of all the United Scottish Lodges.* The ritual of the first four degrees, as practiced in the united Lodges, was adopted, the explanation of the same being made to conform with the actual object of the order. A directory, under the title of a capitular government, was also established at Dresden, in order to lighten the labors of the Heermeister, Von Hund. The seventh Province was now fully organized; up to this time it had been the only one. In 1773, Major Von Weiler, *a spica aurea,* went to France, and instituted at Strasburgh. the fifth province, *Burgundy;* at Lyons, the province *Auvergne;* and at Montpelier, the third Province, *Occitania;* the principal seat, however, remained at Bordeaux. All these provinces recognized the Duke Ferdinand as Grand Master. In 1776, Von Hund instituted the eighth Province of Southern Germany, and constituted several Prefectures. In 1775, a convention was held at Brunswick, at which Prince Charles of Hesse was acknowledged as *Protector Ordinis,* and the capitulary government was transferred to Brunswick for three years. Von Hund, having a presentiment of his approaching end, confided to the Duke Ferdinand all his papers, correspondence, and the rolls and registers of the order, and on the 7th November, 1776, he died.

SUBLIME. The Master Mason's degree is thus styled on account of the grand and sublime doctrines it teaches.

SUBLIME GRAND LODGE. A term applied to the Lodge of Perfection.

SUBLIME KNIGHT ELECT, sometimes called TWELVE ILLUSTRIOUS KNIGHTS. The 11th degree of the Ancient and Accepted rite. This degree completes the series of Elect degrees, viz: Elect of Nine, Elect of Fifteen and Sublime Knight Elect. The legend of this degree specifies that after vengeance had been taken on the traitors, Solomon, to reward those who had remained faithful to their trust, as well as to make room for the exaltation of others to the degree of Elect of Fifteen, appointed twelve of these latter, chosen by their companions, to constitute a new degree, on which he bestowed the title of Sublime Elect, and endowed them with a certain command to provide supplies for the king and his household; to see that the taxes were fairly assessed; to superintend the collection of the revenue; and to protect the people against rapacity and extortion of the tax-gatherers. In this degree is shadowed forth the great principle—free constitutions, without which liberty would often be but a name—the trial by jury of twelve men, whose *unanimous* verdict is necessary to convict of crime. The assembly is called a Chapter. It is lighted with twelve lights, by threes, in the East, West, North, and South; each three forming an equilateral triangle. The presiding officer represents King Solomon, and is styled Thrice Illustrious Sovereign; the two Wardens are styled Inspectors; the Chapter consists of twelve members only. The apron is white, lined, edged and fringed with black, and the flap is black. In the middle of the apron is painted or embroidered a flaming heart. The sash is a black ribbon, worn from right to left, and on which, over the breast, is painted or embroidered, a flaming heart; and over that the words, *Vincere aut Mori*. The jewel is a sword, worn suspended to the sash.

SUBLIME PRINCE OF THE ROYAL SECRET. The 32d degree of the Ancient and Accepted rite, and for many years, or until the institution of the 33d degree, this was the highest degree, or *ne plus ultra* of Masonry. The body is styled a Consistory, and should be held in a building of two stories. The officers are, a Thrice Illustrious Commander, First and Second Lieutenants, a Minister of State, a Grand Chancellor, a Grand Treasurer, a Grand Secretary, and a Grand Captain of the Guard. In the East is a throne,

elevated on seven steps, which is the seat of the Thrice
Illustrious Commander, who wears a robe of royal purple,
and he and the Lieutenants, wear swords. The collar of
this degree is black, lined with scarlet, and in the center, at
the point, a double-headed eagle, of silver or gold, on a red
Teutonic cross. The apron is of white satin, with a border of
gold lace, one inch wide, lined with scarlet; on the flap is a
double-headed eagle, on each side of which is the flag of the
country in which the body is located, the flag of Prussia and
the Beauseant of the Kadosh degree; on the apron is the
camp of the Crusaders, which is thus explained; it is composed of an enneagon, within which is inscribed a heptagon,
within that a pentagon, and in the center an equilateral
triangle, within which is a circle. Between the heptagon
and pentagon are placed five standards, in the designs of
which are five letters, which form a particular word. The
first standard is purple, on which is emblazoned the ark of
the covenant, with a palm tree on each side; the ark has the
motto *Laus Deo*. The second is blue, on which is a lion, of
gold, couchant, holding in his mouth a golden key, with a
collar of the same metal on his neck, and on it is the device,
Ad majorem Dei gloriam. The third is white, and displays a
heart in flames, with two wings; it is surmounted by a crown
of laurels. The fourth is green, and bears a double-headed
black eagle, crowned, holding a sword in his right claw, and
a bleeding heart in his left. The fifth bears a black ox, on a
field of gold. On the sides of the enneagon are nine tents,
with flags, representing the divisions
of the Masonic army; on the angles
are nine pinions, of the same color
as the flag of the tent that precedes
it. The hall of the Consistory is
hung with black, strewed with tears,
of silver. The jewel is a double-
headed white and black eagle, resting on a Teutonic cross, of gold,
worn attached to the collar or ribbon. The members are called Sublime Princes of the Royal Secret.
The moral of the degree teaches
opposition to bigotry, superstition,
and all the passions and vices which disgrace human nature.

JEWEL.

SUPER EXCELLENT MASTER. A degree formerly
conferred in councils of Royal and Select Masters. Its
legend is associated with circumstances that occurred at the
destruction of the first temple. Its presiding officer is styled

Most Excellent King, and represents Zedekiah, the last King of Israel. It is occasionally conferred in a Royal Arch Chapter as an honorary degree.

SWEDENBORG, Rite of. This rite was established by Emanuel Swedenborg, the eminent philosopher, who was born at Stockholm, January 29, 1688, and died at London, March 29, 1772.* His rite was composed of eight degrees, divided into two Temples. The first Temple contained the degrees of Apprentice, Fellow-Craft, Master and Elect. The doctrines of these degrees related to the creation of man, his disobedience and punishment, and the penalties inflicted on the body and soul; all of which is represented in the initiation. The second Temple comprises the degrees of Companion Cohen, Master Cohen, Grand Architect and Knight Commander, and Kadosh. The enlightened Mason

---

* Swedenborg was well versed in the ancient languages; philosophy, metaphysics, mineralogy and astronomy were equally familiar to him. He devoted himself to profound researches in regard to the mysteries of Freemasonry, wherein he had been initiated; and in what he wrote respecting it, he established that the doctrines of the institution came from those of the Egyptians, Persians, Jews and Greeks. He endeavored to reform the Roman Catholic religion, and his doctrines were adopted by a great number of persons in Sweden, England, Holland, Russia, Germany, and lastly, in the United States. His religious system is expounded in the book entitled "*The Celestial Jerusalem, or the Spiritual World.*" If we are to believe him, he wrote it from the dictation of angels, who, for that purpose, appeared to him at fixed periods. Swedenborg divided the Spiritual World, or the Heavenly Jerusalem, into three Heavens; the upper, or third Heaven; the Spiritual, or second, which is in the middle, and the lower or first, relatively to our world. The dwellers in the third Heaven are the most perfect among the angels; they receive the chief portion of the divine influences immediately from God, whom they see face to face. God is the sun of the invisible world. From him flow Love and Truth, of which heat and light are but emblems. The angels of the second Heaven enjoy, through the upper Heaven, the divine influence. They see God distinctly, but not in all his splendor; he is to them a star without rays, such as the moon appears to us, which gives more light than heat. The dwellers in the lower Heaven receive the divine influence mediately through the other two Heavens. The attributes of the two latter classes are Love and Intelligence. Each of these celestial kingdoms is inhabited by innumerable societies; the angels which compose them are male and female. They contract marriages that are eternal, because it is similarity of inclinations and sympathy that attract them to each other. Each pair dwell in a splendid palace, surrounded by delicious gardens. Below the celestial regions is the realm of spirits. Thither all mankind go immediately upon their death. The divine influence, which their material envelope had prevented them from feeling, is revealed to them by degrees, and effects their transformation into angels, if they are predestined to that. The remembrance of the world which they have left is insensibly effaced from their memory; their proper instincts are unrestrainedly developed, and prepare them for heaven or hell. So full as heaven is of splendor, love and delight, so full is hell of darkness and misery, despair and hate. Such were the reveries on which Pernetti and Gabrianca founded their Illuminism.

will find much of the elements of Freemasonry in the writings of Swedenborg, who, for forty-eight years of his life, devoted himself to the cultivation of science, and produced a great number of works, in which he broached many novel and ingenious theories in theology, which obtained for him a remarkable celebrity in several parts of the world. The Marquis de Thomé, in 1783, taking up the system that had been adopted in the Lodge of Avignon, in 1760, modified it to suit his own views, and instituted what afterward became known as the Rite of Swedenborg.

SWEDISH RITE. This rite was composed in 1767, for the Grand Lodge at Stockholm, by Count Zinnendorf, who had created a similar rite for the National Grand Lodge of Germany, at Berlin; he preserving, however, in the Swedish rite something of the religious system of the philosophic Mason, Swedenborg. It is composed of twelve degrees: 1. Apprentice; 2. Fellow-Craft; 3. Master; 4. Elect Master, forming, in the system of Zinnendorf, the Scottish Apprentice and Scottish Fellow-Craft, called also Apprentice and Fellow-Craft of St. Andrew; 5. Scottish Master, called also Master of St. Andrew, or Grand Scottish Elect, and conferring the rank of civil nobility in the kingdom; 6. Knight of the East, or Novice, called by Zinnendorf, the Favorite of St. John, and composed of the Knights of the East, and a part of the Knights of the West, called by Thory, the Brothers Stuart, and said by him to be composed of the degrees of Knight of the East and Prince of Jerusalem; 7. Knight of the West, or True Templar, or the Favorite Brother of Solomon, in the system of Zinnendorf called the Perfect Elect, and also styled True Capitulate, Templar Master of the Key; 8. Knight of the South, Commander, Master Templar, Grand Dignitary, Elect, called also Favorite Brother of St. John, or of the Blue Cordon; 9. Favorite Brother of St. Andrew, or the Violet Cordon, called also Knight of the Purple Cordon; 10, 11 and 12, Brother of the Red Cross, divided into three classes, thus: 10. Dignitary Member of the Chapter; 11. Grand Dignitary of the Chapter, held by the Prince Royal; 12. The Master Regnant, which can be held by the King of Sweden only, whose title is "The Stadtholder," or Vicar of Solomon. This rite was never, we believe, practiced out of Sweden.

SYMBOL. Latin, *Symbolum.* A word derived from the Greek *sumbolon*, from *sumballein*, to suspect, divine, compare; a word of various meaning, even with the ancients, who used it to denote a sign, a mark, watchword, signal, token, seal-ring, etc. Its meaning is still more various in modern times.

TAB. 367

Symbol is generally used as synonymous with emblem. It is not confined, however, to visible figures, but embraces every representation of an idea by an image, whether the latter is presented immediately to the senses, or merely brought before the mind by words. Men, in the infancy of society, were incapable of abstract thought, and could convey truths only by means of sensible images. In fact, man, at all times, has a strong propensity to clothe thoughts and feelings in images, to make them more striking and living; and in the early periods of our race, when man lived in intimate communion with nature, he readily found, in natural objects, forms and images for the expression of moral truths; and even his conceptions of the Deity were derived directly from natural objects. Freemasonry is a complete system of symbolic teaching, and cannot be known, understood or appreciated only by those who study its symbolism, and make themselves thoroughly acquainted with its occult meaning. To such, Freemasonry has a grand and sublime significance. Its symbols are moral, philosophical and religious, and all these are pregnant with great thoughts, and reveal to the intelligent Mason the awful mystery of life, and the still more awful mystery of death.

T.

TABERNACLE. The Hebrew word properly signifies handsome tent. There were three · public tabernacles among the Jews previous to the building of Solomon's

Temple. The first, which Moses erected, was called "the Tabernacle of the Congregation." In this he gave audience, heard causes, and inquired of God. The second was that which Moses built for God, by his express command. The third public tabernacle was that which David erected in Jerusalem for the reception of the ark when he received it from the house of Obed-edom. But it is the *second* of these, called *the* Tabernacle, by way of distinction, that we have more particularly to notice. This tabernacle was of an oblong, rectangular form, 30 cubits long, 10 broad, and 10 in height, which is equivalent to 55 feet long, 18 broad, and 18 high. The two sides and the western end were formed of boards of shittim wood, overlaid with thin plates of gold, and fixed in solid sockets or vases of silver. It was so contrived as to be taken to pieces and put together again at pleasure. It was covered with four different kinds of curtains. The first and inner curtain was composed of fine linen, magnificently embroidered with figures of cherubim, in shades of blue, purple and scarlet; this formed the beautiful ceiling. The next covering was made of goat's hair; the third of rams' skins died red; and the fourth, and outward covering, was made of other animals' skins, colored red. The east end of the tabernacle was ornamented with five pillars, from which richly-embroidered curtains were suspended. The inside was divided, by a richly-embroidered vail of linen, into two parts, the holy place and the holy of holies; in the first of which were placed the altar of incense, the table with the shew-bread, and the seven-branched candlestick; in the latter place were the ark, the mercy-seat, and the cherubim. Besides this vail of fine linen which separated the most holy place, the tabernacle was furnished with other vails of divers colors, viz: of blue, purple, scarlet, and fine-twined linen, (white,) from which are derived the emblematic colors of the several degrees of Masonry. Within the chamber of a Royal Arch chapter, a temporary structure, after the plan of the one built by Moses, may be erected, as a representation of the tabernacle constructed by Zerubbabel, near the ruins of the first temple, after the return of the captives from Babylon, while the people were building the second temple.

TALMUD. A word derived from the Hebrew verb *lamad,* he has learned. It means *doctrine.* Among the modern Jews, it signifies an immense collection of traditions, illustrative of their laws and usages, forming twelve folio volumes. It consists of two parts—the Mishua and the Gemara. The Mishua is a collection of Rabbinical rules and precepts, made in the second century of the Christian era. The whole civil constitution and mode of thinking, as well as language of the Jews, had gradually undergone a complete revolution, and were entirely different, in the time of our Savior, from what they had been in the early periods of the Hebrew commonwealth. The Mosaic books contained rules no longer adapted to the situation; and its new political relations, connected with the change which had taken place in the religious views of the people, led to many difficult questions, for which no satisfactory solution could be found in their law. The rabbins undertook to supply this defect, partly by commentaries on the Mosaic precepts, and partly by the composition of new rules, which were looked upon as almost equally binding with the former. These comments and additions were called the oral traditions in contradistinction to the old law or written code. The rabbi Juda—surnamed the *Holy*— was particularly active in making this collection—150 B. C.— which received the name of Mishna, or second law. The later rabbins busied themselves in a similar manner in the composition of commentaries and explanations of the Mishna. Among these works that of the rabbi Jachanan (composed about 230 A. D.) acquired the most celebrity, under the name of Gemara — Chaldaic for completion or doctrine. This Mishna and Gemara, together, formed the Jerusalem Talmud, relating chiefly to the Jews of Palestine. But after the Jews had mostly removed to Babylon, and the synagogue of Palestine had almost entirely disappeared, the Babylonian rabbins gradually composed new commentaries on the Mishna, which, about 500 A. D., were completed, and thus formed the Babylonian Talmud. Many Masonic traditions are drawn from the Talmud; and it contains a more comprehensive description of Solomon's Temple than can be found anywhere else.

TASTING. One of the five human senses. The sense by which we perceive or distinguish savors; or the perception of outward objects through the instrumentality of the tongue or the organs of taste. This sense is fully explained in the Fellow-Craft's degree.

TATNAI AND SHETHAR–BOZNAI. Words used in a Masonic degree. They are the names of two Persian officers who bore a peculiar enmity to the Jews, and endeavored to interrupt the building of the second temple, which had been commenced by Zerubbabel. Reports of their interference having been made to Darius, the Persian king, that monarch issued a decree commanding the above-mentioned officers not only to desist from interrupting that labor, but also to render such assistance in the work as he should, from time to time, prescribe. *Vide* Ezra v., 3.

TEACHINGS, SYMBOLIC, OF THE DEGREES. Freemasonry teaches by symbols and symbolical ceremonies, and hence each degree, through these agencies, illustrates and inculcates some particular virtue, or commemorates some important event. The following is an analytical summary of the ideas, which the several degrees of the Order seek to enforce; thus in Ancient Craft Masonry:

1. Dependence; the weak and helpless condition of the human family on their entrance into the world; the ignorance and darkness that surround man until the moral and intellectual light of reason and revelation breaks in upon his mind; obedience, secrecy and humility, and the practice of charity.

2. The struggle for knowledge after the release of the mind from the bondage of darkness and ignorance; its attainment, and the reward due to industry and perseverance.

3. Progress in the great duties of aiding humanity from the thraldom of vice and error; man's regeneration; higher sphere of happiness; integrity; mortality of the body, and the immortality of the soul.

4. Order, regularity, and a proper system of discrimination between the worthy and the unworthy; the just reward to the industrious and faithful.

5. Virtue and talent the only proper distinctions of position. All associations of men must, for the sake of harmony and order, be governed by well regulated laws.

6. The completion and dedication of the temple; the spiritual edifice which man must erect in his soul—that "house not made with hands, eternal in the heavens;" an *acknowledgement* that the labors of man's earthly toil are over, and he is *received* into the abode of the just and perfect.

7. The revelation of the divine law; an exhibition of the toils and vicissitudes of man's pilgrimage through life; a realization of the sublime truths promised, when the vails which obscure the mental vision are drawn aside, and man, raised and regenerated, shall enjoy the blessings of peace and joy in the heavenly temple.

8. The mysteries revealed; man rewarded according to his work; the Alpha and Omega—the first and the last.

9. Skill and ingenuity appreciated; justice and mercy accorded to the faithful and worthy.

In the Ancient and Accepted Scottish rite, which is now widely diffused throughout the world, the principles and teachings are:

1. Development of Freemasonry; instructions regarding its laws and uses.

2. Labor, wisdom, and virtue, the true means of securing enduring happiness.

3. Homage rendered to inflexible honor which esteemed duty more than life.

4. Discretion of the wise; watchfulness of the good workman.

5. Perfection of the mind and heart; knowledge of sublime truths, and the tribute of respect due to the virtuous.

6. Necessity of knowing the fountain of so many precious discoveries, and the danger of a vain curiosity.

7. Equity, in judging both the actions of others and our own.

8. A spirit of order and analysis.

9. Zeal and talent; good examples; generous efforts to advance the cause of truth and destroy error.

10. Extinction of wicked passions and perverse inclinations.

11. Reformation of manners, and the dissemination of true and useful knowledge.

12. Persevering courage.

13. Tribute to the memory of some of the first instructors of men.

14. Adoration of the Grand Architect of the Universe.

15. The honor due to the liberators of their country.

16. Joyfulness inspired by the heroism of the Knight-liberators of the East.

17. Advantages promised by Freemasonry.

18. The triumph of light over darkness.

19. Pontificate of the universal and regenerated religion.

20. On the duties of the Masters of Masonic Lodges.

21. The dangers of selfish ambition, and the necessity of sincere repentance therefor.

22. Ancient chivalry propagative of generous sentiments. Devotion to the Order.

23. Oversight of the conservators of Freemasonry.

24. Preservation of the doctrines of the Order.

25. Emulation which creates useful plans.

26. Esteem and rewards due to genius.

27. Superiority and independence given by talents and virtue.

28. Truth harmonized and unvailed with respect to all things which concern the happiness of man.

29. A degree consecrated to Ancient Scotch Masonry.

30. The purpose and aim of Freemasonry in all its degrees.

31. The exalted justice of the Order.

32. Military government of the Order.

33. Administration of the Supreme rite. "Ne plus ultra."

TEMPLARISM, Scottish. This is a form of the Knight-Templar system which does not recognize the three symbolical degrees as its foundation, and, consequently, does not require its members to be Freemasons. It is constituted in two divisions: 1. Novice and Esquire; 2. Knight Templar. The latter is composed of three degrees: 1. Knights of Priories; 2. Knights Commanders, elected from the Knights; 3. Knights Grand Crosses, nominated by the Grand Master. The Grand Conclave assembles four times a year, and the Grand Officers are elected at the March session. They consist of Grand Master, Past Grand Masters, Grand Seneschal, Preceptor and Grand Prior of Scotland, Grand Constable and Mareschal, Grand Admiral, Grand Almoner, Grand Chancellor, Grand Treasurer, Grand Secretary, Grand Prelate, Grand Provost, Grand Beaucennifer, or Standard Bearer, Grand Bearer of the Vexillum Belli, Grand Chamberlain, Grand Steward, and two Grand Aids-de-Camp. With the exception of some slight resemblance to our Templar system, it has no Masonic character whatever, and can scarcely be classed as a Masonic society.

TEMPLE. An edifice erected for religious purposes. As the grand symbols of Freemasonry are a temple and its ornaments, and to construct temples was the business of the original Masons, some remarks upon these structures cannot but be instructive. The word temple is derived from the Latin *Templum*, and this word templum seems to have been derived from the old Latin verb, *Templari*, to contemplate. The ancient augurs undoubtedly applied the name *templa* to those parts of the heavens which were marked out for observation of the flight of birds. Temples, originally, were all open; and hence most likely came their name. These structures are among the most ancient monuments. They were the first built, and the most noticeable of public edifices. As soon as a nation had acquired any degree of civilization the people consecrated particular spots to the worship of their duties. In the earliest instances they contented themselves with erecting altars of earth or ashes in the open air, and sometimes resorted, for the purposes of worship, to the depths of solitary woods. At length they acquired the practice of building cells or chapels within the enclosure of which they placed the image of their divinities, and assembled to offer up their supplications, thanksgivings, and sacrifices. These were chiefly formed like their own dwellings. The Troglodytes adored their gods in grottoes; the people who lived in cabins, erected temples like cabins in shape. Clemens, Alexandrinus, and Eusebius refer the origin of temples to sepulchers; and this notion has been illustrated and confirmed from a variety of testimonies.* At the time when the Greeks suspassed all other people in the arts introduced among them from Phœnicia, Syria, and Egypt, they devoted much time, care and expense to the building of temples. No country has surpassed, or perhaps equaled, them in this respect; the Romans alone successfully rivaled them, and they took the Greek structures for models. According to Vitruvius, the situations of the temples were regulated chiefly by the nature and characteristics of the various divinities. Thus the temples of Jupiter, Juno, and Minerva, who were considered by the inhabitants of many cities as their protecting deities, were erected on spots sufficiently elevated to enable them to overlook the whole town, or, at least the principal part of it. Minerva, the tutelary deity of Athens, had her seat on the Acropolis. In like manner the temple of Solomon was built on Mount Moriah.

TEMPLE BAR. A gate between Fleet street and the Strand, London. This handsome piece of Masonry, demonstrating the architectural skill of the Craft, was erected after the great fire, under the Grand Mastership of Sir Christopher Wren. It is composed of Portland stone, of rustic work below, and of the Corinthian order.

* *Vide* "Treatise on the Worship of Human Spirits," by Farmer, p. 373.

TEMPLE OF HEROD THE GREAT. This temple far exceeded both of its predecessors in magnificence and perfection. It was surrounded with four courts, rising above each other like terraces. The lower court was 500 cubits square, on three sides surrounded by a double, and on the fourth by a triple row of columns, and was called the "Court of the Gentiles," because individuals of all nations were admitted into it indiscriminately. A high wall separated the court of the women, 135 cubits square, in which the Jewish females assembled to perform their devotions, from the court of the Gentiles. From the court of the women fifteen steps led to the court of the temple, which was enclosed by a colonnade, and divided by trellis-work, into the court of Jewish men and the court of the priests. In the middle of this enclosure stood the temple, of white marble, richly gilt, 100 cubits long and wide, and 60 cubits high, with a porch 100 cubits wide, and three galleries, like the first temple, which it resembled in the interior, except that the most holy place was empty, and the height of Herod's Temple was double the height of Solomon's. The fame of this magnificent temple, which was destroyed by the Romans, and its religious significance with Jews and Christians, render it more interesting to us than any other building of antiquity. Each of these temples holds an important place in the symbolism and instructions of Freemasonry, and furnishes the traditions for a large number of degrees.

TEMPLE OF SOLOMON. When Solomon had matured his design of a temple to be consecrated to the Most High, he found it impossible to carry that design into execution without foreign assistance. The Hebrew nation, constantly struggling for its material existence, and just rising to the condition of a civilized people, had made little proficiency in science and architecture, and especially the ornamental arts. There were few artificers and no architects in Judea. Solomon, consequently, applied to Hiram, King of Tyre, for assistance, and that monarch sent him a company of Tyrian architects, under the superintendence of Hiram Abif, by whom the temple was erected. It was an oblong stone building, 150 feet in length, and 105 in width. On three sides were corridors, rising above each other to the height of three stories, and containing rooms, in which were preserved the holy utensils and treasures. The fourth, or front side, was open, and was ornamented with a portico ten cubits in width, supported by two brazen pillars—Jachin and Boaz. The interior was divided into the most holy place, or oracle, 20 cubits long, which contained the ark of the covenant, and was separated by a curtain, or vail, from the sanctuary or holy place, in which were the golden candlestick, the table of the shew-bread, and the altar of incense. The walls of both apartments, and the roof and ceiling of the most holy place, were overlaid with wood-work, skilfully carved. None but the High-Priest was permitted to enter the latter, and only the priests, devoted to the temple service, the former. The temple was surrounded by an inner court, which contained the altar of burnt offering, the brazen sea and lavers, and such instruments and utensils as were used in the sacrifices, which, as well as the prayers, were offered here. Colonnades, with brazen gates, separated this court of the priests from the outer court, which was likewise surrounded by a wall. This celebrated temple certainly reflected honor on the builders of that age. It was begun on the 2d day of the month Zif, corresponding with the 21st of April, in the year of the world 2992, or 1012 years before the Christian era, and was completed in little more than seven years, on the 8th day of the month Bul, or the 23d of October, in the year 2999, during which period no sound of axe, hammer, or other metallic tool, was heard, everything having been cut and prepared in the quarries or on Mount Lebanon, and brought, properly carved, marked and numbered, to Jerusalem, where they were fitted in by means of wooden mauls. So of Free-masonry, it has always been the boast that its members perfect the work of edification by quiet and orderly methods, "without the hammer of contention, the axe of division, or any tool of mischief." The excellency of the Craft in the days of our Grand Master Solomon was so great, that, although the materials were prepared so far off, when they were put together at Jerusalem, each piece fitted with such exactness that it appeared more like the work of the Great Architect of the Universe than of human hands. The temple retained its pristine splendor but thirty-three years, when it was plundered by Shishak, King of Egypt. After this period it underwent sundry profanations and pillages, and was at length utterly destroyed by Nebuchadnezzar, King of Babylon, A. M. 3416, B. C. 588, and the inhabitants of Jerusalem carried as captives to Babylon.

TEMPLE OF ZERUBBABEL. This edifice was built on the site of the first temple, under the direction of Zerubbabel, B. C. 535–15. It was considerably larger than the former one, but very inferior to it in beauty and splendor.

TESSELATED PAVEMENT. The word tesselated is derived from the word *tessela*, diminutive of *tessera*. The pavement which is thus designated is of rich Mosaic work, made of curious square marbles, bricks or tiles, in shape and

RUINS OF THE FIRST TEMPLE.

PREPARATIONS FOR BUILDING THE SECOND TEMPLE
BY ZERUBBABEL.

disposition resembling dice. Various ancient specimens of these have been, from time to time, exhumed in Italy, and other countries of Europe. The tesselated pavement, in the symbolism of Freemasonry, is significant of the varied experiences and vicissitudes of human life.

TETRACTYS. A Greek word—*tetraktus*—meaning four. It was a Pythagorean symbol represented by a delta formed by points, so arranged that each of the three sides consisted of four. The one point, or Monad, represented God; the two points, or *duad*, matter; the three, the worlds which were formed by the action of the one, or Monad, upon the *duad;* and the four points referred to the divine reason and those sciences which are the revelations of it.* On this symbol the initiate into the Pythagorean mysteries was sworn. According to Jamblichus, the oath was as follows:

> "*Ou ma ameterē geneē, paradonta tetraktun,*
> *Pagan aeenaou phuseōs rizoma' t' echousan.*"

"On the sacred *tetraktus*, eternal fountain of Nature, I swear to thee."

This word is nearly related to the Hebrew Tetragrammaton; probably derived from it.

TEUTONIC ORDER. A religious order of knights, founded in 1190, by Frederick, Duke of Suabia, during a crusade in the Holy Land, at the time of the siege of Acre, and intended to be confined to Germans of noble rank; hence its name. The rule of the order was similar to that of the Templars. The original object of the association was to defend the Christian religion against the infidels, and to take care of the sick in the Holy Land. As the order was dedicated to the Virgin Mary, the knights called themselves also "Brethren of the German house of our Lady of Jerusalem." The dress of the members was black, with a white cloak, upon which was worn a black cross with a silver edging. The Grand Master lived first at Jerusalem, but afterward, when the Holy Land fell again under the power of the Turks, at Venice, and, from 1297, at Marburg. The order was abolished by Napoleon, April 24th, 1809. The Teutonic cross forms a part of the decorations of the 27th degree of the Ancient Scotch rite.

---

* The sum of all the principles of Pythagoras is this:—"The Monad is the principle of all things. From the Monad came the indeterminate Duad, as matter subjected to the cause of Monad; from the Monad and the indeterminate Duad, numbers; *from numbers, points; from points, lines; from lines, superficies; from superficies, solids;* from these solid bodies, whose elements are four—Fire, Water, Air, and Earth—of all which transmuted, and totally changed, the WORLD consists."

THEOLOGICAL VIRTUES. Faith, Hope and Charity are thus named, and are said to constitute the chief rounds of the Masonic ladder, by the aid of which the good Mason expects at last to ascend to the perfect Lodge above. These virtues are enforced in various parts of the rituals, and enlarged upon in the first lecture of Craft Masonry. The great duties of man to God, his neighbor and himself, are the precepts most strongly enforced; hence the points to direct the steps of the aspirant to higher honors are Faith, Hope and Charity.

THEOPHILANTHROPISTS. Lovers of God and man— from *Theos*, God; *philos*, friend; and *anthropos*, man. This was the title assumed by a religious society formed at Paris during the French Revolution. The object of its founders was to revive public religious ceremonies, which had altogether ceased during the reign of terror. The temples were appropriately fitted up, and adorned with moral and religious inscriptions, an ancient altar, with a basket containing flowers, as an offering to the Supreme Being; a pulpit, and allegorical paintings, and banners with inscriptions and emblematic devices. The assemblies were held weekly, on Sunday; the exercises consisted of prayer, moral discourses, and singing. The liturgy of the Theophilanthropists was simple and touching. The festivals of nature, love of country, of conjugal fidelity, were scrupulously observed. The society served a very useful purpose in that remarkable period of French history, but soon disappeared on the reëstablishment of Christianity.

THEOSOPHISTS. Those who inquire into the science of divine things. Many eminent Freemasons belonged to this class during the last century. The speculations of the Theosophists, however, were generally of a mystical character. Several Masonic systems were theosophical, as, for example, the rites of Swedenborg, St Martin, Zinnendorff, etc.

THEURGY. The name which the ancients gave to that part of magic which we call *white magic*, or the *white art*. The word is formed from *Theos*, God, and *ergon*, work, as denoting the art of doing divine things, or things which God alone can do. It is the power of working extraordinary things, by invoking the names of God, the saints, angels, etc. Accordingly, those who have written of magic in general divide it into three parts: *theurgy*, which operates by divine or celestial means; *natural magic*, performed by the powers of nature; and *necromancy*, which proceeds by invoking demons. Theurgy, probably, originated with the Chaldeans or Persians, among whom the magi chiefly occupied themselves with it. The Egyptians also pretended to great proficiency in the art. The former considered Zoroaster its author; the latter, Hermes Trismegistus. It occupied largely the attention of the Cabalists, and, in the last century, entered into the speculations of many distinguished Freemasons.

THREE GLOBES, RITE OF THE GRAND LODGE OF. The Lodge of Three Globes was founded at Berlin, September 23d, 1740. On the 24th of June, 1744, it assumed the title of Grand Royal Mother Lodge of the Three Globes; and on the 5th of July, 1772, it took the name of Grand National Mother Lodge of the Prussian States. At first it confined its work to the three symbolical degrees, but afterward added the French, or modern rite. The rite of the Three Globes is practiced by nearly two hundred Lodges.

THRESHING-FLOOR. Ornan, the Jebusite, owned a threshing-floor on Mount Moriah, which David purchased for six hundred shekels of gold. He erected there an altar, and consecrated it to the service of God, by sacrifices and prayers. The Temple of Solomon was afterward built upon it.

TILER. An officer of the Lodge, whose duty is to guard and keep the doors of the Lodge. The name is derived from operative Masonry. A Tiler is one who *covers* the roof of a building with tiles. So the guardian or sentinel of a Lodge is said to tile or cover the Lodge from all inspection or intrusion on the part of the uninitiated.

TRANSIENT BRETHREN. No stranger should be admitted to the Lodge until he has proved himself a Freemason. When he has done this he should be received with cordiality and fraternal courtesy. A traveling brother, away from his home and friends, naturally longs for companionship, and expects to find it around the altars of Freemasonry. Hospitality to strangers is, always and everywhere, a sacred duty, but it is doubly so to Freemasons. The brother from abroad should be greeted with such warmth and brotherly kindness and interest as will make him feel at home, and that he is surrounded with friends, upon whose sympathy he can rely. Lodges are sometimes too remiss in regard to this duty, and many a warm-hearted brother, when visiting a strange Lodge, has been chilled and grieved by the iciness of his reception.

TRAVELING FREEMASONS. As early as the time of Solomon the Tyrian and Sidonian builders traveled to foreign countries, to exercise their calling. They visited Judea and built the temple at Jerusalem. They went to Rome, and furnished the idea and form of the Colleges of Artists and Builders, whose history extended through the whole period of the Roman empire. These Colleges were succeeded by the Building Corporations of the middle ages. All of these societies seem to be identical, possessed the same characteristics, especially the practice of traveling from place to place, to erect public buildings, as their services might be needed. They traveled through all the countries of Europe; the numerous Gothic churches, monasteries, and cathedrals which are there found are the monuments of their skill. Protected by the charters of the clerical and secular powers, and united in one great society for the construction of each great building, as the cathedrals, etc., these societies erected those gigantic monuments—many of them larger than the temple of Solomon—generally termed Gothic, which excite our amazement. We find these traveling societies everywhere. They were composed of members from Italy, Germany, the Netherlands, France, England, Scotland, and other countries, and united under very similar constitutions; for instance, at the erection of the convent of Batalha, in Portugal, about A. D. 1400; of the minster of Strasburg, 1015 to 1439; that of Cologne, 950 and 1211 to 1365; of the cathedral of Meissen, in the tenth century; of the cathedral of Milan, the convent of Monte Cassino, and of the most remarkable buildings of the British isles. That these societies of traveling builders at last gave rise to one, not occupied with actual building—that is to say speculative Masonry, is demonstrated beyond a doubt. Among their symbols were the square, the plumb, the compasses, which are among the most important emblems of modern Freemasonry. They held a convention at Ratisbon in 1459, where it was resolved to constitute a Grand Lodge at Strasburg, of which the architect of that cathedral, for the time being, should be, *ex-officio*, the Grand Master. We have a copy of the constitutions, charges, rules, etc., of this Fraternity in Latin, and some of them are almost, *verbatim et literatim*, the same as many of our own which we designate "the Ancient Charges." An intelligent Freemason who visited Cologne, in 1847, thus writes: "During the interval between 1248 and 1323, there were not only fifty Masters, and three times as many Fellow-Crafts, daily employed, but a large number of Entered Apprentices from all parts of Christendom, who had come to study the operative and speculative branches of the art, and who carried away with them the principles which directed the erection of almost

TRESTLE BOARD OF THE 18TH CENTURY.

every Gothic monument of the age. After the secession of the Masons from the church, the works were suspended, leaving only the choir, with its side aisle, completed." This structure, commenced by the traveling Masons six centuries ago, has, within a few years, been finished after the original plans. Another writer,* remarking on the same class of builders, says: "The architects of all the sacred edifices of the Latin church, whenever such arose—North, South, East, and West—thus derived their science from the same central school; obeyed in their designs the same hierarchy; were directed in their constructions by the same principles of propriety and taste; kept up with each other, in the most distant parts, to which they might be sent, the most constant correspondence; and rendered every minute improvement the property of the whole body, and a new conquest of the art. The result of this unanimity was that, at each successive period of the monastic dynasty, on whatever point a new monastry or church might be erected, it resembled all those raised at the same period in every other place, however distant from it, as if both had been built in the same place by the same artist. For instance, we find, at particular epochs, churches as far distant from each other as the north of Scotland and the south of Italy to be minutely similar in all the essential characteristics."

TRESTLE-BOARD. "As the operative Mason erects his temporal building in accordance with the designs laid down upon the Trestle-Board by the master-workman, so should we, both operative and speculative, endeavor to erect our spiritual building in accordance with the designs laid down by the Supreme Architect." What is here masonically designated the " *Trestle-Board*," artists, poets, and philosophers denominate the Ideal. All things that exist, save God, are created by the ideal, or are reflections of it. The visible creation is God's ideal, wrought out in material forms; and all the works of man are copies of ideal types which he discovers traced on the Trestle-Board of his soul. Every nation exists according to an ideal which is reflected in its life, its institutions, and manners; and the life of man, as an individual, is high or low, as his ideals of life are high or low; or, in other words, it is fashioned after the designs that are traced on the moral Trestle-Board. Societies, also, are constructed from the ideal. If a society have no ideal, it can have no influence, and can exist but for a brief period, because it has no ability to arouse the enthusiasm, or command the respect and allegiance of men. The Masonic

* Hope, "History of Architecture," p. 239.

society has been able to adapt itself to various and changing circumstances of mankind, with facility, because its ideals of society, of benevolence and virtue, rose higher, and shone brighter, as the ages rolled away. It is a part of its mission to keep the minds of its adepts fixed intently upon the designs pictured upon the Trestle-Board, or, to speak more correctly, to establish a perpetual communion between man and the world of glorious ideals.

TRIAD. Three in one. An important symbol in Free-masonry. The number three was thought holy in the earliest antiquity. Numbers, xix. 12, furnishes an instance. This must have its reason in the nature of the number. It repre-sents to us unity and opposition, the principle and its development or opposition, and the connecting unity—syn-thesis. It is the first uneven number in which the first even one is found: herein lie its peculiar signification and perfec-tion. Even in antiquity it could not escape attention, that this number is to be found wherever variety is developed. Hence we have beginning, middle, end, represented in the heavenly rise, point of culmination and setting; morning, noon, evening, and evening, midnight, morning; and in general, in the great divisions of time, the past, the present, and the future. In space, also, this number three occurs, as in above, midst, and below; right midst, and left; and in general, in the dimensions of space, as length, breadth, and thickness, or depth. To the eye, the number is repre-sented in the regular figure of the triangle, which has been applied to numberless symbolical representations; the ear perceives it most perfectly in the harmonic triad. As the triple is also the basis of symmetry, that three-figured form is found in architecture, and in simple utensils, without any particular reference to symbolical or other significations. Of this kind are the triglyphs in architecture, the tripod, trident, the three thunderbolts of Jupiter, the ancient three-stringed-lyre, though the number has in these objects, as well as in the three-headed Cerberus, other more symbolical relations. The Triad, represented by the *delta*, is a signifi-cant emblem in a large number of Masonic degrees.

TRINOSOPHISTS, Lodge of. A body of Masons once, if not at present, very popular and influential in Paris. It was at one time the most intelligent society of Freemasons ever known. It adhered to the ancient Landmarks, but gave clearer and more satisfactory interpretations of the symbols of Freemasonry than are afforded in the symbolical Lodges. It practiced five degrees as follows: 1. Apprentice; 2. Fel-low-Craft; 3. Master; 4. Rose Croix, reformed—*rectifié*—

5. Grand Elect Knight K.∴ S.∴ We have elsewhere given
an account of the Rose Croix degree as it is practiced in this
Lodge. The following extracts from the preliminary instructions to a candidate for initiation into the third degree will
be found interesting, and will serve to illustrate the way in
which these Trinosophical Masons explain the ceremonies
and symbols of Freemasonry. "Man, cast, as it were, by
accident, upon the earth, feeling that he is born free, and
yet seeing himself a slave, seeking the good, and yet often
finding the bad, and not being able to attribute to the same
author both good and evil, imagined that there were two
principles—distinct and separate, eternally antagonistic to
each other. It is thus that the ancient Persians recognized
Oromazdes, the good principle, and Arimanius, the principle
of evil; the Jews, Jehovah and the serpent, and the Egyptians Osiris and Typhon. Masons who form an elect family
in the social order, who study and seek the true and the good,
also have their traditions and allegories. They have the
history of the death and resurrection of H.∴ A.∴, the perfect
workman, assassinated by three wicked fellows, notwithstanding the efforts of the nine good F.∴ C's.∴ to save him. This
legend, it is true, has been mutilated, and made insignificant
and often ridiculous by ignorant expounders of the Masonic
mysteries; but all enlightened Masters know that this
Perfect Master is the *genius of beneficence and truth* both in the
physical and moral order. In the physical order he is the
sun, that glorious luminary which gives life to all nature,
and which makes his revolution in the regular space of
twelve months, which become, so to speak, his eternal and
inseparable companions. These twelve months form the
spring, the summer, the autumn, and winter. The first nine
of these give the flowers, the fruits, warmth and light. They
are the nine good F.∴ C's.∴ who love and wish to preserve their
master. The three last are the authors of the rains, the
frosts, and darkness. It may be said that they kill nature
and the sun himself. They are the three bad F.∴ C's.∴. In
the moral and spiritual order, H.∴ M.∴ is the Eternal Reason
by which all things are weighed, governed, and preserved.
He is also Knowledge, Justice, and Truth, by which the
Eternal Reason is manifested. The good F.∴ C's.∴ are the
virtues that honor and bless humanity; the wicked F.∴ C's.∴
are the vices which degrade and kill it."

TRIVIUM. The name given, in the middle ages, to the
first three of the seven liberal arts: grammar, rhetoric, and
logic. The other four, consisting of arithmetic, music,
geometry, and astronomy, were called the *quadrivium*.

TROWEL AND SWORD. Emblems in the degree of Knights of the East. They are borrowed evidently from a religious and mechanical society, called the *Brethren of the Bridge*, which was founded at an early period in France, when a state of anarchy existed, and there was little security for travelers, particularly in passing rivers, on which they were subject to the rapacity of banditti. The object of this society was to put a stop to these outrages by forming fraternities for the purpose of building bridges and establishing ferries and caravansaries on their banks. Always prepared for an attack from the marauders, they carried a sword in one hand and a trowel or hammer in the other. Ramsay says that they adopted this custom in imitation of the Jews at the building of the second temple; and he endeavors to establish some connection between them and the Knights of the Temple, and of St. John of Jerusalem.

TROWEL, ORDER OF. A Berlin periodical of April, 1791, gives the following account of the formation of this society: "Vasari, in his '*Life of the Painters*,' makes mention of a society of artists, called the 'Brotherhood of the Trowel,' which arose as follows. In the course of the fifteenth century several artists were supping one night in a garden at Florence. By accident their table was placed near a heap of lime, in which a trowel was sticking. One of the guests seized the trowel, and threw, sportively, some lime into the mouth of another guest, exclaiming, at the same time: 'The trowel! the trowel!' This circumstance led to the establishment of a fraternity which chose a trowel for its emblem, and St. Andrew for its patron Saint." It is possible, as Clavel conjectures, that this society might have borne some relationship to the Traveling Masons.

TRUE MASONS, ORDER OF. Baileau, a Masonic mystic, founded, 1778, a Lodge of Hermetic Masonry at Montpelier, and gave it this name. It practiced six degrees: 1. The True Mason; 2. The True Mason in the Right Way; 3. Knight of the Golden Key; 4. Knight of the Rainbow; 5. Knight of the Argonauts; 6. Knight of the Golden Fleece.

TRUE PATRIOTS, SOCIETY OF. In the Latin of the Middle Ages, *patriota* signified a native, in contradistinction to *peregrinus*, a foreigner who did not enjoy the rights of citizenship. As the native, i. e., citizen, was considered to be attached by his interests to the commonwealth, the word gradually received the meaning of a citizen who loves his country. Here, however, it has a wider sense still—the

True Patriots style themselves the friends of mankind. This brotherhood appeared at Frankfort in the year 1787. Its object was to unite all classes of men together, "through the agency of the learned—the society of Freemasons, and other closely-allied fraternities, for the promotion of their mutual interests." The order conferred several degrees, and appears to have had some connection with the Order of Jerusalem, or the Order of Freemasonry, *a priori*.

TRUTH. One of the great tenets of a Freemason's profession. It is the foundation of all Masonic virtues; it is one of our grand principles; for to be good men and true is a part of the first lesson we are taught; and at the commencement of our freedom we are exhorted to be fervent and zealous in the pursuit of truth and goodness. It is not sufficient that we walk in the light, unless we do so in the truth also. All hypocrisy and deceit must be banished from among us. Sincerity and plain dealing complete the harmony of a Lodge, and render us acceptable in the sight of him unto whom all hearts are open, all desires known, and from whom no secrets are hid. There is a charm in truth, which draws and attracts the mind continually toward it. The more we discover, the more we desire; and the great reward is wisdom, virtue, and happiness. This is an edifice founded on a rock, which malice cannot shake or time destroy. In the ancient mythology of Rome, Truth was called the mother of Virtue, and was depicted with white and flowing garments. Her looks were cheerful and pleasant, though modest and serene. She was the protectress of honor and honesty, and the light and joy of human society.

TWELVE GRAND POINTS OF MASONRY. "There are in Masonry," say the ancient lectures, "twelve original points which form the basis of the system, and comprehend the whole ceremony of initiation. Without the existence of these points, no man ever was, or can be, legally and essentially received into the Order. Every person who is made a Mason must go through all these twelve forms and ceremonies, not only in the first degree, but in every subsequent one." Esteeming these points of the highest importance in the ceremonies of the Order, our ancient brethren exercised great ingenuity in giving them symbolical explanations, and refer the twelve parts of the ceremony of initiation to the twelve tribes of Israel. Notwithstanding the value and importance our ancient brethren deemed these points to possess, the Grand Lodge of England thought proper, at the union in 1813, to strike them from its rituals, and substitute three "new" points. Neither of these systems have ever been practiced in this country; the "*four perfect points*" constitute an adequate substitute for either. The symbolism embraced in the explanation of the "Twelve Grand Points" may not be uninteresting or unacceptable to the reader:

1. The *opening of the Lodge* was symbolized by the tribe of Reuben, because Reuben was the first-born of his father Jacob, who called him "the beginning of his strength," the door, as it were, by which the children of Israel entered the world. He was, therefore, appropriately adopted as the emblem of that ceremony which is essentially the beginning of every initiation.

2. The *preparation* of the candidate was symbolized by the tribe of Simeon, because Simeon prepared the instruments for the slaughter of the Shechemites, which excited the heavy displeasure of his parent; and, therefore, to perpetuate abhorrence of his cruelty, candidates for initiation were deprived of all weapons, both offensive and defensive.

3. The *report* of the Senior Deacon referred to the tribe of Levi, in commemoration of the signal or report which Levi was supposed to have given to his brother Simeon when they assailed the men of Shechem at a time when they were incapable of defending themselves, and put them all to the sword, because of the affront which Dinah, their sister, had received from Shechem, the son of Hamor.

4. The *entrance* of the candidate into the Lodge was symbolized by the tribe of Judah, because they were the first to cross the Jordan and enter the promised land, coming from the darkness and servitude, as it were, of the wilderness by many dangerous and wearisome journeys into the light and liberty of Canaan.

5. The *prayer* was symbolized by Zebulun, because the blessing and prayer of Jacob were given to Zebulun, in preference to his brother Issachar.

6. The *circumambulation* referred to the tribe of Issachar, because, as a thriftless and indolent tribe, they required a leader to advance them to an equal elevation with the other tribes.

7. The *advancing* to the altar was symbolized by the tribe of Dan, that the candidate might be taught by contrast to advance in the way of truth and holiness as rapidly as this tribe advanced to idolatry, for it was among the tribe of Dan that the serpent was first set up for adoration.

8. The *obligation* referred to the tribe of Gad, in allusion to the solemn vow which was made by Jephthah, Judge of Israel, who was of that tribe.

9. The *intrusting* of the candidate with the mysteries was symbolized by the tribe of Asher, because he was then presented with the rich fruits of Masonic knowledge, as Asher was said to be the inheritor of fatness and royal dainties.

10. The *investure* of the lambskin, by which the candidate is declared free, referred to the tribe of Naphtali, which was invested by Moses with a peculiar freedom, when he said, "O, Naphtali, satisfied with favor and full with the blessing of the Lord, possess thou the West and the South."

11. The *ceremony of the northeast corner of the Lodge* referred to Joseph, because as this ceremony reminds us of the most superficial part of Masonry, so the two half tribes of Ephraim and Manasseh, of which the tribe of Joseph was composed, were accounted to be more superficial than the rest, as they were the descendants of the grandsons only of Jacob.

12. The *closing of the Lodge* was symbolized by the tribe of Benjamin, who was the youngest of the sons of Jacob, and thus closed his father's strength.

TYPHON. In the Egyptian mythology, a deity, the brother of Osiris. He was considered the author of all the evil in the world. He aspired to the sovereignty of Egypt, possessed by his brother Osiris. His designs were, for a long time, frustrated by Isis, the wife of Osiris; but the latter, while on his return from a tour round the world, was killed by Typhon, who cut his body to pieces, and concealed it. The ceremonies in the Egyptian mysteries were symbolical representations of the various events attending the struggles between Typhon—evil, and Osiris—goodness; their alternate victories and defeats; the destruction of Osiris, and the search for and restoration of his body; the final annihilation of Typhon—evil, and the spread of peace, happiness and virtue over all the world. Typhon is the analogue of the three evil principles personified in the Master's degree. —*Vide* articles "Isis," and "Osiris."

U.

UNANIMOUSLY. In order to secure and perpetuate the peace and harmony of the Craft, it has long been the settled policy of the Masonic Fraternity to receive no person to membership, only by the consent of all the brethren who may be present at the time the ballot is taken. Among the regulations of the Grand Lodge of England we find the following in regard to this subject: "No man can be entered a brother in any particular Lodge, or admitted a member thereof, without the unanimous consent of all the members of the Lodge then present, when the candidate is proposed, and when their consent is formally asked by the Master. They are to give their consent in their own prudent way, either virtually or in form, but with unanimity. Nor is this inherent privilege subject to a dispensation; because the members of a particular Lodge are the best judges of it; and because, if a turbulent member should be imposed upon them, it might spoil their harmony, or hinder the freedom of their communications, or even break up and disperse the Lodges, which ought to be avoided by all true and faithful brothers."

UNIVERSI TERRARUM ORBIS ARCHITECTONIS AD GLORIAM INGENTIS. The introduction to all the decrees and official documents of the Supreme Council of the 33d degree of the Ancient and Accepted rite. It is the Latin for the English phrase: "To the Glory of the Grand Architect of the Universe."

UPRIGHT. Every Freemason remembers the instructions given him in the Lodge at the time of his reception, in regard to the "upright posture." "God created man to be *upright*," i. e., to stand erect. This is the peculiar prerogative of man. All the outward forms and features of the sentient world, whether human or brutal, are created by the nature, disposition or spirit of each race and each individual. The nature of beasts and reptiles is earthly. Prone to the earth, they move horizontally, with downward gaze, or crawl in the dust. To them the ideal world is closed. The glory of the heavens, the grandeur of nature, the beauty of flowers, the wonderful harmonies of sight and sound, which so inspire and elevate man, are unknown to them. Their gaze is downward, and their life is extinguished in the dust. Man, on the contrary, stands erect, and his eyes sweep through the immense regions of space which stretch above his head. His mind, endowed with a divine energy, reaches to the most distant star, and measures it, in weight and size, as accurately as one measures the apple that is held in the palm of the hand? The "upright posture" also has an important moral significance for the intelligent Mason. As it reminds him of his relationship to the celestial powers, and that he is endowed with some of the attributes of the Divinity, and with a life which will endure forever, he is admonished thereby, that he should live in a manner worthy of so illustrious an origin, and so glorious a destiny.

URIM AND THUMMIM. Hebrew words, signifying *light and perfection* or *truth*. They were a kind of ornament placed in the breast-plate of the High-Priest, by means of which he gave oracular answers to the people.* Critics and commentators are not agreed as to what these attributes of the breast-plate were, or the mode in which the divine will was communicated to the High-Priest by means of them. Some exegetical writers have given positive explanations of them, but they are not satisfactory. The breast-plate was undoubtedly of Egyptian origin.

V.

VAILS. Attributes of the decorations and furniture of a Chapter of Royal Arch Masons, which is intended to be a copy of the ancient Jewish Tabernacle. The Tabernacle had

* "And thou shalt put in the breast-plate of judgment the Urim and the Thummim ; and they shall be upon Aaron's heart when he goeth in before the Lord: and Aaron shall bear the judgment of the children of Israel upon his heart before the Lord continually."—Exodus xxviii. 30.

vails of purple, scarlet blue and white—colors adopted by Freemasonry; each one having its symbolical signification.

VAILS, Masters of. In a Royal Arch Chapter there are three officers who bear this title. Their duty is to guard the blue, purple and scarlet vails, and each one is armed with a sword, and carries a banner of a color corresponding to that of the vail before which he is stationed. The Royal Arch Captain acts as Master of the white vail.

VENERABLE. The title of the Master in French Lodges, equivalent to *Worshipful* in English and American Lodges.

VENERABLE BROTHER. A title given to each officer of the Grand Orient of France.

VERGER. An official in cathedrals and churches in former times. In Freemasonry, Verger is the name of an officer who discharges important duties in a Council of Knights of the Holy Sepulcher. His office is analogous to that of the Senior Deacon of a Master's Lodge.

VISITATION. Masonic usage requires that the Grand Master and other officers of the Grand Lodge should periodically visit the Subordinate Lodges, to examine their books and work, and make a general inspection of their affairs. This formal visit is called a visitation. When such an event occurs, the Grand Officers, after being received with the usual honors, take charge of the Lodge. According to the English Constitutions, "the Grand Master has full authority to preside in any Lodge, and to order his Grand Officers to attend him; his Deputy is to be placed on his right hand, and the Master of the Lodge on his left hand. His Wardens are also to act as Wardens of that particular Lodge during his presence." "The Deputy Grand Master has full authority, unless the Grand Master or Pro-Grand Master be present, to preside, with the Master of the Lodge on his right hand. The Grand Wardens, if present, are to act as Wardens."

VISIT, Right of. While the right of a Mason to visit any Lodge, where he may happen to be, is generally conceded, various regulations, limiting this right, have been made at different times, and in divers jurisdictions, concerning the propriety and necessity of which intelligent Masons entertain quite different opinions. By the most ancient charges it is ordered, "That every Mason receive and cherish strange fellowes when they come over the countrie, and sett them on worke, if they will worke, as the manner is; that is to say,

if the Mason have any mould-stone in his place, he shall give
him a mould-stone, and sett him on worke; and if he have
none, the Mason shall refresh him with money unto the
next Lodge." This regulation recognizes the right of a
traveling brother as absolute. But, as early as 1663, it was
ordered by a General Assembly held on the 27th of December of that year, "That no person hereafter, who shall be
accepted a Freemason, shall be admitted into any Lodge or
assembly, until he has brought a certificate of the time
and place of his acceptation, from the Lodge that accepted
him, unto the Master of that limit or division where such a
Lodge is kept." In 1772, the Grand Lodge of England
renewed this statute, and some Grand Lodges in this country
have adopted it. Of course, no stranger can be admitted
to a Lodge without "due trial and examination," or unless he
is vouched for by a known brother present. The Grand
Lodge of England also has the following regulation, which
has been adopted in many other jurisdictions: "A brother
who is not a subscribing member to some Lodge shall not
be permitted to visit any one Lodge in the town or place
where he resides, more than once during his secession from
the Craft." The object of the above rule is to exclude all
drones from the hive of Masonry. Whoever partakes of the
advantages of Freemasonry should contribute something to
its support.

VISITOR. A Freemason who presents himself to a Lodge
of which he is not a member.

VIVAT. A word of acclamation, used in connection with
the battery in the French rite.

VOUCH, Voucher, Vouching. To vouch is to bear witness,
or give testimony, and a voucher accordingly is a witness.
When a person applies for admission to the Masonic society,
his application should bear the signatures of two brethren,
one of whom is called the voucher, because he thus testifies
that the petitioner possesses the required qualifications. So
a stranger can visit a Lodge without trial or examination,
if a brother present *knows* him to be a Mason and vouches
for him.

VOYAGE. A name given, in some countries, to a part of
the trials and labors to which the neophyte is subjected.
The symbolical pilgrimage was common to all the ancient
mysteries, and has, to-day, in Freemasonry, the same significance as in the old rites. This voyage around the altar,
from East to West, has a triple sense—1. Physical; 2. Social;

and 3. Moral. In the first, it refers to the apparent course of the sun and stars from East to West; in the second, it represents the progress of society through toil and suffering and darkness, from the savage to the civilized state, and still onward, from one degree of perfection to another; and, in the third, the advancement of man, as an individual, and his unceasing progress in virtue and intelligence.

W.

WAGES OF A MASON. The operative Mason, in ancient times, received, as compensation for his labor, corn, wine and oil—the products of the earth—or whatever would contribute to his physical comfort and support. His labor being material, his wages were outward and material. The Free and Accepted Mason, on the other hand, performs a moral work, and hence his reward is interior and spiritual. The enlightened brother finds his reward in the grand and gratifying results of his studies, and in the joyful fruits of his Masonic deeds. He sees the glory of the Divinity permeating all worlds, and all parts of the universe reveal to his soul celestial meanings. All nature overflows with beauty, love, melody and song, and unspeakably rich are the delights he derives from communion with her spirit. If he be a child of fortune, and raised above the necessity of labor, he finds the purest pleasure in the practice of charity and the exercise of benevolence; for charity, like mercy, brings its own recompense.

> " It droppeth, as the gentle rain from heaven,
> Upon the place beneath: it is twice bless'd;
> It blesseth him that gives, and him that takes."

If, like our ancient brethren, he is a laborer, his wages are still ample and enduring. Thus, while the ignorant man toils on, drearily, cheered by no bright and living thoughts, his mind destitute of all ideas, and his heart moved by no glad inspiration, the Masonic laborer welcomes his toil with joy, because Freemasonry has taught him that labor is a divine vocation, " *Laborare est orare.*" He goes forth in the morning, and the world on which he looks, swimming in sunbeams, and glittering with dewey diamonds, is less bright and fair than the world that lays in his heart, and which science has illuminated with her everlasting light. The mountains, barren, rocky and storm-blackened, or crowned with sylvan splendors; the valleys, flower-robed and ribboned with meandering streams; the rivers, hastening to the sea, and making music as they go; the trees, and rocks, and flowers ; all the activities of nature, and the great enterprises of man, speak with eloquence to his soul, and reveal to his enlightened spirit the glad secrets of Nature and of Nature's God. These noble, ample and enduring enjoyments are the wages of the true Mason.

WAGES OF THE WORKMEN ON THE TEMPLE. Masonic writers have wasted much time in useless and puerile conjectures in regard to the wages paid to the artists and artisans who were employed in the construction of Solomon's temple. English writers place the sum at about $15,000,000, and Dr. A. G. Mackey thinks that not far from $4,000,000,000! were expended for labor and material. A little reflection will show the unreasonableness of these estimates. A structure like that of the temple could not have cost $4,000,000! All the monarchies of that age, together, could not have raised, by the severest system of taxation, one-tenth part of $4,000,000,000. And how could the Jewish people, a poor and feeble race of shepherds and rude agriculturists, raise such an enormous sum to expend on one public work? The richest modern nation could not do it; and it may be doubted whether *all* modern nations, united, could. So far as Freemasonry is concerned this subject is of no consequence whatever.

WARDER. In the middle ages, a beadle or staff-man, who kept guard at the gate of a tower or palace, to take account of all persons who entered. An officer in a Commandery of Knights Templar; his position is in the West, and on the left of the second division, when formed in line, and is guard of the inner door of the asylum.

WOMAN. As Masonry, at its origin, and through many centuries, was occupied solely with physical labors, in which females do not participate, the instructions of ancient Masonry are only suited to the male sex; consequently women would not find themselves interested in our symbolical Lodges. But there are Masonic rites which unite the wives, sisters, and daughters of Freemasons, who may desire it, to our venerable Order. The rite practiced by the Grand Orient of France, and the American Adoptive rite, or Order of the Eastern Star, are extremely interesting forms of Masonic instruction, and adapted to the circumstance of the female sex. *Vide* art. "*Adoptive Masonry.*"

WORSHIP OF GOD. The highest duty of a Freemason is expressed by these words. The expression of veneration for the Supreme Being, of submission to his will, and of thankfulness for his goodness, though it may be offered in the secret stillness of the heart, will often be conveyed by external visible signs, through which the feelings of awe and love endeavor to manifest themselves in the most favorable and lively manner. These acts of homage to a superior power will be characterized by more or less of rudeness or elevation, as the conceptions of the object of worship are more or less gross or spiritual. Prayer or sacrifice, accompanied with various ceremonies, are the most general external acts by which the feelings of religious veneration are expressed; and while some nations and sects are eager to surround these acts with all the splendor of earthly pomp, others think to render them more worthy of the Being to whom they are addressed, by reducing them to the simplest form. Freemasonry, through all its degrees, and in every part of its ritual, earnestly inculcates this duty of worship.

Y.

YORK RITE. The York rite is the basis of all rites that claim a Masonic character. It derives its name from the city of York, in the north of England, where the Annual and General Assemblies of Masons were reëstablished, A. D. 926, and from which the first Grand Lodge was formed by Prince Edwin, the brother of King Athelstane ; hence the title "Ancient York Masons" is applied to those who are descendants of that branch of the Fraternity. At first there were but three degrees; but, as at present practiced in the United States, there are seven: 1. Apprentice; 2. Fellow-Craft; 3. Master; 4. Mark Master; 5. Past Master; 6. Most Excellent Master; 7. Holy Royal Arch. There are three other degrees—appendages to this rite—viz: the Order of High-Priesthood—an honorary degree conferred on the first officer of a Chapter—and the degrees of Royal and Select Master.

Z.

ZENITH. An Arabic word, used in astronomy to denote the vertical point of the heavens, or that point directly over the head of the observer. The missives and decrees of the Supreme Council of the 33d degree are dated from the *Zenith*, as well as from the *Orient* or *East* as other Masonic organizations.

ZERUBBABEL, *(sown in Babylon,)* a Prince of Judah, son of Shealtiel, of the royal house of David, was the leader of the first colony of Jews that returned from captivity to

their native land under the permission of Cyrus, carrying
with them the precious vessels belonging to the temple for
the service of God. With the aid of Joshua and his body
of priests, Zerubbabel proceeded, on his arrival in Jerusalem,
to rebuild the fallen city, beginning with the altar of burnt-
offerings, in order that the daily services might be restored.
The Samaritans, however, having been offended at being
expressly excluded from a share in the land, threw obstacles
in the way to hinder the work, and even procured from the
Persian court an order that it should be stopped. Accordingly, everything remained suspended until the second year
of Darius Hystaspis (B. c. 521), when the restoration was
resumed and carried to completion, through the influence
of Zerubbabel with the Persian monarch. This subject is
beautifully exemplified in the degrees of the East and Sword
and the Knight of the Red Cross.

ZINNENDORF, RITE OF. This rite was established in the
year 1766, by John William Ellenberger, otherwise known
as Count Zinnendorf. He was Knight Commander of the
Strict Observance, Director of the Lodges in Prussia, member of the Lodge of the Three Globes, and Prior in the
Order of the Templars, with the characteristic of *Eques à
lapide nigro;* was born at Halle, Aug. 10, 1731, and died
June 6, 1782. He was a man of fine talents, but unscrupulous
in his dealings with the Fraternity. In 1768 he founded the
Lodge Minerva, at Potsdam; and the next year the Lodge
the Three Golden Keys, at Berlin, over which he presided
for many years. In 1770 he had twelve Lodges in operation
in various parts of Germany, and on the 24th of June of the
same year they erected a Grand Lodge under the title of
Grand Lodge of all the Freemasons of Germany, "according
to the precepts of Freemasonry in general, and after the
pattern of the Grand Lodge of England." In creating this
rite Zinnendorf pretended to have powers, rituals and
instructions from the Duke of Südermania, and the Grand
Lodge of Sweden; but the Duke and Grand Lodge repudi-
ated him. His rite was based on the reveries of Swedenborg,
and in many respects coincided with the Swedish rite. It
consisted of seven degrees, in three divisions, viz: Blue
Masonry—1. Apprentice; 2. Fellow-Craft; 3. Master. Red
Masonry—4. Scotch Apprentice and Fellow-Craft; 5. Scottish Master. Capitular Masonry—6. Clerk, or Favorite of
St. John; 7. Brother Elected. Clavel says this is the rite
of the National Grand Lodge of Germany, at Berlin.

A DICTIONARY

OF

SYMBOLICAL MASONRY.

BY GEORGE OLIVER, D.D.,

AUTHOR OF "HISTORICAL LANDMARKS," "SIGNS AND SYMBOLS," "HISTORY OF
INITIATION," "REVELATIONS OF A SQUARE," ETC., ETC.

Geo. Oliver DD

PREFACE TO THE DICTIONARY.

IT will be unnecessary to detain the reader for a single moment, by expatiating on the value of a work like the present. Its utility cannot fail to be universally admitted, and the only wonder is, that amidst the endless variety of dictionaries, lexicons, encyclopedias, and glossaries, with which the present age abounds, Symbolical Masonry, as practiced in this country, should have remained so long without an appropriate book of reference, constructed in the comprehensive and accessible form of a Dictionary.

An idea of the absolute benefit arising from such a publication, appears to have been entertained on the Continent nearly a century ago, when M. FLEURY published his "*Dictionnaire de l'Ordre de la Felicité,*" for the use of the Androgyne Lodges, as they were then denominated, or Lodges which admitted, indiscriminately, candidates and members of either sex.

A few years later, PERNETTI published a "*Dictionnaire Mytho-Hermetique;*" and there the matter rested for the remainder of the century. It is highly probable that the speculation was not remunerative, or it would doubtless have been followed up by similar publications on other branches of the science.

In 1805 the attempt was renewed by CHOMEL, who gave to the world an imperfect "*Vocabulaire des Francs-Maçons,*" which was translated into Italian, by VIGNOZZI. This was succeeded by a more compendious work, edited under the superintendence of M. QUANTIN, which he called a "*Dictionnaire Maçonnique, ou Recueil des Equisses des toutes les parties de l'Edifice connû sous le nom de Maçonnerie, etc.;*" and in Germany, about the same period, Bro. G. LENNING published his "*Encyclopadie der Freimaurerei.*" We find also the germ of a dictionary in the "*Nomenclature par Ordre Alphabétique, des Principaux Rites, Coteries, Sociétiés, Secrets et Grades Maçonniques, répandu en France ou dans l'Etranger,*" by THORY in the first volume of the "*Acta Latomorum.*"

The two most perfect productions of this class are the "*Freimaurer Lexicon,*" of GADICKE, and the "Lexicon of Freemasonry," by Dr. ALBERT G. MACKEY, Grand Secretary of the Grand Lodge of South Carolina, U. S. But although these publications are exceedingly well executed, yet their peculiar characteristics serve to render them only partially interesting to the English Fraternity. They dwell too largely on consistorial, capitular, ineffable, and spurious Freemasonry, to be adapted to the taste of an Ancient Craft Mason; and it is, therefore, believed that a vocabulary of terms, peculiar to Symbolical Masonry, and arranged in alphabetical order, for the convenience of expeditious reference, will prove an acceptable boon to the British Freemason.

It will be apparent at a single glance, that the plan I have adopted, is to give the best definitions from the best writers, with the name of the author attached to each article. This method has been preferred, as it was thought questionable whether the Fraternity would have considered the explanations of an individual brother to possess that undoubted authority, with which every book of reference ought to be invested.

On an attentive perusal of the work the reader will find that the definitions have been studiously contracted into as brief a space as possible consistently with perspicuity, in order to increase the number of words, and make the book more generally useful.

My closing advice shall be—he who is ambitious of becoming a good Mason must work, as our ancient brethren worked, with FREEDOM, FERVENCY, and ZEAL.

GEO. OLIVER.

A DICTIONARY

OF

SYMBOLICAL MASONRY.

———◆———

AARON'S ROD. This symbol was introduced into Royal Arch Masonry because it constituted one of the three holy things which were preserved in the Most Holy place of the Tabernacle. It refers to the rebellion of Korah and his accomplices. Moses directed that twelve rods should be brought in, one for each tribe. The princes brought them in, some of them perhaps fondly expecting that the choice would fall upon them, and all of them thinking it honor enough to be competitors with Aaron, and to stand candidates even for the priesthood; and Moses laid them up before the Lord. On the next day the rods, or staves, were brought out of the Most Holy place, where they were laid up, and publicly produced before the people; and while all the rest of the rods remained as they were, Aaron's rod only, of a dry stick, became a living branch—budded, and blossomed, and yielded fruit. In some places there were buds, in others blossoms, in others fruit, at the same time; this was miraculous, and took away all suspicion of a fraud, as if in the night Moses had taken away Aaron's rod, and put a living branch of an almond tree in the room of it; for no ordinary branch would have had buds, blossoms, and fruits upon it all at once.

ABRAXAS. This word occurs in a Masonic manuscript of the fifteenth century. Abraxas is a Basilidean Intelligence, derived from the name of Abraham, and given to Mithras or the Sun, as the representative of the Supreme

Deity, or, in other words, the *Sun of Righteousness.* Basilides was a Pythagorean of Alexandria. The word, being composed of seven letters, referred equally to the seven heavens and the same number of subordinate intelligences, as their governors; for the Basilideans considered the seven planets to constitute the entire universe, and consequently to be God.

ACACIA. There is some difficulty attending the explanation of the sprig of cassia, and in assigning the true reason why it was introduced into the system of Freemasonry. Some say it originated in the Jewish custom of planting a branch of acacia vera (gum arabic plant) on the grave of a departed relative; others in the custom of mourners bearing a branch of it in their hands at funerals. The cassia is not indigenous to the soil of Palestine, and is only mentioned in Scripture as a fragrant herb or spice, the bark being used in ungents, and sometimes employed for embalming; and, therefore, if the legend refer to the branch of a real tree, it could be neither the cassia nor acacia; and this has given rise to an opinion that the branch or sprig is analogous to that alluded to by Virgil, in his description of the mysteries; and consequently was the olive. Others again doubt whether our acacia has any reference to a tree or shrub at all, but means the texture and color of the Masonic apron which those brethren wore which were deputed by Solomon to search for ——, and simply refers to their innocence. If this conjecture be correct, they add, it corroborates the accuracy of the legend which says—"they took a sprig of cassia in their hands (with them)." I am rather inclined to think that the choice of cassia, which is a kind of laurel, was founded on some mysterious reference which it was supposed to possess, either mythological or symbolical. There are, however, great difficulties to be surmounted before the truth can be ascertained.

ACACIAN. Masons, describing the deplorable estate of religion under the Jewish law, speak in figures. "Her tomb was in the rubbish and filth cast forth of the temple, and acacia wove its branches over her monument;" *ακακια* being the Greek word for innocence; implying that the sins and corruptions of the old law and devotees of the Jewish altar had hidden religion from those who sought her, and she was only to be found where innocence survived, and under the banner of the divine Lamb, and as to ourselves professing that we were to be distinguished by our acacy, or as true acacians in our religious faith and tenets.— *Hutchinson.*

ACCEPTED. According to masonic tradition the Masons are said to have acquired the name of Accepted at the building of the second Temple ; for the Fraternity were declared Free by King Solomon ; and the brethren, when the first Temple was completed, were furnished with an honorary jewel or gold medal, with the word FREE inscribed upon it. The posterity of some of the Masons who assisted at the erection of Solomon's Temple having settled on the confines of Judea, were carried into captivity with the Jews, and preserving a knowledge of the sciences of geometry and architecture, even in their fallen fortunes, were liberated by Cyrus, and subsequently declared Free and Accepted, exonerated from all imposts, duties, and taxes, and invested with the privilege of bearing arms by Darius and Artaxerxes, who commanded the governors of the surrounding provinces that they should require no tax or other imposition from any of the priests, Levites, porters, or any that were concerned about the Temple ; and that no man should have authority to impose anything upon them.

ACCOUNTS. All monies received or paid on account of the lodge, ought to be entered in proper books. The fees or dues received on account of, and payable to, the Grand Lodge, or Provincial Grand Lodge, should be kept separate and distinct from the monies belonging to the private fund of the lodge, and be deposited in the hands of the Master instead of the Treasurer of the Lodge, to be transmitted to the Grand Lodge at such times as the laws of the Craft require. The accounts of the lodge are to be audited, at least once in every year, by a committee to be appointed by the lodge.

ACHILLES. Perhaps some worthy people may star when we point out Achilles as a Freemason. What . we hear them exclaim, is it possible that that fierce and ferocious man-slayer, nay, man-eater at heart, for he ex hibited a strong propensity to cannibalism in longing to have devoured the dead body of Hector,—is it possible that he could have been one of our philanthropic society? Yes, we reply, such is the actual fact; and Bonaparte was one too, in the highest degree. But if you will not believe Homer or us, believe your own eyes, if indeed you are a Mason. *Ecce signum!* Behold Achilles giving Priam THE HAND when the latter is supplicating for the body of his slain son.

> " Thus having spoken, the old man's right hand at the wrist
> He grasped, that he might not in any respect be alarmed in mind."

Such is the masonic and literal translation of the text by that illustrious Grecian and brother, Christopher North; and who will say now that Achilles was not a Mason?— *Freemasons' Quarterly Review.*

ACKNOWLEDGED. In the first degree the candidate is said to be *entered;* in the second he is *passed;* in the third he is *raised;* in the fourth he is *advanced;* in the fifth he is *inducted;* in the sixth or Most Excellent Master's degree he is said to be " received and *acknowledged.*" Because the possession of the latter degree is a recognization of higher attainments and greater knowledge of the science of Masonry.

ACROSTIC.
M. Magnitude, moderation, and magnanimity.
A. Affability, affection, and attention.
S. Silence, secrecy, and sincerity.
O. Obedience, order, œconomy.
N. Noble, natural, and neighbourly.
R. Rational, reciprocal, and receptive.
Y. Yielding, yearning, and Yare.

The elucidation of this acrostic having been published in many masonic works, and consequently being well known, it is unnecessary to introduce it here.

ACTING GRAND MASTER. It was the custom and practice of the old Masons, that kings and princes, being Masons, are considered Grand Masters by prerogative during life; and in that case they had the privilege of appointing a deputy to preside over the Fraternity, with

the tit.e and honours of Grand Master. And in the year
1782 a motion was made in Grand Lodge that whenever
a prince of the blood honoured the society by accepting
the office of Grand Master, he should be at liberty to
nominate any peer of the realm to the office of Acting
Grand Master.

ACTIVE. A lodge is called active when it assembles
egularly; and a brother when he is a working member
of such a lodge. Many brethren visit a lodge who never
or very seldom take part in lodge work, either because
they live too far distant from the lodge, or that the
labour is not sufficiently interesting. Every lodge and
every officer ought to strive diligently to avoid the last
imputation, but if they find their endeavours in vain, and
that there is any brother who will not pay due attention
to the work, they ought to endeavour to reclaim him,
first by fraternal remonstrances; if those do not avail, by
punishment. By the death or removal of the members,
a lodge may become inactive for a time, and it is better
that it should be so than that the continuing of the work
should be entrusted to inexperienced officers.—*Gadicke.*

ADAM. That the first parents of mankind were
instructed by the Almighty as to his existence and attributes, and after their fall, were further informed of the
Redemption which was to be perfected by Christ, and as
a sign of their belief, were commanded to offer sacrifices
to God, I fully assent to the creed of Masonry in believing. It is also highly probable that symbolical actions
should have been instituted by them in memory of their
penitence, reverence, sympathy, fatigue, and faith, and that
these might be transmitted to posterity.—*Archdeacon
Mant.*

ADDRESS. Those who accept offices and exercise
authority in the lodge, ought to be men of prudence and
address, enjoying the advantages of a well-cultivated
mind and retentive memory. All men are not blessed
with the same powers and talents; all men, therefore,
are not equally qualified to govern. He who wishes to
teach must submit to learn; and no one can be qualified

to support the higher offices of the lodge who has not previously discharged the duties of those which are subordinate. Experience is the best preceptor. Every man may rise by gradation, but merit and industry are th first steps to preferment.—*Preston.*

ADDRESSING. No brother shall speak twice to the same question, unless in explanation, or the mover in reply. Every one who speaks shall rise, and remain standing, addressing himself to the Master, nor shall any brother presume to interrupt him, unless he shall be wandering from the point, or the Master shall think fit to call him to order; but, after he has been set right, he may proceed, if he observe due order and decorum.— *Constitutions.*

ADMISSION. Not more than five new brothers shall be made in any one lodge on the same day, nor any man under the age of twenty-one years, unless by dispensation from the Grand Master or Provincial Grand Master. Every candidate for admission must be a freeman, and his own master, and, at the time of initiation, be known to be in reputable circumstances. He should be a lover of the liberal arts and sciences, and have made some progress in one or another of them.—*Constitutions.*

ADMONITION. If a brother grossly misconduct himself, let him be admonished privately by the W. M.; try every gentle means to convince him of his errors; probe the wound with a delicate hand; and use every mild expedient to work his reform. Perhaps he may save his brother, and give to society a renewed and valuable member.

ADONAI. The Jews are said to have substituted the word Adonai for the uncommunicable name; but this admits of some qualification. St. Jerome, and after him Bellarmine, doubted the fact, because Jehovah and Adonai were two several names of God, and equally legitimate; and in some instances were appointed to be used in conjunction, as Jehovah Adonai; and the Septuagint uses the word Kurios.

ADONIRAM. This prince was appointed by King Solomon to superintend the contributions towards building the temple, as well as the levy of 30,000 Israelites to work by monthly courses in the forest of Lebanon. For this purpose, and to insure the utmost regularity, an old masonic tradition informs us that he divided them into lodges, placing three hundred in each, under a Master and Wardens, himself being G. M. over all. He was also constituted by the king one of the seven Grand Superintendents, and Chief of the Provosts and Judges.

ADVANCED. In a Lodge of Mark Masters, this term is appropriately applied to the candidate when he is invested with the degree of Mark Master, that being the first step in his progress to higher attainments in the knowledge of the science of Masonry, and of his advancement toward the Royal Arch degree.

ADVENT. We are well assured of the existence of Masonry at the time of the advent of our Lord upon earth, when it received the assistance of those two great lights, who are to this day commemorated in our lodges in gratitude for the kindness received from them. We have reason to believe that the secrecy of our Order was often useful to conceal, and its universal benevolence to preserve, Christian professors, in the early ages of the church, from the malice of their bitter enemies; and it is certain that there are to be found in the writings of the fathers many allusions of an undoubtedly masonic character.—*Archdeacon Mant.*

ADYTUM. In the British and other Mysteries the three pillars of Wisdom, Strength, and Beauty represented the great emblematical Triad of Deity, as with us they refer to the three principal officers of the lodge. We shall find, however, that the symbolical meaning was the same in both. It is a fact that in Britain the *Adytum* or lodge was *actually* supported by three stones or pillars, which were supposed to convey a regenerating purity to the aspirant, after having endured the ceremony of initiation in all its accustomed formalities. The delivery from between them was termed a *new birth.*

The corresponding pillars of the Hindu Mythology were also known by the names of Wisdom, Strength, and Beauty, and placed in the east, west, and south, crowned with three human heads. They jointly referred to the Creator, who was said to have planned the Great Work by his infinite *Wisdom;* executed by his *Strength;* and to have adorned it with all its *Beauty* and usefulness for the benefit of man.

AFFABILITY. The ancient lodges were so many schools or academies for teaching and improving the arts of designing, especially architecture; and the present lodges are often employed that way in lodge hours, or else in agreeable conversation, though without politics or party feeling; and none of them are ill employed; have no transaction unworthy of an honest man or a gentleman; no personal piques, no quarrels, no cursing and swearing, no cruel mockings, no obscene talk, or ill manners, for the noble and eminent brethren are affable to the meanest; and these are duly respectful to their betters in harmony and proportion; and though on the level, yet always within compass, and according to the square and plumb.—*Euclid.*

AGE. It is men of mature age and sound judgment alone who can preserve the Order in its native purity; and those lodges whose officers are careful to act in strict accordance to the laws and to the spirit of Freemasonry will always have a supply of men of mature age as candidates. In the lectures the question of age occurs, but that refers merely to the degree wrought upon. In the ancient mysteries the mystical age of 1, 3, 5, and 7, refer to so many years of probation.—*Gadicke.* The symbolic age of an Entered Apprentice is 3 years, of a Fellow-craft 5, and a Master Mason 7; a Petit Architect 21, and a Grand Architect 27; that of a Knight of the East is 70; a Prince of Jerusalem $5 \times 15 = 75$; a Secret Master, a Maitre Ecossais, and a Prince of Mercy, 81; and a Scotch Knight 500 years. It was by this figurative way of reasoning that the celebrated impostor the Count St. Germain, boasted that he was 500 years old.

AGLA. One of the twelve Cabalistic names of God

The other eleven were: Ehje, Jehovah, Elohim, El, Gibbor, Eloah, Sabaoth, Isebaoth, Schaddai, Adonai, and Makom. It is introduced here because some of our brethren of the last century used the word as an inscription in Hebrew characters for "the lodge" represented on the floor-cloth.

AHIMAN REZON. Dr. Mackey says these words ar derived from the Hebrew *ahim*, brothers, *manah*, to prepare, and *ratzon*, the will or law; and signifies, therefore, literally, "the law of prepared brothers." Others contend that the derivation is from *achi man ratzon*, "the opinions of a true and faithful brother." It was the title adopted for their Book of Constitutions by the section which split off from our Grand Lodge about the year 1740, and denominated themselves, by way of distinction, Ancient Masons.

AIR. Every human being at his birth becomes subject to the action of three elements. He comes out of *water*, passes through the *air*, and when he arrives at maturity, he is under the influence of *fire*. It is only at his death that he can participate of the fourth element *(the earth)*. When he is initiated into the mysteries of Masonry, he is proved by the three elements of *water*, *air*, and *fire* —*Rosenberg*.

AHOLIAB. Of the tribe of Dan. It is observed by R. Bechai, that God chose one out of the lowest tribe (for so they accounted that of Dan), as well as one out of the chief, which was Judah; that Bezaleel might not be lifted up with vain conceit; for great and small are equal before God. And he truly observes, that one of the same tribe of Dan, by the mother's side, was the most skilful person that could be found for the building of the Temple by Solomon. There were several, no doubt, who had a natural genius to such arts as were necessary in this work, but they could not, by their own industry, have attained such skill as God bestowed on Aholiab and Bezaleel; at least not so soon, as to go immediately about the building of the Tabernacle, and all things belonging to it.—*Bishop Patrick*.

AKIROP. The name of an assassin at the building of King Solomon's Temple.

ALERT. As everything in Freemasonry ought to be performed with the precision of perfect discipline, it behoves all the officers of a lodge to be ever on the alert in the discharge of their respective duties, that the brethren may have continually before them an example of order and regularity worthy of imitation ; for it is only by the correct demeanour of the rulers and governors of the Craft, that the machinery of a lodge can be beneficially worked, and its labours conducted with such effect as to produce the blessings of peace, harmony, and brotherly love.

ALEXANDRIA. The inundations of the Nile caused the inhabitants great rejoicings. But it usually happened that when the waters had subsided, and they returned to their agricultural pursuits, the sediment which had been deposited by the retreating river had obliterated their temporary land-marks, which originated violent disputes respecting their several localities. Being at length tired of these annual contentions, and hearing that a lodge of Masons was in existence at Alexandria, over which Euclid presided, the Egyptians resolved to refer all litigated matters to this Grand Lodge. Euclid undertook the task, and with the assistance of his Grand Warden, Straton the philosopher, collected the scattered elements of geometry, and formed them into a regular system, by which means the people were instructed how to measure and apportion their lands, and renew their boundary marks, without any infringement of each others rights or property.

ALLEGORY. The two sons of Abraham, Ishmael, born of Agar his handmaid, and Isaac, born of Sarah the free-woman, contain an allegory in which the name is put for the thing signified or represented by it ; for these two women and their children are, by representation, the two covenants ; the one covenant being that from Mount Sinai, gendering to bondage, which is, by representation, Agar the bond-woman, and so bearing a child which also was in bondage, for that which is signified by Agar, from whom Ishmael descended, is Mount Sinai in Arabia, whence the law was given; and this Agar answers to Jerusalem that now is, and is in bondage with her children to the law, as the bond-woman and her child were to Abraham; but the Jerusalem which is above, is by representation Sarah the free-woman, whose son was born, not according to the flesh, but " according to the promise." " Lo then, brethren, we are not the children of the bond-woman, but the free."—*Whitby.*

ALL-SEEING EYE. Whom the *Sun, Moon,* and *Stars* obey, and under whose watchful care even comets perform their stupendous revolutions, beholds the inmost recesses of the human heart, and will reward us according to our works.—*Lectures.*

ALLUREMENTS. Masonry is one of the most sublime and perfect institutions that ever was formed for the advancement of happiness and general good of mankind; creating, in all its varieties, universal benevolence and brotherly love. It holds out allurements so captivating as to inspire the brotherhood with emulation to deeds of glory, such as must command, throughout the world, veneration and applause, and such as must entitle those who perform them to dignity and respect. It teaches us those useful, wise, and instructive doctrines, upon which alone true happiness is founded; and at the same time affords those easy paths by which we attain the rewards of virtue; it teaches us the duties which we owe to our neighbour, never to injure him in any one situation, but to conduct ourselves with justice and impartiality; it bids us not to divulge the mystery to the public, and it orders us to be true to our trust, and above all meanness and dissimulation, and in all our vocations to perform religiously that which we ought to do.—*Duke of Sussex.*

ALPHA and OMEGA. From eternity to eternity This mode of speech is borrowed from the Jews, who express *the whole compass of things* by א *aleph* and ת *tau,* the *first* and *last* letters of the *Hebrew* alphabets; but as

St. John was writing in *Greek*, he accommodates the whole to the *Greek* alphabet, of which *A alpha* and *Ω omega* are the first and last letters. With the rabbins תאו ועד חו *mealeph vead tau*, "*from aleph to tau*," expressed the whole of a matter *from the beginning to the end; as Adam transgressed the whole law from aleph to tau*, i. e. from the beginning to the end.—*Adam Clarke.*

ALTAR. An altar must be a most holy place to every Christian, and more especially to every true worshipper of God. It was so to the first nations who conceived the idea of a Most High being. High above all the stars they conjectured was his most elevated seat. They fell upon their knees when they worshipped Him, as more emblematical of the immense distance they were removed from Him; and they built altars, upon which they offered fruits and other things, that the smoke might arise towards Him, as a proof of their gratitude. We, as enlightened Christians and Freemasons, make no offerings of fruits upon our altars, neither are they any more to be found upon the tops of mountains, or in the depths of the caverns, but under a cloudy canopy, as emblematical of the heavens, and our offerings are the hallowed obligations of a grateful and pious heart.— *Gadicke.*

AMERICA. The Americans appear to be more generally versed in the principles of the Order than the brethren of this country; which is owing, I conceive, to the genial operation of its local Grand Lodges. Every brother may become a ruler of the Craft, and a Master in Israel, by his own meritorious exertions. The offices of Grand Lodge are open to industrious and worthy brethren who have given proof of their excellence in the art; and this facility of promotion excites a spirit of friendly emulation which operates favourably for society at large. The several Grand Lodges also are engaged in an amicable contest which shall carry out the best interests of Masonry most effectually; and hence we find nothing in Masonry as it is practised there to condemn, but everything to commend. They do not waste their time in talking—debates upon all speculative questions being left to the several committees or boards. The Grand Lodges have to determine merely upon their reports, which are usually found to be drawn up with so much judgment and discrimination as not to be susceptible of any hostile opinion; and hence their members are seldom in collision with each other.

AMBITION. The possession and exercise of authority is a matter of honourable and proper ambition in every brother who really prizes the institution into which he has been initiated, and who wishes to render his Masonry productive of its legitimate fruits—the moral improvement of his mental faculties. It is to be regretted, however, that this ambition, so praiseworthy when exercised within its due bounds, is too frequently indulged, even to an unlimited extent, by brethren who, though in other respects worthy, do not possess the requisite talent or industry to confer distinction. Or, in other words, the ambition is more frequently for the office, than for the qualification to execute it with credit to themselves or benefit to the community over which they have been called on to preside.

AMMI. Say ye unto your brethren, Ammi; and to your sisters, Ruhamah. Although the Israelites, in the days of Hosea, were in general corrupt, and addicted to idolatry, yet there were among them in the worst times some who had not bowed down the knee to Baal. These were always Ammi and Ruhamah; God's own people and a darling daughter. It is probable that God here commissions these faithful few to admonish the inhabitants of the land in general of the dreadful judgments that would be brought upon them by the gross idolatry of the Jewish church and nation. Speak to your brethren, O Ammi (O my people), and to your sisters, O Ruhamah (O darling daughter).—*Bishop Horsley.*

AMPLE FORM. When the Grand Master performs any Masonic ceremony in person it is said to be in "ample form;" if by the Deputy Grand Master it is in "due form;" and if by any other person it is "in form." "Due and ancient form" is often applied in place of the above terms.

ANCIENT CHARGES. To define the authority of Masons in the clearest and most simple manner, our ancient brethren made them the subjects of a series of exhortations ; which is one of the most valuable legacies that in their wisdom they have bequeathed to us. I allude to the *Ancient Charges*, which have been so judiciously incorporated into our Book of Constitutions and which every Mason would do well to study with attention, that they may be reduced to practice whenever their assistance is needed. These charges are sufficiently comprehensive, and embrace an epitome of every duty which the Mason is enjoined to perform. And as a commentary on them, the Grand Lodge has thought proper, in its Constitutions, to enumerate these various duties more minutely, and to make the breaches of them penal, whilst honours and rewards are held out to those worthy brothers who have been distinguished by regularity and decorous conduct.

ANCIENT MASONS. In the year 1739 a few brethren, having violated the laws of Masonry, were expelled from the Grand Lodge, and adopted the bold measure, under the fictitious name of the Ancient York Constitution, of constituting lodges, which were pronounced independent of the Grand Lodge. And the latter, for the purpose of producing a marked distinction between the two systems, resolved at length to adopt the expedient, apparently rendered necessary by the emergency, but extremely ill-judged, of introducing a slight alteration into the system, which might have the effect of detecting the schismatics, and thus excluding them from the orthodox lodges. The resolution was unfortunate, and produced the very evil it was intended to avert. It proved a source of exultation and triumph to the seceding brethren. They loudly exclaimed against what they called an alteration of the landmarks, as an unprecedented and unconstitutional proceeding; accused the Grand Lodge of having deviated from ancient usage, and conferred upon all its members and adherents the invidious epithet of *Modern* Masons, while they appropriated to themselves the exclusive and honourable title of "*Ancient* Masons, acting under the old York Constitutions, cement-

ed and consecrated by immemorial observance." Taking
advantage of this popular cry, they proceeded to the formation of an independent Grand Lodge, drew up a code
of laws for its government, issued warrants for the constitution of new lodges " under the true ancient system
of Freemasonry ;" and from the fees arising out of these
proceedings, they succeeded in establishing a fund of
benevolence, besides defraying the current expenses of
the institution.

ANCHOR. The hope of glory, or of the fulfilment
of all God's promises to our souls, is the golden or precious anchor, by which we must be kept steadfast in the
faith, and encouraged to abide in our proper station,
amidst the storms of temptation, affliction, and persecution.—*Scott.*

ANCHOR AND ARK. The ark and anchor are
emblems of a well-grounded hope and a well-spent life.
They are emblematical of that divine ark which triumphantly bears us over this tempestuous sea of troubles;
and that anchor which shall safely moor us in a peaceful
harbour, where the wicked cease from troubling and the
weary are at rest.

ANDERSON. Dr. Anderson lived in the beginning of
the 18th century, and it is from him that we have the
so deservedly celebrated Book of Constitutions of the
Ancient and Honourable Fraternity of Free and Accepted
Masons. The first part contains the history of the Order,
and the second contains the charges, rules, laws, duties,
&c., together with an historical account of the origin of
the Order. Anderson, in the dedication to the then
Prince of Wales, calls himself Secretary to the Grand
Lodge in London, and states that the work was composed
by the command of the Grand Lodge, from its archives,
traditions, and lodge-books. The first edition appeared
in 1723, a second in 1738; since then various editions
have been published, viz., one by Entick, in 1758, one in
1776, one in 1784, by Noorthouck, and in 1806 the latest.
To the second edition a superior privilege was attached
by the Grand Lodge in London, no other constitution

book being allowed in the lodges but that of Anderson,
and no alteration being allowed to be made in it. Although in this work the history of Freemasonry is carried
back to the creation, yet the information it has been the
means of preserving with regard to the duties of a Freemason, the constitutions of the Order, and the history of
the English lodges, make it a valuable work, and cause
it to be highly prized by every lodge and every brother.
In the first edition no mention is made of the formation
of the Grand Lodge in London in 1717, but is added to
the second edition.   There is a German translation published at Frankfort-on-the-Maine, and various French
editions.—*Gadicke.*

ANGEL OF JEHOVAH.   The Angel of Jehovah
who appeared at the B. B. has been conjectured to be
Michael, the leader of the Host of Heaven, who appeared
also to Joshua and Daniel; but he was really and
truly the captain of our salvation, or Jehovah himself
the Creator of the world, or Jesus Christ, called by
Masons the Grand Architect of the Universe, who only
hath immortality, dwelling in the Light which no man
can approach unto.   This divine Being called to Moses
by his name, and commanded him to approach with
naked feet, because the ground on which he stood was
holy, or consecrated by the divine Presence.   And therefore Moses took off his shoes in obedience to the divine
command, and prostrated himself before the Deity.

ANGERONA.   The goddess of silence.   Both the
Romans and Egyptians worshipped the gods and goddesses of Silence.   The Latins particularly worshipped
Angerona and Tacita, whose image stood upon the altar
of the goddess Volupia, with its mouth tied up and sealed
because they who endure their cares with silence and
patience, do, by that means, procure to themselves the
greatest pleasure.   There is a beautiful female statue,
executed in the finest style of Grecian art, in the Town-
ley Gallery, room iii., No. 22, which some think to be a
figure of this goddess.

ANGLES.   Geometrical figures, as lines, angles,

squares, and perpendiculars, were ranked amongst the
symbols of Druidism, as well as Freemasonry. As the
Druids had no enclosed temples, thinking them inconsistent with the majesty of the gods, so neither had they
any carved images to represent them, and for the same
reason ; but instead thereof rude stones were erected in
their places of worship at some mystic significant distance, and in some emblematical number, situation, and
plan ; sometimes in *right lines*, sometimes in *squares*, sometimes in *triangles*, sometimes in both ; now single, and
fifty paces distant or more from the circles ; or eminently
taller than the rest in the circular line, and making a
part of it like portals, not only to shape the entrance,
but to hallow those that entered ; it appearing, by many
monuments, that the Druids attributed great virtue to
these angular passages between rocks.

ANGULAR TRIAD. At the establishment of the
Royal Arch degree, the angular triad bore a reference to
the three great lights, which at that period were interpreted to symbolize the light of the Gospel and the
sublime Mystery of the Trinity.

ANNIVERSARIES, MASONIC. For Ancient Craft or
Symbolic Masonry the festivals of St. John the Baptist,
24th of June, and St. John the Evangelist, 27th of December.

ANNUITIES. Annuities are granted by many lodges
to aged and distressed Freemasons, and also to the poor
widows of deceased brethren : and this description of
charity is certainly the most useful which any lodge can
exercise. The silent gratitude of the recipient is a sufficient reward to the Order, but it also reaps this benefit,
that the widow will encourage her sons, if she has any
and God may bless and prosper them when grown up, to
assist in giving similar assistance to other suffering breth
ren and widows.

ANOMALY. Freemasonry is mysterious because it
is an admitted anomaly in the history of the earth.
Without territorial possessions—without any other

coercing power than that of morality and virtue, it has survived the wreck of mighty empires, and resisted the destroying hand of Time. Contrast the history of Free-masonry with the history of the nations of the world, and what is the result? The Jews, God's favored people, nto whose custody Masonry was first entrusted by its divine Author, where are they now?—A race of wander ers, scattered over the face of the globe. And th stupendous and magnificent structure—the Temple—at once their glory and the wonder of the world, where is it now?—Not one stone left upon another. Babylon, in her day the queen of nations, has fallen, never to rise again. Egypt, with her kings and philosophers; classic Greece, and Imperial Rome, we now find but occupying their page in the history of the world. But Masonry at this moment shines throughout the world with as bright and undiminished a lustre as when first revealed by God to man.—*Alexander Grant.*

ANTEDILUVIANS. Having been forewarned by Adam of an universal deluge and conflagration, the ante-diluvians erected two pillars, one of brick and the other of stone, which they were of opinion would, one or the other or them, be proof against every attack either of fire or water. They engraved upon these pillars their discoveries and inventions, lest, in a series of ages, the knowledge of science itself should become extinct. Their precaution was not in vain; for, to this day, the stone pillar is to be seen in Syria.—*Josephus.*

ANTI-MASONRY. Anti-masonry was converted into a watch-word about the year 1830, for political pur-poses, and to render the cry more imposing, and more successful, it was alleged that the Fraternity had mur-dered a man of the name of Morgan in 1826 for disclosing the secret. The excitement was kept up with unceasing pertinacity until it numbered nearly 100,000 free and intelligent electors of the State of New York; almost divided the vote of Pennsylvania; planted itself deeply in the soil of Massachusetts; spread itself in others of the New England states in Ohio and elsewhere; while in Vermont, like the rod of Aaron, it so far swallowed up both of the former parties, as to have obtained the control of the state government. Nor was it of factitious partizans or disappointed men that this party was composed. It comprised among its members as great a portion of wealth and character—of talents and respectability—as any party that was ever formed of equal numbers in this or any other country. And where is this great anti-masonic party now? The excitement continued a few years, the hollowness of its principles became apparent, and it suddenly disappeared like a passing cloud, leaving behind it nothing but public shame and contempt.

APOSTACY. In the masonic system we are not only taught something of the history of the material world, but numerous facts pertaining to the moral, which are infinitely more important. Such is the apostacy of our first parents. This melancholy event is explicitly brought to view in so many words, and so strikingly represented, as seldom to fail of making deep and lasting impressions on the heart. The wretched, and destitute, and deplorable situation of Adam, which was the fruit of his disobedience, are affectingly exhibited by the most lively masonic representations.— *Town.*

APOSTATE MASONS. It would be equally useless and vain to deny that we have occasionally found amongst ourselves individuals who have violated their solemn pledges, and sinned against the rites of masonic faith. However we may lament the consequences, we cannot impugn the fact. Still it does not detract from the merit of the institution, any more than the apostates, from Judas Iscariot downwards, who have failed to sully the intrinsic purity of the Christian religion.

APPEAL. As the Grand Lodge, when congregated, is a representation of every individual member of the Fraternity, it necessarily possesses a supreme superintending authority, and the power of finally deciding on every case which concerns the interest of the Craft Any lodge or brother, therefore, who may feel aggrieved by the decision of any other masonic authority or juris-

diction, may appeal to the Grand Lodge against such
decision. The appeal must be made in writing, specify-
ing the particular grievance complained of, and be transmitted to the Grand Secretary. A notice and copy of the
appeal must also be sent by the appellant to the party
against whose decision the appeal is made. All appeals
must be made in proper and decent language; no others
will be received.—*Constitutions.*

APPRENTICE, or first degree in the Order. An
apprentice is respected in every lodge as a brother equally
as much as an older member, and he has not, as might
be supposed, any especially derogatory work to do. He
learns masonic wisdom as far as it can be taught in the
first degree, and he is, therefore, called an Apprentice.
His clothing in the lodge is very little different from that
of the others; and the older brethren dare not place much
value in their being able to wear an ornament or two
more than he does.—*Gadicke.*

APRON. An apron is given to an operative Mason
as a real necessary article; to a Freemason only as a
symbol. If the apron of an operative mason becomes
dirty, this is mostly a sign of his praiseworthy industry;
but when the Freemason does not keep himself morally
pure in all his actions, he stains the pure white of his
apron to his own disgrace. A masonic apron is made of
common white leather, and no brother is allowed to
appear in a lodge without one; it is intended to remind
him of purity of mind and morals; white amongst the
ancients being considered as an emblem of purity of soul.
It is well known that formerly none but those of mature
age were baptized, and they had to be dressed in white,
to show that they had laid aside the lusts of the flesh.
Those brethren who prove by their active benevolence
and industry that they are worthy, receive promotion in
the Order, and their aprons have proper decorations for
each degree.—*Gadicke.*

ARCANA. In the secret arcana of our mysteries, a
series of valuable truths are preserved, which correspond
with the teaching of Christianity, and point to the

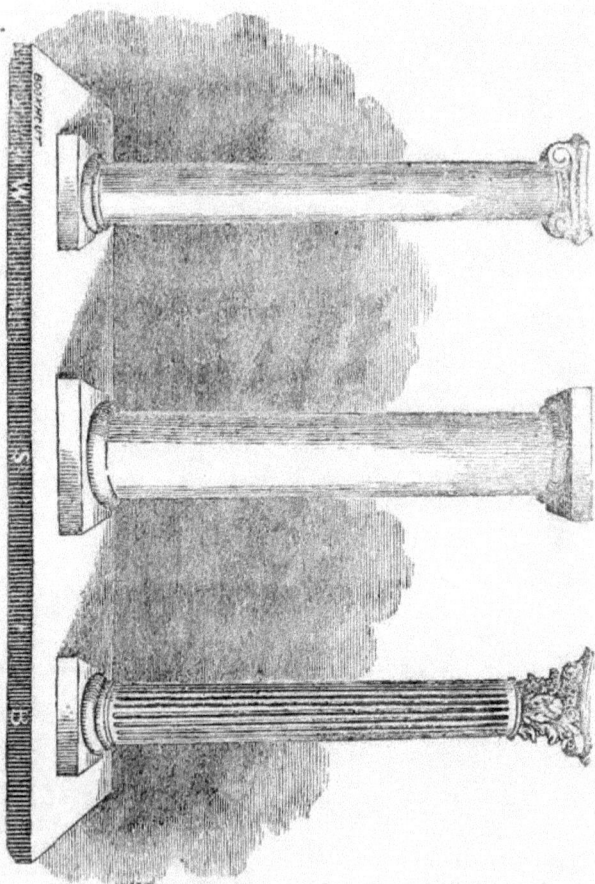

ARCHITECTURE.—WISDOM, STRENGTH AND BEAUTY.

appearance of a Saviour in the world, to atone for human transgression, and carry us from earth to heaven. And being the conservator of such valuable mysteries, it is not surprising that in these days of superior piety and intelligence, it should so rapidly increase in public estimation, and be practised by the wise and good, not merely as a source of rational amusement, but as a means of promoting the blessings of morality and virtue amongst mankind, and augmenting a respect for the institution of religion.

ARCH OF HEAVEN. Job compares heaven to an arch supported by pillars. "The pillars of heaven tremble and are astonished at his reproof." Dr. Cutbush on this passage remarks—"The arch in this instance is allegorical, not only of heaven, but of the higher degree of Masonry, commonly called the Holy Royal Arch. The pillars which support the arch are emblematical ot Wisdom and Strength ; the former denoting the wisdom of the Supreme Architect, and the latter the stability of the universe."—*Brewster*.

ARCHITECTURE. Architecture is one of the first occupations in which man employed himself, and reflection is the first step towards improving the mind. How astonishingly has the science of architecture improved and how honoured and how respected is an experienced architect ! The science commenced with miserable huts ; the next step was to erect altars on which to offer sacri- fices to the gods; of their own imaginations regular dwellings followed next in rotation, after which, in rapid succession, came palaces for their princes, bridges over the most rapid streams to facilitate their commune with each other ; pyramids and towers, proudly pointing to the heavens ; catacombs of nearly immeasurable dimensions for the interment of their dead, and the most gorgeous temples in honour of the Great Architect of heaven and earth. Thus we have adopted the title of Masons from one of the most ancient and most honourable occu- pations of mankind, in allusion to the antiquity of our Order. The working tools of an operative mason have become our symbols, because we can find no better or more expressive ones. No occupation is so widely extended, and in close connexion with others, as that of a Mason; and the various paths by which mankind strive to gain an entrance into the imperishable temple are innumerable.—*Gadicke*.

ARCHIVES. Our traditions state that the hollow or the cylinder of these pillars (J. & B.) was used as archives of Masonry, and contained the sacred rolls which comprised the history of the Hebrew nation, their civil and religious polity, the works of the prophetical and inspired writers, and the complete system of universal science.—*Hemming*.

ARITHMETIC. The science of arithmetic is indis pensable to the architect, and highly prized by him. It is a very ancient science, and was perfected in ancient Greece. Far be it from every Mason to give himself up to the superstitious practice of foretelling human events by the science of arithmetic; but he knows that it is by the assistance of arithmetic that we have discovered the courses of the heavenly bodies; that without its assistance we could not know when the moon would shine, when it would be ebb or flood, when summer or winter would commence.—*Gadicke*.

ARK AND ANCHOR. [*See* ANCHOR AND ARK.]

ARK. The ark of the covenant was a kind of chest or coffer, placed in the sanctum sanctorum, with the two tables of stone containing the decalogue, written with the finger of God, and containing the most sacred monument of the Jewish or any other religion. Along with the ark were deposited the rod of Aaron and the pot of manna. The ark was a symbol of the divine presence and protection of the Israelites, and a pledge of the stability of the theocracy, so long as the people adhered to the articles of the covenant which the ark contained. This sacred chest was made of shittim wood, or the timber of a thorny shrub which grew in great profusion in many parts of the wilderness where the Israelites were directed to encamp, and gave its name to

a particular place, which was hence called Abel Shittim
It is supposed to have been the wood of the burning
bush, which was once held in such veneration in our
Royal Arch Chapters. This timber had a close grain
and consequently was capable of receiving a beautifu.
polish, and, like the cedar, from its fragrance exemp
from the attacks of worms and rottenness. Hence the
ark endured, without losing any of its specific virtues,
from the time of its construction in the wilderness to the
demolition of the Temple by Nebuchadnezzar, a period
of nine hundred years. It was made by Aholiab and
Bezaleel, under the direction of Moses, and according to
the pattern which Jehovah had shown him on the Holy
Mountain; and appropriated to such a sublime office,
that all persons were forbidden to look upon or touch it
under pain of death.

ARRANGEMENT. The appointment and arrangement of a masonic lodge-room in the 18th century were
very different to our present practice. A long table was
extended from one end of the room to the other, covered
with a green cloth, on which were placed duplicates of
the ornaments, furniture and jewels, intermixed with
masonic glasses for refreshment. At one end of this
table was placed the Master's pedestal, and at the other
that of the Senior Warden, while about the middle of
the table, in the south, the Junior Warden was placed.
and the brethren sat round as at a common ordinary.
When there was a candidate to be initiated, the candidate
was paraded outside the whole; and, on such occasions,
after he had been safely deposited at the north-east angle
of the lodge, a very short explanation of the design of
Freemasonry, or a brief portion of the lecture, was considered sufficient before the lodge was called from labour
to refreshment. The song, the toast, the sentiment, went
merrily round, and it was not until the brethren were
tolerably satiated that the lodge was resumed, and the
routine business transacted before closing.

ARTS, LIBERAL. The seven liberal arts and sciences
are Grammar, Rhetoric, Arithmetic, Logic, Music, Ge-

ometry, and Astronomy. They are beautifully explained in the second, or Fellow-Craft's, degree.

ASCENT. The ascent of a Fellowcraft, when he goes to receive his wages, is by a staircase of five divisions, referring to the five noble orders of architecture, and the five external senses or organs which regulate the several modes of that sensation which we derive from external objects. These are the several links of that powerful chain which binds us to the works of the creation, wherewith we can have no connection, exclusive of those feelings which result from the delicate mechanism of the ear, the eye, the smell, the palate, and the touch.

ASHLAR.   [*See* ROUGH and PERFECT.]

ASTREA. The Goddess of Justice dwelt with mortals, but their vices and crimes, which she could not restrain, disgusted her so much, that she was compelled to return to heaven, from whence this charming goddess has never again revisited the earth to preside over the tribunals of mortals, for which reason she is generally represented as hoodwinked. Mythology informs us, that while she was a dweller on this earth, she was so satisfied with the justice of the spirit of Freemasonry, that she took it with her into her sanctuary, where she awaits the brethren of the Order, to bless them with all the pleasures she is able to communicate.

ASTRONOMY is an art by which we are taught to read the wonderful works of God in those sacred pages, the Celestial Hemisphere. While we are employed in the study of this science, we must perceive unparalleled instances of wisdom and goodness, and through the whole of the creation trace the glorious Author by his works.

ASTRONOMICAL. Some of our brethren are inclined to think that our rites are astronomical, and explain the pillars of the lodge thus: Wisdom is the first Person of the Egyptian Trinity ; Osiris, the sun, is the second person, being the Demiurgus, or supposed maker of the world, personating Strength ; and Isis, the moon, the Beauty of Masonry, is the third. But as the first person is not revealed to the initiates of the minor degrees, the trinity for these grades is made up wholly of visible physical powers, adapted to the gross conceptions of the unenlightened; viz., Osiris, Isis, and Orus; that is, the Sun, Moon, and Orion. The cabalistic Jews had some such fancies respecting their patriarchs. Abraham was likened to the sun, as rising in the east; Isaac to the moon, as receiving his light from him; and Jacob to the Zodiac, from his sons constituting so many stars. Therefore, in "Barmidmar Raba," these appellations are given to them. Descending from the heavens to the firmament, the seven planets come after the orbs; these correspond to the seven pre-eminent men until Jacob; *i. e.*, Adam, Seth, Noah, Shem, Abraham, Isaac, and Jacob; or, according to others, commencing with Jacob, Levy, Kohath, Amram, Aaron, David, and Solomon; or Abraham, Isaac, Jacob, Moses, Aaron, David, and Solomon. In either way this number is mystical; for as the sun has three planets above his orb—Mars, Jupiter, and Saturn, and three below it—the Moon, Venus, and Mercury, so Moses is compared to the sun from being in the centre of these last enumerations of patriarchs. Therefore, the sages say—"The face of Moses shone like the sun."

ASYLUM. The Asylum for Worthy, Aged and Decayed Freemasons is a magnificent edifice at Croydon in Surrey. The charity was established by Dr. Crucefix, after sixteen years of herculean toil, such as few men but himself could have sustained. He did not live to see it in full operation, but breathed his last at the very time when the cope-stone was placed on the building. Since the death of Dr. Crucefix, it has been amalgamated with the Provident Annuity and Benevolent Association of the Grand Lodge.

ATHEIST. One who denies the existence of a God, or, supreme intelligent being. The old charges declare that a Mason is obliged by his tenure to obey the moral law, and if he rightly understands the art, he will never be a stupid atheist. A belief in God is one of the unwritten landmarks of the Order. The very nature of the institution is set forth in its rituals as one of the first pre-requisites to the ceremony of initiation.

ATTENDANCE. Every brother ought to belong to some regular lodge, and should always appear therein properly clothed, truly subjecting himself to all its by-laws and the general regulations. He must attend all meetings, when duly summoned, unless he can offer to the Master and Wardens such plea of necessity for his absence as the said laws and regulations may admit. By the ancient rules and usages of Masonry, which are generally adopted among the by-laws of every lodge, no plea was judged sufficient to excuse any absentee, unless he could satisfy the lodge that he was detained by some extraordinary and unforeseen necessity.

ATTRIBUTES. The principal design of the laws of Masonry is to promote the harmony of its members, and by that means create a marked line of distinction be·tween Freemasonry and every other existing society. The attributes of the several degrees were therefore distinctly characterized, that no mistake might occur in their application to the business of the Craft. The brethren of the first degree were expected to distinguish themselves by honour and probity ; the Fellowcraft by diligence, assiduity, and a sincere love of scientific pursuits ; while the few who by their superior virtues attained to the third degree, recommended themselves to notice by their truth, fidelity, and experience in the details and landmarks of the Order.

AUDIT. A committee, consisting of the Grand Officers of the year, and twenty-four Masters of lodges in London district, to be taken by rotation, shall meet between the quarterly communications in December and March, for the purpose of examining and auditing the Grand Treasurer's accounts for the preceding year, and making a report thereon to the Grand Lodge.—*Constitutions.*

AUGUSTAN STYLE. It was during the reign of

Augustus that the learned Vitruvius became the father
of true architecture by his admirable writings. This
imperial patron first employed his Fellowcrafts in repairing or rebuilding all the public edifices, much neglected,
if not injured, during the civil wars. In those golden
days of Augustus, the patricians, following his example,
built above a hundred marble palaces at Rome, fit for
princes; and every substantial citizen rebuilt their houses
in marble; all uniting in the same disposition of adorn-
ing Rome; whereby many lodges arose and flourished of
the Free and Accepted Masons, so that Augustus, when
dying, justly said, "I found Rome built of brick, but I
leave it built of marble!" Hence it is, that in the
remains of ancient Rome, those of his time, and of some
following emperors, are the best patterns of true masonry
extant, the epitome of old Grecian architecture, now
commonly expressed by the Augustan style, in which
are united wisdom, strength, and beauty.—*Anderson.*

AUTHORITY. [*See* ANCIENT CHARGES.]

AXE. In the construction of King Solomon's Temple, every piece of it, whether timber, stone, or metal,
was brought ready cut, framed, and polished, to Jerusalem; so that no other tools were wanted or heard than
were necessary to join the several parts together. All
the noise of axe, hammer, and saw, was confined to Lebanon, the quarries and the plains of Zeredatha, that
nothing might be heard among the masons of Sion save
harmony and peace.—*Anderson.*

B.

BABEL, in the Hebrew language means confusion. The
name of a lofty tower, began to be built by the descendants
of Noah, among whom Nimrod was a leader, on the plains
of Shinar, about 120 years after the flood. It was destroyed by the special interposition of the Almighty.

BABYLON. One of the oldest and greatest cities of the
ancient world, of which Nimrod was the founder. It was
situated in the very heart of the old world. Under Nebuchadnezzar Babylon reached the summit of her greatness.

This king, in the year of the world 3394, destroyed the
city of Jerusalem, including Solomon's temple, and carried into captivity nearly all the people of Judea, who
were retained in Babylon for seventy years, and until
Cyrus, King of Persia, issued a proclamation restoring
them to liberty, with permission to rebuild their temple,
under the superintendence of Zerubbabel, a prince of
Judea; Jeshua, the high-priest, and Haggai, the scribe.

BABYLONISH CAPTIVITY. The Jews had fallen
under the displeasure of the Almighty by deviating from
true masonic principles; and hence they not only fell
into great errors and corruptions, but were guilty of the
most abominable sins; wherefore Jehovah, in his wrath,
denounced heavy judgments against them by Jeremiah
and other prophets, declaring that their fruitful land
should be spoiled, their city became desolate and an
abomination, and themselves and their descendants feel
the effects of his displeasure for the space of seventy
years, which commenced in the fourth year of the reign
of Jehoiachim, A. L. 3398.—*Old Lectures.*

BACK. It is a duty incumbent on every Free and
Accepted Mason to support a brother's character in his
absence equally as though he were present; not to revile
him behind his back, nor suffer it to be done by others
without using every necessary attempt to prevent it.

BADGE. Johnson defines a badge as "a mark of
cognizance worn to show the relation of the wearer to
any person or thing." The badge of a Mason is his
apron—an emblem of innocence and purity. It was
originally a skin of plain white leather. In 1730 it was
regulated in Grand Lodge that the Grand Officers should
" wear white leather aprons with blue silk; and that the
Masters and Wardens of particular lodges may line their
white leather aprons with white silk, and may hang their
jewels at white ribbons about their necks." At present
a Master Mason wears a lamb-skin apron with sky-blue
lining and edging, one inch and a half deep. with a
rosette on the fall or flap. No other colour or ornament
is allowed, except to officers or past officers of lodges.

who may have the emblems of their office in silver or white in the centre of their apron. The Masters and Past Masters of lodges wear, in lieu of, and in the place of, the three rosettes on the Master Mason's apron, perpendicular lines upon horizontal lines, thereby forming three several sets of two right angles, to be made of ribbon of the same colour as the edging of the apron. The Grand Stewards' aprons are distinguished by crimson and silver, and other grand and provincial grand officers by purple and gold.

BALLOT. Ballotting frequently takes place in a Freemasons' lodge, more particularly in admitting a candidate, which is never allowed to take place unless he has a majority of votes in his favour, according to the rules of the lodge; some lodges requiring perfect unanimity, others admitting the candidate when there are not more than three black balls against him. In exercising this privilege, every member ought to give his vote perfectly free from any influence from either the officers of the lodge, or from personal or private motives: he ought at all times to remember that this privilege is given to men who ought to think and act for themselves with this one sole object in view, viz., the credit, honour, and welfare of the Craft in general, and of his own lodge in particular.—*Gadicke.*

BANNERS. When the Israelites marched through the wilderness, we find that the twelve tribes had between them four principal banners, or standards, every one of which had its particular motto; and each standard had also a distinct sign described upon it. They encamped round about the tabernacle, and on the east side were three tribes under the standard of Judah; on the west were three tribes under the standard of Ephraim on the south were three tribes under the standard of Reuben; and on the north were three tribes under the standard of Dan. The standard of Judah was a lion; that of Ephraim an ox; that of Reuben a man, and that of Dan an eagle; whence were formed the hieroglyphics of cherubim and seraphim, to represent the children of Israel.—*Ashe.*

BARE FEET. Nakedness of feet was a sign of mourning. God says to Ezekiel, "Make no mourning for the
dead, and put on thy shoes upon thy feet," &c. It was
likewise a mark of respect. Moses put off his shoes to
approach the burning bush; the priests served in the
Tabernacle with their feet naked, as they did afterwards
in the Temple. The Talmudists teach that if they had
but stepped with their feet upon a cloth, a skin, or even
upon the foot of one of their companions, their service
would have been unlawful.

BANQUET. After the closing of some lodges for
initiations or festival, a banquet is held, that is to say,
the brethren assemble for recreation and refreshment at
a supper. But if the brethren merely meet to eat and
drink, then the appellation masonic banquet would not
be appropriate. Eating, or, more properly speaking,
drinking toasts, and earnest masonic discourses or appeals
for charitable purposes to the brethren, are so blended
together as to produce one beautiful and harmonious
whole evening's amusement; for this reason the officers
of the lodge, at least the Worshipful Master, Wardens,
and Master of the Ceremonies, or his substitute, must be
present. The opening and closing of a masonic banquet,
at which the brethren are clothed, is commonly regulated
by a ritual for that purpose.—*Gadicke.*

BEAUTY. The Freemason is a true admirer of all
the liberal arts and sciences, but he much more admires
a beauty of his own, which stands as fast as the pillars of
the earth—is immovable and immortal. All our working
tools are given to us to find out symmetry, proportion,
and applicability. We are conducted by every step in
our Order to order and harmony, the very being of beauty
We do not crawl in loathsome caverns, but our places of
meeting are beautiful halls. The outward tokens and
clothing of our Order are composed of the most beautiful colours. We refuse neither silk nor metal in our
jewels, we rejoice in the purity of the clothing of our
Order; but more especially we endeavour to make the
spirit of true beauty shine in our assemblies, and not to
allow it to degenerate into a lifeless appearance.—*Gadicke.*

BEAUTY AND BANDS. The application of beauty and bands to the science of Freemasonry was in much esteem with our brethren at the beginning of the present century; but at the reunion, being pronounced inconsistent with the general plan of the Order, it was expunged, and is now nearly forgotten, except by a few old Masons, who may, perhaps, recollect the illustration as an incidental subject of remark amongst the Fraternity of tha period.

BEEHIVE. The beehive is an emblem of industry, and recommends the practice of that virtue to all created beings, from the highest seraph in heaven to the lowest reptile in the dust. It teaches us that as we came into the world rational and intelligent beings, so we should ever be industrious ones; never sitting down contented while our fellow-creatures around us are in want, when it is in our power to relieve them without inconvenience to ourselves.

BEHAVIOUR. A Mason should be always cautious in his words and carriage, that the most penetrating stranger may not be able to discover or find out what is not proper to be intimated; and sometimes he should divert a discourse, and manage it prudently for the honour of the worshipful Fraternity.

BELIEF. The most prominent facts which Freemasonry inculcates directly or by implication in its lectures are these : that there is a God; that he created man, and placed him in a state of perfect happiness in Paradise; that he forfeited this supreme felicity by disobedience to the divine commands at the suggestion of a serpent tempter; that, to alleviate his repentant contrition, a divine revelation was communicated to him, that in process of time a Saviour should appear in the world to atone for their sin, and place their posterity in a condition of restoration to his favor; that for the increasing wickedness of man, God sent a deluge to purge the earth of its corruptions; and when it was again repeopled, he renewed his gracious covenant with several of the patriarchs : delivered his people from Egypt; led them in the wilderness; and in the Mosaic dispensation gave more clear indications of the Messiah by a succession of prophets, extending throughout the entire theocracy and monarchy, that he instituted a tabernacle and temple worship, which contained the most indisputable types of the religion which the Messiah should reveal and promulgate; and that when the appointed time arrived, God sent his only begotten Son to instruct them, who was born at Bethlehem, as the prophets had foretold, in the reign of Herod, (who was not of the Jewish royal line, nor even a Jew,) of a pure virgin of the family of David. .

BENAI. The Benai were setters, layers, or builders at the erection of King Solomon's Temple, being able and ingenious Fellowcrafts, who were distributed by Solomon into separate lodges, with a Master and Warden in each, that they might receive commands in a regular manner, take care of their tools and jewels, be paid every week, and be duly fed and clothed, that the work might proceed with harmony and order.

BENEFITS. The society expends thousands of pounds sterling every year in the relief of the virtuous distressed. Nor can the existence of these benefits be denied, for they are open and undisguised. The relief of widows and orphans, and of aged Masons in want; youth of both sexes educated and trained to a life of usefulness and virtue; the stream of charity disseminated through every class of wretchedness and misery, are indeed so evident, that none can doubt the benefits of the institution; and therefore those who decry it are fighting against truth, and condemn by their writings what their conscience secretly approves.

BENEVOLENCE, FUND OF. The distribution and application of this charitable fund shall be monthly; for which purpose a committee or lodge of Benevolence shall be holden on the last Wednesday of every month. This lodge shall consist of all the present and past Grand Officers, all actual Masters of lodges, and twelve Past Masters. The brother presiding shall be bound strictly to enforce all the regulations of the Craft respecting the distribution of this fund, and shall be satisfied, before any petition be read, that all the required formalities have been complied with. To every petition must be added a recommendation, signed in open lodge by the Master, Wardens, and a majority of the members then present, to which the petitioner does or did belong, or from some other contributing lodge, certifying that they have known him to have been in reputable, or at least tolerable, circumstances, and that he has been not less than two years a subscribing member to a regular lodge.

BETRAYING. By a full and fair exposition of our great leading principles, we betray no masonic secrets; these are safely locked up in the heart of every Mason, and are never to be imparted except in a constitutional manner. But our leading tenets are no secrets. It is no secret that Masonry is of divine origin; it is no secret that the system embraces and inculcates evangelical truth; it is no secret that there is no duty enjoined nor a virtue required in the volume of inspiration, but what is found in, and taught by, Speculative Freemasonry; it is no secret that the appropriate name of God has been preserved in this institution in every country where Masonry existed, while the rest of the world was literally sunk in heathenism; and above all, it is not, neither can it be, a secret, that a good Mason is, of necessity, truly and emphatically a Christian.—*Town.*

BEZALEEL. Bezaleel and Aholiab were not only the most skilful at the building of the Tabernacle, but the most zealous for the work. We are therefore not prepared to see a miracle in this particular; but we are prepared to see something greater, which is, that God claims his own—as his gift, as the wisdom which he had put into them—that we might call the "natural" genius or talent whereby they had been enabled to acquire that master skill in arts which they were now required to exercise in his service. We believe that these endowments were given to them originally by God, and that the circumstances of life which gave them the opportunity of making these acquirements in Egypt, were determined by Him with a view to this ultimate employment in his

service. We see that the services of other persons simi-
larly qualified were required in the same manner, and
on the same ground, although Bezaleel and Aholiab were
the chief.—*Kitto*.

BIBLE. Amongst the great lights of Freemasonry
the Holy Bible is the greatest. By it we are taught to
rule and govern our faith. Without this sacred light we
find no masonic altar. Without it no lodge is perfect ;
neither can any one be legally initiated into the Order
unless he believes in the grand truths which are therein
contained ; unless he supports and is supported by that
blessed book. The square and the compasses stimulate
us to investigate into the truths which are therein contained ; for truth, justice, and mercy, are best supported
by true religion. By it we are taught " In the beginning
was the Word." The sacred writings are a symbolical
chain, by which we are all united in the bonds of brotherly love and universal philanthropy, as John, the meek
and lowly disciple of Jesus, says in his gospel. In this
blessed book is to be found the true rule by which every
real Christian will endeavour to regulate his conduct.—
Gadicke.

BIGOTRY. There are some bigots in their opinions
against Freemasonry. It is, they cry, a bad thing—an
unlawful thing—a sinful thing. Why?—Because we
detest it—abhor it! To pity such, is no mean part of
Christian love, since, I am persuaded, that even in good
hearts the first emotions respecting them were those of
scorn and contempt. Of what use is it to reason with
bigots, whether in religion, morals, or politics?—*Turner*

BLACK. Among the Athenians, black was the colour
of affliction, and white of innocence, joy, and purity.—
The Arabs and blazonry give to black a signification
evidently derived from traditions of initiation. It designates among the Moors grief, despair, obscurity, and constancy. Black, in blazon named sable, signifies prudence,
wisdom, and constancy in adversity and woe. Hence the
mosaic work of a Masons' lodge.—*Symbolic Colours*.

BLAZING STAR. The blazing star must not be considered merely as the creature which heralded the appearance of T. G. A. O. T. U., but the expressive symbol of that Great Being himself, who is described by the magnificent appellations of the Day Spring, or Rising Sun; the Day Star; the Morning Star; and the Bright, or Blazing Star. This, then, is the supernal reference of the Blazing Star of Masonry, attached to a science which, like the religion it embodies, is universal, and applicable to all times and seasons, and to every people that ever did or ever will exist on our ephemeral globe of earth.

BLUE. This durable and beautiful color was adopted and worn by our ancient brethren of the three symbolic degrees as the peculiar characteristic of an institution which has stood the test of ages, and which is as much distinguished by the durability of its materials or principles, as by the beauty of its superstructure. It is an emblem of universal friendship and benevolence; and instructs us, that in the mind of a Mason those virtues should be as expansive as the blue arch of heaven itself

BLUE MASONRY. The three first degrees are clothed in or ornamented with blue, from whence this name is derived. The following degrees have not the same uniformity in their outward appearance. Blue is the colour of truth or fidelity; and it is a remarkable fact that the brethren have ever remained true to the blue degrees, while the authenticity of the other degrees has often been disputed, and in many places altogether denied. Under the reign of William III. of England blue was adopted as the favourite colour of the Craft.—*Gadicke.*

BOARD OF GENERAL PURPOSES. This board consists of a president and twenty-four other members, of which the Grand Master annually nominates the president and ten of the members, at the Quarterly Communication in June; and the Grand Lodge on the same day elects the other fourteen from among the actual masters and past masters of lodges; and they, together with the

Grand Master, Deputy Grand Master, and the Grand
Wardens of the year, constitute the board.

BOAZ. One of the rules of the Jewish Cabala is
called Transposition, and is used by finding an appropriate meaning to a word formed anagrammatically
from any other word. Acting on this rule, Bro. Rosenberg, an eminent Jewish Mason, residing in Paris, thus
improves the names of the two pillars:—"In the first
degree the candidate receives in his preparation the
elements of the sciences; it remains for him to instruct
or to fortify himself by means of the higher sciences.
The word fortify in Hebrew is ZOAB. At the moment
when the young neophite is about to receive the physical
light he should prepare himself to receive the moral
light. The word prepared in Hebrew is NIKAJ. This
word is very important for him who proposes to follow
the path of virtue."

BOND AND FREE. At the grand festival which
Abraham gave at the weaning of his son Isaac, Sarah
detected Ishmael, the son of Hagar the Egyptian bond-
woman, in the act of teazing and perplexing her son.
She therefore remonstrated with Abraham, saying, Cast
out this bondwoman and her son, for the son of the bond-
woman shall not be heir with my son, even with Isaac.—
E. A. P. Lecture.

BOND-WOMAN. Sarah the wife of Abraham being
about eighty years of age, and conceiving herself to be
past child-bearing, endeavoured to procure a son whom
she might adopt, in pursuance of the custom of those
times, by giving to her husband, as her substitute, an
Egyptian slave named Hagar. But when the bond
woman found that she had conceived by Abraham, she
conducted herself with such insolence to her mistress, that
the patriarch was compelled to give her up to Sarah's
correction; and she exercised it so sharply that Hagar
fled into the wilderness, and dwelt by a fountain of
water. She was, however, commanded by the Divinity to
return, and for her comfort a prediction was vouchsafed
which promised to the son that she should bear, and to

his posterity, this remarkable privilege—that his name should never be blotted out.

BOOK OF CONSTITUTIONS. This book contains the written landmarks, rules, regulations, ancient charges, and fundamental principles of the Order ; a detailed exposition of the duties of officers of Grand and Subordinate Lodges, and the rights and privileges of members. In all processions when the Grand Master appears the Book of Constitutions is carried before him, guarded by the Tiler's sword.

BOOK OF THE LAW. The Book of the Law is always spread open upon the pedestal during lodge hours at some important passage of Scripture, during the continuance of the solemn ministrations of the lodge. In the first degree it is usually unfolded at Ruth iv. 7; in the second degree at Judges xxii. 6; and in the third at 1 Kings vii. 13, 14. These usages, however, it may be necessary to add, are arbitrary ; for we find at different periods during the last century that Genesis xxii. and xxviii. were indifferently used for the first degree ; 1 Kings vi. 7, and 2 Chron. iii. 17, for the second; and Amos x. 25, 26, and 2 Chron. vi. for the third. In the United States, according to the instructions contained in   ' Chart, the Bible is opened in the first degree at Psalm cxxxiii.; in the second at Amos vii., and in the third at Ecclesiastes xii.

BRAZEN SERPENT. The brazen serpent was an image of polished brass, in the form of one of those fiery serpents which were sent to chastise the murmuring Israelites in the wilderness, and whose bite caused violent heat, thirst, and inflammation. By Divine command, Moses made a serpent of brass or copper, and put it upon a pole ; and it came to pass that if a serpent had bitten any man, when he beheld the serpent of brass he lived. This brazen serpent was preserved as a monument of divine mercy, but in process of time became an instrument of idolatry; for it being written in the law of Moses, whoever looketh upon it shall live, they fancied they might obtain blessings by its mediation, and therefore thought it worthy to be worshipped. But Hezekiah thought fit to take it quite away when he abolished other idolatry, because in the time of his father they adored it as an idol; and though pious people among them accounted it only as a memorial of a wonderful work, yet he judged it better to abolish it, though the memory of the miracle should happen to be lost, than suffer it to remain, and leave the Israelites in danger of committing idolatry hereafter with it.—*Horne.*

BRAZEN PILLARS. The two pillars on the Tracing-board are the representations of those which stood at the entrance of the porch of King Solomon's Temple, emblems of strength and stability. They are particularly described in Scripture, and were considered of such importance as to be put for the Temple itself when its destruction was threatened by the Almighty. They were composed of cast brass and were manufactured in the clay ground between Succoth and Zeredatha, along with the holy vessels for the temple worship. They were made hollow for the purpose of serving as archives of Masonry, and to hold the constitutional records.

BREADTH. The breadth of the lodge is said to be between the north and the south, for the purpose of demonstrating the universality of Masonry.

BREAST. A Mason's breast should be a safe and sacred repository for all your just and lawful secrets. A brother's secrets, delivered to me as such, I would keep as my own, as to betray that trust might be doing him the greatest injury he could sustain in this mortal life; nay, it would be like the villany of an assassin who lurks in darkness to stab his adversary when unarmed and least prepared to meet an enemy.—*Old Lectures.*

BREAST-PLATE. The breast-plate of the high priest was a square of nine inches, made of the same material as the ephod, and set with twelve precious stones, three in each row, on which were also engraved the names of the twelve tribes. The colours of the banners were identified by these stones, each tribe bearing the same colour as the precious stone by which it was represented in the breast-plate

BRIGHT MASON. If any brothers doubt whether it be really necessary that their masonic teaching should be reduced to practice; if they doubt whether they ought to be peculiarly cautious in their words and actions; or whether, as Masons, they ought to possess a listening ear, a silent tongue, and a faithful heart; they cannot be bright Masons, for the complicated system of Freemasonry is not to be received or rejected as may suit their pleasure or convenience.

BROACHED THURNEL. This was the name of one of the original immoveable jewels, and was used for the E. A. P. to learn to work upon. It was subsequently called the Brute Stone, or rough Ashlar.

BROTHER. In the lodge, Masons always call each other brother; and the poorest among them, even the serving brethren, dare not address them by any other title, although they may fill the highest offices in the state, or even be monarchs. Out of the lodge, in the presence of strangers, the word brother may be dropped; but when a brother meets a brother, even out of the lodge, and no other person is present, then the title of brother must not be omitted. It must be much more agreeable to every brother to be called by that endearing name than to be addressed by the title of your excellency or Mr., as well in the lodge as out of it when no strangers are present. No one hath a brother except he be a brother himself.— *Gadicke.*

BROTHERLY LOVE. This can be manifested in innumerable opportunities not only in the Lodge but also out of it. It is acknowledged by the nearly imperceptible pressure of the hand as much as by the vindication of an innocently accused absent Brother from the throne. It is an essential element to bind the Brethren unto each other; we have pledged ourselves to exercise it, and it is one of the greatest duties of a Free and Accepted Mason to deny it unto no man, more especially to a Brother Mason. To exercise brotherly love, or to feel deeply interested in the welfare of others is a source of the greatest happiness in every situation in life. The king upon his throne would find his situation insupportable if his subjects showed their regard unto him through fear alone and not through love, and so would those also who have a superabundance of worldly possessions. He who does not find his heart warmed with love towards all mankind should never strive to be made a Freemason, for he cannot exercise brotherly love.—*Gadicke*.

BUILDER SMITTEN. It is not to be presumed, that we are a set of men professing religious principles contrary to the revelations and doctrines of the Son of God, revereneing a Deity by the denomination of the God of Nature, and denying that mediation which is graciously offered to all true believers. The members of our Society at this day, in the third stage of Masonry confess themselves to be Christians, " The veil of the temple is rent, the builder is smitten, and we are raised from the tomb of transgression."—*Hutchinson*.

BUILDING. It searcely need to be intimated that operative Masonry was the sole object of the earliest builders; for the scientifical and moral refinements that grew from the profession, and are now implied under the term Freemasonry, could not have taken root until the art and the artists, as well as the institutions of civil society had attained some degree of maturity.—*Anderson*.

BUL. The compounds of this divine name Bel, are of great variety. Bel-us was used by the Chaldeans; and the deity was known amongst the ancient Celtæ by the name of Bel or Belenus, which title, by modern authors, is identified with Apollo. The primitive name of Britain was Vel-ynys, the island of Bel; and the fires lighted up on May-day were in honour of this deity, and called Bel's fire. The inhabitants made use of a word, known only to themselves, to express the unutterable name of the Deity, of which the letters O. I. W. were a sacred symbol. In this they resembled the Jews, who always said Adonai, when the name of Jehovah occurred. Baal was the most ancient god of the Canaanites, and was referred to the sun. Manasseh raised altars to this deity, and worshipped him in all the pomp of heathen superstition; and when these altars were destroyed by Josiah, the worship of Baal was identified with that of the Sun.

BURIAL PLACE.—TIME AND THE VIRGIN.

BURIAL PLACE. The burial place of a Master Mason is under the Holy of Holies, with the following legend delineated on the monument:—A virgin weeping over a broken column, with a book open before her; in her right hand a sprig of cassia, in her left an urn; Time standing behind her, with his hands enfolded in the ringlets of her hair. The weeping virgin denotes the unfinished state of the temple : the broken column that one of the principal supporters of Masonry (H. A. B.) had fallen; the open book implies that his memory is recorded in every Mason's heart; the sprig of cassia refers to the discovery of his remains; the urn shews that his ashes have been carefully collected, and Time standing behind her implies that time, patience, and perseverance will accomplish all things.

BURIED TREASURES. We have a tradition that King Solomon concealed certain treasures beneath the foundation of the temple, which were found when they were opened to build the second temple. It was common in ancient times to secrete treasures in such vaults and caverns.

BY-LAWS. Every lodge has the power of framing by-laws for its own government, provided they are not contrary to or inconsistent with the general regulations of the Grand Lodge. The by-laws must therefore be submitted to the approbation of the Grand Master, or the Provincial Grand Master; and when approved, a fair copy must be sent to the Grand Secretary, and also to the Provincial Grand Master; and when any material alteration shall be made, such alteration must in like manner be submitted. The by-laws of the Lodge shall be delivered to the master on the day of his installation, when he shall solemnly pledge himself to observe and enforce them during his mastership. Every brother shall also sign them when he becomes a member of the Lodge, as a declaration of his submission to them.—*Constitutions.*

CABALA. This was amongst the ancient Jews a mystical philosophy, inasmuch as they professed to possess cabalistical secrets from the earliest ages, even from the days of Adam. There was also a philosophical cabala which had its origin in Egypt. Modern cabalists have introduced many things into this so called science, and have divided it into symbolical and real cabala. In the symbolical cabala the secrets of numbers is taught, and the real cabala is subdivided into theoretical and practical. In the theoretical the sacred writings are explained by a host of traditions, and the practical is, that cabala which has found the most followers as it professes to teach the art of performing miracles. As spiritual errors are frequently the subject of masonic lectures, we could not pass the word cabala without notice.—*Gadicke.*

CABLE-TOW. According to the ancient laws of Freemasonry, every Brother must attend his Lodge if he is within the length of his cable-tow. The length of an E. A. P. cable-tow is three English miles, or 15,840 feet.—*Gadicke.*

CALENDAR. The first intimation we have of this periodical was in the year 1775, when the Grand Secretary informed the Grand Lodge that a Freemason's calendar for 1775 and 1776 had been published by the Company of Stationers without the sanction of the society, and that he apprehended a publication of that kind, properly authorized, would be acceptable to the fraternity, and might be beneficial to the charity. He moved that a Freemason's calendar, under sanction of the Grand Lodge, be published in opposition to that published by the Stationer's Company, and that the profits of such publication be appropriated to the general fund of the society. This motion being seconded, the question was put, and it passed in the affirmative. This calendar was continued till after the union in 1813, but the form in which it was printed being at length found inconvenient, H. R. H. the Duke of Sussex G. M. directed that in future it should be published in the form of a pocket book, and it continues to be published in that form to the present day.

CAMP OF ISRAEL. For so large a multitude of people, and for so numerous an army, it was needful that all the necessary articles of life should be prepared beforehand, or be found ready to purchase. In these respects nothing was wanting to the Israelites. Their bread came down to them from heaven, and they had besides an abundance of every thing that could contribute to magnificence. If we may credit Josephus, they had amongst them public markets and a variety of shops. (Ant. l. iii. c. 12, sec. 5.) The tabernacle being erected, it was placed in the midst of the camp, each of the three tribes stretching themselves on the wings, and leaving between them a sufficient space to pass. It was, says Josephus, like a well appointed market, where every thing was ready for sale in due order, and all sorts of artificers kept their shops, so that the camp might be considered a moveable city.—*Adam Clarke.*

CANDIDATE. A candidate for initiation into Freemasonry, is a person who has been proposed by a Brother, and whose name is written upon the tables of the Lodge, that the brethren may be reminded to make the necessary enquiries into his moral and social character; for which purpose four weeks is generally allowed.—*Gadicke.*

CANDLES. The three great luminaries, are not to be confounded with the three great lights. They are merely candles or torches, or they may be called pillars with torches.—*Gadicke.*

CANDLESTICK. The candlestick in the Tabernacle was manufactured by Bezaleel and Aholiab of beaten gold. It had an upright shaft which stood upon a broad foundation, that its support might be firm and unmoveable, without danger of being overthrown during the process of trimming and cleaning its lamps, which were seven in number, one in the centre, and three on each side, on so many branches that were not equal in length, the outer branches being elongated, that the lights might be all of the same height. The body of the shaft had four bowls, and as many knobs and flowers. Some think that the seven branches symbolised the seven planets, the seven days of the week, and the seven ages of man; but in truth the Christian church is the candlestick, and the light is Christ. The seven lamps are emblems of the gift of the Spirit; the knobs and flowers, the graces and ornaments of a Christian life. As the candlestick gave light to the tabernacle, so we must remain in darkness unless Christ shall enlighten his church. Simeon therefore pronounced it to be " a light to lighten the Gentiles, and the glory of Israel."

CANOPY. In the masonic processions of the Continent, the Grand Master walks under a gorgeous canopy of blue, purple, and crimson silk, with gold fringes and tassels, borne upon staves painted purple and ornamented with gold, by eight of the oldest Master Masons present ; and the masters of private lodges walk under canopies of light blue silk with silver tassels and fringes, borne by four members of their own respective companies. The canopies are in the form of an oblong square, and are in length six feet, in breadth and height three feet, having a semicircular covering. The framework should be of cedar, and the silken covering ought to hang down two feet on each side.

CAPITULAR DEGREES. The appellation, in France, of certain degrees of the Scottish rite, from the fourth to the eighteenth, inclusive, and which the French rite has contracted to four. These degrees are divided into four series, or independent branches.

CAPTIOUSNESS. Captiousness is apt to overset the harmony of conversation. And it is so, not only because it often produces misbecoming and provoking expressions and behaviour in a part of the company, but because it is a tacit accusation and a reproach for something ill taken from those we are displeased with. Such an intimation or even suspicion must always be uneasy to society ; and as one angry person is sufficient to discompose a whole company, for the generality, all mutual happiness cease therein on any such jarring. This failing therefore, should be guarded against with the same care, as either boisterous rusticity and insinuated contempt, or ill-natured disposition to censure.—*Martin Clare.*

CAPTIVITY. The Jews having offended the **Most** High, were delivered over to the Chaldeans to be chastised ; and Nebuchadnezzar let loose his full vengeance

DESTRUCTION OF THE TEMPLE.

JEWISH CAPTIVITY.

upon them. He ravaged the whole country; and the holy city of God, after a protracted siege, during which many traitors went over to the enemy, was abandoned to pillage. They burned the temple, broke down the walls of the city, set fire unto her towers, and carried away the consecrated vessels of gold and silver, the brazen sea and altar, and the two pillars of Jachin and Boaz, which stood at the entrance of the porch. All the princes, the nobility, and every person of consequence, according to the prediction of Jeremiah, were removed into the land of Chaldea; but Nebuzaradan, the chief of Nebuchadnezzar's officers, left behind many families of the lower classes to cultivate the vineyards, and other servile purposes, with strict injunctions to transfer the fruits thereof to Babylon in their season, as luxuries for the tables of the nobility.

CARDINAL POINTS. The cardinal points of the compass have a peculiar signification amongst us, and particularly the east, west, and south. The east is a place of light, and there stands the W. M., a pillar of Wisdom, as a representation of the rising sun; and as that luminary opens the glorious day to light mankind to their labours, so the W. M. occupies this station to open lodge, and to employ and instruct the brethren in Masonry. The south is a station of another important officer, the pillar of Beauty, who is placed in that quarter that he may be prepared to mark the sun at its meridian, to call the workmen from labour, and to recruit their strength by necessary refreshment and rest, that their toils may be resumed with renewed vigour and alacrity, without which neither pleasure nor profit can mutually result. In the west stands the pillar of Strength, to mark the setting sun, and close the labours of the day by command of the presiding officer; because the declining luminary warns mankind of the necessity of repose, else our nature would sink under the effects of incessant toil, unrelieved by rest and recreation.

CARDINAL VIRTUES. They are Fortitude, by which we are taught to resist temptation; Prudence, by which we are instructed to regulate our conduct by the dictates of reason; Temperance, by which we learn to govern the passions; Justice, which constitutes the cement of civil society.

CASSIA. The cassia was anciently a symbol of honour, triumph, life, and resurrection, according to Pierius, who published his Hieroglyphica in 1575, which would be quite sufficient to authorize its introduction into our symbolical legend. When the Master Mason exclaims, therefore, " My name is Cassia," it is equivalent to saying, " I have been in the grave; I have triumphed over it by raising from the dead; and being regenerated in the process, have a claim to life (everlasting)."

CATECHISM. This is the most important document of Freemasonry. The catechism was formerly only communicated by conference from one lodge to another, or from one brother to another; and this is the reason why we have so many different forms of the catechism, although in spirit there is no material difference in any of them. As a religious catechism contains a summary of all that is taught by that religion, so our catechism contains the essence of Freemasonry; but it is not to be understood without the teacher taking great pains in instructing the student, nor without having previously been instructed in a lodge, and being able to reflect upon and remember the instructions there given. Every degree has its own catechismus; and in many lodges it is customary to explain part of it at every meeting, in order that the members may become intimately acquainted with it. -*Gadicke.*

CATENARIAN ARCH. This constitutes the form of a Royal Arch Chapter, and is constructed on the following principles. It is a known truth that a semicircular arch will not sustain its own weight, the crown crushing out the sides; it depends, therefore, on abutment for support. The only arch the bearing of which is true in all its points of the curve, is the catenarian arch. If a slack chain or rope be supported by two hooks, the curve it falls into is what is called the catenarian curve; and this inverted is the mechanical arch of the same name. Such an arch, truly constructed, will stand independent of any collateral aid whatever.— *Noorthouck.*

CAUTION. The Entered Apprentice, at his initiation

in the United States, is presented with a new name, which is Caution, to teach him that as he is then imperfectly instructed in the. mysteries of Masonry, he ought to be cautious over all his words and actions, that nothing may escape him which may tend to afford information to the opponents of Masonry. This is one of the. triad of duties recommended in the first degree.

CAUTIOUS SECRECY. The cautious secrecy of the Craft in early ages was used to prevent the great principles of science, by which their reputation was secured and maintained, from being publicly known. Even the inferior workmen were unacquainted with the secret and refined mechanism which cemented and imparted the treasure of wisdom. They were profoundly ignorant of the wisdom which planned, the beauty which designed, and knew only the strength and labour which executed the work. The doctrine of the pressure and counter-pressure of complicated arches, was a mystery which they never attempted to penetrate. They were blind instruments in the hands of intelligent Master Masons, and completed the most sublime undertakings by the effect of mere mechanical skill and physical power, without being able to comprehend the secret which produced them; without understanding the nice adjustment of the members of a building to each other, so necessary to accomplish a striking and permanent effect; or without being able to enter into the science exhibited in the complicated details which were necessary to form a harmonious and proportionate whole.

CAVE. Solomon had a deep cave dug underneath the Sanctum Sanctorum of the Temple, with many intricacies, over which he fixed a stone, wherein he put the ark and cherubim. They say they did this because, by the Holy Spirit foreseeing that that house would be destroyed, he therefore made a secret place where the ark might be kept, so that its sanctity might not be profaned by heathen hands; and they are of opinion that subsequently Josah secreted therein the ark. They prove it firstly from 1 Kings vi. 9:—"And the oracle within the house [דביר] he prepared to place there the ark," where, by *prepare*, they understand it to mean a preparation for the future; as we see, when previously treating of the ark and cherubim, it says, "And they were there until this day," a term in the Holy Scriptures to signify "to all eternity," as, "And no man knoweth of his sepulchre unto this day," that is, never.—*Manasseh Ben Israel.*

CEDAR. The cedar grows on the most elevated part of Lebanon, is taller than the pine, and so thick that five men together could scarcely fathom one. It shoots out its branches at ten or twelve feet from the ground; they are large and distant from each other, and are perpetually green. The cedar distils a kind of gum to which different effects are attributed. The wood is of a brown color, very solid, and incorruptible if preserved from wet. It bears a small apple like to that of the pine.—*Adam Clarke.*

CEMENT. The lodge is strongly cemented with love and friendship, and every brother is duly taught secrecy and prudence, morality and good fellowship.

CENSER. The censer is a representation of the altar of incense which was made of the acacia covered with beaten gold. In form it was a double cube, and had a crown or rim like the table of shewbread, running round its upper surface. It was of small dimensions, being only one foot six inches square, and three feet high, with elevations at each corner called horns. This altar or censer was placed close to the veil which separated the holy place; that the incense might penetrate into the latter; and for this reason perhaps it was that St. Paul attributes it to the innermost room. It was an emblem or type of Christ, through whom we offer the incense of our prayers. The acacia and gold of which the altar was composed, referred to his human and divine nature; the crown to his regal dignity; and the horns to his power. As no incense could be offered but upon this altar, so no prayers will be accepted but those offered through Jesus Christ. The incense was offered every morning and evening, and our prayers ought to ascend to the throne of grace at the same periods.

CENTENARY. The revolution of a hundred years.

It is usual for lodges which have been established for that ong period to celebrate the anniversary by a commemorative festival.

CENTRAL POINT. Masonry is truly the sister of religion; for she boasts her efficacy in all its native influence, and is continually the assistant promoter of like principles and of like actions. The central point of all her innumerable lines, squares and circles, is the love o. God. And upon this central point she builds her faith; from it she derives her hope of glory here and hereafter, and by it she squares her conduct in strict justice and universal charity. The central point of all true Christianity and of all true Masonry is the love of God. "Masonry is dedicated only to the Gospel."

CENTRAL STAR. The human body of Jesus Christ is the Ark of the Christian Covenant, over which the Shekinah appeared in the cave at Bethlehem, in the form of a supernatural Star in the East, which hence is placed in the centre of our lodges.

CENTRE. The labors of a Freemason must penetrate to the centre of the earth, and his spirit inquire into all the operations of nature, and either be able satisfactorily to explain or humbly admire them.—*Gadicke.*

CEREMONIAL. On our initiation we cannot fail to be struck with the ceremonials, and must think that there is more conveyed by them than appears to the vulgar eye. A due attention to the matter will convince us that our first impressions were just; and by researches to discover their implications, a competent degree of knowledge may be acquired touching the origin of Masonry, the reasons which support its several institutions, the meaning and import of its various symbols, together with the progress of the profession.—*Hutchinson.*

CERTIFICATE. Every Brother who travels, and who wishes to visit the lodges in the cities he comes to, must not only provide himself with masonic clothing but with a certificate. These certificates are granted by the Grand Lodge of England to every one who has been regularly initiated, and contain an account of when and where the bearer was made, and a recommendation to all lodges to admit him to their labours. They are sealed with the seal of the Grand Lodge, and are signed by the Grand Secretary, and the brother to whom they belong. —*Gadicke.*

CEREMONIES. If a person wishes to become a candidate for Masonry, he should make up his mind to watch the progress of all the ceremonies through which he may pass, with attention, and search into their propriety, their origin, and their symbolical reference. He may be quite sure that men of sense and standing in the world—men whose reputation for wisdom and common prudence is of some value, would not subject him to any test which might cast an imputation upon themselves.

CHAIN. All the Freemasons upon the surface of the earth form one chain, every member is a link of it, and should ever strive with the true hand of a brother to strengthen it. No wavering doubt should break it. None should be shut out from it, as is taught in every lodge. What an encouraging thought it is for the newly initiated brother to find himself at once surrounded with the light arising from this great chain. This chain can be no fetter to him, for the hands of brethren prove the contrary.—*Gadicke.*

CHALK. Chalk, charcoal and clay, have ever been esteemed the emblems of freedom, fervency, and zeal, because nothing is more free for the use of man than chalk, which seldom touches but leaves its trace behind; nothing more fervent than charcoal, for when well lighted no metal is able to resist its force; nothing is more zealous than clay, our mother earth, who will open her arms to receive us when forsaken by all our friends.

CHAMBER. It is only in solitude that we can deeply reflect upon our present or future undertakings, and blackness, darkness, or solitariness, is ever a symbol of death. A man who has undertaken a thing after mature reflection seldom turns back. No symbol of death will terrify him, and the words of the sacred writings, "In

the beginning was the light," charm him on to seek the
ight he has lost.—*Gadicke.*

CHAPEL. In every convenient place the architect of
a lodge should contrive secret cryptæ or closets. They
are of indispensable utility, but in practice are not sufficiently attended to in this country. On the continent
they are numerous, and are dignified with the name of
chapels. They ought to be seven in number; 1, a room
for visitors; 2, the Tyler's room; added to which there
ought to be 3, a vestry where the ornaments, furniture,
jewels and other regalia are deposited. This is called
the Treasury or Tyler's conclave, because these things
are under his especial charge, and a communication is
generally made to this apartment from the Tyler's
room. There ought to be 4, a chapel for preparations, hung with black, and having only one small
lamp placed high up near the ceiling; 5, a chapel
for the dead furnished with a table, on which are
a lamp, and emblems of mortality; 6, the master's
conclave, where the records, the warrant, the minutes
and every written document are kept. To this room the
W. M. retires when the lodge is called from labour to
refreshment, and at other times when his presence in the
lodge is not essential; and here he examines the visitors,
for which purpose a communication is formed between
his conclave and the visitor's chapel. It is furnished
with blue, and here he transacts the lodge business with
his secretary. The Ark of the Covenant is also deposited
in this apartment. None of these closets should exceed
12 feet square, and may be of smaller dimensions according
to circumstances. In the middle of the hall there should
be 7, a moveable trap-door in the floor, 7 feet long and
3 feet in depth, the use of which is known to none but
perfect Masons, who have passed through all the symbolical degrees.

CHAPITER. Upon each of the pillars of King Solomon's temple was placed a chapiter or symbolical ornament, five cubits in height, composed of network, chains,
pomegranates, and lily work or opening flowers cast in the
same material of which the pillars were formed. Like
the Palladium of Troy they appear to have been essen-

tial to the well-being of the structure. Thus, at the
time when the temple was abandoned by Jehovah, he is
represented as standing magnificently upon the altar,
and commanding the angel of destruction to strike the
heads or chapiters of these two pillars, and the total ruin
not only of the temple but of Jerusalem and the entire
system of Jewish polity should ensue (Amos, ix. 1). As
their destruction was thus comprehensive and significant,
so was their erection symbolical of the magnitude and
splendour of the Jewish nation under Solomon. And
this reference was embodied in their names.

CHAPLAIN. The Grand Chaplain is appointed by
the Grand Master on the day of his installation. He
should attend all the quarterly communications and
other meetings of the Grand Lodge, and there offer up
solemn prayer suitable to the occasion, as established by
the usages of the fraternity.—*Constitutions.*

CHAPTER. A convocation of Royal Arch Masons is
called a chapter. The presiding officers are a king, a
priest, and a prophet, who are representatives of Zerubbabel, Jeshua, and Haggai. These officers are styled
either by the founders' names as above, or as first, second,
and third Principals. All chapters are under the jurisdiction of the Supreme Grand Chapter in London.

CHARACTER. The character of a man that would
become a Mason must undergo the strictest scrutiny.
He must be a man of strict morality; he must be
humane, benevolent, and charitable to his fellow-creatures; he must be no gambler, tippler, or profane swearer;
he must be no railer against the religion of Christ, or the
professors thereof; he must be a lover of decency and
order; and he must be strictly honest, industrious, and
upright in all his conduct; for such as delight in the
practice of vice are a disgrace to civil society, and are
seldom reformed by the most excellent institutions.
They retain their vices unchangeable as the skin of the
Ethiopian or the spots of the leopard. Such indeed
would never apply for admission into our benign institution, were they acquainted with her solemn principles, as
were not lovers of decency and order.—*Powers.*

CHARGES, ANCIENT. The Charges of a Freemason, as they were collected from the old records of the Fraternity, under the superintendence of Bro. Jas. Anderson, and the learned committee who acted with him, and given to the Craft, through the press, in 1723, by order of the Grand Lodge of England, in 1721, have been, wherever promulgated, accepted, and acknowledged as containing the essence of the fundamental principles, and law of Freemasonry. In them are to be found those undisputed, time-honored principles which constitute the written Landmarks of our Order. They are divided into six general heads, viz: 1. Of God and Religion; 2. Of the Civil Magistrates, supreme and subordinate; 3. Of Lodges; 4. Of Masters, Wardens, Fellows, and Apprentices; 5. Of the management of the Craft in working; 6. Of behavior, which last is subdivided into six parts, detailing the several duties of Masons under all the different relations of life, as a subject of civil government, and as a man.

CHARITIES. Our general charities are the Schools for Boys and Girls, the Fund of Benevolence for Widows and Distressed Brethren, the Annuity Fund for Aged Brethren, and the Asylum for Worthy Aged and Decayed Freemasons and their Widows, and they are all amply supported. In the schools seventy boys and sixty-five girls are educated and clothed. The funded property of the Girls' School is about 16,000l., and its income 1600l. a year, including 150l. annually from the Grand Lodge. The funded property of the Boys' School is not so much, it amounts only to 8500l. and the annual income of about 1150l., including 150l. from the Grand Lodge. The funded property of the Royal Masonic Annuity Fund is 3500l., and the annual income including 400l. from the Grand Lodge, is 1300l. The number of annuitants at 20l. a year each is now thirty. The funded property of the Asylum is about 3450l., and its annual income from other sources 400l. The two latter charities are now united together. The sums annually voted by the Board of Benevolence to distressed brethren and the widows of Masons amount to about 750l., and its funded property is 12,000l., and that of the Board of General Purposes about 6000l.

CHARITY. This is the brightest ornament of our

masonic profession. Happy is the brother who hath sown in his heart the seeds of benevolence, the produce of which will be charity and love. He envieth not his neighbour, he believeth not a tale when reported by a slanderer, he forgiveth the injuries of men, and blotteth them out from his recollection. Whoever would emulate the character of a good and worthy Mason ought ever to be ready to assist the needy as far as lies in his power; and if, in the most pressing time of necessity, he does not withhold a liberal hand, the most heartfelt pleasure will reward his labours, and the produce of love and charity will most assuredly follow.—*Old Lectures*.

CHEQUERED. As the steps of man tread in the various and uncertain incidents of life, as our days are chequered with a strange contrariety of events, and our passage through this existence, though sometimes attended with prosperous circumstances, is often beset by a multitude of evils; hence is the lodge furnished with mosaic work to remind us of the precariousness of our state on earth; to day our feet tread in prosperity, to morrow we totter on the uneven paths of weakness, temptation, and adversity. Whilst this emblem is before us, we are instructed to boast of nothing, to have compassion and give aid to those who are in adversity, to walk uprightly and with humility; for such is human existence, that there is no station in which pride can be stably founded; all men, in birth and in the grave, are on the level. Whilst we tread on the mosaic work, let our ideas turn to the original which it copies; and let every Mason act as the dictates of reason prompt him, to live in brotherly love.—*Hutchinson*.

CHERUBIM. There were four cherubims in the most holy place of Solomon's temple. Two lesser made by Moses of massy gold, and two larger made by Solomon overlaid with gold. Those made by Moses were part of the mercy seat, and inseparable from it those of Solomon seem to have spread their wings over it, being added only for the greater ornament and glory of God's house.—*Bishop Patrick*. See "Signs and Symbols," Lect. 1.

CHIEF POINT. The chief point in Masonry is to endeavour to be happy ourselves, and communicate that happiness to others.

CHILDREN OF LIGHT. Remembering the wonders in the beginning, we, claiming the auspicious countenance of heaven on our virtuous deeds, assume the figures of the sun and moon as emblematical of the great light of truth discovered to the first men, and thereby implying that as true Masons we stand redeemed from darkness, and are become the sons of light, acknowledging in our profession our adoration of him who gave light unto his works. Let us then by our practice and conduct in life, show that we carry our emblems worthily, and as the children of light, that we have turned our backs on works of darkness, obscurity and drunkenness, hatred and malice, Satan and his dominions; preferring charity, benevolence, justice, temperance, chastity and brotherly love, as the acceptable service on which the Great Master of all, from his beatitude, looks down with approbation.—*Hutchinson.*

CHISEL. The chisel, though a small instrument, is calculated to make a permanent impression on the hardest substance, and the mightiest structures are indebted to its aid. It morally demonstrates the advantages of discipline and education. The mind, like the diamond in its natural state, is unpolished; but as the effects of the chisel on the external coat soon presents its latent beauties to the view, so education discovers the latent virtues of the mind, in order to display the summit of human knowledge, our duty to God and man.

CHOICE OF OFFICERS. This is a matter of great concern, for the officers of a lodge are not only bound to advance the welfare of their own particular lodge, but whatever may tend to the good of the Fraternity in general. Therefore no man ought to be put in such election, but such as by his own skill and merit is deemed worthy of performance, *viz.*, he must be well acquainted with all the private and public rules and orders of the Craft; he ought to be strictly honest, naturally humane patient in injuries, discreet in conversation, grave in counsel, constant in amity, and above all, faithful in secrecy.—*Dermott.*

CHRISTIANITY. Masonry is the excellency of Christianity, and every Mason is, if he is in reality a Mason, a true Christian; or at least he is in reality truly religious according to his profession, whether he be Jew or Christian.—*Inwood.*

CIRCLE. The circle has ever been considered symbolical of the Deity; for as a circle appears to have neither beginning nor end, it may be justly considered a type of God, without either beginning of days or ending of years. It also reminds us of a future state, where we hope to enjoy everlasting happiness and joy.—*Gia Lectures.*

CIRCLE AND PARALLEL LINES. In all regular and well-formed lodges there is a certain point within a circle, round which it is said the genuine professors of our science cannot err. This circle is bounded north and south by two perpendicular parallel lines. On the upper or eastern part of the periphery rests the Holy Bible, supporting Jacob's ladder extending to the heavens. The point is emblematic of the Omniscient and Omnipresent Deity, the circle represents his eternity, and the two perpendicular parallel lines his equal justice and mercy. It necessarily follows therefore that in traversing a masonic lodge, we must touch upon these two great parallels, as well as upon the volume of the sacred law; and whilst a Mason keeps himself thus circumscribed, remembers his Creator, does justice and loves mercy, he may hope finally to arrive at that immortal centre whence all goodness emanates.—*Hemming.*

CIRCUMAMBULATION. The ancients made it a constant practice to turn themselves round when they worshipped the gods; and Pythagoras seems to recommend it in his symbols. By this circular movement says Plutarch, some imagine that he intended to imitate the motion of the earth; but I am rather of opinion, that the precept is grounded on another notion, that as all temples are built fronting the east, the people at their entrance turned their backs to the sun; and consequently, in order to face the sun, they were obliged to make a half-turn to the right, and then in order to place themselves before the Deity, they completed the round in offering up their prayer.

CLANDESTINE LODGES. Some years ago there were a number of those so called lodges, but there are none at present. Clandestine lodges are such as have been formed by avaricious Freemasons, who take money from those people who can have no idea of the difference between warranted and unwarranted lodges. They were not warranted by any Grand Lodge, and endeavoured as much as possible to conceal their existence from the Grand Lodges ; their founders formed a ritual from their memories, and by this ritual they made so called Freemasons, but as they could not legitimize themselves for want of certificates and proper information, they were unable to gain admission into any worthy and warranted lodge. Since the lodges have been formed into unions, working under one Grand Lodge, unwarranted lodges have less chance of existing than formerly. A lodge which is held without the knowledge of the magistrates or police of the place may be considered as an unwarranted lodge.—*Gadicke.*

CLASSES. Ancient masonic tradition informs us that the speculative and operative Masons who were assembled at the building of the temple, were arranged in nine classes, under their respective Grand Masters ; viz. 30,000 Entered Apprentices, under their Grand Master Adoniram ; 80,000 Fellowcrafts, under Hiram Abiff ; 2000 Mark Men, under Stolkyn ; 1000 Master Masons, under Mohabin ; 600 Mark Masters, under Ghiblim ; 24 Architects, under Joabert ; 12 Grand Architects, under Adoniram ; 45 Excellent Masons, under Hiram Abiff ; 9 Super-excellent Masons, under Tito Zadok ; besides the Ish Sabbal or labourers.

CLOSING. When it is proper time to close the lodge it is always high midnight, and the brethren then go peaceably home, remembering that the high midnight of life may overtake them without a moment's warning.

CLOTHING. It was ordered by the regulations agreed by the Grand Lodge, March 17th, 1771, that none but the Grand Master, his Deputy and Wardens, who were the only grand officers then in existence, shall wear their jewels in gold pendant to blue ribbons about their necks, and white leather aprons with blue silk. Masters and Wardens of particular lodges may line their white leather aprons with white silk, and many hang their jewels by white ribbons about their necks. Master Masons now are clothed in white, sky-blue, and silver; Grand and Provincial Grand Stewards in white, crimson and silver; and all other Grand and Provincial Grand Officers in white, purple and gold.

CLOUDY PILLAR. When the Israelites were delivered from the Bondage of Egypt, and had arrived on the borders of the Red Sea, the Egyptians thought they were so completely ensnared that their escape was impossible. With inaccessible mountains on each side, the sea in front, and the Egyptian army behind, they appeared to be completely hemmed in. And why did Moses place them in this situation? The road to Palestine was open by the Isthmus; but he declined escaping by that avenue, and led the people southward, and placed thus at the apparent mercy of their enemies. The truth is, Moses had no option in the matter; he followed the direction of the Cloudy Pillar, because he had full confidence that it would conduct him right.

COCHLEUS. A staircase contrived as a screw in the inner wall of the temple.

COERCION. The rules of the Fraternity imperatively declare that no person can be admitted a Mason except by his own free-will and accord. That the candidate is unbiased by the improper solicitation of friends, and uninfluenced by mercenary motives; that he is prompted to solicit the privileges of Freemasonry by a favorable opinion of the institution, and a desire of knowledge; and that he will cheerfully conform to all the ancient usages and customs of the Fraternity. Coercion is, therefore, not tolerated, but is an offense against Masonry.

COFFIN. In all the ancient mysteries, before an aspirant could claim to participate in the higher secrets of the institution, he was placed within the pastos, or coffin, or in other words was subjected to a solitary confinement for a prescribed period of time, that he might reflect seriously, in seclusion and darkness, on what he was about to undertake, and be reduced to a proper state oi mind for the reception of great and important truths, by a course of fasting and mortification. This was the symbolical death of the mysteries, and his deliverance from confinement was the act of regeneration, or being born again; or as it was also termed, being raised from the dead.

COLLAR. An ornament worn about the neck, to which is suspended a jewel appropriate to the office which the wearer occupies in a lodge. The colour varies according to rank.

COLLEGIA ARTIFICIUM. The "Encyclopedia Americana," art. Masonry, derives the Order from the Collegia Artificium of the Romans; and says its members were introduced into this country by the kings Alfred and Athelstan, to build castles and churches. They then united, under written constitutions of the Roman and Greek colleges, and the provisions of the civil law. Their religious tenets being often objects of suspicion to the orthodox catholics, and often differing among themselves, they were not allowed to obtrude in their meetings, and of course they were kept secret.

COLONIAL. It being necessary, on account of the distance of foreign district Grand Lodges, and the consequent delay in their communications with the Grand Lodge of England, that their powers should be more extensive, the Grand Lodge delegates to its foreign district Grand Lodges, meeting under a Grand Master duly authorized and appointed by the Grand Master of England, in addition to the powers before specified, that of expelling Masons, and erasing lodges within the district, subject, however, to appeal to the Grand Lodge of England.—*Constitutions.*

COLOURS. The masonic colours, like those used in the Jewish tabernacle, are intended to represent the four elements. The white typifies the earth, the sea is represented by the purple, the sky-blue is an emblem of the air, and the crimson of fire.

COLUMN. A pillar, usually cylindrical, used for the support of a building. Its construction and ornamentation varies according to the different orders of architecture.

COMMENTARIES. Nothing would elevate the character of a lodge more than a course of historical and philosophical commentaries on the authorized lectures, by an experienced and talented master of the work. If a full and regular attendance of brethren be desirable, this process would ensure it. If the improvement of the mind and the promotion of moral virtue be the objects of our pursuit, this would constitute the most effectual means of recommending them to notice. Whatever is good and valuable in the masonic system would be preserved and maintained by such a practice, and the science would become so unobjectionable in the opinion of the world, that all mankind, if they did not join our ranks, would at least respect our professions, and esteem the motive for our association for the sake of its visible results.

COMMEMORATIVE. Commemorative festivals are incidental to all institutions and systems of religious worship, and are used by Freemasons for the purpose of promoting the interests and increasing the popularity of the Order, of extending the personal acquaintance of the brethren, and of ensuring harmony amongst the members by a social interchange of sentiment, mutual professions of good will towards each other, and benevolence to the Craft at large.

COMMITTEE. It being essential to the interests of the Craft, that all matters of business to be brought under the consideration of the Grand Lodge, should be previously known to the Grand Officers and Masters of lodges, that, through them, all the representatives of such lodges may be apprized of such business, and be prepared to decide thereon, without being taken by surprise, a general committee, consisting of the present and past Grand Officers, and the Master of every regular lodge shall meet on the Wednesday immediately preceding each quarterly communication; at which meeting, all reports or representations from the Most Worshipful Grand Master, or any board or committee appointed by the Grand Lodge shall be read; and any member of the Grand Lodge intending to make a motion therein, or to submit any matter to its consideration, shall, at such general committee, state, in writing, the nature of his intended motion or business, that the same may be read. No motion, or other matter shall be brought into discussion in the Grand Lodge, unless it shall have been previously communicated to this general committee.— *Constitutions.*

COMMON GAVEL teaches us to lop off excrescences, and smooth surfaces; or, in other words, to correct irregularities, and reduce man to a proper level; so that by quiet deportment, he may, in the school of discipline, learn to be content. What the common gavel is to the workman, enlightened reason is to the passions; it curbs ambition, depresses envy, moderates anger, and encourages good dispositions.

COMMUNICATIONS. Four lodges shall be holden, for quarterly communication, in each year, viz., on the first Wednesday in the months of March, June, September, and December, at which none shall be present but the proper members, without permission of the Grand Master, or presiding Grand Officer. No visitor shall speak to any question without leave of the Grand Master, nor shall he, on any occasion, be permitted to vote.—*Constitutions.*

COMPANION. The title by which Royal Arch Masons address each other, and is equivalent to the word Brother in the Lodge. It is supposed to refer to the companionship which existed among the ancient Jews while in captivity, from the destruction of the first temple by Nebuchadnezzar, until their return to Jerusalem with Zerubbabel, by permission of Cyrus, King of Persia.

COMPASSES. The compasses ought to keep us within the bonds of union with all mankind, but more especially with our brother Masons; and may every one whose hands have lifted this great light continue to be guided by it in all his actions! By the compasses the kilful architect is enabled accurately to determine the elative proportions of all parts of the building when he is laying it down upon the tracing-board for the use of the workmen. Without accurate measurement, and thereby acquired symmetry and eurythmy, or beautiful and skilful proportioning of all its parts unto the whole, architectural beauty is not attainable. Without cultivated and amiable conduct—without benevolent feelings and charitable actions towards each other, no endearing bond amongst mankind is conceivable; for so long as mankind confine themselves to acts of justice alone to each other, so long must they be kept asunder by cold civility. It is only the calm affection of pure philanthropy which can unite them in the closer bonds of fraternal affection. A circle or line drawn by the compasses is also an emblem of eternity, and commonly represented by a serpent in the form of a circle.—*Gadicke.*

COMPLAINT. If any complaint be brought, the brother found guilty shall stand to the award and determination of the lodge, who are the proper and competent judges of all such controversies (unless you carry them by appeal to the Grand Lodge), and to whom they ought to be referred, unless a lord's work be hindered the meanwhile, in which case a particular reference may be made; but you must never go to law about what concerneth Masonry, without an absolute necessity apparent to the lodge.

COMPOSITE. The Composite order of architecture is so called from being composed out of the other orders. It is also called the Roman or Italic order, as having been invented by the Romans, conformably to the rest, which are denominated from the people among whom they had their rise.

CONCEALMENT. Keep the door of thy lips nor ever let the frantic moments of revenge wound that which, in sober reflection, perhaps thou wouldst wish, in vain, to spend years to heal. Think the best, but never speak the worst; reverence and imitate the good qualities of others, but to all their defects, whether real or imaginary, be a Mason in secrecy, and thus prove to the world—whose eye is curious, indeed, over Masons—that one of the secrets of Masonry is the concealment of our brother's fault, which, by discovery, could neither be amended nor obliterated.

CONCLUSION. Let us hear the conclusion of the whole matter. Fear God and keep his commandments, for this is the whole duty of man. For God shall bring every work into judgment, with every secret thing, whether it be good or whether it be evil.—*Solomon.*

CONCORD. The Master of each lodge should found his government in concord and universal love ; for as the Great Architect moves the system with his finger, and touches the spheres with harmony, so that the morning stars together sing the songs of gratitude, and the floods clap their hands, amidst the invariable beauties of order ; so should we, rejoicing, be of one accord and of one law, in unanimity, in charity, and in affection, moving by one unchanging system, and actuated by one principle, rectitude of manners.—*Hutchinson.*

CONFIDENCE. What the ignorant call "the oath," is simply an obligation, covenant, and promise enacted previously to the divulging of the specialities of the Order, and our means of recognizing each other ; and that they shall be kept from the knowledge of the world, lest their original intent should be thwarted, and their benevolent purport prevented. Now pray what harm is there in this ? Do you not all, when you have anything of a private nature which you are willing to confide in a particular friend, before you tell him what it is, demand a solemn promise of secrecy ? And is there not the utmost propriety in knowing whether your friend is determined to keep your secret before you presume to reveal it ?—*Harris.*

CONSECRATING. The day of consecration was

annually held as a festival by the brethren of the lodge; and as it is frequently the case that none of those who laid the foundation of the building, and who first taught how it was to be carried on, are in existence, it is a most solemn festival. On this occasion the building must be duly surveyed, and those parts which have become decayed by age must be repaired. When this has been properly done—when the Great Architect of the Universe has been thanked for the blessings he has conferred upon the lodge and its members during the year which has passed—when His assistance has been earnestly implored for the time to come, and when the members have most solemnly pledged themselves zealously to devote themselves to His service—then, and not till then, can they go cheerfully to the banquet; for, by holding a masonic banquet alone, no lodge can duly celebrate this festival.—*Gadicke.*

CONSTITUTING. The following is the manner of constituting a new lodge. A lodge is duly formed; and, after prayer, an ode in honour of Masonry is sung. The Grand Master is then informed by the Secretary that the brethren present desire to be formed into a new lodge, &c. The petition, the dispensation, and the warrant, or charter of constitution, are now read. The minutes of the lodge while under dispensation are likewise read, and, being approved, are declared regular and valid, and signed by the Grand Master. The Grand Master inquires if the brethren approve of the officers who are nominated in the warrant to preside over them. This being signified in masonic form, an oration on the nature and design of the institution is delivered. The lodge is then consecrated according to ceremonies proper and usual on these occasions, but not proper to be written, and the Grand Master constitutes the lodge in ancient form.— *Constitutions.*

CONSUMMATUM EST. The ne plus ultra of Masonry varies in different systems. With some it is one of the Kadoshes, with others the Rose Croix; and with the Ancient Accepte it is the thirty-third degree. With all, however, the possession of it is considered indispensable to those who emulate masonic perfection; and no person can be admitted to it who is not master of all the previous degrees. It concludes with the words—consummatum est.

CONTROVERSY. Masonry is a universal system, and teaches the relative and social duties of man on the broad and extensive basis of general philanthropy. A Jew, a Mahometan, or a Pagan, may attend our lodges without fear of hearing his peculiar doctrines or mode of faith called in question by a comparison with others which are repugnant to his creed, because a permanent and unalterable landmark of Masonry is, the total absence and exclusion of religious or political controversy. Each of these professors practices a system of morality suited to the sanctions of his religion, which, as it emanated from the primitive system of divine worship, bears some resemblance to it, and consequently he can hear moral precepts inculcated without imputing a designed reference to any peculiar mode of faith.

COPESTONE. The uppermost and last-laid stone of a building. Operative Masons, at the completion of the edifice, still observe the custom of celebrating the laying of the Copestone. The Most Excellent Master's degree, as conferred in Royal Arch Chapters, owes much of its impressive ceremonies to " the celebration of the Copestone."

CORINTHIAN. The Corinthian is the noblest, richest, and most delicate of all the orders of architecture. Villipandus supposes the Corinthian capitol to have taken its origin from an ornament in King Solomon's Temple, the leaves whereof were those of the palm tree.

CORN. Corn was a symbol of the resurrection, which is significantly referred to in the third degree of Masonry Jesus Christ compares himself to a corn of wheat falling into the ground, as a symbol of resurrection. St. Paul says, the sower sows a simple grain of corn, no matter of what kind, which at its proper season rises to light, clothed in verdure. So also is the resurrection of the dead. The apostle might, says Calmet, have instanced the power of God in the progress of vivification; and might have inferred that the same power which could confer life originally, would certainly restore it to those particles which once had possessed it. It is possible he has done this covertly, having chosen to mention vegetable seed, that being most obvious to common notice; and yet not intending to terminate his reference in any quality of vegetation.

CORNER-STONE. The principal and important stone in the foundation of an edifice. This stone is usually laid in the north-east corner, and unites the two walls. It is generally deposited in its place with solemn and appropriate ceremonies, and is the depository of mementos of the times in which it is laid, for the use and benefit of posterity. Its position accounts, in a rational manner, for the general disposition of a newly-initiated candidate, when enlightened; but uninstructed he is accounted to be the most superficial part of Masonry. An important symbol in the Mark Master's degree.

COUNTRY LODGES. Country lodges are under the immediate superintendence of the Grand Master of their respective provinces; to whom, or to his deputy, they are to apply in all cases of difficulty or doubt, and to whom all complaints and disputes must be transmitted. If those officers should neglect to proceed in the business, the application or complaint may be transmitted to the Board of General Purposes; and an appeal in all cases lies to the Grand Lodge or Grand Master.—*Constitutions.*

COURSE. In the entire course of lectures attached to the three degrees of Masonry, including the final triumph of the Order in the Royal Arch, such events are held prominently to view as are calculated to remind us of our Christian privileges, emanating from, and connected with, the great promises and advantages which were enjoyed by holy men under the patriarchal and Mosaic dispensations. The creation of the world; the expulsion of our first parents from Paradise, with the consoling promise which accompanied that terrible punishment of sin; the translation of Enoch; the deluge; Abraham and Sarah; Hagar and Ishmael; the offering of Isaac; the peregrinations of Jacob; the deliverance from Egyptian captivity; the wanderings in the wilderness; the building of the first and second Temples, the captivities; the revelation of the cherubic emblem of the Deity; and the annunciation of the Messiah by John the Baptist. The disquisitions on these important points, which embrace also many collateral subjects of equal interest, are recommended by the sublime elucidations of symbol ical machinery with which they are accompanied.

COWAN. From the affair of Jeptha, an Ephraimite was termed a cowan or worthless fellow. In Egypt a cohen was the title of a priest or prince, and a term of honour. Bryant, speaking of the harpies, says they were priests of the sun; and as cohen was the name of a dog as well as a priest, they are termed by Appollonius—"the dogs of Jove." Now St. John cautions the Christian brethren that "without are dogs," (κυνες) cowans or listeners; and St. Paul exhorts the Christians to "beware of dogs, because they are evil workers." Now κυων a dog, or evil worker, is the masonic cowan. The above priests or metaphorical dogs, were also called cercyonians or cer-cowans, because they were lawless in their behaviour towards strangers. A writer of the "Freemasons' Quarterly Review" thus explains the word. "I trace it," says he, "to the Greek verb ακουω, to hear or listen to, from which it is but parcè detorta; and we have high authority for so importing words from one language to another." Our illustrious brother, Sir Walter Scott, makes one of his characters in "Rob Roy" say—"she does not value a lawsuit mair as a cowan, and ye may tell Mac Cullummore that Allan Iverach said sae."

CRAFT. The term applied to persons, collectively in a trade, or mechanical occupation. In free or speculative Masonry it signifies the whole Masonic family, wherever dispersed.

CRAFTSMAN. As a Craftsman you are to encourage industry and reward merit; supply the wants and relieve the necessities of brethren and fellows to the utmost of your power and ability; and on no account to wrong them or see them wronged, but timely to apprise them

of approaching danger, and view their interest as inseparable from your own. Such is the nature of your
engagements as a Craftsman, and these duties you are
now bound, by the most sacred ties, to observe.—*Charge,
Second Degree.*

CREATION. It is the general voice of Scripture
that God finished the whole of the creation in six days
and rested the seventh; giving us an example that
we might labour six days and rest the seventh from all
manual exercises. He who labours with his mind by
worldly schemes and plans on the Sabbath day, is as
culpable as he who labours with his hands in his accustomed calling. It is by the authority of God that the
Sabbath is set apart for rest and religious purposes, as
the six days of the week are appointed for labour.—
Adam Clarke.

CRIMSON. This rich and beautiful colour is emblematical of fervency and zeal. It is the appropriate
colour of the Royal Arch degree; and admonishes us
that we should be fervent in the exercise of our devotions to God, and zealous in our endeavours to promote
the happiness of man.

CROSS. According to an ancient tradition, the Temple of Solomon had three foundations, the
first of which contained seventy stones, five
rows from north to south, and fourteen in
each row running from east to west. The
centre row corresponded with the upright
of a cross, whose transverse was formed by
two stones on each side of the eleventh
stone from the east end of the centre row
of which the upright is formed, and the
fourth stone from the west end of it. This
stone, which hence occupies the place of
the crossing of the beams, was under the
centre of the S. S., where was deposited
the Ark of the Covenant and Shekinah.
This design contained an evident reference
to the cross of Christ, and was so placed that the part
where the heart of Christ would be at the time of his
crucifixion was under the centre of the S. S.

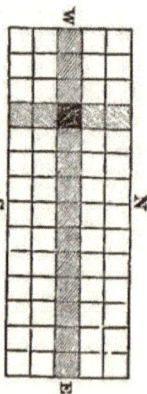

CRUSADES. There is not an instance of the European states uniting in any one enterprise save the holy war; and from thence we most rationally must conceive the present number of Masons, dispersed over the face of Europe, was principally derived. By the Crusades, the number of our society would be greatly augmented; the occasion itself would revive the rules of Masonry they being so well adapted to that purpose, and also professional of the Christian faith, from whence sprang the spirit of the enterprise. After these pursuits subsided, bodies of men would be found in every country from whence the levies were called; and what would preserve the society in every state, even during the persecutions of zealots, the Master Mason's Order, under its present principles, is adapted to every sect of Christians. It originated from the earliest era of Christianity, in honour to, or in confession of, the religion and faith of Christians, before the poison of sectaries was diffused over the church.—*Hutchinson.*

CRUX ANSATA. This sign, originally signifying life, was adopted as a Christian emblem, either from its similarity to the shape of a cross, or from its being considered the symbol of a state of future existence.

CRYPT. A subterranean vault. On the top of the mount of Olives was a vast and very ancient crypt, in "the shape of a cone of immense size; the vertex alone appearing level with the soil, and exhibiting by its section at the top a small circular aperture, the sides extending below to a great depth lined with a hard red stucco." It was an idolatrous construction, perhaps as old as Solomon, and profaned by Josiah. If Solomon built this crypt, he might, as the Jews say he did, construct one of the same kind beneath the Temple, for the reception of the ark, &c., in case of danger; but this must remain undecided till the "times of the Gentiles are fulfilled."—*Calmet.*

CUBE. The cube is a symbol of truth, of wisdom, of moral perfection. The new Jerusalem promised by the Apocalypse, is equal in length, breadth, and height. The mystical city ought to be considered as a new church, where divine wisdom will reign. Isaiah, announcing the coming of the Messiah, said, " He shall dwell in the highest place of the solid rock, and the water which shall flow from him shall give life."

CUBICAL STONE. At the building of the Temple of Jerusalem, an unexpected and afflicting event occurred, which threw the Masons engaged in the work into the greatest confusion. The G. M. (H. A. B.) had sent to certain F. Cs. thirteen stones, and directed that with these they should complete a small square near the cape-stone, being the only portion of the fabric which remained unfinished. Every stone of the temple was formed into a square, containing five equilateral triangles, each equilateral triangle being equal to a cube, and each side and base of the triangles being equal to a plumb line. The space, therefore, which remained to be completed was the last triangle of the last stone, and equal to the eighth part of the plumb-line, or ⅛ of the circle, and ¹⁄₅ of the triangle, which number is in Hebrew יה c the great name of the Almighty. The thirteen stones consisted of all the fragments which remained from the building, and comprised two cubes in two divisions. In the first was contained one cube in an entire piece, and in the second a cube in twelve parts: viz., 4½ parts in 1 piece, 2 parts in 4 pieces, 1 part in 1 piece, and ½ part in 6 pieces; total 12 pieces. The F. Cs. carried the broken cube to S. K. I., who in conjunction with H. K. T. directed that they should be placed along with the jewels of the Craft, on a cubic stone encrusted with gold, in the centre of a deep cavern within the foundations of the temple, and further ordered, that the door of this mysterious court should be built up with large stones, in order that no one in future should be able to gain admission into this mysterious apartment. At the rebuilding of the temple, however, three F. Cs. lately returned from Babylon, in the course of their labours inadvertently stumbled upon this mysterious recess. They discovered the fractured cube, and carried the pieces to Z. J. H., who recognized in the four pieces the XXXX., and accordingly advanced the F. Cs. to a new order in Masonry for having accomplished this discovery.— *Tytlor.*

CUBIT. A measure of length employed by the ancients equal to the length of the arm from the elbow to the tip of the middle finger. Among different nations the length of the cubit differed. The cubit of the Romans was about 17⅔ inches; that of the Hebrews 22 inches, but its length is now generally stated at 18 English inches.

CURIOSITY. Freemasonry has in all ages excited the curiosity of mankind; and curiosity is one of the most prevailing passions in the human breast. The mind of man is kept in a perpetual thirst after knowledge, nor can he bear to be ignorant of what he thinks others know.

CYPHER. It is not customary in Freemasonry to write in cypher, neither is there any law commanding it to be done, although there is a very ancient cypher extant taken from the Square and Triangle. This is also called the Ammonian writing of the ancient Egyptian priests. In the year 1808, Bro. J. G. Bruman, Director of the Academy of Commerce and Professor of the Mathematics at Mannheim, published a programme of a Pangraphia or universal writing, and at the same time an Arithmetical Krypto-graphic, which was to be extremely useful in Freemasonry; but so far as we know this work has never appeared.—*Gadicke.*

CYPHER WRITING. The system of cypher writing has been found so convenient as a depository of ineffable secrets, that it has descended down to our own times, and various methods have been prescribed for its use, any of which will answer the intended purpose; for the interpretation is absolutely impracticable without a key. The simplest kind of cypher consists of a simple transposition of the letters of the alphabet, and appears to have been one of the earliest specimens of this kind of secret communication which was used in modern times, Its mystery, however, is perfect; and the places of the several letters may be so varied as to preclude the possibility of detection.

```
a  b  c  d  e  f  g  h  i  j  k  l  m
n  o  p  q  r  s  t  u  v  w  x  y  z
```

With this key the cypher n serr naq nppregrq znfba, will be found to contain the words—"A Free and Accepted Mason;" but if the key be varied thus:—

a	b	c	d	e	f	g	h	i	j	k	l	m
z	y	x	w	v	u	t	s	r	q	p	o	n

the same words will stand—z uivv zmw zxxvkgvw nzhlm And the key will admit of variations ad infinitum Sometimes the mystery was increased by the junction of four or five words into one. On this plan the abov expression would constitute the forminable word, zuivv-zmwzxxvkgvwnzhlm.

CYRUS. This prince was mentioned by the prophet Isaiah, two hundred years before he was born, as the restorer of the temple at Jerusalem. And accordingly, after the seventy years of captivity in Babylon were accomplished, it pleased the Lord to direct him to issue the following proclamation. The Lord God of Heaven hath given me all the kingdoms of the earth, and he hath charged me to build him an house at Jerusalem, which is in Judah. Who is there among you of all his people? his God be with him, and let him go up to Jerusalem which is in Judah, and build the house of the Lord God of Israel, (he is the God) which is in Jerusalem.

DANCING. Dancing is not a masonic accomplishment, although it usually accompanied the rites of the spurious Freemasonry. The idolatrous Jews made it a part of the worship which they paid to the golden calf. The Amalekites danced after their victory at Ziklag, and Job makes it part of the character of the prosperous wicked (that is, of those who, placing all their happiness in the enjoyments of sense, forget God and religion), that their children dance. The dancing of the profligate Herodias's daughter pleased Herod so highly, that he promised to give her whatever she asked, and accordingly, at her desire, and in compliment to her, he commanded John the Baptist to be beheaded in prison. Notwithstanding this, some Provincial Grand Masters instead of taking the brethren at their provincial meetings to church, as in the good old times of Inwood, Harris, and

Oliver, for the purpose of invoking the blessing of God
on their labours, lead them to a ball in full masonic costume, as the gentry of old used to exhibit their servants
and retainers at an assize or county meeting in blue coats
and badges; whence instead of a praying institution as
Masonry is, it becomes a dancing institution, which it
decidedly is not.—*Freemasons' Quarterly Review.*

DARKNESS. The darkness of Masonry is invested
with a pure and dignified reference, because it is attached
to a system of truth. It places before the mind a series
of the most awful and impressive images. It points to
the darkness of death and the obscurity of the grave, as
the forerunners of a more brilliant and never-fading
light which follows at the resurrection of the just.
Figure to yourselves the beauty and strict propriety of
this reference, ye who have been raised to the third
degree of Masonry. Were your minds enveloped in the
shades of that darkness? So shall you again be involved
in the darkness of the grave, when death has drawn his
sable curtain round you. Did you rise to a splendid
scene of intellectual brightness? So, if you are obedient
to the precepts of Masonry and the dictates of religion,
shall you rejoice on the resurrection morn, when the
clouds of error and imperfection are separated from your
mind, and you behold with unveiled eye the glories
which issue from the expanse of heaven, the everlasting
splendours of the throne of God!

DARKNESS VISIBLE. The light of a Master
Mason is darkness visible, serving only to express that
gloom which rests on the prospect of futurity. It is that
mysterious veil which the Eureka of human reason cannot penetrate, unless assisted by that light which is from
above.

DAVID. The uninterrupted prosperity which David
enjoyed, inspired him with a design of building a sumptuous temple for the worship of the Deity, deeming it
in a high degree criminal to permit the ark of God to
remain in a tabernacle at a time when he resided in a
palace, constructed and ornamented with the utmost
profusion of elegance and splendour. And to this

was further incited by an ancient prediction of Moses. But David as yet was ignorant of the place where the Temple of the Lord was to be erected; for it still remained in the possession of the Jebusites, and on that spot Araunah had established his threshing floor. At this period Mount Moriah exhibited a picturesque appearance, being covered by groves of olive trees; and for this reason it was called " the field of the wood." After David had made the above determination, the Lord directed Nathan the prophet to communicate to him, "Thus saith the Lord, shalt thou build me an house for to dwell in. Whe' thy days be fulfilled, and thou shalt sleep with thy fathers, I will set up thy seed after thee, which shall proceed out of thy bowels, and I will establish his kingdom. He shall build an house for my name, and I will establish the throne of his kingdom for ever I will be his father, and he shall be my son."

DAY AND NIGHT. The sun is the monarch of the day, which is the state of light. The moon of the night, or the state of darkness. The rays of the sun falling on the atmosphere, are refracted and diffused over the whole of that hemisphere of the earth immediately under his orb; while those rays of that vast luminary which, because of the earth's smallness in comparison of the sun, are diffused on all sides beyond the earth, falling on the opaque disc of the moon, are reflected back on what may be called the lower hemisphere, or that part of the earth which is opposite to the part which is illuminated by the sun; and as the earth completes a revolution on its own axis in about twenty-four hours, consequently each hemisphere has alternate day and night.—*Adam Clarke.*

DAY'S WORK. The day's work closed when the sun set in the west. All the expressions used in scripture about hired servants imply that they were hired by the day. This is still the case in the east, where not only labourers, but mechanics, whether they work for a householder or for a master in their own craft, are paid by the day, and regularly expect their day's wages when the sun goes down. It has never come to our knowledge that they work at any trade after sunset, even in winter.

DEACON. The duties attached to the office of a deacon are, " to convey messages, to obey commands, and to assist at initiations, and in the general practice of the rites and ceremonies of the Order." The jewel of their office is a dove, as an emblem of peace, and characteristic of their duties.

DEATH. The heathen nations, before the coming of Christ, wanted the blessing of revelation, and knew nothing of the destination of man after he was laid in the silent tomb. One of their own poets tells us this: "Alas," says he, " when the plants and flowers of the garden have perished, they revive again, and bloom the succeeding year; but we, mighty, wise, and powerful men, when once we die, remain insensible in the hollow tomb and sleep a long and endless sleep—a sleep from which we never shall be awakened." Seneca said, " *post mortem nihil est*." Virgil describes death as an " iron sleep, and an eternal night." (En. x. 745.) But so inconsistent were the heathen philosophers upon these abstruse subjects, which they had received only from dark and uncertain tradition, that in the sixth book of the Eneid, the same poet describes with great minuteness the places of reward and punishment which are assigned to mankind after death, as the consequence of their personal responsibility.—*Bishop Mant.*

DECLARATION. Every candidate, previous to his admission, must subscribe his name at full length to a declaration of the following import, viz.:—" To the Worshipful Masters, Wardens, Officers, and Members of the Lodge of ———, No. —. I, ———, being a free man, and of the full age of twenty-one years, do declare, that unbiassed by the improper solicitation of friends, and uninfluenced by mercenary or other unworthy motive, I freely and voluntarily offer myself a candidate for the mysteries of Masonry; that I am prompted by a favourable opinion conceived of the institution, and a desire of knowledge, and that I will cheerfully conform to all the ancient usages and established customs of the Order. Witness my hand this   day of   . Witness.— *Constitutions.*

DECLARING OFF. When a brother ceases to visit a Lodge, and to pay his monthly subscriptions, he thereby declares himself off the lodge. When a brother requires to leave the lodge for a few minutes, either at labour or at the banquet, he must request leave to do so. Many brethren whose bad conduct is brought before the lodge, and who are afraid that they will be excluded or expelled, take this means of declaring off. We also make use of this expression when any lodge has ceased to assemble for a length of time. A Freemasons' lodge, or assembly of the brethren, is properly tyled when none but brethren are present, and when no stranger can gain admittance. —*Gädicke.*

DECORATIONS. In disposing of the furniture and decorations of a lodge, great discrimination is required; and very frequently the imposing appearance which a lodge ought to present to the eye, is lost for want of due attention to these preliminary arrangements. The expert Mason will be convinced that the walls of a lodge room ought neither to be absolutely naked nor too much decorated. A chaste disposal of symbolical ornaments in the right places, and according to propriety, relieves the dulness and vacuity of a blank space; and though but sparingly used, will produce a striking impression and contribute to the general beauty and solemnity of the scene.

DEDICATION. From the building of the first temple at Jerusalem to the Babylonish captivity, the lodges of Freemasons were dedicated to King Solomon, from thence to the advent of Christ to Zerubbabel, who built the second temple, and from that time till the final destruction of the temple by Titus, they were dedicated to St. John the Baptist. But owing to the losses which were sustained by that memorable occurrence, Freemasonry declined; many lodges were broken up, and the brethren were afraid to meet without an acknowledged head. At a secret meeting of the Craft, holden in the city of Benjamin, this circumstance was much regretted, and they deputed seven brethren to solicit St. John the Evangelist, who was at that time Bishop of Ephesus, to accept the office of Grand Master. He replied to the deputation, that though well stricken in years, having been in his youth initiated into Masonry, he would acquiesce in their request, thus completing by his learning what the other St. John had begun by his zeal; and thus drew what Freemasons call a line—parallel; ever since which, the lodges in all Christian countries have been dedicated to the two St. Johns.—*York Lectures.*

DEFAMATION. To defame our brother, or suffer him to be defamed, without interesting ourselves for the preservation of his name and character, there is scarce the shadow of an excuse to be found. Defamation is always wicked. Slander and evil speaking are the pests of civil society, are the disgrace of every degree of religious profession, and the poisonous bane of all brotherly love. Defamation is never absolutely, or indeed at all, necessary; for suppose your brother has faults, are you obliged, because you speak of him, to discover them? has he no good qualities? sure all have some good ones; make them then, though ever so few, the subject of your conversation, if ye must talk of him; and if he has no good qualities, speak not of him at all.—*Inwood.*

DEGREE. A degree, as the word implies, is merely a grade or step, or preparation, as one grade is but preparatory to another higher, and so on in progression to the "ne plus ultra." A degree sometimes, but not in Freemasonry, means a class or order.

DEGREES. Why are there degrees in Freemasonry? The reason why this question is asked by the men of the world, is because they are men and not schoolboys who are initiated, and because the whole of the Order could be communicated to them at one time. But still there are degrees, or steps, and truly for this simple reason, as there is no art or science which can be communicated at one time, so neither can Freemasonry; and although they are men of mature age who are initiated, yet they require to be proved step by step. Freemasonry is a science which requires both time and experience, and more time than many Masons, especially government officers or tradesmen, can devote to it; the only time they in fact can appropriate to this purpose being their hours of recreation. It is, therefore, good that it is communicated by degrees. Those degrees are communicated in the lodge at the end of certain determinate periods, or immediately after each other, according to the regulations of the lodge, or the candidate's power of comprehension. —*Gadicke*.

DEMIT. A Mason is said to demit from the Order when he withdraws from all connection with it. In the regulations of the Grand Lodge, dated 25th November, 1723, it was provided, that if the Master of a lodge is deposed, or demits, the Senior Warden shall fill the chair until the next appointment of officers.

DEMOCRACY. Symbolical Masonry, under whatever form it may be propounded, is a Catholic institution, democratic in its form and government, and universal in its operation. This is demonstrable from any of the definitions of the Order; from the free election of its chief magistrate, and the inferior governors of every private lodge, annually and by universal suffrage, and from the reputed form and extent of its lodges. If it were deprived of any of the above attributes it would be no longer Freemasonry; and all its beneficial effects upon the mind and manners of men, would be scattered to the winds of heaven.

DEPORTMENT. Since many of our forms and operations are necessarily secreted from common inspection, the generality of mankind will make up their opinion of the society from the deportment of its members. This ought to serve as a very powerful call to every one of us, uniformly and openly to display those qualities and virtues so strongly inculcated and warmly recommended in the lodge. To little purpose shall we commend the institution, and boast the excellence of its principles and purposes, if our lives give not corroborative evidence to our assertions, and prove not the propriety of our encomiums. If we appear neither wiser nor better than the uninitiated, the world will begin to suspect the efficacy of our tenets; and if no good effects are apparent, they will doubt whether any are produced.—*Harris*.

DEPTH. The depth of a lodge is figuratively said to extend from the surface to the centre.

DEPUTY GRAND MASTER. This officer is to be appointed annually by the Grand Master, on the day of his installation, and, if present, is to be immediately installed according to ancient usage. He must have been master of some regular lodge. In the absence of the Grand Master, the Deputy possesses all his powers and privileges.—*Constitutions.*

DESIGN. The initiation into the first or entered apprentice's degree was made to partake, in a slighter proportion, of those trials of physical and moral courage for which the admission into the ancient and chiefly Egyptian mysteries were famous. The second or Fellowcraft's, was rendered interesting by those scientific instructions and philosophical lectures which characterized later parts of the mysteries; though both degrees were made to tend to the glory of that God who had given such wonderful faculties to them and to the welfare of their fellow-creatures. Thus instructed in morals and science, the third or Master Mason's degree led them to that great truth which the sublimest part of even the heathen mysteries, though it too seldom succeeded, was intended to teach, and the faithful believer was assured of a future life and immortality beyond the grave. And, whereas, the heathens had taught this only by the application of a fable to their purpose, the wisdom of the *pious* Grand Mason of the Israelitish Masons took advantage of a real circumstance which would more forcibly impress the sublime truths he intended to inculcate upon the minds of all brethren. Such is a brief outline, intelligible, I trust, to the members of the Order, of the design of that beautiful system which, then established, has long been the admiration of the world, and has stood the test of ages amid every persecution.— *Archdeacon Mant.*

DIAGRAMS. The three most perfect of all geometrical diagrams, are the equilateral triangle, the square, and the equal hexagon. To this we may add an observation, for which we are indebted to our Grand Master Pythagoras, that there exists no other regular equilateral forms, whose multiples are competent to fill up and occupy the whole space about a given centre which can only be effected by six equilateral triangles, four squares and three equal hexagons.—*Hemming*.

DIAMOND OF THE DESERT. Sir Walter Scott, in one of those splendid tales of fiction which have immortalized his name, describes a small spot of verdure amidst an arid waste, which was figuratively denominated the Diamond of the Desert. Amongst Irishmen, too long estranged by political feuds and sectarian contentions, Freemasonry may be esteemed as the moral Diamond of the Desert, within whose hallowed precincts are united men of worth of every class; holding the most antagonistic principles—united by a mysterious and unrevealable bond—joined by a tie of brotherhood which tends to the subjugation of prejudice, the development of charity, and the masterdom of those absurd and irreligious antipathies, which array in hostility creatures of the same God, for all of whom, without distinction, the great sacrifice of Calvary has been consummated.— *O'Ryan*.

DIDACTICAL. The fourth section of the first lecture is called didactical or perceptive. The assertion is fully made out, that morality is the great subject with which Freemasonry is conversant. Hence it follows, that the virtuous Mason, after he has enlightened his own mind by those sage and moral precepts, is the more ready to enlighten and enlarge the understanding of others.— *Hemming*.

DIFFERENCES. All differences or complaints that cannot be accommodated privately, or in some regular lodge, shall be reduced into writing and delivered to the Grand Secretary, who shall lay them before the Grand Master, or the proper board or committee appointed by the Grand Lodge. When all parties shall have been summoned to attend thereon, and the case shall have been investigated, such order and adjudication may be made as shall be authorised by the laws and regulations of Masonry.—*Constitutions*.

DIFFUSION. An ancient masonic tradition relates that our G. M. King Solomon, struck with the universal harmony produced by the admirable arrangements which had been adopted amongst the workmen, conceived an idea of forming an universal bond of brotherly love, which should unite all nations in the pursuit of virtue and science. For this purpose, he admitted into his system those illustrious sages who visited Jerusalem from every part of the globe, and allowed them to participate in his mysteries. And hence, when they returned home they diffused Freemasonry over the whole face of the earth.

DIRECTOR OF CEREMONIES. The Grand Director of Ceremonies is annually appointed by the Grand Master on the day of his installation. He must be a Master Mason, and punctually attend all the ordinary and extraordinary meetings of the Grand Lodge.

DISCIPLINE. At the building of the temple the hours of labour and rest and refreshment were distinctly regulated, and enforced with such strictness that every brother who absented himself from his work, even for the shortest period, was punished by a heavy fine deducted from his wages, because he violated the unity of labour, by which a correct result could be alone accomplished. The precise hours of commencing work and calling off to refreshment, were stipulated in their general contracts, and conducted by known signals and reports, and they were not allowed to exceed them by a single minute. This perfect system of discipline is worthy of imitation amongst the Masons of the present day, if they wish to attain the same excellence in the moral edifice which the Craft is intended to raise.

DISCLOSING. The means devised for promoting the welfare of Freemasonry are the secrecy, the language, and the government of the Lodge. Secrecy is wisely adopted to begin, and continue Masonry, because it is necessary. If the lodge should work in public, who in a short time could be its members? Besides secrecy is, of itself, a virtue; and is taught as such in the lodge, and taught effectually. Men should be able to keep their own secrets, and should never violate the confidence of others. Masonic secrecy is a mysterious thing, but an indisputable fact. The most tattling man, if he be a Mason, keeps this one secret; there is no risk of him.— Enrage, punish, expel—he never tells. Mad, drunk, or crazy—he never tells. Does he talk in his sleep? It is not about Masonry. Bribe him in his wants, tempt him in his pleasures, threaten him or torture him, he is a martyr here—but he never tells.—*Blanchard.*

DISCOVERY. At the building of the Second Temple, the foundations were first opened and cleared from the accumulation of rubbish, that a level site might be procured for the commencement of the building. While engaged in excavations for this purpose, three fortunate sojourners are said to have discovered an avenue supported by seven pair of pillars, perfect and entire, which from their situation had escaped the fury of the flames that had consumed the temple, and the desolation of war which had destroyed the city. This secret vault, which had been built by Solomon, as a secure depository for certain valuable secrets, that would have inevitably been lost without some such expedient for their preservation, communicated by a subterranean passage with the king's palace; but at the destruction of Jerusalem, the entrance having been closed by the rubbish of falling buildings, it had been now discovered by the appearance of a key-stone amongst the foundations of the Sanctum Sanctorum. A careful inspection was then made, and the invaluable secrets were placed in safe custody.

DISPENSATION. Is an instrument which legalizes an act or ceremony, such as opening a lodge without a warrant, forming a masonic procession, &c., which would be illegal without it. The power of granting dispensations is very properly vested in the Grand and Provincial Grand Masters or their deputies, who are the best judges on what occasions it ought to be exercised.

DISPUTES. The candidate at his initiation was formally exhorted that he is never to invest himself with the badge of a Mason should there be any brother in the lodge with whom he is at variance, or against whom he entertains any animosity. In such case it is expected that he will invite the brother to withdraw, in order that the difference between them may be amicably settled; which, if happily effected, they are then at liberty to clothe themselves, and work with that love and harmony which ought always to characterize the Free and Accepted Mason. But if, unfortunately, the differences be of such a nature as cannot be so speedily adjusted, it were better that one or both should retire, than, by their presence, they should disturb the harmony of the lodge.

DISSOLVED LODGES. If the majority of any lodge should determine to quit the society, the constitution, or power of assembling, remains with the rest of its members who adhere to their allegiance. If all the members of a lodge withdraw themselves, their constitution ceases and becomes extinct; and all the authority thereby granted or enjoyed reverts to the Grand Lodge. —*Constitutions.*

DISTRESS. The sign of distress is said, in the book of Raziel, to be derived from the expulsion of Adam from the Garden of Eden. He communicated it, along with the divine mysteries he had learned there, to his son Loth; Loth communicated them to Enoch; Enoch to Methusalem; Methusalem to Lamech; Lamech to Noah; Noah to Sem; Sem to Abraham; Abraham to Isaac; Isaac to Jacob; Jacob to Levy; Levy to Kelhoth; Kelhoth to Amram; Amram to Moses; Moses to Joshua; Joshua to the Elders; the Elders to the Prophets; the Prophets to the Wise Men; and then from one to the other down to Solomon. The sign of distress is very little different from that of the Freemasons.—*Rosenberg.*

DIURNAL PROGRESS. The sun rises in the three stages of its diurnal progress, first in the east to open the day, and dispenses life and nourishment to the whole creation. This is well represented by the Worshipful Master, who is placed in the east to open the lodge, and who imparts light, knowledge, and instruction, to all under his direction. When it arrives at its greatest altitude in the south, where its beams are most piercing and the cool shade most refreshing, it is then also well represented by the Junior Warden, who is placed in the south to observe its approach to meridian, and at the

hour of noon to call the brethren from labour to refreshment. Still pursuing its course to the west, the sun at
length closes the day, and lulls all nature to repose; it is
then fitly represented by the Senior Warden, who is
placed in the west to close the lodge by command of the
Worshipful Master, after having rendered to every one
the just reward of his labour, thus enabling them to
enjoy that repose which is the genuine fruit of honest
industry.—*Hemming*.

DIVINE LIGHTS. To the Tetragrammaton alone
no effect or action can be attributed, nor is it derived
from any. Therefore, all except this venerable name are
applied to other things in Holy Writ; from which consideration, as almost every Cabalist assumes that the
Divine Lights or Sephiroth are emanations of the First
Cause, and appertaining to it, like flames to the fire, or
rays to the sun; or if the divinity of the Lord is infused
into them, then by this mode the philosophers and
Cabalists agree, since by giving this appellation to those
lights, it is given to the First Cause, which is infused
and shines in them.—*Manasseh Ben Israel*.

DIVISIONS. If the Master of a lodge allows a habit
of debate to become prevalent amongst the brethren,
and members, fond of displaying their rhetorical powers,
meet with encouragement from the chair, it is an evil
which carries ruin in its train; divisions disunite the
brethren; parties are formed by a systematic canvass to
carry improper motions into effect, and mutual distrust
is the mildest consequence to be expected; for every
division leaves a certain portion of the members discon-
tented. In the warmth of debate, strong and objectionable phrases and reflections may be indiscreetly used,
which leave a thorn rankling in the bosom of those at
whom they are levelled; and in the end the minority
are certain to relax in their attendance, if not to withdraw themselves altogether from an institution where
their counsels are rejected, and their opinions treated
with contempt.

DOCTRINES. The three degrees blend doctrine,
morality, and science, tradition and history, into a grand

and beautiful system, which, if studied with attention
and practised with sincerity, will inspire a holy confidence that the Lord of Life will enable us to trample
the king of terrors beneath our feet, and lift our eyes to
the bright Morning Star, whose rising brings peace and
salvation to the faithful and obedient to the holy Word
of God. There is, indeed, scarcely a point of duty or
morality which man has been presumed to owe to God,
his neighbour, or himself, under the Patriarchal, the
Mosaic, or the Christian dispensations, which, in the construction of our symbolical system, has been untouched.
The forms and ceremonies, secrets and landmarks, the
types and allegories of Freemasonry, present copious
subjects of investigation, which cannot be easily exhausted. The nature of the lodge, its form, dimensions,
and support; its ground, situation, and covering; its
ornaments, furniture, and jewels, all unite their aid to
form a perfect code of moral and theological philosophy,
which, while it fascinates the understanding, improves
the mind, until it becomes polished like the perfect
Ashlar, and can only be tried by the square of God's
word, and the unerring compass of conscience.

DORIC. The Doric is the second of the five orders
of architecture, and is that between the Tuscan and the
Ionic. It is the most natural and best proportioned of
all the orders; all its parts being founded on the natural
position of solid bodies.

DORMER. The dormer is the window that gives
light to the entrance into the Sanctum Sanctorum.

DOUBLE CUBE. The heathen deities were many of
them represented by a cubical stone. Pausanius informs
us that a cube was the symbol of Mercury, because, like
the cube, he represented Truth. In Arabia a black stone
in the form of a double cube, was reputed to be possessed
of many occult virtues. Apollo was sometimes worshipped under the symbol of a square stone, and it is
recorded that when a fatal pestilence raged at Delphi,
the oracle was consulted as to the means proper to be
adopted for the purpose of arresting its progress, and it
commanded that the cube should be doubled. This was

understood by the priest to refer to the altar, which was
of a cubical form. They obeyed the injunction, increasing the altitude of the altar to its prescribed dimensions,
like the pedestal in a Masons' lodge, and the pestilence
ceased.

DOUBTS. It is a good rule in all doubtful matters
to suspend our opinion at least till positive proof is
obtained on which to found it. Until we have fully
ascertained the real state of the case, let us always be
willing to put the fairest construction it will admit; and
even to hope the best of a thing when appearances are
against it. Where doubt hesitates, let candour prompt;
and where justice balances, let mercy prevail. Even
where we find ourselves obliged to blame the principles
of a certain sect or party, let us not be so uncharitable
as to confound all its adherents and followers under one
general and indiscriminate censure. Especially let us
not charge them with such consequences of their tenets
as they disavow.—*Harris.*

DOVE. This bird was the diluvian messenger of
peace, and hovered over the retreating waters like a celestial harbinger of safety. Thus a lunette floating on the
surface of the ocean, attended by a dove with an olive
branch in its mouth, and encircled by a rainbow, form a
striking and expressive symbol which needs no explanation. If Freemasonry has allowed this bird to occupy a
high situation amongst its hallowed symbols, the reasons
for such an appropriation are fully competent to justify
the proceeding. The dove was an agent at the creation,
at the deluge, and at the baptism of Christ.

DRESS. At the revival in 1717, it was directed—and,
that there might be no mistake about the matter, the
canon was inserted by Anderson and Desaguliers in the
earliest code of lectures known,—that the symbolical
clothing of a Master Mason was—"skull-cap and jacket
yellow, and nether garments blue." After the middle
of the century, he was said to be "clothed in the old
colours, viz., purple, crimson, and blue;" and the reason
assigned for it was, "because they are royal, and such as
the ancient kings and princes used to wear;" and we are

informed by sacred history that the veil of the Temple was composed of those colours; and therefore they were considered peculiarly appropriate to a professor of a "royal art." The actual dress of a Master Mason was, however, a full suit of black, with white neckcloth, apron, gloves, and stockings; the buckles being of silver, and the jewels being suspended from a white ribbon by way of collar. This disposition prevailed until the Union in 1813, when it was ordered that in future the Grand Officers should be distinguished by purple, the Grand Stewards by crimson, and the Master Mason by blue, thus reverting to "the old colours" of our ancient brethren.

DUAD. The duad, representing the number 2, answers to the geometrical line, which, consisting of length without breadth, is bounded by two extreme points. It signifies darkness, fortitude, harmony and justice, because of its equal parts, and the moon because she is forked.

DUPLICATION. The duplication of a cube is the finding the side of a cube that shall be double in solidity to a given cube, which is a famous problem cultivated by the geometricians two thousand years ago. It was first proposed by the oracle of Apollo at Delphos, which being consulted about the manner of stopping a plague then raging at Athens, returned for answer, that the plague should cease when Apollo's altar, which was cubical, should be doubled. Upon this they applied themselves in good earnest to seek the duplication of the cube, which was afterwards called the Delian problem. The problem is only to be solved by finding two mean proportionals between the side of the cube, and double that side; the first whereof will be the side of the cube doubled, as was observed by Hippocrates Chrus. Leaving the consideration of the various methods which have been employed to accomplish the solution of this very important problem, it remains for me to add, that the solution of the cube's duplication constitutes the apex of the Temple; and renders a parallelipipidon, containing 16 linear units, equal to 15 linear units; thus bringing the number 16 or משיח Messiah; the great name Jah comprising the first two letters of the Tetragrammaton or ineffable name of Deity יהוה.— *Tyler.*

DUTY. Freemasonry requires you to be a good and loyal subject; true to your queen; just to your country; peaceable, honest, industrious; temperate in all things, good members of society; kind to your wives and families; courteous to your friends and neighbours; anxious to do good to all men; to love the brotherhood, to fear God, to honour the queen; and whilst you practise the weightier matters required by the law of justice, judgment, and equity, to forget not life eternal by Jesus Christ, the only sure foundation of all your hopes here, and of your eternal happiness hereafter.—*Percy.*

EAGLE. The eagle formed a constituent part of the cherubic symbol. It was referred to the prophet Daniel because he spake with angels, and received visions which relate to all time; and to St. John, who in his gospel treats of Christ's divinity, and soars to heaven like an eagle, in the Book of Revelation.

EAR OF CORN. Some old Masons appear to think that the introduction of this symbol into Freemasonry was intended to perpetuate a remembrance of the transit over the river Jordan by the armies of Israel, when they entered the land of Canaan for the first time, under the command of Joshua. This event, so important in the Jewish history, having taken place at the celebration of the passover, when the promised land was covered with fields of ripe corn, the "ear" was assumed as a symbol of that plenty which gladdened their hearts after a period of forty years in the wilderness, where they had been fed with manna only, and eagerly longed for a change of food.

EAST. The pedestal, with the volume of the Sacred Law, is placed in the eastern part of the lodge, to signify that as the sun rises in the east to open and enliven the day, so is the W. M. placed in the east to open the lodge, and to employ and instruct the brethren in Masonry.

EAVESDROPPER. In the lectures used at the revival of Masonry in 1717, the following punishment was inflicted on a cowan. "To be placed under the eaves of the house in rainy weather, till the water runs in at his shoulders and out at his shoes." The French rather extend this punishment. "On le met sous une gouttière, une pompe, ou une fontaine, jusqu'à ce qu'il soit mouillé depuis la tête jusqu'aux pieds." Hence a listener is called an eavesdropper.

EBAL. The following was introduced into the lectures of Masonry by our brethren of the last century. Moses commanded Israel that as soon as they had passed the Jordan, they should go to Schechem, and divide into two bodies, each composed of six tribes; one placed on, that is adjacent to, Ebal; the other on, that is adjacent to, Gerizim. The six tribes on or at Gerizim, were to pronounce blessings on those who should faithfully observe the law; and the six on Mount Ebal were to pronounce curses against those who should violate it. This Joshua executed. Moses enjoined them to erect an altar of unhewn stones on Mount Ebal, and to plaster them over, that the law might be written on the altar.—*Calmet.*

EDEN. When God created the first man he placed him in the Garden of Eden, to dress it and to keep it. Horticulture or gardening is the first kind of employment on record, and that in which man was engaged while in a state of perfection and innocence. Though the garden may be supposed to produce all things spontaneously, as the whole vegetable surface of the earth certainly did at the creation, yet dressing and tilling were afterwards necessary to maintain the different kinds of plants and vegetables in their perfection, and to repress luxuriance. Even in a state of innocence we cannot conceive it possible that man could have been happy if inactive. God gave him work to do, and his employment contributed to his happiness; for the structure of his body, as well as of his mind, plainly proves that he was never intended for a merely contemplative life.—*Adam Clarke.*

EDICT OF CYRUS. No sooner was the prescribed term of the Israelitish captivity completed, than the Babylonian monarchs were expelled, according to the voice of prophecy; and, the anger of the Lord appeased, he stirred up the heart of Cyrus, King of Persia and Babylon, by communicating to him the Great Secret, to issue a proclamation for the building of the Temple. The people were liberated, the holy utensils restored to the number of five thousand four hundred, which had escaped destruction; and the tribes who consented to return, under their respective princes and chieftains, were led triumphantly into the promised land by Zerubbabel, the prince, Jeshua the priest, and Haggai the prophet.

ELECTING OFFICERS. In most lodges the election of officers takes place upon, or near to, St. John's Day, when either new officers are chosen, or the old ones are re-elected. He who aspires to fill any of the chief offices of the lodge must not only possess the necessary masonic knowledge to enable him to assist in carrying on the lodge work with order and harmony, but he must be a man whose general knowledge, skill, and experience, has gained him the esteem and confidence of his brethren; rank, titles or riches should never be taken into account, unless the possessor is also endowed with the former qualifications; nor, on the other hand, should any brother be elected whose situation in life would not allow him to devote the necessary time to the duties of the lodge without injury to himself, his family, or connections. Should the election have fallen upon any brother who feels himself unable to perform the important duties which would devolve upon him, it is his duty immediately to decline the proffered honour. The welfare of the lodge should be his sole object, and if he feels that he is not able to promote that object so well as he ought to do as an officer, it is much more creditable to him to continue to do his utmost as a private member.

ELECTION. Every lodge shall annually elect its Master and Treasurer by ballot, such Master having been regularly appointed, and having served as Warden of a warranted lodge; and at the next meeting after his election, when the minutes are confirmed, he shall be installed into the chair according to ancient usage; after which he is to appoint his Wardens and other officers.— *Constitutions.*

ELEMENTS. The three elements, water, fire, and air, signify three F. Cs., which conduct us, and are so necessary for our preservation, that our life is at an end the moment they quit the body. Diseases are generally caused by a revolution in these elements. The force o₁ one being increased appears to destroy the body. If the element of fire becomes unnaturally strong, it causes inflammation and fever. If it be the element of water which increases in strength, other diseases, equally dangerous, are brought on. When death takes place, the three elements are again represented by the burning taper, the basin of water, and towels, which are generally placed beside a dead body, and which also represent the three wicked F. Cs., who have destroyed their master.— *Rosenberg.*

EMBLEMS. Freemasonry being confessedly an allegorical system, all its points, parts, and secrets, must partake in common of its emblematical construction. Every doctrine and ceremony has its mystical reference —every landmark its legitimate explanation. But there are often more important antitypes than those which are commonly assigned; and though they do not appear on the surface, are nevertheless worthy of our most serious consideration. Hence arises the necessity in these times of scientific and philosophical research, of maintaining Freemasonry in its proper rank, by investigating the tendency of its numerous details, that we may correctly ascertain whether their import be uniform, and their typical reference valuable.

EMERGENCY. A lodge of emergency may, at any time, be called by the authority of the Master, or, in his absence, by the senior Warden, but on no pretence without such authority first given. The particular reason of calling a lodge of emergency shall be expressed in the summons, and afterwards recorded in the minutes; and no business but that so expressed shall be entered upon at such meeting.—*Constitutions.*

ENDLESS SERPENT. The serpent was symbolical of the divine wisdom, power, and creative energy; and of immortality and regeneration, from the shedding of his skin; and of eternity, when in the act of biting his own tail. Besides these various symbolizations, we are informed that the Egyptians represented the world by a circle intersected by two diameters perpendicular to each other.—*Dean.*

ENJOYMENT. Freemasons are allowed the privilege of enjoying themselves with innocent mirth, treating one another according to ability, but avoiding all excess, or forcing any brother to eat or drink beyond his inclination, or hindering him from going when his occasions call him, or doing or saying anything offensive, or that may forbid an easy and free conversation; for that would blast our harmony. and defeat our laudable purposes.—*Ancient Charges.*

ENOCH. The degeneracy of mankind became so great before the flood, and their perversions of pure antediluvian Masonry so grievous, that, according to our traditions, Enoch feared the genuine secrets would be lost, and swallowed up in the predicted deluge. To prevent which, he hid the grand secret, engraven on a white oriental porphyry stone, in the bowels of the earth; and being apprehensive that the morality and science which had been embodied in Freemasonry with such care would be absorbed in the general destruction, to preserve the principles of the science, he built two pillars near the spot where they were concealed, with an inscription in hieroglyphics, importing that near it was a precious treasure, which had been dedicated to God.

ENSIGNS. On this subject we might refer to the Talmudists, who have gone so far as to define the colours and the figures or arms of the very ensigns. They say, on that of Judah, a lion was painted with this inscription. —"Rise, Lord, let thine enemies be dispersed, and let those that hate thee flee before thee." They gave to Issachar an ass, to Zebulun a ship, to Reuben a river (others give Reuben the figure of a man); to Simeon a sword, to Gad a lion, to Ephraim an unicorn; an ox to Manasseh, a wolf to Benjamin, and a serpent to Dan, though the others give him an eagle. In short they pretended that the ensign of Asher was a handful of corn. and that of Napthali a stag.—*Adam Clarke.*

ENTERED APPRENTICE. Our brethren of the eighteenth century seldom advanced beyond the first degree; few were passed, and fewer still were raised to the third. The Master's degree appears to have been much less comprehensive than at present; and for some years after the revival of Masonry, the third degree was unapproachable to those who lived at a distance from London; for by the laws of the Grand Lodge it wa ordered, that "Apprentices must be admitted Fellowcrafts and Masters only here (in Grand Lodge), unless by a dispensation from the Grand Master."

ENTERING. The lodge when revealed to an entering Mason, discovers to him the representation of the world; in which, from the wonders of nature, we are led to contemplate the Great Original, and worship him for his mighty works; and we are thereby also moved to exercise those moral and social virtues which become mankind as the servants of the Great Architect of the world, in whose image we were formed in the beginning.—*Hutchinson.*

ENTRANCE. In America, "after the lodge has been regularly opened in the third degree, the work is introduced on the entrance of the candidate by the reading of that beautiful and exquisitely touching portion of the penitential hymn of King Solomon, called the Ecclesiastes (xii. 1—7). Remember now thy Creator in the days of thy youth, &c. In the course of the ceremony there is a prayer of deep devotion and pathos composed from some of the most sublime and affecting passages of that splendid sacred drama of Araby, the Book of Job. This prayer includes a portion of the funeral service of the Protestant Episcopal Church, and is full of tenderness and beauty."—*Stone.*

ENVY. None shall discover envy at the prosperity of a brother, nor supplant him, or put him out of his work, if he be capable to finish the same, for no man can finish another's work so much to the lord's profit, unless he be thoroughly acquainted with the designs and draughts of him that began it.—*Ancient Charges.*

EQUALITY. In no society is this more practised

than in the Order of Freemasons, for we are all brethren, and it is said that amongst brethren there must be the most perfect equality. But this word may be misunderstood: we are not all equal in the lodge, inasmuch as some are appointed to rule and govern, so it is the duty of others cheerfully and promptly to obey, and all are equally eligible to be elected to those offices, having first duly performed our duties as private members, and thus enabled to fill them with credit to ourselves and satisfaction to the Craft. We are not all equal by creation with respect to our mental faculties, and more especially we are not all equal in the labour which we have, or ought to have, bestowed upon cultivating those mental faculties to the utmost possible extent. But we ought all of us to be equally zealous in the discharge of our duties as men and Masons, and should all prove ourselves to be perfectly equal in the zeal of our fraternal affection to each other. To be equal to each other in brotherly love, is the principal thing which ought to be understood in our equality. We dare not for one moment lose sight of the rank or station which each individual brother fills in society, yet there may be at the same time a perfect equality amongst men of the most opposite social ranks in the desire to promote every useful work; and this equality will produce the most beneficial effect upon the human heart. Any Mason who would dare to attempt, among the brethren, to claim the precedence which his conventional position in society may give him, would disgrace the philosophy of the Order, and by so doing lay a sacrilegious hand upon that sacred bond by which we are indissolubly united to each other.—*Gadicke.*

EQUILATERAL TRIANGLE. In an old code of lectures I find the following explanation of this figure. An equilateral triangle is perfect friendship. The base of a triangle may be as a duty, the perpendicular as the sincerity of performance, the hypothenuse as the advantage arising from the performance. If the duty of sincerity flow equally, the advantage will flow equally.

ESSENES. Amongst the Jews in Judea and in Syria, some centuries both before and after the birth of Christ,

tt is well known that there were three distinct sects—
Pharisees, Sadducees, and Essenes. This third was the
oldest sect, and they were now and then called Thera-
peutics. The Essenes laudably distinguished themselves
in many respects from the other two sects, inasmuch as
they were less numerous, and proceeded on their way
peaceably, noiselessly, and without ostentation, or forcible
attempts at proselytism; for which reason they were
much less known than the other sects. Fidelity to their
princes or rulers, lawful order, adherence unto truth,
virtue, sobriety, humility, and strict secrecy, were the
chief principles of their code of action. To the punctual
performance of those and other similar duties, viz., the
strictest maintenance of the secrets of their society; of
justice and of humanity every one pledged himself when
he was admitted a member, by a most solemn oath. It
was only by being of mature age, and going through a
three years' probation, during which they were obliged
to lead a temperate, chaste, moral, virtuous, and, in
many respects, a severely self-mortified life, that they
were enabled to gain admission into the Order, when
they received a white dress or apron and a small hatchet
(dolabella), as the signs of their admission.—*Gadicke.*

ESSENTIAL SECRETS. The essential secrets of
Masonry consist of nothing more than the signs, grips,
passwords, and tokens, essential to the preservation of
the society from the inroads of impostors; together with
certain symbolical emblems, the technical terms appertaining to which served as a sort of universal language,
by which the members of the Fraternity could distinguish
each other, in all places and countries where lodges were
instituted.—*Stone.*

ESTABLISHED. Solomon erected his pillars in the
porch of the temple, which he designed should be a
memorial to the Jews as they entered the holy place, to
warm their minds with confidence and faith, by this
record of the promises made by the Lord unto his father
David, and which were repeated unto him in a vision, in
which the voice of God proclaimed (1 Kings, ix. 5), "I
will establish the throne of thy kingdom upon Israel for
ever."—*Hutchinson.*

ESTABLISHED RELIGION. A cheerful compliance with the established religion of the country in which they live, is earnestly recommended in the assemblies of Masons; and this universal conformity, notwithstanding private sentiment and opinion, is the art practised by them, which effects the laudable purpose of conciliating true friendship among men of every persuasion, while it proves the cement of general union.—*Preston.*

EUCLID. An old MS. on Masonry says, "Euclid was the pupil of Abraham, and in his time the river Nile overflowed so far, that many of the dwellings of the people of Egypt were destroyed. Euclid instructed them in the art of making mighty walls and ditches, to stop the progress of the water; and by geometry, measured out the land, and divided it into partitions, so that each man might ascertain his own property." The MS. is incorrect in making Euclid contemporary with Abraham; but it truly adds that he gave to Masonry the name of Geometry.

EVIDENCES. It is not to be presumed that we are a set of men professing religious principles contrary to the revelations and doctrines of the Son of God, reverencing a deity by the denomination of the God of Nature, and denying that mediation which is graciously offered to all true believers. The members of our society at this day, in the third stage of Masonry, confess themselves to be Christians. The veil of the temple is rent, the builder is smitten, and we are raised from the tomb of transgression. Our authorized lectures furnish us such a series of evidences in support of this opinion, as can scarcely be found in the details of any other human institution; for Freemasonry, as now practised, is a speculative, and not an operative institution, although it is admitted that both these might be blended in ancient times. The evidences of the above fact run through the entire system, and are equally conspicuous in every degree.—*Hutchinson.*

EXALTED. This word applies to the ceremony and the position to which the candidate is elevated when he receives the degree of the Royal Arch; for it is declared to be indescribably more august, sublime, and important than all which precede it, and is the summit and perfection of ancient Masonry.

EXAMINATION. If a stranger apply to you in the character of a Mason, you are cautiously to examine him in such a method as prudence shall direct you, that you may not be imposed upon by an ignorant false pretender whom you are to reject with contempt and derision, an beware of giving him any hints of knowledge. But if you discover him to be a true and genuine brother, you are to respect him accordingly; and if he is in want, you must relieve him if you can, or elso direct him how he may be relieved.—*Ancient Charges.*

EXAMPLE. Nothing is more apt to attract the eyes and enliven the countenance than light, especially that which shines in a dark place; so nothing can more excite the observation, engage the attention, or gladden the hearts of beholders, than a fair, bright, excellent character, appearing in the midst of a dissolute and corrupt generation. And as all luminous bodies, in proportion to their own brightness, diffuse their light around them, and at a distance enlighten other bodies; so in a moral and religious sense, a good example is a light shining in darkness, spreading its influence every way, diffusing instruction and knowledge—motives to reform, and encouragement to virtue.—*Harris.*

EXCLUSION. No lodge shall exclude any member without giving him due notice of the charge preferred against him, and of the time appointed for its consideration. The name of every brother excluded, together with the cause of his exclusion, shall be sent to the Grand Secretary; and if a country lodge, also to the Provincial Grand Master, or his deputy.—*Constitutions.*

EXEMPTION. The Masons who were selected to build the temple of Solomon, were declared free, and were exempted, together with their descendants, from imposts, duties and taxes. They had also the privilege to bear arms. At the destruction of the temple by Nebuchadnezzar, the posterity of these Masons were carried into the captivity with the ancient Jews. But the good will of Cyrus gave them permission to erect a second temple, having set them at liberty for that purpose. It is from this epoch that we bear the name of Free and Accepted Masons.—*York Lectures.*

EXPENSES. The whole expense of building the Temple of Solomon was so prodigious, as gives reason to think that the talents whereby the sum is reckoned, were another sort of talents of a far less value than the Mosaic talents : for what is said to be given by David, and contributed by the princes toward the building of the temple at Jerusalem, if valued by these talents, exceeded the value of 800,000,000*l.* of our money, which was enough to have built all that temple of solid silver.—*Prideaux.*

EXPERIENCE. The process of a Mason's experience is gradual, from the rough stone in the north east angle of the lodge, to the perfect aspirant, standing on the five points of fellowship. His progress, however, can only be matured by serious reflection and mental assiduity, without which he will never understand the typical references contained in the degrees he has received, or their tendency to dignify his nature, and make him a wiser and a better man. Still these steps, sublime though they be, are only preparatory to something infinitely more striking, and more directly applicable to the great dispensation on which all our hopes of happiness, both in this world and a better, are suspended. Red Masonry displays the direct prophecies of the Messiah, the star of Jacob, Shiloh, the corner-stone, Moses at the bush, &c. In Military Masonry, all these prophecies are fulfilled, and the Christian system clearly developed ; while in the Rose Croix, it is displayed in all its comely and perfect proportions.

EXPULSION. A Mason offending against any law or regulation of the Craft, to the breach of which no specific penalty is attached, shall, at the discretion of the Grand Lodge, or any of its delegated authorities, or of a Provincial Grand Master, be subject to admonition, fine, or suspension. If fine be the punishment awarded, it shall be, for the first offence, not less than one pound, nor more than five pounds ; for a second offence of a similar nature, within three years, it shall be not less than two, nor more than ten pounds ; and if a brother shall refuse to pay the fine, or be guilty of a third offence within three years of the second offence, he shall be expelled from the Craft.—*Constitutions.*

EXTENT. A Mason's Lodge is said to extend from East to West, in breadth between North and South, in depth from the surface to the center of the earth, and even as high as the heavens, to show the universality of the science, and that a Mason's charity should know no bounds save those of prudence.—*Hemming.*

EXTERNAL. The external preparation of a candidate, which takes place in a convenient room adjoining the lodge, is too well known to need explanation ; and if not, it is a landmark which cannot be inserted here.

EYE. The Eye of God is in every place, for the purpose of taking a strict and impartial cognizance of all human actions. This expressive emblem will remind you that the Deity is watching over all mankind, and will weigh in the balance of truth, every action, thought, and word.

EYE OF PROVIDENCE. A symbol of the W. M. As the eye of the Great Architect of heaven and earth is incessantly upon all his works, so should the eye of the W. M. be upon every thing which passes in his lodge.—*Gadicke.*

EYESIGHT. He who has been temporarily deprived of his sight is reduced to the condition of a new-born babe, or of one of those unfortunate individuals whose natural infirmity renders the presence of a conductor indispensably necessary ; but when there are no outward objects to distract his attention, it is then that with the eye of reflection he probes into the deepest and darkest recesses of his own heart, and discovers his natural imperfections and impurities much more readily than he could possibly have done had he not been deprived of his sight. This short deprivation of sight has kindled in his heart a spark of the brightest and the purest flame.

"The people which sat in darkness saw a great light," (Mat. iv. 16). We must further admit that those who have been deprived of their sight, and who have hopes of being restored to it, strive most industriously and diligently to obtain it; that they have no greater desire, and that they will most readily pledge themselves to do all that can be required of them, in order to obtain that inestimable blessing.

A man who has been deprived of his sight may be introduced into places where he is surrounded by the strangest and the rarest objects, without a possibility of his becoming a traitor. At the same time, those who are in possession of their sight cannot feel the care of their guides so much as those who are hoodwinked, and who feel that without the constant attention of their conductors, they would be much more helpless than they now are; but however many proofs of attention and care they may receive, there is still something left to wish for; and to the question, What is your chief desire, the answer will ever assuredly be, "*Light*."—*Gadicke*.

EZRA. Ezra, or Esdras, the famous Jewish high priest and reformer, was of a sacerdotal family, by some thought to be the son of Jeraiah, the high priest, who was put to death at Riblatha by Nebuchadnezzar, after the capture of Jerusalem; but as Calmet thinks only his grandson or great-grandson. It is believed that the first return of Ezra from Babylon to Jerusalem, was with Zerubbabel. in the beginning of Cyrus's reign, A. M. 3468, of which he himself wrote the history. He was very skilful in the law, and zealous for God's service; and had doubtless a great share in all the transactions of his time.—*Calmet*.

FAITH. Faith is the foundation of justice, the bond of amity, and chief support of society; we live and walk by faith; by it we have an acknowledgment of a superior being, have access to the throne of grace, are justified, accepted, and finally received. A true Christian faith is the evidence of things not seen, the substance of things hoped for; this maintained, and well answered by walking according to our masonic profession, will turn faith into a vision, and bring us to that blessed mansion above, where the just exist in perfect bliss to all eternity; where we shall be eternally happy with God, the grand geometrician of the universe, whose Son died for us, and rose again that we might be justified through faith in his most precious blood.—*Lectures*.

FABRIC. The masonic system exhibits a stupendous and beautiful fabric, founded on universal piety. To rule and direct our passions, to have faith and hope in God, and charity towards man, I consider as the objects of what is termed speculative Masonry.—*Jones*.

FALL OF MAN. When our first parents transgressed by eating the forbidden fruit, they saw what they had never seen before, that they were stripped of their excellence; that they had lost their innocence; and that they had fallen into a state of indigence and danger. They were expelled from the garden of Eden, the ground was cursed for their sakes, and they were condemned to eat their bread by the sweat of their brow. Out of this melancholy defection from purity and peace, a portion of the Royal Arch Degree has been constructed.

FALL OF WATER. There is a certain emblem in the degree of a Fellowcraft which is said to derive its origin from the waters of Jordan, which were held up while the Israelites passed over, and which would naturally fall with great violence when the whole host had reached the opposite shore.

FANATICISM. Fanaticism, or a fanatic, dare not be permitted among Freemasons. We should unanimously strive to obtain that object for which the rules of the Order so powerfully work, and thus there can be no disputes or persecutions among us for diversity of opinion. Every Freemason prays to God in the way his religion teaches him, and he is encouraged so to do in the lodge. If we did not allow the wild dreams of imagination, or the still wilder ones of superstition, to have any effect upon our ideas of God and of godly things, all persecution for difference of religious opinions would fall of themselves. Of fanaticism of whole lodges against each other for a difference in their rituals and systems, there were formerly too many traces; but they have happily for many years entirely ceased. Religious fanaticism cannot have any place in a Freemasons' lodge, for the members of every sect of the Christian Church have an equal right in the Order. If a Roman Catholic is at the head of the lodge to-day, and a Lutheran or a member of the Reformed Church to-morrow, it is scarcely remarked by the brethren.—*Gadicke.*

FEAR GOD, HONOUR THE KING. It is the invaluable distinction of this free country, that such a just and unrestrained intercourse of opinions exist, as will not permit any number of men to frequent any dangerous or disguised society; and that it is impossible any profligate doctrines could be tolerated for a moment in a lodge meeting under regular authority, because its foundation stone is, fear God, honour the king.—*Earl of Moira.*

FEASTS. At regular and appropriate seasons, convivial meetings of the Craft are held for the purpose of social intercourse. Temperance, harmony, and joy should always characterize these assemblies. On the continent and in the United States, an annual feast is held on the anniversary of St. John the Baptist, June 24. That every one may strive to give mirth and happiness to his brother, the Grand Lodge of England, at the quarterly meeting on the festival of St John the Evangelist, in 1720, adopted the following regulation: "That, in future, the new Grand Master should be named and proposed to the Grand Lodge some time before the feast; and if approved, and present, he shall be saluted as Grand Master elect."

FEELING. Feeling is that sense by which we are enabled to distinguish the different qualities of bodies, such as hardness and softness, heat and cold, roughness and smoothness, figure, solidity, motion, and extension; all of which, by means of corresponding sensations of touch, are presented to the mind as real external qualities, and the conception or belief of them invariably connected with these corresponding sensations by an original principle of nature, which far transcends our inquiry.—*Old Lectures.*

FEES. No lodge shall make a Mason for a less consideration than three guineas, exclusive of the registering fee, nor on any pretence remit or defer the payment of any part of this sum; the member who proposes any candidate must be responsible to the lodge for all the fees payable on account of his initiation. All monies payable for register fees, certificates, or quarterage, shall be deposited in the hands of the Master, to be kept distinct from the funds of the lodge; and shall be remitted, with proper lists, at least once a year if in the country, and twice a year if in London.—*Constitutions*.

FEES OF HONOUR. Every brother on his appointment or reappointment to either of the following offices, shall pay these sums:—The Deputy Grand Master, having served the office of Steward, ten guineas, if not, thirty guineas; the Grand Wardens eight guineas each; Grand Treasurer five guineas; Grand Registrar, Secretary, and Deacons, three guineas each; Grand Director of Ceremonies, Superintendent of Works, and Sword Bearer, two guineas each; a Provincial Grand Master twenty guineas, and if he have not served the office of Grand Steward, twenty guineas more; and a Deputy Provincial Grand Master pays two guineas for registering his name in the books of the Grand Lodge.

FELLOWCRAFT. The second, or Fellowcraft's degree, is rendered interesting by those scientific instructions and philosophical lectures which characterize later parts of the mysteries; though both of these degrees were made to tend to the glory of that God who had given such wonderful faculties to them, and to the welfare of their fellow-creatures.—*Archdeacon Mant*.

FEMALES. The only reason why ladies cannot be present in an open lodge of Freemasons, is that their mysteries, being symbolical of labour as performed by man, could not in that case be shared by women; no honest-hearted man could for a moment believe that in mind she was inferior; if a man existed who thought so, let him ask from whom he first imbibed lessons of piety, virtue, and honour. But if ladies could not share our labour of work, there was no reason why they should not enjoy our labour of love.—*Crucefix*.

22

FESTIVALS. The two festivals set apart by Masons of the United States are those of St. John the Baptist, June 24, and St. John the Evangelist, December 27. The annual festival of the Masons of England is celebrated on the Wednesday following St. George's day, April 23, he being their patron saint. The Grand Lodge of Scotland, for a similar reason, celebrate St. Andrew's day, November 30.

FIDELITY. Joining the right hands is a pledge of fidelity; for Valerius Maxemus tells us that the ancients had a moral deity whom they called Fides, a goddess of honesty or fidelity, and adds, when they promised anything of old, they gave their hand upon it, as we do now, and therefore she is represented as giving her hand, and sometimes as only two hands conjoined. Chartarius more fully describes this by observing that the proper residence of faith or fidelity was thought by the ancients to be in the right hand.—*Calcott.*

FIDUCIAL. The fiducial sign shows us if we prostrate ourselves with our face to the earth, we thus throw ourselves on the mercy of our Creator and Judge, looking forward with humble confidence to his holy promises, by which alone we hope to pass through the Ark of our redemption into the mansion of eternal bliss and glory to the presence of Him who is the great I Am, the Alpha and Omega, the Beginning and the Ending, the First and the Last.

FIERY CLOUD. This pillar, or column, which appeared as a cloud by day and a fire by night, was a symbol of the divine presence. This was the Shekinah, or divine dwelling place, and was a continual proof of the presence and protection of God. Whether there was more than one pillar is not clearly determined by the text. If there was but one, it certainly assumed three different appearances, for the performance of three very important offices. 1. In the day time for the purpose of pointing out the way, a column or pillar of a cloud was all that was requisite. 2. At night, to prevent that confusion which must otherwise have taken place, the pillar of cloud became a pillar of fire, not to direct their journeyings, for they seldom travelled by night, but to give light to every part of the Israelitish camp. 3. In such a scorching, barren, thirsty desert, something further was necessary than a light and guide. It appears that this cloud had two sides, one dark, and the other luminous. The luminous side gave light to the whole camp of Israel during the night of passage ; and the dark side turned towards the pursuing Egyptians, and prevented them from receiving any benefit from the light.— *Adam Clarke.*

FINES. A lodge which has been convicted of any breach of masonic law, shall, at the discretion of the Grand Lodge, be subject, for the first offence, to a fine of not less than one pound nor more than five pounds ; for a second offence of a similar nature, within three years, it shall be not less than two nor more than ten pounds ; and if the lodge shall refuse to pay the fine, or be guilty of a third offence within three years of the second offence, the lodge shall be erased and its constitution forfeited. All fines levied shall be applied to the general charity —*Constitutions.*

FIRE. Fire and light were the uniform tokens of the appearances of the Deity. Sometimes shining with a mild and gentle radiance, like the inferior luminaries of a Masons' lodge, and at others flaming fiercely amidst clouds and darkness, thunderings and noise. To Adam he manifested himself in the Shekinah, which kept the gates of Paradise ; to Abel, and Enoch, and Noah, the Deity appeared in a flame of fire. Nor were the appearances changed when he visited Abraham, Isaac, and Jacob. To Moses in the bush, and to the Israelites in the wilderness fire was his constant symbol.

FIRST DEGREE. In this lecture virtue is painted in the most beautiful colours, and the beauties of morality are strictly enforced. Here we are taught such wise and useful lessons as prepare the mind for a regular advancement in the principles of knowledge and philosophy ; and these are imprinted on the memory by lively and sensible images, well calculated to influence our conduct in the proper discharge of the duties of life.

The whole is a regular system of morality, conceived in a strain of interesting allegory, which readily unfolds its beauties to the candid and industrious inquirer.—*Preston.*

FIRST PARENTS. The first parents of mankind were instructed by the Almighty, as to his existence and attributes, and after their fall were further informed ot the redemption which was to be perfected by Christ, and, as a sign of their belief, were commanded to offer sacrifices to God. It is also highly probable that symbolical actions should have been instituted by them in memory of their penitence, reverence, sympathy, fatigue, and faith, and that these might be transmitted to posterity.—*Archdeacon Mant.*

FIRST PRINCIPLES. In the formation of all human societies, there are first principles, which constitute the basis of union. This holds true in all cases. If, therefore, we desire to arrive at simple matters of fact, and form a correct judgment, as it regards the soundness of those fundamental principles, adapted as the basis of such union, or the true objects contemplated in the organization of any society, this is the time when truth appears with the least incumbrance, and the motive of action is seen under the least disguise. In most cases where moral, benevolent, or humane establishments have been formed, these two points are clearly developed.— *Town.*

FIVE. We say that a regular lodge consists of seven Masters, and also of five. The last number is derived from the five senses, inasmuch as the persons who are united to form a lodge should be as perfect as a whole, and work together with as much unanimity as a single man, who is endowed with five healthy senses.—*Gadicke.*

FIVE POINTS OF FELLOWSHIP. The five points of fellowship were thus illustrated in the lectures used by the Athol Masons of the last century:—"When the necessities of a brother call for my support, I will be ever ready to lend him a helping hand to save him from sinking if I find him worthy thereof. 2. Indolence shall not cause my footsteps to halt, nor wrath to turn them aside; but forgetting every selfish consideration, I will be ever swift of foot to save, help, and execute benevolence to a fellow-creature in distress, but more particularly to a brother Mason. 3. When I offer up my ejaculations to Almighty God, I will remember my brother's welfare, even as my own; for as the voice of babes and sucklings ascend to the throne of grace, so most assuredly will the breathings of a fervent heart ascend to the mansions of bliss. 4. A brother's secret, delivered to me as such, I will keep as I would my own, because, if I betray the trust which has been reposed in me, I might do him an irreparable injury; it would be like the villainy of an assassin, who lurks in darkness to stab his adversary when unarmed and least prepared to meet an enemy. 5. A brother's character I will support in his absence, as I would in his presence. I will not revile him myself, nor suffer it to be done by others, if it is in my power to prevent it. Thus by the five points of fellowship, we are linked together in one indivisible chain of sincere affection, brotherly love, relief, and truth."

FIXED LIGHTS. The fixed lights of a lodge were formerly represented by " three windows, supposed to be in every room where a lodge is held; referring to the cardinal points of the compass, according to the antique rules of Masonry." There was one in the east, another in the west, and another in the south, to light the man to, at, and from labour; but there was none in the north, because the sun darts no rays from thence. These constitute the symbolical situations of the three chief officers.

FLOATS. At the building of the temple, everything was prepared with the greatest nicety, the stones were all hewn in the quarries, and there squared, fashioned, marked and numbered; and the timber being cut in the forests, was there framed, carved, marked and numbered also; so that when brought to Jerusalem, there was nothing left to be done but the arrangement of its different parts. The materials being thus prepared, were carried on floats down to Joppa, and thence conveyed to Jerusalem on carriages of curious mechanism provided for the purpose, there to be put together according to the plan of the architect.—*Archdeacon Mant.*

FLOOR. In a symbolical lodge of Blue Masons, the first object which deserves attention is the mosaic floor on which we tread; it is intended to convey to our minds the viscissitudes of human affairs, chequered with a strange contrariety of events. To-day elated with the smiles of prosperity, to-morrow depressed by the frowns of misfortune. The precariousness of our situation in this world should teach us punctuality, to walk uprightly and firmly upon the broad basis of virtue and religion, and to give assistance to our unfortunate fellow-creatures who are in distress; lest, on some capricious turn of fortune's wheel, we may become dependent on those who before looked up to us as their benefactors.—*Dalcho.*

FLOOR-CLOTH. In former times, it was not customary to use a floor-cloth, but the necessary figures were drawn upon the floor with chalk or charcoal, which, when done with, were washed off. This custom was in use here and there till about 1760. Many lodges now use solid bodies for their floor-cloths, and not paintings. Every good Mason knows what they represent, and what a floor-cloth is. The border by which it is surrounded is an important symbol.—*Gadicke.*

FOOT. Indolence should not persuade the foot to halt, or wrath to turn our steps out of the way; but forgetting injuries and selfish feelings, and remembering that man was born for the aid of his generation, and not for his own enjoyments only, but to do that which is good; we hould be swift to have mercy, to save, to strengthen, and execute benevolence.—*Old Lectures.*

FOREIGN BRETHREN. Brethren under the constitution of the Grand Lodges of Scotland and Ireland, as well as of foreign grand lodges, may be relieved by the Fund of Benevolence, on the production of certificates from their respective grand lodges, and satisfactory proof of their identity and distress.—*Constitutions.*

FORM. The form of the lodge should be an oblong

square (▢,) should reach from east to west, and from north to south; up to the clouds and to the centre of the earth. The limits of its influence are not formed by four straight lines, or by two squares placed opposite to each other, but are extended to the utmost bounds of the habitable globe. The lodges must therefore do more than give their workplaces the form of a long square. But if the brethren are assembled in a long square, let them lift up their spirits to the contemplation of the Most High, admire him in the wonders of nature, and extend, as far as in them lies, good and perfect gifts into every clime.—*Gadicke.*

FORTITUDE. By fortitude we are taught to resist temptation, and encounter danger with spirit and resolution. This virtue is equally distant from rashness and cowardice; and he who possesses it, is seldom shaken, and never overthrown, by the storms that surround him.

FORTY. The two perfect numbers, four and ten, being multiplied into each other, produce the number forty, which was also sacred, and bore a reference to the number seven. Thus the probation of our first parents in the garden of Eden, as is generally supposed was forty years; the deluge was occasioned by a rain of forty days and nights, of which event Noah had seven days notice; and the waters remained upon the face of the earth forty days. The days of embalming the dead were forty, and of mourning seventy. The concealment of Moses in the land of Midian was forty years, and he was on the mount forty days and nights. Jesus Christ fasted forty days and nights in the wilderness, to prepare for his ministry; and was tempted of the devil forty days; and the same term elapsed between his resurrection and ascension.

FORTY-SEVENTH PROBLEM. As this figure depends on the connexion of several lines, angles and tri angles, which form the whole, so Freemasonry depends on the unanimity and integrity of its members, the inflexibility of their charitable pursuits, and the immutability of the principles upon which the society is established The position is clear, and therefore in a synthetical sense, we demonstrate that some of our brethren from their exalted situation in life, may be considered as standing on the basis of earthly bliss, emblematic of the greater square which subtends the right angle. Others whom Providence hath blessed with means to tread on the flowery meads of affluence, are descriptive of the squares which stand on the sides that form the right angle. The several triangles inscribed within the squares are applicable to those happy beings who enjoy every social comfort, and never exceed the bounds of mediocrity. Those who have the heartfelt satisfaction of administering to the wants of the indigent and industrious, may be compared to the angles which surround and support the figure; whilst the lines which form it, remind us of those unfortunate brethren who, by a series of inevitable events, are incapable of providing the common necessaries of life, until aided by a cheerful and ready assistance.—*Old Lectures.*

FOUNDATION. The masonic days proper for laying the foundation-stone of a Masons' lodge, are from the 15th of April to the 15th of May; and the 18th of April has been pronounced peculiarly auspicious, because nothing can be more consonant with reason and propriety, than to commence a building in the early spring, that the workmen may have the whole summer before them to complete the undertaking advantageously, in order that they may celebrate the cape stone with confidence and joy.

FOUR. The number four was frequently blended and mixed up with the number seven, and was esteemed to possess similar properties. It signified universality among the Cabalists and Pythagoreans, and formed the holy tetragrammaton of the Jews. This is observable not only in the quadruple cherubic form at the gate of Eden, the four rivers of paradise, and the four artificial ones round the tabernacle, the services of which were conducted by four priests—Moses, Aaron, Eleazar, and Ithamar; the four chariots and angelic messengers in the vision of Zechariah, and the four visions and the four beasts of Daniel, but even our Saviour's prophecy from the Mount of Olives was so constructed as to contain four synchronisms.

FOUR DEGREES. Ancient Masonry consists of ur degrees; the three first of which are, that of the Apprentice, the Fellowcraft, and the sublime degree of Master; and a brother being well versed in these degrees, and otherwise qualified, as hereafter will be expressed, is eligible to be admitted to the fourth degree, the Holy Royal Arch.—*Ahiman Rezon.*

FREE. A word that is often heard among us, but which is circumscribed by the same bounds as the freedom of social life. In our assemblies we have nothing resembling the freedom to act every one according to the dictates of his own caprice; but we are free, or at least, each of us ought to be free, from the dominion of pride, of prejudice, of passion, and of other follies of human nature. Free from the madness of refusing obedience either to the law of the land or the Craft.—*Gadicke.*

FREEBORN. No candidate can be admitted into Freemasonry, or share in its occult mysteries, unless he be a free man, of mature age, sound judgment, and strict morality. Nor can any one, although he have been initiated, continue to act as a Mason, or practise the rites of the Order, if he be temporarily deprived of his liberty, or freedom of will. So essential is it to Freemasonry, that its members should be perfectly free in all their actions, thoughts and designs.

FREEMASON. The explanations of this word, which say the same thing in nearly every living language, are very various. Originally the name was only Mason, but the privileges which were granted unto certain real architects and artists, induced them to adopt the title of Freemasons, to distinguish themselves from those who were merely operative masons. Others again say that Masons should labour free and unconstrained. He who is free from prejudice, and understands how to regulate his life and actions by the working tools of an operative mason, can well explain the meaning of the word Freemason. We may also reasonably suppose that many distinguished persons, who were neither architects nor artists, have been admitted into the Fraternity, and that those persons were afterwards exclusively called **Free** and Accepted Masons; which title they have propagated. —*Gadicke.*

FREEMASONRY. Masonry, according to the general acceptation of the term, is an art founded on the principles of geometry, and directed to the service and convenience of mankind. But Freemasonry, embracing a wider range and having a nobler object in view, namely, the cultivation and improvement of the human mind, may with more propriety be called a science, inasmuch as availing itself of the terms of the former, it inculcates the principles of the purest morality, though its lessons are for the most part veiled in allegory, and illustrated by symbols.—*Hemming.*

FRIENDSHIP. Friendship is traced through the circle of private connections to the grand system of universal benevolence, which no limits can circumscribe, as its influence extends to every branch of the human race. On this general plan the universality of the system of Masonry is established. Were friendship confined to the spot of our nativity, its operation would be partial, and imply a kind of enmity to other nations. Where the interests of one country interfere with those of another, nature dictates an adherence to the welfare of our own immediate connections; but such interference apart, the true Mason is a citizen of the world, and his philanthropy extends to all the human race. Uninfluenced by local prejudices, he knows no preference in virtue but according to its degree, from whatever country or clime it may spring.—*Preston.*

FRUITS. What are the fruits of Masonry? It has often been effectual to save life and property; it has often relieved distress; it constantly teaches the ignorant; it daily wipes rivers of tears from the eye of distress; it has often reconciled the most jarring interests; it has often converted the bitterest foes into the dearest friends.—*Inwood.*

FUNERAL. The public are frequently astonished at beholding a large funeral procession, and cannot conceive how the deceased, who lived in a state of comparative obscurity, could have had so many friends, amongst whom some are of the highest rank in society, and from those friends, one of them advances to the brink of the grave, and addresses the assembled multitude upon life, death, and immortality, in such a touching and feeling manner, that brethren, relations, and spectators, are bathed in tears. He who can flatter himself that he will have such a funeral, and that he is worthy of it, can go down, to the grave in peace, certain that he will receive the reward of all his labours from the Great Architect of the Universe.—*Gadicke.*

FURNITURE. The furniture of a Masons' lodge ought to be disposed with the same scrupulous exactness as the furniture of the tabernacle which Moses made according to the pattern which the Deity shewed him in the mount. The tracing-board should be placed on the Master's pedestal, underneath the bible, square and compasses; the first great light being displayed in Ruth. This is for the first degree. The book of constitutions is placed before the Past Master; the globes in the west; the rough ashlar in the north-east, the perfect ashlar in the north-west, while the Master Masons should take their station in the south-west, and Past Masters in the south-east; the Secretary in the north, and the Treasurer in the corner of Amorites.

G. The situation of this letter, when alone, is well known to all Freemasons. It cannot allude to the name of God alone in the German lodges, or it could not be found in the situation in foreign lodges. It has a closer affinity to Geometry, which is so necessary to an Architect, and geometrical certainty and truth is everywhere necessary.—*Gadicke.*

GEOMETRY. Among the mathematical sciences geometry is the one which has the most especial reference to architecture, and we can, therefore, under the name of geometry, understand the whole art of Freemasonry. In Anderson's Book of Constitutions, Freemasonry is frequently called geometry, and of the latter he saith, that the whole being of the Order is comprehended in

it. Freemasons therefore ought to make themselves
intimately acquainted with geometry. It is not absolutely necessary to be able to delineate geometrical
figures; but it is necessary to be able to deduce all our
actions, works, or resolutions from geometrical principles.
—*Gadicke.*

GHIBLIM. The Ghiblimites were expert operative
Masons, who understood the science of geometrical proportion in its practical references, and were cemented in
their lodges by the morality of its detached and component
parts.

GIRDLE. The girdle, in ancient times, was an universally received emblem of truth and passive duty.
Elijah the Tishbite and John the Baptist, were both
girded with an apron of (white) leather. It was said of
Jesus Christ, that his girdle should represent equally
righteousness and fidelity. And in conformity with these
authorities, his principal disciples exhorted the Christian
converts to gird up the loins of their minds, to be sober
and hope to the end, and to stand firm in the faith, having
their loins girt about with truth.

GIRLS' SCHOOL. This charity was instituted on
the 25th of March, 1788, by the late Chevalier Bartholo-
mew Ruspini, for the purpose of maintaining, clothing
and educating, an unlimited number of the female children and orphans of reduced brethren, belonging to the
ancient and honourable society of Free and Accepted
Masons, and of protecting and preserving them from the
dangers and misfortunes to which distressed young females are peculiarly exposed; with the further view of
training them up in the knowledge and love of virtue, in
the habits of industry necessary to their condition, and
of impressing on their minds a due sense of subordination,
true humility, and the principles and practice of all
social, moral, and religious duties. This charity is supported by voluntary contributions.

GLOBE OF FIRE. In the last century some fanciful
brethren referred the circle and point to the cherubic
form which was placed at the gate of paradise, to prevent

the return of our first parents to that region of never ending happiness and delight, after their fall from purity and rectitude, in the attempt to acquire forbidden knowledge. The "fire unfolding itself," or globe of fire described by the prophet Ezekiel, represented the Deity, and the living creatures on one side, and wheels on the other, denoted his power and goodness.

GLOBES. The terrestrial and celestial globes are the noblest instruments for giving the most distinct idea of any problem or proposition, as well as for enabling us to solve it. Contemplating these bodies, Masons are inspired with a due reverence for the Deity and his works; and are induced to apply with diligence and attention to astronomy, geography, navigation, and all the arts dependent on them, by which society has been so much benefited.—*Preston.*

GLORY IN THE CENTRE. When in the lodge we elevate our thoughts to the Deity, our eyes involuntarily rest on the glory in the centre; then with hearts overflowing with gratitude and love, we bow reverentially before the All-seeing eye of God, which the sun, moon, and stars obey; conscious that it pervades their inmost recesses, and tries our thoughts, words and actions, by the unerring touchstone of truth and eternal justice.

GLOVES. The operative Mason cannot use gloves at his work. but we can, and that too, of the purest white, at ours, thereby intimating that every action of a Mason ought to be pure and spotless.—*Gadicke.*

GOLDEN CANDLESTICK. This utensil was made by Moses for the service of the Temple. It consisted wholly of pure gold, and had seven branches; that is, three on each side, and one in the centre. These branches were at equal distances, and each one was adorned with flowers like lilies, gold knobs after the form of an apple, and similar ones resembling an almond. Upon the extremities of the branches were seven golden lamps, which were fed with pure olive oil, and lighted every evening by the priests on duty. The candlestick was placed in the Holy Place, and served to illuminate the altar of incense and the table of shew-bread, which stood in the same chamber.—*Calmet.*

GOLDEN FLEECE. The masonic apron is said to be more ancient than the badge of any other honourable institution. It was used before the Greeks or Romans had a name. The Argonautic expedition is generally believed to be only a figurative account of the deluge; and the apron is unquestionably older than that event; it was therefore worn before the establishment of the spurious Freemasonry. We are certain from undeniable authority, that the apron was the first species of clothing with which mankind were acquainted, and was adopted before the expulsion of our progenitors from the garden of Eden. When they had violated the original compact, their eyes were opened to a sense of guilt and shame, and they saw that they were naked. Decency suggested the necessary expedient of covering themselves with aprons. It is therefore said with great propriety, that "the apron is more ancient than the golden fleece or Roman eagle."

GOLDEN RULE. Freemasonry recommends the practice of the golden rule, do unto others as you would have them do to you, not so much to preserve the peace and order of civil society, (which notwithstanding it cannot fail to do) as to inspire in our own bosoms, a love of virtue and good will to man.

GOOD MASON. The good Mason is an example to his neighbours, and his name and character are proverbial. Those who are younger venerate him, his companions love him, his superiors extol him. In his family he is high without severity, and condescending without meanness; his commands are gentle—indeed his wishes are his commands; for all are equally ready to answer his desires. To his wife he is the tender husband, not the usurping lord; to his children he is the kind, the providential father, not the domineering tyrant; to his servants he is equally the friend as the superior. Thus ruling, he is obeyed with cheerfulness; and thus his home, whether a cottage or a palace, is, while he is present, the habitation of peace; when there he leaves it with reluctance, and when absent his return is expected with a pleasing avidity.—*Inwood.*

GOSPEL. The Royal Order of Masonry, however secret from its most early foundation to the present moment, has nothing belonging to it, but what is so far from giving birth or growth to the commission of any thing inconsistent with the strictest parts of our holy religion, whether it respects our duty to God or man, that every part of it, if duly followed, has a direct tendency to enforce and to encourage the performance of every one of its most holy precepts; and, "the precepts of the Gospel are universally the principles of Masonry." —*Inwood.*

GOVERNMENT. It is well to give rules for the good government of a lodge; but the best teacher is experience. Points of minor importance, both in discipline and doctrine, are of constant occurrence, which have no precedent, and must be regulated by the judgment of the Master. And on these trifling matters, the welfare and prosperity of a lodge frequently depend.

GRACE. When brother Masons are assembled at the banquet table, where it is their duty to crave a blessing, how joyfully do they hear the words—

> "O source of the purest light! O Lord of Glory!
> Great, incomprehensibly great, are thy handy works;
> Thou gavest to us at the building of the Temple
> Wisdom, Strength, and Beauty!
> Thou gavest to us vitality, pleasure, meat, and drink!
> To thee, therefore, be glory, honour, praise, and thanks.

After the meal the Chaplain again lifts his voice:

> "God be praised! Thou hast thought on us this day also;
> Be praised for this day's blessings;
> Oh! protect us fatherly, according to thy grace and power,
> In happiness and in sorrow, in all our ways,
> And bless this night."

Gadicke.

GRADES OF RANK. Many persons have endeavoured to substantiate their objections to the institution of Freemasonry, from the admitted dogma that its members meet on a level; whence they conclude that the system abolishes all human distinctions, and promises to

disorganise society, and reduce it to its primitive elements. But it does no such thing. There is, in fact, no
other institution where the grades of rank are better
defined and preserved. The W. M. sits in the east. For
what purpose is he placed there? Why, to rule and
govern his lodge. And he is invested with power even
to despotism, should he consider it safe to use it, and
the Wardens are his assistants, not his equals. Each has
a particular duty assigned to him, and beyond that, he
has no right to interfere. The next grade are the Deacons. And what is their duty? Not, surely, to rank in
equality with the Master and Wardens, but to perform
the part of inferiors in office, to carry messages and commands. It is their province to attend on the Master,
and to assist the Wardens in the active duties of the
lodge, such as the reception of candidates into the different degrees of Masonry, and the immediate practice of
our rites. This is the business of the Deacons; and by
its punctual discharge, the office becomes a stepping-
stone to further preferment: for as it is incumbent on a
brother to serve the office of a Warden, before he is
eligible for the chair of a lodge, so it would be well if
the office of a Deacon were preparatory to that of a
Warden. The Treasurer, the Secretary, the Stewards,
the Inner Guard, and the Tyler, have all their respective duties to perform, and rank to support; while the
brethren are bound to obey the will and pleasure of the
W. M.

GRAMMAR. Grammar teaches the proper arrangement of words, according to the idiom or dialect of any
peculiar people, and that excellency of pronunciation,
which enables us to speak or write a language with
accuracy, agreeably to reason and correct usage.—
Preston.

G. A. O. T. U., celebrated in the lectures of Masonry
is the same Jehovah who declared his name to Moses at
the burning bush, appeared on earth at the time and
in the place, which had been foretold by the Jewish
prophets, divested of his external splendour; attested
the truth of his mission by the most stupendous miracles,
and terminated his efficacious atonement by a public

ascension into the cloudy pillar, or Shekinah, which hovered over the Mount of Olives; and the consecutive steps of this great scheme have been embodied in the system of Freemasonry. It can therefore be shown, that the historical landmarks consist of certain prominent facts recorded in the Jewish scriptures, which have been received in all ages, both before and after the advent of Christ, as typical of the Redeemer of man, and of him only.

GRAND ARCHITECT. This Most High Being ought to be duly revered by every brother as the Great Architect of heaven and earth, and his name ought never to be spoken but with the greatest humility and reverence. It is not improper, when we are always speaking of Masonry, to call God the Great Architect of heaven and earth, as we also call him the Lord of lords and King of kings. Every one, even those who are not Freemasons, call him the Creator of heaven and of earth. He has created everything that we can see; and it is certain that he has created many things which we have not power to see; and when the brethren strive to adorn his greatest work—when they assist in carrying on the spiritual temple in the manner he has ordained—they most assuredly fulfil his holy law.—*Gadicke.*

GRAND EAST. Wherever the superior body of the masonic institutions is situated, that place is called the Grand East (Grande Orient); London, York, Dublin, Edinburgh, Paris, Vienna, and Amsterdam, are all Grand Easts in masonic language. Every state in America has a Grand East, and every other place where there is a governing Grand Lodge, is called by Masons the Grand East. The East with Masons has a peculiar meaning. It is well known that the sciences first rose in the East, and that the resplendent orb of light from that quarter proclaims the glory of the day. "And behold the Glory of the God of Israel came from the way of the East, and his voice was like the noise of many waters; the earth shined with his glory. The East Gate shall be shut; it shall not be opened; and no man shall enter by it, because the Glory of the God of Israel hath entered by it. It is for the Prince."—*Dalcho.*

GRAND LODGE. This governing body consists of a Grand Master with a full staff of purple officers, the Grand Stewards for the year, and the Masters, Past Masters, and Wardens, of every warranted lodge. In the Grand Lodge, besides the power of enacting laws and regulations for the government of the Craft, and of altering, repealing, and abrogating them, provided that they continue to preserve the ancient landmarks of the Order, the Grand Lodge has also the inherent power of investigating, regulating, and deciding, all matters relative to the Craft or to particular lodges, or to individual brothers, which it may exercise either by itself or by such delegated authority as, in its wisdom and discretion, it may appoint; but in the Grand Lodge alone resides the power of erasing lodges, and expelling brethren from the Craft, a power which it ought not to delegate to any subordinate authority in England.—*Constitutions.*

GRAND MASTER. This chief officer is generally a person of the highest rank. He is nominated at the quarterly communication in December, and the election takes place in the month of March following. If the Grand Master should die during his mastership, or by sickness, absence, or otherwise, be rendered incapable of discharging the duties of his office, the Deputy Grand Master, or, in his absence, the Grand Wardens, shall assemble the Grand Lodge immediately, to record the event, which Grand Lodge shall appoint three of its members to invite the last preceding Grand Master to act as Grand Master till a new election take place; if he decline to act, then the last but one, and so on; but if no former Grand Master be found, the deputy, or the grand officer next in rank and seniority, shall proceed as principal. If there be a Pro-Grand Master at the time when a vacancy occurs in the Grand Mastership, such Pro-Grand Master shall forthwith act as Grand Master until a new election take place at the usual period.—*Constitutions.*

GRAND OFFICERS. None of the grand officers can be removed, unless for reasons which appear sufficient to the Grand Lodge; but, should the Grand Master be dissatisfied with the conduct of any of his grand officers, ne may submit the case to the Grand Lodge ; and should it appear to the majority of the brethren present that the complaint be well founded, he may displace such grand officer, and nominate another.—*Constitutions*.

GRAND OFFICERS' CLUB. As its name imports none but grand officers are eligible for members; but there is no ballot for admission, it being held that all who are considered worthy of elevation in the Order, have a natural claim to enter, although it is well understood that there is no compulsion to join the club, and that several grand officers do not avail themselves of the opportunity. The Grand Master sometimes honours the club with his presence.

GRAND STEWARDS' LODGE. This lodge has no number, but is registered in the books of the Grand Lodge, and placed in the printed lists, at the head of all other lodges, and ranks accordingly. It is represented in the Grand Lodge by its Master, Past Masters, and Wardens. Being constituted as a Master Masons' lodge, it has no power of making, passing, or raising Masons.

GRAND WARDENS. The Grand Wardens are appointed by the Grand Master annually, on the day of his installation, and if present, are to be immediately installed. These officers should have regularly served the office of Master of a lodge. They cannot act as Wardens of a private lodge while they continue Grand Wardens. When the actual Grand Wardens are in the lodge no others can supply their places; but in their absence the senior Past Grand Wardens present shall act *pro tempore*. If no Past Grand Wardens be present, the Grand Master may direct any Master of a lodge to act as Grand Warden for that occasion.—*Constitutions*.

GRAVE. The Grecian graves were always marked by a shrub called ποθος, or a garland of herbs. In honour of the dead they threw boughs and leaves upon the grave; as Euripides says they did to Polyxena when she died; for in latter times if a man had won a race or the like, they had a custom to bedeck his valiant corpse with boughs and leaves of myrtle, as in Euripides. Elect. v.

510. Whether there was any allusion to the golden bough of Virgil in all this I will not say.

GRAVITY. In a good lodge silence and gravity are recommendations during the hours appropriated to labor. The ordinary business is of too serious a nature to admit of any disturbances; and hence the ancient charges direct that no brother shall behave himself ludicrously or jestingly while the lodge is engaged in what is serious and solemn; nor use any unbecoming language upon any pretence whatever; but to pay due reverence to the Masters, Wardens, and Fellows, and put them to worship. Even the noise of moving the seats or the feet is to be avoided as much as possible; and for this reason sand is not allowed to be strewed on the floor; nor are the brethren permitted to leave the lodge during the solemn ceremonies, lest the noise thus made should disturb the proceedings. The effect of an initiation would be entirely destroyed by any interruption of this kind, and it is easy to understand that the same kind of disturbance would be calculated to distract the attention of the brethren during the delivery of lectures.

GREAT LIGHTS. The Freemasons are enlightened by great and small lights. The Bible, the square, and the compasses, belong to the first; and the sun, the moon, and the Master Mason, or the stars, to the second. The great lights are immortal, and neither limited by time nor space; the small ones are limited by both. The Bible rules and governs our faith; the square our actions; and the compasses keep us in a bond of union with all mankind, especially with a brother Mason. Or with other words, the Bible directs us to elevate our spirits to a reasonable and rational faith; the square teaches so to discipline our minds as to make them correspond with a pure and prompt obedience to the laws of our native land; and the compasses teach us so to cultivate our understandings as to enable us to live in the bonds of social and fraternal union with all mankind, whatever may be their peculiar views on religious or political subjects.—*Gadicke.*

GRIP AND SIGN. In rude times, says a masonic

writer in America, when men, ignorant of chirography, impressed the seal of their parchments with the tooth in their head for a signature, it was usual for Master Masons to give their apprentice a grip or sign, by which he should make himself known to any Mason as a regular E. A. P. to the trade; and another when he had completed his apprenticeship, and passed on to the rank of a journeyman, or F. C.; and a third when, by assiduity and skill, he had become himself a master of the work, took buildings to rear, hired Fellowcrafts or journeymen, and received apprentices. The word, the sign, and the grip, in those days, were the certificate of the Craft to its regularly taught members.

GUIDE. At our introduction into Masonry, we seek for an able guide to conduct us from this dark state of human life into light, and when arrived at that desired point, we are struck with the symbolic representations before us; and under promise of fidelity we begin our career in this secret society of Free and Accepted Masons. We emerge gradually from the lowest vale, and by study arrive at the highest degree of the occult science, or to the greatest mental perfection.—*Husenbeth.*

GUTTURAL. The guttural sign alludes to temperance, which demands a cautious habit of restraint, as may be necessary to preserve us from the risk of violating our obligation and incurring its penalty.—*Hemming.*

HAGAR. Abraham was exceedingly attached to the son of Hagar the Egyptian bond-woman, and as he grew up, the affections of his father increased so inordinately that he earnestly intreated the Lord that Ishmael might be the child of promise. But the request was denied, as being inconsistent with the divine purposes; for children cannot inherit a free and noble spirit except they be born of a free woman.

HAGGAI. This holy prophet and principal of the Sanhedrim, or Royal Chapter, was born during the Babylonish captivity, and returned to Jerusalem with Zerubbabel and Jeshua. He exhorted them to resume the work of the Temple, when it had been interrupted nearly fourteen years, in consequence of the intrigues of the Samaritans, and other obstructions excited to defeat the edict of Cyrus. The prophet represents the people as more ready to build and adorn their own dwellings than to labour in the service of God. He tells them that the unfruitful seasons they had experienced were entirely owing to this cause. He then encourages them with promises of future blessings; and predicts the important revelations that should precede the final advent of the Messiah, when the kingdoms of the world should become the kingdoms of the Lord and of his Christ.

HAMMER. With this small working tool the Master of a lodge governs the most numerous meetings. The blow of the Master's hammer commands industry, silence, or the close of labour, and every brother respects or honours its sound. In so far the hammer is a symbol of the power of the Master. The hammer must never be lost sight of at the meeting of the lodge; and should the Master be unavoidably compelled to leave the lodge-room, he must deliver it to his Deputy or Past Master, or some other skilful brother. The Wardens do not govern the lodge with their hammers, they only direct attention by them to the commands of the W. M.—*Gadicke.*

HAND. When the calamities of our brother call for our aid we should not withdraw the hand that might sustain him from sinking; but that we should render him those services, which, not encumbering or injuring our families or fortunes, charity or religion may dictate for the saving of our fellow-creature.—*Old Lectures.*

HARODIM. The mysteries of this Order are peculiar to the institution itself; while the lectures of the Chapter include every branch of the masonic system, and represent the art of Masonry in a finished and complete form. Different classes are established, and particular lectures restricted to each class. The lectures are divided into sections, and the sections into clauses. The sections are annually assigned by the Chief Harod to a certain number of skilful companions in each class, who are denominated Sectionists; and they are empowered to distribute the clauses of their respective sections, with the approbation of the Chief Harod and General Director, among the private companions of the Chapter, who are denominated Clauseholders. Such companions as by assiduity become possessed of all the sections of the lecture, are called Lecturers; and out of these the General Director is always chosen.

HARPOCRATES. This Egyptian god was unknown to the Greeks till the time of Alexander. They worshipped him under the name of Sigalion, and loaded him with many attributes unknown to the ancient Egyptians. He appears as a young man in an Egyptian mitre, holding a cornucopia, lotus, and quiver, accompanied with the poppy and owl, draped in a long robe, head raiment, branch of persea, the finger on the mouth, persea, cornucopia, lotus, basket on the head. In Stosch, the bust swaddled in a net, persea on the head, globe and serpents on the breast, but the finger on the mouth, and lock of hair distinguish nearly all his figures.—*Fosbroke.*

HEARING. Hearing is that sense by which we are enabled to distinguish sounds, and are made capable of all the perceptions of harmony and melody, with all the agreeable charms of music; by it we are enabled to enjoy the pleasures of society; and reciprocally to communicate to each other our thoughts and intentions, our purposes and desires, and by means of this sense our reason is capable of exerting its utmost power and energy.—*Old Lectures.*

HEART. The heart is the seat of the affections, passions and desires; and by the precept given by Solomon, to keep our hearts, is meant, that we should diligently preserve our good dispositions, and correct our bad ones. All the actions of a man's life issue and proceed from the heart; which is the fountain not only of our natural life, but of our mortal too; so that as a man's heart is, so will his life be: if his heart be kept clean and pure, his life cannot be wicked and vicious; but if his heart be wicked and vicious, his life cannot be kept clean and pure.—*Bishop Beveridge.*

HEIGHT. From the earth to the heavens.

HELPLESSNESS. As a Mason, your first admission in a state of helplessness was an emblematic representation of the entrance of all men into this their state of mortal existence; it inculcated the cherishing lessons of natural equality, of mutual dependence. It instructed you in the active principles of universal benevolence and charity, to make them the solace of your own distresses, and to extend relief and consolation to your fellow-creatures in the hour of their affliction. It required you to free the soul from the dominion of pride and prejudice, to look beyond the limits of particular institutions, and to view in every son of Adam a brother of the dust.— Above all it taught you to bend with reverence and resignation to the will of the Grand Architect of the Universe, and to dedicate your heart thus purified from every malignant passion, and prepared for the reception of truth and justice.

HIEROGLYPHICS. Hieroglyphics were used before the discovery of the art of writing, and through paintings of natural or scientific objects were represented invisible things and ideas, which could not have otherwise been delineated. On account of its importance, and the difficulty of reading it, it was considered sacred. Hieroglyphics must always be understood to be pictorial representations, and a symbol can be both a pictorial representation and an action. From what is here said the Freemason will be able to perceive which of the Masonic objects he has to consider as hieroglyphics and which as symbols.— *Gadicke.*

HIGH TWELVE. We have an old tradition, delivered down orally, that it was the duty of Hiram Abiff to superintend the workmen; and that the reports of the officers were always examined with the most scrupulous exactness. At the opening of the day, when the sun was rising in the east, it was his constant custom, before the commencement of labour, to enter the temple and offer up his prayers to Jehovah for a blessing on the work. And, in like manner, when the sun set in the west, and the labours of the day were closed, and the workmen had departed, he returned his thanks to the Great Architect of the Universe for the harmonious protection for the day.

LODGES MET ON THE HIGHEST HILLS AND LOWEST VALLEYS.

Not content with this devout expression of his feelings morning and evening, he always went into the temple at the hour of high twelve, when the men were called from labour to refreshment, to inspect the progress of the work, to draw fresh designs upon the tracing-board, if such were necessary, and to perform other scientific labours, never forgetting to consecrate his duties by solemn prayer. These religious customs were faithfully performed for the first six years in the secret recesses of his lodge, and for the last year in the precincts of the Most Holy Place. At length, on the very day appointed for celebrating the cape-stone of the building, he retired as usual, according to our tradition, at the hour of high twelve, and did not return alive.

HILARITY. In all Masonic festivals hilarity should be tempered with thoughtfulness and circumspection; and, although we have no objection, in the words of an old Masonic song, to

> "Crown the bowl, and fill the glass
> To every virtue, every grace,
> To the brotherhood resound
> Health, and let it thrice go round,"

yet we would not forget, in the hours of relaxation, to retain decorum in festivity and innocence in mirth, for, when pleasure is chastened by virtue, its relish will be increased, and its zest improved.

HILLS AND VALLEYS. Before we had the convenience of such well-formed lodges, the brethren used to meet on the highest of hills and in the lowest of valleys; and if they were asked why they met so high, so low, and so very secret, they replied, the better to see and observe all that might ascend or descend; and in case a cowan should appear, the Tyler might give timely notice to the W. M., by which means the lodge might be closed, and the jewels put by, thereby preventing any unlawful intrusion.—*Old York Lectures.*

HIRAM. The gavel of the Worshipful Master is so called in England, and on the continent of Europe, in allusion to the perfect order observed by the craftsmen at the building of Solomon's Temple, through the admirable skill and supervision of the operative G. M. Hiram.

HIRAM, KING OF TYRE. When Solomon had determined to build a temple at Jerusalem, he sent an embassy to Tyre, requesting Hiram, the king of the Tyrians, would furnish him with workmen to cut down timber at Lebanon, and stone in the quarries of Tyre, for the construction of that holy edifice. He returned an answer to Solomon's communication, which contained the language of amity and esteem. He agreed to extend the fraternal bond of that charity and brotherly love which was common to both the true and spurious Freemasonry, by furnishing cedars and other timber from the forest of Lebanon for the erection of a temple to the living God, and providing the most expert architects in his dominions for its construction, on the simple condition of receiving certain supplies of provisions in exchange; and he performed his contract with princely munificence and masonic candour. But even this would have been insufficient to produce any satisfactory result, without the presence of a master-mind to animate and direct the proceedings; and the king of Tyre furnished this Master in the person of his chief architect, Hiram Abiff, by whom the re-union of speculative and operative masons was to be consummated.

HIRAM ABIFF. This curious and cunning architect was a widow's son, of the tribe of Napthali, but his father was a man of Tyre, a worker in brass. He was the most accomplished designer and operator upon earth, whose abilities were not confined to building only, but extended to all kinds of work, whether in gold, silver, brass, or iron; whether in linen, tapestry, or embroidery; whether considered as an architect, statuary, founder, or designer, he equally excelled. From his designs, and under his directions, all the rich and splendid furniture of the Temple, and its several appendages, were began, carried on, and finished.—*Anderson*.

HISTORICAL. The historical portion of the Royal Arch lecture refers to three distinct epochs, namely, to the establishment of the Holy Lodge, the Sacred Lodge and the Grand and Royal Lodge.

HOLY FIRE. When Nehemiah was appointed to the government of Judea, with full authority to build the walls of Jerusalem, and to finish the Second Temple, he sent to search for the holy fire, which, before the captivity of Babylon, the priests had hidden in a dry and deep pit; not finding any fire there, but only thick and muddy water, he sprinkled this upon the altar, and presently the wood which had been so sprinkled took fire as soon as the sun began to shine, which miracle coming to the knowledge of the king of Persia, he caused the place to be encompassed with walls where the fire had been hidden, and granted great favours and privileges to the priests.—*Calmet.*

HOLY GROUND. The lodge is situated on holy ground. The first lodge was consecrated on account of three grand offerings thereon made, which met divine approbation. First, the ready compliance of Abraham to the will of God, in not refusing to offer up his son Isaac as a burnt-offering, when it pleased the Almighty to substitute a more agreeable victim in his stead; second, the many pious prayers and ejaculations of King David, which actually appeased the wrath of God, and stayed a pestilence which than raged among the people, owing to his inadvertently having had them numbered; and thirdly, the many thanksgivings, oblations, burnt sacrifices, and costly offerings which Solomon, King of Israel, made at the completion, dedication, and consecration of the temple of Jerusalem, to God's service. These three did then, have since, and I trust ever will, render the ground-work of a Masons' lodge holy.

HOLY OF HOLIES. The innermost and most sacred part of the temple was called the Holy of Holies, and sometimes the Most Holy Place, and was ordained and made on purpose for the reception of the Ark of the Covenant. The whole end and reason of that most sacred place being none other, but to be a tabernacle for it. This place or room was of an exact cubic form, as being thirty feet square and thirty feet high. In the centre the ark was placed, upon a stone rising there three fingers breadth above the floor, to be, as it were, a pedestal for it. On the two sides of it stood two cherubims fifteen feet high, one on the one side, the other on the other side, at equal distances from the centre of the ark and each side wall; where, having their wings expanded, with two of them they touched the said side walls, and with the other two they did meet, and touch each other exactly over the middle of the ark; so that the ark stood exactly in the middle between these two cherubims.— *Prideaux*.

HOLY LODGE. This lodge was opened at the foot of Mount Horeb, in the Wilderness of Sinai, about two years after the exode of the Israelites from Egypt, on the spot where Moses was first commanded to go down into Egypt, and where he was directed to put off his shoes from his feet, because the ground was holy. Here the Almighty delivered to him the decalogue with the forms of the tabernacle and the ark, and here he dictated those peculiar forms of civil and religious polity, which, by separating his people from all other nations, he consecrated Israel a chosen vessel for his service. Over this lodge presided Moses, the great and inspired law-giver; Aholiab, the curious carver and embroiderer, and Bezaleel the famous architect.

HONEY. Honey was universally used as a symbol of death. The ancients made libations to the dead of honey, wine, and blood. Funeral cakes were placed by the Greeks in the mouths of deceased persons to appease the wrath of Cerberus. Thus Virgil, Melle soporatam et medicatis frugibus offam. Ποπανα, or round, broad, or thin cakes, with honey, made a part of the funeral offerings, to Hecate, or the Moon.

HOPE. Hope is an anchor of the soul, both sure and steadfast: then let a firm reliance of the Almighty's goodness animate our endeavours, and enable us to fix our hope within the limits of his most gracious promises, so shall success attend us; if we believe a thing impossible our despondency may render it so, but if we persevere to the end, we shall finally overcome all difficulties.—*Old Lectures*

HOREB. This mountain was remarkable for seven

memorable transactions. The Burning Bush ; the striking of the rock with the rod of Moses; the lifting up of Moses' hands by Aaron and Hur, which produced the slaughter of the Amalekites; the delivery of the law ; the forty days abstinence by Moses ; the demolition of the two tables of stone on sight of the golden calf; and the supernal vision of Elijah.

HOSPITALITY. The white stone mentioned in the Apocalypse, appears to bear some relation to a particular custom among the ancients, with which they commenced and perpetuated a refined friendship. For this purpose the contracting parties took a small piece of bone, ivory, or stone, and dividing it into equal and similar parts, one of the persons wrote his name on one of these and his friend upon the other, and they made a mutual exchange. This little ticket, or "keepsake," was retained as a sacred pledge and remembrancer of an attachment the most sacred and inviolable, entire and permanent, that could be found. Including the word, sign, and token of an endeared fraternity, it was the means of ascertaining the heart's affections after many years' absence, and of securing for him a welcome to the privileges, and a share in the endearments of hospitality and love. Of course the token was carefully preserved. Though, in itself, considered of smallest worth, yet as the memorial of a highly esteemed friend, as it renewed those kind emotions of which he was the object, and called up a history on which the heart delighted to dwell, its value became inestimable, and lest some one else should take the advantage of it, the possessor kept it with great privacy, and cautiously concealed from every one the name and mark engraved upon it.—*Harris*.

HOUR-GLASS. The hour-glass is an emblem of human life. We cannot without astonishment behold the little particles, which the machine contains, pass away almost imperceptibly, and yet, to our surprise, in the short space of an hour all are exhausted. Thus wastes human life. At the end of man's short hour, death strikes the blow, and hurries him off the stage to his long and darksome resting place.

HOURS OF WORK. The masters and officers should always be punctual in their attendance, and observe the hour of meeting with scrupulous exactness; for correct conduct in officers will invariably produce a corresponding accuracy in the brethren. I know nothing which tends more to disgust and sour the mind than the unprofitable employment of waiting impatiently for the attendance of the superior officers, with a probable expectation of being disappointed at last.

HUMANITY. What it is and how variously it can be explained, is not necessary to be stated here. To the Freemason it must be a thing of the heart. All lodges must exercise it towards each other, as also must every brother, not merely in, but also out of the lodge.—*Gadicke.*

I. A. M. According to the cabalistical theologians, Moses, asking the Lord if he would tell him the name of his Divine Essence, received for answer, say "I AM THAT I AM," sent me to you, (the children of Israel), equivalent to saying—What use is it to ask what is inexplicable? "I AM THAT I AM," as the ancient sages say, meant, that he was with them in that captivity, so would he be in others; and therefore He then revealed to Moses the Tetragrammaton; and this He repeated, as He would manifest Himself by its representation of the ten sovereign lights: and by that means would become known, although veiled in them; because His existence will be ever hidden from all, and cannot be explained by any character.—*Manasseh Ben Israel.*

IDEAS. The Jewish system was made up chiefly of ceremonies, types, and figures, denoting intellectual things and moral duties. This mode of teaching morality was at that early period of the world necessary. And why?—Because then not one person in ten thousand beside the priesthood could read. The people were not then able to exhibit thoughts to the eye by means of writing, hence the necessity arose of teaching by signs and symbols, that when these struck the eye they should raise corresponding ideas in the mind, and thus convey moral truths and duties by the sight and by the operation of tools and mechanical instruments. This is the fulcrum on which rests and turns the first and most fascinating part of masonic instruction.—*Waterhouse.*

ILLEGAL SUSPENSIONS. If the Grand Master should be satisfied that any brother has been illegally, or without sufficient cause, suspended, removed, or excluded from any of his masonic functions or privileges, by any private lodge or any subordinate authority, he may order him to be reinstated or restored, and may also suspend, until the next ensuing quarterly communi cation, any lodge or brother who shall refuse to comply with such order.—*Constitutions.*

IMMORTALITY OF THE SOUL. The third or Master's degree leads to that great truth which the sublimest part of the heathen mysteries was intended to teach; and the faithful believer was assured of a future life and immortality beyond the grave.

IMMOVEABLE. The immoveable jewels are the tracing-board, for the W. M. to draw his designs on; the rough ashlar, for the E. A. P. to mark and indent on; and the perfect ashlar, for the experienced F. C. to try and adjust his jewels on. They are termed immoveable, because they are distributed in places assigned them in the lodge, for the brethren to moralize upon. They were formerly called the trasel-board, the rough ashlar, and the broached thurnel.

IMPEACHMENT. In 1842 a singular case occurred at New York, in which the rights and privileges of a Master of a lodge were placed in jeopardy, by the action of his lodge. After the lodge was opened, the Master had occasion to be absent for a short time, leaving the Senior Warden in the chair. On his return, he found that charges had been preferred against himself, and a committee appointed to try him; and the Senior Warden refused to return into his hands the warrant and mallet of the lodge. Complaint being made to the Grand Master by the Master, he directed the Grand Secretary to inform the Senior Warden that it was his direction that he should forthwith return the warrant to the hands of the Master, and that the action of the lodge on that case must be suspended, and the members hold them selves in readiness to maintain their charges before the Grand Stewards' Lodge, which was all promptly complied with by the parties. The ground of his decision was, that the Master of a lodge is only subject to impeachment and trial before his peers, who are acquainted with his duties, but which the members of a lodge cannot know, until they are themselves seated in the oriental chair.

IMPERFECTIONS. The system as taught in the regular lodges, may have some redundancies or imperfections, occasioned by the indolence or ignorance of the old members. And, indeed, considering through what obscurity and darkness the mystery has been delivered down; the many centuries, and languages, and sects, and parties, it has run through, we are rather to wonder it ever arrived to the present age without more imperfections.—*Anderson.*

IMPLEMENTS. A general collection of masonic implements may remind the Master of his power and jurisdiction, while they warn him to avoid the abuse of that power, limiting his jurisdiction and prescribing his conduct. They likewise afford him copious topics of advice to such as assist him in the government of the Fraternity, as well as to all the brethren over whom he is called to preside. He may descant on the excellence of the holy writings as a rule of life; for those writings teach us that, being born upon a level, we should act upon the square, circumscribing our desires within the compass of Nature's gifts, poured from the horn of plenty. Here, also, he may exhort them to walk uprightly, suffering neither the pressure of poverty, nor the avarice of riches to tempt the heart for a moment to swerve from the line of rectitude which is suspended before them from the centre of heaven. The division of time into equal and regular portions, he may also urge as the surest method of securing the greatest good from the opportunities that are afforded us. The subjection of our passions and desires is here likewise taught by the gavel, which is used by the operative builder to remove the excrescences and to smooth the surfaces of the rough materials for a building; while the by-laws of the lodge regulate the deportment of the craftsmen, while assembled for the purposes of social improvement and mental recreation, and while separated from the rest of mankind, and placed among none but brethren.—*Monitor*.

IMPUTATIONS. Individual errors or crimes ought only to reflect discredit on the offending parties, for a gigantic society like ours, whose professors are spread over the face of the earth, and are found in every civilized country on the globe, cannot be responsible for the misconduct of every single member of its body. It is very common to hear those who are not Masons urge this argument with all the force and confidence of conviction. A Mason has misconducted himself most grossly, they will say, and therefore Masonry must be a bad institution. But this way of reasoning is absurd. Take the argument in another point of view, and what does it end in? Why, a general condemnation of all institutions, human and divine. How would it shock our ears were it applied to Christianity. A Christian has been guilty of acts of violence; he has robbed one neighbour, slandered another, and murdered a third; and therefore—mark the consequence—Christianity must be a bad institution. Is not this preposterous? Does it follow because a wicked Christian commits murder, that the Christian religion must necessarily recommend the commission of murder? So Masonry. If some brethren so far forget their solemn obligations as to overstep the boundaries of decency; if they set the censure of the world at defiance, and disgrace themselves in the eyes of God and man, it cannot be urged that the institution recommends this conduct.

IMPOSTS. The members of the secret society of Tyrian artists, who were hired by King Solomon to erect that sacred structure, in order to distinguish them from the Jews, who performed the more humble labours, were honoured with the epithet of Free annexed to the name of builder or mason; and being talented foreigners, were freed from the usual imposts paid to the state by the subjects of Solomon.—*Husenbeth*.

INCOMMUNICABLE. The Cabalistical Jews, and

after them Josephus, and some of the Romans, think that Moses did not ask for the name of God at the burning bush, but for the true pronunciation of it, which they say had been lost through the wickedness of mankind; for which reason the former affirm that the word *gholam*, used by God presently after, being written without a *vau*, should not be rendered for ever, but hid, from the root *ghalam*, to hide; not considering that, if that was the case it should be written *ghalam*, and not *gholam*. Upon this account, the name is by all the Jews called Shemhamphorah, the unutterable name, which Josephus says was never known or heard of before God told it to Moses, for which reason they never pronounce it, but use the word Adonai, or Elohim, or plainly the word Hashem, the NAME, to express it. Thus in their letters and common discourse, instead of saying the Lord bless you, they say the Name bless you.—*Universal History*.

INDENTED TARSEL. This is an old name for the ornamented border which surrounds the mosaic pavement, now called the tessellated border.

INDISSOLUBLE TIE. Masonry annihilates all parties, conciliates all private opinions, and renders those who, by their Almighty Father, were made of one blood, to be also of one heart and one mind; brethren bound firmly together by that indissoluble tie, the love of their God, and the love of their kind.—*Daniell*.

INDUSTRY. Masonry is a progressive science, and not to be attained in any degree of perfection but by time, patience, and a considerable degree of application and industry; for no one is admitted to the profoundest secrets, or the highest honours of this Fraternity, till by time we are assured he has learned secrecy and morality
Williams.

INELIGIBLE. To prevent the introduction of improper persons, it is provided by the by-laws of every lodge, that no person can be made a Mason in, or admitted a member of, a lodge, if, on the ballot, three black balls appear against him. Some lodges wish for no such indulgence, but require the unanimous consent of the members present; some admit one black ball, some two. The by-laws of each lodge must therefore guide them in this respect; but if there be three black balls, such person cannot, on any pretence, be admitted.

INFLUENCE. The influence of Freemasonry can only be supported by an unanimous determination amongst the brethren to preserve in their private lodges the utmost regularity and decorum, an uniformity of rites and ceremonies, and, above all, a resolution to practice, in their several stations, those moral duties which are so strongly recommended, and so beautifully displayed in the private lectures of the lodge.

INITIATED. The initiated, while in the lodge, labour to perfect their own mental faculties, as well as those of the whole human race. Here let us seek the secrets of Masonry, in themselves unpronounceable; neither are they to be communicated by the laying on of hands, in a few fleeting hours. Thoughts, the indulgence in which a few short years ago would have been punished by the sword, the stake, or banishment, are, in our days, loved as philanthropic; and princes now do things for which but a few years back misunderstood philosophers were condemned as mad impostors. But there are thoughts, even in the present day, which the great mass of mankind may mock or curse, but which will in some future period be usefully and beneficially introduced into private life. This has been nearly all, and yet continues to be the chief employment of a genuine Freemason; although in the lodge those subjects are very seldom openly introduced; it is for this reason that the great mass consider the ceremonies to be the true secret, whereas they are in reality but the shell in which they are enclosed —*Gadicke*.

INITIATION. If the brethren, when they enter into this society, do not reflect upon the principles on which it is founded; if they are content to remain in their primitive ignorance, or do not act upon the obligations which they have taken upon themselves to discharge, all I can say is, that the sooner such individuals retire from the Order, the better it will be for the society, and the more creditable to themselves.— *The Duke of Sussex.*

INNER GUARD. The duty of the Inner Guard is to admit Masons on proof, to receive the candidate in form, and to obey the commands of the Junior Warden.

INNOCENCE. That innocence should be the professed principle of a Mason occasions no astonishment, when we consider that the discovery of the Deity leads us to the knowledge of those maxims wherewith he may be well pleased. The very idea of a God is attended with the belief that he can approve of nothing that is evil; and when first our predecessors professed themselves servants of the Architect of the world, as an indispensable duty they professed innocency, and put on white raiment, as a type and characteristic of their conviction, and of their being devoted to his will.—*Hutchinson.*

INQUISITION. The sanguinary tribunals of the inquisition have kept immured and led to the slaughter many an unfortunate Freemason, for daring to seek Light, Science, and Truth, where Darkness, Ignorance, and Falsehood held an arbitrary sway! The *auto da fé*, which, under Philip the Second, was almost quotidian, was instituted to indulge the fanaticism of a barbarous populace, or the capricious ambition of despotic rulers. Not many years ago, a Freemason of the name of Almodovar was burnt in Seville, along with a young woman who had been convicted by the holy office of having carried on an intercourse with an evil spirit, and of knowing the future by heart. Both these helpless victims of ignorance and fanaticism breathed in every feature the most perfect health, so that the hands of the executioner who threw them on the pile trembled all the while. It was in a square, destined to those horrible assassinations, that at the end of a pathetic sermon the two unfortunate beings were conveyed on ass-back. "*Ite missa est,*" was the sign given to throw the wretched creatures on the burning pile.—*Freemasons' Quarterly Review.*

INSECT-SHERMAH. Many of the Jews believe the Temple to have been a divine work. Some of them suppose that the stones were not so framed and polished by human art and industry, but by a worm called samir, which God created for the purpose. And they further feign that the stones came to the temple of their own accord, and were put together by angels. This legend appears to have arisen from a misrepresentation of the word samir, which signifies a very hard stone, that might be cut and polished with great perfection. It was an emblem of the peace and quiet of a Christian church. In masonic lore, the above worm is called " the insect shermah."

INSIGNIA. The presiding officers of a lodge are dis·tinguished by certain geometrical figures, being combinations of those which are called perfect, viz., the square, the equilateral triangle, and the circle; the latter being a general characteristic of grand officers. The compasses (G. M.,) are parts of the triangle; the square (W. M.,) either triangle or square; the level (S. W.,) and the plumb, (J. W.,) are both parts of a square. Now the square, level and plumb, have their separate and specific uses, and are assigned to the three chief officers, as emblems of their respective duties. But the Past Master having already executed them all, and being no longer an operative, is relieved from the burden of bearing a working tool, and invested with a problem of the greatest utility in geometrical demonstrations, he having attained the rank of a ruler in Israel; and therefore the Master's square is relieved by a square silver plate, on which is delineated the forty-seventh problem of Euclid. The compasses are instruments of design, and are thus appointed to the Grand Master. He designs; the P. M. demonstrates; the W. M. governs his particular lodge; the S. W. preserves equality and harmony amongst the brethren; and the J. W. takes care that the proper hours of labour are maintained. Thus a system of arrangement is preserved, which produces order and regularity, and constitutes the Wisdom, Strength, and Beauty of Freemasonry.

INSTALLATION. This ceremony takes place in every lodge at the commencement of the masonic year. The officers are installed, and diligently instructed in their respective duties, from the ancient statutes of the Order. It frequently happens that, on those occasions, the newly installed officers prove to the brethren their qualifications, and it is well for the lodge when they show that they are duly impressed with the importance of the trust reposed in them by their brethren.—*Gadicke.*

INSTRUCTED. The candidate is instructed by the W. M. in his duties as a Mason; the first and most impressive part of which, is to study the Holy Bible, and to practice the three great moral duties to God, your neighbour, and yourself. To God, by holding his name in awe and veneration; viewing him as the chief good, imploring his aid in laudable pursuits, and supplicating his protection on well-meant endeavours. To your neighbour, by always acting upon the square, and considering him equally entitled with yourself to share the blessings of providence, rendering unto him those favours and friendly offices, which, in a similar situation, you would expect from him. And to yourself, by not abusing the bounties of providence, impairing your faculties by irregularity, or debasing your profession by intemperance.

INSTRUCTION. Any person can be made a member of the Order by being initiated; but by so doing, he for the most part only learns to know the ceremonies; and the precise bearing or meaning of Freemasonry he must learn by being afterwards instructed. In many lodges those instructions are written out as a commentary, and are given to the lodge from time to time: at these times the W. M. or lecturer has ample room for explanatory remarks. In other lodges it is left to the W. M. to instruct the brethren upon masonic subjects, according to his own views. These instructions form a principal part of the labors of a lodge, and the candidate must pay great attention to them.—*Gadicke.*

INSTRUCTION, LODGES OF. The importance of meetings under this title is sufficiently apparent, by the provision made for their government and regulation in page 90 of the Book of Constitutions; indeed, to the discipline which pervades, we may say, all of them, the Order is much indebted, as it frequently happens that business of a general nature, which engages the attention of a lodge, prevents a regular practice in the ceremonials of the Order, and the members would require a longer time to become proficient but for the lodges of instruction whose business being confined to the principal discipline required in the ceremonials, lectures, &c., gives a more ample opportunity to those who seek information, as well as a greater scope to those who are emulous of preferment. There are several lodges of instruction in London, which are attended by brethren distinguished by their masonic attainments, the benefits of which all are desirous to impart.

INSTRUMENTAL MASONRY. The instrumental consists in the use and application of various tools and implements, such as the common gauge, the square, the plumb-line, the level, and others that may be called mathematical, invented to find the size or magnitude of the several parts or materials whereof our buildings are composed, to prove when they are wrought into due form and proportion, and when so wrought, to fix them in their proper places and positions, and likewise to take the dimensions of all bodies, whether plain or solid, and to adjust and settle the proportions of space and extent. To this part also belongs the use of various other instruments or machines, such as the lever, the wheel and axle, the wedge, the screw, the pulley, &c., which may be called mechanic, being used to forward and expedite our business, to alleviate our toils, and enable us to perform with a single hand what could not be done without many, and in some cases not at all; and those more properly belonging to our brethren of the second degree, styled Fellowcrafts.—*Dunckerly.*

INSTRUMENTS. There are certain tools or instruments well known to every Master Mason, which have undergone some variations in style and denomination since the revival in 1717. They were then called, setting maul, setting tool, and setting beetle. Later in the century, they had the names of setting tool, square, and rule; which at the union were changed into plumb-rule, level, and heavy maul.

INTEGRITY. As no man will build a house upon a bog or a quicksand, a man of suspicious integrity will be found equally unfit to sustain the character of a true Mason.—*Noorthouck.*

INTERNAL. The internal preparation of a candidate for Masonry, is exemplified by the declaration he is called on to make with respect to the motives which have in duced him to seek its privileges.

INTERRUPTION. There cannot be a greater rude ness than to interrupt another in the current of his dis course; for if it be not impertinence and folly to answer a man before we know what he has to say, yet it is a plain declaration that we are weary of his discourse, that we disregard what he says as unfit to entertain the society with, and is, in fact, little less than a downright desiring that ourselves may have audience, who have something to produce better worth the attention of the company. As this is no ordinary degree of disrespect, it cannot but always give a very great offence.—*Martin Clare.*

INTRODUCTION. The mode of introduction which a Mason ought to use to recommend himself to notice, is a salute of respect to the Master in the chair.

INTRUSTED. When the candidate was intrusted, he represented the tribe of Asher, for he was then presented with the glorious fruit of masonic knowledge, as Asher was represented by fatness and royal dainties.

INUNDATIONS. The inundations of the Nile naturally obliterated the landmarks, which consisted principally of holes dug in the earth at certain distances, forming the boundary lines of each estate or division of property; for I do not find that they used termini, or if they did, they were merely slight stakes, which the waters loosened and washed away. These holes being filled with the alluvial soil brought down from the mountains of Ethiopia, when the waters receded, the whole country presented a level surface, and nothing but the practical assistance of geometry could possibly determine the amount and locality of private possessions. From his superior knowledge of geometry, Euclid was enabled to restore to Masonry its ancient systematic usages and customs, as well as to regulate the affairs of Egyptian agriculture; and he became a general benefactor to the country, "giving." says an old record of the Craft, "to his system the name of geometry, which is now called Masonry."

INVESTED. The investment of the candidate referred to Napthali, and by this ceremony he was considered free; thus the tribe of Napthali had a peculiar freedom attached to them, in conformity with the divine blessing pronounced by Moses just before his death.

INVESTITURE. Among the primitive Masons, the badge of innocence received a characteristic distinction from its peculiar colour and material; and was indeed an unequivocal mark of superior dignity. The investiture of the apron formed an essential part of the ceremony of initiation, and was attended with rites equally significant and impressive. With the Essenian Masons, it was accomplished by a process bearing a similar tendency, and accompanied by illustrations not less imposing and satisfactory to the newly initiated inquirer. He was clothed in a long white robe, which reached to the ground, bordered with a fringe of blue ribbon, to incite personal holiness, and fastened tightly round the waist with a girdle or zone, to separate the heart from the lower and more impure parts of the body. With feet bare and head uncovered, he was considered a personification of modesty, humility, and the fear of God.

INVOCATION. The invocation used in the United States at the dedication of masonic lodges, is as follows:—"Supreme Architect of all worlds! vouchsafe to accept the solemn dedication of this hall to the glory of thy holy name!—Make its walls salvation, and its arch praise. May the brethren who shall here assemble, meet in unity, work in love, and part in harmony. May Fidelity keep the door, Faith prompt the duties, Hope animate the labours, and Charity diffuse the blessings of the lodge! May wisdom and virtue distinguish the fraternity, and Masonry become glorious in all the earth! So mote it be! Amen."

IONIC. The Ionic bears a kind of mean proportion between the more solid and delicate orders. It is said to have been formed after the model of an agreeable young woman, of an elegant shape, dressed in her hair; as a contrast to the Doric order, which was formed after that of a robust man.—*Preston.*

IRON CROW. The crow being an emblem of uprightness, alludes to the erect manner in which the spirit will arise on that great and awful day to meet its tremendous though merciful judge.

IRON TOOLS. Every piece of the Temple, whether timber, stone, or metal, was brought ready cut, framed and polished, to Jerusalem; so that no other tools were wanted nor heard, than what were necessary to join the several parts together. All the noise of axe, hammer and saw, was confined to Lebanon, and the quarries and plains of Zeredatha, that nothing might be heard among the Masons of Sion, save harmony and peace.

ISAAC. Abraham offered his son Isaac in sacrifice, when it pleased the Lord to substitute a more agreeable victim in his stead. As Isaac was an express type of Christ, so this event pointed out the great atonement; Isaac was named by a celestial messenger before he was born—so was Christ; Isaac carried the wood on which he was offered, and Christ bare the cross on which he was crucified; Isaac was offered on Mount Moriah, Christ was offered on an adjoining mountain; Isaac was to suffer by his father's hand, and whose sword was it that pierced Christ? Isaac was redeemed from death three days after Abraham was commanded to offer him up, and Christ was raised from the dead three days after his actual crucifixion. And, lastly, Isaac became the father of the Jews, as Christ is the universal father of Christians.

ISHMAEL. It is probable that Ishmael laughed and jeered at the great bustle which was made at Isaac's weaning, looking upon himself as the firstborn, and by right of that to have the privilege of fulfilling the promise of the Messiah. This gives a good account of Sarah's earnestness for the expulsion, not only of him, but of his mother also; who it is likely flattered him, and bare him up in those pretensions. Many think he did more than mock him, because St. Paul calls it persecution, which Hierom takes for beating. Isaac, who perhaps resenting his flouts, might say something that provoked Ishmael to beat him. And it is very probable his mother encouraged him in this, or at least maintained him in his insolence, which was the reason why Sarah pressed to have them both turned out of doors.—*Bishop Patrick.*

ISH CHOTZEB. Hewers of stone in the Tyrian quarries, preparatory of King Solomon's Temple.

ISH SABBAL. The men of burden, being the remains of the old Canaanites who were employed about the work, amounting to 70,000, who are not numbered among the masons.

JACHIN. In the dome of Wortsberg, in front of the entrance to the chamber of the dead, we see on one side, on the chapiter of a column, the mysterious inscription Jachin; and at the other side, the word Boaz, on the shaft of a pillar. And the figure of Christ, which occupies the top of the portal of the church of St. Dennis, has his hand placed in a position well known to all existing Freemasons.—*Clavel.*

JACOB'S LADDER. Either resting upon the floorcloth or upon the Bible: the compasses and the square should lead the thoughts of the brethren to heaven. If we find it has many staves or rounds, they represent as many moral and religious duties. If it has only three, they should represent Faith, Hope, and Charity. Draw Faith, Hope, and Charity from the Bible; with these three encircle the whole earth, and order all thy actions by the square of truth, so shall the heavens be opened unto thee.—*Gadicke.*

JAH. The inspired writings inform us that the deity was known in idolatrous nations, under his own proper and significant appellation of Jehovah. St. Paul says, that they knew God, though they glorified him not as God, neither were they thankful; but worshipped the creature rather than the Creator. And God himself tells us that they possessed the Tetragrammaton, Tetractys, or sacred name, which amongst the Jews was Jah; for he says, "from the rising of the sun, even unto the going down of the same, my name shall be (or is, according to the translation of Cudworth,) great among the Gentiles And they superstitiously believed that the Name was of such sovereign efficacy, as to enable the possessor to cure diseases, work miracles, and foretel future events."

JEDIDIAH. We have a tradition, that King Hiram has been Grand Master of all nations; and when the Temple was finished, came to survey it before its consecration, and to commune with Solomon about wisdom and art; when, finding the Great Architect of the Universe had inspired Solomon above all mortal men, Hiram very readily yielded the pre-eminence to Solomon Jedidiah, *i. e.*, the beloved of God.—*Anderson.*

JEHOSHAPHAT. Our ancient brethren who reduced the scattered elements of Freemasonry into order at the beginning of the last century, considered the lodge to be situated in the valley of Jehoshaphat; and that in whatever part of the world it might be opened, it was still esteemed, in a figure, to occupy that celebrated locality. Thus it was pronounced, in the earliest known lectures. that the lodge stands upon holy ground, or the highest hill or lowest dale, or in the Vale of Jehoshaphat. This celebrated valley derives its name from Jehovah and Shaphat, which means Christ, and to judge; and as the prophet Joel had predicted that the Lord would gather together all nations, and bring them down into the valley of Jehoshaphat, it was believed by the Jews, (and the Christians subsequently adopted the same opinion) that in this place the transactions of the great day of judgment would be enacted.

יהוה. This word contains the mystery of the Trinity, as the ancient Jews who lived before Christ testify in their traditions. For by י they understand the origin of all things. By ה they mean the Son, by whom all things were made. By ו which is a conjunction copulative, they understand the Holy Ghost, who is the love which binds them together, and proceeds from them. And further, that ה refers to the two natures of Christ, the divine and human.—*Vatabulus.*

JEHOVAH. Most Christian translators of the Old Testament, including our own, generally abstain from introducing the Name in their versions, putting "the Lord" instead of Jehovah, in this following the example of the Jews, who, to avoid any attempt to pronounce the name, read אדני Adonai, instead of it, and of the seventy who set down the word Κύριος in lieu of it. The Jewish notion of this matter is explained in the Talmud, on the authority of R. Nathan Ben Isaac, who is reported to say, "In this world things are not as in the world to come; in this world we write the name of God with the letters יהוה (Jehovah), and read אדני (Adonai), but in the world to come we shall both read and write יהוה."

JEPTHA. There is an old masonic tradition respecting Jeptha to the following effect. When the Ephraimites had assembled together to molest Jeptha, their leader encamped round a certain pillar, which being placed in an elevated situation, commanded a view of the ancient country, where Jeptha was prepared to receive him. After the battle, when the Ephraimites were retreating, Jeptha called a council of war to decide upon the necessary means of intercepting them, where it was agreed that they should be made to pronounce a password on the shores of Gilgal, by which they might be distinguished in the dark as in the light. And as they were unable to pronounce this word, they were immediately slain. This test word having been thus used to distinguish friend from foe, &c.

JESHUA. Jeshua the high priest was a lineal descendant from Seraiah, who held the pontificate when the temple was destroyed, and he became the associate and colleague of Zerubbabel in the furtherance of the great design of building the second temple.

JEWELS. The Freemasons' ornaments are three jewels, the square, the level, and the plumb-rule. Those who are intrusted with them must possess great talents, and whether they can be cautious and worthy guardians of them must be apparent from their previous conduct.

JEWISH MASONS. The true and pure Freemasons'

Lodges allow no Jews to be admitted; for a Jew, according to his faith, cannot lay his hand upon the Gospel of St. John as a proof of his sincerity and truth. Also the doctrine of a Triune God is the most important distinction between Christianity and Judaism, and the chief doctrine of Christianity, so that no Jew can acknowledge this symbol, which is so sacred to a Freemason.—*Gadicke.*

JEWISH SYMBOLS. The Jews had many symbols represented on the Tabernacle and the Temple. Moses placed in the former two cherubims, or sphynxes, as well as ornaments and decorations of flower-work; and figures of cherubims were embroidered on the veil of the Holy of Holies, on the hangings of the sanctuary, and probably on the curtain also. It is evident, therefore, that Moses never intended to prohibit the use of symbols; nor was such a thing understood by the Jews in any age. Solomon did not so understand him, for in his temple the cherubims were represented in the Sanctum Sanctorum, and he decorated the walls with palm-trees, cherubims, flowers, and other figures. The brazen sea rested upon twelve oxen. In Ezekiel's description of the temple are many figures, which, like the Egyptian deities, had heads of animals. The pillars, Jachin and Boaz, were decorated with lily-work, net-work, and pomegranates, as symbols of the peace, unity, and plenty which distinguished the building. Even after the Babylonish captivity the same symbolical system was used. The golden lamp in the second temple, of which a representation is still extant on the triumphal arch of Vespasian at Rome, was placed on sphynxes. In the roof, and at the gate of Zerubbabel's temple, there were golden vines, thickly charged with rich clusters of grapes.

JEWS. The Jews for five hundred years after their delivery from Egypt, have left not a single masonic tradition beyond that recorded in the first degree, and as the second degree treats upon the arts and sciences it certainly came from a different source than the first, for the ten commandments, and more especially the Talmudic explanation of the same, were a bar to the higher studies of the Jews. Nothing sculptured, or otherwise made with hands, whereby the Deity, or eternity was represented, was permitted; and the Rabbinical law saying that the sciences were not necessary, operated so powerfully upon the conscientious part of that people, that they followed the humble employment of a pastoral life. This accounts for the scanty documents we have of the Israelitish Freemasonry.—*Husenbeth.*

JOHN'S BROTHERS. Before the year 1440 the masonic society was known by the name of John's Brothers, but they then began to be called Free and Accepted Masons, at which time in some part of Flanders, by the assistance and riches of the brotherhood, the first hospitals were erected for the relief of such as were afflicted with St. Anthony's fire. Although in the exercise of charity we neither regard country nor religion, yet we consider it both necessary and prudent to initiate none into our mysteries, except those who profess the Christian religion.—*Charter of Colne.*

JOINING. If any member shall be excluded from his lodge, or shall withdraw himself from it, without having complied with its by-laws, or with the general regulations of the Craft, he shall not be eligible to any other lodge, until that lodge has been made acquainted with his former neglect, so that the brethren may be enabled to exercise their discretion as to his admission. Whenever a member of any lodge shall resign, or shall be excluded, or whenever at a future time he may require it, he shall be furnished with a certificate stating the circumstances under which he left the lodge; and such certificate is to be produced to any other lodge of which he is proposed to be admitted a member, previous to the ballot being taken.—*Constitutions.*

JOPPA. There is an old tradition among Masons, that the banks of the river at Joppa were so steep as to render it necessary for the workmen to assist each other up by a peculiar locking of the right hand, which is still preserved in the Mark-Master's degree.

JOSEPH. Freemasons are accustomed to esteem Joseph as one of their greatest lights, because of his numerous practical virtues. He forgave his brethren freely when he possessed the power of punishing them for their inhumanity towards him, he succoured his aged father in his distress, and by his superior wisdom and discernment, he saved a whole people from destruction. These are all masonic virtues of the first class; and having been beautifully illustrated in the character and conduct of Joseph, his example is recommended to our consideration, as an useful lesson more powerful than precept, and more efficacious than admonition.

JOURNEY. Every Freemason, when he is initiated into the Craft, is taught to consider human life as a journey. He would faint with fatigue, lose himself in unknown roads, or fall over high precipices if he was not supported, faithfully conducted, and fraternally warned. By these means he arrives in safety at the end of his journey, and is permitted to receive light himself, that he may be able to support, lead, and warn others when travelling the same road.—*Gadicke.*

JOURNEYMAN. Three or four years since, a paragraph went the round of the press, deriving the English word "journeyman" from the custom of travelling among workmen in Germany. This derivation is very doubtful. Is it not a relic of Norman rule, from the French "jour née," signifying a day-man? In support of this, it may be observed that the German name for the word in question is "tagelöhner," day-worker. It is also well known, that down to a comparatively recent period, artisans and free labourers were paid daily.—*Notes and Queries.*

JUNIOR WARDEN. The Junior Warden is an important officer. The jewel by which he is distinguished is an emblem of uprightness, and points out the just and upright conduct which he is bound to pursue, in conjunction with the Master and his brother Warden, in ruling and governing the brethren of the lodge according to the Constitutions of the Order; and more particularly by a due attention to caution and security in the examination of strange visitors, lest by his neglect any unqualified person should be enabled to impose upon the lodge, and the brethren be thus innocently led to forfeit their obligation.

JURISDICTION. In its general sense, the power or right to exercise authority. All Lodges working within the territorial limits of a Grand Lodge are under its control and jurisdiction.

JUST AND PERFECT. This appellation, which is given to St. John's lodges in general, is of a more important nature than is generally understood by it, for it is not sufficient for a lodge only to be so far just and perfect as to belong to a certain Grand Lodge, to work according to an acknowledged ritual, and to have all its officers and members in their proper places, but it must be just unto all the brethren, and perfect in the exercise of every masonic duty. It is not just when the brethren are deprived of their rights, even of superintending the economy of the lodge, for such a lodge has no independence, and he who is not independent cannot exercise his masonic duties as a perfect Master.—*Gadicke.*

JUSTICE. Justice, the boundary of right, constitutes the cement of civil society. This virtue in a great measure constitutes real goodness, and is therefore represented as the perpetual study of the accomplished Mason. Without the exercise of justice, universal confusion would ensue, lawless force might overcome the principles of equity, and social intercourse no longer exist.—*Preston.*

JUSTIFICATION. We do not hesitate to appeal to the world in justification of the purity of our moral system. Our Constitutions are well known ; we have submitted them freely to general investigation. We solemnly avouch them as the principles by which we are governed, the foundation on which we build, and the rules by which we work. We challenge the most severe critic, the most practised moralist, the most perfect Christian, to point out anything in them inconsistent with good manners, fair morals, or pure religion.—*Harris.*

KEY. This symbol may be improved to impress upon the mind of every brother the importance of those secret which have been transmitted through thirty centuries, amidst bitter persecutions, for the benefit of the sons of light. As we have thus received them, untarnished by the touch of profane curiosity, and unimpaired by the revolution of time and empires, let us deliver them, in all their purity and perfection, to succeeding brethren, confident that they will never be divulged to such as are unworthy.

KEYSTONE. This refers to the keystone of the Royal Arch, called by some the cape-stone, because they erroneously suppose that a knowledge of the principles of the arch is not so old as the building of the Temple of Jerusalem. It was known, however, to the Egyptians several centuries before Solomon flourished, as modern discoveries fully testify.

KING. The first officer in the Royal Arch Chapter, commonly called the First Principal. He represents Zerubbabel, the Governor of Judea, at the building of the second temple.

KING HENRY VI. In the minority of King Henry VI., a very respectable lodge was held at Canterbury, and a coat of arms, much the same as that of the London Company of Freemasons, was used by them; whence it is natural to conceive that the said company is descended from the ancient Fraternity, and that in former times no man was made free of that company until he was initiated in some lodge of Free and Accepted Masons, as a necessary qualification; and it not only appears that before the troubles which happened in the reign of this unfortunate prince, Freemasons were universally esteemed, but even King Henry himself was made a Mason in the year 1442, and many lords and gentlemen of the court, after his example, solicited and obtained admittance into the Fraternity.—*Calcott.*

KING NAME. The name of God includes all things. He who pronounces it shakes heaven and earth, and inspires the very angels with astonishment and terror. There is a sovereign authority in this name; it governs the world by its power. The other names and surnames of the Deity are ranged about it like officers and soldiers about their sovereigns and generals. From this King Name they receive their orders and obey.—*Calmet.*

KINGLY POWER. The kingly power was restored in the person of Zerubbabel, who sprang from the royal line of David, and the tribe of Judah; nor was a vestige thereof again effaced until after the destruction of the city and temple by the Romans, under Titus, in the year 76 of the present era, thus verifying the remarkable prophecy of Jacob, delivered in Egypt above one thousand years before, that the sceptre should not depart from Judah, nor a law-giver from between his feet, until Shiloh came.

KNEE BENT. When we offer up our ejaculations to Almighty God, we will remember a brother's welfare as our own; for as the voices of babes and sucklings ascend to the throne of grace, so most assuredly will the breathings of a fervent heart; and so our prayers are certainly required for each other.—*Ash.*

KNEELING. When we bow the knee, it represents our fall in Adam; and when we rise, having received the benefit of prayer addressed to the throne of grace, it is a type of our restoration in Christ by the grace of God, through whom we are able to lift up our hearts to heaven. The candidate for Masonry is directed to bend the knee with a similar reference.

KNOCK. A candidate for Masonry is said to have complied with the terms of a certain text of Scripture, by having first *sought* in his mind whether he were really desirous of investigating the mysteries of Masonry; then *asked* counsel of his friend, and lastly having *knocked*, the door of Masonry became open to him; and it will be remembered that the door of a Freemasons' lodge does not stand open for every one to enter, neither do we call labourers to the work, but those who wish to work with us must voluntarily offer their services. If he desires to be admitted, he must knock earnestly and manfully. "Ask and ye shall receive, seek and ye shall find, knock and it shall be opened unto you." He who cannot knock in the full confidence of an honourable feeling, and is not convinced in his own mind that he deserves to be admitted, ought not to have the door of the lodge opened to him.—*Gadicke.*

KNOWLEDGE. A man of perfect wisdom and knowledge, accomplished in all his ways, and without the least blame, was painted in the Egyptian hierogly phics with a beautiful face, with wings like an angel, holding in his hands a book, in which he looked, a sword, and a balance, and behind him two vases, one of them full of water and the other of blazing fire, under his right foot a ball with a crab painted on it, and under his left a deep pot full of serpents, scorpions, and different reptiles, the covering of which had the shape of an eagle's head.—*Aben Washih.*

KNOW THYSELF. A brother is said to be a good Mason who has studied and knows himself, and has learnt and practised that first and great lesson of subduing his passion to his will, and tries to the utmost of his power to free himself from all vices, errors and imperfections; not only those that proceed from the heart, but likewise all other defects of the understanding which are caused by custom, opinion, prejudice, or superstition; he who asserts the native freedom of his mind, and stands fast in the liberty that makes him free; whose soul is (if one may so express it) universal and well contracted; and who despises no man on account of his country or religion; but is ready at all times to convince the world that truth, brotherly love, and relief, are the grand principles on which he acts.

LABOUR. An important word in Freemasonry—we may say the most important. It is for this sole reason alone, that a person must be made a Freemason; all other reasons are incidental and unimportant, or uncon- nected with it. Labour is commonly the reason why meetings of the lodge are held, but do we every time receive a proof of activity and industry? The work of an operative mason is visible, if even it be very often badly executed; and he receives his reward if his building is thrown down by a storm in the next moment. He is convinced that he has been active; so must also the brother Freemason labour. His labour must be visible to himself and unto his brethren, or, at the very least, it must be conducive to his own inward satisfaction.— *Gadicke.*

JACOB'S VISION—FAITH, HOPE AND CHARITY.

LABOURER. No labourer shall be employed in the proper work of Masonry; nor shall Freemasons work with those that are not free, without an urgent necessity; nor shall they teach labourers and unaccepted Masons, as they should teach a brother.—*Ancient Charges.*

LADDER. Standing firmly on the Bible, square and compasses, is a ladder that connects the earth with the heavens, or covering of a lodge, and is a transcript of that which the patriarch Jacob saw in a vision when journeying to Padanarum, in Mesopotamia. It is composed of staves, or rounds innumerable, which point out so many moral virtues, but principally of three, which refer to Faith, Hope and Charity; Faith in the Great Architect of the Universe, Hope in salvation, and to be in Charity with all mankind, but more particularly with our brethren.

LAMBSKIN. The lambskin has in all ages been considered as an emblem of innocence and peace. The Lamb of God who taketh away the sins of the world, will grant to those who put their trust in Him, his peace. He, therefore, who wears the lambskin as a badge of Masonry, is reminded of that purity of life and conversation, which it is absolutely necessary for them to observe, who expect to be admitted into the Grand Lodge above.—*Hardie.*

LAMECH. After the sun had descended down the seventh age from Adam, before the flood of Noah, there was born unto Mathusael, the son of Mehujael, a man called Lameeh, who took unto himself two wives; the name of one was Adah, and the name of the other Zillah. Now Adah his first wife bare him two sons, the one named Jabal, and the other Jubal. Jabal was the inventor of geometry, and the first who built houses of stone and timber; and Jubal was the inventor of music and harmony. Zillah his second wife, bare Tubal Cain, the instructor of every artificer in brass and iron; and a daughter called Naamah, who was the first founder of the weaver's craft.—*Ancient Masonic MS.*

LANDMARKS. What are the landmarks? is a question often asked, but never determinately answered. In ancient times, boundary stones were used as landmarks before title-deeds were known, the removal of which was trictly forbidden by law. With respect to the landmarks of Masonry, some restrict them to the O.B. signs, tokens, nd words. Others include the ceremonies of initiation, passing, and raising; and the form, dimensions, and support; the ground, situation, and covering; the ornaments, furniture, and jewels of a lodge, or their characteristic symbols. Some think that the Order has no landmarks beyond its peculiar secrets. It is quite clear, however, that the order against removing or altering the landmarks was universally observed in all ages of the Craft.

LATE HOURS. It is a fact, confirmed by experience, that an indulgence in late hours cannot fail to injure the credit and respectability of a lodge, because it introduces other habits which are not consistent with the gravity and decorum which ought always to characterize the proceedings of Masonry. And hence it is an important part of the W. Master's duty, to discountenance such baleful practice. If the brethren meet for the purpose of business, or to cultivate a knowledge of the science by joining in the lectures, let them pursue their labours with assiduity and zeal during the period prescribed in the by-laws; and should it be necessary for the Junior Warden to perform his office, let the brethren enjoy themselves with decent moderation; but by all means let the Senior Warden discharge his duty honestly and conscientiously, and let the lodge be closed and the brethren depart to their own homes at such an hour as shall excite no unpleasant feelings, nor call forth reproachful observations from the females of their families, whom it is their duty and interest, as well in the character of husbands and fathers, as of Masons, to love, to cherish. and to oblige.

LATOMUS, or LATOMIA. *(A quarry.)* A term sometimes applied to Masons. The title is by no means a correct one. The word *lapicida* is more appropriate, which Bailey defines a hewer of stones; a stone-cutter, or Mason. The word is derived from the Greek, and intended to apply to a cutter and polisher of precious stones.

LAWS OF THE LAND. The Freemason has the greatest respect for the laws of the land in which he lives, and he obeys them with the zeal of a faithful subject. If he is intrusted with the putting those laws in force, his masonic duties remind him to be faithful and diligent in applying them. Should the state command the lodge to be closed of which he is a member, he immediately obeys, and visits no assembly which is not allowed, or at least tolerated by the state. In the event of a brother wilfully violating the laws of his country, the Order itself directs the attention of the magistrates unto him, and he who is punished as a criminal by the laws, is excluded from the Order without exception.—*Gadicke.*

LAWS OF MASONRY. In the Grand Lodge resides the power of enacting laws and regulations for the government of the Craft, and of altering, repealing, and abrogating them, provided that they continue to preserve the ancient landmarks of the Order. No motion for a new law or regulation, or for the alteration or repeal of an old one, shall be made, until it shall have been proposed in, or communicated to, the general committee, which meets on the Wednesday preceding each quarterly communication, nor until it shall have been handed up in writing to the Grand Master. After having been perused and found by him not to contain anything contrary to the ancient landmarks of the Order, the motion may be publicly proposed If seconded, the question shall be put thereon for the opinion of the Grand Lodge. If approved and confirmed at the next ensuing meeting of the Grand Lodge, it becomes a law of the society.—*Constitutions.*

LAW-SUITS. If any brother do you an injury, you must apply to your own or his lodge, and from thence you may appeal to the Grand Lodge at the quarterly communication, as has been the ancient laudable conduct of our forefathers in every nation; never take a legal course but when the case cannot be otherwise decided, and patiently listening to the honest and friendly advice of Master and fellows, when they would prevent your going to law with strangers, or would excite you to put a speedy period to all lawsuits, that so you may find the affair of Masonry with the more alacrity and success; but with respect to brothers or fellows at law, the Master and brethren should kindly offer their mediation, which ought to be thankfully submitted to by the contending brethren; and if that submission is impracticable, they must however carry on their process or law-suit without wrath or rancour, (not in the common way) saying or doing nothing which may hinder brotherly love and good offices to be renewed and continued, that all may see the benign influence of Masonry, as all true Masons have done from the beginning of the world, and will do to the end of time.—*Ancient Charges.*

LEAGUE. It was lawful in ancient times, before the law of Moses was given, to make leagues with strangers to their religion, for their mutual benefit, as appears by the story of Jacob and Laban, Isaac and Ahimelech, (though some doubt whether he was an idolater) and the law of Moses made no alteration. If Hiram therefore worshipped other gods, Solomon might, notwithstanding, make a league with him, (inasmuch as Hiram calls him brother) he being none of the seven nations of Canaan.—*Bishop Patrick.*

LEATHER APRON. The white leather apron is an emblem of innocence, and the badge of a Mason more ancient than the golden fleece, or Roman eagle, more honourable than the star and garter, or any other order that could be conferred upon the candidate at that or nay future period, by king, prince, or potentate, or any other person, except he be a Mason; and which every one ought to wear with pleasure to himself, and honour to the fraternity.

LEAVING. When a brother changes his residence from the place where the lodge is held, of which he is a member, he will act prudently by requiring a written dismissal from the lodge, more especially if there is a lodge in the place where he is going to take up his new abode, and he wishes to become a member of it. In this dismissal it ought to be certified that he had been a diligent workman, and that he had done his duty to the lodge, of which he had up to that period been a member. Should there be any other reason why a member declares himself off the lodge, it ought to be truly stated, for truth should ever be one of the distinguishing characteristics of a Mason. Without such a written testimonial, no strange brother should be allowed to leave one lodge and join another. In places where there are many lodges, a brother may leave one and join another, but ought not to do so without a written testimonial that he has done his duty to the lodge he is leaving; should there be any particular reason for this step, both lodges ought thoroughly to know them. Many brethren leave one lodge and join another, without any notice whatever to the lodge they have left; the consciences of those brethren must be their own accusers or excusers.—*Gadicke.*

LEBANON. The forests of the Lebanon mountains only could supply the timber for the Temple. Such of these forests as lay nearest the sea were in the possession of the Phœnicians, among whom timber was in such constant demand, that they had acquired great and acknowledged skill in the felling and transportation thereof, and hence it was of such importance that Hiram consented to employ large bodies of men in Lebanon to hew timber, as well as others to perform the service of bringing it down to the sea-side, whence it was to be taken along the coasts in floats to the port of Joppa, from which place it could be easily taken across the country to Jerusalem.—*Kitto.*

LECTURE. Literally, a formal or methodical discourse intended for instruction. Lectures have been adopted from the earliest ages as a convenient mode of teaching the elements of every branch of human knowledge. The course of instruction in Freemasonry is divided in parts or sections, which is called a lecture. Each degree is so arranged that the candidate will enjoy the advantage of the theory, the practice, and then the explanation or lecture. Those who are desirous of learning the lectures, with the greatest advantage, must regularly attend the Lodges, and be diligently attentive to the instruction they receive there.

LECTURER. In the symbolical lodges of the Continent and elsewhere, a lecturer is annually appointed, and after the W. M , and P. M., the lecturer has the most important office in the lodge. He, as well as the two first officers, must be perfectly acquainted with Freemasonry, and not only a man who has received a liberal education, but must also possess the true spirit of oratory. His orations or lectures must produce an impression on the minds of his hearers. At the election of a lecturer the electors should bear this in mind, and reflect that he has something more to do than merely read the ritual. If the lecturer has sufficient knowledge to be enabled to teach the brethren Freemasonry, or the bearing of moral truths upon the science in an agreeable and instructive manner, and not in mere mystical forms, he will be willingly listened to by the brethren. Some discourses are appropriated to certain seasons, but even these the lecturer must be able to make interesting, in order that they may not appear as mere repetitions. He who confines himself to these discourses, and the mere reading of the ritual, does not fulfil the duties of his office as he ought.

LEFT HAND. The left hand is mentioned in the system of Freemasonry, as being nearest to the heart. Levinus Lemnius, speaking of the right finger, says that " a small branch of the artery, and not of the nerves, as Gillius thought, is stretched from the heart unto this finger."

LEGEND. Amongst the Jews the type παραβολη, whether expressed dramatically or by words, was a legend or symbol. This method of conveying a striking truth by the use of metaphorical imagery, was employed in their private as well as their public affairs. The symbols, parables, or legends, were, in process of time, multiplied so abundantly, as to form the chief contents of the Mishna and Gemara, compiled by the Rabbi Judah Makkadosh and his successors, which form the text and annotations of the Talmud.

LENGTH. The length of the lodge expresses the extent of masonic love. With this love our profession will never be in danger of acquiring the appellation of hypocrisy, but will bear the test of scrutiny; and however severely tried, will be found a firm possession. With this love our devotion will be the true devotion of the soul, in all its native simplicity and sincerity. This heavenly spark within our bosoms will catch that heavenly flame of divine and seraphic love, which alone can unite the Creator with the creature; and thus alone can be formed and completed, that true felicity of the human soul, the union to its divine original.—*Inwood.*

LESSER LIGHTS. These lights or luminaries are used to light us to, at, and from labour. They are situated in the east, west, and south, in allusion to the apparent course of the sun, which, rising in the east, gains its meridian in the south, and disappears in the west. These luminaries represent emblematically, the sun, moon, and the Master of the lodge.

LEVEL. The level is used by operative Masons to lay levels and to prove horizontals. It is the duty of the foreman or superintendent of every building, frequently to prove the various parts of the building by the level, in the course of its erection, and he who neglects this important part of his duty, lays himself open to severe censure.—*Gadicke.*

LEVY. The timbers for building the temple at Jerusalem, were felled in the forests of Lebanon, where a levy of thirty thousand men of Jerusalem were employed by monthly courses of ten thousand; and the stones were cut and wrought in the quarries of the mountains of Judea, by eighty thousand men, assisted by seventy thousand who bare burthens.—*Hemming.*

LEWIS. This appellation is given to the son of a Mason. Lewis formerly had the privilege of being initiated into the Order younger than any other person, even in his eighteenth year; but they only enjoy this privilege now in those lodges where the law does not prohibit any one to be initiated before he has reached his twenty-fifth year. Lewis must also be a cultivated and morally respectable young man, or the entrance into the lodge will be refused to him as well as to those whose fathers are not Masons.—*Gadicke*

LIFE. The sign of the cross amongst the Egyptians signified life, and was the mark by which the Cabalists expressed the number ten, which was a perfect number, denoting heaven, and the Pythagorean Tetractys, or in communicable name of God.

LIGHT. Light is a symbol of knowledge. May every Mason strive incessantly for light, and especially for the light eternal! When a society is assembled any where to do good, they require an influential person to communicate the light of experience, instruct them, and point out the way they should go, or bring light to them. This may be done symbolically, by suddenly lighting up a dark room with torches. He who thus introduces the light into the lodge, must be a worthy man, and experienced in the Craft.—*Gadicke.*

LILY. This flower was full of meaning among the ancients, and occurs all over the East. Egypt, Persia, Palestine, and India, presented it everywhere over their architecture, in the hands and on the heads of their sculptured figures, whether in bas-relief or statue. We also find it in the sacred vestments and architecture of the tabernacle and temple of the Israelites, and see it mentioned by our Saviour as an image of peculiar beauty and glory, when comparing the works of nature with the decorations of art. It is also represented in all pictures of the salutation of Gabriel to the Virgin Mary, and in fact has been held in mysterious veneration by all people of all nations and times. It is the symbol of divinity, of purity, and abundance, and of a love most complete in affection, charity, and benediction; as in Holy Scripture, that mirror of purity, Susannah, is defined Susa, which signifies the flower of the lily, a name given to the chief city of the Persians, for its superior excellency. The three leaves of the lily in the arms of France, mean piety, justice, and charity.—*Sir Robert Ker Porter.*

LILY-WORK. Lily-work, from its whiteness, denotes peace.

LINE. The universal bond with which every Mason ought to be united to his brethren, should consist of sixty

threads or yarns, because, according to the ancient statutes, no lodge was allowed to have above sixty members;
but it neither depends upon the quality of the thread, nor
the number of the brethren, if the bond which unites us
all is composed of true brotherly love.—*Gadicke.*

LINEAR TRIAD. This figure, which appears in
some old Royal Arch floor-cloths, bore a reference to the
sojourners, who represented the three stones on which
prayers and thanksgivings were offered, on the discovery
of the lost Word; thereby affording an example, that it is
our duty in every undertaking, to offer up our prayers and
thanksgivings to the God of our salvation.

LINK. Refers to Genesis xi.

LION. The lion was a symbol of Jeremiah, because
of the terrible voice of his threatening; and of St. Mark,
because his gospel begins with the voice in the wilderness;
but principally of Christ, who is denominated the lion of
the tribe of Judah, and will ultimately subdue all things
to himself; "for he must reign till he hath put all enemies
under his feet."

LODGE. As men call the house of God a church, and
when religious services are performed in it, say it is church
hours, so also we call the locality in which a lodge assembles, a lodge, and when the brethren are assembled in it,
it is lodge hours. The form of a lodge is an oblong square.
Three well-informed brethren form a legal lodge, five improve it, and seven make it perfect. We may also call a
room in which a lodge is held, a hall.—*Gadicke.*

The earliest description of a lodge that I have met with,
explains it as being "just and perfect by the numbers
three, five and seven." This was subsequently exemplified in the following prescribed form. "A lodge of
Masons is an assemblage of brothers and fellows met
together for the purpose of expatiating on the mysteries
of the Craft, with the Bible, square and compasses, the
Book of Constitutions, and the warrant empowering them
to act." In the formula used at the present day, a further
amplification has been adopted. It is here denominated
an assembly of Masons, just, perfect, and regular, who are

met together to expatiate on the mysteries of the Order just, because it contains the volume of the Sacred Law unfolded; perfect, from its numbers, every order of Masonry being virtually present by its representatives, to ratify and confirm its proceedings; and regular, from its warrant of constitution, which implies the sanction of the Grand Master, for the country where the lodge is held.

LODGES OF LEBANON. Each of the degrees in these lodges had its distinguishing signs, words and tokens, without which confusion and disorder could scarcely have been prevented. The Apprentices messed by seven in a company, and the Fellowcrafts by five. The Masters and Wardens were men of enlightened minds and matured understandings, well skilled in geometry and the rules of proportion. They trained their respective brethren and fellows to the practice of blending moral virtue with the pursuits of science, and inculcated charity or brotherly love, as the distinguishing feature of their profession.

LODGES OF TYRE. In the quarries of Tyre were two lodges of Super-excellent Masters, as supervisors of the work, over which Tito Zadok, the high priest, presided: these were the Harodim. There were also six lodges of Excellent Masters, eight Grand Architects, and sixteen Architects—men of superior talent, who had been selected for their proficiency in the sciences, and placed as superintendents over the workmen. This was a necessary provision; for thus they were enabled to regulate the proceedings of, and to preserve order and arrangement in, the several departments which were assigned to them. There were three classes of Masters in thirty-six lodges, called Menatzchim, and seven hundred lodges of Ghiblim, or operative Fellowcrafts, under Hiram Abiff, their Grand Master.

LOGIC. Consists of a regular train of argument, whence we infer, deduce, and conclude, according to certain premises laid down, admitted, or granted; and in it are employed the faculties of conceiving, judging, reasoning, and disposing which are naturally led on from one gradation to another, till the point in question is finally determined.—*Preston*.

LOVE. The universal charity of a Mason, is like the charity of the Mason's God, and his God is the God of love. Consider the extent of the love of God, and that only, according to his degree, is the extent of masonic charity. In the broad circle of his affections, he encloses all mankind; he, like the God of love, looks through station, clime, and colour, and with one wish of universal good-will, he wishes well to all mankind. With the compass of his mind, he measures and draws the square of his conduct, and within that square, having honestly provided for his own household, he forms his little angles of benevolence and charity, to the distressed of all communities.—*Inwood*.

LOYALTY. As Masons you are required to be, as your ancient brethren have always been, true to your Queen, and just to your country; to teach all within the sphere of your acquaintance to be loyal; to assist readily in putting down all disloyalty or rebellion; to follow temperance, fortitude, prudence, and justice, in your walk through this life; to be good husbands, kind parents, "training up your children in the nurture and admonition of the Lord."—*Percy*.

MADE. This solemn ceremony should never in any lodge be considered as the most important part of a Freemason's work (although it is always a thing of importance to initiate a new member into the Order.) Instruction and charity are the chief works of a Freemason. Initiations are only secondary to these. The day of his initiation must ever be an important epoch to a Freemason, and lead to a serious self-examination. The reflection that in one evening he has become closely united with many thousands of unknown men, is of itself important, even if the initiated should not be able to appreciate the real spirit of the Order. On his initiation the candidate must place himself unreservedly in the hands of the proper officer appointed to conduct him, and submit himself to every proof that is demanded from him, and make no objection to any of the ceremonies he has to go through, but answer every question truly and manfully. When he arrives in the assembly of the brethren he is asked again, and for the last time, if it is his wish to be initiated. In the moment when he is about to receive the first degree, every freedom is permitted to him either to go forward in the ceremony, or return from whence he came; for we must admit that to enter upon an unknown undertaking is a dangerous thing. He who is in earnest will here prove that he holds it to be unworthy of a man not to complete any undertaking which he has commenced after mature deliberation. If he does so, the assembled brethren cheerfully and unanimously pronounce him "worthy," and he is made a partaker of the LIGHT. The solemn obligation taken by the candidate, and the sacred and mysterious manner in which the sacred numbers are communicated, have always been respected by every faithful brother.—*Gadicke*.

MALLET. This is an important instrument of labour, and no work of manual skill can be completed without it. From it we learn that labour is the lot of man, and that skill without exertion is of no avail; for the heart may conceive, and the head devise in vain, if the hand be not prompt to execute the design.

MAN. The man formed a part of the cherubic symbol, and referred to the prophet Isaiah, because of his prophecy of Christ being a man, by his birth of a virgin: and to St. Matthew, because he gives Christ's human genealogy. It was the insignia of Reuben, and denoted reason and religion.

MANNA. A Royal Arch symbol. The manna is called by David "the bread of angels." Some Rabbins believe that it had this name, because the angels are refreshed by divine light, "quod lumen incorporatum est, et factum manna." The Rabbi Ishmael, however, does not subscribe to this doctrine, because the angels being immaterial, do not eat material food; and manna being a material substance, could not be made out of the divine light, which is a spiritual substance. Christian divines, however, think that the mystical manna was called the bread of angels, because it was a type of Christ, whom the angels wished to behold.

MANUAL MASONS. The manual consists of such parts of business as are performed by hand labour alone, or by the help of some simple instruments, the uses whereof are not to be learnt by any problems or rules of art, but by labour and practice only; and this is more peculiarly applicable to our brethren of the first degree, called Entered Apprentices.—*Dunckerley.*

MANUAL SIGN. This reminds us of that deliberate and steady prudence which ought to guard our actions, forbidding us to seal with the sacred pledge of our right hand, what the heart has not sanctioned with its approbation.—*Hemming.*

MANUSCRIPTS. At the revival in 1717, Grand Master Payne had desired that all old masonic records might be brought into the Grand Lodge in order to discover the usages of ancient times; and in the year 1721, Dr. Anderson was employed to prepare a Book of Constitutions. Between these two periods, several very valuable manuscripts concerning the fraternity, their lodges, regulations, charges, secrets, and usages, which had been deposited in private lodges, particularly one written by Nicholas Stone, the Warden under Inigo Jones, were hastily burnt by some scrupulous brothers, under a jealous supposition that committing to print any thing relating to Masonry, would be injurious to the interests of the Craft · but surely such an act of *felo de se* could not proceed from zeal according to knowledge.—*Noorthouck.*

MARK OF CAIN. Some say he was paralytic; this seems to have arisen from the version of the Septuagint "groaning and trembling shalt thou be." The Targum of Jonathan ben Uzziel says, the sign was from the great and precious Name, probably one of the letters of the name Yehovah. The author of an Arabic catena in the Bodleian Library says, "A sword could not pierce him, fire could not burn him, water could not drown him, and air could not blast him; nor could thunder or lightning

strike him.. The author of Bereshith Rabba, a comment
on Genesis, says the mark was a circle of the sun rising
upon him. Abravanel says the sign was Abel's dog,
which constantly accompanied him. Some of the doctors
in the Talmud say, that it was the letter ת thau marked
on his forehead, which signified his condition, as it is the
first letter in the word תשובה teshubah, repentance. Rabbi
Joseph, wiser than all the rest, says it was a long horn
growing out of his forehead!—*Adam Clarke.*

MARK MASONS. The degree of Mark-Master Mason
may be considered as appendant to that of Fellow Craft
although entirely distinct and different from it. The
order and harmony which this degree communicated to
the builders of the temple at Jerusalem, are incalculable;
and, indeed, without it, so many workmen of different
nations would have been in continual confusion. Not
only was each workman thereby known to the Senior
Grand Warden, but every part of the workmanship, for
that stupendous structure, was subjected to the nicest
scrutiny—while every faithful labourer received with
punctuality the rewards of industry and skill. But it has
a speculative allusion infinitely interesting to every
accountable being. It typifies the trial of the great day,
when every man's work will be proved, whether it be
good or bad. That which is imperfect will be cast out,
as unfit for the new Jerusalem, into which "nothing can
enter that worketh abomination or maketh a lie."

MASON. A Mason is a man whose conduct should
be squared by strict rectitude and justice towards his
fellow-creatures; his demeanour should be marked by
the level of courtesy and kindness; while uprightness of
heart and integrity of action, symbolized by the plumb,
should be his distinguishing characteristic; and thus
guided by the moveable jewels of Masonry, he may descend the vale of life with joy, in the hope of being
accepted by the Most High, as a successful candidate for
admission into the Grand Lodge above.

MASON MARKS. Those brethren who have been
initiated into the degrees of Mark-Man and Mark-Master,
perfectly well understand, that the mark which was

conferred upon the ancient craftsman was not arbitrary, but selected from a defined and well-understood series—that the craftsman was not entitled to use any mark until his fitness had been tried, and he had proved himself well skilled in the use of the plumb, the level, and the square. That the distinction of the mark was conferred with peculiar solemnities; and that the subsequent obligation to use the particular mark so conferred, and to affix it to every "perfect ashlar," was not discretionary, but imperative. A knowledge of these facts, combined with a careful examination of the ancient marks, will, no doubt, throw much additional light upon the history or ecclesiastical architecture, as well as prove the firmer connection, and show the union existing in past ages, between practical architecture and symbolical or spiritual Masonry.—*Pryer*.

MASON'S WIND. At the building of King Solomon's Temple, a Mason's wind was said to blow favourably when it was due east and west, because it was calculated to cool and refresh the men at labour.

MASONIC HALL. A masonic hall should be isolated, and, if possible, surrounded with lofty walls, so as to be included in a court, and apart from any other buildings, to preclude the possibility of being overlooked by cowans or eavesdroppers; for Freemasonry being a secret society, the curiosity of mankind is ever on the alert to pry into its mysteries, and to obtain by illicit means, that knowledge which is freely communicated to all worthy applicants. As, however, such a situation in large towns, where Masonry is usually practised, can seldom be obtained with convenience to the brethren, the lodge should be formed in an upper story; and if there be any contiguous buildings, the windows should be either in the roof, or very high from the floor.

MASONIC YEAR. Freemasons date their year according to Mosaic chronology, or from the creation of the world, thus four thousand years more than the common calendar shows. The masonic year does not commence on the 1st January, but on the 24th June. But this way of reckoning is only usual in the writings of the Order.

MASONRY. It is useless to profess a knowledge of Freemasonry, if we do not frame our lives according to it. It is not enough to be acquainted with its doctrines and precepts, if we fail to reduce them to practice. In such a case, our knowledge will rather tend to our dishonour in this world, and will certainly be an additional article of accusation against us in the next. It would be very unreasonable to doubt the beneficial effects of our masonic precepts; but to admit them to be true, and yet act as if they were false, would be unwise in the highest degree. I will not, however, do my brethren the injustice to believe that many of them are capable of such a perversion of reason. And it is my firm persuasion, that they who practise the duties which Freemasonry teaches, in conjunction with the faith propounded in their religion, will inherit that eternal city of God, where they will be associated with a holy and happy fraternity of saints and angels, and enjoy the sweet communings of brotherly love for ever and ever.

MASTER OF THE CEREMONIES. He must be the first at every assembly of the brethren, to see that all preparations are made that are necessary for holding a lodge, and then invite the brethren to enter. He introduces the visiting brethren, and shows them their places. He must enter into conversation with every stranger who comes into the ante-chamber, to discover if he is a brother. In the lodge he must pay attention, and see that everything necessary for the due solemnity is prepared before the lodge is opened, and that nothing may disturb that solemnity while it is open. His seat is so placed, that the W. M. has him in full view, and he can leave it as often as he thinks necessary without asking leave of the W. M. He has the same charge at the banquet, and the serving brethren are generally under his direction. Visitors apply to him first; and it is therefore necessary to fill this office with an experienced Mason, and, if it be practicable, with one who speaks different foreign languages.—*Gadicke.*

MASTER OF A LODGE. All preferment among Masons should be grounded upon real worth and personal merit only, therefore no brother shall be elected Master of a lodge, or appointed to any office therein, merely on account of seniority or rank. The Master, who must have previously been appointed and served as a Warden of some warranted lodge, shall be annually elected by ballot; and at the next lodge, when the minutes are confirmed, he shall be installed in the chair according to ancient usage; he shall then appoint his Wardens and all other officers of the lodge, except the Treasurer and Tyler —*Constitutions.*

MATERIAL LIGHT. Light is one of the most astonishing productions of the creative skill and power of God. It is the grand medium by which all his other works are discovered, examined, and understood, so far as they can be known. Its immense diffusion and extreme velocity are alone sufficient to demonstrate the being and wisdom of God. Light has been proved by many experiments to travel at the astonishing rate of 194,188 miles in one second of time! and comes from the sun to the earth in eight minutes $11\frac{43}{50}$ seconds, a distance of 95,513,794 English miles.—*Adam Clarke.*

MATURE AGE. The Order of Free and Accepted Masons should consist solely of men of mature age, and it is in accordance with this rule that young men and boys are denied admittance. In the ancient charges of the English Constitution Book, under date 29th December, 1729, it is laid down as a rule that no person shall be initiated under twenty-five years of age. The lodges of other countries initiate at an earlier period, and the son of a Freemason, called Lewis, is allowed to be initiated much earlier.

MEET ON THE LEVEL. The level is an emblem of equality, because with God there is no respect of persons, and in his sight all men are equal, liable to the same infirmities, redeemed by the same Saviour, subject to the same death and judgment. This is the sense in which Masons understand the quality of members in tyled lodges They know nothing of that levelling equality which is the idol of the revolutionists of this world; they are taught by their Constitutions to be "peaceable subjects, and obedient to the civil powers," and are enemies

25

to that confusion and anarchy which is destructive of
social happiness. Hence the level distinguishes the Senior
Warden to remind him that while he presides over the
labours of the lodge by command of the W. M., as the
Junior Warden does over its refreshments, it is his duty
to see that every brother meets upon the level, and that
the principle of equality is preserved during the work,
without which harmony, the chief support of our institution, could not be maintained in its purity and usefulness.

MEETINGS. Our meetings, when conducted according to the true spirit of the Order, are characterised by
an emulation to excel in wisdom, and the knowledge of
practical virtue; and that the instruction incessantly
poured from the Master's chair is derived from an ample
and exhaustless mine, stored with the richest gems of
morality and religion, to reform the manners, and cultivate genial propensities in the mind.

MEMBERSHIP. A Mason may withdraw from his
lodge, but the membership remains inviolable. The true
Mason considers, as one of his most sacred duties, the
exact fulfilment of the engagements which bind him to
his rite, the lodge from whence he first received the light
and the masonic body from which he received his powers.
He cannot be relieved from his obligations, except by
the masonic power with which he made his engagements,
and according to the masonic laws which he has sworn
to observe and respect. Every attempt which may have
for its object to compel a Mason, either by persecution
or violence, to quit a rite to which he belongs, is contrary
to the spirit and laws of Masonry.

MENATZCHIM. Overseers and comforters of the
people in working, who were expert Master Masons.

MENTAL. The mental qualifications of a candidate
embrace sanity of mind, a capability of understanding the
obligations and instructions of the Order, that he may be
prepared to perform its duties.

MERCY. A virtue which inspires us with a compassion for others, and inclines us to assist them in their necessities. It is one of the noblest attributes of the Deity, speaking after the manner of men, and explaining what, by supposition, may pass in the mind of God, by what passes in the human mind. The object of mercy is misery; so God pities human miseries, and forbears to chastise severely; so man pities the misery of a fellow man, and assists to diminish it.—*Calmet.*

MERIDIAN. The sun being a fixed body, the earth constantly revolving round it on its own axis, it necessarily follows that the sun is always at its meridian; and Freemasonry being universally spread over its surface, it follows, as a second consequence, that the sun is always at its meridian with respect to Freemasonry.

MERIT. At the building of King Solomon's temple, merit alone entitled to preferment; an indisputable instance of which we have in the Deputy Grand Master of that great undertaking, who, without either wealth or power—without any other distinction than that of being the widow's son—was appointed by the Grand Master, and approved by the people, for this single reason, because he was a skilful artificer.—*Whitmash.*

MESOURANEO. The point within the circle was an universal emblem to denote the temple of the Deity, and referred to the planetary circle, in the centre of which was fixed the sun, as the universal God and father of nature; for the whole circle of heaven was called God. Pythagoras esteemed the central fire the supernal mansion of Jove; and he called it Μεσουρανεο, because the most excellent body ought to have the most excellent place, *i. e.* the centre.

METAL. Many men dote on the metals silver and gold with their whole souls, and know no other standard whereby to estimate their own worth, or the worth of their fellow-beings, but by the quantity of these metals they possess, thereby debasing and degrading those qualities of the mind or spirit by which alone mankind ought to be estimated. He who wishes to be initiated into Freemasonry must be willing to relinquish all descriptions of metal, and all the adventitious circumstances of rank and fortune, for it is the MAN that is received into Freemasonry, and not his rank or riches.—*Gadicke.*

METAL TOOLS. At the building of King Solomon's Temple there was not heard the sound of axe, hammer, or any other tool of brass or iron, to disturb the peaceful sanctity of that holy place. The stones were hewn in the quarry, there carved, marked, and numbered. The timber was felled and prepared in the forest of Lebanon, and conveyed by floats from Tyre to Joppa; the metals were fused and cast on the plains of Zeredathah; after which the whole was conveyed to Jerusalem, and there set up by means of mauls, and other instruments prepared for that purpose.

MIDDLE CHAMBER. The Temple of Solomon stood on Mount Moriah, and occupied the site of the present mosque of Omar, beneath the dome of which is a remarkable rock, fifteen feet above the level of the surrounding platform, evidently left by design for a peculiar purpose, and well answering to the account in 1 Kings vi., where it is stated that "the door for the middle chamber was in the right side of the house, and they went up with winding stairs into the middle chamber, and out of the middle into the third;" thus establishing the fact that the Holy of Holies was on an elevated spot, to which, and to nothing else, can this remarkable rock be referred with the shadow of a reason.

MID-DAY. As often as the Freemason commences his work, it is noon or mid-day, or that time in which the sun has attained its greatest altitude; for the earth being round, the sun is always on the meridian somewhere. The Freemason has the most enlightened and useful works to do; and when high noon is passed, he must be able to give the most satisfactory proofs of the utility of his labour.

MIDNIGHT. It is only when midnight draws near that a freemason thinks of concluding his labour; in fact, his activity and industry should penetrate unto high midnight, or low twelve.

MIDDLE CHAMBER,

MILITARY LODGES. No warrant shall be granted for the establishment of a military lodge without the consent of the commanding officer of the regiment, battalion, or company, to which it is to be attached, being first obtained. No military lodge shall, on any pretence, initiate into Masonry any inhabitant or sojourner in any town or place at which its members may be stationed, or through which they may be marching, nor any person who does not at the time belong to the military profession, nor any military person below the rank of a corporal, except as serving brethren, or by dispensation from the Grand Master, or some provincial Grand Master. —*Constitutions.*

MINERVA. Freemasons use the statue of Minerva, or open temples with her statue therein, as symbols of wisdom. Mythology teaches us that Jupiter opened his scull to bear Minerva, for this reason—she is the symbol of all thoughts that are formed in the head, and the protectress of the arts and sciences. She is generally represented as a young female in Grecian costume, and has an owl or a cock by her side, as a symbol of useful study and watchfulness.

MINUTE BOOK. Every lodge shall have its by-laws fairly written, and shall also keep a book or books in which the Master, or some brother appointed by him as secretary, shall enter the names of its members, and of all persons initiated or admitted therein, with the dates of their proposal, admission, or initiation, passing, and raising ; and also their ages, as nearly as possible, at that time, and their titles, professions, or trades, together with such transactions of the lodge as are proper to be written.—*Constitutions.*

MISCONDUCT. If any brother behave in such a way as to disturb the harmony of the lodge, he shall be thrice formally admonished by the Master, and if he persist in his irregular conduct, he shall be punished according to the by-laws of that particular lodge, or the case may be reported to higher masonic authority.— *Constitutions.*

MOCK MASONS. In the year 1747 some unfaithful brethren, disappointed in their expectations of the high offices and honours of the society, joined a number of the buffoons of the day, in a scheme to exhibit a mockery of the public procession to the grand feast. This, as may well be supposed, furnished mirth to the gaping crowd, and disgust to the society, who, wisely recollecting themselves, determined in future to confine their operations within the limits of their own assembly. They were called Mock Masons.—*Noorthouck.*

MODEL. The Temple of Solomon was erected according to the model presented by God to King David, who nevertheless was not permitted to build this sacred temple himself, because his hands had been stained with blood.

MODERATION. Towards the well-governing of a lodge of Masons, I would recommend moderation in the superior officers and subordination in the brethren; for without mutual good will, equanimity of temper, and reciprocal forbearance, the superstructure will crumble to decay, and the lodge, sooner or later, be inevitably dissolved.

MONAD. The monad is the principle of all things. From the monad came the indeterminate duad, as matter subjected to the cause monad; from the monad and the indeterminate duad, numbers; from numbers, points; from points, lines; from lines, superficies; from superficies, solids; from these solid bodies, whose elements are four, fire, water, air, earth; of all which, transmutated and totally changed, the world consists.—*Stanley.*

MONITORIAL. The monitorial sign reminds us of the weakness of human nature, unable of itself to resist the power of Darkness, unless aided by that Light, which is from above, and we thus acknowledge our own frailty, and that we can do no good acceptable service but through Him from whom all good and just counsel doth proceed, and under whose divine and special favour we can never be found unprofitable servants in His sight.

MOON. The moon is the second lesser light in Free-masonry, moveable, not fixed, and receiving her light from the sun. Changing Wardens lead and assist us, and the moon lights the wanderer on his way by night, but clouds may intercept the light of the moon; for this reason we must not depend upon her, but choose our road by a great and fixed light.—*Gadicke.*

MORAL ARCHITECTS. As moral architects we build temples for every virtue; prisons and dungeons for vice, indecency, and immorality. We are disposed to every humane and friendly office; ever ready to pour oil and wine into the wounds of our distressed brethren, and gently bind them up, (it is one of the principal ends of our institution,) so that when those who speak evil or lightly of us shall behold our conduct, and see by our means the hungry fed, the naked clothed, the sick sustained and cherished—shall see our light so usefully shine—their evil-speaking may be silenced, their foolish prejudices removed, and they may be convinced that Masonry is an useful and a venerable structure, supported by the great and everlasting pillars of Wisdom, Strength, and Beauty.—*Codrington.*

MORAL DUTIES. The science of Freemasonry embraces every branch of moral duty, whether it be applied to God, our neighbour, or ourselves. This peculiarity in the system is expressly inculcated on every member of the Order at his first admission into a lodge; so anxiously has Freemasonry provided against any mistake as to its peculiar tenets. No brother can be ignorant of the great points of masonic duty, although he may be unacquainted with the minuter details. The traditions and peculiar doctrines which are included in the more abstruse portions of the lectures may have remained unexplored; but of its moral and religious tendency he cannot be uninformed.

MORAL LAW. A Mason is obliged by his tenure to obey the moral law; and if he rightly understand the art, he will never be a stupid atheist nor an irreligious libertine. He of all men should best know that God seeth not as man seeth; for man looketh at the outward appearance, but God looketh to the heart. A Mason is therefore particularly bound never to act against the dictates of his conscience. Let a man's religion or mode of worship be what it may, he is not excluded from the Order, provided he believe in the glorious Architect of heaven and earth, and practise the sacred duties of morality.—*Ancient Charges.*

MORAL QUALIFICATIONS. The moral qualifications of a candidate are, that he shall neither be an atheist, an infidel, nor an irreligious libertine; that he must practise the four cardinal and the three theological virtues; he must be an humble believer in the wisdom, power, and goodness of God, because this constitutes the religious creed of Freemasonry, and acts as a check upon vice, and a stimulus to virtue.

MORAL PHILOSOPHY. The moral philosophy of the Order refers to Him whose injunctions to his creatures are peculiarly applicable to the performance of Christian duty. It teaches that we owe a duty to God, which includes reverence for his name and attributes, veneration for his sacred character, and obedience to his just commands. It speaks of a duty to our neighbour; with whom we are directed to act on the square in all the transactions of life. It inculcates a duty to ourselves. We are expected to cultivate self-knowledge and self-respect. For this purpose, an attention to the four cardinal virtues is recommended, as well as the practice of every moral and social duty. Prudence should direct us; Temperance should chasten us; Fortitude support us; and Justice be the guide of all our actions. And in the course prescribed for the regulation of our conduct, we are directed to maintain in their fullest splendour those truly masonic ornaments,—Benevolence and Charity; and to imprint indelibly on our minds the sacred dictates of Truth, Honour, and Virtue.

MORALITY. The morality of Masonry requires us to deal justly with others; not to defraud, cheat, or wrong them of their just dues or rights. But it goes further; regarding all as the children of one great Father, it considers man as bound by piety, masonic morality, and fraterna. bonds, to minister to the wants of the destitute and afflicted; and that we may be enabled to fulfil this high behest of humanity, it strictly enjoins industry and frugality, that so our hands may ever be filled with the means of exercising that charity to which our hearts should ever dispose us.—*Henkle.*

MORIAH. The name of the whole mountain, on the several hills and hollows of which the city of Jerusalem stood, was called Moriah, or Vision; because it was high land, and could be seen afar off, especially from the south; but afterwards that name was appropriated to the most elevated part on which the Temple was erected, and where Jehovah appeared to David. This mountain is a rocky limestone hill, steep of ascent on every side, except the north, and is surrounded on the other sides by a group of hills, in the form of an amphitheatre, which situation rendered it secure from the earthquakes that appear to have been frequent in the Holy Land, and have furnished the prophets with many elegant allusions.— *Horne.*

MORTALITY. Let the emblems of mortality which lie before you lead you to contemplate your inevitable destiny, and guide your reflection to that most interesting of human study—the knowledge of yourself. Be careful to perform your allotted task while it is yet day; continue to listen to the voice of nature, which bears witness that even in this perishable frame resides a vital and immortal principle, which inspires a holy confidence that the Lord of Life will enable us to trample the King of Terrors beneath our feet, and lift our eyes to the bright Morning Star, whose rising brings peace and salvation to the faithful and obedient of the human race.

MOSAIC PAVEMENT. The mosaic pavement was found before the porch of King Solomon's Temple. Fortunate are they who can draw near unto it, as also unto the porch.—*Gadicke.*

MOSES. Moses was learned in all the wisdom of the Egyptians; he was initiated in all the knowledge of the wise men of that nation, by whom the learning of antiquity had been retained and held sacred; wrapped up from the eye of the wicked and vulgar in symbols and hiero- glyphics, and communicated to men of their own order only, with care, secrecy, and circumspection. This secrecy is not in any wise to be wondered at, when we consider the persecution which would have followed a faith unacceptable to the ignorance of the nations who were enveloped in superstition and bigotry. Moses purged divine worship of its mysteries and images, and taught the Jews the knowledge of the God of the Universe, unpolluted with the errors of the nations of the earth, and uncorrupted with the devices and ludicrous ceremonies instituted by the people of the east, from whom he derived his first knowledge of the Divinity.—*Hutchinson.*

MOTIONS. Let the Master of a lodge discourage, on all occasions, that itching propensity which incites a brother to make motions on indifferent or trifling sub- jects. Any motion, on which the lodge is divided, must be to a certain extent injurious, amongst so many various habits, views, and propensities, as usually constitute a lodge of Masons.

MOTIVE OR REASON. He who wishes to enter into the Order of Freemasonry, should first be able to render unto himself a good and satisfactory account why he wishes to take that step. This is not easy. A man who is not a Freemason, can only know the Order by hearsay, or by reading masonic books, and it is rather a dangerous undertaking to join a society, with which a person is totally unacquainted. It is quite different to joining any other select society, who publish their rules and regulations, and the names of all their members, and by those means invite others to join their society. Free- masons on the contrary, try to persuade no one to join their society, do not publish their rules or regulations, and the names of the members are very rarely known, and what is more, the candidate must submit himself to rules and regulations, the purport of which are entirely un- known unto him; it is true, that there is nothing in those rules contrary to the laws of God, or to his duty to his king and country, as a good citizen of the state; but he who is not a Freemason, cannot have any clear idea of what those duties are. What then are the motives sufficiently strong to induce a free man to offer himself as a candidate for admission into a comparatively unknown society. Those parties act the most prudently, who admit that they wish to join the Order, because as a useful and innocent society, it has enjoyed the protection of the state for such a number of years, because so many prudent men are members of the Order, and because, in general, the members distinguish themselves by the propriety of their manners, the uprightness of their business transactions, and the correctness of their moral conduct. —*Gadicke.*

MOUNT OF GOD. The ascent to the summit of the paradisiacal mount of God, by means of a pyramid consisting of seven steps, was an old notion, certainly entertained before the vision of Jacob, for it prevailed amongst the Mexican savages; and the original settlers on the vast continent of America could have no knowledge of this vision, either by tradition or personal experience. The Jewish Cabalists entertained a belief that the paradisiacal mount was the place of residence chosen by the children of Seth, while the contaminated descendants of Cain resided in the plains below; and its altitude was said to be so great, that from its summit might be heard the angels of heaven, singing their celestial anthems before the throne of God!

MOVEABLE JEWELS. The compasses, square, level and plumb, are called the moveable jewels, because they distinguish the officers of a lodge, and are transferable to their successors. They were formerly suspended from narrow white ribbons, which were succeeded by blue of the same width; but the regulation now is, "the collars to be made of light blue ribbon four inches broad; if silver chain be used, it must be placed over the light blue ribbon."

MUSIC. Music teaches the art of forming concords, so as to compose delightful harmony, by a proportional arrangement of acute, grave, and mixed sounds. This art, by a series of experiments, is reduced to a science, with respect to tones, and the intervals of sound only

It inquires into the nature of concords and discords, and enables us to find out the proportion between them by numbers.—*Preston*.

MUSICAL BRETHREN. No lodge is willingly held without songs and music, or a piano at least. If there are many brethren belonging to a lodge who can contribute to the musical entertainment, they form themselves into a musical society, and thus provide both social and sacred musical entertainments.—*Gadicke*.

MYSTERIES. The usages and customs of the ancients in their secret societies are called mysteries. If by mysteries we merely understand a secret religion, then, in the civilized part of the globe, there can be no mysteries, for God may be openly worshipped everywhere; but if by mysteries we understand secret ceremonies and doctrines, then we may say that there are still mysteries among Freemasons. But we do not call our secrets mysteries, and we thereby prove that with us there can be no secret religion. No one among us is a mystagogue, and our outward appearance has nothing mysterious about it.—*Gadicke*.

MYSTERY. The word mystery has given occasion to many improper impressions against our masonic societies. Treason, infidelity, a charge of taking rash and unnecessary obligations, have been laid to their responsibility, yet none of these charges have ever been substantiated by their persecutors. The word mystery has brought down anathemas from over-zealous divines upon the heads of Masons, and has induced merciless governors to use their weapons against the Craft, when, upon a slight inquiry, the church as well as the state might be informed, that devotion to God, obedience to the state, and to all superiors, brotherly love and universal charity, are the principles which separate our Fraternity from all other secret societies which have of late years risen, to the degradation of religion, and to the danger of good order in society and the state.—*Husenbeth*.

MYSTIC. Denotes a secret doctrine which works specially upon the feelings of the heart, or of feelings which cannot be expressed by words. The mystic is a man who believes himself exalted above the material world, and feels himself united with the immaterial and spiritual. We may call mysticism the feeling of faith, or living and moving in supernatural and immortal life. Every man ought to be somewhat mystical, but ought to guard against that coarse mysticism, which believes in intercourse with angels, and to be able to penetrate into the third heaven.—*Gadicke.*

MYSTIC TIE. The sacred and universal principle of the royal art, which unites men of the most opposite tenets, of the most distant countries, and of the most contradictory opinions in one indissoluble bond of affection, so that in every nation a Mason finds a friend, and in every clime a home, has been amply denominated the mystic tie, and the Fraternity are often termed "Brethren of the Mystic Tie."

MYSTICAL LECTURE. The mystical knowledge of the Royal Arch degree, comprehends the form and exposition of the sacred signs, and the nature and import of the Holy Word, and the traditional ceremony to be used in showing and communicating the secrets.

NAKED FEET. The act of going with naked feet was always considered a token of humility and reverence, and the priests in the Temple always officiated with feet uncovered, although it was frequently injurious to their health. The command thus given to Moses, did not represent the civil and legal ceremony of putting off the shoes, as the Jews were subsequently directed to do, when they renounced any bargain or contract, nor yet the sign of grief and sorrow, as when David entered into Jerusalem barefooted; but it was enjoined that Moses might approach that sacred place with reverence and godly fear, as if it had been a temple consecrated to divine worship. Thus the preacher says, "Take heed unto thy feet, when thou enterest the temple of God"

NAME OF GOD. Josephus says that the Name was never known, until God told it to Moses in the wilderness; and that he himself did not dare to mention it, for that it was forbidden to be used, except once in a year by the High Priest alone, when he appeared before the Mercy Seat on the day of expiation. He further adds that it was lost through the wickedness of man; and hence has arisen a difference of opinion, some supposing the Word itself lost; others, the import, or the meaning only; and many, the manner of its delivery; and from hence contend, that Moses did not ask the Almighty for his name to carry to his brethren, but for the true delivery or pronunciation only. How far that might be the case, is to us uncertain; but it is certain that the true mode of delivery cannot now be proved from any written record; first, because it is capable of so many variations from the manner of annexing the Masoretic points, which points were not extant in the days of Moses; and secondly, because the language now in use amongst the Jews, is so corrupt and altered from that in which he wrote, that none of them, except some few of their learned, understand anything of it; for which reason the Jews call it שם המפורש Shem Hamphoreth, the unutterable name. Hence is our learned brother Pythagoras his τετραγραμματον or quaternion.—*Dunkerly.*

NAME OF THE LODGE. Any lodge which may not be distinguished by a name or title, being desirous of taking one, must for that purpose procure the approbation of the Grand Master or Provincial Grand Master, and the name must be registered with the Grand Secretary. No lodge shall be permitted to alter its name without the like approbation.—*Constitutions.*

NAMES OF MASONRY. We still retain all the names by which the science has been distinguished in every age of the world, either in its speculative or operative form; whether it were characterized by the name of Lux, as in the patriarchal age; or Geometry, as it was called by Euclid; or Philosophy, as Pythagoras named it; or Mesouraneo, or any other title; a memorial of such designation has been embodied in the system. We say Freemasonry is a system of Wisdom, Strength and Beauty, and the definition was adopted from our ancient G. M. King Solomon, who called the science Wisdom; which by the Cabalists was subsequently denominated Baphomet. And he defines it thus: "Wisdom is the worker of all things; she is the brightness of the everlasting Light, the unspotted mirror of the power of God, and the image of his goodness. She is more beautiful than the sun, and above all the order of the stars; being compared with the light, she is found before it."

NATURE AND ART. If we take a view of the productions of nature and art on the face of the planet which we inhabit, we shall find that all is replete with the divine principle of the Order. There is not a mountain or valley, a tree, a shrub, or a blade of grass; there is not a magnificent structure of polished marble, rich in the splendid decorations of gorgeous architecture, or a refuse stone rejected from the quarry; there is not an object, animate or inanimate in universal nature, but it is instinct with the genius of Freemansonry; and the learned brother may find an instructive masonic lecture in the wing of a moth, as well as the motions of the august lights of heaven.

NEBUCHADNEZZAR. In the eleventh year of the reign of Zedekiah, King of Judah, Nebuchadnezzar, King of Babylon, besieged, and took the city of Jerusalem, set fire to the temple and city, totally leveling and razing it until it became desolate, and the remnant of the people who escaped the sword he carried away captive to Babylon.

NEGATIVE. When any one is proposed to become a member, or any person to be made a Mason, if it appear upon casting up the ballot that he is rejected, no member or visiting brother shall discover, by any means whatsoever, who those members were that opposed his election, under the penalty of such brother being for ever expelled the lodge (if a member,) and, if a visiting brother, of his being never more admitted as a visitor, or becoming a member; and immediately after a negative passes on any person being proposed, the Master shall cause the law to be read, that no brother present may plead ignorance.— *Old Constitutions.*

NEHEMIAH. Nehemiah was entrusted with a special

commission to rebuild the walls, and renew the fortifications of Jerusalem, and to effect a full restoration of the lands and property which had been seized during the captivity, by the neighbouring nations. When he arrived at Jerusalem, and took possession of his government, he found his country's enemies, the Samaritans and others, headed by Sanballat, Tobias and Geshem, opposing every obstacle that might distress and discommode the Jews. The reparations of the walls and fortifications met with a formidable resistance from those people, who conspired to attack the Jews while engaged in labour, and consequently unarmed; and to this they were encouraged by some traitors within the city. The vigilance of Nehemiah frustrated the scheme.

NEIGHBOUR. Freemasonry instructs us in our duty to our neighbour, teaches us to injure him in none of his connections, and in all our dealings with him, to act with justice and impartiality. It discourages defamation, it bids us not to circulate any whisper of infamy, improve any hint of suspicion, or publish any failure of conduct. It orders us to be faithful to our trusts, to deceive not him who relieth upon us, to be above the meanness of dissimulation, to let the words of our mouths be the thoughts of our hearts, and whatsoever we promise, religiously to perform.—*Codrington.*

NETWORK. Was one of the enrichments with which the chapiters of the two pillars of Solomon's Porch were adorned. From the connection of its meshes, it denoted unity.

NEUTRAL. As all were not of Christ who called themselves Christians in the time of the apostles, so all are not Masons who have been initiated into the Order. A knowledge of signs, words and tokens, without an ability to apply them according to their proper design, can no more constitute a Mason, than the possession of working tools can make a man a carpenter, unless he knows how to use them. There are many erroneous opinions abroad on this point. A person procures initiation, and fancies that is all he wants. There never was a more fatal mistake. Initiation is but the horn-book of

Masonry, and is only of the same use towards a knowledge of its principles, as the alphabet is to those who desire to excel in literary attainments. If this consideration were duly enforced upon every candidate for Masonry, the Order would assume a different aspect, and its genuine lustre would be more universally displayed.

NEW LAW. No motion for a new law or regulation, or for the alteration or repeal of an old one shall be made, until it shall have been proposed in, or communicated to, the general committee, nor until it shall have been handed up in writing to the Grand Master. After having been perused and found by him not to contain anything contrary to the ancient landmarks of the Order, the motion may be publicly proposed. If seconded, the question shall be put thereon for the opinion of the Grand Lodge. If approved and confirmed, at the next ensuing meeting of the Grand Lodge, it becomes a law of the society.—*Constitutions*.

NILE. In the time of Euclid the river Nile overflowed so far, that many of the dwellings of the people of Egypt were destroyed. Euclid instructed them in the art of making mighty walls and ditches, to stop the progress of the water; and by geometry measured out the land, and divided it into partitions, so that each man might ascertain his own property.—*Old Masonic Manuscript*.

NIL NISI CLAVIS DEEST. Attached to the intersecting triangle of the original jewel of the Royal Arch there is frequently the motto of "nil nisi clavis deest," which is a declaration that the wearer of a jewel containing this emblem is desirous of doing his duty, and filling up with justice that link in the chain of creation, wherein the Most High hath pleased to place him.

NINE. Nine being the square of three, is a perfect ternary, beyond which there is no number. It is observed by arithmeticians, says Hume, (Dial. Nat. Rel. p 167,) "that the products of nine compose always either 9, or some lesser products of 9, if you add together all the characters of which any of the former products is composed. Thus of 18, 27, 36, which are products of 9, you make 9 by adding 1 to 8, 2 to 7, 3 to 6. Thus 369 is a product also of nine; and if you add 3, 6, 9, you make 18, a lesser product of nine."

NINE MASTERS. The following are the names of the nine masters who are said to have been elected by Solomon after the death of Hiram Abiff; Moabon, Jachin, Boaz, Ganigam, Azariah, Joram, Jsch'gi, Achal, Obed.

NOACHIDÆ. Sons of Noah; the first name of Freemasons; whence we may observe that believing the world was framed by one supreme God, and is governed by him; and loving and worshipping him; and honouring our parents; and loving our neighbour as ourselves; and being merciful even to brute beasts, is the oldest of all religions.

NORTH. The operative mason is accustomed to lay the foundation-stone of a new building on the north side, and for this reason, all those who have not been initiated amongst us have their place in the north. The light streams from the east unto the north, as all our knowledge has been obtained from the orient.—*Gadicke.*

NORTH-EAST. The foundation-stone of every magnificent edifice was usually laid in the north-east; which accounts in a rational manner for the general disposition of a newly initiated candidate. When enlightened but uninstructed, he is accounted to be in the most superficial part of Masonry.

NUMBERS. We consider the number three, or three times three, as a sacred number; and in all the mysteries of the ancients, the number nine, was most important. Whether we, as Christian Freemasons, still have an ancient explanation of the sacredness of this number, or whether we derive its sanctity from the Holy Trinity, we cannot here determine.—*Gadicke.*

OATH. In Freemasonry a number of men form themselves into a society, whose main end is to improve in commendable skill and knowledge, and to promote universal beneficence and the social virtues of human life, under the solemn obligation of an oath. This liberty all incorporate societies enjoy, without impeachment or reflection.—*Anderson.*

OBEDIENT. To be obedient is one of the great duties of a Freemason, not only to the laws of the Craft, but to the laws of the kingdon or state in which he may reside, to the laws of God, to the laws of morality, but above all, to the laws of true benevolence. He is also bound to be obedient to the commands of his superiors when in the lodge; but every ruler ought to be cautious, and only give such orders as may be cheerfully obeyed by a free man and Mason, and not require a slavish obedience, for in the lodge there are neither lords nor slaves, but truth and justice must there reign in unanimity.— *Gadicke.*

OBELISK. A high, square-sided and sharp-pointed pillar, which is commonly erected in commemoration of some celebrated person or remarkable event. They are to be found among the masonic emblems.—*Gadicke.*

OBJECTS. To communicate the blessings of which we are partakers; to contribute to the successful propagation of knowledge, virtue and peace, of the sciences and arts, and of whatever adorns social life; and to assert the advancement of human happiness, have ever been the great objects of Freemasonry.

OBJECTIONS. Objections have been urged against Freemasonry in all ages of its existence, by those who were jealous of its secret influence, or envied the privileges of the favoured individuals who had been initated into its mysteries. But although refuted over and over again, the same objections recur at stated periods; being reproduced, as it should appear, for the purpose of fanning our zeal and keeping alive our interest in the institution. It is amusing, in studying the history of the Craft, to find the hackneyed arguments which were refuted by Hutchinson, Calcott and others, in the last century, brought forward again and again by new candidates for the honour of an anonymous blow at the immortal giantess. Scarcely any novelty in the form of an objection is to be found. The censures have been chiefly confined to its secrecy, the exclusion of females, the obligation, &c.

OBLATIONS. The oblations which were made by the people towards the erection of the Tabernacle, were so many types of the several graces of Christianity; the gold of Faith, the silver of Hope, the precious stones of Charity; the blue colour of the silks, &c., denoting the lifting up our hearts to heaven, a privilege conveyed to mankind by the meritorious atonement of Jesus Christ; the purple, our warfare and tribulation for the sake of religion; and the crimson, or as the original words (tolag hath shani) signify, the double scarlet, the joint love of God and man.

OBLIGATION. Freemasons in their secret societies, obligate their disciples, similar to the ancient brethren, to keep their doctrines, their engagements, and their transactions, from those who are not of the Order. This obligation is not composed of such tremendous oaths with which we are charged by bigots, who, ignorant as they naturally must be, of the whole of our transactions, unless they had been received into our society, thunder their unholy anathemas and excommunications against us. And thereby make fools approve their rash acts, the world wonder, and the Mason smile at their daring insolence, to condemn their fellow-creatures for imaginary sins against God and religion, which must ultimately be laid to the charge of those triflers with their neighbours' consciences.—*Husenbeth.*

OBLONG. The Tabernacle, with its holy emblems, was a type of a Masons' lodge. It was an oblong square, and, with its courts and appendages, it represented the whole habitable globe. Such is also the extent of our lodges. The former was supported by pillars, and the latter is also sustained by those of W. S. and B. They were equally situated due east and west. The sacred roll of God's revealed will and law was deposited in the Ark of the Covenant; the same holy record is placed in a conspicuous part of our lodges. The altar of incense was a double cube; and so is our pedestal and stone of foundation. The covering of the Tabernacle was composed of three colours, as a representation of the celestial hemisphere; such also is the covering of a Masons' lodge. The floor of the Tabernacle was so holy that the priests were forbidden to tread upon it without taking off their shoes; the floor of the lodge is holy ground.

OBSERVANCES. Almost all the circumstances attending the promulgation of the Jewish dispensations have been introduced into Freemasonry; and the particular observances incorporated with its ceremonial. The Divine appearance at the Burning Bush, the shoes, the rod, the serpent, and the Sacred Name, are equally embodied in the system. The plagues of Egypt, with the signs which attended the divine deliverance of the children of Israel from captivity—the pillar of a cloud and of fire, the mighty winds, the division of the Red Sea, the salvation of God's people, and the destruction of Pharaoh and his host; the wanderings in the wilderness, the delivery of the law, the building of the Tabernacle, and the establishment of the hierarchy, the order observed in the frequent migrations, led by the banners of each tribe, and other important events, all form parts of the complicated system of Freemasonry, and show its connection with the offices of religion.

ODD NUMBERS. Odd numbers were ever esteemed more propitious than even ones, and hence were the conservators of greater virtues. They were sacred to the celestial deities, and represented the male sex, while even numbers were female, and appropriated to the subterranean gods. Hence the monad was esteemed the father of numbers, and the duad the mother, from whose union proceeded not only the triad but the sacred quaternary, which was the origin of the seven liberal sciences, and the maker and cause of all things.

OFFICE. If the superior officers of a lodge be unacquainted with the principles of the institution, it can scarcely be expected to prosper. Should the Master be ignorant of his work, the brethren will soon learn to despise his authority. To speak in the technical language of Masonry, if he be unpossessed of the art of drawing designs, how are the Fellowcrafts to execute, or the Apprentices to be instructed?

OFFICERS. The masonic officers of a lodge are the Master and his two Wardens, with their assistants, the two Deacons, Inner Guard, and the Tyler; to which, for the better regulation of the private concerns of the lodge, may be added other officers, such as Chaplain, Treasurer, Secretary, &c.—*Constitutions.*

OIL. One of the elements of consecration. Oil was anciently considered the symbol of prosperity and happiness. The oil of gladness mentioned in the Jewish writings was a perfumed oil with which people anointed themselves on days of public rejoicing and festivity. Everything that was appropriated to the purposes of religion in the Tabernacle and Temple, were all consecrated with oil. Kings and priests were anointed in the same manner. And our lodges, as temples consecrated to morality and virtue, are also hallowed by the application of corn, wine, and oil.

OLIVE BRANCH. A very great sensation has been created in India by the proposal of the Right Worshipful Brother Burns, Prov. G. M. for western India, to establish a new order, under the designation of the "Brotherhood of the Olive Branch in the East." The proposal was brought forward on St. John's Day, June 24, 1845, when no fewer than eighty brethren, of various nations, were assembled at Bombay; and it has been received by the principal members of the Craft in India with great enthusiasm.

OLIVE TREES. There are some who compare the symbol of a point within a circle to the golden candlestick flanked by two olive trees, mentioned by Zechariah; the candidate representing the circle, the oil the point, and the trees the two perpendicular parallel lines. The former was an emblem of the Jewish nation governed by the central oil, or the Holy Spirit of God; and the olive trees were the two anointed ones, viz., the king and priest, applied by the prophet to Zerubbabel and

Jeshua, who were raised up by divine providence to preside over the temporal and spiritual affairs of the Jewish nation when the second Temple was building, and bearing an ultimate reference to the lights and ornaments of the Christian church.

ON. Under this appellation the Deity was worshipped by the Egyptians, and they professed to believe that he was eternal, and the fountain of light and life, but, according to their gross conceptions, being necessarily visible, the sun was adored as his representative, and was most probably the same as Osiris. If they believed On to be the living and eternal God, they allowed the same attributes to the sun, which they undoubtedly worshipped as the Lord of the creation. Oannes was the God of the Chaldeans, and Dag-On of the Philistines; both of which are derivations of the same name. On was evidently the same deity as the Hebrew Jehovah, and was introduced amongst the Greeks by Plato, who acknowledges his eternity and incomprehensibility in these remarkable words: "Tell me of the God On; which is, and never knew beginning." And the same name was used by the early Christians for the true God; for St. John, in the Apocalypse, has this expression—*O Ὤν, καὶ ὁ ἦν, καὶ ὁ ἐρχόμενος,* which is translated by our authorized version of the Scriptures, by "Him, which is, and which was, and which is to come."

OPENING. The opening of the lodge is a ceremony of great solemnity and importance. Everything is conducted in such a manner as to inculcate respect for those in authority, with solemn reverence and adoration of the Deity, whose blessing and direction on our leaders is invoked, not in a light and thoughtless manner, as some may perhaps infer, but with the gravity and decency of a well-regulated church.

OPERATION. The veil thrown over Masonry renders its operations silent and unobserved; yet the influence of a body spread through all classes of society, pervading every circle, and diffusing (though by its separate members) opinions digested and matured, from remote periods, in the brotherhood, must be powerful in its effect.

OPERATIVE. As operative masons we are taught to hew, square, lay stones, and prove horizontals. We allude by operative masonry to a proper application of the useful rules of architecture, whence a structure derives figure, strength, and beauty, and whence result a due proportion and a just correspondence in all its parts.

OPHIR. Various have been the conjectures concerning the situation of Ophir. Josephus places it in the East Indies, in a country which, by his description, should appear to be Malacca. Bochart contends that it was Taphrobana, or Ceylon. Calmet places it in Armenia; Montanus in America; and Huetius in the eastern coast of Africa. As various have been the sentiments with respect to Tarshish; some consider it as having been near, and others as distant from, Ophir All that Scripture tells us is, that the navy of Tarshish came in once in three years, and furnished Solomon with immense wealth; of which we know not the amount, since we can make no exact estimate of the value of the talents specified.

OPINIONS. Individuals have passed various opinions respecting the purity and usefulness of Freemasonry. One says it is a modern institution, and therefore of little value; another terms it frivolous, and consequently contemptible. A third calls it anti-christian, and warns the public to avoid it as a snare. Others affirm that it is behind the advancing spirit of the times, and therefore obsolete; but let any one candidly judge it by its fruits, which is the great Christian criterion by which all things ought to be tried, according to the divine fiat of its founder (Luke vi. 44). We feed the hungry, clothe the naked, comfort the sick, relieve the distressed, and provide for the fatherless and the widow. Is any one hungry—we give him meat. Is any one thirsty—we give him drink; naked—we clothe him; sick—we visit him; in prison—we come unto him with the messenger of mercy. Whatever may be the opinions of our opponents of such deeds as these, we have the satisfaction of knowing that an approving sentence will be pronounced upon them at the last day.

ORDER. In every order the spirit of regularity should reign, and more especially in the Order of Freemasonry. The Master's call to order reminds the brethren of this in every lodge, and each one acknowledges by the sign, that he is mindful of his duty. Originally the society of Freemasons was not an Order, but a fraternity, and the name Order has been introduced into England in modern times.—*Gadicke.*

ORDERS OF ARCHITECTURE. By order is meant a system of all the members, proportions, and ornaments of columns and pilasters. There are five orders, which are thus classed: the Tuscan, Doric, Ionic, Corinthian, and Composite.

ORGANIZATION. The Dyonitiasts formed one and the same association, as the Jewish Masons who built the Temple of Jerusalem. These latter, beyond doubt, were bound together in an organization which extended beyond Judea. The Bible exhibits them mixing themselves with the Tyrian Masons, notwithstanding the ordinary repugnance of the Israelites towards strangers; and masonic tradition, which must not be contemned, shows that they recognized each other by words and secret signs, similar to those employed by the Masons of other countries.—*Clavel.*

ORIGINAL POINTS. Ancient Masonry admitted twelve original points, which constitute the basis of the entire system, and without which no person ever did or can be legally received into the Order. Every candidate is obliged to pass through all these essential forms and ceremonies, otherwise his initiation would not be legal. They are—opening, preparing, reporting, entering, prayer, circumambulation, advancing, obligated, intrusted, invested, placed, closing.

ORIGIN OF MASONRY. The origin of Masonry is indisputably traced from the creation of the universe; for after the Almighty Architect had finished his great design in making all things good, and, according to geometry, Adam, the first of all the human race, did soon discover this noble science, by surveying the works of God in his state of innocence; and although he fell through disobedience, and was expelled from that lovely arbour into the wide world, he still retained the knowledge thereof, and communicated the same to his offspring —*Multa Paucis.*

ORPHANS. There lived in the county of Essex, a clergyman named Hewlett. He died of malaria. His troubles had been of no common kind. His wife had died of consumption, about three months previously, and nine orphan children were left without a shilling in the world to provide for them. There was a lodge in Rochfort, Essex; they met, took the case into consideration, and before they separated, nine brethren agreed each to take a child to his own home.—*Bushell.*

OUT OF THE LODGE. A Freemason ought to distinguish himself from other men out of the lodge, as well as in it, by uprightness and friendship to the brethren, by a free and unconstrained manner of thinking, and by an unimpeachable purity of living. A brother Freemason shall not only conduct himself in the lodge, but also out of the lodge, as a brother towards his brethren; and happy are they who are convinced that they have in this respect ever obeyed the laws of the Order. A free and unconstrained manner of thinking distinguishes not only an enlightened man, but a man who nobly protects that which is just.—*Gadicke.*

OUTWARD CEREMONIES. A Freemason can neither become a gross sensualist, nor profess to be stoically dead to all sensual pleasures; for it is not necessary that he should deny himself the innocent enjoyments provided for the eye, the ear, and the taste. No man can maintain that he is entirely uninfluenced by outward impressions. To appeal to the bodily feelings or passions, is found the most effectual means of arousing the sympathy and securing the attention of the multitude. It is for this reason that among the ceremonies of Freemasonry, we find outward forms calculated to work upon the inward feelings; these ceremonies are, for the greater part derived from ancient times, and it is very probable that they were more fitted for the state of society then existing, than they are for that which now exists.— *Gadicke.*

OX. The ox forms a component part of the cherubic symbol. It was referred to the prophet Ezekiel, because he sets forth the restoration of the Temple and altar, the emblem of atonement being an ox; and to St. Luke, who commences with the narrative of Zacharias the priest. It also bore a reference to the priestly office of Christ.

PARALLEL LINES. In every well-regulated lodge, there is found a point within a circle, which circle is embordered by two perpendicular parallel lines. These lines are representatives of St. John the Baptist, and St. John the Evangelist, the two great patrons of Masonry, to whom our lodges are dedicated, and who are said to have been "perfect parallels in Christianity as well as Masonry."—*Old Lectures.*

PARTS. An old word for degrees or lectures. In this sense, Freemasonry is said to be consistent in all its parts, which point to one and the same object, prominently kept in view throughout all the consecutive degrees; and that every ceremony, every landmark, and every symbolical reference, constitutes a plain type of some great event, which appears to be connected with our best and dearest interests.

PASSIONS. The end, the moral, and purport of Masonry, is to subdue our passions; not to do our own will; to make daily progress in a laudable art; to promote morality, charity, good-fellowship, good nature, and humanity.—*Anderson.*

PASS-WORDS. Much irregularity has unfortunately crept into the blue degrees, in consequence of the want of masonic knowledge in many of those who preside over their meetings; and it is particularly so with those who are unacquainted with the Hebrew language, in which all the words and pass-words are given. So essentially necessary is it for a man of science to preside over a lodge, that much injury may arise from the smallest deviation in the ceremony of initiation, or in the lectures of instruction. We read in the Book of Judges, that the transposition of a single point over the Schin, in consequence of a national defect among the Ephraimites, designated the cowans, led to the slaughter of 42,000 men.—*Dalcho*.

PAST MASTER. A Past Master, or one who has actually served the office of Master, so long as he remains a subscribing member to any warranted lodge, is, ex officio, a member of the Grand Lodge, and appears to be entitled to many privileges. None but a Past Master can legally initiate, pass or raise. A Master cannot resign his chair except to a past Master. No board of Past Masters can be legally formed, unless three or more installed Masters be present.

PATRONAGE. Many lodges honour the head of the government as their patron without his being a Freemason, and receive from him a public local decree, or protectorium, by which they are not only permitted to hold their lodges, but are also legally protected. It is likewise frequently the case that the patron is a member of the Order.—*Gadicke*.

PAVEMENT. The voluptuous Egyptians, who exhausted their ingenuity in the invention of new luxuries, used in common with painted walls and ceilings, the mosaic pavement, richly tesselated. In the palace of Cleopatra, these pavements were inlaid with precious stones; and in India, the floors of the most sacred temples, or at least of the adyta, were enriched with polished stones disposed in small squares or tessera. which reflected the beams of the sun in a variety of splendid colours. On a similar principle, the floor of a Masons' lodge has been constructed, which is thus in proper keeping with the rest of its decorations; for the design would be imperfect, if a strict regard to uniformity and propriety had not been observed throughout the whole arrangement. This is a striking evidence of the unity of design with which the great plan of Freemasonry was originally constructed. How minutely soever the parts or elements may appear to be disposed, they each and all conduce to the same end, the glory of God, and the welfare of man.

PEACE. A Masons' lodge is the temple of peace, harmony, and brotherly love. Nothing is allowed to enter which has the remotest tendency to disturb the quietude of its pursuits. A calm enquiry into the beauty of wisdom and virtue, and the study of moral geometry, may be prosecuted without excitement; and they constitute the chief employment in the tyled recesses of the lodge. The lessons of virtue which proceed from the east, like rays of brilliant light streaming from the rising sun, illuminate the west and south; and as the work proceeds, are carefully imbibed by the workmen. Thus while Wisdom contrives the plan and instructs the workmen, Strength lends its able support to the moral fabric, and Beauty adorns it with curious and cunning workmanship. All this is accomplished without the use of either axe, hammer, or any other tool of brass or iron, within the precinct of the temple, to disturb the peaceful sanctity of that holy place.

PECTORAL. The general signification or symbolical reference of the pectoral was this:—the four rows of precious stones referred to the four cardinal virtues, and the three stones in each, to the three theological virtues. The twelve stones denoted the precious doctrines of Christianity, promulgated by the twelve apostles; and the Urim and Thummim, the vital spark of these doctrines, was Christ, who bears his church to the throne of heaven, as the high priest bore that mystical oracle on his breast. This utensil has been variously explained, one translating the words Urim and Thummim by elucidations and perfections; another doctrines and truths; others brightness and perfection, justice and doctrine, lucid and perfect, &c. Philo says they were " duas virtutes depictas;" and the seventy translate them by the word *Δηλωσιν* and *Αληθειαν*, manifestations and truth. They were certainly some tangible substances, which were placed in the doublings of the pectoral, as in a purse or pocket, by which responses were vouchsafed to the wearer of the ephod.

PECULIAR RESIDENCE. What was the object of building the temple of Solomon? One purpose, we are informed, was, that is might be a house of prayer for all nations. But this was not its only purpose. God intended to make it the seat of his visible presence, or the place of his habitation. It was not designated, thought an eminent commentator, to be a place to worship in, but a place of worship at, where God was known to have a peculiar residence.—*Scott.*

PEDAL. The pedal is the point on which we receive the first great recommendation of the Master, ever to continue, as we then appeared, upright men and Masons. It therefore denotes the duty of universal justice, which consists in doing to others as we would they should do unto us.—*Hemming.*

PEDESTAL. The altar of the lodge is a pedestal in the form of a double cube, on which is displayed the Holy Bible, to confer upon it the attribute of justice. And why is the open Bible said to be the emblem of justice? I answer in the expressive words of an eloquent writer· Because there is no other virtue of such absolute importance and essential necessity to the welfare of society. Let all the debts of justice be universally discharged; let every man be just to himself, and to all others; let him endeavour, by the exercise of industry and economy, to provide for his own wants, and prevent himself from becoming a burden upon society, and abstain, in the pursuit of his own subsistence, from everything injurious to the interests of others; let every one render unto all their due—that property which he is obliged by the laws of the land, or by those of honourable equity, to pay them; that candour and open dealing to which they have a right, in all his commercial dealings with them; that portion of good report to which their merit entitles them, with that decent respect and quiet submission which their rightful civil authority demands. If justice were thus universally done, there would be little left for mercy to do.

PENAL. The penal sign marks our obligation, and reminds us also of the fall of Adam and the dreadful penalty entailed thereby on his sinful posterity, being no less than death. It intimates that the stiffneck of the disobedient shall be cut off from the land of the living by the judgment of God, even as the head is severed from the body by the sword of human justice.

PENCIL. This is one of the working tools of a Master Mason. With the pencil the skilful artist delineates the building in a draught or plan for the instruction and guidance of the workmen. The pencil teaches us that our words and actions are observed and recorded by the Almighty Architect, to whom we must give an account of our conduct through life.

PENITENTIAL. The reverential sign may be considered as the parent of the penitential or supplicating sign, since it justly denotes that frame of heart and mind without which our prayers and oblation of praises will not obtain acceptance at the throne of grace, before which how should a frail and erring creature of the dust present himself unless with bended knees and uplifted hands, betokening at once his humility and dependence? In this posture did Adam first kneel before God and bless the author of his being; and there too did he bend with contrite awe before the face of his offended Judge, to avert his wrath, and implore his mercy; and transmitted this sacred form to his posterity for ever.

PENTALPHA. In the Royal Arch Degree, the name of God is depicted in the centre of old floor-cloths, by a double interlacing triangle thus ✡, inscribed within a dark circle, representing unlimited space beyond the reach of light, and the top representing the "light shining in darkness, and the darkness comprehending it not." This had been used as a Christian symbol, to denote the two natures of Jehovah, the God-man, for centuries before the Royal Arch Degree was ever thought of. In this form ✶, or the above, it was called the pentangle, or seal of Solomon, and the shield of David, and was employed all over Asia as a preservative against witchcraft, in which superstition the Jews are said to have participated; for they used written charms enclosed in the above hexagonal or pentangular figure, and disposed cabalistically, which were worn about their necks. It constituted the Pythagorean pentalpha, and was the symbol of health.

PERFECT ASHLAR. The perfect ashlar is a stone of a true square, which can only be tried by the square and compasses. This represents the mind of a man at the close of life, after a well-regulated career of piety and virtue, which can only be tried by the square of God's Word, and the compasses of an approving conscience.

PERJURY. Let any unprejudiced man pronounce his opinion of Freemasonry from the experience of the benefits it has conferred on society, and his judgment cannot be unfavourable. Take the great body of Free-masons, and their most determined enemies must admit them to be honourable in their actions, and estimable in private life. Look over the criminal calendar at any assizes, and you very seldom find members of this Order charged with felonious offences, or accused of disturbing social order. Should a Mason be convicted of felony or perjury, he is immediately expelled the Order.

PERPENDICULAR. Geometrically, that which is per-fectly upright and erect, inclining neither one way or the other. Symbolically, inclining neither to avarice nor injustice, to malice nor revenge, to envy nor contempt, in our intercourse with mankind; but as the builder raises his column by the plane or perpendicular, so should the Mason carry himself toward the world; thus will he stand approved before heaven and before men, purchasing honor and felicity to himself as a professor of Masonry.

PERSONAL MERIT. All preferment amongst Ma-sons is grounded upon real worth and personal merit only, so that the lords may be well served, the brethren not put to shame, nor the Royal Craft despised. There-fore no Master or Warden is chosen by seniority, but for his merit. It is impossible to describe these things in writing, and therefore every brother must attend in his place, and learn them in a way peculiar to this Fraternity —*Ancient Charges.*

PETITION. Every application for a warrant to hold a new lodge must be by petition to the Grand Master, signed by at least seven regularly registered Masons; and the lodges to which they formerly belonged must be specified. The petition must be recommended by the officers of some regular lodge, and be transmitted to the Grand Secretary, unless there be a Provincial Gran Master of the district or province in which the lodge i proposed to be holden, in which case it is to be sent to him, or to his deputy, who is to forward it, with his recommendation or opinion thereon, to the Grand Master. Applications for relief must also be by petition, stating the name, occupation, place of abode, and present circumstances of the petitioner; together with the name and number of the lodge in which he was initiated, and the time when he was made a Mason. The applicant, unless disabled by disease or accident, must sign his name to the petition.—*Constitutions.*

PHRASES OF ADMISSION. When a candidate receives the first degree, he is said to be *initiated*, at the second step he is *passed*, at the third *raised;* when he takes the mark degree, he is *congratulated;* having passed the chair, he is said to have *presided;* when he becomes a Most Excellent Master, he is *acknowledged* and *received;* and when a Royal Arch Mason, he is *exalted.*

PHYSICAL. The physical qualifications of a candidate are, that he shall be a free man, born of a free woman, of mature age, and able body.

PICKAXE. The sound of the stroke of the pickaxe reminds us of the sound of the last trumpet, when the grave shall be shaken, loosened, and deliver up its dead.

PILLARS. Every lodge must be supported by three grand shafts, or pillars—Wisdom, Strength, and Beauty Wisdom constructs the building, Beauty adorns, and Strength supports it; also, Wisdom is ordained to discover, Beauty to ornament, and Strength to bear. He who is wise as a perfect Master, will not be easily injured by his own actions. Hath a person the strength which a Senior Warden represents, he will bear and overcome

every obstacle in life. And he who is adorned, like the
Junior Warden, with humility of spirit, approaches
nearer to the similitude of God than another. But the
three pillars must be built upon a rock, and that rock is
called Truth and Justice.—*Gadicke.*

PILLARS OF THE PORCH. It is generally thought
that these pillars were made and erected only for ornament, because they supported no building. But Abar-
binel's conjecture is not improbable, that Solomon had
respect to the pillar of the cloud, and the pillar of fire,
that went before them and conducted them in the wilderness, and was a token of the divine Providence over
them. These he set at the porch, or entrance of the
Temple (Jachin representing the pillar of the cloud, and
Boaz the pillar of fire), praying and hoping that the
Divine Light, and the cloud of His glory would vouchsafe to enter in there; and by them God and His providence would dwell among them in this house.—*Bishop
Patrick.*

PLACED. The situation of the candidate at the
north-east angle of the lodge, was symbolical of Joseph,
who was the father of two tribes of Israel, one of which
was placed at the head of his division of the Israelites
in the wilderness, and bore one of the great cherubic
banners, and the other had two allotments in the land
of Canaan.

PLANS. The tracing-board is for the Master to draw
his plans and designs on, that the building may be
carried on with order and regularity. It refers to the
Sacred Volume which is denominated the Tracing-Board
of the Grand Architect of the Universe, because in that
holy book he had laid down such grand plans and holy
designs, that were we conversant therein, and adherent
thereto, it would bring us to a building not made with
hands, eternal in the heavens.

PLOTS. A Mason is a peaceable subject to the civil
powers wherever he resides or works, and is never to be
concerned in plots and conspiracies against the peace
and welfare of the nation, nor to behave himself unduti-

fully to inferior magistrates. He is cheerfully to conform to every lawful authority; to uphold, on every occasion, the interest of the community, and zealously to promote the interests of his own country.—*Ancient Charges.*

PLUMB-RULE. Without this instrument the operative mason cannot prove that his work is perfectly upright; and the overseer or superintendent of any building must have this tool ever in his hands, that he may prove that his men are working correctly. To proceed straight forward in the paths of virtue and honour, and faithfully to perform those duties the Craft requires of us, demands constant attention on the part of every Free and Accepted Mason.—*Gadicke.*

POETRY OF MASONRY. An intelligible view of the poetry of Masonry may be gathered from its general principles. It inculcates brotherly love amongst all mankind; it tends to soften the harshness of an exclusive feeling towards those who differ from us in our views of religion and politics, although it allows of no discussions on either the one or the other; it suppresses the attachment to class, which is the bane of all other institutions; and, by the purity of its sentiments, it harmonizes the mind, ameliorates the disposition, and produces that genuine feeling of benevolence and Christian charity which "suffereth long and is kind; which envieth not, vaunteth not itself, is not easily puffed up, doth not behave unseemly, seeketh not her own, is not easily provoked, thinketh no evil, rejoiceth not in iniquity, but rejoiceth in the truth, beareth all things, endureth all things."

POINT. A point is an inactive effective disposition or inclination to the several duties of man, and is the beginning of every active duty. It is also the beginning of every advantage, profit, pleasure, or happiness, that flows from the observation or performance of such a duty.

POINT WITHIN A CIRCLE. As in a circle, however large, there is one middle point, whither all converge, called by geometricans the centre; and although the parts of the whole circumference may be divided innumerably, yet is there no other point save that one from which all measure equally, and which, by a certain law of evenness, hath the sovereignty over all. But if you leave this one point, whatever point you take, the greater number of lines you draw, the more everything is confused. So the soul is tossed to and fro by the very vastness of the things, and is crushed by a real destitution, in that its own nature compels it everywhere to seek one object, and the multiplicity suffers it not.—*St Augustin.*

POLITICS. Politics are entirely prohibited from a Freemasons' lodge, and no brother dare attempt to propagate his views upon politics by means of the Order, this being in direct opposition to the ancient statutes. The political opinions of mankind never agree, and they are thus directly opposed to brotherly union. If a peculiar set of political opinions gain the upper hand in a state, or if a revolution take place, or if a country be invaded by a foreign army, the lodges close themselves. Charity to a suffering warrior, let him be a friend or a foe, must not be considered as a political act, for it is the general duty of mankind, and more especially it is a masonic duty.—*Gadicke.*

POMEGRANATE. *Grained Apple.* The fruit is about the size of an orange, of a tawny brown, containing an abundance of seeds; when ripe it opens lengthwise, and is full of juice like wine, which is, when cultivated, sweet and highly agreeable. As an emblem for ornamentation it was highly esteemed by most of the nations of antiquity. Moses was directed to put embroidered pomegranates, with golden bells between them, at the bottom of the high-priest's robe. The two pillars set up at the porch of the temple were ornamented with rows of artificial pomegranates. This fruit, because of the exuberance of its seed, has been selected by Masons as an emblem of plenty.

PORCH. The width of the porch, holy and most holy places, were twenty cubits, and the height over the holy and most holy places, was thirty cubits; but the height of the porch was much greater, being no less than 120 cubits, or four times the height of the rest of the building. To the north and south sides, and the west end of the holy and most holy places, or all around the edifice, from the back of the porch on the one side, to the back of the porch on the other side, certain buildings were attached; these were called side chambers, and consisted of three stories, each five cubits high, and joined to the wall of the temple without.—*Calmet.*

POT OF INCENSE. The pot of incense presents itself to our notice as an emblem of a pure heart, which is always an acceptable sacrifice to the Deity; and as this glows with fervent heat, so should our hearts continually glow with gratitude to the great and beneficent author of our existence, for the manifold blessings and comforts we enjoy.

POT OF MANNA. The pot of manna was placed in the sanctuary to commemorate the heavenly bread, by which the Israelites were sustained in the wilderness; it has therefore been adopted as a masonic emblem, to signify that Christ is the bread of God which came down from heaven.

PURSUIVANT. An attendant or herald, who publicly announced all new-comers at tournaments, etc. In some Grand Lodges, an officer whose name implies similar duties, and who acts as the inner sentinel.

PRACTICE. We may talk of religion, its doctrines, its precepts, and its privileges; we may talk of philosophy with all its train of human perfections, and human acquirements; we may become Masons, boast of its secrecy, its science, and its morals; put on all its gaudy trappings and ornaments, and decorate ourselves with its richest external jewels. But if our religion is destitute of love to God, and of charity towards our fellow creatures; if our philosophy is destitute of philanthropy, or if our Masonry is destitute of the activity of doing good, away with religious profession, it is but an empty name; away with philosophical sentiment, it is but as sounding brass; away with masonic pretensions, they are but as tinkling cymbals.—*Inwood.*

PRAYER. The legitimate prayers of Freemasonry are short addresses to the Great Architect of the Universe for a blessing on our labours. Now who is this Divine Being whom we thus invoke?—Why, according to the interpretation of our ancient brethren, "Him that was carried to the top of the pinnacle of the holy temple," or Jesus Christ. Nor is Freemasonry singular in this interpretation. St. Paul says "Jesus Christ laid the foundations of the earth, and the heavens are the work of his hands," or, in other words, that he is the Great Architect of the Universe.

PRECAUTION. The greatest precautions are used to prevent the admission of unworthy characters; if from want of proper information, or from too charitable constructions, such are introduced, we deeply regret the mistake, and use every proper method to remedy the evil.—*Harris.*

PRECEDENCY. The precedency of lodges is derived from the number of their constitutions, as recorded in the books of the Grand Lodge. No lodge shall be acknowledged, nor its officers admitted into the United Grand Lodge, or a Provincial Grand Lodge, nor any of its members entitled to partake of the general charity or other masonic privilege, unless it has been regularly constituted and registered.—*Constitutions.*

PREFERENCE. Though we give a decided preference to such as have been tried and proved, and found to be worthy, and have in consequence been made members of the masonic family, we are known to profess and practise charity unconfined, and liberality unlimited, and to comprehend in the wide circle of our benevolence, the whole human race.—*Harris.*

PREJUDICE. From prejudice, as well as from ignorance, arise most of the objections against Freemasonry, and all the misrepresentations of its principles and practices. As the origin of such dislike to our institution is so well known, it might be deemed paying too great respect to its evils, to take any notice of them all. In general, it is best to despise the invectives of calumny.

and smile at the impotence of malice; to disdain taking any notice of groundless surmises, and not to give ourselves the trouble of listening to the queries of the ignorant, or of confuting the opinions of the prejudiced and captious.—*Harris.*

PREPARATION. Preparation has several departments, various steps and degrees. We must place our feet on the first round of the masonic or theological ladder, before we can ascend the second; and we must receive the degree of Entered Apprentice before we can obtain the Fellowcraft, and the Fellowcraft before the degree of Master Mason. Then how complete is the analogy between the work of speculative Masonry, and the preparation of the materials for King' Solomon's Temple, and what does the argument by way of analogy demonstrate? Every moral truth which the preparation of the materials of the temple teaches, our masonic preparation also illustrates. It would be wise in us, to think often of the necessity of preparation to be advanced in light and knowledge.—*Scott.*

PREPARED. A man who has been properly pre pared to be initiated into Freemasonry, is a true symbol of a pure and uncorrupted man, such as the Society wishes and requires to have as members. Such an one must be able to appreciate his fellow mortals more by their moral worth and intellectual attainments, than by their rank, power, or riches. Happy are those who wish to be so estimated, for they will do honour to the Craft when clothed in purple and gold.—*Gadicke.*

PREPARING BROTHER. It is the duty of the preparing brother, shortly before the candidate for initiation is introduced into the lodge, to prove if he still continues earnest in his desire to be initiated, what are the reasons which induce him to do so, and if he is willing to submit himself unconditionally to the rules of an unknown society. From this we may perceive that the preparing brother must possess a fine knowledge of mankind. The situation in which he is placed with regard to the candidate, gives him an opportunity of putting a number of questions which could not be put in any other

place, or which the candidate could not answer so fully
and so unhesitatingly as in the preparing-room. The
preparing brother must not terrify the candidate from
seeking admission; his duty is merely to remove any
erroneous ideas the candidate may have formed of the
Craft, as far as may be found necessary.—*Gadicke.*

PRE-REQUISITES. No person is capable of becoming a member unless, together with the virtues afore-
mentioned, or at least a disposition to seek and acquire
them, he is also free-born, of mature age, of good report,
of sufficient natural endowments, and the senses of a
man; with an estate, office, trade, occupation, or some
visible way of acquiring an honest livelihood, and of
working in his Craft, as becomes the members of this
most ancient and honourable fraternity, who ought not
only to earn what is sufficient for themselves and families, but also something to spare for works of charity and
supporting the true dignity of the royal Craft.—*Moore*

PRIEST. The second principal of the Royal Arch.

PRINCIPAL POINT. The principal point of Masonry, is Brotherly Love, Relief, and Truth.

PRINCIPALS. In a Royal Arch Chapter the Companions are supposed to be seated round, in the form of
the catenarian arch, in which the thrones of the three
Principals form the key or cope-stone, to preserve a
memory of the vaulted shrine in which King Solomon
deposited the sacred name of the word. The cope-stones
are represented by the three Principals of the Chapter,
because as a knowledge of the secrets of the vaulted
chamber could only be known by drawing them forth,
o the complete knowledge of this degree can be attained
only by passing through its several offices.

PRINTED WORKS ON FREEMASONRY. The
Mason promises at his initiation, that he will not betray
the secrets of the Order by writing, and notwithstanding
the great number of the so-called printed works upon
Freemasonry which we have, there is not an author ot
one of those works who has been a traitor to the real

secrets of the Craft. When it is maintained by the world that the books which are said to have been written by oppressed Freemasons, contain the secrets of Freemasonry, it is a very great error. To publish an account of the ceremonies of the Lodge, however wrong that may be, does not communicate the secrets of Freemasonry. The printed rituals are not correct, as they are printed from memory, and not from a lodge copy. Inquiries into the history of the Order, and the true meaning of its hieroglyphics and ceremonies by learned brethren cannot be considered treason, for the Order itself recommends the study of its history, and that every brother should instruct his fellows as much as possible. It is the same with the printed explanation of the moral principles and the symbols of the Order ; we are recommended to study them incessantly, until we have made ourselves masters of the valuable information they contain ; and when our learned and cautious brethren publish the result of their inquiries, they ought to be most welcome to the Craft.—*Gadicke.*

PRINTING. No brother shall presume to print or publish, or cause to be printed or published, the proceedings of any lodge, nor any part thereof; or the names of the persons present at such lodge, without the direction of the Grand Master, or Provincial Grand Master, under pain of being expelled from the Order. This law is not to extend to the writing, printing, or publishing, of any notice or summons issued to the members of a lodge by the authority of the Master.—*Constitutions.*

PRIVATE DUTIES. Whoever would be a Mason should know how to practise all the private virtues. He should avoid all manner of intemperance or excess, which might prevent his performance of the laudable duties of his Craft, or lead him into enormities, which would reflect dishonour upon the ancient fraternity. He is to be industrious in his profession, and true to the Lord and Master he serves. He is to labour justly, and not to eat any man's bread for nought; but to pay truly for his meat and drink. What leisure his labour allows, he is to employ in studying the arts and sciences with a dili-

gent mind, that he may the better perform all his duties
to his Creator, his country, his neighbour and himself.—
Moore.

PRIVILEGES. The majority of every particular
lodge, when duly congregated, have the privilege of
instructing their Master and Wardens for their conduct
in the Grand Lodge and Quarterly Communications ; and
all particular lodges in the same Communications, shall
as much as possible observe the same rules and usages,
and appoint some of their members to visit each other
in the different lodges, as often as it may be convenient
—*Moore.*

PROBATIONS. Probation implies progression, and
progression implies reward. If the labour of the Entered
Apprentice is intended to refer to the fall of man, or the
curse pronounced for his disobedience, then the industrious and Christian Mason has an assurance that the time
will come when he will be called from his labour on
earth, to refreshment in heaven.—*Scott.*

PROCESSIONS. Our public processions have been
instituted for many noble purposes. We visit the house
of God in public, to offer up our prayers and praises for
mercies and blessings ; we attend in a body to shew the
world our mutual attachment as a band of brothers ; we
are arranged in a set form to exhibit the beauty of our
system, constructed on the most harmonious proportions,
and modelled by a series of imperceptible grades of rank,
which cement and unite us in that indissoluble chain of
sincere affection which is so well understood by Master
Masons, and blend the attributes of equality and subordination in a balance so nice and equitable, that the
concord between rulers and brethren is never subject to
violation, while we meet on the level and part on the
square.

PROCLAMATION. On the proclamation of Cyrus
the Jews left Babylon, under the conduct of Zerubbabel, son of Shealtiel, the lineal descendant of the princely
house of Judah, attended by Jeshua the High Priest,
Haggai the prophet, and Ezra the scribe, and returned

GRAND MASONIC PROCESSION.

to their own land. In the seventh month of the same year the altar of God was erected, and burnt offerings were sacrificed upon it; and the feast of tabernacles was kept according to the law of Moses. Men were also employed according to the permission of Cyrus, to cut cedars in Lebanon, and bring them by sea to Joppa. In the beginning of the second year, the foundation of the temple was laid by Zerubbabel, the Grand Master of the Jewish Masons, assisted by Jeshua the High Priest, as Senior Grand Warden, with great rejoicing and praise to God.

PROFANE. The word signifies uninitiated. All those who do not belong to the Order are frequently so called. Before a lodge is held, care must be taken that none but the initiated are present, and that the lodge is carefully tiled. In the lodge lists, which are frequently open to the public, there are given the addresses to which all letters for the lodge must be sent, and these are called profane addresses. It would be much more proper to call them "town addresses," for many of the uninitiated translate the word profane as unmannerly or impious.— *Gadicke.*

PROGRESSIVE. There are three steps and three degrees in symbolical Masonry. Each step or degree is an advance towards light and knowledge. There is more revealed in the Fellow Craft's degree, than in the degree of the Entered Apprentice; and there is fulness of light and knowledge in the degree of Master. Mankind, before the appearance of the Messiah, had been partially instructed under the patriarchal and Levitical dispensations. But the world was then comparatively in darkness; more light was wanted, and the Messiah came to give more light, to teach and instruct the world in the mysteries of his kingdom.—*Scott.*

PROMISE. The promise of a Saviour, its reference and fulfilment, is the great mystery of Freemasonry. Some of our most sublime observances are founded upon it, and the distinguishing tokens of recognition in one of the degrees, refer exclusively to that gracious interposition of the Deity in behalf of fallen man : and by virtue of one of these significant signs, if we prostrate ourselves with our face to the earth, it is to supplicate the mercy of our Creator and Judge, looking forward with humble confidence to his holy promises, by which alone we hope to pass through the ark of our redemption, into the mansions of eternal bliss and glory.

PROMOTION. Every man strives for promotion, either in office or in knowledge. It is for this reason that the Apprentice strives for the Fellowcraft's degree; the Fellowcraft for the Master's degree, and the Master for a still higher degree, or state of knowledge. Those who really and zealously strive to obtain a correct knowledge of all that is truly good and valuable in the Craft, will not fail in their endeavours to obtain masonic promotion.—*Gadicke.*

PRONUNCIATION. The name of Jehovah is the fountain and root, produces all others, and itself is derived from none; which is shewn by being written ירד חי ויי חי which is seventy-two; and is adduced by "Bereshith Raba," as one of the highest Names, being taught by the priests and wise men, once in seven years, to their equals in piety and virtue, from the pronunciation being extremely difficult and secret.—*Manasseh Ben Israel.*

PROPAGATION. Our Grand Master Solomon, observing the effects produced by strict order adopted among the Masons employed in his work, conceived the idea of uniting the wise in every nation, in the bond of brotherly love, and in the pursuit of scientific acquirements. He admitted to the participation of this system those illustrious sages, who resorted to Jerusalem, even from the uttermost parts of the East, to be instructed in his wisdom; and they returning to their respective homes, propagated the system of Freemasonry over the whole face of the Eastern continent.—*Hemming.*

PROPER PERSONS. The persons made Masons, or admitted members of a lodge, must be good and true men, free born, and of mature and discreet age and sound judgment; no bondmen, no women, no immoral or scandalous men, but of good report.—*Ancient Charges.*

It is to be lamented that the indulgence subjoined to this wholesome injunction, (no lodge shall ever make a Mason without due inquiry into his character,) should weaken the regard seriously due to it; for as no man will build his house upon a bog or a quicksand, a man of suspicious integrity. will be found equally unfit to sustain the character of a true Mason; and if some corresponding regard to worldly circumstances were included, it would operate more for the welfare and credit of the Society.—*Noorthouck.*

PROPHET. The third principal of the Royal Arch Chapter.

PROPOSING. Proposing a candidate is a thing which requires the greatest care and attention. Through an improper subject, a whole lodge—nay, even the whole Society—may receive a deep wound. No one dare propose a person with whom he is not intimately acquainted, and whose conduct he has not had an opportunity of observing under different circumstances. The person who is about to make a proposition, must have carefully inquired whether the candidate is influenced by the desire of gain or self-interest; for he must not look to the Order as a means of making money, but rather as a means of expending it in charitable objects.

PROSCRIPTION. The severest punishment in the Order. The Freemason who is found guilty of a crime against the regulations of the Order, or the laws of the land, is solemnly proscribed, and notice of his proscription is sent to all lodges, so that he never can gain admission again.—*Gadicke.*

PROTECTION. The true believers, in order to withdraw and distinguish themselves from the rest of mankind, especially the idolaters by whom they were surrounded, adopted emblems, and mystic devices, together with certain distinguishing principles, whereby they should be known to each other; and also certify that they were servants of that God, in whose hands all creation existed. By these means they also protected themselves from persecution, and their faith from the ridicule of the incredulous vulgar.—*Hutchinson.*

PROTOTYPE. Masonry has the Omnipotent Architect of the Universe for the object of its adoration and imitation, His great and wonderful works for its pattern and prototype, and the wisest and best of men of all ages, nations and languages, for its patrons and professors. But though Masonry primarily inculcates morals and the religion of nature, it has caught an additional spark from the light of revelation and the Sun of Righteousness. And though Masonry continues to burn with subordinate lustre, it lights the human traveller on the same road, it breathes a concordant spirit of universal benevolence and brotherly love, adds one thread more to the silken cord of evangelical charity which binds man to man, and crowns the cardinal virtues with Christian graces.— *Watson.*

PROVERBS OR MAXIMS. For the most part having reference to the Order, are in many lodges orally communicated to the brethren, and they are examined in the proficiency they have obtained in discovering the spirit and meaning of those proverbs, before they can obtain a higher degree.— *Gadicke.*

PROVINCIAL GRAND LODGE. The Provincial Grand Lodge of each province is to be assembled by the Provincial Grand Master or his deputy, at least once in each year for business; and which may also be a masonic festival. The present and past provincial grand officers, being subscribing members of any lodge within the district, with the Masters, Past Masters, and Wardens of all the lodges, are members of the Provincial Grand Lodge; and the Master and Wardens shall attend the same when duly summoned, or depute some brethren properly qualified to represent them.—*Constitutions.*

PROVINCIAL GRAND MASTER. The appointment of this officer, for counties and for large populous districts, is a prerogative of the Grand Master, by whom, or, in his absence, by his deputy, a patent may be granted, during pleasure, to such brother of eminence and ability in the Craft as may be thought worthy of the appointment. By this patent he is invested with a rank and power, in his particular district, similar to those possessed by the Grand Master himself.—*Constitutions.*

PROVINCIAL GRAND OFFICERS. These officers are to be annually nominated and installed or invested, according to their stations, in the Provincial Grand Lodge; and when so regularly appointed, they possess, within their particular district, the rank and privileges of grand officers; but they are not by such appointment members of the United Grand Lodge, nor do they take any rank out of the province, though they are entitled to wear their clothing as provincial grand officers, or past officers, in all masonic assemblies. No brother can be appointed a Grand Warden unless he be the Master of a lodge, or has regularly served in that office; nor a Grand Deacon, unless he be a Warden, or Past Warden of a lodge. If Grand Stewards are appointed, the number shall not exceed six, nor shall they take any prominent rank or distinction in the province.—*Constitutions.*

PRUDENCE. The emblem of prudence is the first and most exalted object that demands our attention in the lodge. It is placed in the centre, ever to be present to the eye of the Mason, that his heart may be attentive to her dictates, and steadfast in her laws; for prudence is the rule of all virtues; prudence is the path which leads to every degree of propriety; prudence is the channel whence self-approbation flows for ever. She leads us forth to worthy actions, and, as a blazing star, enlightens us throughout the dreary and darksome paths of life—*Hutchinson.*

PUBLICITY. What is there in Freemasonry, except the landmarks and peculiar secrets, that we ought to be anxious to conceal? Are our doctrines unfavourable to the interests of morality, that we are desirous of hiding them from public observation? Are our ceremonies repulsive to virtue, or our practices subversive to the rules and decencies of society? Nothing like it. We boast of our benevolent institutions; we extol our brotherly love; we celebrate our regard for the four cardinal, and the three theological virtues. Why place our light under a bushel? why refuse to let it shine before men, that they may see our good works have a tendency to the glory of our Father which is in heaven?

PUNCTUALITY. I would impress upon the Masters and Wardens the necessity of being punctual, and always to open their lodges and commence their business at the exact hour mentioned in the summonses, assured that if they persevere in this duty, they will incite regularity in the brethren, and the consequences will be, that their families, and the world at large, will appreciate an institution which thus displays the fruits of sound and wholesome discipline; the lodges will increase in number and reputation, and through their exemplary conduct, Freemasonry will secure a triumphal ascendancy, and excite general admiration and respect.

PUNISHMENTS. Those Freemasons who violate the laws of the country in which they reside, are either suspended, excluded, or proscribed. The lodge, nevertheless, never usurps the place of the magistrate or judge, as it has been formerly accused of doing. It rather directs the attention of the officers of justice to those brethren upon whom remonstrances are of no avail, and whom it is compelled to exclude.—*Gadicke.*

PURITY. White was always considered an emblem of purity. Porphyry, who wrote so largely on the spurious Freemasonry, says, " They esteem him not fit to offer sacrifice worthily, whose body is not clothed in a white and clean garment; but they do not think it any great matter, if some go to sacrifice, having their bodies clean, and also their garments, though their minds be not void of evil, as if God were not the most delighted with internal purity, which bears the nearest resemblance to him. It was even written in the temple of Epidauras— let all who come to offer at this shrine be pure. Now purity consists in holy thoughts.

PURPLE. The colour by which the grand officers are distinguished. It is an emblem of union, being produced by the combination of blue and scarlet, and reminds the wearer to cultivate amongst the brethren over whom he is placed, such a spirit of union as may cement them into one complete and harmonious society.

QUADRANGULAR DIAGRAM. This figure, which

appears on some of the old Royal Arch floor-cloths, reminds us of the seven pair of pillars which supported King Solomon's private avenue, the seven steps in advancing, and the seven seals; for in those days the O. B. was sealed seven times. The entire hieroglyphic, including the linear and angular triads, and the quadrangular diagram, was used in the continental degree of Secret Master, to express the Tetragrammaton, or Sacred Name, which they assert was found written upon the ancient monuments of Jerusalem.

QUALIFICATION. Every candidate for the office of Master must be true and trusty, of good report, and held in high estimation amongst the brethren. He must be well skilled in our noble science, and a lover of the Craft; he must have been regularly initiated, passed, and raised in the three established degrees of Freemasonry, and have served the office of Warden in some regular warranted lodge. He ought to be of exemplary conduct, courteous in manners, easy of address, but steady and firm in principle. He must have been regularly ballotted for, and elected by, the Worshipful Master, officers, and brethren, in open lodge assembled; and presented according to ancient form, to a regularly constituted board of installed Masters.

QUALIFICATION QUESTIONS. These questions are used as tests, to ascertain the progress of a candidate during his passage through the degrees. They are significant; and every one who aspires to the character of a perfect Mason, ought to be acquainted with them.

QUARRELLING. As a Mason you are to cultivate brotherly love, the foundation and cape-stone, the cement and glory of this ancient fraternity, avoiding all wrangling and quarrelling, all slander and backbiting, nor permitting others to slander any honest brother, but defending his character and doing him all good offices, as far as is consistent with your honour and safety, and no farther.—
Ancient Charges.

QUARRIES OF TYRE. The arrangement of the

Tyrian quarries must not be compared with the common stone-pits of this country, but rather to an extensive coal mine. Thus, Shaw describes the quarries of Strabo, at Aquilaria:—"Small shafts or openings are carried up quite through the surface above, for the admission of fresh air, whilst large pillars, with their respective arches, are still left standing to support the roof." Here the lodges were opened in the several degrees.

QUARTERLY COMMUNICATIONS. Four Grand Lodges, representing the Craft, shall be held for quarterly communication in each year, on the first Wednesday in the months of March, June, September and December, on each of which occasions, the Masters and Wardens of all the warranted lodges, shall deliver into the hands of the Grand Secretary and Grand Treasurer, a faithful list of all their contributing members; and the warranted lodges in and adjacent to London, should pay towards the grand fund one shilling per quarter for each member.—*Articles of Union.*

QUARTERLY SUBSCRIPTIONS. Supporting a lodge, paying the serving brethren, and other expenses. which are unavoidable, cause an expenditure which the uncertain fees upon initiation will not meet, and thus renders it necessary for the brethren to contribute a small sum monthly for this purpose; these sums vary in amount in different lodges according to their own by-laws made for the purpose. The balance in the hands of the Treasurer, after paying all necessary expenses, is spent for the benefit of the lodge, or devoted to charitable purposes. No subscribing brother ought to neglect these payments; and he who lives in a place where there is no lodge, and is not a subscriber, acts most unmasonically by neglecting to support the Charities.— Poor brethren, and those who are initiated as musical or serving brethren, are exempt from all contributions; but those who are able to subscribe and do not do so, deserve most justly to be struck off the list of members.— *Gadicke.*

QUATERNARY. The sacred quaternary, or number four, involves the liberal sciences, physics, morality, &c

And because the first four digits, added into each other,
produce the number ten, Pythagoras called the quaternary all number, and used it as the symbol of universality.

QUEEN ELIZABETH.   During the reign of Queen
Elizabeth, the government of the country attempted to
interfere with Freemasonry, but without success.   The
queen was jealous of all secrets in which she was unable
to participate, and she deputed an armed force, on St.
John's day, in December, 1561, to break up the annual
Grand Lodge.   The Grand Master, Sir Thomas Sackville,
received the queen's officers with great civility, telling
them nothing could give him greater pleasure than to
admit them into the Grand Lodge, and communicate to
them the secrets of the Order.   He persuaded them to
be initiated, and this convinced them that the system
was founded on the sublime ordinances of morality and
religion.   On their return, they assured the queen that
the business of Freemasonry was the cultivation of morality and science, harmony and peace; and that politics
and religion were alike forbidden to be discussed in their
assemblies. The queen was perfectly satisfied, and never
attempted to disturb the lodges again.

RAINBOW.   The rainbow was an emblem common
to every species of religious mystery; and was probably
derived from an old arkite tradition, that the divinity was
clothed in a rainbow; for thus he is represented by Ezekiel the prophet: "As the appearance of the bow that is
in the cloud in the day of rain, so was the appearance of
the brightness round about; this was the appearance
of the likeness of the Glory of the Lord."   St. John
saw in a vision the throne of God encompassed by a
rainbow.   A rainbow was in fact the usual emblem of a
divine Saviour throughout the world.   Some Christians,
"from the irradiation of the sun upon a cloud, appre-
hend the mystery of the Son of Righteousness in th
obscurity of the flesh   by the colours green and red
the two destructions of the world by water and fire ; or
by the colour of water and blood the mysteries of baptism,
and the holy eucharist "

RAISED. The expressive term used to designate the reception of the candidate into the third or sublime degree of Master Mason, and alludes both to a part of the ceremony and to our faith in the glorious morn of the resurrection, when our bodies will rise, and become as incorruptible as our souls.

RECOGNITION, SIGN OR SIGNS, WORD, AND GRIP. Wherever brethren meet, in whatever part of the world it may be, whether they can understand each others language or not, if it be by day or by night, if one be deaf and the other dumb, they can nevertheless recognise each other as brethren. In this respect the recognition signs are a universal language, and they are communicated to every Mason at his initiation. Signs and grips can be given so cautiously that it is not possible to perceive them, if they are surrounded by thousands who have not been initiated. To give the word is some what more difficult. By the grip we may make ourselves known to the blind, by the sign unto the deaf, and by the word and grip by day or by night.—*Gadicke.*

RECOMMENDATION. The following is the general form of a petition to the Lodge of Benevolence for relief, which may be altered according to circumstances:—We the undersigned, being the Master, Wardens, and majority of the members present, in open lodge assembled, of lodge No. — called ———, and held at ———, this ——— day of ———, 18 —, do hereby certify, that the within named petitioner hath been a regular contributing member of this lodge for the space of ——— years; and that we have known him in reputable circumstances, and do therefore recommend him to the Lodge of Benevolence for relief, having satisfactory grounds for believing the allegations set forth in his petition to be true.—*Constitutions.*

RECONCILIATION. Freemasonry teaches to suppress private prejudices and party spirit; to forget animosities, and to listen to the voice of reconciliation; to soften into gentleness and complaisance, sympathy, and love; and to prepare for all the duties of universal benevolence.—*Harris.*

RED SEA. That part of the sea over which the Israelites passed, was, according to Mr. Bruce, and other travellers, about four leagues across, and, therefore, might easily be crossed in one night. In the dividing of the sea, two agents appear to be employed, though the effect produced can be attributed to neither. By stretching out the rod the waters were divided; by the blowing of the vehement east wind, the bed of the sea was dried. It has been observed that in the bed of the sea, where the Israelites were supposed to have passed, the water is about fourteen fathoms, or twenty-eight yards deep. No natural agent could divide these waters, and cause them to stand as a wall upon the right hand and upon the left; therefore God did it by his own sovereign power. When the waters were thus divided, there was no need of a miracle to dry the bed of the sea, and make it passable; therefore the strong desiccating east wind was brought, which soon accomplished this object.—*Adam Clarke.*

REFRESHMENT. I like the good old custom of moderate refreshment during lodge hours, because, under proper restrictions, I am persuaded that it is consonant with ancient usage. The following are the routine ceremonies which were used on such occasions by our brethren of the last century. At a certain hour of the evening, and with certain ceremonies, the lodge was called from labour to refreshment, when the brethren "enjoyed themselves with decent merriment," and the song and the toast prevailed for a brief period. The songs were usually on masonic subjects, as printed in the old Books of Constitutions, and other works; and although the poetry is sometimes not of the choicest kind, yet several of them may class amongst the first compositions of the day. Each song had its appropriate toast; and thus the brethren were furnished with the materials for passing a social hour. And I can say from experience, that the time of refreshment in a masonic lodge, up to the union in 1813, was a period of unalloyed happiness and rational enjoyment.

REGALIA. No brother shall, on any pretence, be admitted into the Grand Lodge, or any subordinate lodge, without his proper clothing. If an honorary or other jewel be worn, it must be conformable to, and consistent with, those degrees, which are recognised by the Grand Lodge.—*Constitutions.*

REGENERATION. The cross on which the Messiah suffered was typified by the staff of Jacob amongst the patriarchs; amongst the Jews by the rod of Moses, as an agent of salvation on their deliverance from Egyptian bondage, and during their sojournings in the wilderness; and also by the pole on which the brazen serpent was suspended: and amongst the heathen by the tau-cross, which was appropriated to Serapis, and other deities; and, in its triple form (⛧), constituting a striking emblem of Royal Arch Masonry united with Christianity at the present day. And it is remarkable, that in each and every case, whether of the staff of Jacob, the rod of Moses, the pillar of the brazen serpent, or the tau of the heathen nations, the emblem signified alike the cross of Christ, regeneration, and life.

REGISTRAR. The Grand Registrar is to be appointed annually by the Grand Master on the day of his installation, and, if present, invested according to ancient custom. He shall have the custody of the seals of the Grand Lodge, and shall affix the same to all patents, warrants, certificates, and other documents issued by the authority of the Grand Lodge, as well as to such as the Grand Master, in conformity to the established laws and regulations of the Craft, may direct. He is to superintend the office of the records of the Grand Lodge, and to take care that the several documents issued from his office be in due form.—*Constitutions.*

REGISTRATION. Every lodge must be particularly careful in registering the names of the brethren initiated therein, and also in making the returns of its members, as no person is entitled to partake of the general charity, unless his name be duly registered, and he shall have been at least two years a contributing member of a lodge; except in the following cases, to which the limitation of two years is not meant to extend, viz.: shipwreck, or capture at sea, loss by fire, or breaking or dislocating a limb, fully attested and proved. To prevent injury to individuals, by their being excluded the privileges of Masonry, through the neglect of their lodges in not registering their names, any brother, so circumstanced, on producing sufficient proof that he has paid the full fees to his lodge, including the register fee, shall be capable of enjoying the privileges of the Craft. But the offending lodge shall be reported to the Board of General Purposes, and rigorously proceeded against for detaining monies which are the property of the Grand Lodge.—*Constitutions.*

REGULAR LODGE. By this term we are not only to understand such a lodge as works under a general warrant, granted by the Grand Lodge of the country in which it is situated, and which is acknowledged by, and is in correspondence with, the neighbouring lodges, but also that the Book of the Holy Law shall be unfolded on the pedestal; that it shall be composed of the requisite number of brethren, and the authority of the warrant enforced by the presence of the Book of Constitutions.

REGULARITY. He only is acknowledged as a Free and Accepted Mason who has been initiated into our mysteries in a certain manner, with the assistance of, and under the superintendence of at least seven brethren, and who is able to prove that he has been regularly initiated, by the ready use of those signs and words which are used by the other brethren.—*Charter of Colne.*

. REGULATIONS Without such regulations as Solomon had devised for the government of his servants, without such artificers, and a superior wisdom overruling the whole, we should be at a loss to account for the beginning, carrying on, and finishing that great work in the space of seven years and six months, when the two succeeding temples, though much inferior, employed so much more time; and then we have good authority to believe that the temple of Diana, at Ephesus, a structure not comparable to the Temple of Jerusalem, was two hundred and twenty years in building.—*Hutchinson.*

REINSTATEMENT The Provincial Grand Master

has no power to expel a Mason, though he may, when satisfied that any brother has been unjustly or illegally suspended, removed, or excluded from any of his masonic functions or privileges by a lodge, order him to be immediately restored, and may suspend, until the next quarterly communication, the lodge or brother who shall efuse to comply with such order.—*Constitutions.*

RELIEF. Relief is an important tenet of our procession; and though to relieve the distressed is a duty incumbent on all men, it is more particularly so on Masons, who are linked together by an indissoluble chain of sincere affection. To soothe calamity, alleviate misfortune, compassionate misery, and restore peace to the troubled mind, is the grand aim of the true Mason. On this basis he establishes his friendships, and forms his connexions.

RELIGION. The ancient lodges only admitted those persons into the Order who acknowledged the divinity of Jesus Christ; thus they were to be Christians, either of the English, Catholic, Lutheran, reformed, or modern Greek church. Mahometans, Jews, &c., were excluded, for none of these acknowledged the New Testament as a sacred writing. In modern times some of the French lodges have initiated Jews, but they are not acknowledged by the ancient lodges to be Freemasons.—*Gadicke*

REMOVAL OF LODGES. When any lodge shall have resolved to remove, the Master or Warden shall forthwith send a copy of the minutes of the lodge for such removal to the Grand Secretary, or to the Provincial Grand Master or his deputy, that it may be ascertained whether the above law has been strictly complied with, and that the removal may be duly recorded. If the meeting of a lodge at its usual place should by any circumstance be rendered impossible or improper, the Master may appoint any other place, and consult his brethren on the occasion.—*Constitutions.*

RENUNCIATION. Amongst the Jews, when a person renounced any bargain or contract, he took off his shoe, and gave it to his fellow; which was considered a sufficient evidence that he transferred all his right unto that person to whom he delivered his shoe. It is not easy to give an account of the origin of this custom; but the reason is plain enough, it being a natural signification that he resigned his interest in the land by giving him his shoe, wherewith he used to walk in it, to the end that he might enter into it, and take possession of it himself. The Targum, instead of a shoe, hath the right-hand glove; it being the custom in his time, perhaps, to give that instead of the shoe. For it is less troublesome to pull off a glove than a shoe, and deliver it to another, though it hath the same signification; as now the Jews deliver a handkerchief to the same purpose. So R. Solomon Jarchi affirms—"We acquire, or buy, now by a handkerchief, or veil, instead of a shoe."—*Bishop Patrick.*

REPASTS. The days of meeting are often days of festivity. The repasts are heightened by the temporary equality, which adds much to the mirth of the meeting, and all cares subside for the day. What has been said of certain assemblies, where decency was not respected, is most certainly the invention of calumny.—*Barruel.*

REPORT. The sound of the Master's hammer reminds each brother of the sacred numbers, a thing which ought to induce us readily and cheerfully to acknowledge and obey his commands. He who wishes to gain admittance amongst us must remember the saying, "Knock and it shall be opened unto you." It is only then that he can enter with a sanctified heart.—*Gadicke.*

REPORTS. The reports or signals of Masonry are too well known to every brother to need any explanation. They are arranged on certain fixed principles to distinguish every separate degree.

REPRESENTATION. The public interests of the Fraternity are managed by a general representation of all private lodges on record, together with the present and past grand officers, and the Grand Master at their head. All brethren who have been regularly elected and installed as Master of a lodge, and who have executed the office for one year, shall rank as Past Masters, and shall be members of the Grand Lodge. But if a Past Master shall cease to subscribe to a lodge for the space of twelve months, he shall no longer enjoy the rank of Past Master, or continue a member of the Grand Lodge.—*Constitutions.*

REPRESENTATIVES, or Deputies from one Lodge to another. They may either be representatives of one Grand Lodge in another, or of a St. John' Lodge in a Grand Lodge. In the last case the deputy must endeavour to maintain the rights and privileges of the lodge he represents, and must not allow any resolutions to be passed which may act injuriously to the lodge he represents, or any other lodge. We perceive by this that a deputy should have clear views of the rights and privileges of the lodge he represents, and of the whole Order, or he cannot do his duty as a deputy in bringing any propositions he may have to make before the Grand Lodge. He must also be able to transmit a correct account of the transactions of the Grand Lodge to the lodge from which he is deputed.—*Gadicke.*

REPUTATION. It seems the Masons have great regard to the reputation, as well as the profit, of their Order; since they make it one reason for not divulging an art in common, that it may do honour to the possessors of it. I think in this particular they show too much regard for their own society, and too little for the rest of mankind.—*Locke.*

REPROACH. There are some of persons of so captious and uncharitable a make, that it would be impossible for the most cautious to avoid their remarks, or escape their censures. The exceptious may lay hold of some unguarded circumstance or other, misrepresent what is good, and, by giving it a wrong turn or appellation, spoil both its credit and effect. While the envious and malicious will be sagacious in discovering the weak side of every character, and dexterous in making the most and worst of it. Thus circumstanced, how are we to conduct ourselves? How is it possible to steer clear from blame? It may not be. But if we cannot escape reproaches, we may avoid deserving them.—*Harris.*

RESIGNATION. This word is sometimes applied when a member desires to leave his Lodge. A Mason's obligations to the Order are indefeasible. In the separation of a brother from his Lodge, the word *dimit* should be used.

RESPECTABILITY. In referring to the prosperous condition of the Craft, and the accession which is daily making to its numbers, I would observe that the character of a lodge does not depend upon the number but the respectability of its members. It is too often the case that a lodge manifests too great anxiety to swell its numbers, under the erroneous idea that number constitutes might. It should, however, be remembered, that the race is not to the swift, nor the battle to the strong. So it is in Masonry; a lodge of a dozen men, of respectable standing in society, will exert more influence upon the community than five times the number of doubtful reputation. The latter will be greater in numerical strength, but the former in actual power.—*Tannehill.*

RESTRICTIONS. When the Temple at Jerusalem was completed, King Solomon, being desirous to transmit the society under the ancient restrictions, as a blessing to future ages, decreed that whenever they should assemble in their lodges, to discourse upon, and improve themselves in, the arts and sciences, and whatever else should be deemed proper topics to increase their knowledge, they should likewise instruct each other in secrecy and prudence, morality and good fellowship; and for these purposes he established certain peculiar rules and customs to be invariably observed in their conversations, that their minds might be enriched by a perfect acquaintance with, and practice of, every moral, social, and religious duty, lest, while they were so highly honoured by being employed in raising a temple to the great Jehovah, they should neglect to secure themselves a happy admittance into the celestial lodge, of which the Temple was only to be a type.—*Calcott.*

RESURRECTION. The Master Mason's tracing-board, covered with emblems of mortality, reads a lesson to the initiated of the certainty of death, and also of a resurrection from the dead. Like that of the two preceding contriving to captivate the hearer by strength of argument and beauty of expression, whether it be to entreat or exhort, to admonish or applaud.

RHYME. When lectures were added to the system of Freemasonry, they were sometimes couched in doggrel rhyme; but their verses seldom embodied any of the peculiar secrets. The introduction of the "Master's Part," as it was then called, was expressed as follows The passage has been expunged from our disquisitions, as unmeaning and useless, and therefore there will be no impropriety in introducing an extract here, to show how our forefathers worked. *Ex.* An E. A. P. I presume you have been. *R.* J. and B. I have seen. A M. M. I was most rare, with diamond, ashlar, and the square. *Ex* If a M. M. you would be, you most understand the rule of three, and M. B. shall make you free; and what you want in Masonry, shall in this lodge be shown to thee. *R.* Good Masonry, I understand; the keys of all lodges are at my command, &c., &c.

RIBBON. The ribbon worn by the Companions of the Order, is a sacred emblem denoting light, being composed of the two principal colours with which the veil of the tabernacle was interwoven. It is further signified by its radiated form, and in both respects has been considered an emblem of regal power and dignity.

RIGHT ANGLE. The perfect sincerity of one right line to another, is as the line of that angle, the line of duty being radius. An acute angle is imperfect sincerity. An obtuse angle is injustice. Join sincerity perfectly to any duty, and it forms justice, and is equal to an angle of ninety degrees.—*Old Lecture.*

RIGHT HAND. The proper residence of faith or fidelity was thought to be in the right hand, and therefore this deity was sometimes represented by two right hands joined together; sometimes by two little images shaking each other by the right hand; so that the right hand was esteemed by the ancients as a sacred symbol. And agreeably to this are those expressions in Virgil:—" En dextra fidesque;" as if shaking by the right hand was

He is taught to reverence God's holy name, and never to mention it but with that reverential awe which is due from the creature to the Creator; to implore His aid in all laudable undertakings, and esteem Him as the chief good.—*Scott.*

REVERENTIAL. We are taught by the reverential sign to bend with submission and resignation beneath the chastening hand of the Almighty, and at the same time to engraft his law in our hearts. This expressive form, in which the Father of the human race first presented himself before the face of the Most High, to receive the denunciation and terrible judgment, was adopted by our Grand Master Moses, who, when the Lord appeared to him in the burning bush on Mount Horeb, covered his face from the brightness of the divine presence.

REVISION. A revision of the lodge lectures periodically, to meet the advance of civilization and science, ought to take place under the sanction of the Grand Lodge. Every institution, to be perfect, should be consistent with itself. And hence the insufficiency of the present lectures may reasonably be questioned. It is therefore desirable that the attention of the fraternity should be fairly awakened to the subject, that they may take the premises into their most serious consideration, and endeavour to place Freemasonry on so substantial a basis, as to constitute the unmixed pride of its friends and defenders, and defy the malice of its traducers and foes, if any such are still to be found amongst those who are indifferent to its progress.

REWARD. The brethren are released from their labour to receive their reward. Respect, love, and gratitude, are their reward, and the consciousness of having deserved such must dwell in the breast of the labourer himself. No one can or dare declare himself to be worthy or unworthy of this reward, much less can he claim merit from his brethren.—*Gadicke.*

RHETORIC. Rhetoric teaches us to speak copiously and fluently on any subject, not merely with propriety, but with all the advantage of force and elegance; wisely

degrees, it is an oblong square, circumscribed by a black
border within the four cardinal points of the compass.
The principal figure is a black coffin, on a white ground,
at the head of which is placed a sprig of evergreen, called
cassia, or acacia, which appears to bloom and flourish
over the grave, as though it said—" O death where is thy
sting! O grave where is thy victory!"

RETURNS. Every lodge shall, at least once in the
year, transmit, by direct communication, to the Grand
Secretary a regular list of its members, and of the
brethren initiated or admitted therein since their last
return, with the dates of initiating, passing, and raising
every brother; also their ages as nearly as possible at
that time, and their titles, professions, additions, or
trades; together with all monies due or payable to the
Grand Lodge; which list is to be signed by the Master
and Secretary.—*Constitutions.*

RE-UNION. Freemasonry forms a happy centre of
re-union for worthy men, who are desirous of a select
society of friends and brothers, who have bound themselves in a voluntary obligation to love each other, to
afford aid and assistance in time of need, to animate one
another to acts of virtue and benevolence, and to keep
inviolably the secrets which form the chief characteristic
of the Order.—*Lalande.*

REVELATION. Masonry primarily inculcates morals
and the religion of nature, but it has caught an additional
spark from the light of revelation and the Sun of Righteousness. And though Masonry continues to burn with
subordinate lustre, it lights the human traveller on the
same road; it breathes a concordant spirit of universal
benevolence and brotherly love; adds one thread more
to the silken cord of evangelical charity which binds man
to man, and crowns the cardinal virtues with Christian
graces.—*Watson.*

REVELS. No dark revels or midnight orgies are
practised in a lodge. No words of wrath or condemnation
are heard, and no inquisitorial questions are asked. The
candidate hears of peace, brotherly love, relief, and truth .

an indispensable token of an honest heart And again "Cur dextræ jungere dextram non datur, ac veras audire, et reddere voces?" that is to say, why should we not join right hand to right hand, and hear and speak the truth?—*Anderson.*

RIGHT LINE. A right line is a duty persisted in with constancy, or any uninterrupted advantage, profit, pleasure, or happiness. That which hath no dependence on any other thing to make it perfect in itself, is a right line. Every divine command is a right line, and also the sincerity with which such a command ought to be performed. Every line representing a duty to be performed, may be supposed to contain all the particular branches of that duty; for the branches or parts of any duty, must of consequence make up the whole duty itself.—*Old Lecture.*

RIGHTS. The right of the Entered Apprentice to be advanced, or the Fellow Craft to be raised, depends, in strict principle, upon his proficiency in the degree which he has received. He should be able to exhibit a beautiful specimen of intellectual or moral work, to entitle him to receive wages, or to enter upon the study of higher departments of science.—*Scott.*

RITE. A rite is an item in the ceremonial of conferring degrees, although in some countries it is extended to include a number of degrees and orders, as in the French rite "ancien et accepté," which comprehends the "Maçonnerie Symbolique, Elu, Chev. d'Orient, du Soleil, Kadosh, Rose Croix," &c., with the "Grades dites Philosophiques et Administratifs."

RITUAL. This word imports how a lodge ought to be opened and closed, and how an initiation, passing, or raising ought to be conducted; this may also be called the liturgy of the lodge. The ritual is not the same in all lodges, nay, there are nearly as many different rituals as there are Grand Lodges. Many of those rituals are of quite modern origin, especially that of the Grand Lodge Royal York, Berlin, and that of the Grand Lodge of Hamburgh. The English ritual is the most ancient, and extended itself into every part of the earth but was afterwards superseded in many places by the French, Swedish, and others. Those outward forms and ceremonies, although they differ, yet they do not divide the brethren amongst themselves, but each lodge and its members is tolerant with the members of other lodges; and all lodges are allowed to endeavour and strive to obtain their object by what way they think best. Neither is there any real difference whether some ceremonies are to be performed in this manner, or in that, according to the different rituals, or whether the officers are called this or that. Time and various circumstances have made those alterations in the rituals principally to produce a more lasting impression upon the mind of the candidate at his initiation, and to advance with the improved spirit of the times. Fragments from some of the rituals have been published, especially from the old ones; but there must be more than a dozen rituals published before an uninitiated person could learn how an initiation was conducted, or how a lodge was held. The end to which the ritual leads us is the principal object, or the real secret of Freemasonry, and it would require an adept to discover this from any ritual. There only ought to be one ritual, as was the case in former ages; and the unlucky word system ought never to have been introduced into the Craft.—*Gadicke.*

RIVERS OF EDEN. The four rivers of Paradise had a reference to the cardinal virtues. In Pisor, our first parents revered the fountain of prudence; in Gihon they beheld the sacred stream of justice. The rapid torrent of Hiddekel denoted fortitude, and the Euphrates the mild and steady current of temperance. Happy was their state, while these sacred truths continued to guide their actions; and the Mason will be equally happy who, through life, adheres to the lessons here inculcated. Instructed by prudence, guided by justice, strengthened by fortitude and restrained by temperance, like Adam in the garden of Eden, his services will be acceptable to the Deity.

ROD. The rod of Moses, fearful as the attack of a serpent to the Egyptians. was a sceptre of righteousness to the children of Israel. It was a sign of the divine authority, and a visible demonstration of God's power used to confound the pretended skill of the magicians, to show the omnipotence of the Deity, and to humble the pride of Pharaoh, when he beheld the mighty wonders wrought by so contemptible an agent as a shepherd's staff. But above all, this rod metamorphosed, was a type of Christ's death, to which indeed Freemasonry ultimately points; for as by a serpent death came into the world, so by the death of the Son of God, the serpent, or Satan, was fully vanquished and trodden underfoot.

ROUGH ASHLER. We cannot regard the rough ashler as an imperfect thing, for it was created by the Almighty Great Architect and he created nothing imperfect, but gave us wisdom and understanding, so as to enable us to convert the seemingly imperfect to our especial use and comfort. What great alterations are made in a rough ashler by the mallet and chisel! With it are formed, by the intelligent man, the most admirable pieces of architecture. And man, what is he when he first enters into the world?—Imperfect, and yet a perfect work of God, out of which so much can be made by education and cultivation.—*Gadicke.*

ROYAL ARCH. This degree is more august, sublime, and important than those which precede it, and is the summit of ancient Masonry. It impresses on our minds a more firm belief of the existence of a Supreme Deity without beginning of days or end of years, and justly reminds us of the respect and veneration due to that holy name. Until within these few years, this degree was not conferred on any but those who had been enrolled a considerable time in the fraternity, and could besides give the most unequivocal proofs of their skill and proficiency in the Craft.—*Ahiman Rezon.*

ROYAL ART. It is a royal art to be able to preserve a secret, and we are, therefore, accustomed to call Freemasonry a royal art. To be able to plan large buildings, especially palaces, is also certainly a great and a royal art, but it is still a more royal art to induce men to do that which is good, and to abstain from evil, without having recourse to the power of the law. Others derive the appellation, royal art, from that part of the members of the English Builders' Huts, who, after the beheading of Charles I., 30th January, 1649, joined the persecuted Stuart, inasmuch as that they laboured to restore the oyal throne, which had been destroyed by Cromwell. Anderson, on the contrary, in his English Constitution Book, affirms that the appellation royal art is derived from the fact, that royal persons have stood, and still stand, at the head of the Craft.—*Gadicke.*

ROYAL LODGE. The Royal Lodge was held in the city of Jerusalem, on the return of the Babylonish captives in the first year of the reign of Cyrus; over it presided Z., the prince of the Jews, H., the prophet, and J. the high priest. Now it was that the kingly power was again more visibly restored, and continued till the total destruction of the city and temple by the Romans, under the command of Titus; when Herod, not of their own royal line, nor even a Jew, was appointed king, and hereby was verified that prophecy of Jacob's in Egypt, delivered more than one thousand years before, "that the sceptre should not depart from Judah, nor a lawgiver from between his feet, until Shiloh come."

RUAMMI. The words Ammi and Ruammi, made use of by the prophet Hosea, may be interpreted, *my people,* and *obtained mercy.*

RULERS. The rulers and governors, supreme and subordinate, of the ancient lodge, are to be obeyed in their respective stations by all the brethren, according to the old charges and regulations, with all humility, reverence, love, and alacrity.—*Ancient Charges.*

SABBATH. The institution of a Sabbath was *in signum creationis,* for a memorial of the creation; because, as God rested on that day in testimony that his work was completed, so it was accounted holy, and appointed to be observed as a day of universal repose.

SACRED. We call that sacred which is separated

from common things, and dedicated either entirely or partially to the Most High. The ideas of. truth and virtue, the feeling of a pure love and friendship are sacred, for they elevate us above common things and lead to God. The tenour of sacred thought and feelings is towards religion, and therefore all things are sacred which are peculiarly dedicated to religious services, and carefully guarded from being applied to profane uses, or which, by means of their religious importance and value, are especially honoured and considered indispensable to our spiritual and moral welfare. According to these ideas of what is sacred, the Freemason can call his work sacred, and every brother must acknowledge it to be so. Our labours being separated from the outward world, and founded upon truth and virtue, require brotherly love and philanthropy, and always elevate the spirit to the Great Architect of the Universe. But true inward sanctity every brother must have in his own breast, and not have it to seek in the degrees of the Order.— *Gadicke.*

SACRED LODGE. Over the sacred lodge presided Solomon, the greatest of kings, and the wisest of men; Hiram, the great and learned king of Tyre; and Hiram Abiff, the widow's son, of the tribe of Napthali. It was held in the bowels of the sacred Mount Moriah, under the part whereon was erected the S. S., or H. of H. On this mount it was where Abraham confirmed his faith by his readiness to offer up his only son Isaac. Here it was where David offered that acceptable sacrifice on the threshing-floor of Araunah, by which the anger of the Lord was appeased, and the plague stayed from his people. Here it was where the Lord delivered to David, in a dream, the plan of the glorious temple, afterwards erected by our noble G. M. K. S. And lastly, here it was where he declared he would establish his sacred name and word, which should never pass away; and for these reasons, this was justly styled the Sacred Lodge.

SACRED NAME. This name expresses the eternity of the Godhead, and points to his unchangeableness, as well as his infinite perfections. The Hebrews noted the attributes of the Deity under different names. If they wished to express his divine essence, they used the word Jehovah, if his omnipotence was the theme, it was El, Elah, or Eloah; to express his excellency, they used the word Elion; and for his mercy, Elchannan.

ST. JOHN THE BAPTIST. He was the forerunner of Jesus, a son of the Jewish priest Zacharias and of Elizabeth, who, as a zealous judge of morality and undaunted preacher of repentance, obtained great celebrity, first in his native country, then in the mountains of Judea, and afterwards among the whole nation. His simple and abstemious manner of living contributed much to his fame, and especially the peculiar purification or consecration by baptism in a river bath, which he introduced as a symbol of that moral purity which he so zealously inculcated. Jesus allowed himself to be baptized by him, and from that time forward John said unto his disciples, that he was certainly the Messias. The frank earnestness and the great fame with which he preached even in Galilee, soon brought upon him the suspicion and hatred of the court of Tetrarch Antipas, or King Herod, who imprisoned him, and on the 29th August, in the thirty-second or thirty-third year of his life, caused him to be beheaded. The 24th June, his birth-day, is dedicated to his memory through all Christendom. The patron saint of the Freemasons' brotherhood was formerly not St. John the Baptist, but St. John the Evangelist, whose festival they celebrated the 27th December, upon which day they hold their general assembly, probably induced thereto because at this season of the year the members could be better spared from their business or profession. For this reason also they chose for their quarterly festivals, the Annunciation of the Virgin Mary, Michaelmas, and the festival of St. John the Baptist, which last festival, on account of the better weather and other circumstances having been found to be more convenient for the yearly assembly, was often appointed for the time on which it should be held, so that it has now become nearly general. Many lodges still celebrate the 27th December, and call it the minor St. John's day.—*Gadicke.*

ST. JOHN THE EVANGELIST. St. John the

Evangelist and Apostle of Jesus, whose gospel is so important to all Freemasons, was born in Bethsaida, in Galilee, a son of Zebedee, and a disciple of Jesus, who loved him because he distinguished himself by his gentleness and humility. After the ascension of Jesus, he preached the gospel principally in Asia Minor and at Ephesus, where it is probable that he died in a good old age. He was a man of great energy and poetic fire and life; in his early years somewhat haughty and intolerant, but afterwards an example of love. We have a gospel or biography of Jesus by him, and three of the epistles also bear his name. The gospel of St. John is especially important to the Freemason, for he preached love, and his book certainly contains all the fundamental doctrines of Freemasonry. As a Freemason ought never to forget that he has laid his hand upon the gospel of St. John, so should he never cease to love his brethren according to the doctrine of love contained in that sacred book. Many lodges celebrate his anniversary, the 27th December.—*Gadicke.*

ST. JOHN'S MASONRY. Originally there was only one kind of Freemasonry. But when the Scottish and other higher degrees were introduced, the three first degrees received the name of St. John's Masonry.—*Gadicke.*

SALT. In the Helvetian ceremonies of Masonry, salt is added to the corn, wine and oil, because it was a symbol of the wisdom and learning which characterize Masons' lodges. Pierius makes it an emblem of hospitality and friendship, and also of fidelity. In the Scriptures, salt is considered as a symbol of perpetuity and incorruption, and used as a covenant. The formula used by our ancient brethren, when salt was sprinkled on the foundation-stone of a new lodge was, "May this undertaking, contrived by wisdom, be executed in strength and adorned with beauty, so that it may be a house where peace, harmony, and brotherly love shall perpetually reign."

SALUTE. As operative masons and other mechanics have a so-called sign or pass-word, especially when upon tramp, so had we also formerly a proper form for saluting strange brethren. At present the salutation " from the Worthy and Worshipful Brethren of the Holy Lodge of St. John," &c., &c., is not required from a foreign brother who is paying a visit, because something more is demanded from him than this ancient method of legitimation. The salutation of the brethren should be a salute of peace and love, and strengthened by the sacred numbers. He who does not really love his brother, let him not take him by the hand, let him not feign love. Experience teaches us that every brother is not worthy of love, and that those who meet every one with an embrace, who profess to love every one, lay themselves open to the suspicion that they do not really and truly respect any one.—*Gadicke.*

SANCTUM SANCTORUM. This was the oracle; .d here were four cherubim, two lesser constructed by Moses of massive gold, and two larger made by Solomon and plated with gold. The former were attached to the lid of the Mercy Seat, the latter spread their wings over it as an ornament and protection.

SANHEDRIM. The Sanhedrim was a council of seventy-one or seventy-two senators among the Jews, who determined the most important affairs of the nation. The room in which they met was a rotunda, half of which was built without the Temple and half within, the latter part being that in which the judge sat. The Nasi, or prince, who was generally the high priest, sat on a throne at the end of the hall, his deputy, called Ab-beth-din, at his right hand, and the sub-deputy, or Chacam, at his left; the other senators being ranged in order on each side. Most of the members of this council were priests or Levites, though men in private stations of life were not excluded.—*Calmet.*

SASH. The colour of the R. A. sash is one of the most durable and beautiful in nature. It is the appropriate colour adopted and worn by our ancient brethren of the three symbolical degrees, and is the peculiar characteristic of an institution which has stood the test of ages and which is as much distinguished by the durability of its materials or principles as by the beauty of its superstructure. It is an emblem of universal friendship and benevolence, and instructs us that in the mind of a Mason, those virtues should be as the blue arch of heaven itself.—*Moore.*

SCARLET. This rich and beautiful colour is emblematical of fervency and zeal. It is the appropriate colour of the Royal Arch degree; and admonishes us, that we should be fervent in the exercise of our devotions to God, and zealous in our endeavours to promote the happiness of man.—*Moore.*

SCEPTRE. The old Masons used to say in the R. A. Lecture, "On the top of those staves or sceptres, are the banners of the twelve tribes, which we have for many purposes ; esbecially to commemorate the great wonders wrought for the children of Israel during their travels in the wilderness, when they were first set up as standards around their encampments, and about which each tribe was assembled in due form. The devices thereon were emblematical of what should happen to their posterity in after ages."

SCHAMIR. It is asserted by the Rabbins, that King Solomon received a secret from Asmodeus, an evil spirit, mentioned in the book of Tobit, who had usurped his throne and afterwards became his prisoner. By the use of this, he was enabled to finish the temple without the use of axe, hammer, or metal tool; for the stone schamir, which the demon presented to him, possessed the property of cutting any other substance, as a diamond cuts glass. This, however, is wholly fabulous. Metal tools were used in the forest and the quarry, and it was by a very natural process that the building was constructed without the pollution of these instruments.

SCHISM. It is commonly believed that the prevalence of schism in any institution, is the fruitful parent of many evils, which cannot fail to detract from its purity and excellence. And so it is ; but the evil is not without its portion of good. Experience teaches that if the members of an institution become apathetic, nothing is so likely to rouse them to a sense of duty, as the existence of conflicting opinions, which produce a separation of interests, and divide them into two adverse sections; each of which, like the self-multiplying polypus, will frequently become as strong and prosperous as the parent institution.

SCHOOLS. The Royal Freemasons' School for Female Children was established in 1788, for maintaining, clothing, and educating the female children and orphans of reduced brethren, for protecting and preserving them from the danger and misfortunes to which distressed young females are peculiarly exposed; for training them up in the knowledge and love of virtue, and in habits of industry; and impressing on their minds true humility, and the practice of all social, moral, and religious duties. Already have nearly 600 female children been admitted to this school, since its establishment, and have been apprenticed, or returned to their friends, many of whom have become ornaments of their sex and station, and all of them good and useful members of society. I must also mention the Royal Masonic Institution for Clothing, Educating, and Apprenticing the Sons of Indigent and Deceased Freemasons, established in 1798. The boys are educated at schools near the residences of their parents or friends, are furnished with books, taught to read, write, and arithmetic, furnished with proper clothing, and on leaving the institution, a suitable apprentice fee is granted to them.—*Percy*.

SCIENCE. Freemasonry is a science not to be confined to a few Israelitic traditions learned by heart, as a school-boy learns his lessons; it is a science which embraces everything useful to man; it corrects the heart, and prepares it to receive the mild impressions of the divine code; its moral injunctions, if duly weighed and properly applied, never fail to form its disciples into good members of society. It opens a progressive field for inquiry, and ought never to be driven into narrow bounds by the enactment of a law, saying, thus far will we allow you to go, and no farther, under the penalty of exclusion from its universality.—*Husenbeth*.

SCIENTIFIC MASONRY. The scientific consists in the knowledge of several of the arts and sciences, so far as to enable us to discern the reason for the operations of those before-mentioned instruments, tools and machines, and to the force and momentum of the different mechanical powers; and also to clear up and arrange our ideas in such a manner, as to be able to delineate them so clearly on our tracing-board, that, by the help of a proper scale, the brethren of the second degree may take them off and complete our design, and if intended for that purpose, erect a structure, which when finished, shall contain the greatest degree of strength, elegance and convenience, that the quantity of materials and space allowed will admit of; and this is the part of, or applicable to, our brethren of the highest degree of the Craft of Master Masons.—*Dunckerly.*

SCRIBES. The two scribes represent the two columns which supported and adorned the entrance to the arch; whence is signified their duty of registering, or entering in the records, every act, law and transaction, for the general good of the chapter.

SCROLL. The fine inner bark of such trees as the lime, ash, maple, or elm, was early used as a substance for writing on. As such was called in Latin liber, this name came permanently to be applied to all kinds of books, and has, in a similar connection, been adopted into most European languages. These books, like all others of flexible materials, were rolled up to render them portable, and to preserve the writing. They were usually rolled round a stick or cylinder, and if they were long, round two cylinders, hence the name volume (volumen), a thing rolled up, which continues to be applied to books very different from rolls. In using the roll, the reader unrolled it to the place he wanted, and rolled it up again when he had read it. The book of the law written on parchment, is thus rolled and thus read in the Jewish synagogues at the present time.—*Kitto.*

SKULL AND CROSS-BONES. These are emblems of mortality, and teach the Master Mason to contemplate death as the end of his afflictions, and the entrance to another and a better life.

SCYTHE. The scythe is an emblem of time, which cuts the brittle thread of life, and launches us into eternity. What havoc does the scythe of time make among the human race! If by chance we escape the numerous evils incident to childhood and youth, and arrive in perfect health and strength at the years of vigorous manhood; yet decrepid old age will soon follow, and we must be cut down by the all-devouring scythe of time, and be gathered into the land where our fathers have gone before us.—*Old Lectures*.

SEAL. Every Lodge has its own seal, and a collection of these seals is a very interesting thing, for they each contain either a symbolical or an allegorical allusion to the name of the lodge. Every certificate is sealed with the seal of the Grand Lodge by which it is granted, and as all Grand Lodge seals are well known, it thus prevents false certificates from injuring the Craft.—*Gadicke*.

The component parts of the cherubim are exhibited in the official seal of, I believe, all the Grand Lodges in the world. In that of the Grand Lodge of England, the two large cherubims of Solomon are its supporters, and the four figures are impaled with the Masons' arms on the field. The crest is the Ark of the Covenant, on which the cherubim are again repeated as hovering over the Mercy Seat, to form the superb throne of the Deity.

SEAL OF SOLOMON. The double or endless triangle, in one or other of its different forms, constituted the famous seal of Solomon, our ancient G. M., which was said to bind the evil genii so fast, that they were unable to release themselves. By virtue of this seal, as the Moslems believed, Solomon compelled the genii to assist him in building the Temple of Jerusalem, and many other magnificent works.

SECOND DEGREE. As the darkness of heathenism, or natural religion, preceded the divine revelation vouchsafed to the people of God, so by our initiation into the second degree, we advance still farther into the dawn figured out by the Mosaic dispensation, which preceded the more perfect Christian day. Here the novice is brought to light, to behold and handle tools of a more artificial and ingenious construction, and emblematic of sublimer moral truths. By these he learns to reduce rude matter into due form, and rude manners into the more polished shape of moral and religious rectitude; becoming thereby a more harmonious corner-stone of symmetry in the structure of human society, until he is made a glorious corner-stone in the temple of God.—*Watson.*

SECRECY. Secrecy is one of the first duties of a Freemason, but those Masons err much who think they do their duty by only exercising it in things concerning the Order of the lodge. It is not for this reason only that secrecy is so often inculcated in the lodge as a masonic duty, it is that he ought to use secrecy and caution in all his transactions out of the lodge, and especially where his talkativeness might be the means of causing injury or damage to his fellow-men.—*Gadicke.*

SECRETARY. An important office in a lodge, for it is necessary that it should be filled by a man who can not only make out the common transactions of the lodge, but who is also capable of comprehending the spirit of a lecture, and introducing it into the transactions, briefly and at the same time correctly. To write a protocol correctly, so that in the event of any dispute it may serve as written evidence, is, as is well-known, a most difficult task, and requires great experience. The Secretary must be a Master Mason, and, when necessary, the brethren must assist him as copyists.—*Gadicke.*

SECRET. What can it be? This is a question which has been asked for centuries, and will probably continue to be asked for centuries to come. Ceremonies, customs, moral explanations of allegorical and symbolical instruments and figures which are to be found in a Freemasons' lodge, are, it is true, considered as secrets by some of the brotherhood. But those cannot be the real genuine secrets of Freemasonry; it is impossible; for a Mason may be acquainted with all the ceremonies, usages, and customs of the Craft—he may be able morally to explain every symbolical or allegorical instrument or figure which is to be found in a Masons' lodge—and yet neither be happy in this world, nor have a sure foundation on which to build his hopes of happiness in the world to come.—*Gadicke*.

SECRET SOCIETIES. Freemasons ever endeavour to act up to the principles of the ancient secret societies and if they differ in some points from the practices of those ancient worthies, it is in having improved upon their leading principles, by spreading the truth most extensively over the globe, whilst the schools and academies of learning of our predecessors, were more of local than of universal existence.—*Husenbeth*.

SECT. It must not be imagined that Masonry is a system of religion at the present period. Nothing can be farther from the truth. Such a supposition would reduce it to the level of a religious sect, and utterly destroy its universality. It embraces a view of all the main facts connected with the great plan of human redemption; but leaves the brethren to arrange those facts as may suit their own individual opinion. This is the doctrine of the first ancient charge.

SEDITION. The following clause of exemption from the penalties of the Sedition Act, was highly honourable to the Order:—"And whereas, certain societies have been long accustomed to be holden in this kingdom, under the denomination of lodges of Freemasons, the meetings whereof have been in a great measure directed to charitable purposes, be it therefore enacted, that nothing in this act shall extend to the meetings of any such society or lodge which shall, before the passing of this act, have been usually holden under the said denomination, and in conformity to the rules prevailing among the said societies of Freemasons."

SEEING. Seeing is that sense by which we are enabled to istinguish objects of different kinds, and, in an instant of time, without any change of place or situation, to view armies in battle array, figures of the most stately structures, and all the agreeable varieties displayed in the landscape of nature.—*Old Lectures*.

SEEK. He who is desirous of finding wisdom, must diligently seek for it; and if he would know the real design of Masonry, he must study, and observe, and meditate, on what he hears in the lodge, otherwise the bondage of ignorance will never be removed.

SELF-INTEREST. Let me travel from east to west, or between north and south, when I meet a true brother, I shall find a friend, who will do all in his power to serve me, without having the least view of self-interest; and if I am poor and in distress, he will relieve me, to the utmost of his power, interest, or capacity. This is the second grand principle; for relief will follow when there is brotherly love.—*Dunckerley.*

SELF-KNOWLEDGE. Every Freemason is earnestly exhorted to study himself. He who does not know himself, his moral weaknesses, his desires, his powers of toleration, and his real, not his imaginary, spiritual strength, cannot live as the Order requires that he ought to live, in the bonds of the closest fraternal love with the whole brotherhood; and if an office is intrusted to him in the lodge, he cannot know whether he is capable of filling it with credit to himself and profit to the Craft. It is quite as necessary that a Freemason should be as well acquainted with his moral strength as he is with his moral weakness; for many Masons are inactive in the lodge and in the Craft, merely because they do not know the power which is within themselves. He who has thoroughly studied himself, and is susceptible of all good impressions, will be subject to much less evil than others.—*Gadicke.*

SEMPER EADEM. What is this imperious institution which has spread her wings over the whole continent of Europe, and which, without the slightest dependence on any form of government, has preserved its purity amidst every species of political convulsion, the disasters of empires, and religious wars? What is this immense and influential association whose origin is lost amidst the darkness of antiquity, and whose ramifications branch out amidst the conflicting interests of commercial speculation, diplomatic alliances, and all the social establishments of mankind, in every country of the world, in spite of differences in climate, colour, language and manners? What is the signification of its rites and ceremonies, its usages, and its symbols? What services is it able to render to the sacred cause of humanity? Every reasonable man will answer these questions by a reference to the mysteries of Freemasonry.—*Janvier.*

SENIORITY OF LODGES. The precedency of lodges is derived from the number of their constitution, as recorded in the books of the Grand Lodge. No lodge can be acknowledged, nor its officers admitted into the United Grand Lodge, or a provincial Grand Lodge, nor any of its members entitled to partake of the general charity or other masonic privilege, unless it has been regularly constituted and registered.—*Constitutions.*

SENIOR WARDEN. The duty of the Senior Warden, like that of the Master, is indicated by his jewel of office, which is a symbol of equality, and instructs him that the duties of his situation ought to be executed with strict impartiality, and without respect of persons. Regularity of attendance is an essential part of this office, because if the Master should die, or be removed, or be rendered incapable of discharging the duties of his office, the Senior Warden must supply his place until the next election of officers; and even should the Master necessarily be absent from any single lodge, the Senior Warden must rule the lodge, if no former Master be present.

SEPHIROTH. The term sephira is derived from ‏ספיר‎ sapphire, which, in holy writ, appears to have been considered of the highest brilliancy; the word is therefore generally translated " splendour, " although some writers consider its derivation to be from ‏ספר‎, to number, and render it " enumerations." The former is the most correct, from its supposed origin being, that previous to the creation all space was filled with infinite light, which was withdrawn to a certain point when the Divine Mind resolved to form the universe, thus leaving a spherical vacuum. From the concave so formed, a beam of light issued to the opaque sphere. This light not continuing long in a rectilinear course, diverged at ten different points, forming as many separate concentric circles of light, divided from the supreme light by portions of opaque space, yet leaving in the centre an opaque spherical body; they have therefore termed them sovereign lights. They are named—1, The Crown; 2, Knowledge; 3, Wisdom; 4, Might; 5, Mercy; 6, Grandeur; 7, Victory; 8, Glory; 9, Stability; 10, Kingdom.

SERPENT AND CROSS. Before the Israelites were permitted to inhabit the country assigned to them by covenant from Jehovah to their ancestor Abraham, a compound symbol, which was afterwards introduced into Freemasonry, was publicly exhibited as a type of salvation. I refer to the tau-cross and serpent. The Israelites were subjected to a plague of serpents, as the punishment of sin; and on their repentance Moses was directed to elevate a serpent of brass, that whosoever looked on it might be saved. Hence the cross became an emblem of life and salvation; and being, in a higher degree tripled amongst ourselves, signifies the Tetragrammaton, or Him who made the worlds, even the author of our redemption—Jesus Christ.

SERVITUDE. The stipulated period of an apprentice's servitude is seven years, but less time will suffice, if found worthy of promotion by possessing the qualities of freedom, fervency, and zeal.

SEVEN. Seven is an important number to a Freema son. In ancient times each brother was compelled to be acquainted with the seven liberal arts and sciences; it is for this reason that seven brethren form a symbolic lodge. If two triangles △ are joined together, they form ✦, or six-pointed star, and if this figure is enclosed in a circle, then there are seven points ✹; and it was with this figure that the ancients represented the seven subordinate powers of nature.—*Gadicke.*

SEVEN STARS. An emblem which denotes the number of brethren requisite to make a perfect lodge.

SEVENTY YEARS. This period of the captivity in Babylon must be computed from the defeat of the Egyptians at Carchemish, in the same year that this prophecy was given, when Nebuchadnezzar reduced the neighbouring nations of Syria and Palestine, as well as Jerusalem. under his subjection. At the end of seventy years, on the accession of Cyrus, an end was put to the Babylonish monarchy; Babylon itself became a subject and dependant province, and began to experience those divine visitations which terminated at length in what is so justly called "perpetual desolation."—*Blayney.*

SHEBA. The Queen of Sheba appears to have been a person of learning, and that sort of learning which was then almost peculiar to Palestine, not to Ethiopia; for we know that one of her reasons for coming was to examine whether Solomon was really the learned man he was said to be. She came to try him in allegories and parables, in which Nathan had instructed him. They say she was a pagan when she left Arabia; but being full of admiration at Solomon's works, she was converted to Judaism in Jerusalem, and bore him a son, whom he called Menilek, and who was their first king.—*Bruce.*

SHEEP. The people of God are often typified in the Scriptures under the name of sheep, because of their mild, patient, and inoffensive nature. The lambskin, then, is an appropriate emblem of the innocence of Jesus, and the meekness of his followers. The lamb, too, is of a social nature, and is emblematical of brotherly love. It is easily led. But there are "lost sheep" spoken of in the Bible—those which have wandered far from their fold and shepherd. The apostles were sent to the lost sheep of the house of Israel. Christ called his own sheep by name, and leadeth them out. The sheep should always listen to the shepherd's voice, and follow him and fear. Jesus three times bade Simon Peter to feed his sheep. The repetition of the command is regarded as very beautiful in the Greek dialect. Jesus was called the Lamb of God, not only on account of his spotless innocence, but in allusion to the lamb sacrificed for the passover, he being the true Paschal Lamb, slain from the foundation of the world.—*Scott.*

SHEKINAH. A beam of glory. This beam shone

upon Abel and his sacrifice, and is thought by some to have been the moving cause of Cain's envy. God testified his approbation of Abraham's sacrifice by the same glory, which, like the flame of a lamp, passed between the sacrifices. The pillar of a cloud, and the clouds which filled the Tabernacle and the Temple, were of the same nature; and, according to the Scriptures, were Jehovah, or Christ; for St. Paul tells the Jews that these bright effulgencies vouchsafed to their ancestors, were beams of glory from the eternal Son of God.

SHESH-BAZZAR. Was another name for Zerubbabel, for it was common in the time of the captivity for the great men of Judah to have two names: one of their own country, which was domestic; another of the Chaldeans, which was used at court. Nehemiah had two names, and this of Shesh-bazzar seems to have been a good omen of their flourishing condition; being compounded of two words signifying fine linen and gold. On the contrary, Zerubbabel was a name importing the misery of the people of Israel at that time; for it is as much as an exile or stranger in Babylon, where he was born. Thus pious men, in the midst of the honours they had at court (for Josephus saith, Zerubbabel was one of the guard of the king's body), were admonished not to forget their brethren, but sympathize with them in their miseries.—*Bishop Patrick.*

SHEWBREAD. On the golden table in the Tabernacle of Moses, were placed the twelve loaves of unleavened bread, called the presence bread, because it was perpetually before the face of Jehovah, and some say they were marked with the names of the twelve tribes of Israel; but there is no authority for this conjecture in the sacred writings.

SHIBBOLETH. Shibboleth signifies waters. Thus the Ephraimites prayed the men of Gilead to allow them to pass over, and were asked in return—To pass over what? They could not answer "Shibboleth" without betraying themselves to the enemy.

SHOE. The putting off the shoes some say, was

commanded Moses, that he should thereby sanctify that place by making bare his feet. But the place was holy already, because of God's presence; the place was not holy because Moses put off his shoes, but because it was holy he is bid to put off his shoes. Ambrose thus applieth it—"that because the shoes are made of the skins of dead beasts, Moses should put off all fear of death, for fear whereof he fled at the first from Pharoah." (Comment. in Lucani lvii.) Cyprian says, "that Moses, by putting off his shoes, does not challenge any right in the spouse of the church, but resigneth it to Christ, the head and husband thereof; for this was the custom, that the next kinsman, by putting off a shoe, surrendered his right to his deceased brother's wife."

SHOVEL. The use of the shovel is to clear away rubbish and loose earth; and it morally depicts the mortal state in which the body is laid in the grave; that when the remains of this body shall have been properly disposed of, we, with humble but holy confidence, hope that the spirit may arise to everlasting life.

SHRINE. The place where the Secrets of the Royal Arch are deposited.

SIC TRANSIT GLORIA MUNDI. "Every thing vanishes like an extinguished flame." A most important symbol for a Mason. No earthly glory should be able to captivate him; for he must ever bear in mind the glory of a flame in comparison with which every other glory is vain. Life itself is like a flame, it can be extinguished before it has been scarcely perceived. This beautiful symbol has been adopted by the Knights of the Garter. When the helmet, sword, &c., of a departed brother are solemnly lowered, the herald-at-arms exclaims:—"Sic transit gloria mundi!"—*Gadicke.*

SIGNATURE. Every brother to whom a Grand Lodge certificate is granted must sign his name in the margin thereof, or it will not be valid.—*Constitutions.*

SIGN OF DISTRESS. In a society whose members ought fraternally to love and assist each other, it is to be expected that they should have a sign whereby they could make themselves known immediately to their brethren, in however distressed circumstances they might be placed, and thereby at the same time claim their assistance and protection. This is the sign of distress, in conjunction with a few words. He who falls into the greatest difficulty and danger, and supposes that there is a brother within sight or hearing, let him use this sign, and a true and faithful brother must spring to his assistance.—*Gadicke.*

SIGNS. The science of Freemasonry is still characterized by S. W. and T.; but it is a grievous error to suppose them to be the essence of the system ; they are merely senseless designations of something possessing greater value. The are to the Mason as the wig to the judge, lawn sleeves to the reverend prelate, or the gold-headed cane to the ancient physician—essentials as to form, but unimportant in reality. The sterling value of our doctrines, as well as their universality, would remain uninjured, if these conventional marks of recognition were all abolished. Preston calls them the keys of our treasure ; and so, indeed, they are to a certain extent, but the cabinet might be opened if these keys were lost. The S. W. and T. are merely conventional, though it is not to be denied that great numbers of Masons are satisfied with their possession, and look for nothing beyond them.

SILENCE. The first thing that Pythagoras taught t is scholars was to be silent; for a certain time he kept them without speaking, to the end they might the better learn to preserve the valuable secrets he had to communicate, and never to speak but when required, expressing thereby that secrecy was the rarest virtue. Aristotle was asked what thing appeared to him most difficult; he answered to be secret and silent. To this purpose St. Ambrose, in his offices, placed among the principal foun dations of virtue the patient gift silence.—*Dermott.*

SINCERITY. A search after truth is the peculiar employment of Masons at their periodical meetings, and therefore they describe it as a divine attribute, and the foundation of every virtue. To be good men and true, is the first lesson we are taught in Masonry. On this theme we contemplate, and by its dictates endeavour to regulate our conduct; influenced by this principle, hypocrisy and deceit are unknown in the lodge; sincerity and plain dealing distinguish us; while the heart and tongue join in promoting the general welfare, and rejoicing in each other's prosperity.

SITUATION. The lodge is situated due east and west, for various reasons; but the principal inducement of our ancient brethren to adopt this disposition was, that it might serve to commemorate the great deliverance of the Israelites from bondage, by imitating the arrangement of the Tabernacle which was erected by Moses in the wilderness, as a place of public worship until the Lord should reveal the situation which he had chosen for his Holy Name amongst the tribes in the promised land.

SIX LIGHTS. Royal Arch Masons acknowledge six lights; the three lesser, together representing the light of the Law and the Prophets, and by this number allude to the Patriarchal, Mosaical, and Christian dispensations. The three greater represent the sacred Word itself, expressive of His creative, preserving, and destroying power. These lights are placed in the form of an equilateral triangle, each of the lesser intersecting the line formed by the two greater. Thus geometrically dividing the greater triangle into three lesser triangles, at its extremities, and by their union, form a fourth triangle in the centre, all of them being equal and equilateral, emblematical of the four degrees in Masonry—the Entered Apprentice, the Fellowcraft, the Master Mason and the Holy Royal Arch.

SIX PERIODS. In six days God created the heavens and the earth, and rested upon the seventh, therefore our ancient brethren dedicated it as a day of rest from their labours, thereby enjoying frequent opportunities to contemplate the glorious works of the creation, and to adore their great Creator.—*Webbe.*

SKIRRET. The skirret acting on a centrepin is used

to mark out the ground of a new building. As the skirret has a chalked line attached to it, it points out the straight line of duty chalked out in the Sacred Law of God.

SKY-BLUE. In the cosmogonies divine wisdom creates the world, and the Creator is always coloured blue. Vishnu, according to the sacred books of the Hindus, was born of a blue color. This indicates that wisdom, emanating from God, is symbolized by azure. In Egypt the supreme God, the Creator of the universe, Cneph, was painted sky-blue. In Greece azure is the colour of Jupiter. In China the firmament is the supreme God; and in Christian symbolism the azure vault of heaven is the mantle which veils the Divinity. Azure is likewise the symbol of God the Saviour, the Redeemer of mankind.

SLINKING. It is not only possible, but it has often happened, that men have stole into the Lodge who were never worthy of being admitted members of the Order, but who have managed to get initiated by hypocrisy, and because the members have not had sufficient opportunities to prove them, and to watch their previous conduct. But it is quite impossible for any one who has not been initiated to find his way into a lodge to indulge his curiosity. Every cultivated and moral man knows that initiation will not be denied him if he applies in a proper manner for it, and we are assured that they will never attempt, either by force or fraud, to gain admittance into a society where they have no right to be. Should any one, destitute of moral feeling, attempt to do so, thinking that from printed works he has made himself acquainted with our customs, and can pass himself off for a Mason, he never can get beyond the ante-chamber for he has no certificate, or if he has, it is not his, and this is soon proved; his name is not upon any list, nor does he know anything of how he should answer the questions which will be put to him. An uneducated man has still less chance of stealing into a lodge, for his answer to the first question put to him would discover him at once. If we were as well secured from the first manner of improperly gaining admittance into a lodge as

we aie from the last, the Order would be in a more
flourishing condition than it now is.—*Gadicke.*

SMELLING. With regard to the organ, it is an
impression made on the nose by little particles continually exhaling from odorous bodies; with regard to the
object, it is the figure and disposition of odorous effluvia,
which sticking on the organ, excite the sense of smelling;
and with regard to the soul, it is the perception of the
impression of the object on the organ, or the affection in
the soul resulting therefrom.

SOCIETY. Freemasonry forms a happy centre of
reunion for worthy men, who are desirous of a select
society of friends and brothers, who have bound themselves in a voluntary obligation to love each other; to
afford aid and assistance in time of need; to animate one
another to acts of virtue and benevolence; and to keep
inviolably the secrets which form the great characteristic
of the Order.—*Lalande.*

SODALITIES. Cato the censor, when he was Ques-
tor, instituted sodalities, or fraternities of congenial persons. In the early state of society, when the laws were
too weak to afford protection, individuals had no other
means of securing their lives and property but by entering into such associations, where a number of persons
engaged themselves to vindicate and assist each other.
And they had periodical meetings, at which they enjoyed
themselves merrily. Thus Quintilion said: "Tempestiva
convivia, et perviliges jocos, advocatâ sodalium turba
solutas, et affluens agebam." Confraternities of the same
kind, says Bishop Percy, prevailed in this kingdom not
only during the Anglo-Saxon times, but for some ages
after the conquest.

SOJOURNERS. While preparations were in progress
for building the second Temple, sojourners and pilgrims
from Babylon, incited by the admonitions of the Prophets,
occasionally added to the number of those who engaged
with enthusiasm in these laborious duties; and their
example afforded great encouragement to the workmen.

SOLID. A solid hath length, breadth, and thickness, and is generated by the flowing of a superficies. A solid, then, is the whole system of divine laws, as existing in practice. For if every duty in practice and perfection is a superficies, it will follow that when they are all laid one upon each other, there will be formed a solid; and this solid will be a rectangular triangular pyramid, whose altitude and the length and breadth of its base are all equal. For the length, breadth, and height of the whole law in practice must be perfect.—*Old Lecture.*

SOLOMON. Solomon, son of David, by Bathsheba, was declared by his father to be heir to the throne of the Hebrews, thereby setting aside his elder brother. He enjoyed during a long and peaceful reign, from 1015 to 975 before Christ, the fruits of the deeds of his father. The wisdom of his judicial decisions, as also the improvement and perfection of the system of government he introduced, gained him the love and admiration of the people; and his fame is immortalized by the building of the Temple, which, for size, magnificence, and beauty, far exceeded all the works of architecture ever before seen. This Temple is one of the most sublime symbols in the Order of Freemasonry, for which reason Solomon's name has been introduced here.—*Gadicke.*

SOLOMON'S TEMPLE. This is most important as a symbol to a Freemason, for in its time it was considered as the most regular and most magnificent building. Solomon built this temple at Jerusalem, and it was not only a place for the worship of God, but also a dwelling for the priesthood, and a depository for the ark. David provided a great quantity of building materials, and left an enormous sum of money to pay the expenses of the building, which was carried on in perfect quietness. All the stone and wood were prepared without the city, and then brought to Jerusalem. The foundation was laid in the year of the world 2993; and at that time the Phœnicians possessed the best artists of every description, and in architecture they took the lead of all other nations. In order, therefore, to build his Temple according to the best rules of architecture then known, Solomon requested Hiram, King of Tyre, to furnish him with an architect, and he sent him one who was also called Hiram. Hiram not only possessed scientific knowledge, but also sufficient practical skill in his art to enable him to make everything according to the wish of King Solomon, as well in the building of the Temple with regard to magnificence, as also in originality of formation, and in the appropriateness of the sacred vessels which were necessary in the sacrifices and burnt offerings, and which were all formed in strict proportion, according to the rules of geometry. The walls that surrounded the Temple were 7700 feet in circumference. The large and noble hall stood towards the west, and the Holy of Holies in the east.—*Gadicke.*

SOLSTICES. The symbol of a point within a circle has sometimes been invested with an astronomical reference. Thus it is said that the point in the centre represents the Supreme Being; the circle indicates the annual circuits of the sun; and the parallel lines mark out the solstices within which that circuit is limited. And they deduce from the hypothesis this corollary, that the Mason, by subjecting himself to due bounds, in imitation of that glorious luminary, will not wander from the path of duty.

SONGS OF MASONRY. What may be termed the domestic manners of a society, vary with the customs of the age in which it flourishes; and the fluctuations are accurately marked in the character of its songs. It is unnecessary to enter into a dissertation on the merits of masonic poetry. In this respect I am willing to confess that the Craft does not occupy the first rank in the literature of the day. But our songs are not destitute of poetical merit, if it consist in the display of images which are peculiarly appropriate to the subject under illustration; sentiment which strikes the imagination, and excites new feelings in the mind; pathos which touches a sensitive chord in the listener's heart; and a moral to inspire a love of virtue;—all expressed in chaste language, and divested of extravagancies either in style or matter.

SOUL OF THE WORLD. Philoh says that the Sabbath was the soul instilled into the world by God; which R. Abraham Aben Ezra and Nachmanides properly observe was the benediction which God bestowed on the Sabbath Day, sanctifying it thereby; for by the superior influence of that day, the body is renovated, the strength renewed, and new intelligence and knowledge conveyed to the soul.—*Manasseh Ben Israel.*

SOUTH. The due course of the sun is from east to south and west; and after the Master are placed the Wardens, to extend his commands and instructions to the west and the north. From the east the sun's rays cannot penetrate into the north and the west at the same time. —*Gadicke.*

SPECULATIVE. The masonic system exhibits a stupendous and beautiful fabric, founded on universal piety. To rule and direct our passions, to have faith and hope in God, and charity towards man, I consider as the objects of what is termed Speculative Masonry.—*Stephen Jones.*

SPIRIT OF THE CRAFT. O'er the tesselated pavement of this fleeting and chequered existence, we are fast hastening to the common end of all men; and along the downward track of Time, we are descending, some more smoothly than others, but all with no less sure and quick transition. Let us not, therefore, be unmindful of the merciful ends of our creation and redemption, to "shine as the stars in the heavens," when raised in glorified bodies from the darkness of the tomb, we shall be presented, by our All-sufficient Conductor before the throne of the Almighty and ever-to-be-adored and worshipped Eternal Master of the heavenly lodge above!—*Poole.*

SQUARE. In architecture not only are the corners of the building proved by the square, but all horizontal and perpendicular lines are drawn by it. Without accurate squaring, a building would be weak and tottering in its first stages of erection, and must continue unfinished. Without a well-defined and very clear code of the reciprocal laws and duties of the officers and members of any social, charitable, or scientific society, it is impossible for it to avoid being completely overthrown in a very short time. Perfect legality is the only sure foundation for any society, and by it alone bodies of men are kept within their proper limits; for as soon as arbitrary power and physical force usurp the place of the laws of any society, it speedily becomes defunct; with great propriety, therefore, is the square put into the hands of the Worshipful Master, in order that he may keep the brethren within the square of the ancient charges of Freemasonry. This symbol must at all times, and in all places, be regarded as a great light, and the genuine Freemason is not only reminded by this light to do his duty to his brethren, but to all mankind.—*Gadicke.*

STANDARD. The Israelites in the wilderness were marshalled according to their tribes, each tribe being sub-divided into families. Every head of a sub-division, or thousand, was furnished with an ensign, or standard, under which his followers arranged themselves, according to a pre-concerted plan, both when in camp and when on the march; and thus all confusion was prevented, how hastily soever the order might be given to proceed or to halt and pitch their tents. The four leading divisions were designated by the component parts of the cherubim—a man, an ox, a lion, and an eagle.

STANDARD BEARER. Grand Standard Bearers may be appointed by the Grand Master as occasion shall require; they must be Master Masons, and are to carry the standard of the Grand Lodge, Grand Patron, and Grand Master, on all grand ceremonies. They are not, however, by their appointment, members of the Grand Lodge, nor are they to wear the clothing of a grand officer. Any grand officer appointed to have a standard, may appoint a Standard Bearer whenever it shall be necessary, who must be a Master Mason.—*Constitutions.*

STAR. A star, in hieroglyphical language, always denoted a God. Thus, when Balaam predicted that a star should arise out of Jacob, and a sceptre out of Israel, he referred to the law-giver, or Shilo, of whom that patriarch had already spoken. A star out of Jacob and a God out of Jacob would, therefore, be parallel expressions. And who could that God be who should bear the sceptre of Israel as King of kings and Lord of lords but the theocratic King of Israel, Jehovah, the Messiah, or Christ?

STARS. The Master Mason, like the starry firmament, ought to be able to enlighten the younger brethren. Seven stars remind us that seven brethren make a perfect lodge. Stars are also employed principally as symbols of great intellectuality, and this symbol has been perpetuated from the most remote antiquity. The decoration of most spiritual and temporal orders consists of a star.—*Gadicke.*

STATUTES OR DUTIES. Every lodge has its statutes, with which every brother should be well acquainted, and which ought frequently to be read in open lodge. They treat upon the duties of a Freemason both in and out of the lodge, upon the duties of the officers, on the management of the lodge, the duties and privileges of the brethren towards each other, and of the locality in which the lodge is placed.—*Gadicke.*

STAVES. In the year 2513, while Moses was tending the flock of his father-in-law Jethro, at the foot of a mountain, he was commanded by the Almighty to go down into Egypt, and deliver his brethren from their galling captivity. The Deity then asked him—"What is that in thine hand?" And he said, "A rod." And the Lord said unto him—"Cast it upon the ground." And he cast it upon the ground, and it immediately became a serpent, and Moses fled from it. And the Lord said unto Moses—"Put forth thy hand and take it by the tail." He did so, and it resumed its original form. This is the origin of our R. A. staves.

STEP. In the system of Masonry, the candidate is presented at each step with three precious jewels. As an E. A. P., he receives "a listening ear, a silent tongue, and a faithful heart." As a F. C., it is "faith, hope, and charity." And as a M. M., he receives "humanity, friendship, and brotherly love."

STEPS. The reflecting man is cautious how he takes a step, and it is not indifferent to him whether they are directed to the east or west, north or south. His desire is to be continually progressing, and he does progress, even though he is compelled occasionally to wait, or even to take a by-path. But to him the three grand steps, which symbolically lead from this life unto the source of all knowledge, are of the utmost importance. He advances with a firm step, and he never turns back —*Gadicke.*

STEWARD. The stewards are those officers who have charge of the expenditure of the lodge in refreshment, &c. Every lodge has two.—*Gadicke.*

STONE OF FOUNDATION. The masonic foundation stone is said to have been inscribed with the awful Name or Word, which is confided to the perfect Master when he has arrived at the highest dignity of the science. The characters were placed within an equilateral triangle and circle, as a symbol of the Divine Being under whose protection this consecrated stone was placed, and hence it was frequently termed the stone of life. The Rabbins believed that, from the potency of this Word, the stone was invested with oracular powers, and many other singular virtues.

STONE PAVEMENT. The stone pavement is a figurative appendage to a Master Masons' lodge; and, like that of the Most Holy Place in the Temple, is for the High Priest to walk on.

STONE SQUARERS. These were the Dionysiacs, a society of architects who built the Temple of Hercules at Tyre, and many magnificent edifices in Asia Minor, before the Temple of Solomon was projected. They were the Masters and Wardens of the lodges of Masons during the erection of this famous edifice.

STRENGTH. It is not necessary that the strength of a Warden should consist of the physical or bodily; it should be of the spiritual. A pillar has strength to bear. He who assiduously goes through the difficult path of life—courageously bears up against all its disappointments—manfully and unflinchingly speaks the truth,

even before the thrones of kings and princes,—he possesses true strength.—*Gadicke.*

STRIKING OFF. Prohibiting a lodge to assemble,
or striking a lodge off from the Grand Lodge list. It is
an event of a very rare occurrence that a lodge is struck
off the list, or prohibited from assembling. This may
be done by command of the State; and when this is the
case, the brethren are bound to obey the law without
murmuring, or complaining that their sphere of usefulness is circumscribed. But when a lodge is struck off
from the list of the Grand Lodge under which it held its
warrant, it must be because it has fallen into irregularity,
or has violated the rules of the Craft to such a degree as
to bring down upon it the greatest punishment the Grand
Lodge can inflict.—*Gadicke.*

STRING. Our traditions say that when Hiram Abiff
went into the H. of H. to offer up his orisons to God at
the hour of high twelve, the ark of the covenant had
not been removed thither, for that took place at the
dedication, after which no one was permitted to enter
but the H. P., and he only once a year, on the great day
of expiation, at which time he had a string, or belt, round
his waist, which extended into the court of the Tabernacle, that he might be drawn from the S. S., in case
sudden death should occur whilst he officiated there.—
Dalcho.

SUBORDINATION. The rulers and governors, supreme and subordinate of the ancient lodge, are to be
obeyed in their respective stations by all the brethren,
according to the old charges and regulations, with all
humility, reverence, love, and alacrity.—*Ancient Charges.*

SUBMISSION. Your obedience must be proved by
a close conformity to our laws and regulations; by
prompt attention to all signs and summonses; by modest
and correct demeanour whilst in the lodge; by abstaining from every topic of religious or political discussion;
by a ready acquiescence in all votes and resolutions duly
passed by the brethren; and by perfect submission to
the Master and his Wardens, whilst acting in the discharge of their respective offices.—*Hemming.*

SUCCOTH. When a sufficient quantity of stone and timber had been provided for the building of the Temple, the brethren were assembled in the extensive plains between Succoth and Zarthan, where the whole materials were arranged, squared, and carved; having been first carefully measured under the architect's own eye, and the shape delineated by darker lines; each lodge having its peculiar mark and number, that specimens of imperfect workmanship might be known and submitted to general reprobation.

SUMMONS. The brethren must be invited by summons from the Secretary on every lodge night; which summons must contain the place where, and the time when, the lodge is to be held, as well as what degrees will be wrought.—*Gadicke.*

SUN. The sun rises in the east, and in tne east is the place for the Worshipful Master. As the sun is the source of all life and warmth, so should the Worshipful Master enliven and warm the brethren to their work. Among the ancient Egyptians, the sun was the symbol of divine providence. Schiller says, "the sun darts his beams equally into every part of infinity."—*Gadicke.*

SUPERFICIES. The flowing of a line generates a surface. A surface, therefore, is perfect duty. Duty is either theoretical or practical. The sum of theoretical duties is the whole system of divine commands. Practical duties are those commands as existing in practice.— *Old Lectures.*

SUPERINTENDENT OF WORKS. The grand superintendent of the works ought to be a brother well skilled in the science of geometry and architecture. He is to advise with the Board of General Purposes, on all plans of buildings or edifices undertaken by the Grand Lodge, and furnish plans and estimates for the same; he is to superintend their construction, and see that they are conformable to the plans approved by the Grand Master, the Grand Lodge, and the Board of General Purposes; he is to suggest improvements when necessary. in all the edifices of the Grand Lodge; and on the first meeting of the Board of General Purposes in every year report on the state of repair or dilapidation of such edifices, and make such farther reports from time to time, as he may deem expedient.—*Constitutions.*

SUPPORT. The lodge is supported by three pillars, which are called Wisdom, Strength, and Beauty; because no piece of architecture can be termed perfect, unless it have Wisdom to contrive, Strength to support, and Beauty to adorn.

SURFACE OF THE EARTH. Reminds the Freemason that his activity should be universal, that hills or mountains in his way should not be able to turn him from the straight path of duty, but that in the midst of the greatest dangers and difficulties, he should proceed steadily, though cautiously, on his way to light and truth.—*Gadicke.*

SUSPENSION. If any brother be summoned to attend the Grand Master or his deputy, or his Provincial Grand Master or his deputy, or any board or committee authorized by the Grand Lodge, and do not comply, or give sufficient reason for his non-attendance, the summons is to be repeated, and, if he still persist in his contumacy, he shall be suspended from all masonic rights, and the proceeding notified to the Grand Lodge —*Constitutions.*

SWORDS. In ancient times, every brother was obliged to be armed in the lodge to protect himself, in case the lodge was assaulted, and as a symbol of manly strength. At present, swords are not necessary in many lodges, and in others, they are only used as symbols of obedience, in case that one should be necessary, and to be regarded as the sword of justice. For the protection of his fatherland, every faithful brother ought to draw the sword of defence cheerfully, but he ought never to stain it with a brother's blood, even though that brother is a foe.—*Gadicke.*

SWORD BEARER. The Grand Sword Bearer is appointed annually by the Grand Master, on the day of his installation. His duty is to attend the quarterly communications, and other meetings of the Grand Lodge.

SYMBOL. Every Apprentice knows what to understand by this word, and he also knows that a pillar upon a good foundation may stand firm, although nearly broken. The inscription further says to him, "Let no one despair under his trials, when his anxious strivings after the only true good are impeded at every step ; the man determined to advance in the paths of virtue must be firm as a well-founded pillar, even when it is broken above half-through."—*Gadicke.*

SYMBOLICAL. Freemasonry being confessedly an allegorical system, all its points, parts, and secrets must partake in common of its emblematical construction. Every doctrine and ceremony has its mystical references —every landmark its legitimate explanation. But there are often more important antitypes than those which are commonly assigned, and though they do not appear on the surface, are nevertheless worthy of our serious consideration. Hence arises the necessity, in these times of scientific and philosophical research, of maintaining Freemasonry in its proper rank, by investigating the tendency of its numerous details, that we may correctly ascertain whether their import be uniform, and their typical reference valuable.

SYMBOLICAL LECTURE. The forms, symbols, and ornaments of Royal Arch Masonry, as well as the rites and ceremonies at present in use among us, were adapted by our predecessors at the building of the second temple. Thus to preserve in our minds the providential means by which that great discovery was effected, as in our hearts the lesson of that high morality, we, as members of this exalted degree, ought to practice, we have recourse to the explanations of the symbolical lecture. —*R. A. Lecture.*

SYMBOLICAL MACHINERY. The learned Faber, speaking of the construction of the Apocalypse, has the following very important remark : "In the representation of a pure church, an ancient patriarchial scheme of symbolical machinery, derived most plainly from the events of the deluge, and borrowed, with the usual perverse misapplication, by the contrivers of paganism, has been reclaimed (by Christianity) to its proper use." What is this patriarchial scheme of symbolical machinery, from which the heathen contrived and borrowed their spurious Masonry? What can it be, but a system of truth, appended to the original plan of divine worship, which was revealed by God to the first man? It was indeed primitive Freemasonry, veiled in allegory, and illustrated by symbols.

SYMBOLICAL MASONRY. Symbolical Masonry, under whatever form it may be propounded, is a catholic institution, democratic in its form and government, and universal in its operation. This is demonstrable from any of the definitions of the Order, from the free election of its chief magistrate, and the inferior governors of every private lodge, annually and by universal suffrage, and from the reputed form and extent of its lodges. If it were deprived of any of the above attributes, it would be no longer Freemasonry; and all its beneficial effects upon the mind and manners of men, would be scattered to the winds of heaven.

TABERNACLE. The Tabernacle appears to have been constructed on the plan of the Egyptian temples. It is true that, strictly speaking, it ought not to be looked upon as a piece of architecture, being only a vast tent. But by reflecting on it more closely, we shall perceive that the Tabernacle had a great relation with architecture. In the government of the Hebrews, the Supreme Being was equally their God and King. The Tabernacle was erected with a view to answer to the double title. It served at once for the temple and the palace.

TACITURNITY. Taciturnity is a proof of wisdom, and an art of inestimable value, which is proved to be an attribute of the Deity, by the glorious example which he gives in concealing from mankind the secret mysteries of his providence. The wisest of men cannot penetrate into the arcana of heaven, nor can they divine to-day what to-morrow may bring forth.

TASSELS. Pendant to the corners of the lodge are four tassels, meant to remind us of the four cardinal virtues; namely, temperance, fortitude, prudence and justice; the whole of which, tradition informs us, wee rconstantly practised by a great majority of our ancient brethren. The distinguishing characters of a good Freemason, are virtue, honour and mercy; and should those be banished from all other societies, may they ever be found in a Mason's breast.—*Hemming.*

TAU CROSS. The emblem (⊓) forms the principal distinction of a Royal Arch Mason's apron and jewel. Being placed in the centre of a triangle and circle, both emblems of the Deity, it would appear that it was originally intended to typify the sacred name, as the author probably of eternal life; being tripled in the Christian system, because the life to come, according to the light of revelation, is superior to the elysium of the heathen; or perhaps in allusion to the three heavens mentioned by St. Paul. It has been referred to the three great lights of Masonry, expressive of the creative, preserving, and destroying power of God.

TEMPERANCE. By temperance, we are instructed to govern the passions, and check unruly desires. The health of the body, and the dignity of the species, are equally concerned in a faithful observance of it.

TEMPLE. The Temple of Solomon was only a small building, and very inferior in point of size to some of our churches, its dimensions being only one hundred and five feet broad, and one hundred and fifty feet long. Its splendour and superiority lay in the richness of its materials, and ornaments, and the cloisters and other buildings with which it was surrounded. It was built of white marble, so excellently put together, that the joints could not be distinguished, and the whole building looked as though it had been cut out of one entire stone. The timber was cedar and olive wood covered with plates of gold, and studded with precious stones of many hues.

TEN. The number of perfection. The great triangle generally denominated Pythagorean, because it served as a principal illustration of that philosopher's system. This emblem powerfully elucidates the mystical relation between numerical and geometrical symbols. It is composed of ten points, so arranged as to form one greater equilateral triangle, and at the same time to divide it into nine similar triangles of smaller dimensions.—*Hemming*.

TESSELATED. The tesselated border was anciently called the Idented Trasel. A learned Scottish Mason, in a letter to the author, thinks that the proper term is tasselated border. The simple and original meaning, he says, is to be found in books of heraldry, and is nothing more than an indented bordure of a shield, or coat of arms. In Masonry, the border is the margin of the masonic floor-cloth, or tableau of the lodge, the tassels being appended as ornaments.

TESSERA HOSPITALIS. This was a token or tally amongst the ancient Greeks and Romans, divided lengthwise into two equal parts, upon each of which one of the parties wrote his name, and interchanged it with the other as a sign of hospitality. The production of this, when they travelled, gave a mutual claim to the contracting parties and their descendants, for reception and kind treatment at each other's houses, as occasion might require. It is supposed that an allusion to these is intended in the Book of Revelations, where it is said, "to him that overcometh will I give a white stone, and in the stone a new name written, which no man knoweth, save he that receiveth it."

TESTS. One cogent reason why our brethren of the last century adopted a series of tests to distinguish the cowan from the true and faithful brother, is found in the fact that the entire system of speculative Masonry is contained in the Holy Scriptures. The Old Testament presents us with its history and legend, its types and symbols; and the New Testament with its morality, and the explanation of those allegorical references, which were a sealed book until the appearance of the Messiah upon earth, and the revelation of his gospel. Now, as the particular tests where all this information might be found, were freely circulated amongst the brethren in manuscript, if not print, a few stray copies might get into the hands of the uninitiated, and a superficial knowledge of our references might be thus attained; and without some written tests as a means of detecting imposture, a bold man, even with such slight pretensions, might have succeeded in introducing himself into a lodge where the officers were careless about the admission of visitors, and the Senior Entered Apprentice was remiss in the discharge of his duties; and once there, he would see enough to qualify him to repeat the experiment, and thus would become enabled to reveal the truths, which were not bound upon his conscience by any obligations to secrecy.

TETRAGRAMMATON. The Jews are quite aware that the true pronunciation of the Word is lost, and regard it as one of the mysteries to be revealed in the days of the Messiah. They hold, however, that the knowledge of the Name of God does exist on earth, and he by whom the secret is acquired, has, by virtue of it, the powers of the world at his command; and they account for the miracles of Jesus, by telling us that he had got possession of the Ineffable Name. Rightly understood, they seem to mean that he who calls upon God rightly, by this His true name, cannot fail to be heard by him. In short, this word forms the famous tetragrammaton, or quadrilateral name, of which every one has heard.—*Kitto*.

THEORY. The theory of masonry contains something of the whole of science; the operative part of Masonry is the practice of all the virtues, of all the sciences. Therefore, to be initiated only into the theory of Masonry, is at least to be in the way of learning well; and if we follow on to exercise the practice of Masonry, it will as assuredly lead us into the way of doing well; and both to learn and to do well, is the whole of our religion, whether as men, as Christians, or as Masons.—*Inwood*.

THIRD DEGREE. In the ceremonial of the Third Degree, the last grand mystery is attempted to be illustiated in a forcible and peculiar manner, showing by striking analogy, that the Master Mason cannot be deemed perfect in the glorious science, till by the cultivation of his intellectual powers, he has gained such moral government of his passions, such serenity of mind, that in synonymous apposition with Mastership in operative art, his thoughts, like his actions, have become as useful as human intelligence will permit; and that having passed through the trials of life with fortitude and faith, he is fitted for that grand, solemn, and mysterious consummation, by which alone he can become acquainted with the great secret of eternity.—*Crucefix.*

THREAD OF LIFE. By which the masonic key is suspended.

THREE. A sacred number in Freemasonry, with which all labour is commenced and finished. This number reminds us of the three great lights, the three kingdoms of nature, the Holy Trinity, or of the words of Christ : " Where two or three are assembled in my name, there will I be in the midst of you." We may also consider ourselves as the third party in unity and love, whose duty it is to exercise those two cardinal virtues. The Christian can also take the number three as the grand distinguishing doctrine of his faith. There are three principal parts in a man, body, soul, and spirit. Faith, love, and hope, support and adorn life.—*Gadicke.*

THREE GRAND OFFERINGS. These were all performed on the sacred mountain of Moriah. First, the offering of Isaac, when it pleased the Lord to substitute a more agreeable victim in his stead. The second consisted of the many pious prayers and ejaculations of King David, which appeased the wrath of God, and put a stop to the pestilence which raged among his people, owing to his inadvertently having had them numbered. And the third, of the many thanksgivings, oblations, burnt sacrifices, and costly offerings, which King Solomon made at the dedication and consecration of the Temple

THREE SENSES. The three senses, hearing, seeing

and feeling, are deemed peculiarly essential amongst Masons, and held in great estimation. Their nature and uses, form a part of the instruction in the Fellowcraft's degree.

THREE STEPS. The three steps delineated upon a Master's carpet, are emblematical of the three principal stages of human life, youth, manhood, and old age.

TIME. The central point is a symbol of time, and the circle of eternity. The latter, like the universe, being unlimited in its extent; for time is but as a point compared with eternity, and equi-distant from all parts of its infinitely extended circumference; because the latter occupied the same indefinite space before the creation of our system, as it will do when time is extinguished, and this earth, with all that it contains, shall be destroyed.

TOASTS. The brother whose duty it is, as a visitor, to return thanks, must be extremely careful not to say too much, or he is easily led away into an extemporaneous lecture, to which it is not so easy to find a becoming end; the opposite fault of repeating a few set phrases, like a parrot, ought to be equally as carefully guarded against. If both old and young members are at the same table, the young never attempt to press before the old. And before the close, the toast, which is so dear to every good Mason, should never be omitted; viz. "our sick and afflicted brethren," neither ought the serving brethren ever to be forgot.—*Gadicke.*

TOKENS. Signs, tokens, and words do not constitute Freemasonry, but are local marks whereby they know each other, and may be altered, or entirely done away, without the least injury to scientific Freemasonry. It is with many Freemasons too absurd a belief, and a still more absurd practice, to build our science upon so shallow a foundation as signs, tokens, and words, which I fear constitute with some the only attainment they look for in Freemasonry. That certain signals may be necessary, I do readily allow; but deny that such a mechanism shall constitute a principal part of our institution.— *Husenbeth.*

TONGUE. A Mason should use his tongue to protect, but never to betray.

TRACING-BOARD. The tracing-board is for the Master to draw his plans and designs on, that the building, whether moral or literal, may be conducted with order and regularity.

TRADITION. It is well-known that in former times, while learning remained in few hands, the ancients had several institutions for the cultivation of knowledge, concealed under doctrinal and ritual mysteries, that were sacredly withheld from all who were not initiated into a participation of the privileges they led to, that they might not be prostituted to the vulgar. Among these institutions may be ranked that of Masonry; and its value may be inferred from its surviving those revolutions of government, religion and manners, that have swallowed up the rest. And the traditions of so venerable an institution claim an attention, far superior to the loose oral relations or epic songs of any uncultivated people whatever.—*Anderson.*

TRAITOR. Ancient Freemasonry inflicted very severe punishment for the least treason to the Order; nevertheless, we have accounts of men who have proved traitors, even as we find accounts of such traitors to the mysteries of the ancients. With the increase of enlightenment and rational reflection, it is admitted that a brother may both speak and write much upon the Order without becoming a traitor to its secrets. How an initiation is conducted, how a word or grip is given, gives no key to the true secret of the Order; but we nevertheless disapprove of such disclosures, for this reason, that the uninitiated could only form a useless chimera from them.—*Gadicke.*

TRANSFERRING. If a lodge be dissolved, the constitution shall be delivered up to the Grand Master, and shall not, on any account, be transferred without his consent. If the brethren holding a warrant for a lodge render themselves unworthy of longer possessing it, the Grand Master may, after the Grand Lodge shall have

decided on that fact, transfer such warrant to other
brethren, whom he may think deserving, with a new
number, at the bottom of the lodges then on record.—
Constitutions.

TRAVEL. Our ancient brethren are masonically
said to have travelled from west to east, in search of
instruction; and it is an undeniable fact that all knowledge, all religion, all arts and sciences, have travelled,
according to the course of the sun, from east to west.
From that quarter the Divine glory first came, and thence
the rays of divine light continue to diffuse themselves
over the face of the earth. From thence came the Bible,
and through that the new covenant. From thence came
the prophets, the apostles, and the first missionaries that
brought the knowledge of God to Europe, to the isles of
the sea, and to the west.—*Adam Clarke.*

TREASURER. The old founders of the lodges must
have intended to collect large sums of money, or very
small sums must in those days have been considered large
treasures, for they have given the title of treasurer to
the brother who has charge of the lodge funds. Every
lodge has a treasurer, and it is his duty not only to take
care of, but to collect all the lodge dues. Part of the
expenditure of the lodge is fixed, and part is voted by
the Master Masons for charitable purposes. Those lodges
which are in the habit of practising the charitable virtues, inculcated so forcibly in Freemasonry, seldom are
in possession of large funds; and lodges which pride
themselves upon being rich, seldom enjoy a great reputation in Freemasonry.—*Gudicke.*

TRIANGLE. A geometrical figure, which every
Freemason knows; and he must in particular study that
triangle which has three equal sides, or which is called
an equal sided triangle. The ancient Egyptian priests
expressed the origin of all things by the triangle; and
when they afterwards wished to describe the Godhead in
its various attributes, they also adopted the triangle.
The kind, good, gracious, and merciful God, they delineated by the water triangle ∇ ; and the just and angry
God, by the fire triangle $\triangle$. The triangle considered as

a geometrical figure, is composed of three things, which united, form one whole, viz., of three particular points and angles, by the union of which the triangle itself is formed, as one whole, or complete figure. It is for this reason that it has been adopted as the symbol of the Triune God. If we unite a ▽ with △ we have a six pointed star ✡ as a symbol of the perfect Godhead, in all his attributes and works. If we surround this figure with a circle ✪ there will be seven points in it, if we include the centre point of the circle, which represent the sacred number seven.—*Gadicke.*

TRIPLE TRIANGLE. One would be apt to suspect that they (the Druids) had a regard for the sacred symbol and mystical character of medicine, which in ancient times was thought to be of no inconsiderable value; this is a pentagonal figure, formed from a triple triangle, called by the name of Hygeia, because it may be resolved into the Greek letters that compose the word. The Pythagoreans used it among their disciples as a mystical symbol denoting health, and the cabalistic Jews and Arabians had the same fancy. It is the pentalpha, or pentagrammon, among the Egyptians, the mark of prosperity. Antiochus Soter, going to fight against the Galatians, was advised in a dream to bear this sign upon his banner, whence he obtained a signal victory.—*Stukely.*

TRIPLE TAU. This figure forms two right angles on each of the exterior lines, and another at the centre by their union, for the three angles of each triangle are equal to two right angles. This being triplified, illustrates the jewel worn by the companions of the Royal Arch, which by its intersection forms a given number of ngles; these may be taken in five several combinations, and reduced, their amount in right angles will be found equal to the two Platonic bodies, which represent the four elements and sphere of the universe.—*R. A. Lecture.*

TROWEL. The trowel is appropriated to the Master's degree, because, as the lectures say, it is as Master Masons only we constitute the recognized of the masonic family. Again, this implement is considered as the appropriate working tool of the Master Mason, because, in operative masonry, while the E. A. P. prepares the materials, and the Fellowcraft places them in their proper situation, the Master Mason spreads the cement with a trowel, which binds them together. In speculative Masonry the Master of the lodge is the cement which unites the brethren, and binds them together in peace, harmony, and brotherly love.

TRUE. The Mason should not only be true to the brotherhood and the Order, but to all mankind. Every Mason ought to act in such a manner as to render it unnecessary to doubt his truth. Flattering words, which are only calculated to entrap the weak and the unwary, do not strengthen that truth which is expected amongst brethren. We must be able to depend with as much confidence upon the word of a Mason as if he had given us a written undertaking.—*Gadicke.*

TRUTH. Truth is a divine attribute, and the foundation of every virtue. To be good and true, is the first lesson we are taught in Masonry. On this theme we contemplate, and by its dictates endeavour to regulate our conduct; influenced by this principle, hypocrisy and deceit are unknown in the lodge; sincerity and plain dealing distinguish us, while the heart and tongue join in promoting the general welfare, and rejoicing in each other's prosperity.—*Preston.*

TUBAL CAIN. Before the general deluge there was a man called Lameck, who had two wives, the one called Adah, the other Zillah; by Adah he had two sons, Jabell and Juball; by Zillah he had a son called Tubal, and a daughter called Mahmah. These four children found the beginning of all the crafts in the world. Jabell found out geometry, and had divided flocks of sheep and lambs; he built the first house of stone and timber. Juball found out music. Tubal found out the Smith's trading or craft, also the working of gold, silver, copper, iron, and steel.—*Ancient Masonic Manuscript.*

TUSCAN. The Tuscan being the first, is the most simple and solid of the five orders. It was invented in

Tuscany, whence it derives its name. The simplicity of the construction of this column, renders it eligible where solidity is the chief object, and where ornament would be superfluous.

TWENTY-FOUR INCH RULE. An instrument made use of by operative masons to measure and lay out their work; but we, as Free and Accepted Masons, are taught to make use of it for the more noble and glorious purpose of dividing our time. It being divided into twenty-four equal parts, is emblematical of the twenty-four hours of the day, which we are taught to divide into three parts, whereby we find a portion for the service of God, and the relief of a worthy distressed brother; a portion for our usual avocations; and a portion for refreshment and sleep.—*Lectures.*

UNANIMOUS. A ballot is unanimous when there are no black balls. This unanimity must be founded upon the proper exercise of the rules and regulations laid down for our guidance in this important part of our duty, and a perfect unanimity in the opinions of the brethren on the moral character of the candidate.—*Gadicke.*

UNIFORMITY. All lodges are particularly bound to observe the same usages and customs; every deviation, therefore, from the established mode of working is highly improper, and cannot be justified or countenanced. In order to preserve this uniformity, and to cultivate a good understanding among Freemasons, some members of every lodge should be deputed to visit other lodges as often as may be convenient. If any lodge shall give its sanction for a lodge of instruction being holden under its warrant, such lodge shall be responsible that the proceedings in the lodge of instruction are correct and regular, and that the mode of working there adopted has received the sanction of the Grand Lodge.—*Constitutions.*

UNIVERSE. The universe is the Temple of the Deity whom we serve. Wisdom, Strength, and Beauty are about his throne, as the pillars of his works; for his Wisdom is infinite, his Strength is in omnipotence, and Beauty stands forth through all his creation in symmetry and order. He hath stretched forth the heavens as a canopy, and the earth He hath planted as his footstool; He crowns his temple with the stars as with a diadem;

and in his hand He extendeth the power and the glory; the sun and moon are messengers of his will, and all his law is concord. The pillars supporting the lodge are representative of these divine powers. A lodge, where perfect Masons are assembled, represents these works of the Deity.—*Hutchinson.*

UNIVERSALITY. The universality of Masonry is thus described by a masonic writer of the last century: "Leaving holy ground, we trace Masonry amongst the Eastern Magi, and in the renowned learning of Egypt. From whence, like other sciences, taking a westerly direction, it was brought by that European apostle of Masonry, Pythagoras, from whose propagation it reached the British isle. Its principles were respected and disseminated by Brahmins, philosophers, artists, and saints, and diffused the light of science to the remotest corners of the earth. It taught natural religion, philosophy, subordination, and arts on the banks of the Ganges, in the hieroglyphics of Egypt, the sanctuaries of Eleusis, the schools of the sages, the caves of the Druids."

UNIVERSAL LANGUAGE. An universal language has been much desired by the learned of many ages. It is a thing rather to be wished than hoped for. But it seems the Masons pretended to have such a thing among them. If it be true, I guess it must be something like the language of the pantomimes among the ancient Romans who are said to be able, by signs only, to express and deliver any oration intelligibly to men of all nations and languages.—*Locke.*

UPPER CHAMBER. Our lodges are formed in upper chambers, and carefully guarded by tyled doors and drawn swords. The highest of hills and the lowest of valleys are situations least exposed to unauthorized intrusion. Thus Masons are said to meet in these situations, to commemorate a remarkable custom of the ancient Jews in the building of their temples, schools, and synagogues; and as by the Jewish law, whenever ten of them assembled together for that purpose, they proceeded to work, so it was with our ancient brethren, who formed themselves into a lodge, whenever ten operative masons were assembled, consisting of the Master, two Wardens, and seven Fellow-Crafts.

UPRIGHT POSTURE. To walk and act uprightly before heaven and before men is to add still great luster to the Mason's character; to do justice and to have charity, are excellent steps in human life, but to act uprightly, gives a superlative degree of excellence, for in that situation we should become examples in religious, in civil, and in moral conduct, which are among the great principles of our noble institution.

USAGES. The usages and customs of Masons have ever corresponded with those of the ancient Egyptians, to which they bear a near affinity. Their philosophers, unwilling to expose their mysteries to vulgar eyes, concealed their particular tenets, and principles of polity and philosophy, under hieroglyphical figures, and expressed their notions of government by signs and symbols, which they communicated to their priests, or magi alone, who were bound by oath not to reveal them.

VAULT. Vaults are found in every country of the world as well as in Judea, and were used for secret purposes. Thus Stephens, speaking of some ruins in Yucatan, says—"The only way of descending was to tie a rope around the body, and be lowered by the Indians. In this way I was let down, and almost before my head had passed through the hole, my feet touch the top of a heap of rubbish, high directly under the hole, and falling off at the sides. Clambering down it I found myself in a round chamber, so filled with rubbish that I could not stand upright. With a candle in my hand, I crawled all round on my hands and knees. The chamber was in the shape of a dome, and had been coated with plaster, most of which had fallen, and now encumbered the ground, the depth could not be ascertained without clearing out the interior."

VIRTUES. In all ages it has been the object of Freemasonry, not only to inform the minds of its members, by instructing them in the sciences and useful arts, but to better their hearts, by enforcing the precepts of religion and morality. In the course of the ceremonies of initiation, brotherly love, loyalty, and other virtues are inculcated in hieroglyphic symbols, and the candidate is often reminded that there is an eye above, which observeth the workings of his heart, and is ever fixed upon the thoughts and actions of men.—*Laurie.*

VISITING BRETHREN. If a Freemason is a member of any lodge, he has a right to be admitted into all other lodges as a visiting brother, but he must be either introduced by a member of the lodge, or he must be able to legitimize himself by producing his Grand Lodge certificate, and proving himself by his work.

VOTES. All matters are to be decided by a majority of votes, each member having one vote, and the Grand Master two votes; unless the lodge, for the sake of expedition, think proper to leave any particular subject to the determination of the Grand Master. The votes of the members always to be signified by each holding up one of his hands, which uplifted hands the Wardens are to count, unless the number should be so uneven as to render counting unnecessary.—*Constitutions.*

WAGES. The tradition respecting the payment of the workmen's wages at the building of Solomon's Temple, may or may not be accurate, as I am ignorant of the authority on which the calculations are founded. Indeed the probabilty is, that the tradition has been fabricated in a subsequent age, without the existence of any documents to attest its authenticity. The men were paid in their lodges by shekels, a silver coin of about half-a-crown of our money; and the number of shekels per day was regulated by the square of the number of the degree which each order of men had attained. Thus with respect to the Entered Apprentices only, there were ten thousand in work, and twenty thousand at rest. These men, at the rate of one shekel per head, would receive daily £1,250, or, during the seven years and seven months of building the Temple, £3,458,750. In the higher grades, the men were not only remunerated for their labor, but also for their superior ingenuity and artistical skill.

WARDENS. Every lodge has two, and they stand next in rank to the M. W. Their places are so situated, that they are enabled to superintend the execution of the commands of the W. M. Experienced brethren, who have a sufficient knowledge of strength and beauty, and who are at all times ready to use the level and the plumb-rule, ought always to be chosen as Wardens, that they may be enabled to conduct the business of the lodge in the unavoidable absence of the W. M. or his deputy.

WARRANT. In former times a lodge formed itself without any ceremony, wherever a sufficient number of brethren dwelt to form a lodge, and one of the neighboring lodges formed it for them. But in 1722 the Grand Lodge in London determined that every new lodge in England should have a patent, and since that time all those brethren who wish to form a new lodge, strive to obtain a warrant from the Grand Lodge. The new lodge then joins the Grand Lodge as a daughter lodge, binds itself to work according to its system, and to keep within the ancient landmarks. Then is such a lodge called just perfect, and regular.— *Gadicke.*

WATCH-WORD. The Word is not to be understood as a watch-word only, after the manner of those annexed to the several degrees of the Craft, but also, theologically, as a term to convey to the mind some idea of that Great Being who is the sole author of our existence, and to carry along with it the most solemn veneration for his sacred Name and Word, as well as the most clear and perfect elucidation of his power and attributes that the human mind is capable of receiving.

WEST. Where the sun closes its daily race, there the thanks of the inhabitants of the world follow it, and with the ensuing morning it again commences its benevolent course. Every brother draws near to the evening of his days; and well will it be with him if at the close of his labors he can look forward with hope for a good reward for his work.— *Gadicke.*

WHITE. This color has ever been regarded as emblematic of purity and innocence. In the York rite the apron is always of this color, though the trimming varies in the symbolic and chapitral degrees. "Let thy garments be always WHITE," etc.— *Solomon.*

WHITE STONE. The white stone is an inestimable gift, promised to every one who lives a moral and virtuous life. White is an emblem of purity, and the new name conveys a title to be admitted within the veil, and honored with a seat near the living God in that palace which is described by St. John as a perfect cube, whose walls and foundations are garnished with all manner of precious stones, all hewed, squared, and polished by the masterly hand of the T. G. A. O. T. U.

WIDOW'S SON. Hiram, the architect, is described in two places of Scripture; in the first he is called a widow's son, of the tribe of Naphtali, and in the other is called the son of a woman of the daughters of Dan; but in both that his father was a man of Tyre; that is, she was of the daughters of the city of Dan, in the tribe of Naphtali, and is called a widow of Naphtali, as her husband was a Naphtalite; for he is not called a Tyrian by descent, but a man of Tyre by habitation.—*Anderson.*

WINDING STAIRCASE. When the Fellow-Crafts went to receive their wages, they ascended a winding staircase, the steps of which, like all the Masonic symbols, are illustrative of discipline and doctrine, as well as of natural, mathematical, and metaphysical science, and open to us an extensive range of moral and speculative inquiry. In their delineation, the steps, which count odd numbers, should be more particularly marked as one, three, five, seven, eleven; and in ascending them the Fellow-Craft should pause on each alternate step, and consider the several stages of his progress, as well as the important lessons which are there inculcated.

WISDOM. Those alone are wise who exercise the powers of the mind in secrecy, and who, without any selfish object, endeavor to promote the universal happiness of mankind, whom neither fortune nor misfortune are able to drive from a calm and steady progress through life. To possess Masonic wisdom it is not necessary to be very learned, or to have a most penetrating genius; the man of good plain common sense may be more masonically wise than the most learned man in existence. It is not the act of a wise man to make a great profession of wisdom; and the secrets of our Lodges ought to teach us how to exercise our Masonic wisdom.—*Gadicke.*

WORKING TOOLS OF FREEMASONS. They are of three kinds, viz: ornaments, furniture, and jewels. What we understand by these are things without which we are unable to perform any manual labor as ought to be expected from working tools; but if we take them as symbols, then they have a most important signification.

WORLDLY WEALTH. Masonry regards no man on account of his worldly wealth and honor. The poor as well as the rich may knock at the door of our temple, and

PORCH OF THE TEMPLE AND WINDING STAIRS.

gain admission. All are welcome if found worthy to receive light. This is strictly spiritual: "Seek, and ye shall find; ask, and ye shall receive; knock, and the door shall be opened unto you."—*Scott.*

WORSHIPFUL. A title of respect given to justices of the peace, etc., and in the same sense to symbolic Lodges, and also to the present and Past Masters of the same.

WORSHIPFUL MASTER. He who has attained the third degree in Freemasonry is a Master; and where they do not work in the so-called high degrees, has attained the summit of his profession. None but F. Cs. who have been found worthy can obtain this degree. As a M. M. he has a voice in all the consultations of the officers of the Lodge, and he may, if possessed of sufficient Masonic skill, be appointed to any office in the Lodge, even that of W. M. This is the highest preferment a Mason can obtain in St. John's Masonry, through the three degrees of which every candidate for the P. M. degree must have passed. If there are members in the Lodge who have the higher degrees, they are generally elected W. M.; but although it is by no means necessary to possess those degrees to enable a brother to be elected to the chair, it is absolutely necessary that he should be a man of good moral character, and extensive Masonic information; he is then elected by his brother M. Ms. for one year. The greatest care and caution ought to be used by the brethren at this election to prevent the Lodge being injured by the election of an improper person. He must also be well acquainted with the Order, its doctrines, its secrets, its history, and constitution, and must possess the power of communicating his own reflections upon all these subjects, in a clear comprehensive form, to the brethren.

YEAR OF MASONRY. The birth of Christ is commonly given to the autumn of the year 5 before Christ, which is an apparent anomaly, which may require a few words of explanation. The era of the birth of Christ was not in use until about 532 A. D., in the time of Justinian, when it was introduced by Dionysius Exiguus, a Scythian by birth, and a Roman abbot; and which only began to prevail in the West about the time of Charles Martel and Pope Gregory II., A. D. 730. It has long been agreed by all chronologers that Dionysius made a mistake in placing the birth of Christ some years too late; but the amount of the difference has been variously estimated at two, three, four, five, and even eight years. The general conclusion is that which is adopted in our Bibles, and which places the birth of Christ four years before the common era, or more probably a few months more. In Masonry we add 4000 up to the birth of Christ, and that sum constitutes the reputed year of Masonry.

YORK MASONS. The brother of King Athelstan, Prince Edwin, being taught Masonry, and taking upon him the charges of a Master Mason, for the love he had to the said Craft, and the honorable principles whereon it is grounded, purchased a free charter of King Athelstan for the Masons; having a correction among themselves, as it was anciently expressed, or a freedom and power to regulate themselves, to amend what might happen amiss, and to hold a yearly communication and general assembly. That accordingly Prince Edwin summoned all the Masons in the realm to meet him in congregation at York, who came and composed a general Lodge, of which he was Grand Master; and having brought with them all the writings and records extant, some in Greek, some in Latin, some in French, and other languages, from the contents thereof that assembly did frame the Constitution and Charges of an English Lodge, and made a law to preserve and observe the same in all time coming.

ZEREDATHA. The pillars and other brass work were cast in the clayey ground between Succoth and Zeredatha. In the Hebrew the words for "clayey ground" are "in the thickness of the ground." That is, the earth was stiff and glutinous, and upon that account more fit to make moulds of all kinds.

ZERUBBABEL. The son of Salathiel, of the royal race of David. Cyrus committed to his care the sacred vessels of the temple, with which he returned to Jerusalem. He is always named first, as being the chief of the Jews that returned to their own country, where he laid the foundations of the second temple. When the Samaritans offered to assist in rebuilding the temple, Zerubbabel and the principal men of Judah refused them this honor, since Cyrus had granted his commission to the Jews only.

ABOUT THE AUTHOR

Robert Macoy (October 4, 1815 – January 9, 1895 was born in Armagh, Ulster Ireland, but moved to the United States at the age of 4 months. He was a prominent Freemason, and was instrumental in the founding of the Order of the Eastern Star and the Order of the Amaranth. He also founded what may be the largest Masonic publishing, regalia, and supply house currently active.

Growing up in America and having attained a considerable degree of education, Macoy entered the printing craft as soon as he was old enough to work. He spent most of his life in that business and in Masonic activities in New York City. In 1849, he started a Masonic supply and publishing business, which, under the name, Macoy Publishing & Masonic Supply Company, is still in active operation. Macoy was initiated in Lebanon Lodge No. 191 in New York City, January 20, 1848, passed, January 27, and Raised February 3 of that year. On August 15, 1855, he withdrew to affiliate with Adelphic Lodge No. 348. He was elected Deputy Grand Master of New York in June, 1856 and re-elected in 1857. He was exalted in Orient Chapter No. 138, Royal Arch Masons, September 5, 1849 and became a member of Adelphic Chapter No. 150 on December 24, 1855. He was also affiliated with Union Chapter No. 180, Americas Chapter No. 215, and De Witt Clinton Chapter No. 142. He also received the Cryptic degrees and was a charter member of Adelphic Council No. 7, Royal and Select Masters. He was elected Grand Recorder of the Grand Council on June 4, 1855. He was also knighted in Palestine Encampment No. 18 of New York City, in February, 1851, and in March withdrew to join Morton Encampment No. 4. On April 28, 1874, he affiliated with DeWitt Clinton Commandery No. 27 Knights Templar, where his membership continued for 20 years. He received the Scottish Rite degrees sometime prior to December 9, 1850, for on that date he received the 33rd Degree, Sovereign Grand Inspector General. In 1866 Macoy published A Dictionary of Freemasonry, which comprised his own work *("General History of Freemasonry" and "Cyclopaedia of Freemasonry")* as well as George Oliver's Dictionary of Symbolical Masonry of 1853.

www.ingramcontent.com/pod-product-compliance
Lightning Source LLC
Chambersburg PA
CBHW021804270326
41932CB00007B/47